# LeRoy Collins Leon County
# PUBLIC LIBRARY

*This book has been donated in honor of*

My good friend Louis Keefer

*by*

Elmer Horne

**From Maine to Mexico: With America's Private Pilots in the Fight Against Nazi U-Boats** Copyright ©1997 by Louis E. Keefer. All rights reserved. Printed and bound in the United States of America. No part of this book may be reproduced in any form or by any means, electronic or mechanical, including photocopying, recording, or by any information storage retrieval system without written permission from the publisher. For information contact: COTU Publishing, P. O. Box 2160, Reston, VA 20195-0160, Telephone (703) 742-8260

First edition
4 3 2 1 97 98 99
ISBN: 0-9644740-1-8
Library of Congress Catalog Card No: 96-72081

Dust Jacket Design by John K. Underwood, III

## Acknowledgments

This book has been a pleasure to research because the people who helped me — nearly five hundred of them — were so wonderful to work with. More than half are quoted, and the others gave me help of all kinds. Without this help, there would be no book.

Special thanks are owed to Colonel Lester E. Hopper, former CAP National Historian, who for two days helped me explore his personal collection of photographs and other materials, and with his wife, Carol, introduced me to the delights of "Cajun Country" living and eating. The work of Colonel Hopper and the National CAP Historical Committee, which he chaired from 1980 until 1995, was a constant inspiration.

Special thanks also go to the reviewers of particular chapters: Harry P. Bridges, Isaac W. Burnham II, Frederick K. Creasey, Dolly L. (Heberding) Feigenbaum, George E. Haddaway, Paul R. Loux, Jr., and Frank S. Myers. The book is far better for their collective contribution. If errors have slipped through, blame me, not them.

Many librarians and archivists also provided help, among them: Cynthia Beeman, Administrator, Local History Programs, Texas Historical Commission, Austin, TX; Judy Bolton, Louisiana and Lower Mississippi Valley Collections, Louisiana State University, Baton Rouge, LA; Donaly E. Brice, Supervisor, Reference Services, Texas State Library, Austin, TX; Jeffrey Brown, Reference Services Branch, Maine State Archives, Augusta, ME; Glenn R. Conrad, Secretary-Treasurer, Louisiana Historical Association, Lafayette, LA; Constance J. Cooper, Ph.D., Manuscript Librarian, The Historical Society of Delaware, Wilmington, DE; Deborah Dyer, Curator, Bar Harbor Historical Society, Bar Harbor, ME; Bette M. Epstein, Archivist, New Jersey State Archives, Trenton, NJ; Jonathan Gerland, Archivist and Judith Linsley, Education Coordinator, both of the Tyrrell Historical Library, Beaumont, TX; Randy L. Goss, Archivist Supervisor, Delaware State Archives, Dover, DE; Lynne D.

Joshi, Reference Libarian, Hagley Museum and Library, Wilmington, DE; David Kerkhof, Librarian, Suffolk County Historical Society, Riverhead, NY; Ling Lu, Reference Librarian, State Library of Massachusetts, Boston, MA; Michael Steinitz, Survey Director, Massachusetts Historical Commission, Boston, MA; Dorothy S. Svenning, Archivist, Falmouth Historical Society, Falmouth, MA; Frank Wheeler, Senior Archivist, Georgia Historical Society Library, Savannah, GA; Stefanie A. Wittenbach, Assistant Director for Library and Information Services, The University of Texas at Austin, Austin, TX; and Bob Wyllie, Research Volunteer, Coastal Georgia Historical Society and Museum of Coastal History, St. Simons Island, GA.

Much is owed also to three steadfast but recognition-resistant helpers whose initials are A. B., L. J., and B. R.

# Contents

Acknowledgments
Preparing for War ............................................. 1

**February 28 - March 11, 1942**
  1. Atlantic City, New Jersey ............................. 7
  2. Rehoboth Beach, Delaware ......................... 37
  3. Lantana, Florida ....................................... 61
  4. Parksley, Virginia ..................................... 85
  5. Flagler Beach, Florida .............................. 111

**May 12 - June 24, 1942**
  6. St. Simons Island, Georgia ...................... 133
  7. Miami, Florida ....................................... 157
  8. Charleston, South Carolina ..................... 177
  9. Grand Isle, Louisiana .............................. 197
 10. Beaumont, Texas .................................... 231
 11. Pascagoula, Mississippi .......................... 257

**July 8 - July 23, 1942**
 12. Brownsville, Texas .................................. 279
 13. Sarasota, Florida .................................... 303
 14. Panama City, Florida .............................. 317
 15. Corpus Christi, Texas .............................. 347
 16. Manteo, North Carolina .......................... 373

**August 6 - September, 1942**
 17. Riverhead, New York ............................... 403
 18. Falmouth, Massachusetts ........................ 429
 19. Portland, Maine ..................................... 451
 20. Bar Harbor, Maine .................................. 475
 21. Beaufort, North Carolina ......................... 499

Epilogue ......................................................... 525
Bibliography ................................................... 527
Index ............................................................. 529

This book is respectfully dedicated to the twenty-six airmen who lost their lives while serving in the CAP Coastal Patrol during 1942 and 1943.

# Preparing for War

Many aviation historians give most of the credit for the birth of the Civil Air Patrol to Gill Robb Wilson, former World War I pilot, president of the National Aeronautics Association, innovative director of the New Jersey Bureau of Aviation, and editor of the *New York Herald Tribune* aviation page. His autobiography, *I Walked With Giants*, still unfinished at the time of his death in 1966, reveals the thinking that led to the creation of the Civil Air Patrol. His 1936 tour of Germany had left him certain that the dictator Adolf Hitler was preparing for war and that, while the democratic nations might have greater resources than Germany, they might lack the time to tap them quickly enough:

> It was at this point that I began to think of the private and business pilots and the miscellaneous aircraft fleet as shock troops to gain time should the United States coasts be attacked. I had never heard anyone suggest that this segment of aviation might be a national resource. At first blush, the idea seemed ridiculous. But at first blush, the idea of founding an air force on a soaring campaign must have seemed equally ridiculous to most Germans. I had never heard anyone mention the light-aircraft industry as the backbone of a premilitary training program, yet the more I thought of it, the more logical it seemed to be. If gliders served Germany, would not the light-plane family serve us even better? It was too early to introduce the idea of a comprehensive civil pilot-training program as yet, but the time would come.

Wilson's long career in civil aviation had left him completely convinced that most American sports and business flyers would embrace the concept. A first step was to put dimensions on the service that might be rendered:

> I set about a research program of my own in New Jersey [classifying the pilots, mechanics, airfields, and aircraft that would be available]. This was not difficult, since as director of aviation I personally knew almost everyone and had inspected every aircraft in the state. The picture that emerged from my survey was interesting — about 130 licensed pilots whom the military establishment could not use, including a few women. And few of the aircraft could be used in any standardized military training program. My own Fairchild 24 was one of the few fully instrumented and radio-equipped aircraft in the privately-owned fleet. But these people had one unique knowledge. They knew the Jersey coast and the nearby reaches of the Atlantic Ocean as they knew the palms of their hands. They were accustomed to murky weather. Most of them were not instrument pilots and did not go "over the top" to any extent, but they could crawl around underneath when the crows were walking.

Gill Robb Wilson persuaded other state aviation directors he knew — Fred Sherif of Montana, Floyd Evans of Michigan, Les Morris of Connecticut, Earle L. Johnson of Ohio, Harry Coffee of Oregon, A. B. McMullen of Florida, and others — to make similar assessments. They also favored establishing a "Flying Minute Man" organization that could be called upon with short notice to perform vital air services. The next question was exactly what were these vital services? Wilson's first thought was of a past need that might recur. The remark of a former German U-boat commander who had brazenly come ashore on an Atlantic City beach during World War I stuck in Wilson's mind: "Your East Coast is the best submarine hunting ground in the world." In his memoir, Wilson went on to observe:

> Patently, coastal reconnaissance would be a ready-made job for a swarm of private planes and their coast-wise crews. Presently, they were forbidden to fly beyond gliding distance of the shore; but this could be extended seaward to cover the coastal sea lanes without facing impossible hazards. They could maneuver at wave-top altitude in murky weather much better than heavy military planes. And in the last analysis, military patrol initially would be unavailable because neither Army nor Navy would have the necessary planes and crews. The civilians might not be able to do combat with submarines, but they could carry smoke bombs to mark their sightings; and their very presence would be a threat to submarines.

Once Wilson's "Flying Minute Men" concept became public, he spent weeks and months in Washington talking up the significance of air power, and the immediate need to organize civilian aviation for defense purposes. Wilson, who served as the president of the National

Aeronautics Association, enjoyed the strong support of such powerful private citizens as Thomas H. Beck, president of the Crowell-Collier Publishing Company, Guy P. Gannett, publisher of a chain of New England newspapers, and Earle L. Johnson, Ohio industrialist and dollar-a-year Director of Aeronautics for that state. During this period, well before the Japanese attack at Pearl Harbor, Wilson and his supporters won over General Henry H. "Hap" Arnold and key Air Corps staff but there the matter rested because, as Wilson later recalled:

> For some reason I never clearly understood, "Hap" was in high disfavor at the White House. He had provided me with a letter approving the establishment of a civilian air cadre for emergency service and set forth the particular functions it could serve. Further than that he dared not go. The organization could be created only by executive order of the President. We had drawn up the substance of such an order, and it had lain at the White House for months although the war in Europe was now under way and the United States was aiding the Allies in every way possible short of joining them. We had sought to get action by the President through his son James, who was sympathetic to our proposal, but James's efforts had been unavailing. Then one day I received a call from Frank Gannett, the publisher from Maine. Mrs. Roosevelt was to be in Maine for several days, and he would have the opportunity to visit with her at length. If I could brief him on exactly what we wanted and how we sought to serve, he would take the matter up with Mrs. Roosevelt and ask her intervention with the President.

Shortly afterwards — whether or not because of "intervention" by Mrs. Roosevelt is unknown — on December 1, 1941, President Roosevelt signed an executive order establishing the Civil Air Patrol, and visionary Gill Robb Wilson's brainchild became fact at last. The newly appointed Director of Civil Defense, New York's Mayor Fiorello La Guardia, appointed Wilson, Thomas Beck, and Frank Gannett as a committee, with Wilson as the executive officer, to get the organization moving. Wilson was delighted when "Hap" Arnold appointed his old friend, Brigadier General John Curry, as first national commander. Earle Johnson then received an Air Corps commission and became Curry's executive officer, later assuming command himself when Curry was needed elsewhere. After helping to establish the nation's first coastal patrol base at Atlantic City, Gill Robb Wilson took no further part in the Civil Air Patrol. But his was the driving force when it was needed most.

How fortunate it was that America's pilots and aircraft owners had made this much preparation! With extremely limited funding and equipment, the all-volunteer Civil Air Patrol and its hastily established coastal patrol bases quickly became the nation's first line of defense against a determined and dangerous enemy. The havoc wreaked by the German U-boats stalking our Gulf coasts in 1942 and 1943 has been described by many historians. Robert E. Neprud's *Flying Minute Men: The Story of the Civil Air Patrol*, authorized by the Civil Air Patrol and the United States Air Force and published in 1948, did not dwell on ship tonnages and lives lost, but drew a compelling picture of the brashness of the German attack and of the American helplessness before it:

> There was a time early in 1942 when Nazi submarines were bagging two or three vessels a day along the East Coast and in the Gulf of Mexico. The entire 1,200-mile sea frontier from Halifax to the Florida Keys was protected by some antiquated subchasers, five old Eagle boats, three ocean-going yachts, fewer than a dozen Coast Guard ships, four blimps, and a handful of airplanes. During those first deperate months after the United States was plunged into war, the Navy was spread far too thin to keep the Nazi sharks at bay — and the tankerman who sailed past Cape Hatteras alive counted himself lucky. Twelve vessels went down in January, 42 took the plunge in March, and by May the toll of shipping was so terrible that no figures on losses were released to the public. For several humiliating weeks, all coastal vessels were ordered to put up in harbors until convoys could be organized.
>
> Danger lurked along the waterfront. Mysterious blinkers contacted offshore craft at night; enemy agents rubbed shoulders with sailors in bars and restaurants, alert for news of ship movements; short-wave sets concealed in attics and basements relayed information from towns and cities along the coast. Eight Nazi saboteurs, schooled in the arts of death and destruction, were actually intercepted by alert Coast Guard sentries. Four Nazis landed on a Florida beach, and the other four near the eastern tip of Long Island after disembarking from submarines in rubber boats.
>
> The 245-foot transatlantic monsters, spawned in the pens at Lorient, Bremen, and Wilhelmshaven, became brazenly impudent. They sank a ship in the mouth of the Connecticut River, potted two more in the Saint Lawrence, and crept up into the Lower Mississippi to threaten shipping plying out of New Orleans. Before dim-outs were ordered along the coast, the U-boats turned the waters off brightly lighted resort cities into shooting galleries, ramming torpedoes into sharply silhouetted tankers and merchantmen within sight of the boardwalk crowds. Sometimes, in order to conserve their "tin fish," subs blasted shipping with their two formidable four-inch guns … On occasion, U-boat crews even hung out their wash and took sunbaths on deck when their crafts surfaced to charge batteries.

This was the desperate situation when, with much skepticism and little real support, the armed forces permitted the coastal patrol a ninety-day trial period in which to prove its worth operating from only three bases: Atlantic City, New Jersey; Rehoboth Beach, Delaware; and Lantana, Florida. To the surprise of none of the volunteers who served, the experiment succeeded, and during the next eighteen months more than three thousand men and women left their homes, their jobs, and their loved ones to staff twenty-one different coastal patrol bases. During tens of thousands of missions, coastal patrol crews flew more than 24,000,000 miles over water, spotted 173 submarines, dropped bombs or depth charges against 57 of them, and were officially credited with sinking or damaging at least two. These accomplishments were paid for with the loss of 90 planes and the lives of 26 coastal patrol members, most of them drowned or frozen to death at sea.

This is the story of these unheralded volunteers as told by two hundred and seventy-five survivors of the fight — the pilots, observers, mechanics, radio and plotting board operators, linemen, guards, and office workers who served. Now in their seventies, eighties, and even nineties, these men and women tell of their satisfaction in serving their country, their excitement over daily base activities, their ingenuity in improving the often primitive conditions in which they lived and worked, and their dedication in returning to the fight after harrowing crashes and ditchings of small planes in the ocean. They deserve the heartfelt gratitude of the whole nation.

Atlantic City Municipal Airport — or Bader Field — was surrounded on three sides by water and marshland. Convenient to downtown hotels, a number of coastal patrol personnel got their daily exercise by walking to the field across a causeway bridge over the Intracoastal Waterway (source: 1952 United States Geological Survey map).

# 1
# Atlantic City, New Jersey

The first coastal patrol base in the United States was officially activated on February 28, 1942 at Bader Field, Atlantic City, New Jersey. The newborn Civil Air Patrol had just a ninety-day test period during which to convince the skeptical armed services that its Coastal Patrol could play a significant role in repulsing the German submarine menace. The task involved considerable risk and Frank A. Burnham in his book, *Hero Next Door*, described what the volunteers faced:

> The Atlantic is not a friendly ocean even where it laps against the sun kissed shores of Florida. It is a grey, green, sometimes even black, angry body of water especially during the winter months. Even today with modern electronic navigation systems, emergency locator transmitters, life rafts, survival suits and much, much more reliable aircraft and engines, experienced pilots are loath to fly much beyond gliding distance of the beach. In the winter and spring of 1942, the fledgling CAP's handful of volunteers, male and female ranging in age from 19 to 81, faced this same ocean with little but plain guts to sustain them.

## Gill Robb Wilson

One account of the early days at Atlantic City is found in aviation pioneer Gill Robb Wilson's autobiography, *I Walked With Giants*:

> Pearl Harbor triggered the beginning of anti-submarine action by the Civil Air Patrol. General John F. Curry sent me to Atlantic City to organize the activity. The municipal government turned over Bader Field as a base of operations. The call for immediate volunteers and their planes brought out some twenty teams of pilots and observers. We were a motley crew, and no two aircraft were the same. One of the planes was an antique bird-cage Sikorsky, but the crew consisted of a test pilot from Martin and a retired old mate from the Coast Guard. Another was a Grumman Widgeon amphibian flown by Tom

Whitney, a millionaire retired stockbroker. Tom was a notable big game hunter. Other planes, I recall, were a Stinson Reliant, an ancient Bellanca, a Cirrus Fairchild, several models of Wacos, a Curtiss Robin, and a bathtub Standard. Charley Peyton, my assistant at the New Jersey Department of Aviation, came down to oversee maintenance. We set up an operations office in one of the decrepit old sheet-iron hangars.

Regular patrols began on the tenth of March. After several days of morning and afternoon flights as far north as Long Island and as far south as Delaware Bay, the crews of sister ships flying together off Asbury Park, New Jersey reported a sinking freighter. One crew was sure it had also detected the feathery wake of a submarine's periscope. Their reports were quickly relayed to the Navy's Eastern Sea Frontier headquarters on Long Island. Instead of prompt acknowledgment and thanks, an ensuing telephone call to Wilson revealed the Navy's complete ignorance of the Civil Air Patrol's mission:

> "Are you the man in charge of a group of civilian pilots at Atlantic City?" a voice asked. I replied in the affirmative. Then the voice let me have it with both barrels. One of my pilots had made a scatter-brained report of a ship sinking. It was obviously false, but they had to send out destroyer patrols to check on it. The whole coast was in an uproar. That's what came of civilian meddling! It must be put to a stop immediately! And so on and on, in high indignation. When I could get a word in edgewise, I assured the Admiral that the report was accurate.... Obviously, the Navy had never heard of us.

**Wynant C. Farr**

In *Sank Same*, William B. Mellor's 1944 account of the coastal patrol, the arrival of the first patrol volunteers at Bader Field was met with derision by members of the Air Corps 104th Observation Squadron based there. As Wynant C. Farr, who would command the base over the next eighteen months and become an Air Medal winner, taxied what the Army pilots thought a too-fragile Fairchild 24 up to the hangar, one of them supposedly remarked, "So that's what's going to show us how to chase Jerry's pig boats away! One trip over the ocean and that one-lung Maytag will be ready to go back to country club flying."

Another coastal patrol arrival was millionaire broker Thomas C. ("Tommy") Eastman in his Grumman Widgeon, a sturdy little twin-engine amphibian. After landing, he was met by his new commanding officer: "Well, Tommy," said Farr, "this is it." Surveying the rough turf of the field, the bumpy gravel runways, pockmarked with little lakes of rain water, and the high tension wires bordering the south side of the field, Eastman replied. "*This* isn't much."

Subsequent arrivals included a Stinson Reliant, several Waco biplanes, a Piper Cub (which was too underpowered for patrol work), another Fairchild 24, another Grumman Widgeon, and an ancient Sikorsky amphibian. Except for the Grummans and the Sikorsky, none of the these planes were designed for over-water flight and few could fly more than five hundred miles nonstop. Mellor described them as an aerial "Coxey's Army," and declared that "no task force ever took up so dangerous a military assignment with as strange a mix of components as did CAP Coastal Patrol Base No. 1."

"Big Brass" at Atlantic City, 1943: left to right, Colonel Harry Blee, Army Air Corps; Major Wynant C. Farr, Base Commander; Capt. Allen Muthig; Capt. Pete Johnson; and 1st Lt. Randall M. Custer (courtesy Frederick K. Creasey).

Major Wynant Farr himself looked rather unmilitary. Most of his flying, noted Mellor, had been done on "sunny weekends when he could get away from his cardboard factory in New York and slip up to the Walden airport near his country home at Monroe in the Catskills for a two or three hour hop." Farr's staff, however, would soon find him a tough, demanding boss, intent on maintaining military-style discipline and fulfilling the base's mission. Among other early Atlantic City arrivals listed in *Sank Same* were:

> Isaac W. Burnham, II, the Manhattan broker who answered to the name of "Tubby," though he hadn't been a pound overweight since

he was a boy.... Al Muthig, a cigar-chewing mechanic who quit his job at the DuPont Fabrikoid plant in Newburgh, New York, climbed in his Stinson 105, and flew to Atlantic City to join the coastal patrol; long-faced Rudie Chalow, an automobile repairman [but also an aircraft mechanic] and back-lot flier from Vineland, New Jersey; Jim Knox, a hulking six-footer from Buffalo, whose hobby was photography; Floyd "Eggy" Eggenweiler, tall aviation mechanic from Lehighton, Pennsylvania; and Bob Stephenson, who came out of the American Rolling Mills in Ashland, Kentucky, and whose greatest delight was playing church organs.... Henry Arthur Graef, better known as "Bud," a former Minneapolis insurance adjuster; and scholarly, gray-haired J. Gordon Gibbs, of Marion, Massachusetts, who instantly won the nickname of "Kitty" when it became known at the field that he was the owner of the Katherine Gibbs Secretarial Schools.

## Isaac W. Burnham, II

*Though base commander Farr must have hated to see him leave, Isaac Burnham soon was ordered by CAP National Headquarters to leave Atlantic City and to establish a new base at Parksley, Virginia. In 1996, the 87-year-old Burnham recalled some of his duty in New York State and at Atlantic City:*

I'd learned to fly around 1937, had my own plane, and after the war began I flew all over the state recruiting pilots for the Civil Air Patrol — Buffalo, Albany, Syracuse, Rochester, and so on, wherever there was an airport. On the national level, more than 100,000 men and women signed up. It was said some German spies joined, but everyone was finger-printed and checked by the FBI and that would have been difficult.... We had several excellent women pilots who flew as co-pilots. When the Germans heard them talking on the radio they started to taunt us from Radio Berlin saying we needed women to protect ourselves. This resulted in the Air Corps barring all women from further flight duty in the CAP coastal patrol.

We lived in Atlantic City hotels for a dollar a night for a few months, weren't paid, and had no life vests or life rafts. We were instructed on over-water navigation by Ted Weems and by Ed Link, inventor of the Link Trainer. What shocked us all was being expected to fly no higher than a thousand feet over the water, but of course that was only proper, since so little surface detail could be seen from any higher altitude. We had about a hundred people — roughly thirty pilots, thirty observers, and forty ground personnel. We mostly flew Fairchilds and Stinsons, Cessnas and Beechcrafts, but not the smaller Aeroncas or Piper Cubs. They were too under-powered for patrol work. I left after a few months to establish a new base somewhere south of Rehoboth, Delaware.

\* \* \*

During Atlantic City's eighteen months of operation, more CAP members served there than at any other base — at one time or another, more than four hundred. Many served for only the minimum enlistment of thirty days or for only a few months before enlisting — or taking jobs as civilians — in one of the military services or simply returning home to their regular jobs. Some volunteers were reassigned to help establish or maintain strength at other bases.

**Frederick K. Creasey**

*Frederick K. Creasey of Charleston, West Virginia, became CAP pilot number 5-4-30 on December 1, 1941. The "5" stood for the Fifth Service Command, of which West Virginia was part, the "4" meant the state was the fourth in the Command, and the "30" placed Creasey as being the thirtieth Mountain State pilot to enlist. Creasey had been a dedicated flyer for a long time. He first took flight instruction at the Charleston Seaplane Base, and then had more lessons at Wertz Field, where he soloed in a J-2 Piper Cub. With six friends he established the "Charleston Flyers" and became one of the co-owners of a Luscombe all-metal monoplane that cost $1,400, each man putting up two hundred dollars:*

To start with I served with the Charleston squadron based at the old Wertz Field. After I'd flown several simulated lost plane searches, my Charleston squadron commander, David M. Giltinan, asked me to consider serving at Atlantic City. I took a leave of absence from my job at Owens-Illinois Glass Company and arrived together with my Charleston squadron mate, Omar Crim, at Bader Field on May 10, 1942. When I reported to Major Farr, his first comment to an aide was, "Well, he does have shoes on!"

Along with most of the other flight personnel, I stayed at the Cosmopolitan Hotel on the boardwalk at the south end of downtown. I paid two dollars a day for the evening meal and miscellaneous services. Except for the men on duty, we all ate dinner together every evening. We wore full uniforms, were carefully groomed, and were most military in every way. The non-flight personnel — the men and women who maintained the planes, operated the radio and teletype equipment, maintained the plotting boards, handled the myriad administrative details, and guarded the base — were welcome to have joined us if they wished, but usually did not. Many were from Atlantic City or nearby towns up and down the coast and simply went home to their families when their work day was done.

We were responsible for patrolling the area from New York harbor to Delaware Bay. Mostly we flew three-hour patrols twice a day — one going out at dawn, another returning at dusk. We occasionally ran short of flight personnel, and I might fly as much as nine hours a day. At first we flew without any days off. Later on as more pilots and observers arrived, we got some breaks. I got up very early to walk downtown for breakfast. Some fellows could fly on an empty stomach, but I couldn't. After breakfast I walked across the bridge from downtown to Bader Field, a fifteen-minute hike. Few of us owned cars and this was virtually our only exercise.

Ben Berger, a pilot from Denver, Colorado, was killed on Easter Sunday, 1943, while practicing landings at Bader Field. Twenty minutes earlier he had been playing Ping-Pong (courtesy Frederick W. Creasey).

Like most newly-arrived pilots, I served a "breaking-in" period as co-pilot and flight observer, which meant handling the radio and keeping a sharp watch for survivors of sunken ships, floating debris, suspicious small craft, drifting mines, and — most crucial of all — scanning the water for any tell-tale signs of enemy U-boats. A periscope wake was hard to see, especially if there were any whitecaps, so we seldom cruised at more than five hundred feet, and often, in bad weather, we flew at even lower altitudes. I soon was flying as pilot-in-command with the newer arrivals as co-pilots.

I remember that we had at least three planes go "into the drink," but fortunately no lives were lost. The base's only fatal accident happened on Easter Sunday, April 25, 1943 at the base itself. Ben Berger, a pilot from Denver, Colorado and I were playing Ping-Pong when a deep voice from the ready room squawk box told Berger to go out and shoot some landings and build up his time on our low-wing Bellanca. Twenty minutes later, Berger crashed into a bridge abutment and was killed. I'll never forget losing him that suddenly. One minute we were together having fun, the next, he was gone.

Frederick and Virginia Creasey of Charleston, West Virginia. He flew the second highest total patrol hours of any Atlantic City pilot and she was one of the teletype operators (courtesy Frederick K. Creasey).

Among my several forced landings, luckily none in the water, was one that was particularly memorable. While about eleven miles off Beach Haven, some thirty miles northeast of Atlantic City, I noticed the oil pressure in our Waco dropping fast. I turned for shore immediately and made a lucky landing on a small island at the mouth of Great Bay Inlet. What made it so dicey was that I'd forgotten to jettison our two-hundred pound depth charge, and came in with it still hanging from the plane. To top it off, once we were out of the plane and walking along the beach, here came two Coast Guardsmen on patrol with a huge dog.* As we approached one another, one of the Coast Guardsmen shouted, "Don't come any closer! This dog will kill you. He makes no noise, he just kills!!" We quickly identified ourselves and got back to our base without further incident.

* In 1943, about 24,000 Coast Guardsmen were involved in beach patrols covering 3,700 miles of Atlantic, Gulf, and Pacific coasts. About 2,000 dogs, mostly German shepherds, Doberman pinschers, and Airedales, were used before they were phased out in favor of horse-mounted beach patrols. See *Guardians of the Sea*, Robert E. Johnson, Naval Institute Press, 1987.

About a year after I arrived in Atlantic City, my wife Virginia joined me and became one of the base teletype operators, for which she was paid five dollars a day (I earned eight dollars a day). She served until the base closed, then returned to her job in Charleston, while I moved on with various other base personnel to Hadley Field from which we flew night-time missions for the radar and searchlight batteries ringing New York City. In March 1944, I was sent to the Suffolk Army Air Base on Long Island to tow sleeve targets.

I was the first of our group to actually pull a target. Another pilot had been scheduled for the first flight, but excessive vibration while he was releasing the target caused him to bring the plane back in. When I took it up, I found that if I put the plane into a real steep turn before my winch operator let out the target there wasn't any vibration. I don't know why, but it worked. Perhaps the addition of the heavy winch and cable had thrown off the plane's balance. I pulled targets only ten days, and then was released from the CAP and went into the Air Corps as an instructor. Of my two years with the CAP, I'm proudest of the fact that at Atlantic City I flew 987:15 hours of patrol missions — second highest of anyone there — and thereby became an Air Medal winner.

## Charles E. Seiferd

*Charles E. Seiferd, a pilot-observer from Springfield, Missouri, served at the Atlantic City base from April 14, 1943 to August 31, 1943 and also won the Air Medal. He arrived less than two weeks before Ben Berger was killed:*

On the days that we weren't flying dawn patrol, we were required to be at the airport pretty early and I was there, scheduled to take an afternoon patrol. Ben invited me to go up with him. Although I really wanted some flight time in the Bellanca, for some reason I declined. The official cause of the accident was never determined, but I believe Ben dropped too low in the flight pattern and went into a bridge piling while trying to pull up.

I learned to fly in the Civilian Pilot Training program (CPTP), and for a time before the war I was a member of a Springfield flying club. Four of us owned a J-3 Cub, NC 31081. After Pearl Harbor, the government began appropriating such planes for use as Air Corps trainers. We didn't have an option. We *had* to sell it. I was the manager of radio stations KWTO-KGBX and married but thought it would be a good thing to join the CAP, so I did. When I first got to Atlantic City I stayed in the Haddon Hall Hotel, then when my wife joined me, we took an apartment in Chelsea Village, a complex for married personnel. She went to work for a radio station whose call letters I can't recall right now.

I was there a little over four months but logged 202:5 hours of patrol time, which without my knowledge turned out to be just enough to earn me the Air Medal. I don't recall many people by name, but I remember our commanding officer, Wynant Farr, because of his pronounced Brooklyn accent, saying things like the "choiping boids" and all that. Since I was from the south — look at a map and you'll see that Springfield, Missouri is farther south than Richmond, Virginia — maybe every New York accent sounded that way to me.

What I remember best is how people seemed to know so little about the nearness of war to our shores. There were some sunken ships right off the coast. We used the hulks as navigational check points. But the local people didn't seem to notice. When the base closed, I drove to Texas to be checked out as a candidate civilian flight instructor for the Air Corps. But they didn't need me and I was discharged and returned to Springfield. I got back into the radio business, starting my own station — call letters KICK — which I named "Kickapoo Prairie Broadcasting." For some time, I flew for fun now and then, but I never owned a plane. I have four sons, one of them a champion aerobatics pilot. He owns a Pitts Special and gives me a ride sometimes. I still love it.

\* \* \*

In mid-summer of 1942 the base scored its first strike against a German U-boat. As summarized many years later in the January 1984 "Civil Air Patrol News," the results were uncertain (and remain so to this day):

> On July 11, 1942, when another aircraft sighted a sub but had to return to base for fuel, pilot John Haggin and observer Wynant Farr sped to the area, flying 300 feet above the white caps. Tracking the oil trail gleaming in the sun, they played a waiting game, stalking the U-boat until it came up to periscope depth. Haggin put the aircraft into a shallow dive, dropping the first charge just in front of the sub. Shock waves buffeted the Widgeon as it curved for a second run and they saw large quantities of oil bubbling up. The second charge brought debris to the surface and Civil Air Patrol Coastal Patrol Base No. 1 had damaged its first sub, if not sunk it.

Within a few days of the July encounter, base commander Farr and pilot Haggin received the following letter from CAP national commander Earle Johnson:

> The action taken off Atlantic City the other day was the most pleasant happening that has occurred since the Civil Air Patrol was organized. It made everyone at Headquarters very happy. I took your letter to General Arnold and he in turn read it to the Senate Appro-

priations Committee in an off-the-record session. It pleased him immensely. We are going to see if something can be done to secure some sort of a medal for you both. From the standpoint of the morale of the whole organization, it is too bad that an incident of this kind cannot be publicized, but some day the story will be told and the general public will realize at that time what a great job you and all the other members of the Civil Air Patrol on task forces are doing.

For a time, the government kept Coastal Patrol efforts relatively secret from the public — or at least tried to. In the LIFE magazine photo-story for April 27, 1942, "The Civil Air Patrol: America's Private Pilots Are Mobilized for War," the Coastal Patrol was the only CAP activity *not* listed. That extra responsibility might easily have been surmised: the caption under a photo of flight personnel racing to their planes to begin an early morning patrol referred to a "city on the Atlantic," and the New Jersey resort town's skyline was clearly prominent in the background. LIFE told its readers:

> Today more than a third of the nation's 100,000 civilian pilots are at war on the home front. They are the Civil Air Patrol, composed of the men and women who flew for fun in the days of peace. As many of them are too old to pilot fighting planes, they are actively experimenting as the third arm of U.S. air power. Flying their own planes, they are carrying vital freight, transporting military officials, testing spotter networks, towing targets for anti-aircraft units, patrolling defense area reservoirs, forests and barrens.

## Luverne A. Kraemer

*Luverne A. Kraemer, from Deadwood, South Dakota, was both a pilot and a mechanic and joined the CAP just after Pearl Harbor. He spent all his spare time around airplanes. After working a late afternoon shift at the Homestake Mining Company (4:30 to 11:30 p.m.), he would rise early the next morning and go to the local airport to work in the shop until his next shift at the mining company. In March 1942 he went to Wichita, Kansas to help build B-29s for Boeing. Three months later he had a pilot's license, and in April 1943 he volunteered for the coastal patrol in Atlantic City. Today, at eighty, Kraemer has his own airstrip and "flies every day the weather permits":*

At first I rented a house, but then my wife quit her job with Beechcraft, also in Wichita, and we found an apartment in Atlantic City. By mid-1943 the German submarines had been chased so far out into the ocean that I never saw one. We mostly escorted convoys or individual ships from Cape May to New York harbor. We'd go out about twenty-five miles, find a ship, then circle round, from time to time reporting to the base where we were. I recall a really scary experience one morning when the ocean was kind of glassy smooth, there was no wind, and the ceiling was so low the light was funny. Suddenly I saw a ship that looked like it was in the sky. The sea and sky were so indistinguishable I'd lost all sense of the horizon and was probably in a shallow dive without knowing it. It has scared me more in retrospect than at the time.

Luverne A. Kraemer and an unidentifed enlisted man hold a one-hundred pound demolition bomb. Though unarmed and unlikely to explode if dropped, such a bomb demanded their respect (courtesy Luverne A. Kraemer).

When I returned from dawn patrols, I didn't sit around waiting for something to do. I sought Major Farr's permission to work in the shop, and he said okay. Rudy Chalow was the chief of maintenance, and I noticed he always had planes in the shop, usually two or three at a time. He was pleased with any help he could get, but I'd had a couple of years experience, and that was even better. Besides that, there was always some class to attend, in things like Morse Code, first-aid, military courtesy, and such. Morse Code and I definitely did *not* get along. The only time we used it, and that was very infrequently, was to read a message from a ship. We also had to drill and do calisthenics, which the older guys hated. Major Farr was a go-getter, and when he said to go do something you did it! But he was okay. I liked him. Nobody liked the red shoulder boards, or epaulets, we wore on our uniforms. On any stroll along Atlantic City's famous Boardwalk, we took many a smart-aleck comment about maybe being Russians or Chinese. We got to a point where we didn't want to go out. Some people removed their epaulets in order to look like Air Corps men or simply went out in civvies. When the base closed, I went down to Maryland to tow targets for a while, then came back up to New Jersey* and did more of the same. After I became a civilian again in 1945 I held some jobs in aviation then was a fixed base operator here in Deadwood for twenty-seven years. I believe there's nothing like flying, and I can't wait to get out of bed every morning and get to it!

\* \* \*

The first issue of "Plane Stuff," a mimeographed base newsletter, appeared August 8, 1942. The lead news was that military ranks would soon become effective and should make "living with the Army a great deal more pleasant," since Air Corps and Civil Air Patrol personnel would need to recognize and to salute each other as two equal services. Gossipy "personals," an admonition to personnel to stay healthy by regular exercise, and some suggestions from the maintenance department to guard against engine, propeller, and leading edge wear by following proper procedures were among the other features:

> When an aircraft is stationary, a quick advance of the throttle causes a small whirlpool or tornado to form directly under the engine. This sucks dust and small cinders up into the air intake and moving parts of the engines causing considerable wear. When "revving up," pour the coal to her at least as slowly, if not slower, than you would on a normal take-off.... Do not be in too great a hurry to follow your lead ship into the air. Allow time for the dust and small pebbles to settle.

Half a year later, "Plane Stuff" had become five times longer, with editorials by the commanding officer — "The Farr Corner" — complete reporting of important base activity, and cartoons. In the March 6, 1943 issue, recalling the base's first patrol, Major Farr reminisced about the early days and commended his staff for its excellent performance despite numerous hardships.

---

\* Tow Target Unit #1 began flying out of Hadley Field, New Brunswick, New Jersey on January 3, 1944. Twenty-nine Atlantic City base members served there: commanding officer, Wynant Farr; operations officer, Allen Muthig; intelligence officer, Frank Schweinfest; pilots and observers Reuben Babcock III, Omar W. Crim, Frederick K. Creasey, Randall M. Custer, Ray R. Fisher, Robert A. Hogue, Russell R. Johnson, John F. Lankalis, Jack T. Martin, Asa L. Miller, Robert E. Stephenson, and Earle B. Wilkinson; and fourteen mechanics and other personnel.

## Marilou Crescenzo

*Marilou Crescenzo met her future husband, Floyd E. Eggenweiler, at the Atlantic City base, although they weren't married until the base had closed and they had been transferred elsewhere. Born and raised in Atlantic City, Crescenzo and her friend Helen Klimek were still students at the New Jersey College of Commerce when Gill Robb Wilson's private secretary recruited them for jobs at the base. Within months Miss Crescenzo became Master Sergeant Crescenzo and took charge of the office. In a 1984 interview by Colonel Lester E. Hopper, CAP National Historian, she remembered the first arrivals:*

The base newsletter, "Plane Stuff," was a pleasant source of coastal patrol and general war news, personal gossip, and corny humor (source Hopper collection).

The men came in on the fourth, feeling almost like they were on a lark. And on the fifth, they were taken out to see the routes that they would be patrolling, from the mouth of New York Harbor down to the mouth of the Delaware. That was the end of feeling like it was a lark, because the *Gulf Pride* had been torpedoed the night before, and the men looked down on debris, floating bodies, life jackets, this horrible oil slick — it was a very sobering experience for all of them.... Most of the men that came in, I think, were very patriotic. Most of them were over age for the draft, but some were draftable. They were well-to-do men. They had nothing whatever to gain from being there, and still they came in with their planes and put in long hours, and I always admired them terrifically for it.

Atlantic City Airport at that time was way past its prime. The three hangars were three big tin buildings that had originally been put up for the annual new car shows. Before the big convention hall was built in Atlantic City, they used to throw these metal buildings up on the beach to show the new cars, and they had been put out at the airport as hangars. We always said that we had the only airport in existence where every time the wind blew we'd holler, "get the planes *out* of the hangar!"

Marilou Crescenzo, left, with her friend, Helen Klimek, seated beside her in a group photograph taken August 31, 1943. Both reported to Frances R. Glassman, tech section head (Hopper Collection).

Crescenzo found the base an exciting place to work. When an Army plane crashed and burned on the runway, ground crewmen rushed out with fire-fighting equipment and foamed down the ship. After they stopped, the fire flared up again and this time, as the tracer bullets began to fly, Crescenzo hid under the tail of another aircraft for shelter. Some of her other memories are less frightening and more humorous:

> Our national operations officer, Colonel Blee, had been a balloon pilot or a balloon observer in World War I, and one day a Navy blimp came over in the middle of a horrible rainstorm. Colonel Blee declared, "That blimp's in trouble. I'm an old blimp man. I know that blimp's in trouble." So everyone went out to grab landing ropes to get the blimp down in the storm. A fellow named Wallace, who was the man who trained everybody in Morse Code and things like that went out and as he was watching the blimp's blinker light, Colonel Blee asked him, "What are they saying?" Wallace replied, "They say, why are all you damn fools standing out in the rain?"

Then there was another time when Rudie Chalow and my future husband Floyd Eggenweiler (we called him "Eggie") went in the drink after going out to practice bombing a sunken ship. The plane belonged to Al Muthig, who was our operations officer, Wynant Farr's buddy, and my pet. It was a beautifully maintained Waco, and he was very fussy about it. The navigation lights stayed on for two days even under water. The fellows would fly over it and they could see the navigation lights, and Muthig kept saying, "My plane's still in operation. I should still be getting paid for it" (they got so much for every hour of operation). He'd say, "It's down there. You can see it. I should be getting money." He was really funny about it....

The base tower operator was Annette ("Ann") Ackerman, another Atlantic City girl. Ann was a beautiful girl. She looked sort of like Rita Hayworth. She was absolutely gorgeous, and one of the coolest characters you ever heard in your life. I believe Johnny Haggin's wife was also a tower operator, but the girl I remember particularly is Ann Ackerman. She was quite well known by everyone flying up and down the coast... she kept her head so beautifully in any sort of emergency. We had planes ditching, we had planes cracking up on the beach, and Annie's voice would come over so calmly, "Give your position, please. Send in the clear." And it just calmed the men down, just to hear her, you know.*

When we were relocated to Hadley Field as Tow Target Unit #1, our men shared a barracks at Camp Kilmer with a detachment of U.S. Rangers in training there. They were rough and tough fellows who blackened their faces with lamp black, and carried hunting knives in their boots. One night as they were having their evening's entertainment attacking each other with their knives and throwing each other across the cots at one end of the barracks, our Lieutenant _____ came walking back from the latrine in his robin's egg blue pajamas, and a robin's egg blue robe with white tassels. Lieutenant _____ was always a perfect gentleman and never under any circumstances relaxed his high standards. As he went past the Rangers, he very courteously bid them, "Good evening, gentlemen. Good evening." I'm told that you never saw such shocked faces in your life as those Rangers had at the sight of this apparition strolling by!

Not long after we got there, Colonel Blee flew into Hadley with our new commanding officer, a fellow from Florida named Gresham. The runway is very short, and one of Gresham's pilots flipped the plane

---

* Of the twenty-one bases, Atlantic City had the second highest number of men (thirteen) who experienced forced ocean landings. They were Jack E. Bagon, L. D. Binder, R. Binder, Rudy Chalow, Thomas C. Eastman, Floyd E. Eggenweiler, Wynant Farr, J. P. Knox, Clifford Poley, Tom J. Sanschagrin, William A. Scott, William O. Smith, and Robert E. Stephenson. Source: *Civil Air Patrol Historical Monograph Number One, "Duck Club,"* by Colonel Lester E. Hopper, 1984.

over in landing. Fortunately, no one was hurt, and it turned out to be pretty funny. Here's this plane lying on its back, the wings out flat on the ground, and the door opens. Colonel Blee is a very dignified man, so when he gets out, he very carefully adjusts his hat, brushes off his uniform, and with great aplomb steps out of the airplane and walks right down the wing, crunch, crunch, crunch, crunch. I guess he figured it was already damaged, so what the heck.

\* \* \*

The final issue of "Plane Stuff," August 29, 1943, contained a great many fond good-byes and congratulations, including these kind words for the local citizenry:

> In our final farewell it is not at all improper that we say to Atlantic City and its people with whom we have associated for eighteen months "You are swell folks. You made our stay most pleasant. We sincerely trust that when we come back on a visit very soon after the conclusion of this world wide unpleasantness that we can more fully enjoy the hospitality which was extended to us, but which, through duty's tour was denied us. May Gracious Providence abide with you."

Notwithstanding this kind acknowledgment, not many resort residents even knew the Civil Air Patrol existed. How could fewer than a hundred men and women with red epaulets possibly stand out among tens of thousands of soldiers sent there to prepare for overseas duty? The Army Air Corps leased major hotels and converted them to barracks — among them the Shelbourne, Traymore, Breakers, Brighton, and St. Dennis. Lobbies, dining rooms, and halls were stripped of rugs, carpets, draperies and other adornments, and bedroom furniture was replaced with standard Army issue. Atlantic City's "Convention Hall," large enough to have been host to the world's first indoor football game, was regularly used for mass calisthenics. Between 1942 and 1945, more than 400,000 trainees passed through the building. While such military occupation was a financial blessing for the city, the handful of Civil Air Patrol personnel were just a part of the crowd.

## Chester F. Low

*Chester F. Low, born in New York City, joined the Royal Canadian Air Force (RCAF) in 1941, and despite the poor eyesight that should have disqualified him, stayed there a year, mostly in the Chatham, New Brunswick air observer school. When the medical examiner's oversight was discovered, Low was grounded. Given the choice of staying in the RCAF in a non-flying role or resigning and returning home — which as a United States citizen he could do*

— *he came back home. Unable to satisfy Air Corps visual acuity tests, Low, at the tender age of eighteen, joined the coastal patrol at Atlantic City in October 1942 and served as an observer until the end of that year:*

I was bitterly disappointed that I was not in combat. I was young and full of piss and vinegar and wanted action. In my disappointment, I may have acted somewhat patronizing toward the coastal patrol even though I knew they were making a good job of their assignment. In other ways, I also felt a bit out of place. I'd had an excellent education in the then first-rate New York public school system and some of the pilots seemed to me to be ill-educated and not even very nice. Even now I think of my three months at Atlantic City as an unhappy hiatus in a "safe harbor," a reaction that was probably sheer disgust at being "out of the real war" and had nothing to do with the coastal patrol. In my youthful desire to fight, I was impatient to do something that seemed more demanding. But then came the biggest machination of my life — getting into the Army Air Corps under false pretenses: I obtained and memorized the basic 20-20, 20-30, and 20-40 eye-test charts and located an *Ishihara* test for color blindness at an optical shop in Manhattan when even the Air Corps no longer could find any. It cost fourteen dollars. The *Ishihara* was developed at the University of Tokyo in the 1930s, and still remains the most exact test of color blindness. That's how I passed the Army Air Corps tests and entered the Air Cadet program in January 1943. I completed that training as a navigator and served in the Pacific Theater of Operations. When I finally "came clean," a flight surgeon gave me an honest eye test, then a waiver to continue flying with glasses.

## Irwin D. Minter

*Irwin D. Minter was born in Minneapolis, Minnesota in 1924 and was the youngest pilot at the Atlantic City base. Fascinated with aviation and airplanes, as a teenager he began bicycling to Wold-Chamberlain Field where, in exchange for washing and cleaning planes, he got free flying lessons. He earned his pilot's license at fifteen, and flew all of his life. His widow, Jean Minter, speaks of the many highlights in his long career in aviation:*

From the time Irwin was a small boy, he loved aviation. After he had his license he flew at every opportunity, and did everything from barnstorming to crop dusting. By 1942 he was a co-pilot in Alaska for Northwest Airlines, then for a time was a flight instructor for Parks Air College in St. Louis. He served with the coastal patrol in Atlantic City from June 25, 1942 until October 10, 1942. In that short time he flew enough patrols to win the Air Medal. He once reported seeing a submarine that was later sunk by the military. One of his favorite memories of Atlantic City was going to the Steel Pier to hear the big-name bands, one of them being Glenn Miller's.

In his early teens Irwin D. Minter of Minneapolis, Minnesota, washed planes in return for flying lessons. He was a pilot all his life (courtesy Jean Minter).

After Irwin left the coastal patrol, he became an Air Transport Command pilot, flying across the Himalayas between Burma and China. He took part in the evacuation of Merrill's Marauders and in the liberation of Shanghai from the Japanese. When he returned to civilian life he continued flying in the Air Force Reserve while attending the University of Minnesota. Recalled during the Korean war, he served in a Special Air Missions group until 1952, then left the Air Force and founded a company that built houses and apartment complexes throughout the state. He loved flying to them in his twin-engine Cessna 310.

### Gustavus ("Gus") S. Simpson, Jr.

*Gus Simpson, Jr., from Margate, New Jersey, was a 22-year-old engineering student enrolled in the ROTC, and looking forward to graduating and getting his second lieutenant's bars. Looking for a summer job, he "jumped at the chance" when he heard the coastal patrol wanted someone knowledgeable about weapons and military behavior. For five dollars a day he became a base guard, a weapons instructor, and a military customs advisor, happy to work seven days a week:*

I was about as low on the totem pole as one could get. Since I was only there for two months in the summer of 1942, I didn't make many social connections with the people at the base, but I got to know a few pilots by name. One was Joseph H. Dotterweich, a pharmacist from Buffalo, New York. He was great. He took me up in his plane, and even let me fly it, but only once, because you can't imagine the mess I caused! No matter, Joe stayed friendly and took me flying again, but he did the piloting. I was just as happy.

Another pilot, whose name I just can't recall, wanted to train me as his bombardier. Was I ever excited when he entered the armory one day and said, "Let's go!" En route to the target, a sunken tanker not far offshore, he explained that he'd dive and drop a one-hundred pound practice bomb (the weight of which was mostly sand) that would splatter green dye where it exploded. He said he'd tell me when to pull the bomb release. Then, at about a thousand feet, he put his beautiful Stinson Voyager into a dive, and seconds later yelled, "Pull!" The bomb separated from the plane, but so did the bomb release mechanism — I had pulled the darned thing completely away from the airframe! What a mess. My career as a bombardier was over.

There wasn't much to guard duty. The perimeter of the field was large, much of it delineated by water, and thus requiring no fences. Certain unkind souls called our watery surrounds "swamps," but we natives knew them as the "meadows." There may have been a fence along Albany Avenue, but I don't recall a guarded main gate or anything like that except that the Air Corps guarded its part of the field, and generally disdained our operation. During the day, I sometimes served as a substitute O.D. since that allowed the assigned O.D. to fly or do something else worthwhile. All "officer of the day" meant was carrying a holstered sidearm — in my opinion, a silly task perhaps intended to make the coastal patrol seem more "military."

The most tragic thing that happened while I was there concerned a popular young pilot, only slightly older than myself. One day when I had charge of the armory he came in and offered to relieve me while I went outside for a smoke. Since I knew him, and I knew Major Farr liked him, I saw no reason not to let him take over. I was outside the hangar watching our planes take off on patrol when I heard a shot. I ran back inside and found him with a bullet wound in his temple. He died on the way to the hospital. It was so sad. He was well liked and good looking. Why did he do it?

I know the coastal patrol was ill-regarded by some people, but to me all those men were outstanding. Many would have been Air Corps pilots but for needing glasses, or being color-blind, or being too old. For these men, the coastal patrol was a blessing. They could fly, do needed work, and maintain a high degree of self-respect. It was as dedicated a group of Americans as I later found on active duty as an Air Corps officer during the final years of the war.

**Carl M. Kloth**

*Carl M. Kloth was an aircraft mechanic at Atlantic City from March 1942 until March the following year. He became involved in the coastal patrol in an unusual way. The co-owner of an aircraft school he had attended called to see if he might want "two or three weeks of aircraft work" for which he would receive expenses "eventually, but not right away." He agreed, and within the week was told to be at the Cleveland Airport with one hundred dollars and not more than sixty pounds of tools and forty pounds of clothes. With four others, he boarded a Stinson Reliant without even knowing where he was headed. En route, he recognized Pittsburgh and the Allegheny Mountains but after landing could only guess that they were somewhere on the East Coast:*

We were whisked from the airport to a small hotel and interviewed. The man said they'd be glad for me to work for them, and drove me to a rooming house. By now it was suppertime, and I went out to dinner with some other fellows. Next morning, we were driven to a little restaurant for breakfast, and then to the airport where yet another man interviewed me. He wanted to know what CAP group I had joined back home, and when I said, "What's the CAP?" he was really floored. I was enlisted in the CAP post-haste and the rest of the day was spent getting acquainted with the aircraft maintenance crew and learning the routine for fueling and daily inspections of the aircraft.

My second day was more organized. I met Rudy Chalow, who was in charge of maintenance, and Albert Hildredth, who would be my partner. Al and I were to do the major repair work and oversee other work. I left my rooming house that night and moved into a private home with Al and Rudy. The house belonged to an elderly widow who had donated rooms in response to a Red Cross request. I lived there the whole year I was in Atlantic City. We ate at nearby restaurants like the "Kent" on Atlantic Avenue.

A fourth person in our group, Philip Catona, came from Hammonton, New Jersey, and took care of aircraft radio repairs. The base was brand new when I joined, but as time went by more planes and flight crews arrived, and local men and women were enlisted as our stock clerks, fuel handlers, parts cleaners, and office workers. A pair of brothers from Margate, New Jersey, William and Robert Datz, joined us as aircraft mechanics.

After a time, apparently to make the coastal patrol seem more closely affiliated with the armed forces, someone decided to give us ranks and put us into uniforms. Rudy was made a second lieutenant, Phil a master sergeant, Al and I staff sergeants, and the Datz brothers buck sergeants. We were ordered to the quartermaster supply depot to draw uniforms appropriate to our ranks. We got two caps, two pairs of pants, two ties, and two shirts. After a tailor added the red epaulets to the shirts, we were issued all the appropriate insignia and told where to sew it on. Did we look neat!

Wynant Farr, second from left, Howard Sterne, fourth from left, and others pause to study a coastal map. The "Tommy Gun" at Sterne's right shoulder was probably only for the photographer's benefit (courtesy Richard G. Sterne).

Monday evening, Rudy, Phil, and I headed for our favorite restaurant for dinner. Just outside we were nabbed by a bunch of MPs: not only had we failed to salute a passing officer, but why was this officer, meaning Rudy, fraternizing with lowly noncoms, and what the hell were the red epaulets, anyway? We were arrested and put in the brig and it took several hours to win release. This happened one or two more times, until word got around to the MPs to let the guys with the red epaulets alone. When cold weather came we had some more trouble, because we hadn't been issued winter overcoats, and had to wear whatever civilian coats we had over our uniforms.

I particularly remember many of the pilots and their planes. When I first arrived at Atlantic City, we had two Grumman Widgeon amphibians, one owned by Tom Eastman, the other by Bill Zelcer. There was also Karl Fischer's low-wing Bellanca, Wynant Farr's and Howard Sterne's Ranger-powered Fairchild 24s, and half a dozen Stinson Voyagers. Eastman usually flew his Widgeon himself, while Zelcer let his son-in-law fly his. Sometimes when the son-in-law flew mornings, on his return he'd buzz the Boardwalk and chase the early bathers off the beach. Once or twice he also "forgot" to lower his wheels and made belly landings. We'd assemble all hands, tip the plane up on its nose, and hold it there while the landing gear was cranked down. The gravel runways did a pretty good sandpaper job on the bottom of the hull and the floats.

In March 1943 I received my draft board notice to report to the reception center in Cleveland. After failing to pass the physical, I called Atlantic City to see if they wanted me back. I was told things had slowed so much I wasn't needed. I wasn't really sorry to hear that. When I had first joined everyone pitched in together to solve problems and finish jobs. The pilots, observers, mechanics, and linemen all banded together to do what was needed. As soon as uniforms and ranks became the order of the day, flight crews no longer fraternized so closely with mechanics and ground crews. Something was definitely lost, and our job wasn't as much fun as before.

**Robert J. Datz**

*The Datz brothers, William A. and Robert J., studied diesel engineering at a school in Philadelphia, but halfway to their graduation the school went bankrupt and they were left seeking an alternative. They enrolled at the Rising Sun School of Aeronautics, also in Philadelphia, and there got their Aircraft and Engine (A&E) mechanic's licenses. Aware that the CAP was seeking mechanics, they joined up almost immediately as CAP members #2-2-1018 and CAP # 2-2-1019 on March 23, 1942. They commuted from home to the Atlantic City base daily. William Datz died a few years ago on the West Coast, but Robert Datz talks about some of his own experiences:*

I reported to the base as a licensed A&E mechanic and mostly worked on our two Grumman Widgeons. The Widgeon was a beautiful two-engine amphibian that could carry a 325-pound depth charge effortlessly. Since I was right out of school and only twenty, I was glad to have an older more experienced mechanic by the name of Victor Eble "coach" me through my first days. Victor was a small, very pleasant man, but he may have been a German national, and one day he just was no longer there. The Widgeon was easy to work on except for one thing: If you didn't have a factory-supplied special wrench, one of the engine's spark plugs could not be reached without removing the carburetor, a time consuming task to say the least. I still remember that. I think the depth charge on the Grumman was hung between the hull and the starboard engine, but after more than fifty years, you know, details can escape you. The mounts were installed by Air Corps armorers. I remember flying up to Roosevelt Field once or twice to work on some CAP float planes, and that was a nice change of pace.

Sometime in the fall of 1942, Congress lowered the draft age from twenty to eighteen, and some of our fellows started to get drafted. But pretty soon a deal was cut whereby if we enrolled in the Air Corps Reserve we would be deferred for as long as the CAP needed us. So I signed up. I wasn't even twenty-one yet and my mother had to sign certain papers, too. When the base closed I went to Hadley Field for a time with the tow target unit, but in early 1944 I was called to active duty with the Air Corps. After a year's extra training, I ended up with the 30th Bomb Group in the Pacific, working on B-24s. I went in as a private, and had just made corporal, when I was appointed crew chief over a bunch of mostly staff and technical sergeants. By then, the end of the war was near and nobody cared much about rank.

## Ray C. Custer

*Ray C. Custer was a 21-year-old pilot from Pittsburgh, Pennsylvania whose service at Atlantic City began just two months before coastal patrol activity ended. After learning to fly on a Taylor Cub (predecessor of the better-known Piper Cub) and soloing at eighteen, he tried to join the Air Corps. When he was rejected because of a dental problem, he took a job at Westinghouse Electric in East Pittsburgh. In 1943 the commanding officer of Pittsburgh's CAP squadron suggested that he go to Atlantic City, and he did.*

One of my first assignments was flying as Tom Eastman's flight observer in his Grumman Widgeon. He was much older than me, and a great guy. We carried a depth charge on every mission, but never dropped it — everything had quieted down by this time, and all we ever saw were some whales. Tom always landed the Widgeon on the field, rather than on the brackish water of the surrounding bay. Its salt content would have been very corrosive. I was up about three hours every day, and my only "hairy" experience was returning to base once in a Waco, trying to arrive before fog blotted out the field. When the fog grew thicker and thicker, we flew lower and lower, eventually dropping down to a hundred feet or so. When we should've seen the sandy beach but still saw only water, I became a little concerned. After four or five minutes, however, we recognized some landmarks and realized that we were flying down Great Bay somewhere north of Atlantic City. After that, getting back to base was easy. We didn't enjoy today's avionics, so our navigation was only by compass and wristwatch, with a few half-sunken ships for check points.

I was single at the time, and had a room in a motel close enough to walk to the field every morning. I wasn't at the base long enough to form close friendships and I don't remember too many people. I do recall that once back in Pittsburgh my father was visited by two FBI agents. A nasty neighbor had seen me at home in my coastal patrol uniform and had reported me for wearing an Air Corps uniform when he knew I was not in the Air Corps. Nothing came of it.

## John F. Lankalis

*John F. Lankalis, one of the base pilots, was born in 1916 in a small coal-mining town in Pennsylvania, a first-generation American of Lithuanian descent. Liking speed, he not only learned to fly as a teenager, but became a serious bobsledder who on weekends drove to Lake Placid, New York to pursue the sport. When he reported for active duty with the coastal patrol on July 26, 1942 — to serve until August 31, 1943 — he was married, had two children, and owned and operated a restaurant. His son, John F. Lankalis, II, with the assistance of his father's sister, Margaret Lankalis Nichols, describes one of his father's close calls:*

After the Atlantic City base closed, some pilots were reassigned to Hadley Field in New Brunswick, New Jersey to tow targets for anti-aircraft gunnery practice. Most of the flying took place over the Atlantic Ocean. One day as it was turning dusk and a snow storm was approaching, a stray shell hit and severed the tow wire connecting the target to my father's plane, and somehow knocked out his navigational equipment. He was now in a snow storm at night over the Atlantic Ocean with no sure way of getting a land bearing.

True to my father's nature he chose a direction and continued flying. By doing so he reckoned that they had a chance, even if a slim one. After several hours of flying, he saw some lights and went to check them out. They came from an airport at Lancaster, Pennsylvania. After landing and getting a good night's sleep, he and his co-pilot next morning found their airplane gassed up and ready to fly. My father was a spirited man who lived his whole life with the same enthusiasm and eagerness he showed as a coastal patrol flyer. He was an extraordinarily brave man and much deserved the Air Medal he received after the war.

Pilot John F. Lankalis and his wife Edith. Lankalis was nearly lost at sea when he became lost in a snow storm (courtesy John F. Lankalis, II).

## Randall M. Custer

*Randall M. Custer earned his pilot's license in 1940 through the CPTP while a student at the University of Cincinnati, and in early 1941, with help from his parents, he bought a Taylorcraft and became a "weekend" pilot. The next year after failing, at six feet and one hundred-twenty pounds, to meet Air Corps weight standards, he chose to serve with the coastal patrol while trying to get heavier. He served at Atlantic City from May 31, 1942 through August 31, 1943 and then in the group that went to Hadley Field to tow targets and fly tracking missions. In 1989, he told the CAP New Jersey Wing historian, Major Gregory F. Weidenfeld, what Bader and Hadley Fields were like:*

> As I recall it, Bader Field had two main runways, a twenty-five hundred foot east-west runway, and a sixteen hundred foot north-south runway, both unpaved. One hangar was in good condition and had a concrete floor. Another one was in rather rundown condition and had only a dirt floor. The field was surrounded on three sides by water, and anyone who wasn't familiar with landing over water had a tendency to come in too high.

At first, we were housed in the Chelsea Hotel on the corner of Morris Avenue and the Boardwalk. We soon learned to avoid strolling the Boardwalk, because it was so swarming with Air Corps recruits that it was just one salute after another, and believe me, your arm got tired! Sometime in the summer or early fall we were moved to the Cosmopolitan Hotel on Atlantic Avenue just south of the monument and traffic circle. The Cosmopolitan was about a block from the beach and we had the whole thing. I was assigned a room with Francis (Fran) Morgan, a pilot from Dunkirk, New York. In the spring of 1943, most of us left the hotel and rented apartments or rooms in the area. I teamed up with Fran and Paul (Deacon) Wallace, a pilot from Anderson, Indiana, in a two-bedroom apartment with a view of the airport. We were there until the coastal patrol ended in August.

Randall M. Custer was six-feet tall but much underweight for the Air Corps (courtesy Randall M. Custer).

During his sixteen months at Bader Field, the twenty-five-year-old Custer flew 719:40 hours as pilot-in-command and approximately 250 hours as an observer. These numbers easily qualified him for one of the coveted Air Medals belatedly awarded in 1948.

As things seemed to wind down in the summer of 1943, the question was what will we do now? Stay on active duty or go home? Most of the base personnel wanted to return home after their service with the coastal patrol, but someone had the idea that we should serve as tow target pilots, only not at Atlantic City. Major Farr himself selected who would give it a try — about twenty-five or thirty of us —

and Hadley Field just outside New Brunswick, New Jersey, and near Camp Kilmer, was chosen as our new base. Someone was dispatched to see what Hadley Field was like, and suffice it to say, that's exactly what they found: a field.

At one time, it had been a small airport used in the air mail service. It was all-grass with ill-defined, short runways and bounded on two sides by wooded sections. There was a hangar across the road on the north side, and an operations office and radio shack next to it. All the planes would be tied down and only those receiving routine maintenance would be housed inside the hangar. The base would need a lot of work. That fall we moved up to the Camp Kilmer Bachelor Officers Quarters and were told that while the Army Corps of Engineers would give us the equipment to fix up the base, we'd have to do the work ourselves. That included bringing in gravel and stone to stabilize the runways and then compacting it with a roller. We all took turns hauling gravel in the Army truck, and I well recall wrestling

The final issue of "Plane Stuff" included this cartoon of a trash bin filled with a sunken submarine, a tattered Nazi flag, and a Hitler-faced rat.

with its eight forward and four reverse gears. Finally, around December, we were officially designated Tow Target Unit #1, although that was something of a misnomer because we did not in fact pull any targets. What we did was to fly tracking missions around the northern New Jersey and New York City areas to provide the anti-aircraft batteries practice in picking up and following us as though they would be firing at an enemy aircraft. We flew daily random patterns throughout the area, a somewhat boring and routine assignment. That spring, we added night missions as well. A single plane would fly over New York City and Long Island between 9 p.m. and midnight at no less than ten thousand feet altitude. This was danger-

Stinson Reliant and un-extended sleeve target. Various tow target units on the east and west coasts were staffed largely by former coastal patrol personnel, several of whom were killed pulling targets (courtesy Frederick K. Creasey).

ous mainly because Hadley Field had no runway, boundary, or landings lights of any kind, and we had to depend strictly on our aircraft landing lights. We finally got several high-intensity flood lights that we placed on either side of the ends of the runways, but we still had the problem of coming in over the pitch-black wooded areas. I flew half a dozen night missions and they were uncomfortable. You didn't dare ever look down because a searchlight could momentarily blind you with potentially fatal results.... In May of 1944, I managed to get into the Cadets (I was still underweight but got a waiver for it) only to have flight surgeons at Keesler Field, Mississippi, discover a hearing problem that effectively busted me out of the program. I went through radio and radar schools, then spent the rest of my Air Corps career at Wright-Patterson in Dayton, my home town.

Established as a ninety-day experiment, the Atlantic City, Rehoboth, and Lantana coastal patrol bases proved their worth almost from the first day. Long before the trial period was completed, the planes and the men and women serving at these three bases had demonstrated their effectiveness at helping to repel the enemy at the nation's shores. Within six months, similar anti-submarine bases had been established all the way from Maine to Mexico and more than three thousand patriotic Americans had volunteered to man them.

---

Base officers, pilots, and observers who served at least one month at CAPCP #1 and who are not elsewhere mentioned in this chapter include: Nels C. Anderson, Mason L. Ashford,* Nathan Bakalar, Edouard W. Ballentine,* Harry Berg, Russell W. Berndt, Robert S. Blythe,* William D. Brown, Edgar B. Cahn, Lorimer F. Cain, Albert R. Chambers, Donald M. Chisholm, Harold E. Cobb, Charles E. Compton, Stanley E. Cortright, Frank Crall, Briggs Cunningham,* Bertram S. Cutler,* Harold S. Davidson, Howard V. C. Davis,* Roloff M. Dewsnap,* Marlin W. Easton,* William G. Eckman, Jr., Frederick O. Fillingham, Adolf K. Fischer,* Richard J. Fleck,* Duane C. Frasier,* Charles H. Gartrell,* James M. Gibson,* Edward F. Gorski, Albert G. Gray, Edmund L. Harvey, Marvin H. Huckins, Lawrence W. Irvin,* Vernon R. Jeffries,* Stewart A. Joyce, Merle C. Keepers,* Jonathon B. Kenworthy, William P. Kilgore, Albert F. Kloer, Robert P. Laible, James H. Laidlaw, Patrick R. Larkin, John M. LeBailly, Jerome S. Leeds, Roy W. Lenck, James R. Lewis, Charles R. Lontz, Frederick J Lyon, Jefferson G. McKee, Dale R. Madsen,* Harold A. Meade,* Theodore H. Merckens, Washington T. Miller,* Edward K. Mills, Jr.,* Martin Mills, Noble D. Mitchell,* Thomas H. Morgan,* Walden W. Morrison, Burton H. Nagel, Paul F. Nagle, Fred V. Nash, Stuart F. Neely, Thomas J. Newbold, Howard T. Okes, Walter J. Orton, Jr.,* Robert C. Owen, Joseph T. Payne,* Charles L. Payton, Emmett Pedley,* John H. Perry, Jr.,* Gino Piermattei,* Arthur R. Pulin, Leon F. Rasczewski, Stanley H. Reaver,* Fred S. Robbins, Frederick V. Rosenberger,* Charles R. Ross, George A. Ruhl,* Hubert H. R. Ryder, William M. Schnell, John K. H. Schuler, George G. Scobie, Harry A. Shubin, Henry J. Sloan,* Peter G. Sloan, Clarence H. Smith, John A. Smith, Walter B. Smith, Winfield R. Smith, William F. Springer, Leslie E. Steen,* Ray L. Stepphens, Edward L. Sterling, Edgar E. Sullivan, Jr., Rex Sullivan,* Jacob L. Sutton, Marion R. Swaney, Robert E. Thomas,* Rolla E. Thompson,* Albert F. Titus,* Robert D. Underwood,* Earl J. Vallen, Richard P. Wallace,* William R. Wallace, Edward F. Walsh, Norman Warren, Henry K. Willis, Jr., and Verner V. Young. Asterisk indicates Air Medal winner.

36  From Maine to Mexico

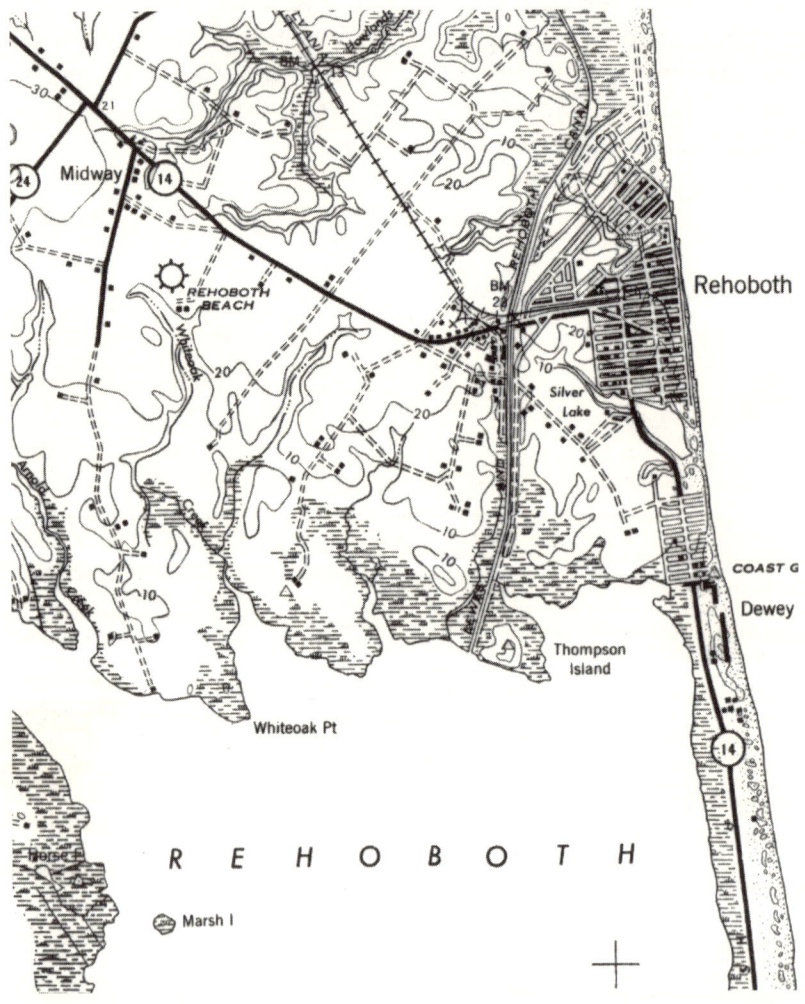

This 1938 U.S. Corps of Engineers map shows the Rehoboth Beach airfield symbol about two miles due west of the beach resort. The coastal patrol seaplane base was at Whiteoak Point on Rehoboth Bay.

# 2
# Rehoboth Beach, Delaware

Though the coastal patrol base at Rehoboth Beach, Delaware was activated the same day as the Atlantic City, New Jersey base — February 28, 1942 — its first patrols went out on March 5, five days sooner than did Atlantic City's. Located roughly half way between the Atlantic City base and another to be established later at Parksley, Virginia, the Rehoboth Beach base was well placed so that its flyers could cover the area north to Cape May, New Jersey, and south to Ocean City, Maryland. Today the town is a bustling summer resort, the small airfield turned into a shopping center and housing development. But for a year and a half in the early 1940s many people along the Delaware coast became used to seeing the coastal patrol's little planes going out to sea each day in all kinds of weather.

The Rehoboth Beach base got its fast start because of Delaware's advanced state of preparedness. Shortly after the attack on Pearl Harbor, the Delaware Wing of the CAP was organized by its first Wing Commander, Holger Hoiriis, assistant to Richard C. DuPont, president of All-American Aviation. Hoiriis devoted his whole attention to CAP work. Allison F. Fleitas was named Wing Adjutant, and Hugh R. Sharp, Jr., became Wing Training and Operations Officer. Through the early days of the CAP, Delaware led the nation in its percentage of pilots enrolled for duty. Courses of instruction were begun, and all members were required to take First Aid. Those unqualified to operate aircraft radios were given a radio course, and studies were required in navigation and meteorology. On January 23, with four squadrons formed and the training program well under way Wing Commander Hoiriis announced that "the Delaware Wing is ready for duty."

### Roland W. ("Tom") O'Day

*Tom O'Day was born in 1912 near Denton in Queen County, Maryland, then moved to Delaware with his parents when he was five. His first taste of flying came in 1931 when he sold rides for a barnstormer who let him fly a little on their way from town to town. Later, he took flying lessons in a Porterfield and bought a J-3 Cub, planning to be a commercial pilot, until his fully grown 5' 4" height finally precluded that possibility. For O'Day, flying with the CAP was an answer to a dream: "Doing what I wanted most to do as well as taking an active part in our nation's defense." An Air Medal winner, O'Day's recall of the base at Rehoboth is exceptional:*

No amount of imagination could have visualized us Rehoboth recruits as semi-military personnel. We were of all sizes and ages — some skinny, others portly, some lame, others wearing thick glasses, and some with hearing problems. Most of us, including for a time one woman, were student or private pilots. Some had commercial and instructor ratings. Many of us had just clawed our way through the great depression, but still believed in our country and wanted to defend it. We all felt that our flying experience could help.

Major Holger Hoiriis, a Norwegian with the distinction of flying the first paying passenger across the Atlantic Ocean,* came down from his job with All American Aviation at Wilmington, Delaware to be our base commander. I had the honor of flying with him once as his observer. He was one of the great "olden-time" pilots and did things differently than today's instructors might suggest. On this flight I recall our dropping down to check the number of a buoy. He simply pushed the stick forward and dove at the thing — no cutting the throttle and losing altitude gradually — and we pulled out practically on the water.

Hugh R. Sharp was our first operations officer and selected our pilots with great care. Considering that we were all untested volunteers, his caution was justified. When Hoiriis died, Sharp became our base commander and Allison F. Fleitas was named operations officer. I became airdrome officer by taking upon myself, with much help from Ralph J. Fidance, another pilot, the task of correcting some of our "didn't have" situations. Because Rehoboth Beach was a summer resort, and all its hotels were closed when we arrived, our first priority was to find

---

* In June 1931 Hoiriis (who answered to the nickname "Hold Your Horses) had flown Otto Hillig of Liberty, New York, from Harbor Grace, Newfoundland to Copenhagen, Denmark where Hoiriis was knighted by King Christian. He would serve at Rehoboth despite a serious kidney ailment that kept him in continual pain. In August 1942 he was promoted to major. The night his men pinned the gold oak leaves on his shoulders, he drove home, proudly showed them to his family, then entered the hospital at Somers Point, New Jersey, where he died.

living quarters. That problem was solved when a local lady opened her unheated and uninsulated boarding house for us until we could find rooms and apartments elsewhere. The airfield situation was more desperate. While we had a hangar, an underground fuel tank and pump, and an adequately-sized sod field, we had no heating system, no shop equipment, no operations office, and no sanitary facilities.

Roland W. ("Tom") O'Day always wanted to be an airline pilot but couldn't meet the height requirement. He joined the Coastal Patrol where he won an Air Medal instead (courtesy Henry E. Phipps).

We began by partitioning-up the hangar, this part for an operations office, that part for rest rooms, another for a radio and control room, and so forth. Next we searched salvage yards until we found some steam radiators and a coal-burning steam-heating system to install at the base — not too good, but better than none and at no cost. We then added showers and more toilets, which meant drilling a well and installing a septic system. As our complement grew so did our need for a lunch room and a larger maintenance shop. Hugh Sharp's father agreed to pay for constructing one, but an existing building was found and purchased for next to nothing. My father and two of his friends dismantled it, moved it, and rebuilt it on the base. A lunch room was added and Hugh Sharp's mother paid for its furnishings. To provide a proper shop floor, we borrowed an old one-half yard cement mixer and an ancient dump truck to haul beach sand to the field, and mixed and poured our own concrete. We put salt into the cement to keep it from freezing while it cured. Everyone shared these muscle-building exercises, and God bless the wives who ran the lunch room!

But our work still wasn't done. We had also to create a separate seaplane base for the Fairchild 24 float planes that several pilots brought in. One of our older flyers was Tom J. Sanschagrin, a New Hampshire native of French descent and a first world war Navy veteran. It was commonly believed that a beer was never brewed that he wouldn't drink, or an airplane built that he couldn't fly. Tom took over the management of the seaplanes and the training of their pilots, and the O'Day volunteers went to work building a supply shack and a mooring dock along the Indian River. Thankfully, we never found out if the float planes could have survived landing on a rough sea, but just having them gave us confidence. On patrols, a float plane flew as sister ship to a land plane whenever possible.

Captain Everett M. Smith was our engineering officer and chief mechanic. "Ev" had served with the Flying Tigers in China before our entry into the war, and the men he recruited as base mechanics often possessed some of his own mechanical ingenuity. Starting with practically no equipment, they bought some, borrowed some, and then made what they couldn't buy or borrow. They made flotation tanks and installed them in the rear of our aircraft, installed snap hinges on the cabin doors, and painted the tail sections of our aircraft bright yellow. The idea was that in case of a ditching at sea, the doors would easily pop off so the crew could get out quickly, and the weight of the engine would hold the aircraft's nose down while the tail stood up like a beacon. We owe a great debt of gratitude to Ev Smith and his mechanics for work well done. I personally flew well over a thousand hours over the ocean without one scary moment because of mechanical failure.

Another fellow who made a fine contribution was Lieutenant Charles C. Ports, our communications officer. When Chuck first arrived with his wife and children from Akron, Ohio, where he had served on one of the early Goodyear blimps, our aircraft radios had very limited range. In no time at all, he increased their range ten-fold. I don't know how he did it, but I felt much safer knowing that I could reach the base when I had to. The success of our entire operation depended on our staying in constant touch with the base and telling them what we saw so they could call on the Army or Navy for appropriate action.

Our objective was to cover our entire patrol area from Five Fathom Bank on the north to Winter Quarter Shoal on the south during all daylight hours. Our first flight of the day left before dawn in order to reach the eastern edge of our patrol area by sunrise. Our last flight of the day returned as it was getting dark. The weather was rather unpredictable, especially the low-lying fog that might form at any time. At times we would get completely lost, and would head west and come in over the beach, sometimes practically down on the sand. Our radio antennas were weighted trailing types, unwound for a hundred feet for sending and receiving, and then retracted for landing. I can just imagine the expression on the face of some unknown surf fisherman when his line became snarled with ours and went air-born! Despite some uncertain weather, however, I can recall only one day in eighteen months when we did not fly at least one mission.

The attitudes of local citizens were sometimes puzzling. Perhaps they didn't really appreciate the danger involved in what we were doing, since the military, the government, and the news media withheld any information considered to be helpful to the enemy. Some citizens did not accept the seriousness of the U-boat attacks, resented the mandatory blackouts along our coastline, and even seemed to think of us as "playboys" evading the draft. When the base closed I was taken into the Air Corps as a buck private, had further training, and eventually served as a flight engineer in the Air Transport Command. I still think of myself and my coastal patrol comrades as ordinary, everyday Americans doing the best we could with what we had.

### Henry E. ("Ed") Phipps

*Ed Phipps was born in Baltimore, Maryland in 1913 and graduated from Baltimore Polytechnic Institute at age eighteen. He learned to fly in 1939 at Baltimore's Logan Field, joined the CAP in December 1941 and became personnel officer of the Logan Squadron the following summer. Too old to fly in any of the regular armed services, in November 1942 he left his position with the General Automatic Heating Company (where ultimately he would work for forty years), and served as a pilot at Rehoboth until the base closed. Phipps recalls being put to work immediately and logging over five hundred hours of patrol flying in ten months:*

The first thing they did when a new man reported to the base was to make sure he could fly over water without losing the horizon and his sense of perspective. I reported November 7, 1942, and my first logbook entry was dated the next day, though it was already my fourth flight. The first three were as an observer, and given for orientation purposes. I didn't log my time as an observer. Some people logged everything as flight time. I didn't do it that way. Nevertheless, when the base closed, I had logged over three hundred hours as pilot-in-command, more than enough to earn the Air Medal.

When I first arrived, the base was keeping flights in the air throughout all the daylight hours. Under normal circumstances, flights were of two hours duration, although under specific circumstances they were sometimes extended. Then the procedure changed, and we began running only two regularly scheduled flights a day — a three-hour dawn patrol, and a three-hour evening patrol. In addition we might have other in-between-hours patrols responding to specific requests, such as for escorting the numerous ten-ship convoys that passed through our area, or even accompanying a single vessel. Various special orders and other information came through in code from the Naval Air Station at Cape May and were received and decoded by our intelligence officer.

Ed Phipps (left) and Glen Cook togged out in rubberized "zoot suits" ready for a patrol. The suits were not watertight, but in the water would help the airman retain body heat just a little longer (courtesy Ed Phipps).

At first I recall that we flew with only our Mae Wests. Later on we got the so-called barracuda bags. Though there weren't any barracudas at our latitude, we called them that anyway. They were simply canvas bags attached to truck inner tubes, and designed to let you stand in them about chest deep to the water. As the winter came on and the water got colder we were issued rubberized "zoot suits," something used by the U.S. Merchant Marine as survival gear. Flying in them was a big change from what we were used to, but we all adapted to them, and they undoubtedly saved a couple of men's lives.

When I came home from Rehoboth, I went to work as a civilian procurement inspector stationed at the Glenn L. Martin Company where

I inspected airplane parts for the rest of the war. After the war ended I returned to my civilian job and continued to fly both for business and pleasure. I stayed active in the CAP Cadet Training Program and as a check pilot on the PT-17s and the L-2s which the Army gave to the CAP. I was appointed as training officer for the Maryland Wing in 1949. Though my business flying ended with my retirement in 1983, I still fly a rented Warrior or Skyhawk now and then and feel privileged to enjoy that pleasure.

**Glen P. Cook**

*For some years before he joined the coastal patrol at Rehoboth, Glen P. Cook had worked in his father's photography shop in East Greenbush, Massachusetts. Cook learned to fly in 1939, but was still working toward his private license when his local draft board "caught up" with him:*

When I went in to see them in August 1941, I explained that I was taking flying lessons, and needed more time to get my license. The draft board gave me extra time, but a string of bad weather kept me from flying much. I was given another ninety days, but that was through the winter and the weather was even worse. Finally I was given April, May, and June, and then July, August, and September, to get my license, or else! At the last possible second, I showed the draft board my license and a telegram from Rehoboth ordering me to report for active duty at once. The draft board gave me a further deferment for as long as I remained on active duty with the CAP.

I made my first patrol, as an observer, the same afternoon I arrived at the base. Out on a mission, bang! It was that quick. And that fast pace kept up. From mid-September 1942 when I arrived, until the base closed, I flew 306 patrols as a pilot and totaled over seven hundred flight hours for which in 1948 I won the Air Medal.

In addition to flying, I served as one of the teletype operators and taught meteorology at night. Flying was always the main thing, however, and some experiences are unforgettable — like the day we lost Harold Swift and almost lost Harvey Cannon. That happened on March 6, 1943. I was flying the lead plane, and Harvey and "Swiftie" were in the sister ship. I saw them go down. Both got out of the plane and into their one-man life rafts okay, but the sea was rough and the wind rising so somehow they drifted apart before they could rope their rafts together. I continued to circle in an ever-widening ellipse until the base ordered me back. They had sent out the base's Sikorsky amphibian and, as we were flying at about seven hundred feet in extremely poor visibility with the clouds right down on top of us, they didn't want to risk the two planes having a mid-air collision. By the time the Sikorsky arrived, the downed men had drifted too far to be located again. A cold front came through that night, and the next morning Swift was found in his raft frozen to death, and Cannon, while alive, was in bad shape and suffering frostbitten heels. He soon recovered and began flying again.

When the coastal patrol ended, I returned to East Greenbush to help dad in the photography shop, and I subsequently made that my life's work. I'm still going full blast as a professional photographer, taking pictures all day and working in the dark room nearly every night. We Rehoboth folks have a reunion each year that's great fun. In 1993, someone invited a former German submarine officer, one of the very few survivors who served in our coastal waters during the war. We got to talking, and it turned out that our paths actually had crossed without either of us knowing it. By comparing our log books, we determined that his sub had been sowing mines in the mouth of the Delaware Bay the same day I'd been flying across it on patrol. We'd been looking for him, while he'd been looking out for us. But he spotted us first and dived before we could see him.

## Henry W. ("Jim") Tegg

*Jim Tegg arrived at Rehoboth from Media, Pennsylvania, a Philadelphia suburb. Born in 1910 in Hyde Park, Massachusetts, he had his first airplane ride in 1925, and while still very young flew a J-2 Cub, an American Eaglet, and a Gypsy Moth ("my first self-learned lesson from the Gypsy Moth: keep hands and arms inside cockpit because the red-hot exhaust pipe runs right alongside"). After four-years as an apprentice photo-engraver, a Philadelphia firm hired him as a journeyman, and he became expert in the* Benday *and* Tinto-O-Graph *printing processes.\* By the late 1930s he had obtained his commercial pilot's license and owned a plane that he kept at Buckman Field in Chester, Pennsylvania:*

One day I received a call from Arnold McNeal seeking volunteers for the coastal patrol. I had a good job and all was going well, and maybe I shouldn't have left, but as a patriotic citizen I went to the big boss, and we decided it was a worthy cause, and since I could have my job back at any time, I left. My own plane had been requisitioned by the govern-

---

\* Benjamin Day (1838–1916) was the son of Benjamin Henry Day (1810–1889), the founder and first publisher of the *New York Sun*. The younger Day invented a system using celluloid sheets for shading plates to print maps and illustrations in color. The so-called Ben Day or *Benday* process was replaced by the *Tint-O-Graph* process. Tegg made the original Sunday color plates for such comic strips as "Blondie" and "King Arthur" from which printing "mats" were distributed to more than one hundred and fifty newspapers.

ment to be used for training fledgling pilots so I flew it to Grand Rapids, Michigan for delivery, then reported to Rehoboth.

Henry W. Tegg left his job as an expert photo-engraver to fly for the Coastal Patrol and qualified for the Air Medal while serving as Operations Officer at Rehoboth (courtesy Ed Phipps).

The first plane I flew on a mission was Stinson NC 26265, and that was on April 10, 1942. I flew it three more days in a row, and then again on May 10, which was the end of Stinson NC 26265. Returning from an early flight to check the weather, with Sykes Ewing as co-pilot, I came over the airport at 6:10 a.m. on a very black morning. After passing beyond the car lights which lit the field for a short way, I leveled off and in pitch blackness "landed" well off the ground. The impact was greater than we had realized, because when I got out, the left-hand door fell off. The plane had to be taken off the line for repairs. In time our commander Hugh Sharp promoted me to Captain and made me base operations officer. But I continued to fly over-water patrols, totaling more than a thousand hours and winning the Air Medal.

Several months after I got to Rehoboth, I was sent to Parksley, Virginia to help Isaac Burnham get that base going. I don't know how helpful I was, but I recall being a party to a practical joke pulled on Major Wyant Farr, Burnham's former commander at Atlantic City. Farr had come down to see Parksley, and Burnham was returning to New York with him. A midnight train from Norfolk stopped to let Burnham and Farr board. Earlier that night some of us had gone hunting for bullfrogs and I had two in an old flour sack. When Farr wasn't looking, we snuck them into his small suitcase. We figured that when Farr opened it later to get something, two angry, flour-covered bullfrogs would leap out and create havoc throughout the blacked-out car. We waited weeks to hear what happened, half expecting to be court-martialed, but nothing came of it.

When the coastal patrol ended, I spent some time in Trenton, New Jersey as a final inspector on Martin TBMs, then had a chance to be a civilian instructor on AT-6s at Camden, Arkansas. After doing that for a while, I decided I preferred some real action. I enlisted in the Air Corps and was assigned to evaluating the effects of aircraft cannon, finally ending up on Okinawa in the 319 Bomb Group, 438th Squadron, a Douglas A-26 Invader outfit. When I came home I returned to Philadelphia, then later went to Boston to work for the now-defunct *Boston Post*, and still later for a commercial engraving house. I've been retired here in South Carolina for twenty-four years now.

## George W. Townson

*Another early arrival among the Rehoboth pilots was George W. Townson, then vice-president and chief pilot for a Philadelphia fixed base operation that ran a government contract flying school and was a distributor for Stinson and Aeronca airplanes. In March 1942, his boss "volunteered him" to fly for the coastal patrol and agreed to pay him his regular salary plus room and board. The following is his account of going to Rehoboth, and one of his experiences flying patrols:*

> On March 16, I flew to Rehoboth with another man who was volunteering both his Stinson Voyager and himself for patrol duty. I stayed up most of the night before we left painting the CAP logo on the sides of the fuselage and on the wings. The logo had the letters "U.S." proudly showing in white block letters. After we landed, the base commander, Hugh Sharp came out to greet us. After shaking hands, he pointed to the "U.S" and said, "the first thing we have to do is paint that out. We're not 'U.S.' anything."
>
> The Stinsons we flew had very modest instrument panels: needle, ball, airspeed, and altimeter. The altimeter was very insensitive. The first mark on the dial, about an eighth of an inch from zero, was "about" one hundred feet. We had only a "wet" compass, not a gyroscopic one, and our radio had a "good day" range of about twenty miles.
>
> Besides looking for subs and/or survivors of ship sinkings, one of our duties was to report the weather — visibility, ceiling, and the wind direction and velocity. The "crab angle" we had to have to keep our plane parallel with the beach, together with our ground speed, let us compute the latter two measures. Not really accurately, but close enough for the next patrol to use (as I think about it now, a dawn weather observation would not seem to be of much value to a

pilot in the next patrol two hours later after the sun had come up). All the time I flew these patrols, my strongest wish was that I would not land my airplane in the sea.

George W. Townson often flew the first, pre-dawn patrol of the day in order to report on what weather the dawn patrol could expect. Even then, the weather might change before that patrol took off (courtesy George W. Townson).

I had some anxious moments one day about ten miles off the coast of New Jersey. My engine began to shake and bang loudly. Instinctively I pulled on carburetor heat, but that made no improvement. The oil pressure and oil temperature gauges were in the normal range, but the tachometer needle was bouncing between 2300 rpm and 800 rpm. I tried the magnetos, and found no problem if I only ran on the left magneto, so I flew to the nearest landfall that way. My co-pilot had already called in a mayday, and Rehoboth wanted me to land on Cape May. If I did, our only two mechanics will have to drive up to Chester, Pennsylvania, cross the Delaware River on a ferry, then drive down to Cape May, about a one-hundred-mile trip.

Since it is only thirteen miles from Cape May to Lewes, Delaware, just above Rehoboth, I decided to fly back to base, and climbed to 3,000 feet. From that altitude I felt I could glide to land even if I lost engine power completely. Our Stinson on the ground in New Jersey would be out of service for sub patrol and our maintenance crew would be tied up there as well. I felt that if I could get back to base, the engine could be "made well" with a magneto change. In fact, the flight to Rehoboth proved uneventful. Once on the ground, the right magneto was removed, and found to have a defective oil seal. Oil had gotten onto the distributor rotor and caused the plugs to fire out of sequence.

Going down at sea was always highly risky, not only to the downed crew, but to their rescuers as well. One of the coastal patrol's first fatal crashes happened to an experienced aircrew from Rehoboth. At 4:50 p.m., July 21, 1942, thirty-seven-year-old pilot Henry T. Cross and his nineteen-year-old flight observer, Charles E. Shelfus, both of Columbus, Ohio, went down in their Fairchild 24. Responding to a distress call, commander Hugh R. Sharp, with Edmond I. Edwards as co-pilot, got to the crash site within an hour and landed the base's Sikorsky S-39 Amphibian in heavy seas. Sharp later described the rescue:

> Dropped smoke bombs and landed at 17:50. Sustained crushed port wing float in landing. Sea rough, wind-northeast-fresh. After landing was unable to locate survivor for several minutes on account of rough sea. Finally sighted Pilot Cross at several hundred yards distance while he and Amphibian were on crests of waves. Encountered some difficulty in making the downwind turns to reach the victim ... On our second try, however, we were successful in grabbing hold of the victim who was unable to hold on to the rope which was thrown to him because of his injury. The observer, Lt. Edwards, however, lifted Pilot Cross from the water and helped him into the ship, which was no easy task because of the rough water and the violent pitching of the Amphibian.
>
> Remained in water at location searching for Observer Shelfus until 18:20. There being no signs of Shelfus and with Cross in serious condition, it was deemed wise to get to shore as soon as possible. As the sea was too rough for takeoff, we started taxiing on westerly course at 18:20. At approximately 18:25 port wing float sank. Observer Edwards went out to starboard bomb rack for balance.... This was no easy task for Observer Edwards for he had stripped off almost all of his clothing in order to give it to pilot Cross. At intervals all during the night, he was completely immersed in the seas during which waves flowed over the starboard wing float to which the bomb rack was attached, and to say the least, he was far from comfortable from cold after the sun went down.
>
> Laid course for coastal buoy No. 3 planning to tie up to it for the night, not having sufficient gas to taxi to Chincoteague, the nearest harbor. By tying to the buoy, our position could be reported by radio so that a fast Coast Guard boat could rush Cross to shore for medical aid. On approaching No. 3 buoy, we were met by Coast Guard picket boat. Condition of sea made transfer of Cross unwise. Seaplane was taken in tow by picket boat at 19:50 and towed to Chincoteague, arriving about 23:45. An ambulance from Parksley, Virginia was waiting at the dock to take Cross to the hospital in Salisbury, Maryland. Due to the serious condition of Pilot Cross it required one hour and

ten minutes to transfer him from the Amphibian to the ambulance. Cross arrived at the Salisbury hospital at 02:15.... Pilot Cross sustained several fractured vertebrae, also numerous cuts and bruises.

Two months later, in a special White House ceremony, President Franklin D. Roosevelt himself pinned the Air Medal on Sharp and Edwards, the first CAPers and the first civilians ever so honored. In a 1983 interview with Colonel Lester E. Hopper, Hugh Sharp recalled the circumstances with amusement:

> We waited in the waiting room for quite some time to get into the august presence of the president. We apparently caught him a little by surprise, because he was picking his teeth at the time. But he recovered from that very gracefully. He invited us in and he was very gracious, congratulated us and pinned on the medals.... I think the president was confused. He said "This is the first time this medal has been awarded." So we took it that we had number one. I'm sure that's not right [the president meant to say it was the first time it was ever awarded to civilians].

\* \* \*

The Air Medal was established by executive order of May 11, 1942 for use by all branches of the United States military. The award may be won by individuals for meritorious achievement in either single acts of merit, or for sustained operations against armed enemies of the United States. Awards presented to Civil Air Patrol members were uniquely engraved with name, rank, and years of service such as "John Doe, 1st Lieut., Civil Air Patrol, Active Duty, 1942-43." Using as the criteria two hundred hours of over water flight (as compared to the one hundred hour requirement by the Army), 824 Civil Air Patrol flight crewmen were finally recognized by a series of General Orders beginning on April 14, 1948, and by certificates signed by President Harry S. Truman.

## Hugh R. Sharp

*Hugh R. Sharp had his first airplane ride in an OX-Jenny in 1919. Ten years later he soloed in a Warner Fleet, then, while both were still in college he and Richard DuPont bought and learned to fly a primary glider. When his friend DuPont later set several world's records in soaring, Sharp liked to say he'd taught him to fly. In 1936 Sharp and his brother Bayard secretly bought a Taylorcraft. When their dad learned of it, he flew into a terrible panic. They dubbed the plane "Pappy's Panic," and painted that name on its side. Soon thereafter Sharp bought a Fairchild 24 while his brother bought a Stinson Reliant. By then their father was no longer perturbed about their flying.*

Sharp joined the CAP after Gill Robb Wilson called Sharp's old college friend Richard DuPont, and asked him to get something going in Delaware. DuPont chose Holger Hoiriis, who'd been his chief pilot at "All American Aviation" before being grounded for medical reasons, to become head of the Delaware CAP Wing, and Hoiriis named Sharp his operations officer:

> I was given the job of trying to find a place to put such a [coastal patrol] base, and what would we do when we got there, and so forth. Nobody had the faintest idea of what we were really supposed to do.... I don't remember being too quiet about it. Yes, we were told not to say anything when we went down to Rehoboth the first time to look at it, and not to say why we were coming, that's true. Anyhow, Holger and I flew down to Rehoboth and landed there on the airport and we went in and looked around and everybody was very suspicious about what we were doing, because everything was sort of grounded at that time and everybody was very suspicious of our flying around. We just kind of pretended that we had some sort of clearance to do it, and I think we really did, because you weren't supposed to fly.... But we went down and we decided that Rehoboth Airport was a usable place.
>
> I think the community thought we were a bunch of fellows trying to play like we were on a secret mission. It was pretty obvious it wasn't secret, because they could see almost everything we did. I think they sort of pooh-poohed us at first, but over the months that they got to like us. Some of the kids were pretty rambunctious and got into some scrapes and troubles, which we had to smooth over with the town authorities from time to time. But I don't think it was anything more than just fun. There was never any kind of destruction or any of that kind of thing down there. And it was a good bunch of guys by and large. We never had any real trouble.

\* \* \*

In his 1983 interview, Hugh Sharp went on to talk about the area patrolled by the Rehoboth base and the kind of weather they encountered. He called it pretty dreary, but added that most pilots became very adept at flying in bad weather with only needle, ball, airspeed and compass, and found their way back to base even without direction-finding equipment. Sharp told of acquiring the Sikorsky S-39:

> Paul DuPont owned the plane and I called him one day to ask if he'd like to sell it. He declined, but I said I'd like to have it anyway to keep at Rehoboth in case of emergency, and I was coming over to see if it was flyable. So Holger and I and Ev Smith, our chief mechanic, went over to Seaford where the plane was kept. We looked it over

and it looked reasonable, so I said, "Let's see if the engine will start." We cranked it up and it sounded pretty good, so we checked the mags and taxied it around to see how it felt. We left Smitty in our car, and took it up to the end of the field and gave it the gun, and the first thing we knew we were in the air. And so I said, "We're up here, so we might as well keep going." We flew around some, and I said, "Let's take it over to Rehoboth." And we just kept going. And Smitty came back in the car.

Hugh Sharp was the first civilian ever to win the Air Medal — personally presented to him by President Franklin D. Roosevelt (courtesy Jim Tegg).

Asked about what kind of discipline he maintained around the Rehoboth base, Sharp admitted he was no military man. His idea was to take good care of his staff and let their own patriotism take care of the rest. Such training as might be necessary was given, but he had no interest in drill for drill's sake:

> Frankly, we were too busy doing what we were supposed to do. Any time off that the boys got, I wasn't going to march them around the field for no good purpose that I knew of, and so we didn't really pay much attention to that until we got several directives reminding us that we were not doing our duty, and then we'd go out, and I got a Victrola with a loud speaker and a marching record, and we'd march up and down a time or two, but really our drill was not much. We had a fellow who was in charge of the guard unit, and he was an ex-Army man, and he loved to drill people, to get people out there and call the commands, but nobody took it terribly seriously.

With an attitude like that, and having learned to be a leader by leading — he flew the base's first patrol — Hugh Sharp was both respected and popular. And he had a good sense of humor. Here he describes leaving Washington National Airport after having been decorated by the president:

> We were in a long conga line of airplanes going out to take off, and in front us were several of what at that time we thought were perfectly tremendous airplanes, C-54s. One of them was cleared to Gander, and one of them was cleared to someplace in the West Indies, and another was cleared for a non-stop flight to England. The fellow in front of us was kind of parked, so he could see us behind him. He called the tower and asked, "What the heck is that back there?" The man in the tower said, "I'm not sure, I'll ask." So he called us, and we told him we were a Sikorsky S-39. The fellow in the airplane ahead said, "Tell that fellow to take off ahead of me. I want to see if it really will fly." I have to admit the S-39 was one of the silliest-looking airplanes you ever saw.*

## Bruce H. Bird

*In 1942, twenty-year-old Bruce H. Bird was a "hangar bum" at the airport in Lehighton, Pennsylvania, working on the planes while attending ground school and taking flying lessons. He had nearly finished a $65 course for his first solo when he learned of an opening at Rehoboth. Before leaving to drive down with his friend Jim Ingram, he went to an Army-Navy store to buy the uniforms he would need: three shirts, three pairs of trousers, two jackets, and several caps and ties, just enough to let him begin his guard duties as soon as he arrived:*

We went down there in Jimmy's 1937 Chevy. He owned an open cockpit Bird biplane, which he kept at Lehighton Airport, but it would have been too cold to fly in during the winter so he left it behind. Jimmy was a good pilot with lots of air time, but until he began flying patrols, he headed our guard unit. I took with me an old twelve-gauge shotgun, because the base didn't furnish any weapons. (I still have it and occasionally fire it.) I stood guard with it loaded with triple-ought buckshot, but never fired it. If someone approached us during the night, we were required to challenge them — "Halt! Who goes there? Advance and be recognized."

---

* After its courageous career in the coastal patrol, the amphibian went on flying for many more years through frequent changes of ownership. From 1957 until 1963 the tough old veteran lay wrecked in Alaska, but was finally rescued and shipped to the Bradley Air Museum in Connecticut. This oldest of all surviving Sikorsky aircraft, built in 1930, has been restored and can be seen in the New England Air Museum.

Though there was concern about spies and saboteurs, and things were supposed to be pretty hush-hush, the base was hardly a secret. Many local people worked there, and various suppliers came and went. Still, we remained extremely strict about letting people onto the base. Every car or truck had to stop at the entrance gate and each person in them had to be identified — in the mornings there might be four or five people in a car and we had to record the names and arrival times of each. Horace Waddington, a veteran of the Delaware State Prison in Wilmington, was our sergeant of the guard.

Life at a coastal patrol base was not all hard work. Here Bruce H. Bird (standing center) and buddies have fun on the beach with some local girls and Mrs. Mary Ann Sullivan, owner of the Mary Ann Inn, bottom center (courtesy Bruce H. Bird).

I lived at the Mary Ann Inn, which was owned and operated by Howard and Mary Ann Sullivan. They were very nice people and a real pleasure to live with. The Inn was a large three-story building with a screened-off porch. The screens were made of aluminum to avoid rusting out from the salt spray. The Sullivans had a daughter named Betty who married a soldier named Jim Steele. Because I had some sheet music and often played the popular wartime songs on the piano in the Sullivan's living room, they asked me to play at Betty's wedding. I played "Here Comes the Bride" and other selections. I hear she and her husband had six children and were quite happy. I was also the Inn's unofficial "waker-upper." I'd go out in the long hallway before people were up and play Tommy Dorsey's theme "Only Occasionally" on my Selmer Bundy trombone. It was all too easy to sleep soundly there. I still can hear those waves breaking on the beach as I lay in bed.

The field and planes were guarded on a twenty-four basis, and we all rotated our shifts and posts regularly. One post was along the flight line, another at the administration building and the hangars, and another down at the bomb shack where the bombs were stored. A man and his two sons, I think their name was Wolfe, guarded only the seaplane base. They liked it there with the float planes. I checked it out one night and it was absolutely pitch dark except for the flicks of their flashlights. Every post was a little eerie in the winter what with howling winds and the distant wail of offshore fog horns. In the summer, the mosquitoes could be a curse.

What I remember most vividly are the four men we lost at sea. Charles Shelfus, Harold Swift, Del Garrett and Paul Towne. I also remember several crashes right at the base, one of them coming when General Smedley D. Butler's son, Smedley, Jr., cracked up a Monocoupe in the trees near the bomb shack.* I left before the base closed to volunteer for the paratroops. After I was hurt on a training jump, I wound up at Fort Oglethorpe, Georgia as a military policeman. I served a total of forty-three months before my discharge.

## Joseph W. Thoroughgood

*After graduating from Rehoboth Beach High School in the class of 1942, Joseph W. Thoroughgood worked as a base guard for several months before enlisting in the Army. Because of the area's manpower shortage, C. O. Hugh Sharp gave him the very devil for leaving, but Thoroughgood did what he thought was best:*

I was a mere private in the coastal patrol, and wore the regular khaki uniform, which I had to pay for myself. Guards carried whatever they had — shotguns, hunting rifles, even revolvers. I carried my father's single-shot twelve-gauge shotgun. We didn't have M-1s or other Army weapons. We were there mainly to prevent tampering with the dozen or so planes that were tied down on the field at night. We worked day duty as well, but I mostly remember the nights. The field was rather small and the runways quite short. It's gone now, replaced by a housing development. I didn't earn much, maybe five dollars a day, but a couple

---

* Major General Smedley Darlington Butler (1880–1940), U.S. Marine Corps, was a commander in France in the First World War. Notable for violent opinions and flamboyant quarrels, he campaigned following his retirement for isolationism and against war. His autobiography, *Old Gimlet Eye*, as told to Lowell Thomas, appeared in 1933.

of the pilots took me along for rides when they did practice bombing runs over Rehoboth Bay, and that was a thrill. Most guards had little to do with the pilots, but I remember Logan Grier of Milford, Delaware because he was so easy to talk with. I went on to fight in Italy for two years with the 85th Infantry Division and picked up two Purple Hearts.

## Arthur L. Hairgrove

*Arthur L. Hairgrove was a twenty-two-year-old from Dover who also signed up as a guard. He found such duty very tame:*

Rehoboth was a quiet, peaceful little town in those days, with not nearly so many people around as there are today. Dover wasn't far away and I'd been to the beach down there many times. I was single and boarded with Mr. and Mrs. Moore on Rehoboth Avenue about the second block down. The beach was a big attraction, and I spent a lot of time swimming and fooling around in the water. The job didn't pay much, but enough to get along. I got to fly as an observer a couple of times, maybe an hour or two down the coast. I really liked it and I'd have liked to be a flyer, but didn't have money for lessons. Later, I joined the U.S. Merchant Marine and took training at Hoffman Island (now Gateway National Recreation Area) near Staten Island, New York. I didn't care much for coastal service on oil tankers, so I left and enlisted in the Army, and served overseas with the Third Armored Division.

## Arthur T. ("Tom") Worth

*Tom Worth was born and raised in Wilmington, Delaware, and in 1940, at age twenty, earned a license in the Civilian Pilot Training Program at the University of Delaware. He took lessons at Bellanca Field, not far from the campus, in a two-place, side-by-side, 55 hp Taylorcraft. While earning his BA degree in 1941, he built up his flight time, and had two hundred hours when he reported to Rehoboth:*

I served from early March 1942 until late August 1943. Living in a resort town wasn't easy. Everything was closed from Labor Day through the next Memorial Day. Most hotels and rooming houses were open only in season. One restaurant opened at eight a.m., too late for breakfast, and closed at six p.m., too early for dinner — so I rented a small apartment and did my own cooking. Later on, Howard Carter's wife, Virginia, and Charles Ports' wife, Mildred, and several other ladies, ran a restaurant on the base to coincide with our flying hours.

The over-water flying in winter was probably the most disliked thing about coastal patrol. At first we didn't have the rubberized zoot-suits, so that a water landing in cold weather didn't afford good survival odds. Even a warm-weather ditching could be bad if the seas were rough, or the landing not very good. This was the constant hazard that was part of the job. Being twenty-three years old, however, I was too young to worry much about it.

Besides his flying, Tom Worth remembers spending a lot of time at the beach and canoeing in the Atlantic Ocean. Here he stands on the float of one of the base's several Fairchild 24s (courtesy Ed Phipps).

For off-duty fun the young unmarried guys like me had the beach, some boats, and lots of girls. I used to visit Rehoboth while at the university, and I already had friends there. One fellow kept a canoe on Silver Lake, and we'd drag it out through the surf to the ocean. Another guy kept a fifteen-foot sailboat down at the seaplane base. I remember swimming one day with some girls vacationing at the beach. They wore a kind of thin, rubberized suit, a new style like the rubber gloves you'd wear to do dishes. The surf was rough and as one girl started for the beach she fell and was tumbled around pretty hard. When she got up, the top of her suit was loaded with sand and water. The material began to rip apart and by the time she got up to us on the beach, it was in bits and pieces, and she was partially naked. One kind soul went to her aid with a blanket. So much for that new style!

That reminds me of the time that Tom O'Day and some of the other guys skinny-dipped after dark off Rehoboth Avenue. No one was supposed to be on the beach then — the entire coastline was patrolled by Coast Guardsmen on horseback— so they undressed and left their clothes on the boardwalk before dashing down to the water. After enjoying a good frolic, the guys came back to find their clothes gone. No one knows who took them or why. With the blackout in effect they got back to their quarters without discovery but they never recovered their clothes.

I mostly flew Fairchild 24s with either the Warner 145-horsepower engine or the Ranger 165-horsepower engine. We kept several 24s on floats down at the seaplane base and sometimes used them on patrols. When fully loaded, however, their take-off performance — especially on hot summer days — wasn't very good. They'd take half of Rehoboth Bay to get off the water and sometimes they didn't make it at all.

More than the flying and the fun times, and winning the Air Medal, what I remember and cherish the most about the Rehoboth coastal patrol are the friendships formed there, friendships that continue more than fifty years later. Believe it or not, our group had its first reunion in 1948, and we've had one every year since then. They've been a great way to renew acquaintances and to make new friends as well. Though each year someone else passes away we expect to continue meeting once a year for as long as possible.

## Maury H. Betchen

*Maury H. Betchen grew up in the Atlantic City and Philadelphia areas and in 1940 worked as a line mechanic for TWA when it was still flying Lockheed Electras and Douglas DC-2s. By the time he was recruited for the Rehoboth Beach base by head mechanic Everett Smith, he was both a licensed pilot and an A&E mechanic. Betchen's wife went with him and worked for the U.S. Corps of Engineers in Lewes, Delaware:*

With help from my family, who were fairly affluent, we rented a big summer home on Silver Lake in Rehoboth. It was a sprawling Spanish villa design, and we rattled around in it. It was very nice, but we couldn't afford to heat it. Being young and newly married, my wife and I often had dinner in front of the fireplace and then rushed upstairs and into bed to stay warm.

We worked long hours at the base. As much as we could, actually, because there was always so much to do — modifying airplanes to meet overwater safety needs (such as installing quick release doors, flotation tanks, bomb rack adapters, and a myriad other things) and doing major engine and aircraft overhauls. We'd have to send some instruments away to be fixed, but mostly we repaired them ourselves. CAA rules and regulations sometimes were overlooked when need be. We just did the jobs and kept the aircraft flying. I was dedicated and enjoyed what I did. So did we all. We had to improvise a lot — like the hot air blower we jury-rigged to warm up aircraft engines on cold mornings and the power crank we used to turn over the props until the engines caught. They may have seemed like crazy contraptions, but they worked, and that was the thing.

Another sort of innovation was the the result of at least two pilots taking off on dark mornings without removing their aileron locks. With great skill and tremendous luck, they managed to stagger around in very wide circles, line up with our runway, and land without damage. To prevent this happening again, we attached lines from the aileron locks to the tie-down lines, so that the locks would pull off automatically if a forgetful pilot forgot to take them off. This scheme may have pulled off a couple of ailerons, too, but better that than a pilot taking off with locked ailerons.

Smitty ran the shop with an iron hand, but he was great. He came up with most of the ideas and we worked them out as a team. There were only two A&E mechanics besides Smitty and me, and they were local auto and farm machinery mechanics. The pilots were of two general kinds — the unmarried guys who caroused around town a little, maybe having a beer or two and raising a ruckus, and the older guys and those who didn't qualify for the military, who were steadier and pretty much stuck to business, Major Sharp was a gem of a commander, a real gentleman and regular guy. He ran the base informally without any regimentation. None was required. We all knew what to do and we did it. Sharp was a wealthy man, but you'd never know it to see him. He was "old money," but never sloppy. He'd wear a sweater with holes in the elbows and not worry about it. And he flew regularly, too, which many base commanders never did.

I was there almost eighteen months, as were most base personnel. A few drifted in and out, but most stayed the course. Rehoboth has grown and changed a lot in the last fifty years. It had its boardwoalk when we were there, but it was reasonably deserted then. There were no big summer crowds or anything like that. Some soldiers were stationed in the firehouse. I don't know what they did. And there were some Coast Guard people who patrolled the beaches with dogs, then later with horses. The local folks paid little attention to us. They knew we were there, of course, but they didn't have any special entertaments or dinners for us that I remember.

\* \* \*

The memorial tablet erected by former base members on the 25th anniversary of the base's activation. Over the names of their comrades, the inscription reads, "In fond memory of our friends and brother pilots lost at sea from Civil Air Patrol Base #2 Rehoboth Beach, Delaware" (courtesy Ed Phipps).

Those who remained at Rehoboth for the duration remember the four planes and eight crewmen who were forced down at sea — four of them rescued, four of them lost. The very last coastal patrol plane ever to ditch at sea also involved Rehoboth personnel. Walter L. Grier, Jr. and Walter A. Fullerton, Jr. went down on July 31, 1943, but were rescued within an hour and a half and returned unhurt to Cape May.

---

Base officers, pilots. and observers who served at least one month at CAPCP#2 and who are not elsewhere mentioned in this chapter include: John B. Andrews,* Edward R. Arn, William E. Blythe, Albert W. Brown, William G. Caufield,* John W. Chew, Jr.,* John O. Cogswell,* Greensbury P. Dukes, Jack B. Escott,* Robert A. Escott, Jr.,* Lee Fishman, Gilbert Goldman, Roy W. Harmon, John L. Haverstick, William E. James,* Jr., Charles W. Lawson, Irvin V. Leight,* Lawrence K. Lunt, Philip F. Masterbone, Harry T. Mitchell, Walter P. Mullikin,* Thomas F. Neblett, William B. Nicholson,* Jr., Gordon C. Prince,* Henry H. Proctor,* John D. Reed, Clarence L. Roberts, John M. Robinson, Jr.,* Robinson A. Rogers,* Warren O. Smith,* Howard N. Stayton, Jr., Alfred E. Suess, Jr.,* Alex J. Sziky,* Albert J. Thompson,* Arthur H. Tully, Jr., Howard Turpin, Jr.,* William C. Vance,* John H. Vaughn,* Carl L. Virdin,* Stephen A. Walker, Forrest P. Wenyon, Henry H. Wilder, Jr.,* and Laurence E. Willson.* Asterisk indicates Air Medal winner.

60   From Maine to Mexico

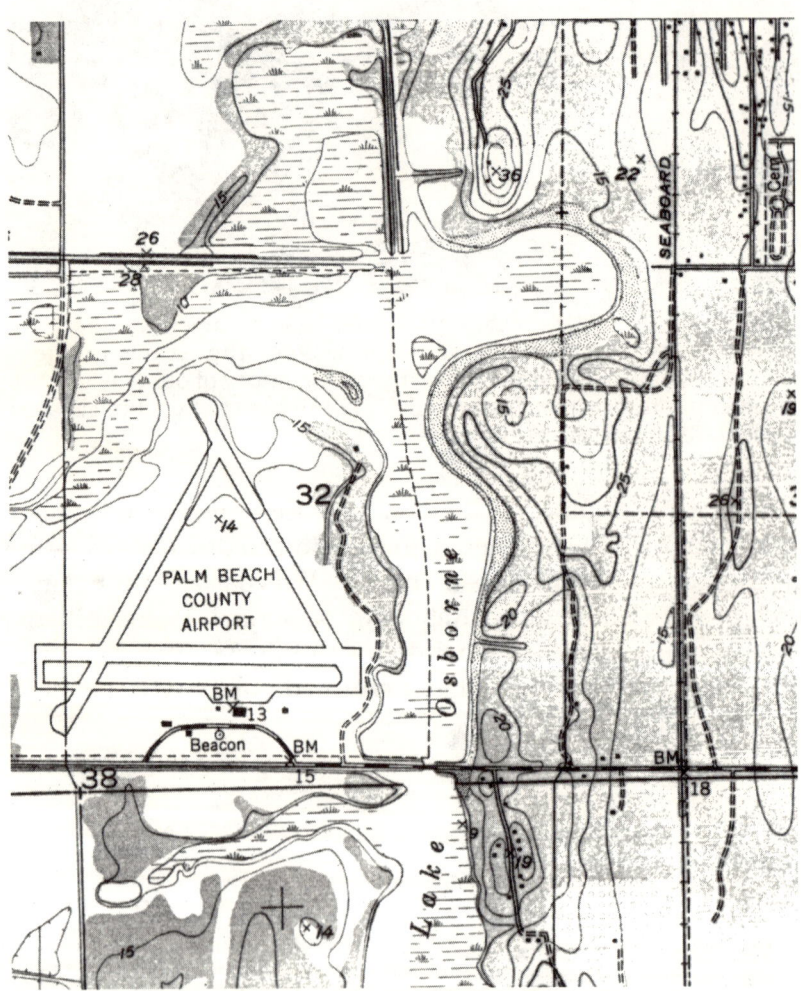

Lantana Airport just after the war when it was named Palm Beach County Airport. Like many Florida airfields, it was surrounded by water (including Lake Osborne to the east) and swamps alive with alligators and six-foot diamond-back rattlesnakes (source: 1956 United States Geological Survey map).

# 3

# Lantana, Florida

In 1940, after the German war machine had swept through France and the war in Europe seemed more threatening to America, Congress authorized the armed services to begin establishing air bases along the east coast. Taking over certain existing airports was the quickest means of doing so, and among the Air Corps acquisitions was Palm Beach Municipal Airport. On the north side of the field it installed hangars, streets, utilities, hundreds of buildings, and other requirements of a military base. All general aviation and airline activities were moved to the south side of the field. This greatly expanded airport — renamed Morrison Field in honor of local flyer Grace Morrison* — became a jumping-off point for some 6,000 planes and 45,000 pilots headed for war zones by way of the South America-to-Africa route. Over 2,500 civilian workers helped Air Corps personnel speed those planes and pilots along.

In early 1941, after General Henry J. L. Miller, chief of Air Corps Maintenance Command, estimated that Florida had only a tenth of the aviation resources that would be needed to protect it should America be attacked, local aviation leaders formed the "Florida Defense Force." Since its proposed operation and structure did not fit into normal state militia or National Guard requirements, the FDF was established under an Office of Civilian Defense umbrella. The First Air Squadron of the FDF was officially set up at the Palm Beach Airport on May 28, 1941

* Grace K. Morrison, the first woman pilot in the Palm Beach area, died in a car accident in 1936 just before the airport was first dedicated. She is credited with forming the Palm Beach County Airport Association and leading the lobbying for the federal funding assistance that made airport construction possible. Morrison Field is now Palm Beach International Airport.

with 26 officers and 41 enlisted men who performed various search and rescue and coastal patrol activities until the squadron was absorbed by the Civil Air Patrol.*

## Owen Gassaway

*Though the Lantana base was initially located at Morrison Field, it was soon moved to a brand new and otherwise unoccupied airport at Lantana, a town thirteen miles to the south. The story of how this airport came to be built during 1939-1941, with a future coastal patrol very much in mind, is told by Owen Gassaway, who was then the youngest mechanic in the First Air Squadron. Today — after an amazing fifty-five year association with the same airport — Gassaway is president of Lantana-based Florida Airmotive, one of the busiest general aviation service and supply companies in the United States. Still spending much of every day at the airport, Gassaway flies his beautifully restored Stinson Voyager whenever he has time. Complete with standard coastal patrol insignia and Mosley-designed CAPCP #3 base logo painted near the nose, his NC 34645 also carries a big number "1" on the tail denoting his self-appointed leadership at the airfield. Gassaway recalls:*

Before the war began, I worked in a bicycle-motorcycle shop in West Palm Beach owned by Wesley B. Jackson who was then active in the "Florida Defense Force," a kind of Florida home guard, patterned after one that had been set up in England by pilots ineligible for military duty. Wes Jackson and his group were patrolling and watching the coast line long before Pearl Harbor came along, and soon began thinking of having an airport of their own — especially as Morrison Field became increasingly busy. When I had time, I hung around this bunch at the airport, working as a kind of volunteer mechanic.

As it happened, John Prince, one of the county commissioners, a pilot as well as the Palm Beach County engineer, knew of some desirable land near Lantana and a deal was made to acquire it. Then federal funding was sought to match county support. Fifty years ago, a number of the wealthiest and most influential people in the country lived in Palm Beach and they made things happen. As a result, Lantana became the first — and only — airport in the U.S. to be built with funds from the "Our Town Airport" Civil Aeronautics Authority model airports program (the program ended when we entered the war). When fully com-

---

* Those who continued on as CAP members assigned to CAPCP #3 included Harry Hood Bassett; Rex E. Bassett, Jr.; J. M. "Jake" Boyd; Ralph J. Cohn; Cecil Z. Cornelius; Emerson H. "Rusty" Gates; E. Wesley Jackson; J. Art Keil; Ted F. Keys; Henry F. Lilienthal; Orville H. Loy; E. John McCann; Zack T. Mosley; John Prince; M. E. "Doc" Rinker; Arthur R. Sprott; David R. Thompson; Charles Weeks, Jr.; and Wright "Ike" Vermilya, Jr.

pleted in 1942 the new airport boasted a modern hangar, an operations center with a small tower, and a canteen. Its thirty-five hundred foot long and two-hundred foot wide runways could accommodate any airplane then flying.

Except for wartime service in General George S. Patton's Third Armored Division in Europe, Owen Gassaway has been associated with the Lantana Airport since its opening in 1942 (courtesy Owen Gassaway).

War came while the airport was under construction, and the Florida Defense Force became part of a local Civil Air Patrol squadron. They immediately got busy painting their planes in the coastal patrol colors, buying uniforms, and getting organized for what would be expected of them. They remained at Morrison Field only until the Lantana airport was ready. The new field was really in the sticks. Getting there seemed like driving half way to Miami!

Knowing I'd soon be drafted I considered joining the Air Corps. But while I was still hanging out at Morrison Field, I heard so many Air Corps people disparage that service, that instead I volunteered for an all-Florida tank repair company then being organized. I ended up in Europe as part of General George Patton's Third Army. When I returned after three years, I found that Wes Jackson, my ex-boss, had sold his cycle shop and gone into the aviation business at Lantana Airport. He called and invited me to became his partner. He handled everything to do with the flying end and I handled everything on the ground. I got my A&E and then my DMI — designated maintenance inspector — licenses, and so I could do it all. Wes Jackson was killed in 1957, and I've been here ever since.

The Lantana base was officially activated March 30, 1942, about two months after the Atlantic City and Rehoboth bases. Wright ("Ike") Vermilya, Jr., the chief organizer of the First Air Squadron, was named commanding officer, and dispatched the first CAP patrols on April 2. Vermilya was an excellent choice for commander. He had left college during World War I to serve in the U.S. Army Air Service, and later held National Guard and Air Service Reserve commissions. He held CAA license number thirty-five, was one of the nation's earliest licensed glider pilots, and was a pioneer air mail pilot as well. Experienced with running fixed base operations in Cincinnati, Little Rock, and West Palm Beach, and with over twelve thousand hours of air time, "Ike" Vermilya was well equipped to direct one of the busiest of all the CAP's coastal patrol bases.

Like others, the Lantana base received general guidance as well as specific directives from CAP national headquarters, located first in Washington, then later in New York. Though base commanders enjoyed a considerable latitude in making day-to-day decisions, many matters such as the selection, training, and assignment of personnel were dictated by national headquarters. For example, Operations Directive No. 23, dated June 22, 1942, indicated that only "properly qualified" members with official identification cards could serve in the coastal patrol, and that members had to sign this "Active Duty Oath" upon reporting:

> I, as a member of the Civil Air Patrol, an agency of the United States of America, having been assigned to active duty with Civil Air Patrol hereby voluntarily enlist subject to any and all orders of the National Commander of Civil Air Patrol to a term of continuous active service for the term of _____ months, commencing _____ 194_ and I hereby agree to be available for duty continuously and at all times during said term.
>
> During said term and any extension thereof, I do solemnly swear that I will bear true faith and allegiance to the United States of America; that I will serve them honestly and faithfully against all their enemies whomsoever; that I will fully and faithfully perform all duties assigned to me and obey the orders of the President of the United States and the orders of the officers appointed over me subject to the rules and Articles of War.
>
> In the event that I shall not report or be available for active duty at any time during said term or any extension thereof which I shall voluntarily undertake, or if I shall not faithfully and fully perform all duties assigned to me, I hereby consent to the revocation and cancellation of my license to own, operate and service any aviation and radio equipment.

Directive No. 23 also spelled out the basic table of organization for each base, the "succession of command," and the required qualifications of personnel. The maximum complement per base was seventy-six men and women — a Base Commander, an Operations Officer, an Engineering Officer, and an Intelligence Officer; fifteen pilots and fifteen observers (including pilot-observers); an Assistant Operations Officer, an Assistant Engineering Officer, an Assistant Intelligence Officer, and an Airdrome Officer; five mechanics, two apprentice mechanics, and two radio mechanics; an administrative section head, four clerk-typists, and two plotting board operators; four linemen; and sixteen guards.

Base commanders and their Operations and Assistant Operations Officers were required to be pilots but the remaining officers (other than the pilots themselves, of course) could be non-pilots, although pilots were preferred. Pilots had to hold an effective Civil Aeronautics Administration Airman Certificate as a Private Pilot, or higher, and to have the following qualifications:

> Shall have officially logged a minimum of 200 hours as a pilot [and] Shall hold an effective Federal Communications Commission Restricted Radiotelephone Operator Permit [and] Shall have a practical working knowledge of Air Navigation and be skilled in the use of the Air Navigation Computer in the solution of ground-speed and radius-of-action problems and in the calculations involved in the preparation of complete flight plans. [the qualifications for Observer were the same except for needing only 30 hours solo flight time as a Student Pilot or 30 hours as an observer on air missions]

## Alexander D. Thomson

*Alexander D. Thomson served as a pilot in the Lantana coastal patrol from October 10, 1942 until the base closed on August 31, 1943, and accumulated enough hours to be awarded the Air Medal after the war:*

While I was growing up in Duluth, Minnesota, my parents used to come down to Lantana to visit friends, and later they moved to the area. After the Japanese attacked Pearl Harbor, I took a job as an aircraft sheet metal worker at the Morrison Field Air Corps base not far from Lantana. I started taking flying lessons at the Lantana Airport, earned my private license there, and then bought a Stinson Voyager. When I joined the CAP it seemed natural to contribute its use for coastal patrol work, and I placed no restrictions on that. Any qualified pilot could fly it. I flew it a lot myself but I also flew Fairchild 24s and Wacos. I wasn't involved in any unusual incidents, and never saw any submarines. I do remember being instructed that if we ever saw one on the surface, we were to turn and fly the other way. We were no match for their deck guns.

My wife and I lived at Ocean Ridge, a few miles south of the base. I don't recall any particular social events at the base, like dances and that sort of thing. I went into the Air Corps about when the base closed, and fortunately was still young enough for flight training. Later on, I became an instructor on B-25s at the Air Corps base at Albany, Georgia. Still later, I was an instructor on A-26s at the Del Rio, Texas, Air Corps base. I had enough "discharge points" to quit the service just after V-J Day. When I returned home, I started up a Stinson dealership at the Lantana Airport. Now and then, I still see friends from the coastal patrol, and we talk about our good old days chasing subs from our shores.

## Charles Weeks, Jr.

*One of those friends, fellow pilot Charles Weeks, Jr., was born in Palo Alto, California in 1919, moved to Florida in 1934, and learned to fly at Morrison Field. He was with the Florida Defense Force when it became part of the Civil Air Patrol, served at Lantana from October 1942 until November 1943, and was awarded the Air Medal:*

I was young and single and loved to fly. I flew every plane they had at the base, most of them owned by the wealthy older fellows living in West Palm Beach. Though I also flew Fairchild 24s, and Stinson Reliants with Wasp 450 hp engines, I mainly flew Stinson 10-As with Franklin 90 hp engines. I'd usually only fly one four-hour patrol a day, but sometimes would trade with someone — fly his patrol the same day, so he'd take mine on another day — and end up in the air for as much as eight hours by sundown. That was a little tiring even for a young guy. In twelve months I totaled about a thousand hours on patrol.

Lantana was a good field. It had thirty-five hundred foot paved runways and clear approaches, and it was about ten miles from where I lived. A canteen was operated by a group of women volunteers from West Palm Beach who put on excellent breakfasts and lunches for everyone. Sleeping quarters were available for pilots on the next morning's dawn patrol who wished to stay at the field overnight. I don't recall much socializing — parties and dances and such — but I do remember having occasional close-order drill. Wright Vermilya, our commanding officer, ran a well-disciplined base and we did what we had to do without thinking too much about it. Despite those long hours on patrol I personally never saw a submarine. On several occasions, however, I did see bubbly wakes that may have meant a sub had just submerged

— there were plenty around. On our late afternoon patrols north to Melbourne, it became standard procedure for us to land at the Naval Air Station at Banana River and stay overnight. We'd eat a Navy dinner and head for the bachelor officers quarters to sack out, so we could rise early and fly back to Lantana on the dawn patrol. After my many missions carrying bombs and depth charges on anti-submarine patrol, I signed up in the Air Corps.

Colorful decals, such as this featuring the Lantana coastal patrol insignia, were distributed at the 1995 Aircraft Owners and Pilots Association meeting, one session of which paid tribute to all coastal patrol flyers during World War II (courtesy Owen Gassaway).

Charles Weeks briefly recounted some of his extensive Air Corps record in a 50th anniversary (1941–1991) brochure about Lantana Airport history:

> I took my flight test for the Air Corps at Morrison Field in a twin engine Cessna known jokingly as the "Bamboo Bomber" because it was mostly made out of wood and fabric.... I was sent to the 26th Transport Group at La Guardia Field, New York. This was a little frightening to a country boy! After two weeks I got further orders to report to Brownsville, Texas for Officer Training School.... After a few weeks of flying in UC-64s we were transferred to the 6th Ferrying Group located at Long Beach, California. Our next transfer was to Palm Springs where our main effort was to learn instrument flying in BT-13s, known as "Vultee Vibrators."... I was transferred to the Air Transport Command and after further training in Curtiss Commandos (C-46s), I wound up stationed at Casablanca, North Africa. My regular run was from Casablanca to Cairo, with stops at Tangier, Algiers, Tunis, Tripoli, and Benghazi. Additionally, I made four flights across the Pacific on the "Purple Project," San Francisco to Manila, transporting paratroopers to invade Japan.

After the war, Charles Weeks flew thirty-four years as a corporate pilot. Flying remains a great part of his life. Now and then he goes over to Lantana Airport to fly — with an undeniable sense of *deja vu* — Owen Gassaway's beautifully restored Stinson 10-A with its special coastal patrol paint job.

## John S. Prescott

*At eighteen, John S. Prescott, a native of Fort Lauderdale, was the youngest of the Lantana pilots:*

I saw an ad in the newspaper saying the coastal patrol wanted a hundred pilots, and since several of my friends including Charlie Weeks got into it, I did too. Charlie took me under his wing like a guardian angel. He was like a father figure. But even at my young age, I had a lot of hours, so they made me a pilot right away, and I never had to spend any time as an observer.

There were a lot of subs around when I first reported. Sightings were not at all unusual, but our little Stinson 10-As were no match for them. If we saw one on the surface, we were told to stay far, far away. They had a deck gun that could hit Hollywood, California. One of our regular patrols was north to the Banana River Naval Air Station. The Navy told us, "Come on up, the food and bunks are free." [The Naval Air Station is gone now, and in its place is the Cape Canaveral Rocket base.] They had PBYs and PBMs, and sometimes they'd let us go up with them. They were looking for the same guys as we were — Schicklegruber's subs!

The Lantana airfield was very comfortable. I remember a bunkhouse that could sleep forty men. When we returned from a dusk patrol too tired to drive home, and knew we had to get up early for the following morning's dawn patrol, we slept there. It was a pretty plush bunkhouse because Lantana was a very rich base. "Ike" Vermilya was our boss — a flyer-soldier from the first world war — and a gentleman. Art Keil took command when Ike was absent. I remember a number of fellows pretty well. One was Arthur R. ("Yardbird") Sprott, a big bean farmer from Delray Beach who owned one of those spin-proof Ercoupes and could fly like a son-of-a-gun. Sprott was a good buddy of Rex Bassett, who had his own electronics business in Fort Lauderdale. He built long range radios that could pick up our signals many miles at sea.

When the base closed, I went into the Air Transport Command and began ferrying P-47s and P-51s from California to the east coast. We usually flew in a large group and landed at Newark Airport. From there the planes would be sent to England. Later on I flew "the Hump" across the Himalayas, a scary assignment as anyone will tell you. But I had some real good flying time with the coastal patrol, and easily had enough hours to be awarded the Air Medal. When I look back, my missions at Lantana were often more exciting than any I had with the Air Corps.

## David R. Thompson

*David R. Thompson grew up in West Palm Beach ("across the lake" from Palm Beach Island) and at age twenty was one of the youngest men at the Lantana base. He had only a student pilot license, but someone suggested he go and see what the coastal patrol was all about and he volunteered on his first visit. By the time the base closed he had earned his private license and flown enough hours to win the Air Medal:*

I started off working in the radio shack and flying occasionally as a flight observer. One exciting experience was flying a mission with Jack Prescott, who was piloting Jimmy Donahue's Stinson Reliant gullwing. I was in back where I could stretch my legs. When suddenly the engine started to run rough, I told Jack he ought to quit fooling around with the magnetos. He replied, "I haven't touched them." I said, "Well start touching them! The prop is barely turning." Then Jack said, "I don't know what the hell is wrong. There's plenty of fuel, plenty of everything." We'd both totally forgotten the three-hundred and fifty pound depth charge we were sitting on.

Then the engine stopped for a few seconds before Jack got it restarted and we headed straight for the beach. It started and stopped two or three more times, and rather than take a chance on getting all the way back to Lantana, we called Morrison Field — maybe ten miles closer — requesting a clearance to land there. We planned landing into the wind, from west to east, but the tower told us that the west end of the

Lantana base member Zack Mosley was a cartoonist and pilot long before the coastal patrol was organized. His continuing comic strip, "Smilin' Jack," was undoubtedly its most effective promoter (courtesy Jill Mosley).

runway was closed for repairs. Not wanting to risk crashing in the urban area while we went around to find another runway, we explained we weren't a large aircraft and didn't need more than fifteen-hundred feet at most. They said, "Okay, land at your own risk." After landing we thought of the depth charge, and I jumped out and put a pin in the thing so it couldn't possibly explode. The engine problem we had had was that the last time the plane was overhauled, somebody forgot to put the lock washers on the bolts attaching the magnetos, and engine vibration had finally loosened them to where the electrical contacts became intermittent. Some of our fellows were pretty well-to-do. Among them was Wiley Reynolds, the son of a wealthy banker, and Hood Bassett, who subsequently became the chairman of the board of the Southeast Bank of Florida. Bassett, who's now dead, was also something of a war hero, parachuting into Nazi-occupied France to work with the French underground.

The Lantana base had a canteen in a new, unlived-in house down past the hangar. It had a very pleasant screened porch, but lacked cooking facilities. Socialite Red Cross ladies served coffee and doughnuts, sandwiches and cold drinks, much like a U.S.O. They were more accustomed to maids and servants serving them, but they were very cordial

In this and the previous panel, Mosley explains the CAP's origin and its various assignments. The pilot standing in a barracuda bucket hoping the circling sharks will let him alone depicted a real danger to be faced.

to us. Some of the things I've read in recent years — particularly *Operation Drumbeat\** — have made me question very seriously whether the U.S. Navy's Admiral Ernest J. King couldn't have allocated more naval resources to fighting the submarines off our coasts. The loss of some coastal patrol pilots might have been avoided if he'd responded differently. As for me, I never thought of the coastal patrol as really dangerous. I figured, what the heck, I could swim and I had a Mae West, so the only thing to worry about was the damned sharks. At age twenty, I just enjoyed the hell out of it all!

\* Michael Gannon, *Operation Drumbeat: The Dramatic True Story of Germany's First U-Boat Attacks Along the American Coast in World War II* (Harper & Row Publishers, New York: 1990). Among other coastal patrol statistics cited — 86,685 missions flown, 244,600 hours flown, 82 bombs dropped against enemy submarines, two submarines definitely damaged or destroyed, 5,684 special convoy missions performed at Navy request, 90 airplanes lost, 26 men killed, and seven men seriously injured.

A number of interesting and often humorous stories of the Lantana base can be found in the excellent 1992 memoir co-authored by David Thompson and his wife, Sandra. *Palm Beach: From the Other Side of the Lake* offers unusual insights into the flora and fauna of south Florida and the somewhat unique hazards of the area for coastal patrol flying. Here are two excerpts:

> [Our] little Stinson planes didn't have bathroom facilities aboard, and we would have to set down occasionally to relieve our situation. On one run we landed at Vero Beach on a Navy practice field to answer the call of nature. As we approached, we saw about eight or ten gobs with big, wide brooms sweeping the runway ahead of us and had to pay keen attention to put the planes down without hitting them. We set the planes down and were able to taxi close enough to spot the problem. There was an army of armadillos on the runway, and the Navy boys were sweeping them off. If a plane came in hot and hit even one of those tough armor-covered critters it would wipe out easily. The Navy practiced simulated carrier landings on the strip, and it was an ongoing problem to keep the runways free of the crusty menaces.
>
> [On one dawn patrol] the planes began slipping and sliding all over the runway and could not take off. The pilots couldn't figure out what was happening and came back in to report the difficulty they were experiencing. It was a chilly morning after a warm night, and when an inspection was made of the runway it was discovered that the warm asphalt had attracted lots of rattlesnakes. The snakes had come out of the brush around the airport in search of a warm haven and found it on the asphalt.... A Jeep went out with a rifleman and returned with the hood covered with dead rattlers. Some of the critters had ten rattles. They were huge. The sensation of slipping and sliding and bumping over the rattlers must have been very strange.

David and Sandra Thompson's book also provides glimpses into the wealthy lifestyles of some pre-war Palm Beach families several of whose sons were volunteer flyers at the Lantana coastal patrol base. One incident describes David Thompson's introduction to his friend Hood Bassett's mother:

> Most of our flying was trouble-free and routine, but occasionally a problem would arise. We had a plane go into the ocean due to a piston rod breaking. I received the emergency message. The plane went into the ocean just east of Hood Bassett's mother's house, which was located behind the Bethesda-by-the-Sea church in Palm Beach. We lost little time getting over to help the crew when the report came in that they had made it safely to shore with the use of Mae Wests. I

asked for permission to use the phone at the Bassett's to call for a support unit to come and salvage the plane to be trailered back to the airport. Once a plane went into the drink it was pretty much a goner. The salt water would do a job of destroying the engine and the interior, and the plane was lost unless the owner wanted to spend a lot of money rebuilding and renewing it. Mrs. Swenson, Hood's mother, became aware of the commotion and had her butler invite the soaking wet crew into the house for coffee. The house was magnificent and the guys were dripping salt water. The fact that no one was hurt allowed for a bit of joking about the incident, and it was decided that it was a hell of a way to get an invitation to have coffee at Hood's mother's mansion.

## Wiley R. Reynolds

*Wiley R. Reynolds was born in New York City, raised in Michigan, and became a Florida resident in 1937. After taking a complete Civilian Pilot Training Program ground school course for only seven dollars, he went through the other CPTP courses "all on Uncle Sam," and had his private pilot's license before Pearl Harbor. As shown on his Air Medal certificate, Reynolds was a Lantana pilot from April 2, 1942, the day the base was activated, until August 31, 1943. Forty years later, he told of the dunking that earned him a membership in the Duck Club:*

> Engine started missing and losing power at about 1500 ft. Dropped a couple of smoke flares to get wind direction. Saw small craft below and circled near. Occupants of craft signaled to us to drop our 100 lb. demolition bomb. As I got close to the water I pulled on full flaps, shut off ignition and hauled back on controls. Ocean was calm. Plane nosed over, then settled back to float about 8 minutes before sinking in 150 ft. of water. Landing craft picked us up in about 5 minutes. My observer, who did not know how to swim, kept cool, inflated his one man raft and held on to plane wing and raft. I opened door on left side and swam around to my observer. All this time my cousin, Harry Bassett, and Alex Thomson were circling in a companion plane calling base but could not be heard at Lantana due to local thunderstorms. We arrived in Fort Pierce about an hour later.

In 1996, Reynolds expanded on this experience:

As for my ditching incident, I'm still amazed at the calm displayed by my 57-year-old observer, Ralph Cohn, considering his age and the fact that he couldn't swim. Most people in that situation would have panicked. I nearly did myself, because when I swam around to his side of the plane, I looked down in the water and saw what appeared to be the gaping jaws of a large shark. I quickly realized that it was cloth bag in which Ralph's life raft had been stored. It was suspended open-end up just beneath the surface of the water. I had seen sharks pulled from the water with open maws and I may have been thinking of that, because sharks abounded in the coastal waters.

After I got back to base and described the noises the plane's engine was making, they explained that the engine had probably "swallowed a valve." In any case, I knew that we were losing power, and since there was a Navy boat just below us, I thought it prudent to ditch. We all flew each other's planes. Ted Keys put my plane down, and I had put someone else's plane down. It sank in eight minutes. I had been married for a year and my bride didn't worry much about my flying. When I called her after I'd gone into the water, she said, "Oh, you had a chance to try out your ditching system!" (I'd been the base's safety officer and had begun a system of practicing ditching on dry land.) She said that it was only later that it had suddenly dawned on her that I'd really crashed into the Atlantic Ocean. I flew all the various shifts, including the dawn patrol, for which I had to rise at about four o'clock in the morning. We had a nice canteen at the field and I'd usually have coffee and a couple of donuts to start the day. In May of 1942, every morning when we went out we'd see a torpedoed ship and the black smoke boiling upwards. The main idea seemed to be just to keep our planes out there. If the U-boats saw any kind of plane they had to crash-dive, because they knew that even a little plane might summon a bigger plane. They just didn't like airplanes at all. We weren't permitted to take photos. I wish we had been, because they'd have been unforgettable.

I tried to enter the Air Corps well before the base closed, but was denied a release by the CAP. At that time, the coastal patrol was far more important than adding yet another Cadet to the large stream of trainees already in the mill. I did finally enter the production line, but ended up going through basic training twice while waiting for an opening to take flight training. By then the war was almost over and I never did get in any flying. When the war ended I came back to my family, and to work at my father's bank, the First National Bank in Palm Beach. At age seventy-eight I'm supposed to be retired but I still spend a lot of time in my office.

\* \* \*

Membership in the "Duck Club" was limited to the coastal patrol flyers who survived a ditching at sea, a form of recognition for the airmen who came so close to losing their lives. Colonel Lester E. Hopper has described the award's origins in the 1984 CAP Historical Monograph Number One, *Duck Club:*

Long a tradition in European armies the recognition of individuals for special acts had its beginnings in the United States Military with the Badge for Military Merit. Orders creating the Badge for Military Merit were issued by the Continental Army on August 7, 1782. A simple heart-shaped piece of cloth, it was awarded to all ranks involved in acts of unusual gallantry. George Washington wrote when he established this first award, "The road to glory in a patriot army and free country is open to all." Certainly, it is then fitting that the form taken some 160 years later to recognize Civil Air Patrol's patriots would be a simple cloth device.

Some form of recognition was badly needed to help the sagging morale of the civilian airmen so valiantly fighting the Axis Submarine fleet in our coastal waters. Already, by March of 1943, some 51 aircraft had been lost at sea resulting in 16 fatalities and 87 aircrew men surviving the harrowing experience of a crash on water. It was at that time that Lieutenant Colonel L. A. (Jack) Vilas conceived the award to be presented to all who survived. Designated the "Duck Club" the idea paralleled the Army Air Corps famed Caterpillar Club [for a forced parachuting from an airplane]. The name of the actual designer has been lost in the pages of history, but it has been commonly thought that Colonel Vilas was the designer.

Utilizing the prevailing Blue Civil Air Patrol Disc as a background, the emblem portrays a red duck sitting on the water which is represented by a series of blue wavy lines. Civil Air Patrol Bulletin, Volume II, Number 15 of April 9, 1943 specifies that it is to be worn below the flap of the left pocket of the shirt or blouse. Subsequently, CAP Rules specified both the two and a quarter-inch diameter cloth badge and a one-inch metallic version. The metallic version was produced in blue and red enamel over sterling silver by Bastian Brothers of Rochester, New York.

## Zack T. Mosley

*The best-known member of the Lantana coastal patrol was Zack T. Mosley, creator of the popular cartoon strip, "Smilin' Jack." An airplane owner and pilot since the mid-thirties, Mosley became involved with the First Air Squadron of the Florida Defense Force in early 1941, and was a booster of the CAP concept from its inception. Several chapters in his 1976 book,* **Brave Coward**, *recall his flying experiences and other aspects of the Lantana base:*

> In February, 1942, Andy Sprague, my assistant at that time, and I, set up a studio in West Palm Beach, so I could continue writing and drawing "Smilin' Jack," mostly at night. That way I could pursue Civil Air Patrol duties in the daytime. Not long afterward, I was permitted to build a studio alongside the top of the hangar at the Lan-

tana, Florida, Airport. It was a beauty and looked like a control tower. Then I could practically live at the C.A.P. base.

On February 28, 1942, we started patrol flight training. On April 2, 1942, we received official orders to fly on active duty offshore. By now I had almost conquered my fear of flying, but to fly out over the Atlantic Ocean in a small single-engine LAND plane was a different "pail of witch water." The "BRAVE COWARD" in me reared its ugly head again. I was a bit scared, but I wasn't ALONE. Our squadron of nervous "pucker pants" pilots and observers winged waterward.

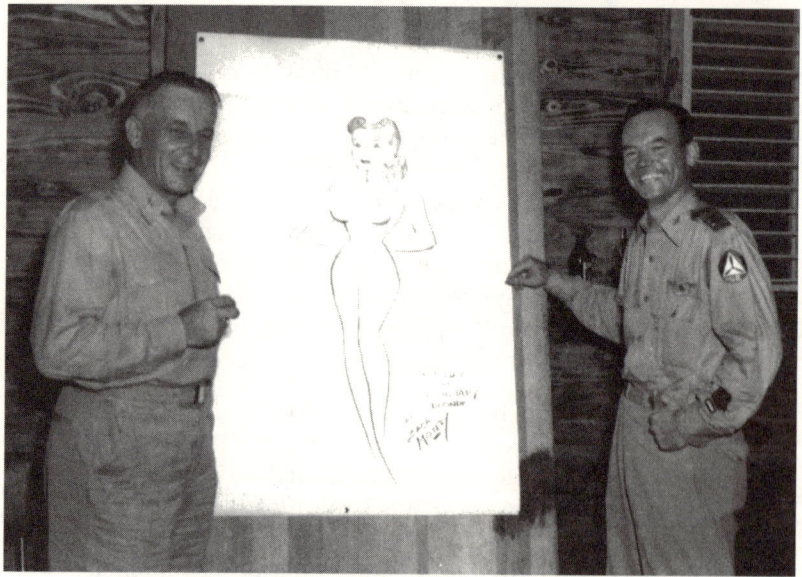

Zack Mosley showing an unidentified senior officer a preliminary sketch outline of one of his "Li'l Miss De-Icer" drawings. Mosley visited various other coastal patrol bases and gave away autographed prints of his drawings (courtesy Jill Mosley).

During his stint at Lantana, Mosley visited other bases, drew numerous "Smilin' Jack" strips aimed at educating the public as to the hardships and dangers faced by coastal patrol flyers, and generally acted as a goodwill emissary and morale builder on the organization's behalf. Aware that critics doubted if coastal patrol members ever did anything dangerous, he would invite them to meet him at their convenience forty miles off Cape Hatteras, in a single-motor land plane, at four hundred feet above the ocean. He called the following his "classic frightening story" with a humorous twist:

While flying the dusk patrol from West Palm Beach to Melbourne, Florida on April 24, 1942, the THING that we feared most, HAPPENED! "Bean Sprout" Art Sprott, flying his "fugitive-from-a-canning-factory" Ercoupe, was my wing man on that flight. We were out of sight of land, darkness was not far away, and one helluva wide thunderstorm area was just ahead in our flight path. My observer, Johnny Prince, tried to radio Sprott that we should head back for shore, but the static was too bad. We wing-waggled to him to turn back, but Sprott just kept heading further on out to sea to try to fly around that inferno of lightning and thunderheads. Johnny and I reasoned that if an engine failed and a plane crashed near darkness far out at sea, any injured pilots would probably never be found. I said to Johnny, "Sprott must not be as big a coward as I, but I think he's a bigger damned fool. He isn't going to turn back, but I think we should try to find the coast. What say you?" Johnny said, "AMEN, and good luck to Sprott and his observer!" We must have had a premonition, and it was the best decision we ever made.

Just about the time we sighted land, the RPM gauge dropped to about 1500 rpm, and I thought it was carburetor ice. So I pulled the heat full on and pushed full throttle, but the rpm didn't increase. The oil pressure was decreasing, engine-head temperature was rising, and we were losing altitude. We were down to about 300 feet as we neared the beach, but it looked too rough to attempt to land, especially since my Rearwin had a "stiff-legged" landing gear. We knew we'd roll up into a ball. In the distance we spotted the new Vero Beach Airport, which was under construction. We headed across town toward one runway that was partially finished. The plane was shaking, the cowling was jumping, smoke was pouring out, and the engine was making one hell of a noise, but it was still clunkin' at about 1000 rpm!

After landing and stopping just short of some heavy construction equipment still sitting on the runway, Mosley and Prince exited the plane as quickly as they could, convinced that it would catch fire at any second. Just then an automobile came roaring up, and a dapper man with a flat-brimmed straw hat jumped out and said — almost with disappointment it seemed to the startled flyers — "Oh, you two pilots are still alive — er — can I be of any assistance, take you somewhere?" Needing a drink more than anything, the two flyers allowed the man to drive them to a bar where he introduced them to the bartender and some of his other friends, bought them a double rums on the rocks, and left. Then, according to Mosley:

> The bartender and crowd starting laughing, and Johnny and I asked, "What's so funny? The laughing bartender said, "When you two went over town at about 200 feet in that smokin', clunkin' plane, a lot of us thought you would crash for sure, and our friend with th' straw hat rushed out to 'tag' the bodies. He is a local UNDERTAKER! Hah, hah, hah!"

In addition to his well developed sense of humor and cartoonist's skills, Zack Mosley was an excellent and serious pilot. He flew over three hundred hours on regular patrols, and was awarded the Air Medal in 1948. He died in 1993 at the age of eighty-seven.

## Henry McLemore

Mosley and John A. ("Art") Keil, base intelligence officer, once gave well-known newspaperman Henry McLemore a hop from Daytona Beach down to Lantana in Mosley's handsomely maintained Stinson 10-A. McLemore's August 9, 1942 humorous account of the trip was carried in papers throughout the country. Although his comic exaggeration may have been carried too far, his point that the airmen of the coastal patrol were doing a dangerous job with minimal resources was well made. Some excerpts:

> The two C.A.P. captains — Zack Mosley and Art Keil — brought me down in a ship that looked as if it were on lend-lease from the Smithsonian Institution. I wouldn't be at all surprised, in fact, if its motor wasn't stolen from Eli Whitney's cotton gin.... Its instrument panel would make the face of a Mickey Mouse watch seem complicated, and the few dismal little instruments on the dashboard didn't work. The airspeed indicator showed 8 miles per hour as we were airborne and 210 when we cleared a pine thicket so closely that I could have robbed a sparrow's nest had I chosen to.... We came down as the crow flies — but didn't beat any crows who were following the same flight plan. We had an exciting time with a pelican near Fort Pierce and we were proudly holding our own until the pelican changed his prop-pitch and left us as if we were standing still. Two sea gulls buzzed us, but we were more maneuverable and we turned inside of them.

McLemore began and ended his story, "Hats Off to Civil Air Patrol, Nothing Too Tough for Fliers Searching for Subs," with an honest tribute to the coastal patrol and the risks its fliers ran:

> Let me tell you that I have never met flyers for whom I have more admiration and that goes for the hot fighter pilots I have watched take off for sweeps over France and Germany, and the bomber boys who fly the giant Fortresses in the face of enemy flak and fighters.... Anytime you want to sing a song to some unsung heroes, lift your voices to these middle-aged men, all volunteers, who are doing a hazardous job with equipment that would make Pratt and Whitney have gooseflesh that [Donald] Douglas could see all the way from California.

By present definitions of age brackets, the columnist would be wrong to call most coastal patrol flyers "middle-aged." Records show that the average age of these pilots, disregarding the higher-ranking and somewhat-older base officers who usually did not fly regular patrol missions, was probably nearer the early- or mid-thirties. But then average life spans have increased, and in this earlier era, the mid-thirties were considered older than they are now. Men of thirty-eight and older were even excluded from the draft, a limit that might now be debatable but was hardly questioned then. One has only to think of today's astronauts, many of whom are well into their forties and fifties.

Coastal patrol planes were never this decripit, nor were Ryan ST look-alikes ever used for patrol, but the drawing may have made the patrols seem more "daring" to the public (courtesy Jill Mosley).

## Wallace R. King

*All of the flight crewmen at Lantana knew Mosley, and he drew some of them into his "Smilin' Jack" cartoon strips, among them 28-year-old pilot Wallace R. King, then of Lake Worth, Florida, whom Mosley thinly disguised as "King Wolf." A Missourian by birth, King grew up in Florida and learned to fly a J-3 Cub in the late 1930s. Before the war he drove for a transfer company and flew only occasionally. But when he joined the coastal patrol, he had both a private license and enough experience to begin flying as pilot-in-command from the start. By the time the base closed, he had totaled a thousand hours on patrols. King and fifty-one other Lantana flyers won the Air Medal. Only the men from the Atlantic City base won more:*

The base was about twelve or thirteen miles from Lake Worth and I slept at home every night. I flew mostly Stinson Voyagers and never had a close call, though I once had a scare when my engine quit out over the ocean. It wasn't anything. The engine cut out, but cut right back in again. One of the magnetos went bad. We got into trouble with thunderstorms once or twice, but we'd just head on in, and find the beaches. Fog was sometimes a problem, but usually it wasn't very thick and you could go right down into it — as long as you could see the runway.

We thought we saw a sub once. We were on patrol off Stuart, and saw the ocean bubbling, like a sub had just crash-dived, so we dropped a bomb on the spot. The Coast Guard had a boat nearby and they came to investigate. A couple of days later, the base got a message from headquarters to "quit bombing sunken ships." Apparently the ocean had been rough enough to roll a ship around on the bottom, and let a lot of air escape to the surface.

I think I'd been at the base about six months when everybody was sworn into the Air Corps reserve. And so, when the base closed, I was transferred into the Air Transport Command and flew for them as a civilian for a year. After that, I was a test pilot for Raytheon for a while before I was finally taken into the Air Corps and sent to Keesler Field, Alabama for basic training. I later served with the 7th Liaison Squadron in the Pacific. After the war, as a civilian again, I did some crop dusting in old Stearmans in New Jersey, New York, and Maine, then worked for Piper Aircraft at Vero Beach for sixteen years. I've enjoyed every kind of flying there is, and I still go up with a friend now and then.

\* \* \*

Nobody ever got rich serving in the coastal patrol or in any other CAP service. There were no salaries or wages, only daily expense allowances, or "per diems." These allowances were scaled to a position in the base table of organization: commanding officer, $10; operations and assistant operations officers, engineering and intelligence officers, flight surgeons, and pilots, including pilot-observers, $8; non-pilot observers, assistant engineering and intelligence officers, airdrome officer, radio operators, mechanics, and radio mechanics, $7; the administrative section head, $6; plotting board operators, clerk-typists, apprentice mechanics, linemen, and guards, $5.

The government also awarded expense allowances to the owner of each base aircraft. Such allowances, revised several times, were based on aircraft horsepower and whether bombs were carried. An August 29, 1942 payments schedule allowed the owner of a 90-120 hp non-bomb-carrying plane $4.40 an hour for operation and maintenance, $3.50 an hour for depreciation, and $2.75 an hour for crash, accident, and liability insurance, a total of $10.65 an hour. The owner of a 400-445 hp non-bomb-carrying plane (the largest used) was allowed $20.00, $10.00, and $11.00, respectively, a total of $41.00 an hour. When bombs were carried, the insurance allowances were doubled. As a practical matter, all allowances for operations and maintenance were received by the base and pooled for use on all base aircraft as needed. The allowances for insurance were received by the base and dispersed only for that purpose. Only the depreciation allowances were actually paid to plane owners. Most owners accepted the hourly allowances as more than fair and some even saw them as a low-cost way to own and operate an airplane largely at government expense.

## Ralph S. Boynton

*When he joined the Lantana base in July 1942, Ralph S. Boynton was a twenty-one-year-old living in Lake Worth with his parents. His father, who had been an engineer for General Electric in Boston, Massachusetts, in 1909 helped to found the town of Fellsmere, Florida. When his health failed, and his doctor advised him to move south, he returned to Florida and settled in Lake Worth. Ralph Boynton still lives in the house his father built in 1929 when he was four years old:*

I was hired as an apprentice mechanic, but I wasn't really much of one. I was more like the number one windshield cleaner and battery and oil level checker. I was there just a month or two and then joined the Navy. When I first reported, the squadron was located at the south end of Morrison Field. I remember a few names, such as Ted Keys, who had a nice low-wing monoplane and Art Sprott, who took me for a ride in his plane. Seems it hadn't passed its hundred-hour check because of some engine problem, which I assume he did not believe, so before he let us work on it he wanted to check it out himself. He asked me to come along and I did. I think someone had found some kind of unusual metal shavings in the crankcase. I also remember driving to Vero Beach with another mechanic to replace the engine on a plane that had a forced landing there. I had no tools of my own and did not wear a uniform. I was just a young kid who nobody paid much attention to.

But I always thought the coastal patrol was doing a good job helping to keep the subs away from the immediate coastline. At one point they'd been sinking three or four ships a night. I recall lying on the beach with a gang I hung out with and seeing a ship sunk right in front of us. It was heading north, just inside the Gulf Stream, when it was hit by a torpedo and broke in two. We all jumped in our cars and drove down to the Boynton Inlet to be there when the lifeboats arrived. This incident was one reason I joined the Navy. Well after the war was over, and I'd returned home, I received an honorable discharge from the Civil Air Patrol. By then I'd nearly forgotten it, except for these things I've just mentioned.

## Thomas G. Coleman

*Thomas G. Coleman was a thirty-year old service technician who lived in nearby Lake Worth. Born in Alabama, he had come to visit his sister who lived in West Palm Beach and stayed in Florida for fifty-five years:*

Before the war, a friend and I bought a used 40 hp Taylorcraft and learned how to fly. One day after my engine had stopped and started a few times, but I had gotten down safely, I thought, "What the heck am I doing? I've got a wife and two kids, and this paying for gas and oil and insurance is just too expensive, anyway." So I quit. Later I became a chicken farmer selling chickens and eggs around town. When the coastal patrol started, I worked eight hours a day at the base, shoving airplanes around, and then kept my chicken business going the rest of the time. I got either Friday or Saturday off to make my deliveries.

At the base, I was a lineman and did whatever was needed to be done. I worked the same total hours each day, but at different times, like coming in to help get the dawn patrol off the ground, or maybe coming in around eight o'clock. It varied. Naturally, I got acquainted with a number of the pilots, including Zack Mosley. He was a great guy. He put some of us in his comic strip, not by our real names, but he'd tell us what to look for. Often, he'd tell us the story of a whole strip, and he'd laugh as much telling it as we laughed hearing it. He was well liked by the linesmen and guards and mechanics because he never threw his weight around. I remember a day when he returned from a patrol with a bullet hole in his plane. He had no idea where it had come from, and we never found out.

I was there the day the English pilot flew an A-30 into Lantana thinking it was the Army's Morrison Field. That was a pretty hot aircraft and when he saw he'd run off the end of the runway into Lake Worth, he ground-looped the plane deliberately. Except for bursting a tire it did little damage, but he remained overnight for repairs. In the morning, he blasted down the same runway, just barely making it out of there. I believe he'd come in from the Bahamas — Nassau being less than two hundred miles from Lantana. They say that the A-30 was not a popular plane, and that we had given them to the English because we didn't want them. They also say that the English pilots swore to kill the designer after the war. I stayed at the base until it closed, and thought I was helping the war effort to the best of my ability. I'd already served four years in the U.S. Navy, 1931-1935, as a hospital corpsman, and had no desire for further military service.

* * *

It was within the Lantana base's patrol area that a bizarre incident led to the arming of coastal patrol planes with demolition bombs and depth charges. After pilot Thomas C. Manning and observer Marshall E. Rinker spotted a submarine on the surface near the mouth of the Banana River, they also noticed that in its haste to escape by submerging the sub had rammed its nose into a mud bank and remained stuck there. Ensuing events are recounted in *Flying Minute Men:*

> The CAP plane circled overhead for 42 agonizing minutes while Rinker and Manning watched the mired monster squirm in the sand like an ugly worm. Rinker was on the radio every minute of that time, calling for bombers, destroyers, sub chasers — anything! But before help arrived, the sub worked itself loose and disappeared in deep water. Weak with excitement and disappointment, Manning and Rinker flew home to Lantana, moaning and cursing about "the big one that got away." Major "Ike" called CAP headquarters in Washington and scorched the wires with his report: "That's one that we could have chalked up for a sure kill if we'd had bombs!" he shouted. "You see that we get 'em, and pronto, so we don't get caught with our pants down like that again. General [Hap] Arnold, learning of the incident at Cape Canaveral and of similar experiences by other CAP fliers along the coast, soon afterward directed the arming of all patrol planes.

---

Base officers, pilots, and observers, who served at least one month at CAPCP#3 and who are not elsewhere mentioned in this chapter include: E. C. Adams,* Thomas A. Alban,* H. G. Allen, Richard Z. Atkins,* W. J. Bailey,* John J. Barber, S. A. Belcher, M. T. Bevington,* T. V. Billings, Frederic E. Boyd,* Rhodes C. Boynton, Grady H. Brantley, Kenneth L. Brodbeck, Walter L. Carey,* Emerson C. Cook, Clarence C. Coston,* Briggs S. Cunningham,* Alfred N. Deacon,* Arthur R. Deacon, Lindsay N. Eve, Edward A. Forbes, R. R. French, James H. Garnett, Everett T. Garret, Kristoffer M. Granning,* Theodore Hardeen, Jr.,* Caleth W. Heard, Willis H. Hitt,* Virgil G. Humphries, Chester F. Jackson, Edgar W. Jackson, Russell P. Kelly,* George E. Kent, Jr.,* Albert P. Krueger, William M. Layman,* Ernest E. Lehmann, L. M. Lennard, Edgar C. Loy,* W. H. Maier, Robert L. Mosley, Charles A. Munn, Ector C. Munn,* Samuel I. Oldham,* Albert L. Perry,* John H. Quincey, Edward V. Quinn,* Jay F. Reeve,* Richard P. Robbins,* James O. Rose,* John H. Rothrock,* James A. Sapp, Jr.,* Daniel J. Stack, Jr., W. F. Thomas, Adam G. Thomson, Jr., James L. Turnage, Charles A. Van Wormer,* William K. Weber, Quenton M. Wilson,* and Bernard A. York.* Asterisk indicates Air Medal winner.

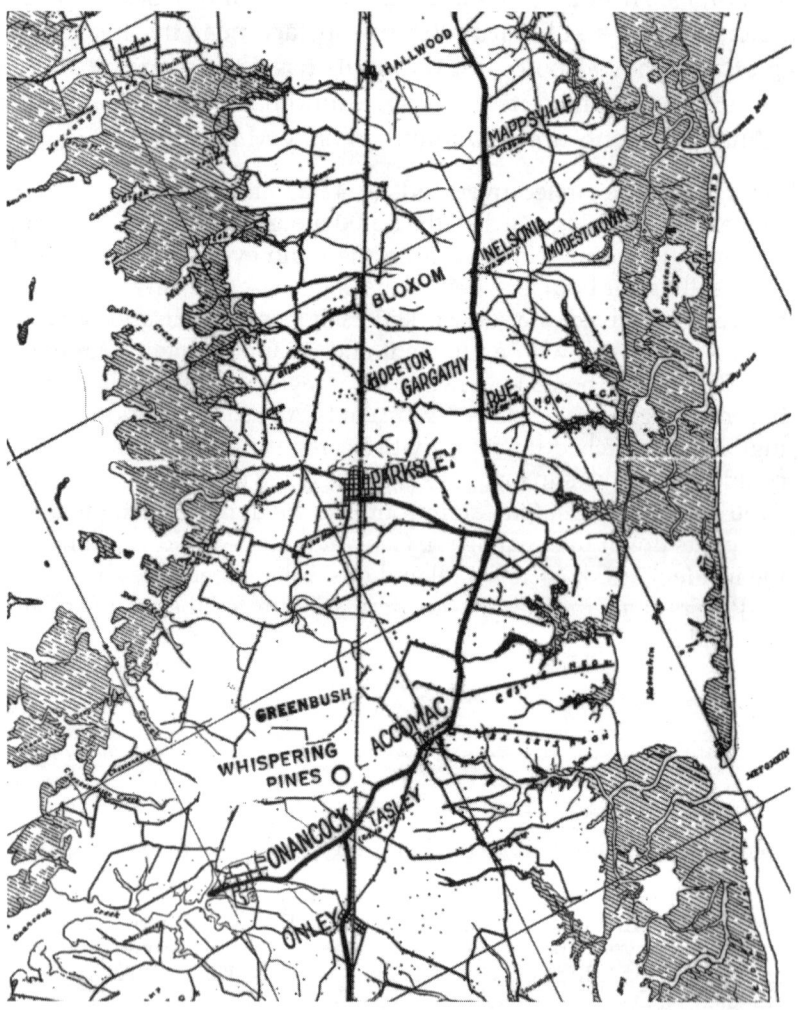

The town of Parksley, Virginia is located near the center of the "Delmarva" (Delaware-Maryland-Virginia) penisula only a few miles from the Atlantic Ocean to the east and the Chesapeake Bay to the west. The "airfield" used by the coastal patrol was just west of town, and does not even appear on this 1938 map distributed by the Eastern Shore of Virginia Chamber of Commerce.

# 4
# Parksley, Virginia

When the CAP first arrived the Parksley "airport" was little more than a rough cow pasture dotted with pine saplings and bounded by dangerous drainage ditches. After seeing what he would have to work with, the newly appointed base commander, Major Isaac W. Burnham, II, who had been transferred down from Atlantic City, wired the men assigned to him to "bring enough money to last you a month, and picks and shovels, because there'll be no landing field until we've built one." Major Burnham, age thirty-four and known to friends as "Tubby," was the much-respected founder and chief executive officer of Burnham & Company, a New York brokerage firm.

In the mid-1930s, the Parksley airport had been the brainchild of several local citizens who bought and developed the land for a private field. Supported by Works Projects Administration (WPA) funding, many unemployed Parksley people found jobs grading runways and building a small wooden hangar. Though a few privately-owned planes had been based there, and a barnstormer flying a Ford Trimotor once came through offering sightseeing hops over the town for a dollar, the venture was not a commercial success. The airport soon closed except for emergency use. In his short history of the base, written just before it closed, Burnham tells what he and his men found when they arrived:

> One farm house occupied by a farmer and his family. One chicken house occupied by five thousand baby chickens. One old well occupied by questionable water. One so-called hangar capable of holding one Cub airplane and quantities of water and dust because of its complete lack of weather-proofing. Two so-called runways, one 1400 feet long, the other 1600 feet long, obstructed by trees on three sides

and large drainage ditches on all but one side. There was no gasoline available, no oil available, no electricity, no telephones, in fact, no "nothun."

Upon my arrival Mr. Barton [Harry Barton, the farm's occupant] was very friendly, and he immediately whisked me to town to meet Mayor William Lewis of Parksley. I soon found out that the Mayor was one of the nine partners who owned the Airport, and that he was more than anxious to get a good tenant. Mr. Barton was paying the corporation all of $5 per month for rent, and they were perfectly willing to get rid of him if they could get $25.00 per month rent from the Government.

Left to right: Commanding Officer Isaac W. Burnham, II, Flight Surgeon Adam D. F. White, and Operations Officer, Alfred C. Nowitsky who was killed in a post-war plane crash (Hopper Collection).

Although I knew that the Civil Air Patrol at the time had no funds whatever and had only received authorization to pay a limited number of personnel certain small stipulated amounts daily for expenses, I had been informed that some money would be available for the purpose of starting a new Base. Apparently, this money was to come from the Tanker Protection Fund. The tanker companies had banded together and set aside a fund of money to be distributed to Civil Air

Patrol Bases to pay for those things which couldn't be begged, borrowed, or stolen.

After talking to the Mayor, I spent some time at Parksley with the Power Company and the Telephone Company. I found that Parksley was a town of approximately five hundred inhabitants and that it was a very prosperous little agricultural center. It seemed to me that facilities were available as well as the man-power to set up a Base. At the time I was worried about the housing situation because there was a United States Coast and Geodetic Survey Group in the vicinity, and most of the men were boarding in Parksley. No housing seemed to be available until someone suggested that possibly our men could stay at the Parksley Volunteer Fire Department, which had the most modern building in Parksley. After a hasty conference with the head of the Fire Department, I came to the conclusion that we could rent the second floor of this building, and use it as a temporary barracks.

Acting on the authority of the national Commander Earle L. Johnson, Burnham induced Captains Rudolph Smutney and Harold Cobb, and Lt. Robert H. Minton, to leave Atlantic City and join him in Parksley to set up the base. Once the base radio receivers and transmitters became operational, and the base mechanics, guards, and administrative staff were on the job, the flight personnel and planes began arriving. In his history, Burnham continued:

The pilots and observers straggled in each day by plane, and I was happy to note that we were getting a fine class of men and, in general, airplanes that were in very good condition. We had "Pappy" [James J.] Sutton, who came from Lake Charles, Louisiana, with "Louie" DiCarlo as his observer. "Pappy" and "Louie" only stayed here for thirty days, but all of us will remember them as two grand guys. They were oil men from way back as could be noted by the fact that neither of them had a full set of fingers. They left after their short stay and went back to Louisiana to help open the Base at New Orleans. That was the system in those days. Give them a month of experience, and then let them help to open another Base. It is our understanding that "Louie" DiCarlo since leaving this Base has had two forced landings in the Gulf of Mexico.

Twelve months and much hard work later later Burnham and his staff proudly announced to the world:

The Farm House is now an Operations Building ... [with] ... heat and light, telephones, teletypes, two radio receivers, two radio transmitters, a canteen, an Administration Office, an Operations Office, and S-2 Office, and a Storage Room. The Chicken House has been renovated only after the five thousand chickens were allowed to grow large enough to be ready for market and now has in its place a Radio Shop, a Photography Section, Pilot's Lounge, Lockers for personnel, three showers, and toilet facilities for men and women.... The old Hangar had its roof raised and a concrete floor added. Then to this another hangar was added, all built and planned by Base Personnel with the use of practically no strategic materials. This Hangar has complete steam heat, an oil room, a complete supply room (with supplies), insulation, and will hangar ten planes. It has been constructed so that the sand and dust of the Airport will not blow inside ... [and] ... so that it is easy to paint our planes during cold weather.... A two thousand gallon gasoline tank with Bowser filter was installed.

With help from the Virginia State Road Commission and the WPA, the airfield itself was vastly improved: the three grass runways were extended to two thousand feet by leasing adjacent farmland, trees were felled on the sides of the runways, and the drainage ditches were filled-in. Having heard of what had been accomplished, Zack Mosley visited the base, then featured it, with its farmhouse headquarters and hen house radio shack, in a "Smilin' Jack" comic strip. He also gave each pilot a drawing of his favorite female character, "Li'l Miss De-Icer," inscribing it, "Happy landings to the Parksley 'Wolves.' Hope this li'l de-icer helps keep th' frost outta th' fire house." While they completed work on the airfield, most of the squadron's pilots, eventually numbering some twenty-five to thirty, lived on the second floor of the town fire house. There they slept and ate, read newspapers, wrote letters, played gin rummy, and otherwise relaxed after a long day's flying.

### Isaac W. Burnham, II

*More than fifty years later, in 1996, the former base commander provided further information about the establishment of the Parksley base, and its sometimes thorny relationships with the region's population:*

I was in Atlantic City for several months before I was asked to open a base somewhere on the coast between Salisbury, Maryland and Cape Charles, Virginia. Flying down through Virginia along the coast where there were no airports, I saw a pretty sizable piece of land, and dropped down and landed. The owner came out with a shotgun and threatened to blow our heads off if we didn't get out. He really didn't know that a war was going on, but when I showed him my credentials he let me stay there. This was at Parksley, Virginia. They were never really very friendly to us, looking at us as intruders. Most of them were uneducated southern farmers, and when a bunch of pilots descended on them from various states and even Canada, they thought we were mostly spoiled rich kids. Most of us were lots tougher than they thought.

An unpleasant incident took place at a dance we held just before we closed the base. We had engaged a Negro band of six men from Salisbury, Maryland, and shortly after they started playing, the Negro cook's son who had just been drafted, came out on the floor to jitterbug with his girlfriend. One of the local men promptly broke a soft drink bottle over his head, and severely injured him. After we ejected all the local people from the dance, they organized outside, chanting, and threatening to lynch some members of the band. We sent our four Army armorers home to don their uniforms and return armed with rifles and pistols and then invited the local men to return to the dance. We warned them there would be arrests if there was more violence.

When they returned one of them backed me up to the bar, cursing me as a "nigger lover," and was about to hit me with a bottle when my men grabbed him. He was arrested, and ultimately served time in the brig at Langley Field. This ended the unpleasantness, and the dance went on. I mention this because it's important to understand that things were not always pleasant for us. There were unpleasant incidents because we virtually took over that little town. Our local relationships were basically pretty good because most of us boarded in local homes and made friends that way. I lived with a Mrs. White, a lovely woman who had a big house where six of us stayed. She couldn't have been more charming. It was the local tough guys who were troublemakers.

## Paul R. Loux, Jr.

*Paul R. Loux, Jr. was born in Bucks County, Pennsylvania, and graduated from high school in 1939 in New Cumberland, a small town near Harrisburg. For a time, he attended the Rising Sun School of Aeronautics near Philadelphia full-time, but ran short of funds and switched to night school, graduating in March 1942 as a licensed A&E mechanic. The way in which the 21-year-old Loux got his first job seemed surrounded by secrecy:*

I was determined to begin work with my new license right away, and my best prospect was to report to an anonymous office on the sixteenth floor of Philadelphia City Hall. When I did so, there wasn't even a name on the door. Today, you'd think it was some covert operation. Nobody told me much about the job itself, just to go buy an Army uniform and report to Parksley, Virginia. I really had no conception of what I was getting into. Once there, it wasn't long before I was named assistant engineering officer. I had the qualifications and they had the need. My job was keeping the airplanes flying. We averaged about twenty aircraft of all types at the base — a collection to befit a museum.

The big job was establishing an inspection schedule, developing a reliable source of parts and supplies (each base had to have its own), supervising a dozen or so mechanics and service technicians, and performing some of the maintenance work myself. We did almost everything ourselves, including recovering jobs. It was easy enough to tell when the fabric was going bad. We had a little spring-loaded device with a sharp-nosed plunger that you held up against the fabric. If when

Off-duty and standby personnel playing penny-ante poker in the shade of the old apple tree (Hopper collection).

it was released the plunger pierced the fabric, you knew it was rotten. If it only made a dent, the fabric was okay. We covered a whole wing once. In those days, you could buy something like a fitted slip cover to slide the wing into. Then you'd sew it up as tight as you could get it, and spray it with water to shrink it some more. Then, after one coat of dope, you'd sew it at three-inch intervals to each rib and then finish off with many more coats of dope. It was very time-consuming!

I recall one of our planes going down due to a failed oil pump. I believe that it was Trowbridge Heaton's plane, a Stinson Voyager 10-A, but the pilot that day was Arthur R. Myers of Lemoyne, Pennsylvania and the observer was Raymond E. Cooper of Topeka, Kansas. The 10-A's Franklin engine had its oil pump up inside the oil sump, attached to the crankcase with four coarse-threaded, quarter-inch bolts. They had so short a "meet" in the crankcase, they could loosen and snap off. Should that happen, the pump would drop into the sump and stop working. An oil-starved engine would then quickly freeze up and stop. We don't know for sure if this is what happened because the plane sank, but it seems likely. Fortunately, a life raft was dropped by the sister ship and the men were picked up by a Coast Guard craft within an hour, and eventually returned to the base unharmed.

Floyd Stawls was flying that sister ship and he told me that as he was putting the raft out the left door to drop to the guys on the water, it tripped the bomb release located just below the door. Fortunately, the bomb was unarmed and dropped harmlessly into the water. When Floyd got back to Chincoteague, the armorers noticed the bomb was gone, and assumed Floyd and his observer had dropped it on a submarine.

Another of our jobs was adding bomb racks to the planes. At some bases, that was done by mechanics at nearby Air Corps bases. We did it ourselves. Our very short runways made it dangerous to take off and land carrying explosives so we got permission from the Navy to use a corner of the Chincoteague Naval Air Station to mount and dismount the bombs and depth charges there rather than at our field. While the explosives were at Parksley we had some Air Corps personnel there to look after that ticklish job.

In the fall of 1942 I married a girl from Washington, DC and brought her down to Parksley. We found an apartment with a lady in town. The folks there were very kind to all of us, and I liked them and their little town a great deal. There wasn't much to do, however, and the only "base party" I can remember was on New Year's Eve 1942 at the firehouse. Earlier that fall, I had enlisted in the Air Corps reserve and that kept the draft board away as long as I was with the coastal patrol. After Parksley closed at the end of August 1943, and I'd taken a job as a mechanic for the Lynchburg, Virginia Air Transport Service, I received notice to report for active duty, and did so on December 27, 1943. I wanted to fly, but instead they sent me to gunnery school at Tyndall Field near Panama City, Florida. I did so well they kept me on as an instructor. After the war I learned to fly on the G. I. Bill, and many years later ended my aviation career as a flight engineer for Pan American Airlines.

## Arthur R. Meyers

*Arthur R. Myers, Air Medal winner, was another Pennsylvanian, and a relative latecomer to Parksley, arriving there April 1, 1943. He left behind his 1941 Taylorcraft, too under-powered for coastal patrol work, and flew a friend's Stinson SR-4 to the Virginia base instead. Twenty-two and single, he bunked first in the firehouse, then found a room in a widow's home near the airfield. It was close enough to walk, but usually he drove to the field. Most of his flying was done in Fairchild 24s and Stinson 10-As, one of which he had to ditch when the engine quit just off Wachapreague Inlet:*

On one of our patrols Ray Cooper and I spotted a Russian freighter heading northeast. Standard procedure called for us to identify the ship, then fly at least fifteen miles away, and in code give its position, direction, and speed. We advised Parksley that we'd remain on escort but after several patterns around the ship, I noticed our oil pressure heading for zero. I asked Ray if he'd rather try for shore or go to Russia. Wide-eyed and without hesitation he answered emphatically, "shore!" I was half-kidding, because I'd already started a turn toward the beach, a good twenty-two miles away. Ray called our sister ship, and they relayed our situation to base.

The Stinson 10-A purred along for a while as I held only enough power to maintain altitude. Our sister ship advised that we were trailing smoke, and we started to lose altitude. By using different combinations of fuel mixture and carburetor heat, I kept the engine going for a few more seconds before it stopped with a sudden squeal. We were down to three hundred, so a nice controlled turn into the wind put us at wave tops. The wind was about six knots off shore, so the waves were mere swells. After our wheels brushed through the first crest, I hauled back hard, and the little Stinson settled in pretty easily.

The hardest part was getting out. When the plane stopped, we were about twenty degrees nose-down. The water outside ran from the wing's leading edges diagonally across the door windows with the wing's trailing edges up out of the water. We couldn't open the doors because of the pressure of the water, so we waited a few seconds, pulled the quick release door pins, and waited for the water inside to reach chin level. When it did, we were able to kick off the doors and get out. Both Ray and I actually went back inside to try and find our life rafts but couldn't. We climbed atop the plane and inflated our life vests while our sister ship's crew dropped us their rafts.

After we were in them and roped together, the planes started coming — a whole string of them, seven in all, forming a line from the Wachapreague Coast Guard Station about eleven miles away. Captain Bobby Silverman in his magnificent Ryan SCW flew low, cut the throttle and yelled something that sounded like, "looks like you guys are hungry." What he didn't realize was that his trailing radio antenna, with its heavy lead weight on the end, had gone bouncing past our rafts only a few yards away. The Coast Guard picked us up an hour and seventeen minutes after we ditched. Our plane had flown nine minutes on failing oil pressure, and floated eight minutes more. And that's how Ray and I became members of the Duck Club.

I think what happened was this: the 10-A's Franklin engine had long oil supply lines from the bottom of the crankcase up along the cylinders and out to the rocker boxes, a long reach without support. An air-worthiness directive was put out to put clamps on the crankcase where the lines turned sharply to keep them from vibrating and cracking off. On our pre-flight check that day, I saw we had no such clamps. I asked our mechanic about them and he said, "Oh sure, they came in yesterday, and we'll install them when you get back from patrol." Well we got back, but the 10-A is still sitting out there on the ocean floor.

But that created a new hazard. By this time, the new Naval Air Station had become a busy place. A Navy torpedo squadron was training here in Grumman TBFs, big planes with big heavy props that could reduce our little aircraft to splinters in the blink of an eye. When we landed there, we had to break into the traffic pattern pretty much by judgment. We did not maintain radio contact with the Navy tower and they seldom bothered to clear our landings with signal lights. If we thought it was clear, we just went ahead and landed. But we also scooted off the active runway at the first intersection because we never knew what might be close behind us!

Once or twice I served an eight-hour shift at the Norfolk Information Center where representatives from Navy, Air Corps, Coast Guard and CAP together kept track of all the sea and air activity within a hundred mile radius. Markers were constantly rearranged on a huge plotting table to show the locations of all the ships and planes in the area. We knew that a marker labeled "2OS" (two observation slow) was one of our planes because we knew when and where they were dispatched. Manteo and Parksley alternated in providing personnel for this job.

I flew three hundred and sixty hours in my five months there. It was not at all tiring, either. In fact, it was delightful! In 1948, we held a reunion at Parksley to receive our Air Medals. I remember Major Burnham coming up to me and saying, "I didn't get much of a chance to know you then, you were always out flying." When the base closed, I returned home, then went into the Air Corps, where I served for twenty-seven months. I've remained in aviation all my life, still give flying lessons, and get up now and then in my own little home-built.

## Edward R. ("Jack") Fuller, II

*Another of the first arrivals was Jack Fuller of Richmond. Since he was already a member of the Richmond squadron of the "Virginia Protective Force" when the CAP was formed, a switch to CAP coastal patrol duties at Parksley seemed natural. Invited to try it for a month, he stayed from April 16, 1942, when the base was activated, until August 31, 1943, when it closed. He logged more than eight hundred hours of over-water flying, and was later awarded the Air Medal:*

We had two main jobs — convoy patrols and beach patrols. If there were any convoys in the coastal shipping lanes we got their coordinates from Norfolk Navy Base people and we went out to intercept them. Then, for as long as we could, we'd fly to either side or out in front of them to look for subs. If there were no convoys that day, we'd usually just go out and fly set patterns along the shipping lanes. We had a dawn patrol that left at first light, and an afternoon patrol that went out after lunch. If we were short-handed on a given day, we'd fly both patrols.

We also flew beach patrols covering the shoreline between Virginia Beach and Rehoboth Beach looking out for derelict naval mines and spent torpedoes. Sometimes there were dead bodies. We'd fly real low, maybe only twenty feet off the deck. That was exciting. By comparison, convoy patrol flying could just about put you to sleep. Going along for hours in the warm sunshine and hearing the drone of the engine was about like taking a snooze in a greenhouse. But if that engine so much as coughed, you were instantly alert!

## Frederick Stanger, Jr.

*Yet another of the pilots who helped open the base was Frederick Stanger, Jr. Born and raised outside Philadelphia on "the main line," Stanger earned his private pilot's license in 1940 at the Flying Dutchman airport near Paoli, Pennsylvania. Ralph Earle, who would later become commanding officer at the Riverhead coastal patrol base, and who was a friend of Stanger's uncle, called him one day to ask if he'd like to go down to Parksley, Virginia, and fly anti-submarine patrols. Stanger was more than happy to give it a try:*

Earle arranged that I meet Robert Silverman at the Flying Dutchman and fly down to Parksley in Silverman's Ryan SCW, a beautiful all-metal low-wing job that was sometimes used in the movies to look like a Japanese Zero fighter. There wasn't much there when we arrived — just this old farmhouse and thousands of chickens. We got there the day the base was officially activated, and the first patrols went out the very next day. Of course, you know how everyone pitched in to convert the farmhouse and its outbuildings into a functioning headquarters. There was just one wooden hangar, so most of the planes remained outdoors overnight. Everything was crude but workable. At first, like most of the others, I lived in the firehouse in town. The second floor was fixed up with bunks and showers, a little mess hall, and even a room for Ping Pong and card games. I think a game of "twenty-one" was kept going continuously. We had breakfasts and dinners at the firehouse, but snacked at the base for lunches. There was even room enough at the firehouse for occasional dances and other social affairs, too.

Later on, I shared an apartment with Murray Keeler — we called him "Ruby" after the famous star of Broadway musicals. "Ruby's" family owned some kind of textile factory in Rhode Island, and he brought down his own Fairchild 24. We rented from a woman whose husband was stationmaster at the local railroad depot. That was a busy line in those days, bringing troops down from the north to the ferry at Cape Charles, on their way to board ships for Europe.

Frederick Stanger, Jr. (left) and Robert Silverman working on Silverman's Ryan SCW. While aircraft owners were not required to do any mechanical work on their planes, for many it was a labor of love (courtesy Frederick Stanger, Jr.).

One of the funniest things I remember is when the first contingent of Virginia CAPers arrived. After they landed and taxied their planes up to the hangar, they got out and strolled over to the farmhouse evidently expecting that there'd be some enlisted men to go out and get their luggage. After some awkward moments when they began to realize that we didn't *have* any enlisted men, and that none of us were going to give them a hand, they went back and got their things themselves. We sort of fought the Civil War all over again, all eighteen months I was there. You see, Major Burnham was a New Yorker, and most of us early arrivals were "Yankees" from up north. It didn't matter that we soon were outnumbered by the boys from Richmond, we'd been there first and opened the base, and it was a *Virginia* base.

Major Burnham was the best base commander of them all. He was a great administrator, with a wonderful knack for handling people, the best C.O. I ever had in all my time in the service. We had some Stinson Voyagers, Waco cabins, at least the one Fairchild 24, and the four or five Monocoupes that were loaned to the base by the Monocoupe Corporation. Nobody liked to fly the fast little Monocoupes but kids like me and Ed Fuller, he at twenty, and myself at nineteen, being the youngest pilots on the base. The Monocoupes were dangerous. I think we cracked them all up, one by one.

I remember alternating — four hours as pilot, then four hours as observer. I went down there with about two hundred hours flying time. While I was there, I logged about five hundred hours as pilot and another five hundred as observer, and later was awarded the Air Medal. I was checked out on everything they had, and we hardly ever flew the same plane twice in a row. Of course, the fellows who brought their own planes flew them, and nobody else was allowed to. Mostly we flew convoy escort. There were two convoy lanes, one about fifteen miles offshore, the other thirty miles offshore. We covered the sector from Assateague Island down along the barrier islands as far as Cape Charles at Hampton Roads. I still recall flying the two-hundred-ten degree heading! I only once thought I saw a periscope wake, just before a U-boat submerged, and I reported it by radio, but I don't know if the Navy came out to investigate or not.

The most important thing is that we never had any fatalities at our base, and we accomplished what we set out to do. Not one ship was ever sunk in our patrol sector after we opened the base at Parksley, and I am very, very proud of that. After the war was over, a friend and I ran a charter service between Philadelphia and Bar Harbor, Maine, but then I got into real estate and haven't flown for forty-five years. Could I still get in a plane and go? Sure I could!

### Ferrell E. Weatherman, Jr.

*Some pilots came from considerable distances. One of them was Ferrell E. Weatherman, Jr., an Air medal winner from Hutchinson, Kansas, who had earned his private pilot license in the Civilian Pilot Training Program (CPTP) at the local junior college. Responding to the call for volunteers, he and four other CAPers boarded an old Waco cabin plane one Sunday morning to head for points unknown. Somebody handed them an envelope and told them to open it after they were aloft. They expected to head west, but the sealed order said* head east, to Virginia. *After stopping overnight, probably in Kentucky or West Virginia, they got some maps to see where Parksley was. When they called Washington CAP headquarters for directions, they were told "just head across Chesapeake Bay, pick up the railroad tracks that run between Washington and Cape Henry, and turn right." The trip was mostly in vain because the old Waco could not pass CAP acceptance standards. Everyone flew back to Kansas except Weatherman.\**

At first I lived in the firehouse with the other fellows. It was okay. We slept on cots, had showers and toilets, and a little kitchen toward the back. But then Ray Cooper, another pilot from Kansas, and I got together and rented a room from a Mrs. Johnson, remaining there until the base shut down. In the flying department, my closest call came in January 1943. My observer, Lee Savage, and I were returning from convoy escort in a Stinson 10-A against a fifty-knot wind, when our four-cylinder Franklin engine quit. I had just switched fuel tanks, so I went back to the first tank and she restarted for me — but only on three cylinders. We were at about a thousand feet, but I couldn't hold altitude. Rather than go into "slow flight" our sister ship kept S-turning back and forth to keep from outpacing us.

Our mayday call soon brought two Army 0-47s and a Navy PBY-5 for company. We were down to maybe two hundred feet when we came up on an oil tanker. Parksley told us that we might want to put down right there, if we thought the tanker would help us. I said we could at least make the beach, and kept going. The nearest airfield was Chincoteague Naval Air Station, at that time still under construction. We made the beach just above the trees and I thought we had it made, but Lee wasn't so sure. We were lucky. The only thing finished on the whole base was one cement ramp and when the engine suddenly quit dead, that's where we sat down. After we got out of the plane, a sentry came over to advise us. "You know, we're not open for business yet," he said. And I replied, "Well you are now!" When our mechanic came over from Parksley, he found all our plugs badly fouled. We figured that whoever filled our tanks last had done so out of a barrel which once had contained used engine oil. After our experience, some big changes were made in the way fuel was handled!

I was single when I arrived in Parksley, but I soon met a local girl, Sally Wessells, and eventually married her. She wasn't old enough to get married right away, so when the base closed, I went on down to

---

\* Before the war, the Civilian Pilot Training Program, not to be confused in any way with the Civil Air Patrol, was a dual-purpose federal program promoted by the Civil Aeronautics Authority not only to boost the aviation industry, but also to provide trained pilots in the event of war. Through 1939–1942 the CPTP trained more than 125,000 pilots. See*To Fill the Skies with Pilots: The Civilian Pilot Training Program, 1939–1946,* by Dominick Pisano, University of Illinois, 1995.

North Carolina with one of the other Parksley pilots, my friend James L. Fletcher, where we took jobs at an Air Corps base. Despite our flying experience, he was made a mechanic and they put me into the control tower. I didn't like seeing so many young kids crack up around the field, and I left to go back to Parksley where I picked up Sally and we eloped to the Poconos. I had a number of flying jobs after that, but ended up employed by the National Air and Space Administration here on the eastern shore of Virginia. I never did return to Kansas.

On a hot summer day in Virginia, the shade of a Waco's upper wing made a good place to pause for a quick picture while a lineman refueled the plane (courtesy Frederick Stanger, Jr.)

### Richard L. Yuengling

*Richard L. Yuengling, a 28-year-old from Pottsville, Pennsylvania flew his own plane down to Parksley in mid-1942, bringing his pregnant wife with him. Like everyone else, they rented a small room in a private home. Mrs. Yuengling was familiar with and enjoyed Virginia's Eastern Shore because for years she and her family had taken summer vacations at the beach on Wallops Island near Chincoteague, not far from Parksley. She remembers Parksley well:*

When he was on dawn patrol, Dick had to rise at five o'clock to get out to the field. I slept in until later, then I'd walk over to the drugstore where I could take a booth and have orange juice and coffee, then read a morning newspaper. It was the only place in town that served food of any kind. For our evening meals, my husband and I ate upstairs in the firehouse. I think the local ladies did the cooking, and we were served family style. After the baby came (I went home to Pottsville for the delivery), we took him along in his bassinet. In the evenings, Dick and I might play gin rummy or just read. Parksley wasn't very exciting, but it was a nice period in our lives.

After the base closed, Dick was taken into the Air Corps. He wanted to fly, of course, but they said he was too old to be a pilot. Instead they sent him to gunnery school and he flew in Europe as a turret gunner on a B-17. That was aggravating to him, because he had many more hours flight time than his twenty-year-old captain. In a way, after Dick began bombing missions over Germany, the coastal patrol suddenly seemed like child's play. Yet it wasn't really. That was dangerous, too. The coastal patrol flyers did a fine and necessary job, and I'm sure that Dick was proud of serving with them and earning the Air Medal.

## Alvah B. Killmon

*In contrast to Weatherman and the other base personnel who came from distant places, most of Parksley's guards and linemen were local men. Alvah B. Killmon, the youngest of them, was an 18-year-old who had just graduated from high school in nearby Bloxom. He took a job as a guard and felt lucky to get it, because there were not that many jobs to be had at that time:*

I was hired by Lieutenant Ralph G. Holt, who was in charge of the guards. There weren't any particular qualifications that I was aware of. I just filled out an application and was hired. I didn't think I'd make it, but I thought I might as well try. I lived at home and drove to work in my dad's Model A. Most of the time I stopped in Parksley to pick up one or two others guards on my way to the field. The fellows that rode with me at one time or another are all dead — Billy Justice, Nat Johnson, Henry Wessells, and Dorsey Matthews. Sergeant of the Guard Burleigh Taylor is gone, too. They were mostly older men — Wessells was already in his sixties. We had to buy our own uniforms and supply our own weapons. I carried a twelve-gauge shotgun loaded with double-ought buck shot. There were four guard posts: one on the road to town, one at the hangar, one at the door to our headquarters building, and the fourth out under the trees where the bombs were kept. We started off taking eight-hour shifts, and then they reduced that to six hours. I don't believe that anybody ever challenged anyone except perhaps on the road to town. We knew everyone that lived out that way, and people that lived west of the base had to divert around the base because one of the runways went across the road just near the headquarters building.

Corporal Alvah B. Killmon lived in nearby Bloxom and had just graduated from high school when he took a job as a base guard (courtesy Alvah B. Killmon).

If there were any base parties, I didn't know about them. The guards weren't involved much with the rest of the people, as I recall. We received little information at all really. I guess they felt we didn't need any. There was a snack bar in the headquarters building, but I didn't use it because I had all my meals at home. In January 1943 I was drafted, one of the first boys from the area to go after they dropped the draft age from twenty to eighteen. I went into the Air Corps and after a certain amount of training I wound up in the Aleutians as a radar operator, and served there until late 1945.

I should tell you about our base mascot, "Tailwind." He adopted us and when he came there, his right hind leg had been broken and he could only get around on three legs. The pilots collected money and took him to a vet to have him fixed. The vet had to break his leg again in order to set it, and then he was fine. After the base closed my wife got him from Burleigh Taylor. Tailwind lived for several more years after I got home from the war, and we had him until he died.

## Sidney L. Sherwood

*Another of the airfield guards was Sidney L. Sherwood, who lived half a mile from the base on the road into Parksley. Twenty-eight years old, with a wife and two children, ages six and seven, he started work there a month after the base opened and stayed until it closed, Sherwood still thinks of it as a happy time and a good place to have been employed:*

My family and I lived about a half mile from the airfield along the road into Parksley, and I don't know what I was doing or how I happened to be home that day, but I saw all these airplanes flying around, and wondered, "What in the world is coming off?" So, being kind of nosy, I went on down to see for myself. Well I ended up working there as a guard. I was signed up to work from seven in the evening 'til seven in the morning, a twelve-hour shift, for three dollars a day. There were only a few planes then and only two of us guards. When my pay check finally came, it figured out to five dollars a day, and I felt like I'd gotten a raise right off. Times were still hard where we lived, and with a wife and two children, I was very pleased to get that job. I think it must have been the same for most of the local folks.

Later, I worked regular eight-hour shifts, rotating the hours with other guards, and also rotating the posts — the hangars, the ammo dump, and so on. We had to buy uniforms and supply our own weapons. I had a twelve-gauge shotgun but I never even bothered to load it. It was quiet out there at the airport and nobody expected any problems. I could have walked to the field from our house, but I was lazy, so I drove as far as I could and parked on the shoulder and walked the rest of the way. The road past the airport was actually blocked off — one of the short grass runways had been extended across it — and anyone living west of the field had to follow a long detour to get into town.

I remember some people better than others. Like myself, all the guards were local fellows. So were most of the linemen and mechanics. My brother John L. Sherwood, Jr., was a lineman, and so was Franklin N. Ewell, who's now my next-door neighbor. I recall "Doc" White as being very nice, and Irene Hillman, who was Major Burnham's secretary. When the base closed I went down to Newport News to work in the shipyards. When peace came I went to work for the electric power company and stayed there 'til I retired. I'm eighty-two now, and some days I still go out "cruising timber" with a friend — measuring about how many board feet could be got out of stand of trees, and how much the lumber company ought to pay for them.

\* \* \*

## Nancy B. Taylor

*Most of the secretaries, clerk typists, radio operators, and plotting board experts were young women from Parksley and nearby communities. Nancy B. Taylor and her sister May R. ("Bobbie") Taylor were from Onancock, a small town on the Chesapeake Bay a few miles southwest of Parksley.*

When the war began, I was working for a Gulf Oil bulk distributor keeping books and that sort of thing for about fifteen dollars a week. Mainly I went up to Parksley for the better money they paid. I was interviewed by Major Burnham but there weren't any tests or anything. I worked for a couple of months as a clerk-typist, but I wasn't very good at it, so they switched me to radio operator.

Part of Parksley's smartly uniformed office staff. Second from left is May R. ("Bobbie") Taylor and next to her, center, is her sister Nancy Taylor (courtesy Frederick Stanger).

The radio room was in the old farmhouse, and my sister Bobbie and I worked together as a team on it each taking a different shift. The plotting board was upstairs somewhere, and those girls listened to the position reports on their own speakers. We had little contact with the flight crews except when they were out over the ocean on patrol.

I didn't have a car at the time, so I took a room in Parksley, and hitched a ride to the field with somebody each day. I met Daniel Breene, a handsome young pilot from Pennsylvania, and we began going steady. There wasn't a lot to do in Parksley, so we saw a lot of movies. There was only one theater in town, but the shows changed every other day. I thought he really loved movies. That's one of the reasons I married him!

After we were married in my church down in Onancock, Daniel never went to another movie. I guess he loved me, not the movies. We lasted fifty years anyway and he died just a few years ago.

There was a time he nearly cost me my job because of a mayday call he *didn't* make. Out on patrol something happened to his plane, and on his return to base he had to land on Cedar island, from where he called our operations officer from a Coast Guard station. I hadn't reported anything, because I didn't know anything had happened, but the operations officer jumped all over me saying "you missed the mayday call, you missed the mayday call." Daniel didn't admit not making a mayday call until later. The December 1942 "Sub Sniper" showed his photo with the caption, "Daniel A. Breene, just a great big overgrown kid who is a swell flier and who is just as good at getting into hot water (and out)." Well, that was my Daniel.

## Billings L. Mann

*Billings L. Mann, another Air Medal winner, served at Parksley from May 24 until November 1, 1942, doing double duty as a regular patrol pilot and as the assistant operations officer. Born in Providence, Rhode Island, he graduated from the New York Military Academy at Cromwell-on-Hudson and learned to fly in 1933 first in a Kitty Hawk biplane (manufactured in Providence) and then in a Gypsy Moth. His CAP serial number, #1-6-3, marks him as having been the third CAP volunteer in Rhode Island, and he was one of the wing's organizers. The 28-year-old Mann, who left his wife and young children behind, explains "I guess I just got patriotic":*

Because I had a lot of hours, I was named assistant operations officer at Parksley almost from the time of my arrival. That meant scheduling people and flights, while juggling fluctuations in aircraft availability. I also took my turn at patrols, flying everything on the base. I don't remember having any forced landings or other excitements, but I accumulated enough hours to qualify for the Air Medal. I never lived at the firehouse, but got a room immediately in a private home.

Well before the base closed, I went back to Providence, where I received a promotion to Major and was appointed executive officer for the Rhode Island wing. I stayed with CAP right up to V-J Day, but then resigned in order to resume my personal affairs. My father had just died and I had to take over the presidency of a business. I continued to fly for fun, right up to about five years ago, and over the years have owned several planes, including an Aeronca C-3, a Gypsy Moth, and a Waco. Looking back to that time, the CAP started as a somewhat disorganized operation, but developed into quite an efficient one.

## Thomas P. Lawrence

*Thomas P. Lawrence was a 25-year-old student pilot from the Norfolk area when he arrived at Parksley. As early as October 1941, he had been active with the "Civilian Flying Corps" of the Virginia Protective Force, a new kind of state militia organization with an air arm. By the time the base closed he had gained his private license and flown 280 missions and upwards of eight hundred hours on patrol for which he would win the Air Medal:*

Like just about everyone else, I slept for the first weeks in the firehouse. Then David H. Jones, a Richmond fellow who we all called "Jonesy," and I rented a beach cottage on Hunting Creek. I didn't have a car but he did, so we had no trouble getting around. A favorite eating place, when we had a few dollars and wanted to put one on, was Taylor's Inn down in Onancock. The people there served native foods family-style, and were quite famous on the eastern shore. We'd get a gang together and have a ball down there. Except for Paul Loux, our chief mechanic, with whom I'm still close friends, the fellows I knew best at Parksley are all dead, and I've been out of touch with the rest.

Two events stand out in memory — a crash and a forced landing. The first occurred at the end of a patrol with "Ruby" Keeler. In landing our Cessna Airmaster in a crosswind, he stood the plane on its nose, busting the prop and damaging a wing. We both scrambled to get out as fast as possible because we could see smoke coming out from under the engine cowling and I could see some gasoline running down. Getting out was not easy. The Airmaster didn't have any wing struts, but for strength had an extra-large wing spar that went straight through the cabin from side to side. Space was cramped and our tail-up position didn't help much, either. We got out uninjured but shook up.

The forced landing occurred toward the end of a patrol in a Stinson 10-A. The engine got a little rough and then stopped because a rocker arm had broken. We dumped our bomb off Parramore Island and sat down on the beach near a Coast Guard station. After our mechanics came out and made repairs, "Jonesy," who was our chief pilot, flew the plane off the beach and back to base. Our boys made a number of forced landings on the beaches, and what you tried to do was land as near the water as you could because that's where the sand is firmest. After it's had a good soaking by a high tide, it's as hard as concrete.

## Robert P. Northam

*Robert P. Northam, a Parksley man who was employed at the base for its first six months, recalled the rough and ready maintenance equipment he used until improvements were made and a new steam-heated hangar built:*

I was working at a grocery store in town making eighteen or twenty dollars a week, when Major Burnham came in one day, and invited me to work at the base for five dollars a day. I jumped at the chance. But I soon discovered that some facilities were pretty primitive. We almost lost the whole base one morning when a careless fellow poured gasoline, which he mistook for kerosene, into the hangar coal stove to start it up and warm the planes slated for dawn patrol. Only some very fast action saved the day. What I remember best, though, is how everyone pitched in to do whatever had to be done. A person's income and background didn't matter. The wealthy guys who owned the planes and others like myself all got along real well. We played cards, and held dances in the hangar, and everybody mingled with everybody else.

\* \* \*

In his base history, Major Burnham described each pilot's indoctrination to patrol procedures and the geographical limits of the patrols. He said his flyers's main enemies were monotony and boredom:

> It was Rudy Smutny's job to teach the boys how we wanted to patrol our area.... He decided to take each man on a flight in his own plane, and for days on end Smutny was in the air personally practically the entire day. Our area was about 85 miles long and ran from the point 25 miles at sea, known as Winter Quarter Shoals, down to the harbor at Norfolk. At the beginning, we were responsible for an area extending 30 miles at sea. Later, this area was extended to 60 miles. I spent most of my time in operations, watching over our faltering radio and teaching our ground personnel their various duties.
>
> We have been here since May 1942, and we have yet to sight a submarine. We have flown 10,000 hours on patrol in search of submarines and trouble and have seen nothing of the enemy. True, we have seen two ships that were sunk by enemy mines off the Norfolk harbor and one ship on fire after a collision at sea. We have seen a few dead bodies of victims of sinkings, and we have picked up life rafts, life boats, debris, et cetera, from sinkings outside of our area. There have been submarines in our area. Intelligence reports of the Army and Navy have proved that, but since we have been here, there has not been one sinking by enemy submarine in our patrol area. Whether this is due to our continual efforts, plus the Army and the Navy efforts from Norfolk, is something we will never know, but our work has been very boring for the men, and it has always amazed me that their morale has stood up so well. If we had come upon the enemy once in a while, it would have relieved the boredom.

\* \* \*

## Clarence Lee Savage

*In the early days of the coastal patrol, many lessons were learned the hard way. In early June 1942, while flying routine patrol out of Parksley, pilot Jacob R. Schlager of Sewickley, Pennsylvania, observer Clarence Lee Savage, a native of Chincoteague, and student observer James L. Fletcher of Parksley had to ditch at sea when Schlager's Fairchild experienced an engine failure due to vapor lock. After two hours, the plane's left tank had gone bone-dry while the right tank refused to feed. Major Burnham ruled that, in the future, pilots would fly from alternating tanks rather than from both tanks simultaneously, and that student observers would henceforth be excluded from actual missions. Fortunately, in this case, all three men were rescued, but the result might have been different. Savage, born in 1906, still recalls many of the details of that ditching and much else besides:*

My granddaddy and daddy were oyster men and clammers, so I practically grew up on and in the water. Bobbing around in the easy swells waiting to be rescued didn't bother me at all. Our sister ship was circling around and I knew that they'd called for help. But thank the good Lord it was a warm summer day. Had it been winter, the story would have had a different ending. I remember that Major Burnham suggested I take a day off, but I told him that I wasn't at all shook up, and I flew patrol again the next day.

My flying began years before when I used to deliver seafood to New York. I'd wanted a plane for a long time so one day I stopped at this little airport at Hightstown, New Jersey, and asked if any airplanes were for sale. A man said, "Well, I can let you have that J-3 Cub over there for a thouand dollars." I said I'd take it if he'd throw in flying lessons, and he agreed to do so. I asked when I could start, and he said, "Right now, if you want." A few New York runs later, I soloed and then I flew the plane down to Chincoteague and landed in a small field next to the cemetery. That was the first time anyone on the island knew I had a plane

When I began flying for the coastal patrol, I continued to live at home and drove back and forth from Chincoteague every day, about a half hour or so. I could've stayed in town at the firehouse but I couldn't leave my mother's wonderful cooking. I flew every type plane they had, and I never missed a day. When the base closed, I wound up in Memphis, Tennessee, in accident investigation and safety for the Air Corps. I met my wife-to-be in Memphis and after the war we came back to Chincoteague and raised a family. I was in the family seafood business all my life, but for three or four years, I also ran a seaplane base and probably gave flight instruction to half the young men on the island, home from the war and taking advantage of the G. I. Bill. In 1948, I was awarded the Air Medal, along with a bunch of others from Parksley.

### William Edward ("Willie") Mears

*Young Willie Mears lived in Parksley and was thrilled to deliver the morning newspapers to the pilots and other men living in the fire house:*

They were usually up and out to the field by the time I brought the papers. I just threw them on the bunks for them to read in the evenings. I didn't get to know any of the pilots too well. With all the pretty girls in town, those fellows hadn't much reason to notice eleven-year-old boys. My special thrill came the day one of the pilots took me out to the field to let me see and touch his plane. I considered it an enormous privilege.

Parksley's closing on August 31, 1943 was the occasion for a big party. Most of the flyers went into the Air Corps or worked for the armed services as civilian flight instructors (courtesy Frederick Stanger, Jr.).

I knew there was a war on, and that this was a real air base, no matter how small! The only Army Air Corps personnel assigned to Parksley were the members of the four-man ordnance crew sent down from Langley Field. The crew chief, Staff Sergeant Peter Marangas, and his recent bride, Ann, rented a furnished partment in our house. Ann's mother had come over from Italy on the *Lusitania* before World War I and Peter's parents were from Greece. Ann was a wonderful cook, and we learned to love the highly spiced exotic smells coming down the stairs. After the war, my mother and father visited them in Brooklyn.

\* \* \*

The final paragraph in Major Burnham's history of the base expresses the pride of accomplishment he felt for the entire organization:

> As our duties come to a close, we can look back upon the past as a period in which all of the personnel at this Base did their jobs to the limit and extent of their ability. From May 17, 1942, to the closing day, August 31, 1943, this Base never received one single word of criticism as to its manner of operating or its conduct in carrying out its missions from either the Army, the Navy, or National Headquarters of the Civil Air Patrol. It did receive many evidences of appreciation for the work done, and there are enclosed, herewith, copies of some of these letters of commendation.

Fifty years after the coastal patrol took it over, the farmhouse headquarters was still standing, needing only a fresh coast of paint to look familiar to the men and women who served there (photo by author, 1992).

Two of these commendation letters especially merit repeating. Both were on the occasion of the Parksley base's first anniversary, the first signed by Captain R. S. Crenshaw, U.S.N., Assistant Commandant for

Operations at the Naval Operating Base, Norfolk, the second signed by Rear Admiral Manley H. Simons, Commandant of the Fifth Naval District, Norfolk:

> I wish to extend a greeting to the Parksley Patrol at the end of a year of fine work. Your continued interest and perseverance in the daily grind has been most commendable and is sincerely appreciated. We have counted on your patrols in the coverage of convoys, in patrol of the Coastal waters and in special investigations, as an integral part of the defense of the Coast and shipping. When you make no report we feel confident that the area you covered is clear, and when you report something we prick up our ears and act on it at once. We have learned to place dependence in what you say. Keep up your good work. [signed Crenshaw]

> Although there is only one candle on your birthday cake tonight, it does not indicate by any manner or means the value of the service you have performed for the United States and the Navy. Giving of yourselves unstintingly such as you have, has built the Civil Air Patrol into an organization well worthy of carrying the American battle flag. First, I want to congratulate you on your efforts to be of service and then I want to thank you for the work which you have done. [signed Simon]

When the war ended, the Parksley base lasted for a time as a private airfield, but finally reverted to farmland in the early 1950s. Willie Mears remembers helping his father plow up the runways so corn could be planted. Today, the field looks much as it did in its earlier farming life, and the skeletal remains of the old hangar can be seen crumbling in the undergrowth near the road. Having made its vital contribution to the 1942-1943 war effort, the airbase has returned to its more natural state. Only a farm family and some baby chicks are needed to turn back the clock to the first year of the war.

---

Base officers, pilots and observers, who served at least one month at CAPCP#4 and who are not elsewhere mentioned in the text of this chapter include: William H. Baker, William G. Bell,* Henry R. Bergman, John R. Betters,* Warren W. Bourdier,* Henry H. Cromartie,* Frederic W. Deisroth,* Frank Drennan, Earl C. Evans,* Robert S. Fisher,* William A. Gooch, John T. Griffin, Aubrey B. Hilliard,* Burton B. Howell,* David Klee, Ralph S. MacKenzie,* Paul V. Meehan,* Leonard J. Messina, Alfred C. Nowitsky,* Calvin Pardee III,* Arthur C. Pottorff, James T. Rutherfoord, Jr.,* James V. Smith,* Charles H. Steel, Jr., James J. Sutton, and Willis S. Young.* Asterisk indicates Air Medal winner.

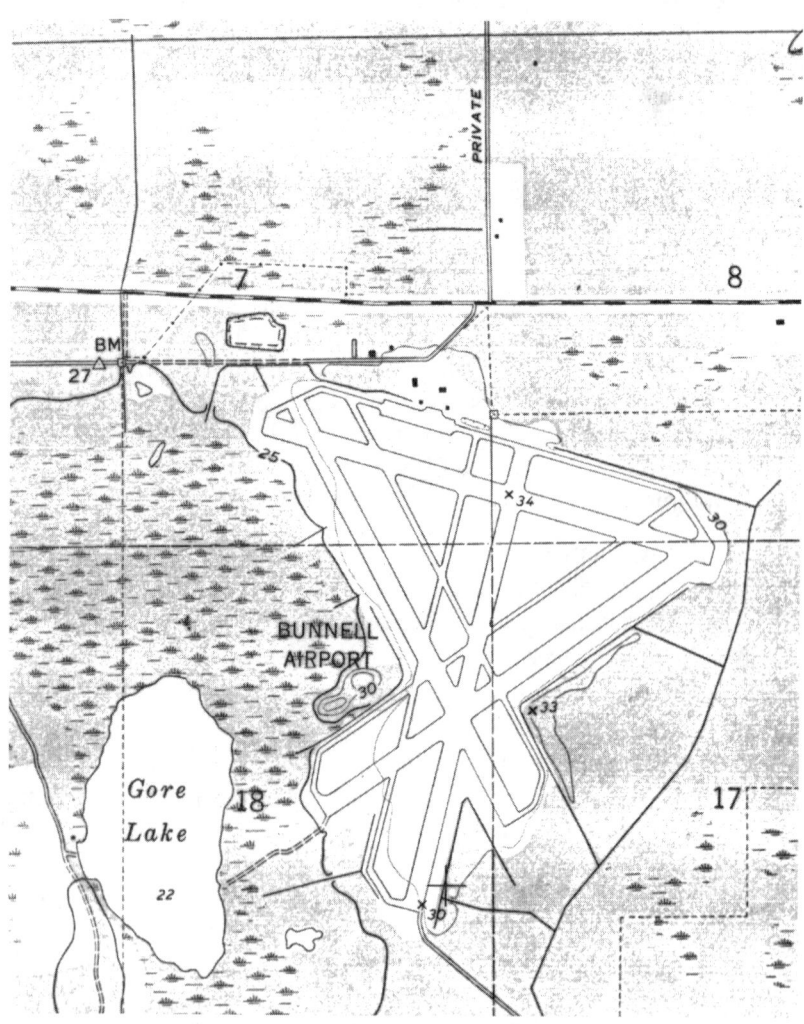

In the years following the war, the old coastal patrol base was much improved and renamed Bunnell Airport. Located about five miles due west of Flagler Beach, the airfield remained a mere 25-30 feet above sea level and was still surrounded by low-lying swamps and marshes (source: 1956 United States Geological Survey quadrangle map).

# 5

# Flagler Beach, Florida

The coastal patrol base at Flagler Beach, Florida* was first established at Daytona Beach on May 12, 1942, and later relocated to Flagler Beach when the Daytona Beach Municipal Airport proved unsuitable as a military base. The commander was Julius L. Gresham, a forty-two-year-old Daytona Beach businessman active in civic and social affairs, and a member of the Aircraft Owners and Pilots Association and the National Aeronautics Association. A former U.S. Marine, and charter member of the "Quiet Birdmen," an association of early aviators, he was well suited to his command. Gresham was commissioned Captain on July 1, 1942, and Major on March 15, 1943.

As at other bases, the first days were hectic and makeshift. Though there were paved runways, there were no buildings. As an expedient, sheds and shacks left by building contractors were torn down, hauled in, and reassembled near a lone hangar on the field. The Florida Defense Force provided three tents and cots on which flight crews might rest between flights. The local Red Cross chapter ran a canteen from 4:30 a.m. until the work day ended. Men who hadn't done manual labor for years developed well-callused hands.

The base history written by First Lt. Claude Y. Nanney, Jr. of Union Mills, North Carolina, describes the preparations made for the first patrol on May 19, 1942, only a week after the base was activated:

*Somewhat ironically, the little town of Flagler Beach, with a present population of under five thousand, is the only town in the Sunshine State named for the great developer, Henry Morrison Flagler (1830–1913). Flagler, friend of John D. Rockefeller, built the Florida East Coast Railway, established steamship lines, dredged the Miami harbor, and built palatial hotels, all to encourage the growth of Florida as a winter playground.

At noon the flight board was written up, assigning planes and personnel for the first mission. Albert Crabtree, with his once natty uniform smudged with grease and grime, and David Booher, a Jacksonville orchestra leader, were posted as pilot and observer, respectively, to fly Albert's Ranger Fairchild No. 2 on the first mission. The time was to be 1330, and their code name was "Lime," as this base was to use fruits as code symbols. This provoked Dave to remark that he sure hoped the flight wouldn't be as sour as the fruit it represented. Harry Clinton as pilot and Ed Walton as observer were to follow at 1334 with Harry's Culver Cadet No. 5; their code was "Plum" — according to Harry, "Plum good." Bill Tyree as pilot and Bill Chastain as observer were to fly Tyree and Hammons' Warner Fairchild at 1340. Ben Handler as pilot and Shelburne "Sub" Carter were scheduled to fly the Melbourne run beginning at 1500.

Major Julius L. Gresham proved to be an excellent base commander (Every photograph in this chapter is from an album kept by the late Edna McGrath, one of the base secretaries, and kindly made available for this book through the courtesy of her daughter, Marti Cheesboro).

After a briefing by commander Gresham, operations officer Robert P. Boynton, assistant operations officer Clarence Simpson, and intelligence officer Lawrence W. Grabe, the flyers were ready:

> Struggling with their kapok life preservers; checking their so-called flotation gear, which consisted of a canvas bag, an automobile inner

tube, and a kapok life preserver; plotting their courses, and generally acting nervous, they filed out of the operations building to the waiting planes. They seemed to sense the danger of their work, but they also seemed to know that this was counter-balanced by its importance.... this was war, total war, and for the first time each man realized that the opportunity to participate in it directly had come. With the good-natured horse play that Dave Booher exhibited during his entire tour of duty with the Base, he patted the ground, stroked the cowling of No. 2, climbed aboard, and waved back with "to hell with Hitler, here we come!" written in a broad smile.

* * *

Patrols continued regularly throughout the summer and into the fall, but on October 28, 1942, without the slightest interruption of its missions, operations were moved to a little used field at Flagler Beach. There was a new all-metal hangar that housed six planes and contained a supply room and several small offices. A separate administration building provided additional offices, a pilot's lounge, and a canteen. A few days after the move, base personnel received a hurricane notice from the U.S. Weather Bureau and hastily evacuated all flyable aircraft to a field in Americus, Georgia. The planes that were not flyable were dug into deep holes so that their wings were almost on a level with the ground, possibly a first in the annals of hurricane precautions for airplanes. The storm threat did not materialize.

In a foreward to his base history, C. Y. Nanney, Jr. wrote that he hoped "this record will in the future serve to... reassure each and everyone that there was one hell of job to be done and that one hell of a good job was done."

Nanney's base history gives an unusually complete account of all the mishaps that befell base aircraft. Of the thirty-nine planes assigned to the base at one time or another, three were lost at sea, four were damaged in major ground accidents, and three were damaged in minor ground accidents. None of these incidents resulted in serious injuries. The planes had been numbered as they arrived at the base, and replacements for crashed or retired aircraft were given the same numbers:

**Baker Fox 2,** NC 15987 Ranger Fairchild 24 — Owner: Albert Crabtree. Assigned May 17, 1942. Number 2 has three "firsts to its credit. It was the first plane assigned [the number "1" was not used] the first plane to go on a mission, and the first plane to be lost at sea. On October 28, 1942, at 1442, a few miles off and NE of St. Augustine, due to motor failure, No. 2 made a crash landing at sea with Lieut. Albert Crabtree, pilot, and Lieut. Francis McLaughlin, observer. Neither man was injured, and were picked up by the Coast Guard after remaining afloat in their life jackets and rubber raft, dropped by the Navy, for an hour and thirty minutes. Both the weather and the surface of the sea were very rough at the time of the crash.

**Baker Fox 5,** NC 28987 Bellanca Low-Wing — Owners: Gresham and Clinton. Assigned August 10, 1942. It became the second plane to make a crash landing at sea. Fifteen miles east of Daytona Beach Pier at 1020, November 22, 1942. Lieut. Lew Rhodes, pilot, and Lieut. Gates Clay, observer, were forced to crash land due to motor failure. The plane floated eight minutes before sinking, and the launching of the old-style life vests and flotation bags was made without incident. They remained in the water for one and a half hours. A Navy PBY Patrol Bomber effected the rescue by landing nearby in the calm water. Lieut. Earl Folsom and Flight Observer Moore Bryson were flying the sister ship.

**Baker Fox 13,** NC 36733 Stinson Voyager — Owner: Albert Crabtree. Assigned November 16, 1942. This ship was lost at sea by reason of motor failure, 9 miles NE of Matanzas Inlet, on the morning of February 24, 1943, 1013, with Lieut. Wesley C. Wallace, pilot, and Lieut. Robert Wimp, observer. Neither were injured and were rescued by a passing freighter 40 minutes later. They were taken off the freighter by a Navy Crash Boat and put in at St. Augustine. Lieut. Earl Folsom and his observer, Flight Officer Carl Langston, were the crew of the sister ship. This was Lieut. Langston's second experience in seeing his sister ship go into the "drink."

\* \* \*

## Wesley C. Wallace

*Mrs. Wesley C. Wallace recalls her late husband's early love affair with airplanes, the excitement of the day he ditched, their duplex apartment near the airport, and his pride in being an Air Medal winner:*

We were both from North Carolina. I was born and raised in Raleigh, and Wes was from Garner, a few miles to the south. I knew him from the time he was twelve, and first started messing around with airplanes out at the old county airport. He'd run home from school to do his chores, then walk two or three miles to the airport, which was run by Mr. and Mrs. Meyers. They didn't have any children so they sort of adopted Wes, taught him to fly, and sometimes took him with them on short trips.

When he was older, his daddy wanted him to become an engineer for the Seaboard Railroad. To please him, Wes worked there some, but that job only provided money for more flying. When he finished work in the afternoon, he'd scoot to the airport on a motorcycle and spend all the rest of the day there until it was dark. His mother always caught him coming in and would ask, "Where have you been, Wes?" — like she didn't know. He and a friend later built a little plane and earned their private licenses. Wes was a quiet man, and didn't talk much about things, so I never knew the details. Then we were married, our baby boy was born, and Wes signed up for the coastal patrol at Flagler. Once he got settled, I joined him.

He'd gone on duty one morning as usual, but then later on I heard all of these planes taking off one after another, evidently heading for the ocean. I thought, "Oh my goodness, what in the world's going on!" I learned that afternoon, when the fellow who lived across from us — also a patrol pilot and a very nice man — dropped by to visit. He liked our little boy, and stopped by frequently. He spent a few minutes bouncing our baby on his knee, then told me that Wes had gone down, but was okay. Wisely he'd waited until Wes had been brought into Saint Augustine to tell me. I hadn't known or suspected a thing until then. I guess I'm glad that I didn't.

Besides having to care for our son, I was pregnant with our daughter, and everybody sort of looked after me. Flagler Beach was just a tiny little place then. A country store was handy, about a block from the beach, and the couple that ran it sort of adopted me after I started going over there to buy milk. They were always around to help. If anything happened I'd look up, and they'd be standing in the door. Wes and I didn't enjoy much social life. We mostly liked to read, and keep track of what was going on in the world. When the base closed we returned to Raleigh and Wes went back to railroading. The work really didn't suit him, and he went into the sound systems business. He continued to fly some for fun, and we had some great trips together, but he never got into the aviation industry itself. Wes was a good person, a very nice person. He passed away four years ago.

One of the most exciting crashes involving base aircraft occurred on the airfield itself, and was witnessed by many base personnel. The plane was **Baker Fox 20,** NC 14622, a Waco owned by Wes Bailey and Jack Tamm:

> In taking off from the Flagler Beach Field on the morning of November 2, 1942, the heavy load and rough runway caused the landing gear to buckle at a point in the landing gear strut that was later determined to be a partial old break. Pilot Dave Booher and Observer Wes Bailey considered themselves in a bad state of affairs with their landing gear gone, a full load of bombs, gas, and other equipment. They flew out over the ocean and jettisoned their bombs ... [and flew until they exhausted most of their fuel supply, then] ... A low and slow power-on approach was started, and the tenseness of those that lined the runway was plainly visible. Dave eased 'er in on the good wheel and was doing all right for a few hundred feet on the ground, but suddenly the bad side dropped, and with it there was plenty of action. The ship lurched to one side, dug in the prop, nosed over, and skidded first on one wing, then the other. This was the end of No. 20, but Dave and Wes extracted themselves with the help of a dozen hands, shook their shaggy heads, reached for the bottle someone provided, and that was that.

Descriptions of three other accidents at the Flagler base round out the picture of the kinds of mishaps that might occur at any busy coastal patrol base. They also exemplify the skills and ingenuity of the engineering staffs who made the planes flyable again:

> **Baker Fox 22,** NC 28927 Monocoupe — Owner: Claude S. Wells. Assigned June 16, 1942. This plane is also one of the few originals still on the flight line, and was the first plane on the Base to figure in an accident. Lieut. Wells and his observer, Edward J. Walton, cracked-up "22" in a cross-wind take-off on the Jacksonville airport, June 22, 1942, time 1330E. There were no injuries to speak of, but the plane turned turtle and washed-out the wing tips, prop, cowling, vertical fin, and landing gear. The plane was completely rebuilt and returned to the flight line to fly many hours of patrol missions. An interesting sidelight to this accident was Flight Officer Walton's anxiety to return to the Base at Daytona Beach. Commercial transportation was

too slow for him, so he hitchhiked to the Base from Jacksonville in nothing flat. Eddie was to figure in the second Base accident, which was also a Monocoupe, and did not fare so well in that one, mentioned later.

**Baker Fox 23,** NC 28928 Monocoupe — Owner: M. W. Graham, Jr. Assigned June 16, 1942. Baker Fox 22 and Baker Fox 23 were sister ships, having been built at the same time and carrying consecutive numbers. Baker Fox 23 was the second ship attached to the Base to meet with an accident. On the morning of August 17, 1942, Lieut. Earl G. Folsom and his observer, Edward J. Walton, attempted a take-off with a strong cross-wind, and veered off the runway and missed a pile of marl that the contractors were using in the construction of runways. They missed the marl by inches, but it was enough to flip them over, and the result was a total wash-out. Earl suffered a fracture of the right arm and minor cuts and bruises, while Ed came out with a cut wrist, lacerated face requiring several stitches, cut leg, and a gang of bruises. This was Ed's and the Base's second accident. The ship was scrapped, as it was beyond repair.

Pilot Claude S. Wells badly damaged his Monocoupe during a crosswind take-off at Jacksonville Airport, but neither he nor his observer were badly hurt.

**Baker Fox 23,** NC 32291 Stinson Voyager — Owners: Gresham and Boynton. Assigned October 14, 1942. This ship replaced the original "23" and flew patrol until June 19, 1943, at which time it, too, met the fate of its predecessor. On that date Lieut. Chas. F. King parked on the flight line of the Daytona Naval Air Station and, with motor idling, a Navy SNJ taxied head-on into "23" and chewed it up like matchwood. The propeller of the SNJ cut through the cockpit, and only because Lady Luck was in the seat beside him kept Charlie from a sad fate. He was not even scratched, but that was the end of the Voyager. Lieut. Wells was co-owner with Major Gresham at the time of the crash.

## George A. Wolcott

*Twenty-five-year-old George A. Wolcott of Daytona Beach reported to the Daytona Beach base on July 29, 1942, and remained with CAPCP #5 through its relocation to Flagler Beach and its eventual disbanding. A pilot since 1937, he owned a 40 hp Piper J-2 Cub. By mid-1942 he'd also flown for three months as a co-pilot in one of National Airlines Stinson trimotors:*

Major Julius Gresham, the base commander, kept begging pilots he knew, like myself, to come out and fly for him. I figured I might as well do that as what I was doing. I was married and had a family, but my wife wasn't real concerned about the possible dangers of my flying over water. And of course I'd be home every night. I could fly most everything they had on the field then — the low-wing Bellancas, the Wacos, the Stinson 10-As, the Fairchilds, and so forth. But I mostly flew a Monocoupe. It was a hot little airplane and I think they let me fly it because of my considerable experience.

After soloing in 1937, George A. Wolcott flew for fifty years, accumulating more than twelve thousand hours in the air. He was considered one of the base's better poker players.

When I joined the coastal patrol, the U-boats were still sinking ships just off the coast. I remember the morning my sister ship and I were fired upon by one. We were heading east for a routine patrol when we saw something in the water at a distance. As we came closer at about a thousand feet, suddenly there were dirty white puffs ahead — a submarine's deck gun was banging away at us. Since we were no match for them, we got real brave and got the hell out of there! We reported this to our base, and they called the Navy, but what happened after that I don't know. We continued our patrol well away from that sub. The only time you could possibly get close enough to drop your bomb was when you caught a U-boat submerged. We never did.

We started at Daytona Beach, as you know, but as Navy activity there increased, we moved up to a much smaller airfield near Flagler Beach. The grass runways were no problem, but the fact that it was unlighted made it so risky landing there at dusk that we sought and got the Navy's approval permission to land at Daytona Beach if a patrol arrived after dark. In fact, the Navy even gave us an instrument flying course. Any morning that we didn't have patrol duty, we could fly down to their base and take a couple of hours on the Link trainer. I did that a few times though I believe that I already had my instrument rating.

I don't remember many details of my time at the two bases. We had various training classes — such as to learn the Morse Code, some military drill and some calisthenics. Of course I best remember our daily patrols up and down the coast between Jacksonville and Melbourne. While I certainly do *not* consider myself a hero, I flew enough hours to win the Air Medal. At the end of my stint I became a flight instructor in the Air Corps, and then strange to say, they put me into the Cadet program flying ST-13s and AT-6s. I resigned when the war ended but continued flying, and in fifty years or so I've logged about twelve thousand hours.

**James S. Lawrence**

*James S. Lawrence of Winter Park, Florida was another Flagler flyer who entered the Air Corps, having served in the coastal patrol only from May 31 to August 10, 1943, or not quite three months. Only twenty-two years old, flight observer Lawrence admits to some boredom with what by then were uneventful patrols. Like many other volunteers, he was also annoyed by the lack of respect shown him by people who had no idea what the coastal patrol was all about:*

It was those red epaulets mainly. You'd go into a bar and somebody would ask, "What the hell are those things?" Sometimes we'd say we were with the Russian Air Corps, and then there might be some verbal unpleasantries. There must have been ten thousand WACs, soldiers, sailors, Air Corps guys, and Marines in that part of Florida, and I always felt like the CAP was sort of frowned on. That was a real downer and there wasn't much we could do about it because in theory our anti-submarine patrol work was a secret. It was extremely annoying that we couldn't properly respond to our critics.

I didn't like the "politicking" at the base, either. I never got to fly as much as I wanted to because the rich guys always seemed to get first shot at the missions. Maybe that was because they usually flew their own planes and wanted to build up the maximum time on them. As a result I wasted more time than I wanted to hanging around the base playing cards. That wasn't what I went there for. So I left. I had a stretch of instructing Cadets before I became one myself, but the war ended before I completed the program.

\* \* \*

When he wrote the base history, C. Y. Nanney, Jr., did a particularly good job of presenting vignettes on base personnel. Some of the allusions might be obscure but they nevertheless reveal the wide variety of backgrounds possessed by the men and women who served in the coastal patrol. Following are some examples of Nanney's "Slips, Stalls, and Spins" and more will come later:

> Landon Alison, besides being an able-bodied seaman, is one of Arthur Murray's top-notch dance instructors, and used to winter among the elite in Miami and points south.... Charlie Thigpen is a gentleman farmer near Montgomery, Ala., in addition to operating Montgomery's Municipal Airport.... "Cracker" Graham was a big-time baseball player once, and a darn good one, too.... Ben Handler washes all the clothes in Sarasota and surroundings.... Ben was one of the first from the Base to join the ATC.... He was followed by Earl Folsom, Harry Clinton, Dave Booher, and Jack Tamm.... Lieut. Horner and Major Gresham attended Horner's Military Academy in Charlotte, N.C., at the same time.... No one will forget how Capt. Dix and Capt. Grabe came back from Atlantic City after being "educated," and tried to change our methods of drilling.... Pappy McElvey, the keeper of the books, had a long career behind him, and was a long-time opera singer, journalist on *The Phildelphia Ledger*, and hotel owner-manager in Ocean City, N.J.

## Landon E. Alison

*Landon E. Alison was born in Gainesville, Florida and entered the Air Corps when he was twenty-seven, just under the age limit for pilots. After finishing primary flight training and winning his wings, he went to Randolph Field, Texas, and there sprained his back so badly while working out on a trampoline that he had to accept a medical discharge. He returned to Florida and joined the coastal patrol:*

I was single and living at home with my parents during the year or so I served at Flagler. Like me, most of the pilots lived in Daytona Beach and drove back and forth to the base. Other people may have lived in Flagler Beach, but it was still a small place of maybe only two thousand people and available housing would've been scarce. I was a flight observer the whole time, never a pilot-in-command, but when the base closed I had flown two thousand hours, more than enough to win the Air Medal.

When the Flagler Beach Base closed, Landon E. Alison joined the U.S. Merchant Marine. He and his ship took part in the D-Day invasion of France, June 6, 1944.

We didn't provide convoy escorts, but flew only specified patrol patterns, usually at three thousand feet, so we'd have the altitude to glide back to land if we lost our engine. I went out with many different pilots, but perhaps most often with John Tamm. We're still good friends and see one another often. The base didn't have any social events that I recall, but we played a lot of poker. I wasn't much good at it then but I do well now. You know why? Because my older brother, an Air Corps flyer, told me one day, "Landon, poker's like anything else. If you're going to gamble, get yourself a good book and read it!" So I did — I think it was one of John Scarne's books to tell the average G.I. how to avoid being taken by card sharks — and I've been successful ever since.

When the base closed I joined the U.S. Merchant Marine, and spent the rest of the war crossing and recrossing the Atlantic. One of my ships was a participant in the June 6, 1944 landings in France. We stood offshore, landing supplies and flying a "barrage balloon" tethered on a steel cable to deter strafing attacks by enemy aircraft. I learned after the war — I hadn't noticed it at the time — that we had an obscuring ground fog much of the time, and that the balloons floating just above it made great aiming points for the Germans. We got the hell bombed out of us! The Merchant Marine was *far* more dangerous than the coastal patrol. But I still think that the CAP was terrific and that we did a wonderful job. After the war I was glad to return to peaceful pursuits.

## John R. Tamm

*An Air Medal winner, John R. Tamm was born in Chicago, Illinois in 1920 and spent most of his younger life in nearby Evanston. After living for a time in Atlanta, Georgia, he came to Daytona Beach, where he learned to fly in J-3 Cub and Aeronca Chief float planes. He flew coastal patrols even before the Flagler Beach base was officially established, but his first job there was as radio operator:*

I was one of the only ones with a qualifying radio license, albeit only a minimal one, and was sent down to West Palm Beach for training before taking over my duties at the base. After a couple of months, I graduated to flying patrols as an observer, and then to being a pilot. I served from May 14, 1942 until July 14, 1943, and had about eight hundred hours total flight time when I left. We had some guys go into the water, but I didn't. It was nothing to land on the beach. We did that all the time just because it was fun. Those long stretches of packed sand, five hundred feet wide, were too inviting to pass up. You just had to watch out for the cross winds coming from the west over the dunes.

On one of our patrols my observer thought he saw a sub, so we went over and dropped a bomb where he thought it had been. I don't know whether the bomb was improperly armed or what, but it didn't explode. Our bomb sight was very simple — two paper clips attached "just so" to the fuselage. We practiced at about a thousand feet until we could hit a target by lining up the target with the two clips. The pilot kept his right hand on his observer's knee and when he squeezed, his observer released the bomb. A more sophisticated method used a periscope-like device linked electrically with a light on the instrument panel that lit when the pilot had the target centered. To do real damage to a submarine, we'd almost have had to drop our small bombs down the conning tower and we all knew how impossible that would've been.

I was married and lived at home, and while the base remained at Daytona Beach it was only a two-mile drive at most. Once the base moved to Flagler Beach, it was like fifteen miles or so. Reporting for the dawn patrol meant driving that distance uncomfortably in the dark with slitted headlights. Our main recreation at the base was playing cards in the day room, and an old western game called "Red Dog" was the favorite for a long time. Major Gresham was a popular commander. He'd been a Marine in the first World War, and seemed to enjoy the element of command. We did a certain amount of policing-up the area, and some occasional marching drills. Because we had so many older men, well beyond draft age, the exercising and drill was not overdone. I was one of the younger men and had no complaints at all.

John ("Jack") Tamm was a pilot, but because he was also an experienced radio operator, he was sometimes pressed into service at the microphone.

About a month or so before the base closed, I drove down to West Palm Beach, where I passed the Air Corps physical and flight tests for a service pilot's rating. For a time I was based there but eventually went to the China-Burma-India war theater to "fly the Hump."* I came home

* Massive supplies of arms and equipment were delivered to Chiang Kai-shek's Chinese Nationalist Army by flying over the Himalayan Mountains from bases in Burma. So dangerous was this that "more than 1300 pilots and crew members were lost and more than 500 transport planes crashed trying to make it." See *Flying the Hump* by Jeff Ethell and Don Downie, Motorbooks International, 1995.

when the war ended but stayed in the Air Corps Reserve, attaining the rank of Colonel. I finished up my college degree, then went on to become an attorney. I'm still in practice with my son, who lets me make the coffee every morning!

\* \* \*

More of C. Y. Nanney's "Slips, Stalls, and Spins":

"Uncle Joe" Bond, who was born Mar. 14, 1867, and served in the Spanish-American War, was, at 76, the oldest man to serve on the Base. He was one of the guard detail, and was always on his post for tour of duty.... The youngest man was Eugene Philips, who was barely sixteen when he reported for duty.... Arnold "Elephant Jockey" Glass, a long, tall Texan, was the biggest man on the Base, while Gates Clay was the smallest.... Lieut. Simpson, better known as "Slippery," used to live in Buffalo, N. Y., and once sold Niagara Falls to a tourist. He is still selling real estate. Billy Jinks, the proprietor of the Greasy Spoon, has been a professional boxer, a bookie, and a gambler, by his own admission; what else, nobody knows.... Laurels go to Lieut. Horner as Poker's most ardent admirer, and he won ocasionally, too.

## David F. Gray

*In October 1942 David F. Gray, from Greenfield, Ohio, accepted a position as plotting board operator just after the base moved to Flagler Beach. Married and living in Daytona Beach, he took the job to kill time while awaiting appointment as a Naval air cadet. He had been told by Navy recruiters that they would soon be accepting married men into the program, but that was not to be. After four months with the coastal patrol, Gray was accepted as a Cadet in the Army Air Corps, later became an Air Force career officer, and retired as a lieutenant colonel:*

What I did was so simple that no special training was needed. I listened to the radio, and as our patrol planes radioed in, I marked their positions on a horizontal plotting board about twenty feet long and six feet wide, just like a big banquet table. The board showed the coastline and the coastal waters as far out as our planes went, the whole thing gridded into squares for easy reference. The observers used clipboards with maps showing similar grids. We usually sent out two flights of two planes each, one to the north, the other to the south. I marked their positions in grease pencil that could be easily wiped off when new reports came in. I didn't get information on any other planes or ships. All I did was keep track of our own planes

The plotting board and radio room were on the second floor over the base administration offices. Nobody ever came up to look over my shoulder, and it was very routine. It was a one-man job from dawn to dusk, the same for the radio man, J. P. Borden. We became friends and entered the Cadet program together. If either of us needed to do something, each filled-in for the other. I kept no plotting board record, but J. P. kept a strict log of each radio message received. I have no idea of what might have happened to this information.

When somebody didn't show up as scheduled, I was lucky enough to fly some missions as a back-up observer. This was strictly unofficial, and, of course, I never received the higher per diem of a flight-observer. And no record of my hours was kept. But it was fun, and at least once, scary. The pilot, I think, was Art Stone and the plane was his own Monocoupe whose engine had the cute little habit of shutting down every thirty minutes — stopping cold. But nobody told me that, and when it did I looked quickly at Art and he just said, "Don't worry about it." I said, "What do you mean, don't worry about it? We're fifteen miles out over the ocean." He explained, "Well the engine quit because it has some warped valves. They'll cool off in a few seconds and it'll start running again." And it did.

I remember another special day when somebody spotted a mine in the shipping lane, one of those spiky things you see in the movies. Next thing we knew, Army and Navy airplanes were coming from everywhere — Jacksonville, Orlando, the Naval Air Station at Banana River — to try to explode it with machine gun fire. I couldn't see any of this but followed events on the radio. Everybody made pass after pass without result. I thought surely there'd be a mid-air collision sooner or later, but finally somebody finally blew it up and the planes returned to their bases. We didn't have planes in our area. If we had, we'd have told them to stay clear!

I wore a uniform on duty, and I think I held the rank of sergeant. We did some close-order drill and Major Gresham sometimes gave it himself. He had been an automobile dealer and everyone knew of him before there was any CAP. A nice guy, he was one of the first commercial pilots in the country, holding license number six or something like that. I look back on the coastal patrol as having done the very valuable service of forcing the German U-boats to keep their heads down during daylight. The coastal patrol could see and report them if they tried to operate on the surface. Staying submerged all day posed operational problems for them and advantages for us.

\* \* \*

## Charles B. French

*Charles B. French was born and raised in Daytona Beach, and after the war began tried to join the Air Corps and become a pilot. Rejected for his color-blindness, he joined the coastal patrol. French was thirty years old and an experienced automobile mechanic, so he was first brought into the maintenance section to head the parts shop. When the base moved from Daytona Beach to Flagler, he became assistant engineering officer and was promoted to lieutenant:*

I was not an aircraft mechanic, but I did have my own tools, so besides supervising the parts shop I also did some mechanical work on the planes. We had a nice hangar up at Flagler, with a smooth concrete floor which was easy to keep clean and was well-equipped. Our hours

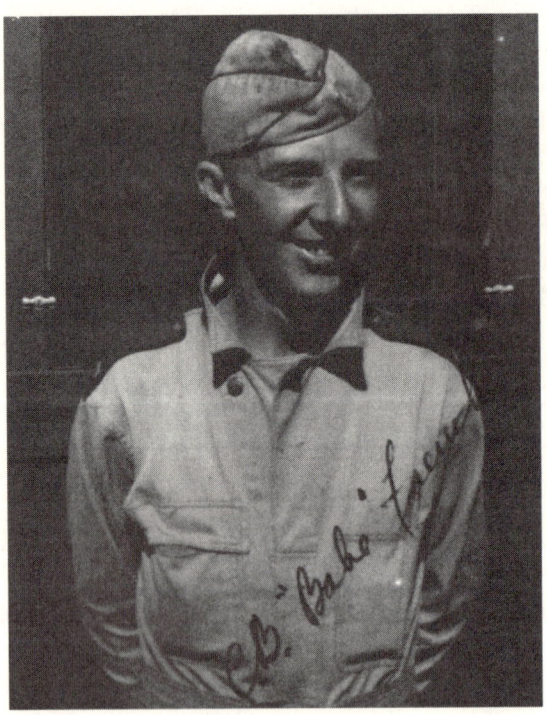

The base history described pilot Charles B. French as loving cats and purring kittens, "especially those with Army WAC uniforms on."

could be very long. I carpooled with another mechanic and usually got up around 3:30 a.m. to get to the field in time to help the dawn patrol get going. The twenty mile drive on route U.S. 1A, the so-called "scenic route," took about forty-five minutes of squinting into the total darkness of a coastal blackout. There weren't any set hours. We might get home as late as midnight.

Our engineering officer was J. Gilbert Angell, who had been an instructor in mechanics at the Daytona Beach Vocational School. We were required to have G.I. shorts and trousers, but usually just wore dungarees, or shorts when it was really hot. We handled all routine maintenance and repair jobs everything right at the base, except that if we found an engine problem we couldn't handle we'd take it out to be worked on locally, and if we found a major problem we'd have to return the engine to the factory. Our mechanics didn't specialize on particular planes but worked on them all. There was no reason to have a favorite. I never worked on a plane that didn't have some devilish area difficult to work on, and the other mechanics probably all felt that way, too.

Altogether, I served at Flagler from May 20, 1942 until August 31, 1943, when the base was deactivated. Then I was with the contingent — virtually everyone except for the guards, linemen, and clerks — who went as a group to Otis Field near Falmouth, Massachusetts, where we were redesignated as Tow Target Unit #5. After the war I worked for an aviation parts company in Peoria, Illinois, but after a serious bout with pneumonia returned to my warmer home in Daytona Beach to work in an automobile dealership. I got into management and stayed with them until I retired. I feel good about my time at Flagler and think I learned a lot there, particularly with regard to managing men.

## Clyde K. Hull

*Clyde K. Hull was born and raised in Ormond Beach, Florida, and was working for a lumber company when the war began. As a member of the Florida State Guard he spent the first six months of the conflict guarding other airports before being transferred closer to his home to guard the Daytona Beach municipal field. Later, he was assigned to full-time duty with the CAP, and served for a year at Flagler Beach.*

I was born in 1912, the year the *Titanic* sank. As you can well imagine, since this was long before the big land boom of the nineteen-twenties, Ormond Beach was just a cross roads then and it wasn't so much bigger in 1942. I was married, and living at home, and commuted to the base at odd times, depending on what shift I worked. On guard duty, I carried a loaded English Enfield rifle on guard duty. I got to know everyone there including the pilots and all the top officers. It wasn't at all like in the Army, you know, it was more like a family. We kept necessary discipline, but nothing excessive.

A few months after the base closed, I was transferred to Otis Field in Falmouth, Massachusetts with the tow target unit there, where first I was promoted to a mechanic, then, after getting in many hours in the air as a winch operator, I was promoted again to flight officer. This was considerably more interesting than standing guard all the time. My job was playing out targets on a one-eighth steel cable and reeling them back in when the firing practice was done. We used an electric winch. The thing would have been impossible to do by hand. The maintenance on them was done by the base mechanics. I had nothing to do with that.

Sergeant Mary Upchurch was a clerk-typist in the technical section, and a close friend of Edna Gordon McGrath, for whom she inscribed this photograph.

It was a little dangerous at times. I remember once when we were out around Sandy Hook, and down low to give the anti-aircraft boys something to shoot at, we saw tracers *ahead* of us. That was definitely a very serious no-no. Speak of your salty language, you should've heard my pilot telling people on the ground where they might go! Another incident was even more frightening. We were at altitude with a long tow for some fighter planes to shoot at. Some of those boys were real hotshots, and it wasn't unusual for one to see how close he could come across in front of us, just to see our wings wobble in the turbulence. This time, one cut right through our cable with his propeller. His plane went down but he parachuted safely. Luckily for us, the cable broke, or we'd have gone down too and probably would've been killed. To top it off, the fighter group commander came over to our base and wanted to know what the h__ we thought *we* were doing! When our commanding officer explained, he went back and had choice words for *his* pilots.

Eight Civil Air Patrol tow target units (TTUs) were activated in late 1943 and began operations by the end of January 1944. Planes pulled either a "sleeve" or a "banner" target at the end of a steel cable that could be played out from an electric winch for up to five thousand feet. When providing a target at higher altitudes for the big 90 mm anti-aircraft guns, the entire cable might be used. If the flight called for simulating a low-level strafing mission for the 20 mm and fifty-caliber machine guns, then one thousand feet of cable might be safe enough. Towing targets could be scary because live ammunition was used and the trainee's marksmanship might be wildly erratic. One story circulated about the recruit, who after his first practice firing asked his sergeant, "What the heck was that long round thing behind the plane we were shooting at?"

* * *

The eight Tow Target Units were: TTU #1 at Hadley Field, Brunswick, NJ; TTU #5 at Otis Field, Falmouth, MA; TTU #7 at Glendale Army Air Base, Glendale, CA; TTU #12 at Gibbs Airport, San Diego, CA; TTU #15 at San Jose Airport, San Jose, CA; TTU #17 at Hyde Airport, Clinton, MD; TTU #20 at Gray Field, Ft. Lewis, WA; and TTU #21 at Monogram Field, Driver, VA. Later in 1944 when Hadley Field closed and most of its TTU #1 personnel were released, the remaining personnel, augmented by transferees from other tow target units, formed TTU #22. This new unit, which for a time was based at the Newark Air Force base, flew temporary assignments both in the New York area and as far away as Fort Bragg, North Carolina and Sault Ste. Marie, Michigan. Some of its personnel later moved to Clinton, Maryland, then ended their CAP service at the Baltimore Army Air Base restoring the planes that had been leased to the CAP before returning them to their owners.

Virtually the entire complement of the Flagler base was redesignated as TTU #5 and relocated to Otis Field, near Falmouth, Massachusetts in December 1943. Those making the move included commanding officer Julius L. Gresham; operations officer Arthur S. Dix; engineering officer James G. Angell; intelligence officer Lawrence Grabe, pilots Shelbourne W. Carter, A. G. Clay, Shelley E. Edmondson, Donald T. Speirs, Wesley C. Wallace, and Claude S. Wells; mechanics Byron W. Bailey, W. A. Bock, C. B. French, Clyde K. Hull, George C. Kloppell, and James R. Strange; radio operators Charlie A. Pool and K. F. Rowell; technical section head John J. McElvey; and clerk-typists George M. James and Mary Upchurch. Operations began January 16, 1944. A few months later Gresham was promoted to head all of the target towing units on the east coast, as described in *Flying Minute Men:*

The four basic units were consolidated under a single command, with fourteen detachments which towed for the Harbor Defense gunners and for ack-ack batteries all the way from Portland, Maine, to Key West, Florida. Gresham's headquarters was first set up at Hyde Field, Maryland, and later transferred to Baltimore Army Air Base. Major overhauls were performed at Baltimore, where 45 mechanics and a half dozen radio technicians were constantly on duty. An old ship could be flown in and a reconditioned one flown out in the space of a few minutes. All CAP missions in the East were flown under the operational control of the First Air Force at Mitchel Field.

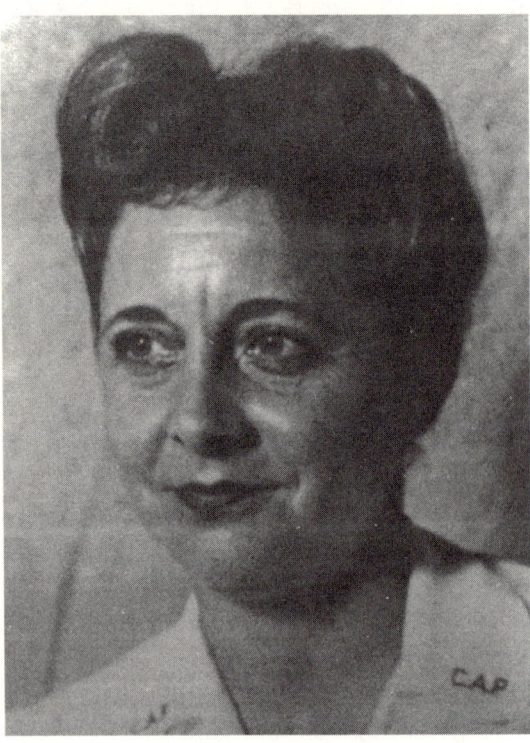

Edna Gordon McGrath was a secretary at the Flagler Beach base from April 26, 1943 until its closing August 31, 1943.

The final paragraph of "Slips, Stalls, and Spins" gave credit to the Navy and the Coast Guard and reminisced one last time:

Orchids to the men of the Naval Air Station at Banana River for all their many courtesies.... The Coast Guard at Cocoa Beach always had good food, but their courtesy was accepted once too often! Remember? That was the day the Interceptor Command like to have gone crazy.... The day Wes Wallace and Bob Wimp went into the drink with "13" was a perfect day for vocal "May-Days," as Wimp squalled so loud a radio was not necessary. The Radar thought there was a tidal wave approaching.... We could never have made the grade had not Leroy Morrison fetched each day a batch of his mother's tasty pies.... Capt. Dix was a lover of fine music, as it will be recalled that he bought and paid for that famous old piece, "Sweet Violets," for the juke-box.... Enuf said, eh?

On August 27, 1943, commanding officer Julius Gresham commended each man and woman who had served at the base:

> It is with genuine sincerity that I take this opportunity to highly commend and extend my personal thanks to each and everyone for your untiring service that made the operations of this Base the success that it was. You made self sacrifices in as many ways as there were individuals on the Base, and each sacrifice was real and close to your heart. A great number of you voluntarily offered your services at a time when they were most needed, and most of you would never have been called upon otherwise. To me, that was the American way of serving — serving in a manner just as important as the Marine, Soldier, or Sailor who met the enemy on Wake Island, in Africa, or on the Coral Sea. And, I might add, just as perilous. When the final victory is won, no small part of it will be yours. Again, I say simply, "Thanks, fellows — thanks a million!" With personal good wishes for your future, I am, yours very sincerely, Julius L. Gresham, Major, Civil Air Patrol, Commanding, CAP Coastal Patrol, No. 5.

---

Base officers, pilots, and observers who served at least one month at CAPCP #5 and who are not elsewhere mentioned in this chapter include: Isaac C. Beatty III,* Eugene D. Coleman,* Robert W. Davis, Henry A. Freeman,* Harman Furman,* H. D. Gilley,* George M. Green, Ralph B. Hayes,* Ernest G. Helms,* Junius M. Horner, Jr.,* F. M. Longley, Thomas J. Parker, Jr., John W. Ragland, Clarence Simpson, Joel S. Spice,* James E. Staples, Daniel H. Wallace, Frank G. Wickersham, Frank A. Winchell, and George W. Wright, Jr.* Asterisk indicates winner of Air Medal.

Malcolm McKinnon Airport was situated on the southern end of St. Simons Island just north of the small town of St. Simons. Though most of the base personnel lived in the town, it was just a little too far to walk to the base (source: 1950 United States Geologic Survey map).

# 6

# St. Simons Island, Georgia

Georgia's one hundred mile long Atlantic coastline, from South Carolina to Florida, is marked by seven major barrier sea island groups that Spanish explorers of the 1500s called the "Golden Isles." Many of the unpopulated islands are publicly-owned wilderness areas or wildlife sanctuaries, but others are well-developed retirement and tourism centers. St. Simons Island and its companions, Little St. Simons Island and Sea Island, are located near the center of the chain, seventy miles south of Savanna, about half way to Jacksonville, Florida. The city of Brunswick is on the Georgia mainland opposite St. Simons Island.

The St. Simons coastal patrol base used Malcolm McKinnon Field, about two and a half miles from the village of St. Simons on the southern tip of the island and about eight miles from Brunswick. Glynn County owned the land, but leased it to the Navy. Patrol planes operated from the original airfield even as it was being developed as a Naval Air Station. In its early stage what the base most lacked was office space, a shortage soon alleviated by the actions of a well-meaning army general. How the general became involved has been described by Major Thomas H. Daniel, Jr., who commanded the base from its formal activation on May 12, 1942 until it closed. Major Daniel's account is included in John H. Batten's short 1988 history of the base:

> At the beginning of our patrols (when the planes flew in from all around the United States) all of the lights on St. Simons Island, and the adjoining islands, had to be extinguished. This included all the lights on the automobiles and houses that fronted on the ocean or could be seen from it. For additional security, the main hotels, namely,

The King and Prince* on St. Simons and the old Arnold House (which was owned by my great-aunt) were closed, as were all the restaurants, except during daylight hours. The Red Cross served us sandwiches out of tents for at least a month. By that time, I had contacted the owners of The Cloister Hotel, where we could obtain dinner at a real discount. The owners of The King and Prince were also contacted and free rooms were given even though the lobby and other common space was covered with sheets and the remainder of the hotel was closed.

One day Major General Eric Fisher Wood appeared at the base notifying me he was based at Ft. McPherson in Atlanta and wanted to see the operations of the base. The guards and all of the personnel had the strictest instructions from National Headquarters that no person be allowed on the base whether in uniform or not. I went to the guard gate myself, and after talking to the general and seeing his credentials I informed him I would have to get permission from National Headquarters before I could allow him on the Base.

While we were waiting for approval, I took him to lunch at The Cloister Hotel. The request for permission was granted and after Major General Wood saw the efficiency and necessity of our operations, he learned to respect what the Civil Air Patrol's units were doing for the safety of the American shipping lanes.... [later] ... he sent us three portable one-story buildings. One for personnel and operations, one for engineering, and one for a mess hall. He sent one staff car at first, and another one later, four or five jeeps, several two-ton, six-wheel trucks and a larger one to be used in our ammunition dump (all four-wheel drive). He also nicknamed the CP-6 operation the "suicide and sandwich squadron."

Major Daniel must have had a real knack for making friends quickly, because he formed yet another excellent working relationship with William Daniel Thomas, the commander of the Naval Air Station scheduled soon to take over the airport. Thomas did not object to the coastal patrol's continued use of the runways, and even promised to give them priority. There was plenty of runway capacity: two 4,000-foot paved runways and another paved runway 2,800-feet long. Though trees lined the field on three sides, runway approaches were adequate, and the two longer runways had contact lights. At first the St. Simons flyers were razzed by the Navy pilots for their red epaulets, but after they located

---

* Both the Cloister Hotel and the King and Prince Hotel are still popular. High-season rates at the world-class Cloister, which, with its Spanish-style buildings and immaculately landscaped grounds, covers virtually all of the southern tip of the more exclusive Sea Island, start at around $400 per night for two. Rooms at the King and Prince Hotel remain more moderate.

several Navy pilots down at sea then aided with their rescue all that changed. As the military activity increased, however, the coastal patrol became increasingly squeezed for space on the field. Major Daniel again came up with a solution — create a coastal patrol base off of the Naval Air Station, but close enough that its patrol planes could still reach and utilize the excellent NAS runways:

> After we got the buildings and materials from the Army, there was no place to put them and still operate. I went to Bill Jones, who owned several acres of land adjoining [but across the road from] McKinnon Field. I asked for permission to clear out the heavy undergrowth and trees for our buildings to be assembled. He not only gave us permission, but additionally told us there was an artesian well with a constant flow of approximately 300 gallons, or better, a minute of water within 100 ft. of the paved road that separated us from the airport runway. Therefore, we built a village of our own ... CP-6 men and women built the base by themselves, and during the short construction period not a single patrol was altered.

## Ernest G. Helms

*Ernest G. Helms was in the aviation business in Reading, Pennsylvania when the Japanese attacked Pearl Harbor. Wishing to continue in aviation even after most civilian aviation had been curtailed, he tried for the ferry command, but though he held a commercial license he failed to qualify because he wore glasses. After he discovered the CAP's need for planes and pilots Helms flew his Fairchild 24 to St. Simons Island a few weeks after the base was activated. In time, he was named executive officer, remained at the base until it closed, and in 1948 was awarded the Air Medal. In 1983 he told Colonel Lester E. Hopper of some of his experiences at St. Simons:*

> After I became executive officer, I continued to take my turn at flying patrols just like everyone else. I might sometimes fly my own plane, but more often than not, I flew somebody else's plane — whatever was assigned to me. We had the usual collection of mostly Stinsons, Wacos, and Fairchilds. I think all the bases had a similar hodge-podge. I don't think the location of the base had any bearing on what types of planes it used.

> I was on patrol in somebody else's plane one day, when the engine started running real rough. I just made it back to the beach. My co-pilot and I had pulled the plane back up past the high tide line, and the mechanics who came out to see what was wrong later told us that a bearing had burnt out. We were probably lucky the engine hadn't flown apart. I'm sure that similar beach landings must have been made by pilots at all the bases.

I had a lot worse scare another time when my observer — Rufus King from Atlanta, Georgia — and I ran into some fog just a few miles off the coast. Our flight instruments were really worth about nothing, but I tried to climb out over the top of the overcast, and fell off into a spin. I knew we were only maybe eight hundred feet or so above the water, and that I had to straighten out the nose and dive down in order to recover from the spin. I came out in the clear just above the water, but started back up, and was immediately into the fog again. I decided to keep a steady climb and broke above the fog into the clear. I called base to tell them our predicament and where we were and they said descend through the stuff until I broke into the clear again. I'm not bragging on myself, because there was really little choice, but it took a lot of nerve to come down blind like that. We were lucky and stayed on the deck all the way back to the base.

Major Thomas H. Daniel, Jr. cut a dashing figure as base commander. The six-man Army tents in the background housed unmarried enlisted men (Hopper collection).

I don't remember much about living conditions at St. Simons. I recall that if you stayed in what we called "tent city" right at the base, that lodging was free. If we stayed in a hotel in Brunswick, about ten miles away, we paid for it out of our pockets. We went in to Brunswick for whatever recreation we could find — mostly to go a movie or have a nice dinner out. Since you ask, I'd say that what the CAP proved was that a bunch of private pilots with diverse backgrounds and aircraft could actually band together and perform a really difficult job with considerable success. In the beginning the military didn't think it could be done, but we proved them wrong.

## Jack W. Metz

*Jack W. Metz, an aircraft mechanic from Albany, Georgia, served at CAPCP #6 from September 1942 until its closing. After his graduation from the Roosevelt Aviation School as an aircraft and engine mechanic he worked at Dart Aero Tech in Albany, one of many private schools then under contract to provide Air Corps primary flight training. When another mechanic joined the coastal patrol at St. Simons, Metz went with him:*

We did all our own maintenance and overhaul on the aircraft and engines, and had a fairly decent repair shop. I brought my own tools. They weren't furnished to us. Our main problem was that we often couldn't get material or parts. We made exhaust stacks out of stove pipe and you can guess how long they lasted. We were paid once a month, and this was a real problem, because the checks were always late anyway. We'd first send a voucher to the government and then have to wait another month to get the money.

I remember being broke, and using stale shrimp as bait to catch enough fish for my wife to cook a meal. We had fried fish, baked fish, fish cakes, and fish chowder. I came in from the base one evening and my wife was sitting on the bed crying. She looked up at me and said, "If I have to eat fish one more time I'll turn blue." I told her to dress, we were going out for dinner. There was a bar and a restaurant down on the ocean front, and we went in and sat down. When the owner came over, I told him to bring us a bottle of whiskey and two of the best steaks in the house. I went on to say that we'd all been keeping the bad guys off his back, and that it was time for him to put out something and he agreed. Some of our pilots and other mechanics were in there drinking ten-cent beers, and when they saw him bring our whiskey, they came over asking if I had received some money. Next thing I knew we had a party going, and all on credit. We were paid soon after that, and from then on it was arranged that a Brunswick bank advance our monthly pay checks for a one-dollar fee.

Shortly after my wife and I arrived, I started playing the piano in a band that appeared Friday and Saturday evenings at the King and Prince. It was actually what they called a "bottle club." They couldn't sell liquor, so you brought your own and bought set-ups at the bar. We mostly played "big band" and jazz, and had a piano, bass, drums, and trumpet. Sometimes I'd go in on Sundays just to play requests. Sort of anything to make a few extra dollars. I'd roll the piano around to individual tables when I did that. My wife and I had an apartment made from half a garage, and the downtown consisted of several restaurants and shops, a drug store, a hardware store, and several "touristy" type places. I thought the local people were very nice.

At first the Navy wasn't very cooperative. We'd been flying and docking our planes off the Navy runway, but as soon as they finished the barracks for their own operation, they made us move. We went across the road into a swamp and built our own base, consisting at first only of tents and an operations shack. We then had to tow our aircraft across the road in order to take off from the Navy runways. On one occasion our boys dropped a number of bombs and depth charges on a suspected U-boat but none exploded. An investigation revealed that our fuses were rusty and obviously hadn't been well maintained. The Army sergeant in charge was busted and shipped out the same day.

As I said, at first the Navy wouldn't give us any parts or help on things we needed, but that changed after an incident concerning a downed Navy plane. During a gunnery run, an F4-F went down in the ocean and a sea fog moved in. Other Navy pilots were grounded by their commanding officer who didn't want to risk any more of his aircraft looking for the F4-F. They came over to our base to try and borrow ours. Our C. O. wouldn't allow that but he did send our fellows out in the fog to search. They located the downed pilot, dropped him a life raft, and watched him climb aboard it. But when the Coast Guard picked him up — this was in February — he'd already died of exposure. Even so, after this, the Navy gave us anything we wanted.

We had one gentleman by the name of Jim Williams who was a pilot. Jim was quite heavy and stuttered. Coming back from southern patrol almost down to Daytona Beach, he'd often land at Jekyll Island to answer the call of nature. The sand was hard and smooth and easy to land on, and various pilots did the same thing. One day Jim had landed and done his business and had started his takeoff roll when a coast guardsman came out of the bushes and cut loose on him with a submachine gun. Needless to say, Jim had a *lot* of trouble reporting that on the radio. We never found out why the man fired at him, or even for sure if he really was a coast guardsman.

## Elmer E. Wachter

*Elmer E. Wachter was another mechanic at the base — in his own words, a "greaseball." Born and raised in Frederick, Maryland, he received his A&E training in Trenton, New Jersey at the Luscombe School of Aviation and at eighteen years of age went to work for Dart Aero Tech in Albany, Georgia, where British air cadets were being trained in PT-17s. But working strictly on Stearman trainers day after day became very boring, and when a chance came to join the coastal patrol in November 1942 Wachter grabbed it:*

I got what I wanted. We had twenty six planes and it seemed like they were all different. We had Cessnas, Fairchilds, Wacos, and Stinsons, and at least one Bellanca. When I first arrived, which was just after the base opened, most of them needed lots of work. We had one other A&E and four helpers, and we worked twelve hours a day getting the planes ready to go in the mornings and putting them to bed at night. John M. Cloud from Athens, Georgia was our first engineering officer. Until the Navy took over and upgraded the airport to support the training of F4-F fighter pilots, we had Malcolm McKinnon Field to ourselves. But when the Navy said, "Okay, you can still use the runways, but you've got to take your planes and personnel somewhere else," we moved into the pine trees across the road and established our maintenance operation in two old barns. It was a rough go, but we managed. We were a very small outfit, many wearing two or more hats, and there were wonderful people there.

At first I lodged at the King and Prince, a kind of motel-hotel-inn, later was lucky enough to rent a little trailer attached like a wing to a big old house near the edge of a swamp and three or four miles from the base. A nice old lady had used it for her study, but besides that reading room, it had a bathroom, kitchenette, and bedroom, and for eighteen dollars a month rent I felt very snug. That summer I married a girl I'd known in Frederick and we lived there happily together until I left the base. Unfortunately, we didn't see much of each other, because I left for work very early every morning and often didn't get home until late at night. I rode to and from the base on a "victory bike" I bought for thirty-five dollars. The long driveway to our house and trailer was loose gravel, so I had to walk the bike through it. At night I walked *very* carefully to avoid stepping on the snakes.

I remember a number of people fairly well. There was Walter Nicholai, a pilot from Philadelphia, and a real perfectionist. He owned a beautiful all-metal, low-wing Ryan-SCW, and when it failed to hit the top engine speed he wanted, he decided to try a new propeller. He gave the old one to me, and I've kept it all these years. It's still on the wall of my den. And I recall Rufus King, an insurance salesman from Atlanta and a stutterer. I can still hear him caution me, "Ta-ta-take good care of this engine, because if it qu-qu-quits, it'll get awful qu-qu-quiet up there." Our commanding officer, Tom Daniel, also was in the insurance business in Atlanta and owned a low-wing Bellanca. It was murder to work on, but a good airplane

Before I married, I mostly had my meals at Pomeroy's Restaurant down at the city pier. There was a little complex there — the lighthouse, several restaurants and shops, a bank, and a drugstore. St. Simons wasn't that fancy in those days. Sea Island, just across a small bridge, was more costly. My wife and I stayed there at the Cloister a couple of nights. Cumberland Island was home to some even wealthier businessmen, such as the Carnegies. Everyone had his own big mansion and they shared a private airport. Everything around the area was so spread out that you either had to bicycle or bum a ride, you couldn't just walk. Fortunately, the Georgia State Police gave us two "junker" squad cars with bald tires in which to get around. Though I'd been warned very carefully not to exceed thirty mph, I hit a dare-devilish forty mph one day and blew a tire. I invented some wild story to cover up my mistake.

In April 1943 I left the base to become a Cadet. My departure was not altogether pleasant, because my boss didn't want to let me go, forecasting a dim future for me in the infantry. But I thought I could make the Air Corps and I did. I finished flight training in December 1944, but missed going overseas because by then bomber crews were no longer needed. After the war, my basic love of flying kept me in the Air Force Reserve for twenty eight years. I ended up flying C-124s world wide and completed my service as C. O. of the 756th Material Airlift Squadron of the 459th Military Airlift Wing at Andrews Air Force Base, Maryland, resigning with the rank of colonel. The coastal patrol experience helped me in many ways throughout my Air Force career. I'm very proud to have been associated with the grand bunch of people at St. Simons.

## Brooks W. Lovelace

*At age seventeen, Brooks W. Lovelace of Atlanta dropped out of high school when he was asked to enlist in the coastal patrol, but later went on to become a commissioned officer in the Air Corps serving both in World War II and in Korea:*

I went down to St. Simons in January 1943 and stayed until July. I was first a security guard, then after a few weeks, the night teletype operator and a driver in the motor pool. Usually only two or three messages came in then — orders for next day's search and rescue or other special missions, names of ships entering our patrol area, and so forth. Most messages arrived uncoded — I really don't recall, some could have been coded — between 4:30 and 5:00 a.m. I acknowledged receiving them and put them where our operations officer would see them when he reported for duty. Each midnight I took a Jeep over to the Naval Air

Station weather station to get the latest weather forecast, and talk with the meteorologist on duty. I got to know him well enough that he taught me how to send up weather balloons and read certain meteorlogical instruments for myself.

After a while I was told that if I wanted to add some flying time as an observer they'd let me. So during my off time I flew fairly often. My first flight was with Wyly F. Flint in a Waco N, an early tricycle-gear plane. Since ours was the faster of the two-plane patrol, we "hen-sailed" behind the lead plane, making broad sweeps back and forth — something like a hen searching for feed — to avoid overtaking it. With its 285 hp Jacobs engine, the Waco-N was powerful enough to carry a two hundred and fifty pound depth charge, the one with a blunt concrete nose. We were continually hampered by parts shortages and an inability to obtain them. None of our Fairchild 24s ever flew, only one of our three Waco Ns, and there was one Stinson Reliant that never flew. Our Ryan SCWs and a half dozen Stinson Voyagers did almost all the work.

Not a lot of people remember that a Liberty ship was small enough to use parts of the Intracoastal Waterway* where the U-boats couldn't get at them. But the Waterway was discontinuous in the St. Simons region, and such ships had to go outside, around the island, where they were fair game for the subs. That's why we were always told when a Liberty ship was due. Ten miles from Brunswick, at Glynco,** was a Navy blimp station and they did some patrol work, too. But as far as attacking a submarine, they were handicapped — far too slow and obviously vulnerable to anti-aircraft fire from a surfaced sub.

By the time I reported, the Navy had occupied the field and relegated our operation to the pine woods across the road. We had a bunch of tents back in the palmetto scrub, a motor pool, a mess hall, and several administration buildings. We eventually established ourselves across the road from the Naval Air Station, about mid-way along the northeast-southwest runway, and tied down our aircraft along the north side of the clear zone for the east-west runway. We continued to use the NAS runways but were required to get their tower clearances

* Over 2,500 miles long, partly natural, partly man-made, the Intracoastal Waterway provides sheltered passage for both seagoing vessels and small pleasure craft traveling along the Atlantic and Gulf Coasts. It was built by the U.S. Corps of Engineers, not to guard shipping from enemy attack, but as protection against major storms.

** Squadron Fifteen (eight airships) of Fleet Airship Wing One, Headquarters, Lakehurst, New Jersey came on line February 1, 1943. Airship bases usually were named for the nearest town, but since there was already a "Brunswick" Naval Air Station in Maine, Glynco Naval Air Station was named for its Glynn County location.

for taking off and landing. The Navy had some Wildcat F4-Fs training there, but I don't think we had any traffic conflicts with them. Since neither the Navy nor we flew at night, the field was unlighted, and for me that led to quite an exciting adventure. I was on teletype duty one night when I thought I heard a plane land. I went out in one of our trucks and there was this B-25 off the runway stuck in a shallow drainage ditch. I pulled them out with my winch and for two days while the B-25 was being repaired I carted them around here and there in our Jeep. They apparently were quite grateful, because when the bomber was ready to fly again they invited me to go along for the test ride. Well, I was a kid and when I had a chance to get on a military plane, man, I was gone! They put me up in the nose, and then they buzzed that field over pretty good. After we came back, they said they'd been trained with the B-25 group that Jimmy Doolittle led over Tokyo, but were among the crews that had been scratched at the last minute.

Brooks W. Lovelace was called "Whitie" around the base because the sun had bleached his blonde hair white. The car is an Austin "Bantam" convertible owned by airdrome officer Thomas B. Sutton of Atlanta (courtesy Brooks W. Lovelace).

After I left St. Simons, I was accepted into the Cadet program, and first spent about five months in college at the University of Toledo before going to flight school. By that time, the Air Corps was saying that it had too many pilots, and would some of us like to try something else. I opted for flight engineering and ultimately made second lieutenant in that specialty. I left the Air Corps in 1946 as a B-29 flight engineer, was recalled in 1952 as a B-36 flight engineer, then stayed in until 1969, retiring with the rank of major. Between tours, I went back and got my diploma, obtained an A&E license, and later was employed as a mechanic with Southern Airways and Delta Airlines. After retiring I worked as professional with the Boy Scouts of America and Rockwell International in Albany, Georgia.

## Joe O. Mangum

*Joe O. Mangum was a pilot at St. Simons from May 1942 until December of the same year. Born in 1921, he learned to fly at age sixteen in Atlanta. His family owned a plane, but it wasn't suitable for patrol work, and when he joined the coastal patrol it was left behind:*

Some one that I knew from hanging around the Atlanta Airport called me one day and told me about the coastal patrol operation and the plans for St. Simons. When he asked if I'd be interested in serving I said I'd think it over. That afternoon I called and said okay. I was single and unemployed and had no one to talk it over with except myself. I roomed in a boarding house down there, and at first didn't know a soul. One of the fellows I met there was Cliff Zimmerman, a young banker from Atlanta. He became my flight observer throughout my time at the base. When it closed, Cliff ended up in our army ground forces.

I must have had four or five hundred hours flight time when I reported at St. Simons, and about twelve hundred when I left, plenty enough for the Air Medal. Nothing ever happened to me — I was lucky in that regard — but two of my sister ships were lost. The first was a low-wing Bellanca flown by James Knott of Atlanta. Coming back from a patrol he lost power off Sapelo Island, and while he managed to make the beach he overshot it somewhat and went on into Doboy Sound. Neither Knott nor his observer were hurt, but the plane ended up about half-in and half-out of the water, and the thing about salt water is that it quickly ruins a plane. I doubt the Bellanca ever flew again.

The second time I lost a sister ship was real bad. We were going out for dawn patrol, and I took off second. It was still almost pitch black, with no lights at all and I was about four hundred yards behind. Once we were both airborne I watched their navigation lights as they made a slight turn to the left, then a sharp turn to the right, then down. They went in from about seventy-five feet, and it's a miracle they survived. I returned to the base but don't remember if I went out again or not. I suspect — I don't know for sure — but I suspect the pilot had little night flying experience and just got disoriented.

When I left St. Simons in December, I went with Delta Airlines.

Because the airline was carrying military cargo for the Air Corps, the Air Corps gave me instrument training, the only rating I didn't already have. A year later, the draft boards came after the airline's younger men like myself, but Delta intervened. They told the Pentagon that, if we were drafted, they'd have to shut down cargo operation, and that ended the draft threat. I flew for Delta until 1983 — some forty years. I'm sorry to say I haven't kept track of any of my coastal patrol friends. They were a good bunch of men, and we worked quite well together, but I haven't seen or talked with any of them since then.

Captain James P. Knott, a pilot from Atlanta, Georgia, and clerk-typist Laura Jane McClain in the base Operations Room. On wall at right is the daily assignments blackboard (Hopper collection).

CAP Colonel Batten's short base history provides additional information on the accident and ditching record at St. Simons:

> Early in the base's career several aircraft were lost in the ocean by engine failure. The first was in the vicinity of Sapelo when a Bellanca monoplane had to ditch. 1st Lt. Feldher Sommer of Racine, Wisconsin, executed two night landings on a small emergency strip on Sapelo to bring the crew back to base after their radio distress signal was heard. [J. O. Mangum believes that this may have been before all patrols were made with pairs of planes.] ... no personal injuries of consequence were encountered except for the accident to Lt. Ernie Jenkins [with observer Roy Weakland] on a takeoff emergency which occurred on a pre-dawn patrol. The aircraft stalled and spun in and Lt. Jenkins, seriously injured, spent months in an Atlanta hospital.

## Wyly F. Flint

*Colonel Batten's history fails to mention the ditching by pilot Wyly F. Flint from Meadville, Pennsylvania, and his observer Earl Gaston of Brunswick, Georgia. Flint's written crash report dated August 21, 1942, two days after the crash, provides details:*

> Left Malcolm McKinnon Airport, St. Simons Island, Georgia , at 1026, August 19, 1942 — circled field and joined sister ship piloted by John Sweitzer. Flew East approximately fifteen miles and headed South on regular patrol. The motor was running fine, oil pressure and temperature was normal. After flying South approximately one hour on irregular course, our motor missed four times at different intervals. We headed West and after three or four minutes we were beginning to lose rpm and finally cut back to 700 rpm — we were flying at 1100 feet when motor began missing and at 400 feet we dropped demolition bomb unarmed, at approximately 40 feet above water we cut switches and started in for crash landing. At 10 feet above water I gave the ship full flaps and hit the water at about 35 mph — time 1125 — position approximately 7 miles East of St. John's Lightship.

> Was able to get out of plane safely and inflate my life vest, but we were unable to get the flotation gear from the airplane due to the fact that it sank approximately 3 minutes after crash. After being in the water approximately 30 to 35 minutes we were picked up by Naval Vessel from Mayport, Florida. Weather conditions — hazy — visibility 2 to 3 miles. All positions reported were made from dead reckoning. COMMENTS: Believe cause of motor failure was due to carburation [sic] trouble. Observer Gaston did a fine job of handling radio equipment and cutting me loose from antenna wire. [signed Wyly Francis Flint]

Colonel Batten's history also fails to mention the ditching of pilot Lex D. Benton of Atlanta and his observer, Claude B. Guest of Winder, Georgia. According to a newspaper account, their plane was forced down by an oil leak, and they then floated from dawn to dusk in their Mae Wests before being rescued thirty miles off Savannah. Although Benton only served at St. Simons Island for six months he was named base intelligence officer and won the Air Medal in 1948 for flying over two hundred hours of anti-sub patrols. He stayed in the CAP following the war, and in 1960, by-then Colonel Benton was presented with the CAP Meritorious Service Award for his leadership as Georgia Wing Commander, October 1952 to February 1960.

Altogether, the St. Simons Island base had fourteen men downed at sea who lived to tell about it. Besides those not previously mentioned were 1st Lts. Edward H. Egbert and George E. Dickson; 2nd lieutenant

Clifford B. Zimmerman; flight observers Harold R. Harris and Walter H. Salter; and enlisted men Charles E. Johnson and H. Rubin.

Captain Wyly F. Flint went from the St. Simons coastal patrol to "flying the Hump," crossing the jagged snow-capped Himalayan Mountains more than two hundred times. He was sent home in a state of exhaustion (courtesy Frank Flint).

After most reported ditchings, Washington CAP headquarters was quick to officially welcome the men involved to the Duck Club. Flint's letter from National Commander Earle L. Johnson, dated August 26, 1942, read:

> To Mr. Wyly Francis Flint — It is recorded at National Headquarters that in the service of the Civil Air Patrol you were in an airplane which had a forced landing on water while on an active duty mission. Just as everyone who has ever bailed out an airplane is one of the fellowship of the Caterpillar Club, it is our thought that every member of the Patrol who shares your experience shall be a member of the Duck Club. In token of your experience in this select fraternity, I enclose herewith an emblem which you are entitled to wear on the left pocket of your uniform, half an inch below the flap. With it goes my congratulations that you are still with us to talk about it and the hope that you will wear it to show that the Patrol is proud of you.

Roughly a year later, with national CAP Headquarters relocated to 500 Fifth Avenue, New York City, now-Captain Wyly F. Flint drew top-level attention again for his heroism in an attempted at sea rescue:

To Captain Wyly Francis Flint — You are hereby cited for distinguished service in flying as pilot with Lt. Peter D. Biegun under extremely hazardous conditions for a number of hours in the attempted rescue of a Navy pilot who had gone down at sea. In token of this citation, I enclose the Blue Triangle Emblem which is to be worn point down above the left pocket of the shirt or blouse. My heartiest commendation and that of the entire Patrol go with this token. By direction of National Commander JOHNSON: [signed] JACK VILAS, Lt. Col., AC, Executive Officer.

Following his coastal patrol service at St. Simons Island, May 24, 1942 to August 11, 1943 — for which he won the Air Medal in 1948 — Flint flew for the China National Aviation Corporation based in Calcutta, India. In sixteen months, he crossed the Himalayas almost two hundred times, accumulating 1,420 hours flying time in the process. He was relieved of the duty in mid-December 1944 for reasons of "fatigue and war weariness," and sent home to Meadville. With the withdrawal of his occupational deferment, the local draft board in mid-May 1945 actually summoned him for a pre-induction physical — which he failed to pass. After this, he resumed his duties with the family lumber business, which he eventually took over and directed until his death.

## Fletcher R. Shurley

*Fletcher R. Shurley was a local boy, born and raised in Brunswick, the largest town on the island. He learned to fly in the Civilian Pilot Training Program at Malcolm McKinnon Field:*

When the coastal patrol first took over, there was nothing there but a hangar and a CAA weather station. A small back room back inside the hangar served as operations headquarters. I was rated as a pilot-observer, which meant I flew in either role as scheduling demanded. I particularly remember intelligence officer Thomas Carnegie from Kingsland, Georgia who owned a roadside business there, a place called "Tommy's Chi-Chi." His family owned Cumberland Island. And who could forget flying with Rufus King, a pilot so huge at 280 pounds that he nearly filled the cabin of his Fairchild 24 by himself. I could barely squeeze my small frame in beside him.

We had a team of Air Corps ordnance men who came down from Hunter Field to check out our newly installed bomb racks and release mechanisms before we began using them on missions. Two of them were underneath a Stinson 10-A loaded with two bombs, arms and hands forming a cradle to catch the bomb on the right side while a man inside pulled its release. An instant too late someone shouted out, "Don't forget the right release works for the left bomb and vice versa!" The bomb on the left hit the concrete with a thud, while the two embarrassed armorers looked at each with their arms outstretched foolishly under the bomb on the right. That really scattered everyone.

We used a little island — Egg Island it was called — as a target for practice bombing. We hit it pretty frequently, but then we weren't flying very high or very fast. The Stinson 10-A cruised around 95 mph, I think, and for that matter its top speed wasn't much higher. It was a good little airplane all the same, and burned fuel very economically. Sometimes Tom Carnegie and I flew an inland mission to check out a Japanese-American village in the rice-growing area along the Little Satilla River about ten miles upstream from Jekyll Island. He knew some of the people and their shrimp boats, and we swung low just to see if anything unusual seemed to be going on. There never was.

**Aubrey R. Bates**

*Aubrey R. Bates was a forty-year old flight observer originally from Tifton, Georgia, and one of the older men at the base. He and his wife, Helen, and their two young children moved from Athens, Georgia to live in Brunswick while he served at the coastal patrol base. Bates died in 1992 at age ninety, but his widow remembers certain events of 1942-1943:*

Aubrey was a supervisor for Western Union working in Athens when we met and were married in 1937. I know that he got into flying well before the CAP came along but I don't remember any of the details. He had a Cub and a Waco cabin plane at one time. I remember, because after the CAP, he was in the Eighth Air Force in England when I got a letter from him saying to sell the Waco. He gave me the suggested asking price, but I "upped" it and got my price, too. He didn't talk much about coastal patrol flying, but I did worry about his safety. There were some accidents, as you know, and with two small children I couldn't help but worry.

We went out to the base a lot of times. There was nothing secret about it being there. Aubrey took me and our two-year-old son up for a ride once, and baby screamed to high heaven. Now and then, friends came over for a little party, but our social life was limited. In the Air Force, Aubrey served in communications, probably because of his Western Union background. At one point, he had a serious bout of pneumonia, and he was sent home for a while. After he went back to duty, he seemed to serve all over the country. A few months ago I drove by where the base used to be. I thought I could see the old hangar back in the pines, but I'm not sure. It'd be a miracle for it to survive this long.

## Richard N. Bromley

*When he first heard of the coastal patrol, twenty-seven-year-old Richard N. Bromley of Philadelphia owned a Taylorcraft on floats and thought there would be nothing to over-water flying. When the coastal patrol refused his Taylorcraft he sold it and bought a Stinson Reliant with a 225 hp Lycoming engine. Bromley had nearly four hundred hours of flight time, but his navigator for the trip to St. Simons got them lost, and he made an unscheduled stop at Washington National Airport:*

I didn't have any trouble finding the patrol base, however, and people there had reserved a room for me at the Golden Isle beach hotel. Later I went in with two other boys and rented a house on Sea Island, definitely the more upscale as compared to St. Simons Island. Because of the war, vacancies were common and rentals easy to find. We always ate out. Nobody wanted to fool around with cooking. The "Nineteenth Hole" just across the road from the base was basically a bar, but it served food as well, and was especially handy if we'd just returned from patrol and wanted a fast meal. The "King and Prince" was popular and there were lots of little "Southern" restaurants around town.

When I got there, the chief mechanic found my Stinson had a defective brake that required repair, so I flew whatever other planes were assigned to me. I spent a year and a half there — from the opening of the base to its closing, and had more than enough hours for the Air Medal. I experienced several forced landings on the beach for lack of fuel to get back to base. The beaches were beautiful, and nobody thought anything of landing on them if necessary for any reason. Eventually I became one of the operations officers, assigning people and planes to patrols. Everyone pretty much pitched in to do whatever was needed, and the Navy allowed us to use their runways without giving us a lot of grief.

When the base closed, eight of us went to El Paso, Texas to serve in the border patrol. Our group included Tom Daniel; our engineering officer, Alfred Earl; our operations officer, F. A. Baker; our plot board operator, Eva S. Clayton; and three pilots besides myself. It was a really useless duty! We'd fly up and down the Rio Grande and *maybe* we'd see someone crossing it. But we couldn't do anything about it except to radio-in what we'd seen and I never knew if anyone we saw was ever caught or not. The chances of an enemy agent's entering this country in so careless a manner seemed very remote. The El Paso base shut down within months of our arrival, and I left the CAP to take a position in the research department at Sperry Rand on Long Island. After the war, I went back to Philadelphia to work in my family's textile business.

\* \* \*

The border patrol, more correctly, the "Southern Liaison Patrol" formed in mid-1942, flew dawn to dusk surveillance along the United States-Mexican international boundary from Brownsville, Texas to Douglas, Arizona — more than a thousand miles — until April 1944. As described in *Flying Minute Men,* its purpose was to help protect the United States from enemy infiltration:

> This territory could have been an open gateway for scores of agents, saboteurs, and currency smugglers if left half-guarded during the war years. With fewer border patrolmen available for duty along the wild mesquite country of southern Texas, the danger of a fifth-column invasion from the south was very real. Cracks in the protective wall had to be cemented, and vigilance increased a hundred-fold. This was exceedingly difficult. The draft was draining available manpower, and Army units were being moved out for pressing combat duties. Replacements of trained and experienced men in this work were too few to make up for losses and to shoulder the additional burden.

Two main Southern Liaison bases were established, one at El Paso, Texas (SLP #2), the other at Laredo (SLP #1). Halfway between them was a smaller, unnumbered base at Del Rio. A separate reconnaissance base was established at Marfa. Refueling facilities were provided at Brownsville for the Laredo unit, and at Douglas for the El Paso group. *Flying Minute Men* suggests the border patrol's usefulness:

> Light planes were ideal for border patrol. Pilots hedge-hopped along creek beds and ravines, enabling observers to comb the brush on the banks for fugitives who might be hiding during daylight hours. When automobiles were spotted careening down obscure back roads toward the International Boundary, CAP crews sometimes flew low enough to read the license plates.... They were captured at the border and found to be enemy agents. Another time, the observation of automobile tracks and other signs of activity around a deserted hay barn on an abandoned ranch led to the discovery of a radio station which was being operated by enemy agents.... The finale for the "Cactus Kids" came in April of 1944 after more than eighteen months of daily operations. During this period the CAP pilots flew 4,720 patrol missions plus 1,397 special missions, which added up to a total of 30,033 hours in the air with only two fatalities. These operations resulted in the observation and reporting of 176 suspicious aircraft and 6,874 out-of-the-ordinary activities along the border.

\* \* \*

## Edward E. Witte

*Edward E. Witte was the assistant engineering officer at the St. Simons base. Prior to that, the twenty-one year old native of Albany, Georgia had worked for a defense contractor who operated flying schools for the Army Air Corps in Albany and Augusta, and in Penca City, Oklahoma:*

I'd been a member of the CAP squadron in Albany when I learned that the assistant engineering officer at St. Simons had enlisted in the Air Corps and would soon leave. I had my A&E license, and was put in touch with commanding officer Thomas Daniel who agreed that I'd become his new assistant engineering officer. I was replacing Elmer Wachter, a fellow from Hagerstown, Maryland with whom I'd attended the Luscombe School of Aeronautics in Trenton, New Jersey. We both got our A&E licenses there.

Four of the base mechanics, including Jack Metz, running off a batch of moonshiner's "white lighting," coastal-patrol style. Working a still came naturally to such skilled improvisers (courtesy Jack Metz).

I can't recall the exact date I reported, but my young bride and I almost had second thoughts when we saw the operation. As I think back on it, it was like a scene from the "MASH" television series — dirt and sand streets; tents for enlisted personnel, supply, and communications; Quonset huts for operations and maintenance shops; and no hangars. At least we officers found places to live in various homes on the island. We didn't do any major repair work for lack of a hangar, and even the routine maintenance we did on the flight line depended on having favorable weather. Our maintenance crew was constantly having to pull wheels and brakes because of the sand. Spark plugs were a problem because of the humidity. We used a dehydrator to keep the new plugs dry.

Some of the St. Simons gang, including base commander Tom Daniel in white jacket nearest camera, enjoying themselves after work. The bartender's CAP insignia was entirely unofficial (Hopper collection).

Avionics were very simple. Each aircraft was equipped with a trailing wire antenna that was pulled off a reel by a small drag cone played out beneath the fuselage. I heard of one patrol where a Stinson Voyager lost power and gradually dropped so low the drag cone caught in the waves. It acted like a sea anchor, finally pulling the plane down about a hundred yards off shore. Fortunately the crew got out safely and simply waded in. The Navy pulled the plane up on the beach, and we eventually got it flying again. Those of us renting rooms on the Island got rides every morning and evening with one of our ground crewmen, who drove either a Jeep or a command car depending on the weather and how many passengers he expected. For the life of me I can't remember many people but I think our communications officer was Austin Baumann, and there was a fellow named Peter Biegun who was our "Mad Russian" and would fly anything with wings. I also remember our executive officer, Ernie Helms, a man from Pennsylvania.

The last day before the base closed everybody was elated. Everything that would fly got off the ground, and they all played follow the leader, hedge-hopping all over St. Simons Island and the town of

Brunswick. Only our J-3 Cub was left. Peter Biegun had been away from the base and when he returned he asked me if the J-3 could fly. When I said yes, he said. "Let's go!" We caught up with the rest of the crowd and then I never had such a wild ride in my life — what a day! We were proud of our work and of our uniforms, which, except for the added red epaulets and CAP insignia, were the same as regular Air Corps uniforms. We never were treated with anything but great respect, and I have to say that serving in the coastal patrol was an experience I'll never forget — even though I haven't thought much about it for over fifty years now. I stayed in aviation all my life, retiring from Hawthorne Aviation in 1986 after some thirty nine years with them.

\* \* \*

While some coastal patrol bases reported no U-boat sightings at all, the St. Simons Island base had several of them. Colonel Batten's base history suggests the enormous frustration of the air crewmen who encountered the enemy without having the means of attacking him:

> Capt. Sam Baker was flying off Cumberland Island the spring of 1942 when he saw a sail boat with nice rigging. After a few seconds he noticed that the boat was sailing straight into the wind and the sails were being blown to the stern rather than forward as normally would be the case. The code name for a submarine was "one zed unit." When Capt. Baker approached the sail boat it suddenly submerged leaving all of its sails awash on the surface. Baker then realized it was "one zed unit" and so notified the base. At that time bomb racks had not yet been installed. On another occasion, a submarine was sighted stuck in the mud off Sapelo Island. Lt. Erwin Bosarge radioed headquarters that he had spotted one zed unit submerging. Again, as this occurred before bombs were installed, nothing could be done after radioing Savannah for military assistance.
>
> Shortly thereafter base headquarters received a phone call from a man living on a small island north of Sapelo Island called Horses Neck.... The informant accused base headquarters of not having come out to sink a submarine that was in his yard. [no such sighting was reported by any patrol] A flight was dispatched at once. While the submarine had gone, there was evidence that the crew had been ashore, but had departed very quickly when suspicions had been aroused.... Before bombs were provided, Lt. James King [later the commanding officer of the Bar Harbor coastal patrol base] spotted a submarine in Ossabaw Sound and reported it by way of CAA communications to the Naval Air Station at Savannah, where this report was disregarded as representing an overactive imagination. The sub was actually seen to turn around in the Sound and make its way out to sea once more.

## John S. Rowland

*A number of CAPCP #6 men came from the state of Wisconsin. Besides John H. Batten, pilot and incidental base historian, there were pilots James B. King and Frank F. Sommers and pilot-observer John S. Rowland. All had belonged to the Racine CAP Squadron and knew each other well. King was later transferred to Bar Harbor, Maine as base commander. J. David Rowland was ten years old when his dad was at St. Simons Island but remembers hearing stories of his coastal patrol days and of a flying career that started long before:*

Dad was born in Racine in 1902 and learned to fly in the 1920s. He knew such people as Steve Wittman, Billy Mitchell, and Eddie Rickenbacher. Steve Wittman became an air racing hall-of-famer and Mitchell, son of a Wisconsin senator and chief of the Army Air Service, sacrificed a bright military career to try to alert the Congress and the American people to the need for a strong air force. After I was born, mother asked dad to give up flying, but he took it up again in the late 1930s as the European situation deteriorated and it seemed only a matter of time until the United States might be embroiled in war. He tried in the worst way to enlist in the Air Corps, but a recruiter in Milwaukee told him he was "too old" and should "go on back home."

About this time he and several of his friends started the Racine CAP squadron. Soon thereafter, three of them — pilots Archie R. Fuller and Walter M. Petersen, and pilot-observer Clarence J. Nielson — went to Bar Harbor, while my father and three others went to St. Simons Island. They reported in May 1942, the same month the base was activated. Dad returned home some time before the end of the year, but not before he had flown many hours of over-water patrol.

At forty, Dad was still young enough at heart to enjoy a prank. Out on a patrol one day with John Batten, they dropped one of their hundred-pound bombs on an innocent sea turtle. They knew they shouldn't, but were bored, and gave in to temptation. The turtle swam away unharmed. I recall, too, Dad's telling of the razzing they got from some of the military personnel at the Naval Air Station, and the naval air trainees singing a parody of "Mademoiselle from Armentiers" as they marched — "The CAP will win the war, parlez-vous. The CAP will win the war, parlez-vous. The CAP will win the war, so what the hell are we here for? Rinky-dinky, parlez-vous."

When Dad left the coastal patrol, he came home and got an instructor's rating at what was then the Racine-Horlick Airport, where he then began teaching would-be air cadets the fundamentals of flight in little Piper Cubs. (Later, this field was renamed Racine Commercial Airport, and then Batten Field, after John Batten. It has always been a private field used primarily by the several large corporations based in Racine.) After the war, I remember a 1946 Fourth of July parade which featured members of the local CAP squadron, led by my Dad because he was the only one with real military training, having as a young man attended Tennessee Military Institute. Dad gave up flying about 1950.

Several base members came from CAP Squadron 622-1 in Racine, Wisconsin. Here that squadron takes part in a "Victory Parade" shortly after V-J Day and the end of the war (courtesy J. David Rowland).

Base officers, pilots, and observers who served at least one month at CAPCP#6 and who are not elsewhere mentioned in this chapter include: Russell A. Alger,* Julius M. Allen, Erwin H. Besarge, Arthur A. Bieder,* David C. Black, Jr.,* George A. Bland, Billy M. Burckhalter,* John W. Clayton, A. G. Cochran,* Norton A. Davidson, Jr.,* George E. Dickson,* James D. Duckworth,* Clarence B. Gowen, Gordon M. Guilbert, Daniel W. Henderson, John J. Humphries, Williard B. Joy, Kelly W. King,* Roy L. Larson,* C. F. Luce,* MacLean Marshall,* Walter Nicolai,* Hugh M. Nunnally, John N. Reid,* Francis L. Roma, Jr., Wilford A. Rose,* Floyd M. Shepherd,* George E. Shivers,* Joseph M. Smallwood,* Harry Smith, Horace D. Smith, Alexander P. Solomon, III,* Thomas B. Sutton, Millard E. Winchester, Orval J. Winover, and John M. Woods.* Asterisk indicates Air Medal winner.

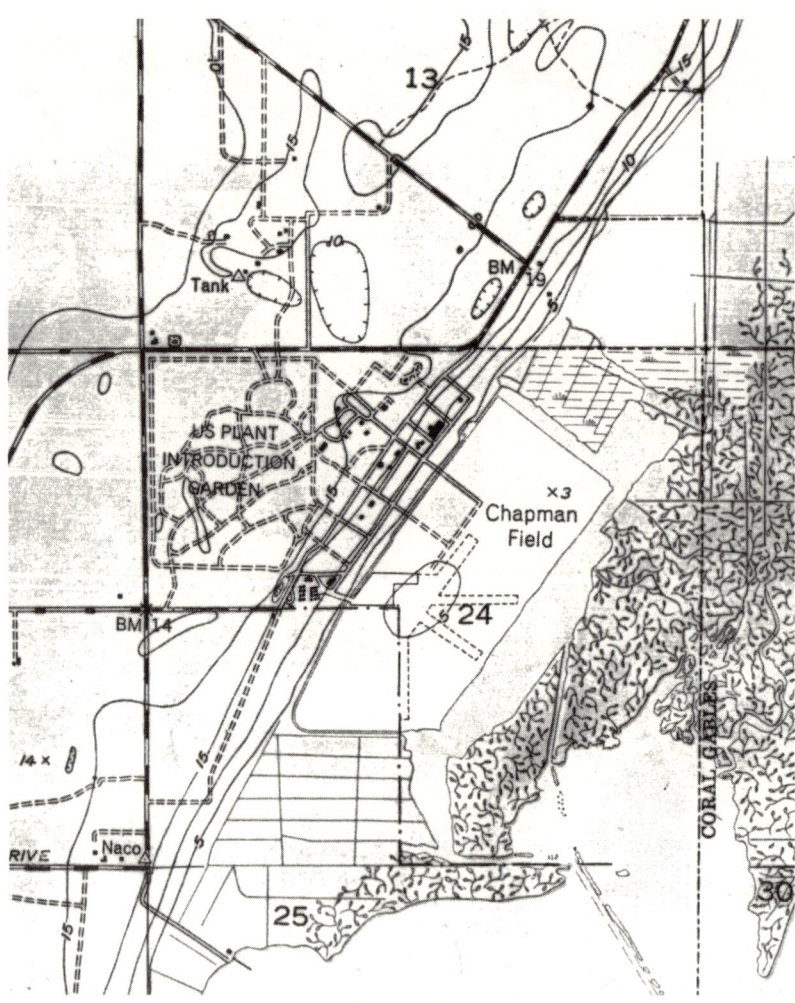

Chapman Field was surrounded on the west and north by open grassland, small farms, and two-lane roads; on the east and south by tidal flats and lots of water (source: 1950 United States Geological Survey map).

# 7
# Miami, Florida

The incomplete blackouts of the early months of the war and an unusual ocean floor topography led to particularly aggressive German submarine activity off the south Florida coast. The disregard for strict blackout regulations was, in the eyes of many, a national disgrace, but a fault that could be, and was, eventually corrected. That the region's ocean floor dropped off so quickly, so close to shore was simply good fortune for the submariners who could stay submerged in the deeper water until night, then surface close enough to land to fire their high-explosive torpedoes into the sides of ships silhouetted against the skyline.

In response, private pilots and aircraft owners in the Miami area organized two CAP squadrons that actually began flying anti-submarine patrols before the coastal patrol was fully organized and operational. The planes flew alone rather than in teams of two, and some were distinctly underpowered by comparison to the coastal patrol's subsequent minimum requirement of 90-horsepower. The first squadron, based at Amelia Earhart Field in Coral Gables, was commanded by Robert D. Beilman. The second squadron, based at the Sunny South Airport in the northern part of the Miami area, was largely thanks to the work of Charles Darnes. These squadrons merged to become CAPCP #7, officially activated on May 13, 1942.

The 42-year-old Lloyd H. Fales was chosen to command the new base. He had attended the highly regarded Massachusetts Institute of Technology, worked for the International Business Machines Company from 1920 to 1928, and owned and ran the Viking Airport and Seaplane Base in Miami until 1937. He then retired because of bad health, but came back in 1941 to participate in the fledgling Civil Air Patrol in Miami. He had six hundred hours flight time before he took over the Miami base. Major Fales received the Air Medal in 1948.

## Robert D. Beilman

*Robert D. Beilman was born and raised about forty-five miles east of Scranton, Pennsylvania some eighty-five years ago. He soloed in an American Eagle with the 90 hp Kinner engine. Years later, after moving to Miami, he met John Paul Riddle, co-founder of the Embry-Riddle School of Aeronautics, who introduced him to Sam Belcher, Florida Director of Aviation and owner of Belcher Oil Company. Beilman and Belcher became friends and founded B&B Aircraft, a Luscombe aircraft dealership for the state. Belcher put up the money, while Beilman ran the company. When war came, and put B&B out of business, Beilman joined the Civil Air Patrol, then organized and took command of the first CAP patrol group in southern Florida — the "Coral Squadron":*

At a recent Aircraft Owners and Pilots Association meeting in Atlantic City I talked with a number of former coastal patrol members who thought the first anti-sub patrols in Florida were flown out of the Lantana base. I said they were wrong. Although the Miami base was officially activated after the Lantana base our "Coral Squadron," the nucleus for the Miami base, was out there looking for subs before the Lantana base got going.

During this initial period we flew whatever we could get hold of. I flew my own plane, a 65 hp Luscombe, and several squadron members owned early-model Stinson Voyagers with 75 hp Continental engines. The improved 10-A version with the 90 hp Franklin engine appeared in April 1941 and we had some of those, too.* We patrolled well beyond the Gulf Stream, as far as thirty miles out. We also did search and rescue exercises and other missions.

When the Miami coastal patrol was formally activated, Lloyd Fales was named base commander and for the relatively short time I served there I took my regular turns flying assigned missions. Although I was never involved in any ditchings or forced landings, several of my friends were. I recall Henry Cushman going down somewhere off Fort Lauderdale in his sporty Monocoupe, and Bob Royce ditching in somebody's seaplane, then spending the night floating around in a life raft off Molasses Reef. I don't recall who their co-pilots were.

---

* Stinson Voyagers flew two-thirds of all CAP wartime missions and were undoubtedly the workhorse of the coastal patrol. Many non-CAP flyers owned Voyagers, among them millionaire Howard Hughes, speed racer Roscoe Turner, ventriloquist Edgar Bergen, and aerobatics ace Al Williams. Williams, who flew the Grumman biplane, "Gulfhawk II," now hanging in the National Air and Space Museum, named his Voyager, "Gulfhawk, Jr."

When the base relocated down to Chapman Field, I left the coastal patrol and went with the Pan American Airways ferry service, delivering A-20s, B-25s, and A-26s to Europe. I did that from about April until November 1942. When the Air Transport Command took over, civilian pilots like myself were given a choice: go into the military or go with the airlines. I went with Pan American and for about thirty years flew just about every plane they owned, totaling thirty thousand hours or so. But I continued to fly, and still do.

## Robert G. Royce

*Robert G. Royce learned to fly before the war in his father's J-3 Cub float plane, earning his pilot's license at sixteen, a commercial license at eighteen, and both instructor's and instrument ratings at nineteen. After enlisting in the Air Corps he joined and served in the coastal patrol until being called up:*

I began my flying with the coastal patrol in a Fairchild on floats, a fairly large single-engine plane owned by my father and another man and based at Chalk's Flying Service along the Biscayne Causeway. I don't recall its model designation, but it had only one seat up front, with no instruments or controls for a co-pilot. My observer was usually Gene Bozarth, a fellow about my father's age and a good friend of mine and of my father's. Gene took the wide rear seat and enjoyed visibility to either side of the plane. All of our missions were made without a sister ship. On one, I landed with Gene to inspect one of those big metal life rafts the freighters and tankers all carried. No one was on it, but we wanted to see whether there were any notes or anything. We wound up removing and taking home a load of emergency provisions to be added to those in the life rafts carried by other Miami coastal patrol planes.

The only time I came close to a major disaster was during a take-off just before dawn. I saw the guy wires to a radio tower on the 79th Street Causeway just in time to avoid them. That could have been real bad. Gene and I both became Duck Club members, however, when we had an engine failure down around Molasses Reef. I landed into the wind as always, but if I'd known just how rough the water was I'd have tried to set down cross-wind in a trough. It was a hard landing and damaged one of the floats so badly it sank, then dragged the plane under with it. Gene and I got out all right, inflated our life preservers, and swam to the hulk of a nearby sunken freighter sitting on the bottom with most of her main deck awash. She had probably been torpedoed, and beached on the reef intentionally. We climbed aboard, found some mattresses in a cabin and settled down for the night. We were spotted early next morning and someone dropped us a note to say that a boat was on the way.

During the evening my father, who was also a pilot, had wanted to come out looking for us because we were obviously overdue, but the Navy said "no way," because they'd end up shooting him down if he went poking around out there after dark. The rescue boat took us to Islamorada, and I took a bus back to Coral Gables from there. I was single and living at home with my parents, and they were most relieved to see me! When we resumed flying, it was from Chapman Field. In February 1943 I was called into the Air Corps, and was assigned to Palm Springs, California to fly B-17s, B-24s, and B-25s from there to the east coast. Then I went to C-47 school, and flew one of them to Prestwick, Scotland, where I was stationed for a year to do more ferrying, first to points in southern England, and then to France.

A group of linemen and mechanics with Major Lloyd H. Fales, base commander, kneeling at far right, and Robert F. Barres standing fifth from left (courtesy Robert F. Barres).

After the war I stayed in the reserves for a while, but left just after the Korean police action began. I had married in 1948 — the same year they gave me the Air Medal for my CAP service — and didn't think Korea was so good an idea. A friend and I then started a small charter airline — Argonaut Airways. We bought a couple of war surplus C-47s for ten thousand dollars each, and he flew one and I flew the other. Our two mechanics flew as co-pilots. We flew to places in South and Central America, the Caribbean, and all along the U.S. east coast. We weren't particularly successful, though the plane purchases were a great bargain. Only a few years later, the engines alone were selling for six thousand dollars each. We sold out, and I went into the fuel oil business in

Jacksonville. For a time, my dad and I owned a Republic Seabee amphibian, but as family and business grew, I had less time to fly, and finally gave it up.

## Dr. Herman L. Anderson

*Herman L. Anderson was a 30-year-old dentist who flew half days — one week he'd be a sub-hunter in the mornings and a dentist in the afternoons, then the following week he'd reverse the sequence. He had been flying since 1937, the same year he got his dental degree from Atlanta Southern Dental College (now part of Emory University):*

My family came to Florida from Kansas City, Missouri during the big land boom of the 1920s, when I was fifteen. Those were the wonderful years of the great aviation heroes and most young men like myself were crazy for airplanes. After finishing dental school, I became a part-owner of a Taylorcraft, and later bought a Luscombe Silvaire of my own. When the war came I sold it to the head of the American Red Cross in Cuba — I've forgotten his name — but continued to work on a commercial rating at Embry-Riddle, which I completed while serving with the coastal patrol. I joined the patrol at its inception, and remained active until the patrol ended, flying both from the municipal airport (the patrol's original base) and from Chapman Field.

I remember several interesting things. One day, some distance out over the Atlantic from Alligator Point, my observer and I saw a small boat with three men in it. We dropped a hastily-written note inside a cork float attached to a streamer telling them how to signal us depending on who they were. They retrieved the float and indicated they were the survivors of a sinking. We then flew to the nearby lighthouse and flew close enough to the keeper to attract his attention, and he went out with his motor launch and rescued them. Before we left them, we'd dropped flares near their drifting boat so they could be spotted more easily. We learned later they were off a fishing trawler that had been stopped by a submarine. They were ordered to stand off in their small boat while German sailors boarded the trawler and took all the fresh food and other supplies they could use. The trawler had been blown up with an explosive charge the Germans had left behind. We also heard the three survivors were particularly grateful for our dropping the flares, because they'd used them to light the first cigarettes they'd enjoyed for three days. They said they'd counted fifteen planes pass over them before we stopped to help.

On another occasion we spotted one of our own patrol planes in the water with two men atop it. They must just have gone down, because their plane sank just as we were circling and radioing-in their position. They had their life jackets on and were rescued unhurt, but they may have been lucky we came by when we did. The pilot was my friend Joe Schuchter, but I can't remember his observer's name. My observer was Wilbur Groth, who now lives in California. Schucter lives here in Florida.

On yet another patrol I remember seeing a military plane losing altitude in the distance. That caught my attention, so I followed it. It was flying faster than I was but when I saw its depth charges drop and explode I thought the plane was attacking a sub. Actually, it was dumping them before ditching. By the time we got there, three men had gotten out and were floating around in life jackets. One's head was rolling limply as though he'd been injured. We called in their position and I assume they were rescued. We couldn't remain long enough to be certain but I like to think we may have saved their lives, too.

Barracuda buckets, more often called "barracuda bags," supposedly were for protection from hungry barracuda and sharks, but whether they ever saved any airman's life cannot be confirmed (courtesy Mrs. Gus Halwardson).

Unlike the common practice at other bases, we did not fly in pairs, but always alone. We experienced many ditchings but never lost a man, so our system must have worked. If we had anything called "barracuda bags," I don't recall them. I've gone swimming when barracudas were around but they never worried me. They are a curious fish and easily attracted to shiny objects such as a belt buckle or a wristwatch, but they seldom attack a person. My wife was also a pilot, by the way, and an aviation enthusiast, which meant that I had real support at home for what I was doing. She didn't work but with others she organized a canteen at the base, and showed up early every morning to serve coffee and doughnuts for the fellows on the dawn patrol.

As the base was winding down, I got my notice from the draft board. The Navy was about to take me as a dentist when someone noticed my flying credentials and decided I should become a flight instructor. I wasn't so sure that's what I wanted, however, and I seriously considered joining the Pan American Airways ferry service with Bob Beilman, another pilot and friend at the base. But I went with the Navy, was sent to a Navy instructor's school in Texas, and then spent a year at a training facility in Olathe, Kansas teaching kids to fly Stearmans. Just before the end of the war, I was assigned to fly multi-engine flying boats. After my discharge I continued flying, and bought and sold a Stearman, a Luscombe, and a couple of Howards. Though I quit flying at eighty, I'd be happy to have any of those planes back right now!

## Marshall B. Harper

*Marshall B. Harper was born in Millersville, Georgia, and moved with his family to Florida when he was nine. After earning his private license via the CPTP at Compton Aviation in Fort Lauderdale, he joined the Civil Air Patrol, took more advanced training at Embry-Riddle, then reported for active duty at Chapman Field:*

I had a wife and two little girls, and was classified 3-A in the draft, so I might never have been drafted. Chapman was roughly a twenty-five mile drive from my home, but that was no problem. I guess I was one of the latecomers, and by then everything was routine. Nevertheless, we often had to fly twice a day. We had some ditchings but no men had been lost. Chapman Field didn't have much but one hangar, two grass runways, and a headquarters building. It'd been a training base for the Army Air Service in 1918, and to tell the truth I don't think it had changed very much in the years since then.

I mostly flew the Stinson Voyager. Ours had originally been equipped with racks for two one hundred pound bombs, but we only carried one. We called the Voyager the "ground hog" because it was so hard to take off with us and our equipment and only one bomb. We flew beyond Key Largo and well down toward Key West. Some of the men who were there before me may have seen some subs, but I never did. The Germans knew we were there, all right.

Not long before the coastal patrol shut down we often flew down to Homestead Army Air Base to learn instrument flying on Link Trainers, predecessors of our modern flight simulators. We all had about thirty-six hours on the trainers and that was a good thing, because later on it may have saved my life. We weren't kept very well informed and had no idea where we might go next, but we saw an increasing number of U.S. Navy planes and blimps* patrolling through the same areas that we were. When our missions suddenly ended, most of us, except for the guards, linemen, and clerical staff, were transferred to TTU #7 based at the Glendale Army Air Base in Glendale, California.

A fast Cessna Airmaster framed by the interplane struts of a Waco. Pilots were discouraged from carrying cameras, and only a few in-flight photographs are anywhere to be found (Hopper collection).

Pulling targets was a different kind of flying and a pleasant change from the routine patrols we'd been doing in Florida. But the Los Angeles area is ringed by mountains and for anyone who learned to fly over

* Squadron 21 (fifteen airships), Fleet Airship Wing Two, located at Richmond, twenty miles southwest of Miami, Florida, was commissioned November 1, 1942. Its patrols ranged from the northern coasts of Haiti and the Dominican Republic through the Florida Straits — the U-boats' main route from the Atlantic into the Gulf and Carribean — and well into the Gulf itself. NAS Richmond also served as the major repair base for airship squadrons based in the Gulf Coast, Caribbean, and Southern Hemisphere. *Blimps and U-boats: U.S. Navy Airships in the Battle of the Atlantic,* J. Gordon Vaeth, The Naval Institute Press, Annapolis, Maryland, 1992, provides an excellent account of the Navy's LTA (lighter-than-air) service in World War II.

level country that can be a problem. We flew lots of search missions to try and find flyers who'd gone down in those snow-covered mountains. I remember the time when Charlie Bible and I were out looking for a Lockheed C-45. We didn't find that plane, but we did find a twin-engine Beechcraft that'd been missing for months. We were lucky enough to spot the sparkle from a silver wingtip not covered by snow.

My earlier Link training may have saved my life one day when I got caught on top, trapped above a solid layer of clouds where I couldn't see the ground. Knowing the hazards of the mountains below, I flew a compass course due west, well out over the Pacific, then let down through the overcast, counting on breaking through into clear skies before reaching sea level. I had to trust my instruments completely in clouds and fog. Without the Link training I might not have done so, but gotten disoriented and spun-in.

\* \* \*

By January 1944, Marshall Harper and nineteen others from the Miami base, including commanding officer Lloyd H. Fales, had moved to the Glendale Army Air Base in California and been redesignated TTU #7. Sixteen others joined the unit from other bases, seven from the Panama City, Florida base.* The four tow target units established on the west coast were later consolidated under Major Fales, and his headquarters moved from Glendale to San Jose. A dozen different detachments provided good practice for anti-aircraft batteries stationed around various cities on the west coast, and for anti-aircraft training detachments near several Army camps.

## Robert H. Hurt

*Robert H. Hurt, from Marion, Alabama, took a job in 1936 with Eastern Airlines in Miami, and remained in their employ for "forty-four years and five months" before retiring. There he was trained and soon specialized in sheet metal work. He took flying lessons, got his private license, and had logged about a hundred hours by the time he was married in 1941. Having an occupa-*

---

* From the Miami base, besides Harper and Fales: engineering officer Claude E. Demonbreun; intelligence officer Clifton K. Hyatt; pilots Charles L. Bible, Frank L. Bowman, Carl L. Boyson, Albert W. Broome, Wilbur H. Groth, Jack R. Hoolsema, Wilbur Horton, Blaney M. Johnson, Charles T. McCrimmon, William A. Robinson, Joseph R. W. Schucter, and Ward A. Vilas; and mechanics Joseph J. Brennan, Richard H. Haughn, L. E. Leitner, and Emil P. Pellini. From the Panama City base: pilots Joseph Azis, Edward P. Bruch, Jr., Carl S. Clark, and Francis E. Kissell; mechanics John Reaver and Franklin B. Wetzel; and technical section head Mabel Bennett. From various other bases: pilots Samuel W. Catoe, James D. Duckworth, David T. Farrelly, Oliver P. Fullerton, Floyd Shepherd, Rex Sullivan, and George A. Turner; radio operator Norman H. Larrabee; and clerk Ann McDonald.

*tional deferment from the draft, he volunteered for part-time, unpaid service with the coastal patrol:*

I lived about six miles from the coastal patrol base, and worked there in the afternoons after putting in my regular hours with Eastern. Sometimes I'd work into the evenings and at night. I was what they called a "service technician," or simply lineman, meaning that I gassed the planes, checked their oil levels, and otherwise made sure they were ready to fly. I did some fabric and dope work, and since I had my aircraft license I also helped repair various parts. I was at the base from May 23, 1942 until May 7, 1943. My friend Gus Halwardson, a volunteer pilot, was another Eastern Airlines man. I think half of them out there at the base were. I'm still in touch with Russell P. Egan, another volunteer mechanic from Eastern. Russ was a neighbor for years, but now lives in Tampa. Like Russ, a lot of people have moved out of the Miami area. My wife and I had some swell property back in Alabama, but we've stayed here largely because our son and his family are nearby. I'm active in things like my church, the EAL retirees association, golfing, and raising palm trees. I have a half acre and a greenhouse on it with about two hundred palms inside. It's a good life.

## Russell P. Egan

*Russell P. Egan was born in Lakeland, Florida in 1918, but grew up in Tampa, where he graduated from the Hillsboro High School. Having been a captain in his high school ROTC, he served for a time with the Florida State Militia before going to work for Eastern Airlines in Miami. There fellow co-workers such as Bob Hurt told him of the coastal patrol operation at Chapman Field and suggested that he volunteer some of his time as they were doing:*

As I recall, I finished my regular shift at about 3:30 p.m. and drove straight down to Chapman Field. Most of the roads were two-laners and it took about an hour. The field was right up against Biscayne Bay near Shoal Point, just below South Miami and east of Rockdale. A small field only three feet above sea level, Chapman had little to commend it except that it was exclusively the CAP's domain. I was listed on the coastal patrol roster as a mechanic, though at Eastern I was a sheet metal worker, and I didn't need an A&E license for that. I remained at Eastern for over forty years, by the way, twenty-five of them as a master mechanic in the sheet metal fabrication department.

At the time, however, I was working toward my "A" license, and knowing how to work with fabric covering was part of the requirement. It's interesting, but tedious. First you have to lay a kind of linen tape along the fuselage stringers — or lay it down on the tops and bottoms of the ribs if you're covering the wing. Then laying your large sheets of linen covering fabric along a section of fuselage or wing, you take enough stitches to hold it to one stringer or rib while you pull that fabric tight to the next stringer or rib and tack it there as well. Then you stitch on the covering permanently, stitching back and forth with heavy linen thread, one man pushing the needle through from one side, and his partner pushing it back from the other side. I don't recall shrinking the linen with water before applying dope, as model airplane builders would do. I think we began brushing on the dope right away. I only worked a few hours each evening, maybe from 4:30 p.m. to 7:30 p.m., and it seemed like forever getting that job done. I wasn't paid for my efforts there, but we got some nice pats on the back and kind words of encouragement. I really admired the fellows who flew out over the ocean. They were the ones who deserved the credit.

**Robert F. Barres**

*Robert F. Barres, a native of Miami, had just turned seventeen when on April 4, 1943 he joined the coastal patrol as a security technician. Aiming for a career in the U.S. Merchant Marine, he had previously attended a Miami technical school where he earned his radio and telegraph certificate for sending code as a radio operator. After a short time with Pan American Airways as a base radio operator — he failed to qualify as a flight crewman because he wasn't old enough — he turned to the coastal patrol:*

I lived with my parents and had a long commute, down 27th Avenue and across 36th Street to the Embry-Riddle flying school, and then by jitney to Chapman Field in South Miami. Door-to-door it must have taken about two hours. I carried a thirty-two revolver when I was on duty. When I first went into the store to buy it, I was told I needed a permit, and I had to be twenty-one to get a permit. So the base gave me a letter that I took to the police department, they fingerprinted me, gave me the permit, and I went and bought the gun. It had a six-inch barrel, and I installed larger grips to fit my hand better, and it looked like a bigger weapon than it was. Night guard duty was kind of scary. In our total blackout, everything was pitch black, and I was just an imaginative kid. A trained saboteur could've easily overcome our entire undermanned guard unit. We rotated posts and shifts. I think there was a perimeter fence and I recall for sure the guard's shack at the main gate. All the posts were manned twenty-four hours a day and we wore uniforms and all that. Mine included a pistol belt and a holster, which I also paid for myself.

When I was off duty, I liked to hang around the training shack where the pilots had to learn the Morse Code. One day I was sitting in there, sending away, when somebody said, "Hey, you're pretty good at that, you ought to work for our radio department." And so I did. I remained a corporal, with the same pay, and began by doing little things like replacing the lead weights on the planes' trailing radio antennas. Some crews forgot to reel them in before landing and they would snag on something, snapping off the weights. I only recall one other person by name, Sergeant Leo F. McReady, another guard like myself. It would be fun to find out what happened to everyone.

A very young Robert F. Barres posed for this "mug shot" used on his I.D. card. Without the card, he could not have gained admittance to the base (courtesy Robert F. Barres).

I almost had the dubious distinction of an ocean ditching on the last day the base operated. One of the pilots I'd gotten to know invited me up as his observer, and I said sure. Out over the Atlantic, we began to have some engine trouble, and he called in to say he thought we might have to go down. He told me when we hit just to get out as quickly as I could while he deployed our automobile inner tubes. As it happened, we didn't ditch, but after we landed one of our radio operators said she'd thought she'd have to add another chapter to her book.

A few days after the base closed, I enlisted in the Coast Guard. Because of my technical school background and coastal patrol experience, I was made a third-class radioman immediately. I was assigned to operate a radio at Coconut Grove where the Pan Am flying boats used to come in. Soon afterwards I began flying anti-sub patrols in Coast

Guard PBYs, PBMs, and Vought OS2U Kingfishers as an aviation radioman. Our patrol missions for the next two years were just the same as the CAP had been flying. I was discharged fairly early — January 17, 1946 — because I piled up a lot of "points." (Any flight beyond the three-mile limit counted as overseas duty). I took flying lessons after the war and remained active with the Florida Wing of the CAP while working for the CAA and then the FAA for over thirty years.

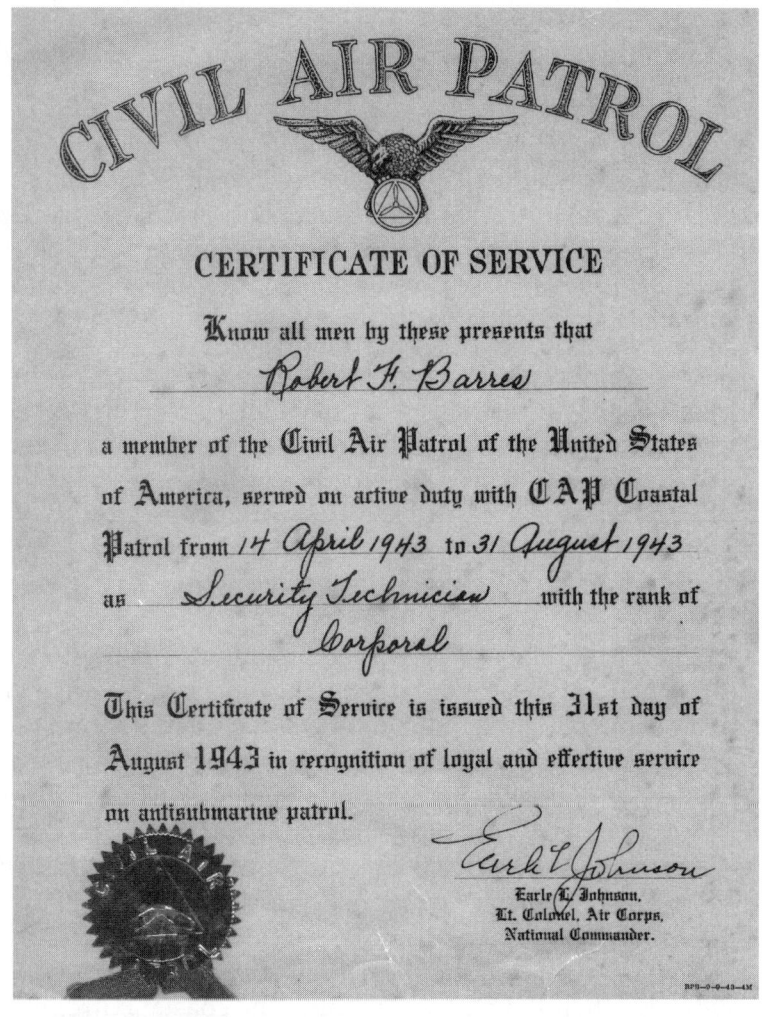

Certificates of Service, with gold embossed seal and red ribbon, were issued to everyone who served at a coastal patrol base for over thirty days (courtesy Robert F. Barres).

Pilots and flight observers were supposed to be reasonably proficient in taking Morse Code either by radio or by blinker light and in recognizing international signal flag codes. Some were but many were not. An April 1, 1943 report on the qualifications of thirty-nine officers and flight personnel at the Miami base showed that four had no skill at the Morse Code, eleven could take five words a minute (the passing level), fourteen could take from six to ten, and only ten bettered ten words a minute. The ratings for reading blinker lights were consistently lower and no one rated higher than "fair" on signal flag recognition.

**Wesley C. Randles**

*Before the war, twenty-five year old Wesley C. Randles had been a radio engineer with station WSUN in Saint Petersburg, later held a similar post with station WILD in Miami. Tiring of a midnight-to-eight a.m. stint there, he went to work for Eastern Airlines at the 36th Street municipal airport, where he worked from four p.m. until midnight instead. Early in 1942, he learned that a number of airline employees were volunteering services to the fledgling CAP organization, and decided to help out, too:*

I believe I started going down to Morrison Field long before the coastal patrol base was officially activated, May 13, 1942. I remember helping one of the regular CAP radiomen set up the base radio before patrol operations began. I went down about nine in the morning and worked until three, then reported to Eastern at four. I worked as an unpaid volunteer, though the CAP furnished my uniform. My chief recompense was getting extra gasoline for the drive from Eastern down to Morrison Field, a distance of ten miles.

The biggest part of my work was helping to maintain the radios in the aircraft. That they were of different makes and models wasn't really any problem. In those days a transmitter was a transmitter, and the only real difference was what frequency you were using. The same was true of the receivers. If there was some minor problem, I worked inside the aircraft. If it was bigger, I'd remove the radio and carry it to our radio shack to work on it. At the outset, the radio equipment was pretty poor, and we were plenty busy getting it into working condition. Sometimes I went out with the patrols so I could listen to the radios and see if any frequencies were out or couldn't be heard properly.

I have to say that the way I remember the coastal patrol was as a very makeshift kind of operation. The whole thing was something like the old barnstorming days — meager facilities, grass landing strips, old airplanes, and for that matter a lot of somewhat older pilots. That field wouldn't be adequate even as a private-use airport by today's higher standards. But everyone pitched in and made it work, and that was what counted. Later in the year I left Eastern and my CAP volunteer activities to take another radio engineering job with Raytheon, and I stayed with them for thirty-eight years until I retired.

A wonderful photograph of some fifty men and women of the Miami Coastal Patrol. On the hangar is painted "Chapman Field - Alt. 3 Ft." (courtesy Robert F. Barres).

## Clifton T. Bowes

*Clifton T. Bowes was born and raised in Miami and lived there with his wife during his tenure as a full-time pilot with the coastal patrol. He'd learned to fly as a student at the University of Florida, not by taking formal flight lessons but because his roommate owned a J-2 Cub, and let him fly it. Later, another friend let him fly his Kinner Bird biplane. In 1941 after earning his business degree at Tulane University, he returned to Miami, bought a J-3 Cub for nine hundred dollars, then joined an informal group of flyers who met once a week to practice over-water patrols:*

The United States wasn't in the war yet, but to some of us it seemed just a matter of time, and we could see how vulnerable our coastlines were. We'd fly the beaches and down along the keys, and became quite familiar with the area. After we entered the war and the CAP was established, our patrols were flown for a while from Amelia Earhart Field, maybe for three months or so. We didn't move to Chapman Field, an old abandoned first World War training field, until after the Embry-Riddle School had moved there and re-sodded the field for its students.

It wasn't much of a field, but it was adequate for the type of aircraft we had at the time. I flew all the various shifts — dawn patrol, mid-day, dusk — and probably every airplane at the base. We thought we saw a periscope wake a couple of times and dropped a bomb once, but never learned the result. The Navy simply was never forthcoming about our efforts. Our base was somewhat unique in that we had such a high percentage of part-time pilots and observers. I think about half of us — twenty or so — were full-time and about an equal number part-time. As a result not many of us totaled huge amounts of time in the air, but I certainly had more than enough to get the Air Medal after the war, and I'm sure others did, too.

Air Medal awards for qualifying members of CAPCP #7 were authorized by Department of the Air Force general order #14 dated April 16, 1948. Here Major General Lucas B. Beau, USAAF, addresses award winners and their families in a ceremony held in the Palm Beach Airport hangar for members of all Florida east coast bases (courtesy Mrs. Gus Halwardson).

The German submarines were still sinking ships when I began flying, and it was not unusual to wake up in the mornings and see these big plumes of oily black smoke rising out over the water. I think we did more search and rescue work than submarine patrol, because our first task would be to look for survivors. To help get their crews get off safely, ship skippers often headed their sinking or disabled ships straight for shore, and some reached water so shallow they settled on the bottom. I had a speed boat, and sometimes after a patrol I'd head out toward the burning or scuttled ships. Once I found pineapples bobbing around and almost sank my boat with the number I picked up. I took them home and my wife and I and friends were eating pineapples for weeks.

I spent a lot of time taking advantage of the free instruction on the Link Trainers at Homestead Air Corps Base. As I remember it was possible to get an instrument rating after twenty hours of Link Trainer time, ten hours of actual instrument flying with an instructor, and a flight test by a CAA examiner. I got to know a number of Air Corps fellows down there and was sometimes invited to fly with them on trips to Trinidad in Curtiss C-46 Commandos, logging something like a hundred hours on them. They called it "the fireball run," because the early C-46s were not real dependable airplanes. The ones used later to "fly the Hump" had improved propellers and performed more reliably.

When the coastal patrol drew to an end, I left the CAP and was employed by National Airlines, which had a contract with the Air Transport Command. I stayed with National after the war and flew for them thirty-four years — they were the only employers I ever had! I retired in 1976, the year that Pan American bought them out. When I left I'd flown over thirty-four thousand hours in every type of aircraft they had, up to and including the Boeing 747. On the side, for a few years, I owned and operated a flight school at Opalocka, and ran a business called International Air Service. That little Cub I had before the war? Well, the Army bought it from me for nine hundred dollars, just what I'd paid for it. But they didn't take into account that it'd just had a major overhaul and been re-covered, so I feel like I was kind of "taken." They were supposed to resell it to me after the war, but I never heard from them again.

## Jack L. Meyer

*Jack L. Meyer was employed as a security technician just weeks before the base closed. A 16-year-old graduate of Miami High School, where he'd been a CAP Cadet, Meyer had long had the aviation bug, and the lure of working around Chapman Field with the coastal patrol planes and pilots was reason enough to leave another job for the assignment:*

I didn't know the base was soon to close, and it wouldn't have mattered. I'd have taken the job anyway. I'd known Chapman Field since childhood, when I'd go there and maybe see a Martin bomber or some other exciting Army plane. Chapman was a small out-of-the-way field that'd been there for years and years. Embry-Riddle ran a big operation there giving Cadets their first five or six hours flight training in J-3 Cubs. The field was fifteen miles from my house, but I had an old

Willys sedan and got all the gas I needed for my "essential" job. The Willys four-door was widely advertised as America's "economy car." And it was — a car so basic, for example, that to adjust the driver's seat called for unbolting it from the floorboard, moving it, then re-bolting it.

I remember guard duty as a dusk-to-dawn affair and that we had little guard towers at strategic points around the base. We were quite remote, many miles south of Miami, and right up against Biscayne Bay. But just being there to see the dawn patrol depart was worth it. Most of our planes were either Stinson Voyagers or Fairchild 24s, and once in a while one of them would go into the water somewhere. After one of our planes had been pulled out after a ditching in Biscayne Bay, I took a piece of fabric from the tail as a souvenir (the fabric had to be replaced anyway). I've kept it all these years.

When the base closed, I was accepted into the Army Specialized Training Program as a 17-year-old reservist and sent to North Carolina State to study engineering.* After several terms and becoming eighteen, I was sent to Fort Benning, Georgia for basic training. Rather than return to college as was usual, I opted for Officer Candidate School and wound up as a platoon leader in the 86th Infantry Division in the Philippine Islands. To our mutual surprise, some of my former ASTP classmates ended up in the 86th, too. Years later, at age forty, I obtained a private pilot's license, and bought a Mooney airplane to use in my engineering business and for fun as well.

\* \* \*

The Miami coastal patrol base suffered no fatalities, but led all bases in the number (seventeen) of pilots and observers who survived crash landings in the Atlantic. They were: captains Ted F. Keys, Eugene M. Bozarth, Ward A. Vilas, Joseph R. Schuchter, Jr., Hugh E. Ridgley, and Charles A. Baner; 1st lieutenants Henry B. Cushman, Thomas C. Manning, Robert G. Royce, Earl E. Penn, Jesse N. Atlass, and Wilber H. Groth; 2nd lieutenants Carl M. Pearson, Harris A. Coller, and Robert E. Scholtze; flight observer William H. Sanders; and C. L. Marvel. All except Vilas, Penn, Pearson, Scholtze and Marvel were high-hour airmen who won the Air Medal, which suggests that membership in the Duck Club was perhaps mostly a matter of time and probabilities.

---

*More than 200,000 highly talented young Americans were ordered to attend 227 Army Specialized Training Program colleges and universities in 1943-1944. When the program was sharply curtailed as a means of getting the Army to full fighting strength prior to the D-Day invasion many thousands of ASTPers found themselves suddenly in the infantry. See the author's *Scholars in Foxholes: the Story of the Army Specialized Training Program in World War II*, McFarland Publishing, 1988.

Not surprisingly, then, it was the Miami coastal patrol base that took credit for developing the often-mentioned and ostensibly life-saving "barracuda bucket." An issue of the *Barracuda Bucket*, the official journal of Florida CAP Wing 41, explained the anachronistic contraption:

> This name of this publication, "Barracuda Bucket," stems from antiquity —well, if you want to call the old bootlegging days antiquity. In those days the rum runners used to cross the rough, tough Gulf Stream with gunwales of their oft-times frail and flimsy craft awash because of the load they carried. Sometimes accidents happened. Because of the frequency of these accidents, many of the 'leggers carried a home-made lifesaving rig, known as the barracuda bucket.... It consisted of an old inner tube, from which a shroud of canvas hung, and into which the survivor could climb, float, and still be protected from that most vicious of all fish, the barracuda.
>
> In the early days of the CAP, when it was still being organized at Morrison Field and was starting patrol duty on a wing and a prayer, the modern life rafts were not available. But the barracuda bucket served. It was adapted to CAP use by Thorne Donnelly, then communications officer of the CAP patrol squadron, now commander, USNR. Included in the equipment was an emergency kit bag of some 16 items calculated to keep the CAP flier from being hungry, thirsty or too unhappy. It held water, chocolate bar, mirror, flashlight, first aid material, fish line and similar items. You could call it the foxhole of the sea.

---

Base officers, pilots. and observers who served at least one month at CAPCP#7 and who are not elsewhere mentioned in this chapter include: Arthur L. Arnold, Jr.,* Charles A. Baner,* James M. Bates,* John B. Bauer, Robert H. Bell, William B. Bell, William H. Bittorf,* Warren L. Bratcher, Albert W. Van H. Burgin, Royce Chalmers, Harris A. Coller,* Greenville F. Curtis,* James M. Davis,* Ulysses J. Desjardins,* James Enrico, Richard K. Fitch,* Elmer R. Flodin,* Howard W. Goll, Dewey Guay,* Calvin C. Haworth,* Stanley S. Hayden,* Henry W. Hollingsworth,* Wynne B. Howard, Jr., James E. Jack,* George D. Lilly, Harmon B. McDonald, Jr.,* Francis E. Maguire, William W. Moore, Roy R. Morton, Kenneth E. Nolen, Sidney L. Oliver, Peter Ordway, Clarence G. Parramore, Jr.,* Graham Place, Armand V. Renuart, Hugh E. Ridgely,* William A. Robertson, Jr.,* Hope Root, Elbert L. Sauls,* James H. Shaughnessy, Clarence A. Terry, Addison Thompson, Ariel F. Vilas, Lawrence G. Walters,* James E. R. Wirick, Jr.,* Sidney J. Wood,* and George N. Woods. Asterisk indicates Air Medal winner.

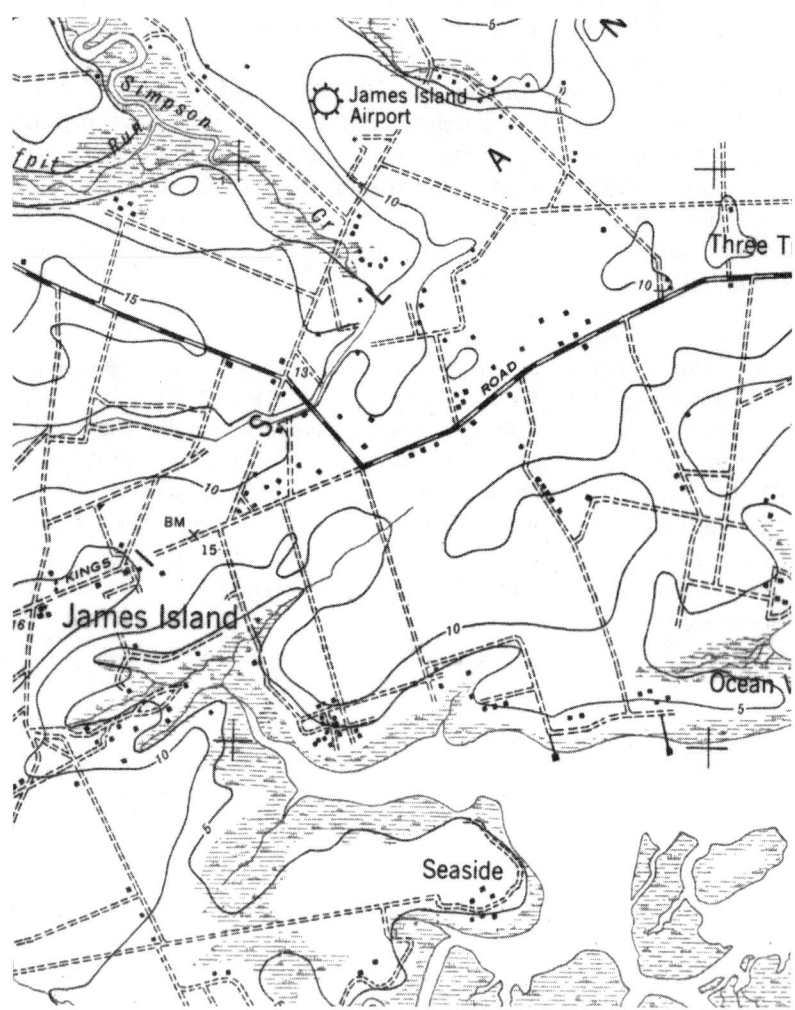

Seven years after the Charleston coastal patrol base (top center) was closed, and the field renamed James Island Airport, its setting was still extremely isolated. Surrounded on three sides by tidal marshland, most of the field was less than ten feet above sea level (source: 1950 United States Geological Survey map).

# 8
# Charleston, South Carolina

No city in the South better represents the ante-bellum style of living than Charleston, South Carolina. In 1690, it was the fifth largest town in North America, and by 1772, the wealthiest. Though it suffered during the Civil War, it had been spared destruction by General William Tecumseh Sherman in his fiery march to the sea because Confederate forces evacuated the city before the dreaded Yankees arrived. Charleston's beauty and traditions set a standard that is still admired the world over.

The Charleston coastal patrol base was located not in the city itself, but on nearby James Island, just to the south.* An old 108-acre cotton field was leased from its owner Frances H. Dill Rhett and, with help from the South Carolina Aviation Commission, graded out and properly drained for all-weather operation. Some old CCC buildings were rebuilt on the site and a recreation and classroom building added later. The coastal patrol was the field's sole occupant. The Charleston Naval Air Station, operating PBYs and blimps, was located on the Cooper River north of Charleston.

Major Sidney B. Mahaffey, a native of Lancaster, South Carolina, commanded the Charleston base from its activation until July 30, 1943. He was a well-respected leader who did his fair share of flying, and was thought to be an excellent pilot. Though he won the Air Medal for more

---

* It was from Fort Johnson on the northern tip of James Island at 4:30 a.m. on April 12, 1861 that the first shot was fired against Fort Sumter, triggering the terrible conflict between North and South. The shot burst almost directly over Fort Sumter, and was a signal for other Confederate batteries to open fire. The town of "Secessionville" was located only a few miles from the CAP airfield.

than two hundred hours of over-water flying, the 1948 award was made posthumously: he had been killed in a freak accident while towing aloft a glider on Mother's Day, May 12, 1946. Piloting an under-powered plane that may have been unsuitable for such work, he was unable to climb and spun-in. The plane plunged into a grove of trees, burst into flames, and Mahaffey was burned to death.

**Whitemarsh S. Smith, Jr.**

*One of the pilots who arrived shortly after the base was activated on May 23, 1942 was Whitemarsh S. Smith, Jr. of Charleston. Only twenty-two years of age, he'd earned a private pilot's license in 1938 via the CPTP at the College of Charleston. He had flown a total of 135 hours when he joined the coastal patrol (having been turned down by both the Air Corps and the Navy because of a heart murmur). From May 30, 1942, through August 31, 1943 Smith totaled 876 hours, fifth highest of any pilot at the base, and in 1948 received the Air Medal:*

When I got there, they'd just graded and scraped the field, and there was very little grass. There was no hangar, only tie-downs. We were lucky during that first summer that no major storms came to knock around our planes. For my first two weeks I flew as a flight observer with the late C. Norwood ("Norm") Hastie of Charleston. This let me learn the locations of checkpoints and patrol lanes and qualified me to fly as the pilot-in-command. The Atlantic Ocean is quite shallow in the Charleston area, and the usual convoy route for smaller, more shallow-draft ships followed the twenty-fathom contour about ten miles offshore, while the route for larger ships followed the forty-fathom line about twenty-five miles out. I mostly flew Stinson 10-As, but sometimes a Monocoupe, a Rearwin Cloudster, or a Cessna Airmaster, the last mainly for beach patrol.

In February 1943, we lost an airplane and two men off Myrtle Beach. Both were South Carolinians. Clarence L. Rawls, the pilot, was from Charleston and I think Drew L. King, his co-pilot, was from Spartanburg. I knew them both. That morning we'd been looking over the planes we'd been assigned to fly that day, and I'd noticed my plane, number thirteen, had a crack between two laminations of its wooden prop that I could slip a dime into. When I refused it, Rawls spoke up and said "I'll fly the airplane, there's nothing wrong with that propeller." Well it went to pieces on him later in the day — he called in to say that's what had happened — and he had no choice but to ditch. He and his observer got out and into their barracuda bags okay, but the water temperature was fifty-six degrees and they died of hypothermia within thirty minutes.

Their sister ship continued to circle their location until its fuel ran low and it went into Myrtle Beach to refuel. They'd ditched in "C" grid and I was down in "H" grid, but I was told to head up there and find them, and I did. By that time there was no sign of life. They didn't look up and wave. Their heads just rested on their Mae Wests. I stayed with them as long as possible before heading into Myrtle Beach for fuel. I flew out again but there was nothing anyone could have done. The wind was blowing real hard, and the whitecaps were streaking steady spray. The Beaufort Naval Air Station sent out a Kingfisher float plane, but it was much too rough for it to land, and no PBY was available. Both bodies were recovered by a Coast Guard crash boat. After that we all declared we wouldn't fly again until we were equipped with individual rubber life rafts. The Air Corps came through with them in three days.

Base commander Major Sidney F. Mahaffey, a native of Lancaster, South Carolina, crashed and was killed shortly after the war while towing a glider (courtesy Samuel W. Pilgrim, Jr.).

I was involved in a couple of minor accidents myself. In the first, I'd just come back from patrol and had reached land when my carburetor iced up. I went into an inadequate field without enough room to slow down after landing so that my only choice was to put the nose between two trees and let the wings be torn off to stop us. Neither my co-pilot or I were hurt, and a truck arrived shortly from the base and carted away the wreckage. The little 10-A never saw service again.

Another time, and again we were flying a 10-A over land, a piston went through the cylinder wall at three hundred feet and my engine locked up. You can't do much in that case except come down. I spotted a good field, but found it full of people picking beans, so I slammed the plane into a hog pen. We flipped over and were hanging upside down. I got out right away, but noticed my observer still hanging there. I went back and asked what the hell he was doing, and he said he was picking up the dimes that had fallen from his pocket. Seems he'd been the big winner at the gin rummy game back at the base. When he got out, I wrote a message to our sister ship on the slate board we carried: NOBODY HURT. SEND SOMEONE FOR US. The pilot waggled his wings and flew off, while my observer retrieved the rest of his dimes.

I don't recall that there was any particular social activity around the base. We had a nice little kitchen at one end of the administration building, and we used to gather there for coffee and chit-chat. One of our radio operators cooked nice breakfasts and lunches, for which everybody chipped in dimes and quarters to buy the bacon and eggs, bread and butter, sweet rolls, and coffee. Although our recreation room was a pleasant place in which to sit and read newspapers and magazines, I never felt I needed any "recreation." Flying *was* my recreation. I really loved it. I was also dating someone I'd known all my life, a girl who lived only two blocks away from my parents' home. We were married half way through my time at the base, then made a home of our own.

One other thing I remember pretty well was the time I saw the biggest convoy I'd ever seen, a hundred and ten ships stretching the span of the horizon. I was the observer that day, sitting there somewhat awestruck, when suddenly I also saw other planes and some little white specks streaking past, maybe a hundred yards in front of us. They were tracer bullets, and for each one we could see we knew there were ten more we couldn't see. The other planes were off a British carrier escorting the convoy and evidently we just weren't welcome. Seeing our one hundred pound bomb, and lacking radio communications, they were warning us off the only way they could. Though they should've known who we were, we didn't remain to dispute their suggestion that we leave.

I never saw a submarine or even a suspicious object, but I doubt the planes we flew would have frightened a German U-boat anyway. We took a small sandbar in the Stono River that ran past our base and outlined a hundred-yard circle on it. Then we dropped a bunch of practice bombs trying to hit that bulls-eye. Few even landed inside the large ring around the bulls-eye. The aiming system was antiquated: we had a peep-sight outside the port window, and while flying straight and level, when the target was where we wanted it we tapped the co-pilot on the knee and he pulled the bomb release. I never dropped a bomb on a mission, but I suppose someone did. Some whales may have been bombed, but that was about all.

## Samuel W. Pilgrim, Jr.

*Another young pilot was Samuel W. Pilgrim, Jr. of Rock Hill, South Carolina, who learned to fly at age sixteen in an old Standard biplane and then in a Taylorcraft (Pilgrim didn't get a driver's license for a car until he was twenty-one). He later purchased a $300 Taylorcraft which he says he would dearly love to have today. "She was such a beauty!" Pilgrim instructed in the CPTP, and had nineteen hundred hours flight time before joining the Charleston Base:*

I was single and lived in a boarding house on James Island about four or five miles from the base. About all the men lived on James Island because it was handy and there was plenty of housing. Everett L. Cotton, who also came from Rock Hill, lived in the same boarding house as I did. Others lived right at Folly Beach, which was then, and still is, a good place to swim. Sadly our old airfield has been converted into a housing development. Four of us from the base went into the drink, and for me it was a close call. My observer, Robert H. Miller from Charlotte, North Carolina, and I were out looking for oil slicks or submarines or whatever, flying the "low" plane at about two hundred feet off the ocean. Our sister ship, the "high" plane, was up at about fifteen hundred feet. This was standard practice to facilitate line-of-sight radio communications with the base — the farther out to sea we were, the higher the "high" plane would fly. During a patrol we'd usually trade off, one plane flying low for a while, then flying high for a while. This helped keep us sharp and relieved the monotony a little.

On this particular day, we spotted a life preserver in the water. I went around and made a second pass at about fifty feet to be sure there wasn't a body in it, and in pulling back up to two hundred feet I felt a severe jolt. I went to push over and level off and there was no control. We went into a three-quarter spin to the right, and there was only time to tell my co-pilot to brace himself, we were going in. We hit the water hard at a forty-five degree angle. The plane was demolished, and I have no idea how we ever got out. When I regained conciousness I was floating on an elevator, and didn't see Robert anywhere. Then I saw two fingers wrapped around the rudder three feet away. I got around to the other side and saw his arm sticking up but his head and the rest of him was under water. When I pulled him up by his hair I saw that his face was all bloody. His glasses had broken, and he was cut up around his eyes pretty badly. He was blinded all the time we were out there. I was trying to hold us both up when I realized I hadn't inflated my Mae West. After I did that — and Robert's, too — I tied us together just as what was left of the plane sank, though the tires and various lighter parts continued to float all around us.

We drifted for about four hours before a U.S. Marine Corps PBY from Parris Island found us just before it got dark. The water was too rough for a landing, so the crew dropped a large life raft, and it drifted straight downwind to us. It was upside down, and I had to separate Bob and myself to turn it over. After I got in, I pulled Bob in after me, and his feet were no more out of the water than a hammerhead shark cruised by, making a pass on a still-bleeding Robert. The raft had a whistle and some plugs for sealing leaks, but no flashlight for signaling, no food or water, and no first-aid supplies. We spent all night watching the flares dropped by the Air Corps planes searching for us. They were dropping them at the crash site, and by then we were several miles downwind. We were picked up next morning by the Coast Guard.

Samuel W. Pilgrim, Jr. was one of several coastal patrol volunteers from Rock Hill, South Carolina, and one of the youngest pilots on the base. This photo was obviously taken before he sewed on his red epaulets (courtesy Samuel W. Pilgrim, Jr.)

Our sister ship had called in a mayday. They really didn't see what happened, only that we were suddenly gone, and that there were pieces of an airplane all over the water. Our accident was probably due to structural failure. The bomb racks were fastened directly to the lower longerons, and over time might have worn and over-stressed them. When I pulled up sharply the fuselage probably deformed just enough to put slack in the cable controls to the elevators.

I continued to fly patrols, of course, but I left the base late in 1942 to join the Navy. I got my draft notice and had to act quickly. With the C. O.'s okay I flew over to the Atlanta Naval Air Station and signed up with the Navy. They were glad to get me because of my coastal patrol experience and my having both an instructor's and a commercial rating. I spent twenty-four years as a Navy pilot and retired as a Lieutenant Commander. While serving at Pensacola in the 1960s —*twenty years after leaving the coastal patrol, and doubtless the result of some bureaucratic snafu* — I was called out of formation one day and given the Air Medal I'd earned at Charleston. I turned seventy-five last year and wish I could do everything all over again!

## Vernon S. Hickman

*Vernon S. Hickman was a fixed base operator in Charlotte, North Carolina, the center of the state's textile industry. He'd only heard of the coastal patrol after several bases had been opened and when Dexter Martin, the commander of the South Carolina Wing, invited him to join the Charleston base as its engineering officer, he did so. In a 1983 interview with Colonel Lester E. Hopper he described some of his duties:*

> Our base was on James Island about five miles south of Charleston. It was an old landing field, that's all it was. We set up barracks and equipped them with bunks and made them as comfortable as we could. We had buildings for administration, engineering, operations, and radio — but no hangar. We did have a recreation hall and a good mess hall, however, and in general we were just about the same as any other military post at the time. There were three sod runways, each 150 feet wide, and 2,300, 2,700, and 3,000 feet long, respectively. I think we were about eight feet above sea level, but on the western side of the island and somewhat sheltered from storms at sea.

> I was a pilot but spent nearly all my time on engineering and maintenance matters. We had a very busy base, and air time accumulated so fast on our aircraft that our mechanics were doing major overhauls on one or another plane about every four days. I flew only on occasion, mostly as an observer, to fill-in for somebody. The radio group was separate, not under engineering. We learned a lot of things as we went along. For example, not much was known then about carburetor icing, and how to detect it before it built too much. We found that by putting in a manifold pressure gauge, we could sometimes detect icing quicker — a carburetor temperature gauge wouldn't tell the whole story. A manifold pressure drop of maybe an inch would alert you to pull on heat. We also modified many of the carburetor heaters to get more heat into the systems.

> We lost one crew at sea, probably due to icing. [Whitemarsh Smith's account of this loss is the correct one] Ironically, if they'd hit the water a mile or two further out they would have been in the Gulf Stream, where the water was warmer. In close, the water was much colder and they only lasted about forty-five minutes. There were *many* times

a plane just made the beach on the eastern side of James Island. We had one that landed on the beach with a broken crankshaft. One of our crews met them there with a replacement engine, installed it, and had them on their way in only an hour or so.

We were close to Charleston and found most of our recreation there. I remember a place downtown, supposedly only one of six in the country, that served draft Mickelob beer. I think it was fifteen cents for a big schooner. For another fifteen cents you could get a great big heaping bowl of steaming shrimp. We'd sit there and peel them and dip them in some seafood "dunk" while we talked and told stories. We'd also go swimming from the Atlantic beaches that were just a few miles away.

Major Jack R. Moore was our base commander for a while, and a fine fellow whom I got to know very well. We were next-door neighbors over on Folly Beach. My wife and her sister, and Dorothy Moore and her sister, had a bridge foursome going all the time. When Jack and I returned from work in the evenings, we had long talks about going into the aviation business together back in Portland, Oregon, his hometown. In fact, once our part in the war was over, Jack and I and Ernie Helms, another CAPer we got to know when we moved from Charleston to the border patrol base in Marfa, Texas, went to Portland and started Western Skyways, a major fixed base operation in the northwest.

## Carl R. Hinnant

*Carl R. Hinnant of Ridgeway, South Carolina, twenty-three miles north of Columbia, had three years at Clemson University and had been flying since the mid-1930s. While serving as a trooper with the South Carolina Highway Patrol he failed four times to meet the Air Corps weight requirement for his height by six pounds or less. Expecting soon to be drafted, he joined the Charleston coastal patrol base soon after it opened:*

I was signed on as a service technician to start with, and left before I got a promotion, but I flew a good bit as an observer — unofficially, that is — and on occasion a pilot would let me take the controls. The shipping lanes off Charleston were fifty miles out, and we usually flew about forty miles out. We could see the ships sometimes, but we were not flying convoy escort, just regular search patterns north and south from the Charleston area. Unless a ship was entering or leaving Charleston harbor, we never got up close to them.

I'd been a state trooper in the Charleston area, and kept an apartment in town where I had a lot of friends. I had a car, and commuted fifteen miles to the base. If I were flying dawn patrol the next morning,

I'd sleep in the base recreation room, which had cots and blankets. I was only twenty-one and that was no hardship. I remember Cornelius ("Neely") Thompson as our boss, and he was a fine officer. Before the war he had been running the Grayline boat tours out to Fort Sumter and elsewhere. He also ran a couple of tour buses. His brother Allen Thompson was the base intelligence officer.

When Base CAPCP #8 ceased operation, Carl R. Hinnant went into the Army Transportation Corps. Here, during a leave in April 1944, he visits with his sister Olive before taking part in the invasion of Europe (courtesy Carl R. Hinnant).

As far as I know, "Sonny" Pilgrim is the only pilot I flew with who's still alive. I went out as his observer several times. I wasn't with him when he had to ditch, but I remember the time when we almost went into the trees on takeoff. It was a hot August day and that Stinson 10-A just didn't want to leave the ground. "Sonny" sort of jumped it over those trees then stayed close to the ground for a ways to get up full flying speed. If we'd carried a bomb that day, we wouldn't have made it. Later that day, we almost went into the drink. We were fifteen miles at sea heading north to Georgetown — we could see the smoke plume from the paper mill — when the engine quit cold. It started again just as suddenly, but after that we turned toward the beach and hugged the coast all the way back to Charleston. After landing, we rolled the plane over to Captain Bill North, our chief A&E, and told him to red tag it

We lost two men at sea. Clarence L. Rawls was an old-time pilot, as well known for auto racing as for flying. They say that in 1922 he drove a racing car up the steps of the state house. The other fellow was D. L. King of Spartanburg, South Carolina. They both froze to death in the water. When their bodies were found and retrieved, Rawls was floating upright, still clinging to King, who was horizontal in the water. King had already ditched once before, going down with Thomas J. DuBose of Columbia. Both were fine fellows — I'd known Clarence even before Civil Air Patrol days — and it was a terrible loss for everyone at the base. I left the CAP about April 1943 and went into the Army Transportation Corps as the first mate, and later the captain, of a sea-going tug boat, and participated in the invasion of Normandy on June 6, 1944. After the war, I flew a little for sport, but that was tame compared to what went before.

**Harry R. Arnold**

*Harry R. Arnold of Spartanburg, South Carolina served as a radio mechanic at the Charleston base from the spring of 1943 until the coastal patrol shut down at the end of August. Then in his early thirties, Arnold owned a radio business in Spartanburg and, ineligible for regular military service, wanted to do his share for the war effort. His widow, Florence Arnold, tells this about her late husband:*

We had been married in 1937 and had a two-year boy when Harry went over to Charleston. I don't remember the exact date, but it was some time after Drew King, a pilot and friend from Spartanburg, was killed in a plane crash there, and that happened on February 2, 1943. Harry came back for us after a couple of months and we all moved into a great big house at Folly Beach. It was the second street back from the water, and we could watch the breakers from a front balcony. The house was so big we allowed Walt Norment, a mechanic, and two other men whose names escape me, to board with us. I fixed breakfast for everyone each morning and sometimes that would be quite early.

Harry worked on the radios, and I believe he went out with the pilots on occasion to check how the radios worked after he had fixed them. He didn't talk about it much and I didn't worry about him. I remember Major Jack Moore, our commanding officer. I believe he was fairly wealthy, and I recall going to some parties thrown for base personnel. There weren't any social events at the base itself, but mostly visits back and forth in people's homes. Sometimes we'd get a baby sitter and Harry and I would drive into Charleston to see a show or to shop or whatever. We enjoyed the area and stayed until the base closed.

But then Harry was selected to go to California with an advance party of some sort to set up a new base. I don't know what it was intended for, but apparently plans were canceled, and Harry drove back to Texas, where he was first stationed at Laredo and then at Marfa. We lived at Fort D. A. Russell, an old cavalry post, and German prisoners of war from a nearby stockade worked around the airbase for us. Several others from Charleston transferred into the border patrol the same time as we did. I remember Rose Katz and her husband Lewis best, because she went with me when I drove home to Spartanburg to visit my mother. I found our Texas adventures more exciting, because it was all so different than South Carolina, where we were hardly away from home.

## Robert M. Bouknight

*Robert M. Bouknight was a twenty-year-old from West Columbia, South Carolina, fresh out of Palmetto School of Aeronautics in Columbia where he was permitted to graduate as an engine mechanic a month earlier than the rest of his class so he could join the coastal patrol. He and another Palmetto graduate, Brady F. Corley, and John J. Crawford, a mechanic from Wadesboro, North Carolina, drove to Charleston together and lived in the same boarding house:*

I think we got there pretty much at the beginning, but none of us stayed to the end, that is, when the base closed. It was my first job, so I kind of learned as I went along, working on the whole variety of planes they had there. We heard repeated rumors of sub sightings, hangar talk, you know, and that's probably all it was. I remember the day when Captain William W. North took me up for a ride — my first time off the ground — and that was probably the most excitement I had.

Brady Corley was the first of us to leave. That left me without wheels, so I moved out to the airfield and lived in one of the cabins, like a CCC barracks they'd brought in. I cooked a little on hot plate. Later on, there was also a cafeteria at the base, so I didn't starve. I bought a Harley motorcycle and left the base during October 1942 to work at the Columbia Army Air Base. In the spring of 1943, a couple of us were accepted for the Cadet program. I got through the first phase of flight training, but washed out in the second. I was then trained as a gunner on B-17s and B-29s, but when I could not conquer my chronic air sickness they pulled me out of that and reduced me to a private. I served briefly at a Philippines airbase, and was discharged in March 1946.

## Brady F. Corley

*Brady F. Corley, who arrived at the Charleston coastal patrol base just after his eighteenth birthday, was an engine, but not an aircraft mechanic ("just the 'E' of the 'A&E'"). He and Robert Bouknight had been neighbors and friends even before they went to the Palmetto School of Aeronautics together:*

Bob and John Crawford and I may have driven down to Charleston in my car — I really don't remember whether it was mine or John's. But

I know that later on John had his own car, too. We lived in this boarding house on Wentworth Street in the old part of Charleston, down near the battery. It was one of those huge ante-bellum mansions, and I believe there were at least fifteen of us there, mostly workers from the naval base. We had most of our meals there, and they made up paper bag lunches to take with us to the base. I remember buying a khaki shirt and khaki trousers but I'm not sure I ever wore them. For work, we wore dungarees, even shorts and T-shirts in the really hot weather. We were very non-military, very relaxed in that way.

At first we had a really old bunch of airplanes. They were kind of maybe-they-went and maybe-they-didn't. After a while, we began getting newer planes that didn't need so much work. Captain North was our engineering officer. His son was an apprentice mechanic and at sixteen was the youngest man on the base. I remained at the base to the end of August, then went to work at the Columbia Army Air Base. The experience at the base really helped me, most of all, when I finally joined the Air Corps and was able to skip basic training completely. I got to Warner-Robins Field one night, and was out working on the flight line the next night. I spent a year there, but was disqualified for overseas duty because of a bad back, so they sent me to Atlanta which was a major refueling stop for the ferry flights heading to the war theaters. I was discharged in early 1946.

## John A. Rast

*Like his friends Everett L. Cotton and James R. Tucker (and several others at the base), John A. Rast came from Rock Hill, South Carolina. Following his graduation from high school he went to business school for two years then worked for his brother in a family-owned business. Twenty-four-years-old and single, Rast became active with a local CAP group in Rock Hill:*

I guess some of us got to talking about the coastal patrol, and someone said, "I'll go if you'll go." We discussed it for some time, and I think I joined at least partly out of curiosity. As a child, I'd had polio, which left me with just a slight limp, but enough to make me 4-F and ineligible for the draft. Since I wanted to do something for my country, the coastal patrol seemed like a good thing. I had a job I didn't particularly like anyway, so I just went. At the time, money was still scarce, and five dollars a day sounded pretty good.

But I really didn't know what I was getting into. The base was an empty field out in the middle of nowhere — I don't know what it'd been used for before — with a one-story wooden building for headquarters. It was built like a summer cottage, with no inside walls and no insulation, and a little space heater for warmth. We didn't need heat during the summer, but as winter came on, it got very cold inside. Another building had some bunks and showers in it. To start with, I lived in a rooming house near the base with some of the other boys. We'd get together and go out for meals, just like we did in civilian life. While we wore our uniforms, it wasn't like the Army, and nobody worried about relative rank and that sort of stuff. We were all just good buddies.

I was hired as a clerk-typist, but in fact I did a little of everything, more or less anything anyone asked me to do. I was a corporal, way down the line and about the last thing they had. I did some typing, but then began working the teletype machine. Someone decided an operator was needed around the clock, and asked for volunteers for the night shift. One eager-beaver who tried it lasted one night. Then I agreed to give it a try, and it suited me fine. All I had to do was listen for a "ding," sort of like a telephone ring, then check the message. If there was an emergency, I was to call someone, but it never happened. Most messages were just routine orders for the following day, which I'd tear off and put in the C. O.'s office. I mainly just slept all night, or talked back and forth with other night operators in the same "message loop."

Since I slept most of the night, I mostly stayed up and around all day. I might go over to the bunkhouse for a nap, but usually I hung around the base, afraid that I otherwise might miss something exciting. Nobody ever asked me to go up for a ride in an airplane. To tell the truth I didn't want to. I watched too many planes barely clear the trees on take-off and figured that was not for me! I remember once when seven or eight British fighter planes landed at the base — evidently thinking it was the Charleston Army Air Base. Once they got proper directions they took off again. Until we recognized their nationality, we were concerned when we saw them coming down at us. They were off some aircraft carrier on convoy escort. I left the base in November 1942, and got a job in the payroll department of a textile mill. It was a very long time ago, but it would be nice if a reunion could be arranged.

## Hugh L. Meyers

*Hugh L. Myers was born near Greenville, South Carolina, and took a job as a service technician at the base in the spring of 1942. He took a room only a mile away and rode a bicycle to work every day. His duties were driving a gas truck, fueling the planes returning from patrol, pulling through their props to help start their engines, and tying them down at night:*

We had some real bad weather down there. I remember one patrol that ran into such strong headwinds they couldn't get back to base until after dark. We had to take all the cars and trucks on the base and line up facing the runway with their lights on to show the planes where to land. I watched them as they touched the ground and I doubt they rolled twenty feet. It was a job getting them tied down securely. During the winter of 1942-43. one of our planes went down off Myrtle Beach. By the time the Coast Guard picked up the crew both had frozen to death. Another pilot I knew told me about flying a patrol right over the wave tops and then suddenly seeing nothing but bubbles. He and his observer were picked up okay, though. In April 1943, I joined the Navy, and was discharged in December 1946 as a torpedo man third-class.

Hugh R. Myers of Greenville, South Carolina worked on the flight line as a service technician, commuting to work by "Victory Bicycle" (courtesy Samuel W. Pilgrim, Jr.).

## Grey M. Minshew

*Born in Marion, South Carolina, Grey S. Minshew grew up in the Charleston area, and served as one of the two base teletype operators from October 25, 1942 until August 10, 1943. She was granted a week's leave in early February by base commander Sidney Mahaffey, and returned to duty as Mrs. William Rhett. After Rhett's death in 1964, she remarried and is now Mrs. Grey Geissler:*

There were six of us girls altogether and we carpooled with other people from Charleston in order to save gasoline. I lived near the Francis Marion Hotel and my ride to work either picked me up at the corner or stopped near my house and beeped softly to avoid waking neighbors. Maude Cox, who was older than the rest of us, worked on the plotting board. Patricia Thomas was Major Mahaffey's secretary while Marie

Passailaigue was the clerk-typist. Angus W. Hagins, our operations officer, had a daughter named Marian who came in after high school as a part-time clerk-typist.

The first ones to arrive at the base were expected to put a huge frying pan on our old wood-burning iron stove and cook two dozen eggs for the boys heading out on dawn patrol. We felt they should always leave with a full stomach so that, if they went down, they'd have a better possibility of surviving. We also gave them Hershey bars and other snacks. Our kitchen and dining room were at one end of the barn that was our administration building. I mean, it really was a barn! The outside had been covered with tar paper to help keep out the wind, but inside everything was raw wood, unfinished and unpainted. We all brought tables, chairs, typewriters, and other office equipment to furnish the rooms.

The plotting board and teletype machine, the radio room, and two little cubby holes for our clerk-typists were located at the opposite end from the kitchen, and Captain Malcolm McCrae's S-2 office — which was always kept closed for flight crew briefings and debriefings — was situated at about the middle of the building right beside the commanding officer's office. I was at the teletype machine virtually all day long. We were interconnected to Mitchel Field on Long Island, and at the end of each day we had to send them a summary of our day's activity. During the day we were in constant contact with the Carolina sub-sector headquarters in the Fort Sumter Hotel in Charleston. We got to know all the flight crews and their wives and soon gave each one a code name. One wife, a real nervous wreck, always wanted to know the moment her husband returned safely from a patrol. We'd call her, let the phone ring so many times, then hang up. That was our signal that her husband was back on the ground and all right.

We were a tight-knit group on James Island, and I still remember how devastated we were when C. L. Rawls and D. L. King died at sea off Myrtle Beach. I know the coastal patrol served a serious purpose but we laughed at ourselves, too. While the flight crews were in the debriefing room after a patrol we would start our usual joke around, "Was it a sub or was it a whale?" Because it was so easy to confuse them, our S-2 officer Malcolm McRae always admonished crews when they called in a possible sub sighting, "Now go back and look again!"

When some of the men teased me for never having been up in an airplane, "Neely" Thompson invited me to come fly with him, saying, "Now Grey, you'd better dress properly, and wear slacks." Well, back then ladies didn't wear slacks, so next morning I came to work in my riding jodhpurs. He flew me over my family home on Johns Island and it was quite a thrill. In fact, it scared me to death! I remained at the base until it closed, then worked for the Charleston Shipbuilding and Dry Dock Company. After the war, Mr. Rhett and I moved to Beaufort and started a family here.

## James A. McEvoy

*James A. McEvoy was a young Charlestonian who had dropped out of high school to work at Hawthorne Aviation and in his father's garage. Before he served as a "gas boy" at the base, he helped to prepare it for occupancy:*

You could say the base was there, and there was a building on it, but it had no telephone service. My daddy was hired to cart the utility poles to where they'd be put up. The phone company gave us the poles, and we loaded them on a flat trailer using daddy's wrecker, then unloaded them at designated points along the route to the airport. The utility company dug the holes and put them in. It was a big job. We must have hauled a couple of hundred poles.

Once the planes came, I signed up as a service technician, which meant I fueled the planes, added oil as needed, washed the windshields, and things like that. I also pushed the planes round, tied them down, and so on. Fueling the planes was hard work: climbing up and down ladders with a heavy hose to place in the wing tanks, filling and moving around five-gallon jerricans, and such as that. I had the morning shift, so I had to get up at three a.m. in order to help the dawn patrol get going. I lived on Oak Street in Charleston, and since others were heading for the base at the same hour, somebody'd always pick me up. My shift was done by 2:30 or 3:00 p.m. and I'd hitch a ride back to town.

## Harry H. Tucker

*Harry H. Tucker was born and raised in Pageland, South Carolina. He learned to fly in 1941 in a J-3 Piper Cub at the Plaza Airport in Charlotte, North Carolina. Later he bought an Aeronca Chief and flew out of the Lancaster, South Carolina airfield operated by Sid Mahaffey, who soon would be named commander of the Charleston base. After rejection by the Army, Navy, and the Air Corps because one of his legs was slightly shorter than the other, due to an automobile crash, Tucker joined the coastal patrol as the next best thing:*

I was lucky. My uncle lived in Charleston, and he let me move in with him and his family. He and his wife and his two daughters treated me like a king — a nice room, the most delicious meals I've ever had, and family friendship, all for the exorbitant price of twenty-five dollars a month! It was only six or seven miles to our base on James Island.

Charleston folks were very nice to anyone in service, and seemed intrigued with our "uniforms with the red shoulders." I believe I joined the base quite a time after it opened, and since there were plenty of pilots I was a pilot-observer for all the time I was there, despite my private license and several hundred hours of flight time.

Pilot Harry H. Tucker lived in Charleston with his uncle and his uncle's family, and remembers swimming at Folly Beach, not far from the base (courtesy Harry H. Tucker).

There weren't many promotions and military rank wasn't really important. Our commanding officer was a major, the operations and engineering officers were captains, most of our pilots were first lieutenants, and pilot-observers were second lieutenants. Taking off in a ground-loving 90 hp Stinson Voyager could be pretty exciting: fully loaded with forty gallons of fuel, a five-gallon jug of yellow marker dye, two truck inner-tube flotation devices, and the rest of our gear, including a one-hundred pound bomb beneath the fuselage, we bounced across our bumpy field on a hot day when the air was thin and kind of lurched into the air much like Charles Lindbergh's overloaded *Spirit of St. Louis* taking off from Roosevelt Field for Paris. He had high tension lines to cross, while we had a row of trees.

We weren't heroes. We were just a bunch of guys doing a job. It was dangerous, but it could be humorous, too. I was in the base radio room when one of our planes called in from pretty far out to say that he was running low on fuel. Sometimes we'd go out seventy-five miles to bring a ship into Charleston harbor, and that's what he was doing. Base radio told him to stick with it a little longer, that a relief plane was on the way. Ten minutes later he called in again, and base told him they'd let him start home in a few minutes. He burped real loud and said, "You better let me come in right now, because I've got more gas on my stomach than in the tanks." They did, and he made it.

During long patrols beyond sight of land, aircrews might feel pretty lonely without sister ships. In addition to the reassurance they provided, four sets of eyes were better than two for spotting subs (courtesy Theodore E. Sellers).

One of the exciting things we did was drop the daily newspaper to the Charleston pilot boat. The crews stayed out there a week at a time guiding ships in and out of the harbor with very little communication with the outside world — certainly nothing like they would have today, with TV, voice-mail, and "fax" machines. We'd fly real low and try to put the paper right on their deck. We dropped some in the water, too, but the papers were wrapped in plastic and floated so that they could be picked up.

There weren't any planned recreational activities that I recall. We swam at Folly Beach a good bit. Charleston had plenty of bars and such, but I didn't drink much and I don't think anybody else did either. Like

I say, it was a pretty low-key operation, and we weren't trying to make a name for ourselves or anything like that. Still, I think it was very unfair of the government to deny active-duty CAP veterans the same benefits other veterans receive under the G.I. Bill. It would be good if Congress could yet correct that oversight. Not long before the Charleston base closed, I obtained my commercial and flight instructor's ratings, then became a civilian flight instructor for contingents of Air Corps Cadets arriving each sixty days to study at Winthrop College for Women in Rock Hill, South Carolina. My job was to give them ten hours instruction on Piper Cubs but not allow them to solo before they went on to a primary flight school at either Orangeburg, Camden, or Bennettsville, South Carolina. The Cadets were quartered in a dormitory campus just between two of the girls's dorms — a pleasant assignment for all concerned.

When this Piper Cub program was canceled, I went to Marietta, Georgia and became a pre-flight inspector at a B-29 plant, following the construction of one particular plane from start to finish, then taking the first test flight in it. When the war ended, I came home and stayed in family businesses until I retired. I continued to fly for pleasure and owned several airplanes, including a surplus Fairchild PT-19, a Luscombe tail dragger, and a neat little all-metal, low-wing, retractable-gear Swift. I'm 78 years old now and don't fly anymore but I still remember.

---

Base officers, pilots, and observers who served at least one month at CAPCP#8 and who are not elsewhere mentioned in this chapter include: Homer C. Aenbacher,* J. D. Ardamis,* G. C. Ballard,* C. E. Barfield,* K. C. Bates,* Donald H. Bender,* James E. Bobo, Jr., W. M. Caldwell,* Jacob B. Carroll, Jr., Lloyd W. Cathey,* Joseph C. Cauthen, Jr., Albert E. Coggins, Jr.,* William S. Crane,* Frank M. Culler,* Thomas J. DuBose,* James O. Dunlap, William R. Dunlap,* Charles W. Gray, Jr., Glenn E. Haines,* John W. Hamilton,* Robert J. Harrison,* Edward V. Hill,* William T. Hodges, George R. Hurd,* Thomas H. Johnson, Jr., Richard W. Kapp,* Richard F. Lackey,* Robert D. Lucas, John F. McLaughlin,* William E. Roberson, William S. Scott, Joseph J. Scruggs,* Raymond A. Seelig, Harry C. Shackelford, Jr., Charles M. Simon, N. A. Simrill,* Hyman D. Smith,* Walter B. Stafford, Jr., Karl F. Steel,* Claud A. Strickland,* William J. Suter, John A. Taylor,* Horace B. Thomas, Jonas Weiland, and James R. Williams.* Asterisk indicates Air medal winner.

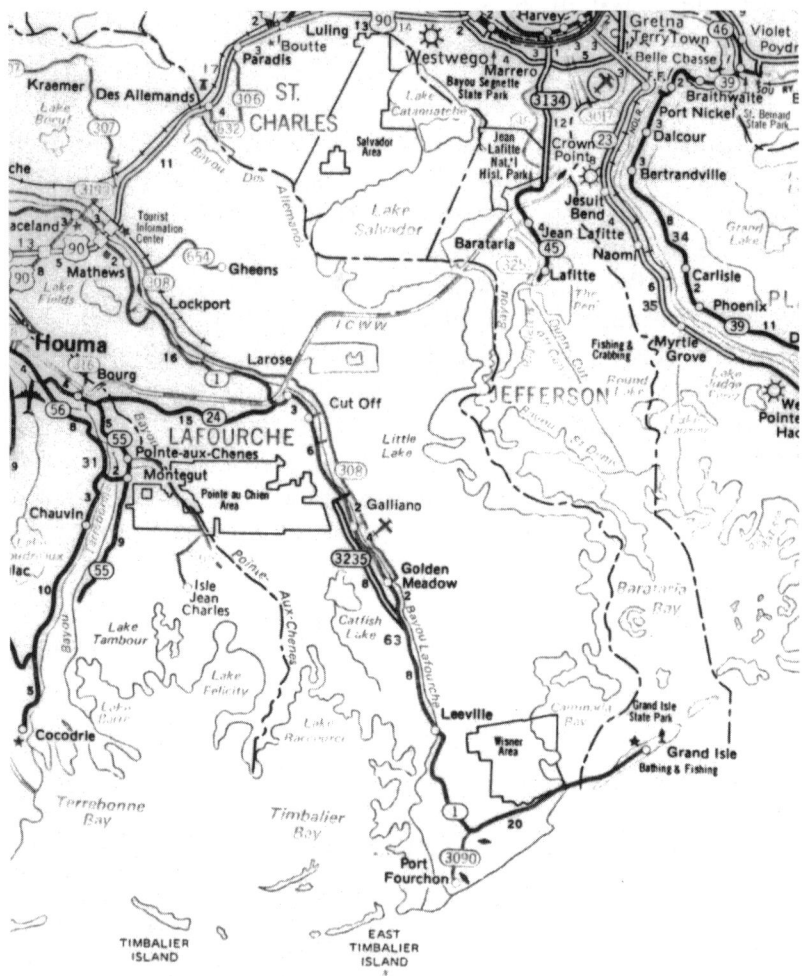

This recent tourist map shows the still somewhat roundabout driving trip from New Orleans (top) to the end of the road at Grand Isle (bottom center). No trace of the coastal patrol airfield remains — runways and buildings all having been replaced by Grand Isle State Park and privately owned beach homes.

# 9
# Grand Isle, Louisiana

Grand Isle lies at the southern tip of Louisiana's Bayou Country, a continuous expanse of low-lying land between the Mississippi River and the Atchafalya Basin, generally to the south and west of New Orleans. Three quarters of the region consists of marshes and swamps. The watery isolation from built-up urban areas attracts hunters, trappers, and fishermen, but few vacationers other than those wanting to experience the language and folkways of traditional Cajun culture. The volunteers who came to Grand Isle to establish a coastal patrol base — especially those from more northern states — found there a physical and social setting unlike most of them had ever experienced before.

Guidebooks describe the eight-mile long, one-mile-wide island as having been the major attraction on Louisiana's Gulf Coast since the later 1800s. Far too vulnerable to hurricanes to support an upscale resort, Grand Isle has instead been an attraction for more casual visitors who simply enjoy the salt air and warm waters of the Gulf beaches. The area abounds with waterfowl — egrets, cranes, ducks, geese, and, of course, brown pelicans, the official state bird of Louisiana — and such fur-bearing animals as otter, nutria, and muskrat. Gulf waters still produce shrimp, crabs, oysters, and other fish in abundance. This semitropical paradise of live oaks and bald cypress, Spanish moss* and purple water hyacinth, is marred only by the presence of poisonous snakes, sleeping alligators, and hungry mosquitoes.

* The Spanish dubbed it "Frenchman's wig," while the French supposedly called it *barbe espagnole,* or "Spanish beard." Around 1900, Spanish moss (actually a member of the pineapple family) was used for upholstery stuffing. The black inner fiber filled the seats of many a Model T Ford.

When the coastal patrol base was activated on June 25, 1942, Grand Isle was just a small village with a general store, several cafes, a combination grade and high school, a church, the modest homes of the resident Cajun families and two old hotels, the Brown and the Oleander — the former abandoned, the latter still popular with vacationing fishermen, but very old and rundown. By plane Grand Isle was about 50 miles from New Orleans. By car or truck it was twice as far, and the washboard roads made it nearly an all-day drive. Many of the arriving volunteers, even those from other parts of Louisiana, felt as if they were coming into another world.

The first arrivals were Lts. Jackson C. Pryor, William L. Heim, Joseph C. Greiner, and Raymond R. Fisher, and Sgt. Andrew W. Cohen. A history of the base, *Joe — Submarine Hunter, 1942-1943: A True Story of Grand Isle Patrol Activity*, written by Lt. Stuart M. Speiser, the Assistant Intelligence Officer, provides a fascinating source for stories of subsequent events. What Pryor and his party found at Grand Isle could hardly have been more unpleasant. The "hotel" in the following paragraph was the Brown, rather than the Oleander, and it was the Brown that became base headquarters:

> Base #9 consisted of a miniature swamp with a shell road crossing it, and a dilapidated old "hotel" with its back door not 20 yards from the Gulf. It was 2 stories high, and had about 16 small rooms, each 10 feet square. The floors and walls were rotting; the place was rat-infested. It was unwired, unwindowed, and unscreened; the odor from the outhouse which served as the sole relief station was so strong that even the flies stayed away.

With the help of the local French-speaking fishermen who volunteered to help build the base and later to serve as guards and linemen, the five-man advance party soon created a fully functioning airbase:

> The CAP pioneers and the natives rebuilt walls and ceilings, installed new plumbing, cleaned out the rats, windowed and screened the place and erected a power plant. By far the hardest job of all was erecting the antenna for radio station WXBS. Three 90 foot poles had to be placed behind the Administration Building, and repeated efforts to give them a solid foundation in the soft sand beach put gray hairs in the heads of the workers. Largely through brute strength they were finally anchored 10 feet into the sand. Two "hams" from Arkansas, Leo Brians and Ray Beam, donated their services and radio equipment; WXBS went on the air in a few weeks. Pemberton McRae took over the job of trying to make WXBS audible between the bellowing Pensacola Naval Air Station on one side and the New Orleans tower on the other. The road department of the State of Loui-

siana was helpful in clearing the runways and the parking area for planes. The swamp area was drained to an extent which permitted planes to be tied down. The rough roads were leveled off and runways 900 feet long and 40 feet wide were made available.

## William L. Heim

*In a 1983 interview with Colonel Lester E. Hopper, William L. Heim, who had learned to fly in a J-2 Cub near his hometown of Little Rock, Arkansas, remembered arriving at the base-to-be:*

It was July the 26th, 1942, when I got there. I didn't see much of anything — just an old gasoline truck, a red Ford stick-bed truck, and this big old administration building that at one time must have been some kind of old hotel or something down on one end of the island. It was just a shell road [that we landed on].... Yeah, and after we got it completed that's still all we had. We had one nine hundred foot, one twelve hundred, and I think, I don't know what the middle one that we bulldozed up in there, how long it was, but I presume it was about a thousand feet.

William L. Heim and his brother Michael L. Heim were both from Little Rock, Arkansas. William was a pilot-observer and Michael was the base engineering officer (Hopper collection).

William Heim remembered that eight or ten people were working there when he arrived, including Major Byron A. Armstrong, the commanding officer from New Orleans. Most of the base's personnel actually were still in New Orleans flying their patrol missions from the lakefront airport. They usually passed right over Grand Isle on their way out to sea. Once the base was ready for them, all of the planes and pilots transferred to Grand Isle:

> Oh man, they had some of those airplanes, lord, they'd about had it before we got 'em. Some of them were as old as could be.... A little later someone came in with a gullwing Stinson and then we got some more eighty and ninety horse power Stinsons, the small ones you know. We had those and probably more Fairchilds, and Wacos, and Stinsons than anything else.... But the airplanes were old, and parts weren't available. So they sent my brother Mike and I back to Little Rock because Mike, he had a lot of metal lathes and things like that, that he loved, that was his life, that machinist thing.... I think we brought an electric welder with us too.... we brought everything because we had to close our business down.... It wasn't long before Mike got some of those old clunkers up in the air, one after another. Then I think we got them all flying except one, I believe.

After a few months at the base, Heim got two weeks off and returned to New Orleans to complete the requirements for his private pilot's license. Back at Grand Isle, he resumed patrol duty, mostly escorting convoys:

> They had a regular roster. If you flew dawn patrol they'd probably put you on the last flight. They tried to give you a little break in between.... If they had enough guys to go around, you just got maybe one flight a day. And some of them were longer than others, depending on how big the convoy was. Pascagoula would bring it so far, we'd take it from there, and somebody else from Beaumont would get it a little further on.... We had a day or two off occasionally, but I don't remember just how that was. It didn't matter, we weren't going anywhere anyway. Men that really liked to fly, like we did, enjoyed just doing that.

By the time the base closed, Heim had accumulated twelve hundred hours flying time (for which after the war he received the Air Medal). Meanwhile, he and his wife had rented a little house in Golden Meadow, and generally seemed to enjoy themselves:

> I was twenty-five I believe at the time. It wasn't bad down there. In war time and like a lot of other times you just have to do the best you can with what you have. So we made out all right. We didn't eat the fanciest, but we had food and I didn't see anybody shrinking up much.... My brother and I made a friend of every native on that island. A lot of people not that far south as us appeared to feel a little superior to these people. Those people down there were just as important to me as anybody else. When we were coming in on a flight,

if the time of day was right you could see all the fish migrating into Barataria Bay or one of the big bays. Shark going through them occasionally. I knew the fishing hole would be there. So everybody'd go up there and go fishing. Man, we'd catch a gang, and not once have I ever had to clean a fish.... Native guys did that, and I wasn't asking them, they just did.

* * *

The base remained primitive for some time. The first "hangar" was a large canvas sheet stretched down to the sand from a telephone pole. The ground crews not only fought blowing sand and bugs but also had to walk two hundred yards for fresh water. They often worked late into the night with only flashlights, and an oil and driftwood fire for warmth. Some men had to walk the three miles between village and base, because there was no arranged transportation. Though such needs would finally be met, the first weeks and months at Grand Isle posed a tremendous challenge.

**Alvin H. Gautreaux**

*One of the ground crew who remembers working under that canvas sheet is Alvin H. Gautreaux. A native of New Orleans, he graduated as an airplane mechanic from the Del Gado Trade School just before the Army took it over to offer the same training to its own enlisted men. While Gautreaux trained there, the head instructor was Major Byron A. Armstrong, who was shortly to command the coastal patrol base at Grand Isle.*

After talking with Armstrong about the CAP, I joined up. It didn't pay so well, but in the early forties nobody made big money. I was a young man without any obligations, and since I was getting ready to go into the Navy, it seemed like a good way to get some experience. Several of us from Del Gado signed up — my friends Raymond Dunn and Johnnie Mura were two of them. In the beginning, the Grand Isle group was based at the New Orleans lakefront airport, and flew coastal patrols from there. That continued for some time, then we moved the base right down to the Gulf. I didn't have my A&E license so I worked only on engines, not airframes. My work was supervised by Louis Trosclair and William Lum, both licensed mechanics.

I stayed at the Oleander Hotel with about twenty or twenty-five other fellows. The married ones lived elsewhere in rented houses and cottages. I think we paid about eighty-five dollars a month for three meals a day and a cubby-hole-sized room with a lavatory. The community bathroom was down the hall. Mr. and Mrs. Ludwig owned and operated the place, and I remember that she made the best tapioca that

I've ever tasted. We got to be good friends and I'm sorry to say they've both passed on.

We were pretty hard on that old hotel. It was already beat-up, but we certainly didn't do it any good. We had some times there I'll never forget. When we felt like raising hell, we'd take a big fat snake and run back and forth over it with a truck, then toss it into the lobby. Once we chased a milk cow inside. The hotel's still there, but it's in even worse shape than it was then.

The locals were happy to have us there because it meant jobs for a lot of them, and we spent most of our paychecks there. Though some of the older Cajuns could hardly speak English, they made good security guards, and we all got along together very well. We had a very democratic base, in that the wealthy fellows never looked down their noses at the rest of us. One of the pilots owned a big construction company in New Orleans, for example, and often rented one of the nightspots to throw parties for everyone.

About my only souvenir of Grand Isle is a check for $1.10, which was my share of a $218.72 check to the base from the Rubber Reserve Corporation for the salvage of 1,367 pounds of rubber. This came about because, when our patrols spotted bales of rubber washed up on the little islands around the Gulf coast, we sent out a boat to retrieve them, then we'd truck them to New Orleans. Real rubber was extremely scarce during the war because the Japanese had captured Malaysia and cut off our main supply. The $218.72 was divided equally among all former members of the base. I was already overseas when the check was delivered to my home. I thought it'd make a good keepsake, so I kept mine.

I was only twenty-two when I was at Grand Isle, but I don't begrudge a minute of my time there. It was actually pretty good living. I fished some on my off days though mostly I went back up to my home in New Orleans. I didn't have a car, but someone did, and three or four of us would pile in and go on up whenever we could. I left long before the base closed, because I could see I'd soon be drafted and I wanted to enlist in the Navy. As it happened, after Navy boot camp, my experience at Grand Isle made me eligible for a rating as an aviation machinist's mate. I went to the South Pacific to work on PBY patrol planes. When I came back from the war, I married Emelia Crosby, whom I'd met at Grand Isle while she was still in high school. Last year, we celebrated our fiftieth anniversary!

\* \* \*

As the number of planes at the base increased so did the urgent necessity for a proper hangar. Arthur N. ("Pop") McAninch of Little

Rock, Arkansas, the 45-year-old Intelligence Officer who had been an architect in civilian life, drew up the plans. Construction was ready to begin when, during the night of August 28, Major Armstrong received word that a hurricane was on its way, and all planes and personnel were to leave the island at once. Next morning, the airfield was two feet deep in flotsam-filled water. Only the fact that the hurricane by-passed the island saved it from worse. The materials for building the hangar were scattered all over the island. Once base personnel could return, they began rebuilding the base — and the new hangar — well aware that other, possibly worse, storms might follow. Two months later, on October 25, the historic canvas hangar was lowered from its telephone pole as the engineering department moved equipment and personnel into the sumptuous quarters of a permanent hangar.

**William J. Fandison**

*William J. Fandison had begun working on airplanes at the New Orleans Airport in 1938, and later earned his pilot's license there. He was twenty-six-years-old when he came to Grand Isle, and his stories of the base — as told to Colonel Lester E. Hopper in 1982 —confirm its primitiveness. When a pilot wanted his plane washed down, Fandison had to ask with what. Surely not salt water from the Gulf, which for a time was all they had other than rainwater collected for cooking and drinking purposes. Shortages of everything made mechanical innovations a must. One of them involved roadside Coca Cola signs and old metal barrels. Cut down to suitable size, the signs were installed between the cylinders of radial engines to keep them cool. The barrels were cut up and used to build "heaters" to capture heat from a plane's muffler and direct it inside the plane's cabin. Without such heaters the aircrews could become quite cold in the mostly unheated planes brought to the Florida base. Once the base was "fixed up," though, Fandison recalls enjoying the life there, including fishing, partying at the casino, and flying patrols. He considered the Bayou Country people tops:*

> The people down there were great. When you left the island and came up to New Orleans, no matter where you stopped off, if you went in to have a cup of coffee or a hamburger or something those people wouldn't let you pay for anything. I'd go in, or a couple of us would go in, and order a hamburger and a soft drink and a guy would come out with a steak and french fried potatoes. We'd say we didn't order that. And they'd say that man over there said to give it to you. That's the way they were.

As a pilot, Fandison flew both escort and patrol duty. Much of his escort duty involved ships headed to or from New Orleans:

I don't know how other bases worked, but when there was a transport coming on down the river we would get a coded message that night and the next morning they'd tell us to fly over there and meet that ship or two ships or three ships. They would be be coming out to the Gulf and we'd take them as far as maybe Sabine River and another squadron would pick them up ... probably Beaumont. While you were scouting for submarines you never saw them, because they laid out in the mouth of the river, in the murky water. If they got out in the clear water you could see them. Eight hundred or a thousand feet you'd see the whole submarine. But you know in that murky water you wouldn't spot them unless they'd come up. If they'd come up the only alternative we'd have was to get as far away from them as we could and call in to a squadron at the New Orleans Air Corps Base....You know at our 90 miles an hour, and with the guns the subs had, it would have been tough on us.... Some of the boys said they sighted some. It's possible that they did. I don't know. Could have been a log floating down there. Nothing came of it you know. Couldn't locate them.

## Nicholas F. Denham

*Nicholas F. Denham and his brother, Charles T. Denham, six years older, were a coastal patrol team, and both won the Air Medal. Born in Kansas City, Missouri, they grew up in President Harry Truman's hometown of Independence. Charles was the elder and learned to fly in the Army Air Corps in 1929. Nicholas began flying only after the war began, and this is his story:*

My brother Charles was an early CAPer and said they needed help at the coastal patrol bases. He suggested I learn to fly and that we volunteer for coastal patrol duty as a team. So I took lessons and got a student license, and we joined up. At first, they intended to send us to Falmouth, on Cape Cod, but my brother said winter's coming on, and the water up there will be pretty cold if we have to go into it. He said let's try for a warmer spot, and they said, okay, report to Grand Isle on October 1.

Before all this, I had been a schoolteacher, and had a friend who thought we should join the Navy. I felt I might soon be drafted, and since I wanted a choice of service branch, I agreed. However, the recruiting officer told me that the only post for which I was qualified was as chief of a naval gun crew on a merchant ship, and he didn't think that was a good place for a married man. He implied I might not come back. So I declined and ended up doing something even more dangerous.

My wife Dorothy wasn't too keen about my coastal patrol duty, because she understood I'd be flying well out over the water. My brother and I flew down in his plane, taking a mechanic and the mechanic's wife with us. We shared a room in the Oleander Hotel, and we were all crowded up pretty good in there. Everyone shared a common bath down the hall. But we really didn't need air conditioning, because with the windows open, the Gulf breezes blew right through from one side of the building to the other. It wasn't so hot down there anyway. Missouri can be a lot hotter.

1st Lt. Charles T. Denham (left) and his younger brother Flight-Observer Nicholas F. Denham, September 30, 1942. Nicholas recalls that during the month before the Grand Isle base was opened, thirty-three ships had been sunk in the Gulf (courtesy Nicholas F. Denham).

As a flight observer I was paid five dollars a day. As a pilot, my brother received eight dollars a day. We paid for our own room and board at the hotel, and took three meals a day there. For lunch, they often served us a spicy-hot crab gumbo. We called it "gumbo with the spider in it," meaning the crab. I was about five feet, ten inches and weighed one hundred and thirty-five pounds or so, definitely thin, and I didn't gain any weight there. We flew whatever was required of us. Sometimes, one shift a day, sometimes two, and sometimes we'd get a day off. We did whatever was asked of us. All of the submarine attacks took place before my brother and I reported for duty. It had been bad. As assistant intelligence officer, I had access to the various classified documents. I was told that thirty-three ships had been sunk in the Mississippi Delta area in the thirty days before our base was opened.

Though by my time, there probably wasn't a German U-boat within a thousand miles of Grand Isle, we still took security precautions, including a total blackout every night. We didn't use the headlights on our cars, just the parking lights, which were very dim. This led to at least one accident. One night I was a passenger with an officer driving down to the airstrip, about two and a half or three miles from the Oleander Hotel. He drove very fast, following what passed as a road only from the faint reflection of light on the crushed shell surface. Without warning, we hit a herd of horses, killing one and badly injuring two others. Apparently the guy just didn't see any point to driving slowly, even without headlights. The station wagon took weeks to repair.

We had to be careful, too, when on guard duty because of the possibility of sabotage. We carried a sidearm, in which we were given some training, and all took turns at being the Officer of the Day. We had some close order drill, which I didn't mind, but just considered part of my duty. So yes, there was a certain amount of military discipline, but such things as inspections were rare.

As for the flying, we actually had what amounted to three runways, sandy-sod and crushed shell. I remember the longest as being about fifteen hundred feet and the shortest about five hundred feet. Every landing was a "spot" landing or you didn't get in. We made lots of five hundred foot landings! Most of the ships had landing flaps and they helped a lot. We had Stinson Reliants and Voyagers, some Wacos and a Fleetwing amphibian with a single engine mounted on a tripod above the fuselage. My brother and most of the pilots were qualified to fly everything including the amphibian. It was used not only for rescue work, but also for regular patrols.

The story in *Joe — Submarine Hunter* about my brother and I having to make an off-field landing on our first patrol is correct. We were following our sister ship in to land, when a squall line came through. They got down but we could not. We had forty-five minutes of gas left, and no knowledge of the surrounding terrain. Fortunately, the veteran Gibson Autin had been sent with us to show us the ropes, and he knew the area well, directing us to a safe landing on a stretch of Mississippi River levee hardly higher than the surrounding swamp. We forgot to reel in our trailing wire antenna in landing and lost it, so we couldn't radio anyone where we were. Chuck and Autin walked to a nearby town to call in while I sat with the plane for about an hour battling mosquitoes. After a while it cleared up and we took off and flew back to base.

One day out on patrol with Ray McClain as pilot, our engine started coughing and then stopped — probably due to carburetor icing. We were down to where we were about to dump the plane into the water when the engine started up again. We landed with about a gallon of gas left in the tank we were using, and the vent on the other tank was sealed with ice, so that we couldn't have used it if we'd wanted to. We carried a life raft rolled up into a bundle that would float. If we'd ditched, it would've been my job to open the rear door and push that bundle into the water, then catch up to it and inflate it using a cartridge of compressed air. I'm glad I never had to do all that. We knew there were sharks in the Gulf, but there were also plenty of porpoise and they say whenever they're around, the sharks won't hurt you.

Chuck's wife and my wife Dorothy joined us in Grand Isle after a month, and the four of us shared a furnished rental house — more like a fisherman's shack, really. In due course the C.O. asked me if Dorothy could type and take shorthand and when I said yes, he said they'd like have her services in the office. I told her and she couldn't get down to the office fast enough. By then my brother and his family had left the base, and she was left to spend whole days by herself because we didn't have children at this point. She worked for five or six months, mostly as a teletype operator.

We didn't have a car, though my brother and several of the others did, and since there wasn't any bus service either, we were at the mercy of others to give us a ride up to New Orleans or Houma once in a while. We had parties for base personnel now and then and we socialized at a local honky-tonk called "Tony's." There wasn't any rowdiness or stuff like that. It was more like a private club, with movies every night.

It was all a *very* happy time for me. Our top officers were great guys, and we felt we were really doing some good in the war. We realized it was serious business, but we loved flying and didn't mind the risk. Both Chuck and I went into the Navy after the coastal patrol base closed, he for about four months and I for about a year. He died in August 1994 at age ninety.

* * *

Though the Denham brothers escaped dunking, seven other Grand Isle flyers became members of the famous Duck Club: Louis J. DiCarlo, Frank J. Serwich, Raymond B. McClain, M. M. Garvin, William K. Jenkins, Earl A. Dimitry, and Michael L. Heim. One of them, Louis DiCarlo, was eligible twice-over. His first ditching occurred September 17, 1942 while on late afternoon patrol. Oil began coming from the firewall of their Rearwin Cloudster, so DiCarlo turned for the nearest point of land immediately, while his flight observer Frank Serwich radioed in a "mayday" and reported their position. The following is from *Joe — Submarine Hunter:*

The oil pressure started to sink slowly as DiCarlo tried to climb the ship. He reached 1,000 feet when the pressure dropped to zero. Serwich continued to try to reach the base, but never got a "Roger" on his report. A few seconds later parts started to fly from under the cowling and then the engine flew to pieces. DiCarlo glided down toward the water, leveled off, then brought the nose up and made a tail-first landing on the waves. They struck with a terrific impact and the glass jug which held the silver marker slick fluid broke at once, splattering the pilot and observer with bright silver paint. At the same time the antenna wire whipped around the front of the ship, and caught around DiCarlo's neck, momentarily strangling him. Serwich quickly pulled out his hunting knife and severed the wire.

In the 35 seconds between the time the ship hit the water and the time that is sunk beneath the waves, both men fought their way out of the ship and inflated their Mae Wests, dragging along the canvas motor hood which had been laying in the back of the plane. They each clenched opposite ends of this canvas between their teeth, which kept them from being separated as they swam clear of the wreckage. DiCarlo guided the pair away from the muddy Mississippi water, because he knew the current would carry them out to sea. Through the dark, swelling waters the two men swam, tying their Mae Wests together so as not to become separated.

According to a contemporary account, the 38-year-old DiCarlo was an "almost sickly looking man," and the 37-year-old Serwich was a rail-thin six-footer weighing but a hundred and fifty pounds. Anxious Grand Isle personnel gave them little chance to survive the night. Still, they fought on:

> DiCarlo and Serwich were in the water two hours now, still moving toward land and steering clear of the Mississippi current. Both men were weakening, but continued to lie on their Mae Wests and paddle with their hands toward shore in the complete darkness. As time wore on Serwich, the weaker of the two, became nearly exhausted, and DiCarlo had to pull and shove him along to keep him from giving up right there. Just about when DiCarlo was ready to give up, they sighted the seawall and with what was more guts than strength they hoisted themselves up and lay there exhausted. They had been swimming for four and one-half hours.

> As they lay on the seawall several small boats passed, not hearing their shouts. Finally they were able to attract the attention of a small Coast Guard boat, which flashed its searchlights up and down the seawall. As the searchlight swung up and down, it suddenly hit bright silver objects that shone like Greek gods in the black night. The two men were still covered by the marker fluid, which they can thank for

saving them from cold and exposure on the seawall. They were picked up by the Coast Guard and taken to Burwood, where because they had lost all identification, they were placed under technical arrest. A telephone call to the base soon verified who they were, and that same phone call was received amidst great jubilation by the members of the base.

Though perhaps less dramatic, DiCarlo's second "dunking" again showed his courageous qualities. Following is an excerpt from Civil Air Patrol Accident Report number 6, dated May 22, 1943:

Early on December 18, 1942 after experiencing radio trouble in Fairchild NC 29013 Pilot DiCarlo accompanied by Observer Michael L. Heim found it necessary to return to Grand Isle for repairs. Subsequent to the necessary repairs to their radio DiCarlo and Heim encountered a rough engine while attempting to take off. They returned to the hangar where the engine was found to be safe for flight. So for the third time on that fateful day DiCarlo taxied for departure. This time he made it, but not for long. At about 200 feet, already over the Gulf, the Fairchild's engine stopped completely. Unable to make it back to land, DiCarlo skillfully effected another water ditching. Upon impact the aircraft flipped over trapping both he and Heim. Freeing himself from his seat belt he noticed that Heim was having difficulty releasing his seat belt. Only after assisting Heim in the removal of his seat belt did DiCarlo leave the aircraft and swim to the surface and safety.

## Louis DiCarlo

*Today, Air Medal winner Louis DiCarlo is an energetic 86-year-old living in Texas, less than one hundred miles from his Lake Charles, Louisiana birthplace. He says that at first some pilots joined the Civil Air Patrol because their costs of flying were defrayed by the government, and because the uniforms made them feel "macho." When serious flying began, most of the "weekend warriors" dropped out. In the spring of 1942 DiCarlo was assigned, not to Grand Isle, but to Parksley, Virginia:*

We stayed in private homes in town, and our base headquarters was an old farmhouse near a runway cut through a pine forest. I wasn't there long, but I especially remember the day the Army and Navy got after a U-boat that had sunk a ship right off Virginia Beach near Norfolk, and another time when we helped to escort a thirty-mile-long convoy of ships that included everything from battleships and aircraft carriers to a seagoing floating dry-dock.

When the U-boats started operating in the Gulf, I was sent to Louisiana to help set up the Grand Isle base. I remained there from midsummer 1942 to mid-summer 1943, when I was assigned to the Del Gado Flight School in New Orleans to teach aircraft field maintenance. During all this time, my pay was eight dollars a day, but I was spending fifteen. After I went to New Orleans, I was turned down for government housing because I was still a Civil Air Patrol volunteer receiving a monthly government paycheck. I wrote Air Corps Colonel Harry Blee, the CAP operations chief, and told him I was quitting. He told me if I did I'd be drafted. I was called up two days later, but I failed the physical — as I knew I would — and became the first CAPer (I think) to tear up his draft card.

Technical Sergeant Addis H. McDonald of North Little Rock, Arkansas displays a life jacket found in the Gulf and said to have German inscriptions. Similar finds were made along the east coast as well (Hopper collection).

My flying at Grand Isle was interesting. I had to ditch twice and saw some things during patrols that I remember well. Two weeks after the troopship *Robert E. Lee* was sunk at the mouth of the Southwest Pass, for example, I found one of its life rafts, floating empty, eighty miles to the southwest. On another occasion, I saw a Navy mine sweeper at work, and thought I saw a periscope following it at the same speed. I called in my "sighting," but was told to forget it. What I took for a periscope wake was actually the track from a spotter-buoy that marked the end of the paravane the mine sweeper was pulling. I made an even worse booboo once by reporting a sunken cargo ship floating upside down in clear water as a submarine.

Two of Grand Isle's other Duck Club members, Earl A. ("Doc") Dimitry, a 35-year-old ophthalmologist from New Orleans, and 50-year-old William K. Jenkins of Shreveport, were rescued from Gulf waters thanks to inspired cooperation between their sister ship and one of the tankers in the convoy they'd been escorting. After spotting the downed flyers in high seas — their Waco sank almost immediately — Ray R. Fisher and William R. Sprott, both of Little Rock, Arkansas, dropped a marker bomb from their Fairchild 24 and flew to seek help from the nearest tanker, about a mile away. *Joe — Submarine Hunter* describes what happened next:

> By frantically diving and zooming on it [they] were able to show the crew that their sister ship had gone down. Sprott and Fisher were jubilant as they watched a lifeboat being lowered from the deck of the tanker. But the smiles were frozen on their faces when they saw that the angry seas completely swamped the lifeboat as soon as it touched the water. The waves slapped it aside like a boxer hitting a light punching bag; Sprott and Fisher first realized at that point what those two men were going through in the water, with nothing but Mae Wests holding them up.
>
> A few minutes later another lifeboat was lowered, this time from the other side of the tanker. With great difficulty a rescue crew got the boat under way, and Fisher led them toward the spot marked by the slick. It took that crew forty minutes to negotiate that mile of mountainous waves; they reached the two men just about the time when they were ready to give up all hope of rescue. They were brought back to the tanker and thence to Burwood, where, after three days treatment for shock and exposure, they returned to the base, ready to go out on patrol again.

## Lawrence G. Englert

*Another brother team at Grand Isle was Fred S. and Lawrence G. Englert. Born and raised in New Orleans, both were pilots, but Lawrence, though rated as an observer, worked during his short stay at Grand Isle mainly as a service technician driving the base's gasoline truck. Both began flying in the 1930s, and joined the CAP while the coastal patrols were still being flown from New Orleans. Lawrence Englert tells of his first truck trip to Grand Isle:*

I think it was in August 1942 while working the ground crew at Shushan [the lakefront airport] that my captain told me that after I'd finished the work I was doing I should take the gas truck and head for Grand Isle. I said, "Where the hell's Grand Isle?" I was assigned as the driver but took along two passengers: Willie Lum and William Fandison.

All we had were the clothes on our backs. Luckily, the truck broke down immediately, and when a mechanic came out to fix it we went home and packed a change of clothes.

After a while we stopped at Raceland for a cup of coffee, and discovered that we had only about fifty cents among us. We went inside a cafe where everyone was drinking, and one man asked where we were headed. I just looked at him, and he said, "Well, I know you men can't talk, but come on, I'll buy you all something to eat," and we had hamburgers and coffee. We didn't get to Grand Isle until about two-thirty in the morning, and it was pitch black because of the blackout. Somehow we found the Oleander and checked in for the rest of the night.

While I was there, I worked ground crew starting at 5:30 a.m. One of my jobs was chasing cows off the runway for the dawn patrol. Unfortunately, after a few weeks, I contracted amoebic diarrhea, and was ordered home for hospital treatment. I was in the Touro Infirmary for four weeks, but I felt just as sick when I came out as when I went in. After a year of three-times-a-week treatment without improvement I found a satisfactory diet that worked for me, and I healed myself. I never was able to report back to Grand Isle.

My brother Fred, who was awarded the Air Medal after the war, was the only Louisiana man killed while flying for the Civil Air Patrol. It was after Grand Isle closed. One day, he was working ground crew at the lakefront airport in New Orleans when an Army Colonel came round asking for the best pilot on the base. He wanted someone who could safely fly him low enough that he could drop flour-bombs on his soldiers taking training at nearby Camp Plauche. They told him my brother Fred was the man. "I'll take him," said the Colonel, and told Fred, "Let's go," but Fred said, "Hang on while I sign some insurance papers." Later, they crashed into the Mississippi River. The plane was never recovered, but they found Fred's body three days later.

## Mrs. Norman T. Ozenberger

*As the base became fully functional, new volunteers continued to arrive. Two of them were newlyweds. Norman T. Ozenberger and his wife Lois had been married just two weeks before in Emporia, Kansas. After their two-week honeymoon, they departed from Kansas City flying as passengers with two other men reporting to Grand Isle in their Stinson. Mr. Ozenberger served as an aircraft mechanic, his wife as a secretary. Mrs. Ozenberger recalls:*

Grand Isle, as you know, is about seven miles long and one mile wide, and is connected to the mainland by a small bridge. All the roads on the island were of ground-up seashells, which fortunately helped you see your way at night, because the island was kept totally blacked-out. We'd ride on the car fenders to help drivers find their way. Norman and I lived at the Oleander Hotel as did other coastal patrol and Coast Guard people and their families. We had our meals there, too, with grits and chicory coffee for breakfast, which we sometimes had to prepare for ourselves if the cooks were hung-over. We called the waitresses "Octane" and "Propane," though I don't know why.

Norman T. and Lois Ozenberger went to Grand Isle only a month after their marriage, he as a mechanic, she as a base secretary-typist (courtesy Norman T. and Lois Ozenberger).

Our evening's entertainment was to gather with the Coast Guard families at one of the two "honky-tonks" to drink, dance, and eat fresh shrimp right off the boats. The government sometimes was very slow to pay us, and at one point Norman and I were practically down to our last dime when the checks came in. Fortunately, the hotel carried us in such times. I think he made seven dollars a day, and I made five dollars. We worked for twelve days, then had three days off, which we frequently spent in New Orleans.

The Cajun people on the island were friendly and sociable. Many worked at the base, but mostly they fished, and spent their days catching shrimp and working the oyster beds. I remember Nat Pedro, a sort of dare-devil pilot, meeting the oyster boats at the dock and sitting down right there to fill up with raw oysters as soon as they unloaded. We visited the island in 1980, but the airport was gone, and in its place was a regional park. We found a couple of old ladies in a restaurant who remembered the CAP days, and had a nice chat with them, but except for the remains of the Oleander and our administration building, nothing else was left.

## Addis Holly McDonald

*Another autumn arrival was 36-year-old Addis Holly McDonald of North Little Rock, Arkansas, the base communications officer. When he reported for three-months active duty at the end of October, he had never before been separated from his wife of fifteen years and their two sons. In a 1983 interview, McDonald told CAP historian Colonel Lester E. Hopper of the surprises he found at Grand Isle:*

> That Oleander Hotel was just a clap board building built in a kind of L-shape. There were two porches, one at the lower level, and one at the second floor level. The rooms were just little cubicles with a lavatory and a small bed. My only furnishing was an orange crate to set my books and other things on. We had our meals at the Oleander, too. The proprietors, Opey and Renae Ludwig — they were great — tried their best to make a home for us. They had a native colored boy, that was the cook, and after you got used to their cooking, why it was bearable. I had a little trouble getting used to black strap molasses. But all in all it wasn't too bad.

\* \* \*

When one of the other radio operators moved to another base, McDonald signed up to stay with the coastal patrol for the duration of the service. Maintaining the base radio transmitting and receiving equipment and all the radio sets on the planes was a painstaking job:

> We had lots of radio trouble down there. We furnished our own equipment and tools such as tube testers and volt meters. We had built us a cabinet in there and tried to protect our equipment from salt air. Salt atmosphere is deadly to electronics. But if we could keep one ship going, with the radio gear operating correctly, we'd let two ships go out together to fly. Lots of times, both planes had contact with the base and with each other, but we wouldn't break a flight up on account of radio failure, if one of them was still operating.

At home, McDonald's wife had been working long hours as a seamstress to send him money while he waited for his government pay:

> My wife, she sewed, she made enough to keep groceries on the table and also to pay my board bill on the island. It cost me about a dollar a week or something like that for laundry on my uniforms. But in hot weather we just wore our shorts and undershirts. The weather was so blamed hot anyway, and they wasn't strict about what we wore when we was on duty in the hangar.... I was told they didn't know who was going to finance the thing, whether it was going to be the Office of Civilian Defense or the Army.

## Addis Eugene McDonald

*About two months after Christmas, 1942, McDonald brought his wife and two sons to the base. His oldest son, Addis Eugene, remembers the move:*

Dad drove my mother Edna and my six-year-old brother Audrey and me down there in our 1936 Ford. We leased a house from Hamilton Landry, and since we had no electricity, we lighted it with wind-charged 32-volt Delco batteries. Mom cooked with butane gas, and did the ironing with flat irons heated on the stove. Dad built a radio that operated off the battery system, and since we didn't get a newspaper down there, all our news came from that radio.

My brother and I were immediately enrolled in a small parochial school for all grades. Most of the kids were French-speaking sons and daughters of the local fishermen, but courses were taught in English, and there was no language problem. My "high school" classmates and I all had classes in one room: we had four or five kids in 8th grade, none in the ninth, only one in the tenth — myself— and three in the graduating class, which was the eleventh grade. The area was so thinly populated, the next nearest school was at Golden Meadow, some thirty-two miles away.

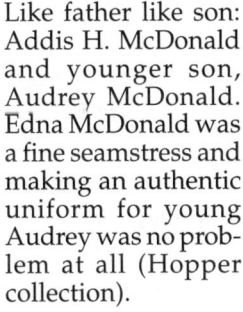

Like father like son: Addis H. McDonald and younger son, Audrey McDonald. Edna McDonald was a fine seamstress and making an authentic uniform for young Audrey was no problem at all (Hopper collection).

I worked on Mr. Landry's shrimp boats the following summer. We had all the fish, oysters, shrimp, and crabs that we could eat, even that first winter. All of our fresh meat and other foodstuffs came down from up north. I felt the "culture shock," all right, in the lack of certain amenities, the changes in daily diet, attending such a little school, hearing French spoken all the time, and all that. It wasn't bad, just different.

There certainly wasn't much for entertainment. I remember "Tony's Place," a combined bar and movie theater sharing one long room in a real narrow building. When movies were shown. they'd lower a canvas curtain halfway down the room's length, and a bed sheet movie screen was hung from that. The floor was level, and the benches and stools in the back had longer legs so the people in back could see. Dad maintained the projector, but it was never entirely dependable.

**Ray B. McClain**

*Another volunteer who brought his family to Louisiana (but only as far as New Orleans) was Ray B. McClain, a self-styled "farm boy" from Zionsville, Indiana, just north of Indianapolis. The 31-year-old McClain already had his commercial license, over fifteen hundred hours air time, and was a CAP member when a close friend, M. M. Garvin, another CAPer, asked him, "If I buy a plane will you come down to Grand Isle with me and fly it?":*

Garvin and I, my pregnant wife Helene and our 11-month-old son, and Fred Englert, another CAP pilot, took off for Louisiana in Garvin's Waco cabin plane NC 14609 on Thursday, November 19, 1942. We were so late getting away that we stopped in Memphis overnight and went on to New Orleans the next day. I left my wife and son there, and continued with Garvin and Englert the next morning to Grand Isle. There we were ordered to return to New Orleans immediately to pick up some radio equipment. Returning to Grand Isle, we had a rude shock.

I remember two runways at Grand Isle, one short, about nine hundred feet, and the other a little longer, maybe fifteen hundred feet. Before coming down, we were advised the prevailing winds favored using the longer runway but on arrival the wind had shifted and we had to use the shorter one. So I just flew kind of leisurely out over the Gulf to get lined up. I was only a country boy and had never seen the ocean before, so I did a little sight-seeing. There was no hurry about getting in. I guess I was a few hundred yards out on final when the engine quit.

Well, I slowed down as much as possible and pan-caked into the water well short of the runway. I did the best I could, but you know you can't slow down a big four-place aircraft much below seventy, and I'll tell you, that water's mighty hard when you hit it at that speed. We had quite a load, too. We didn't go over on our back. But the wheels caught, and that heavy engine dipped way deep in the water before bobbing back out again. I spent about sixteen days in the hospital with head and facial injuries. The other two fellows, Garvin and Englert, weren't hurt. I think what surprised and startled me the most was the taste of saltwater! When you've grown up on a farm in Indiana like I did, you wouldn't expect salt water when you take a dunking. It was some great introduction to the coastal patrol!

Left to right, Lts. Raymond B. McClain, Samuel R. Vitelaro, and Allen House standing in front of the remains of Waco NC 14609 after its salvage from the Gulf in early 1943. Once immersed in salt water for any length of time, a plane was virtually impossible to restore (courtesy Raymond B. McClain).

That was my only ditching, but I came awful close to another one. On Sunday morning, March 7, 1943, I was flying Lucien Troxler's Waco NC 13421 maybe forty miles out, south of the base, when the engine started to run pretty rough. I figured the carburetor might be icing up — that was a common problem with the 220 hp Continental engines — so I asked my observer, Nick Denham, to call the base and tell them our problem, and to have them tell our sister ship we were returning to base and to have them waggle their wings if they got the message. We didn't have air-to-air radio on our aaircraft. That came along later I believe. I remember that we'd no more than turned north when the engine quit cold just like you'd turned off the switch. I told Nick to radio the base that we were going down.

We had the only life raft on the base, and Nick got in the back seat to prepare for ditching. At the very last minute that big old Continental came back on just like it left off, and we got back to base safely. I was very glad, because I certainly was not looking forward to another dunking. They talk about the Gulf water being warm and all, but at that time of year it wasn't. It wasn't warm when I went in the first time, either, which was back in November before the air temperature turned wintry.

In fact, I remember that base as really a cold spot. At first, I lived in the Oleander Hotel, a kind of run-down place where fishermen came for a vacation. The only heat came from little electric stoves in the hallways that were turned off at 10 p.m. because the generator they operated from made so much noise nobody could have slept. That place was so cold that when I came in from dusk patrol, I often just threw something over what I'd been wearing and went to bed wearing a double layer. It wasn't particularly hot even in the summer, what with cooling breezes coming off the water.

Not only did Grand Isle lack electricity — the base had to generate its own power — but there was no fresh water other than that captured during a rain and piped to a storage cistern. Additional water was trucked-in from up north. While I was staying at the Oleander I got pretty well acquainted with Mr. Ludwig, the hotel's proprietor, and I asked him once why they didn't sink a well. He said they did. "Went down seven thousand feet and the water was even saltier than it is in the Gulf itself," he told me.

It was really a different world down there. It was all just a big open place then, not like today, when all you see are houses. I don't recall any deer or other wildlife, but it was not unusual to have to chase cows off the runways. Waterfowl were everywhere, but we didn't find them a hazard to our flying. The natives spoke "Cajun" among themselves, but could speak English, too. Language was never a problem. I remember that people were buried above ground, just like in New Orleans. Altogether, you'd have to say it was pretty different, maybe even "exotic." My wife lived in New Orleans all the time I was at Grand Isle, but I'd go see her and my son on my days off. I flew a lot, but not every day. We all got along very well, though I do not recall the base commander, Captain Melvin G. Smith, as particularly outgoing. I think he may have resented me because, while he was older, I had actually flown more and he only had a private license as compared to my commercial license. It was awkward for both of us.

I was watching from shore the day Louis DiCarlo went into the water for the second time, and I saw him rescue his observer from the wreck. He went in right after take-off. Louis was just a little guy, and probably wouldn't have weighed more than one hundred and twenty pounds. To do what he did that day he must have been endowed with super strength, and he should have received a medal for bravery.

I always think back to all that water. It was always there. You started your take-off at the water's edge, and you finished your landing roll-out at the water's edge. We wore Mae Wests, but never the waterproof zoot suits the flyers at the northern bases wore. I didn't experience any hurricanes, but in 1969 *Camille* swept away everything on Grand Isle except the Oleander, and even it was damaged pretty badly. By the time I reported in November, 1942, the danger of ship sinkings had virtually ended. I never saw a U-boat nor any evidence of one, except for the superstructures of certain ships sunk earlier that year. Sticking up out the water, they made dependable navigation checkpoints. The natives used to tell stories of seeing subs cruising right up the Mississippi River toward New Orleans. "What could we do?" they'd ask, "the U-boats had all the guns. We had nothing to fight them with." I also heard stories of how one sub had nosed up and grounded itself on Grand Isle, presumably seeking to replenish its food and water supplies.

After we were there, the Coast Guard established a small craft base a stone's throw from our coastal patrol base, but the nearest Navy base was at New Orleans.* They had some North American 0-47 observation planes, big pot-bellied mid-wings, and when they came down our way, they often buzzed our base. We had a good operation down there, and I'm proud to have served, but it's over fifty years ago now, and there's so much I've forgotten!

**Omar W. Crim**

*Omar W. Crim was a West Virginian with a long and colorful history of flying. The diminutive Crim (5' 8" and 115-pounds) joined the U.S. Army as a reserve officer in 1933, served at several CCC camps, learned to fly, and in 1940-1941 ferried warplanes from British factories to Royal Air Force bases in England and Scotland. When he returned to Charleston, West Virginia as something of a celebrity, he said after a radio talk show he was "much more frightened on the air than I ever was in the air."*

---

* Airship Squadron Twenty-Two, with its four airships uniquely nicknamed *Jeanne LaFitte, Dominique You, Nez Coupé,* and *Gambi,* was established at the newly commissioned Houma Naval Air Station, midway between Grand Isle and New Orleans, on May 15, 1943.

Crim was among the several flyers who served at two or more different bases. His "certificate of service" dated July 1, 1945, shows him at Atlantic City from May 9 until July 6, 1942 and at Grand Isle, Louisiana from then until July 9, 1943, when he returned again to Atlantic City to serve until the base's closing. Crim's trademark was versatility. At Atlantic City, he flew both as a pilot and an observer. At Grand Isle, he doubled as a pilot and an engineering officer. During much of 1944, he pulled sleeve targets for Tow Target Unit #1 based at Hadley Field, New Jersey, then at Suffolk County (Long Island, New York) Army Air Corps base. In December he began work as an aviation mechanic at the old Baltimore Army Air Field. He remained with CAP until mid-1945, serving his final six months in West Virginia. In 1948 he was awarded the Air Medal.

Omar W. Crim, "Our Family Hero." Crim served first at Atlantic City, and after Grand Isle, returned to pull targets at Suffolk County Army Air Corps base (Crim collection, West Virginia State Archives).

Crim's log books and his collection of aviation memorabilia can be found in the West Virginia State Archives. Among them are scribbled notes about his early flying days. Some are touching reminders of the often primitive state of civil aviation when many CAP members first began flying. This is one excerpt:

> I was bit by the flying bug during the early twenties but wasn't able to do anything about it except read of the aces of World War I and dream. Here in [the] Kanawha Valley [near Charleston, West Virginia] there wasn't any decent place for an airport, but in the early twenties there were some open fields. One place was on an island in the middle of the river, but it was hard to get to, so only a few flights [were made] from there. Now the island is covered with a chemical plant.

## Walter E. Blocker

*Unlike the pilots from other states, few if any from Louisiana brought their families to Grand Isle. Instead, they might take a few days leave at home, or invite their families to visit them at the base. Mrs. T. J. Williamson remembers that her father, Walter E. Blocker of New Orleans, did both:*

My father was about thirty-nine when he went down to Grand Isle. My mother and younger brother and I remained in New Orleans, but I recall going down there as a young teenager — I was probably about fifteen years old — to visit him and look at the airplanes. I didn't fly with him then because that was against regulations, though I had done so earlier when he was a part-time instructor at the New Orleans lakefront airport. He flew his own airplane to Grand Isle and lived in the Oleander Hotel.

My father dearly loved flying and that was his life after he got into it. He continued to fly after the war, but I think his eyesight gradually failed and he had to give it up. He owned a number of planes over the years, one of them a Stearman biplane in which I flew with him from Virginia to New York. It was the first open cockpit plane I'd ever flown in, and I really felt like I was big time! On one occasion with me as a passenger, he did some barrel rolls with it, and as we turned upside down I heard and felt the seat belt go "ker-chunk," and I thought, "Oh my God, I'm gone!" I grabbed the intercom and told my dad that the seat belt was broken, but he laughed and said "Don't worry, it's okay." I was scared just the same. Father died in 1967 when he was only sixty-four, but he was always proud of his coastal patrol work.

\* \* \*

According to *Joe — Submarine Hunter*, old movies were only one of the entertainments to be had at "Tony's Place." After shelling out thirty cents for admission and seating themselves on hard wooden benches, it was not unusual for viewers to notice that as the evening wore on the screen grew dimmer and the sound more faint:

> Tony's system was to get a big crowd in the "Playhouse" for the movie, then when the 1898 projection equipment went out, as it invariably did, to furnish other forms of entertainment. Customers trapped in the rear for an hour and frantically seeking relief, usually staggered up front to quaff a few drinks of Tony's 90 octane swamp-juice and to give the dice a few futile rolls.

But Tony's Place had some stiff competition about two blocks away, a place called "Adam's," a large casino with wooden tables up front near the bar, and a dance floor and juke box in the rear. Base members needed all the recreation they could find because, taken altogether, Grand Isle was undoubtedly the most primitive coastal patrol base of them all. When the fictional "Joe" and a new recruit dropped by the casino they found that:

> Most of the gang were gathered there, downing a few beers and discussing their lot on this new outpost. It was the consensus that the place was another Bataan; but the tone of all the conversation was jovial, the men preferring to poke fun at the island and themselves, rather than face the grim fact that they would have to live on greasy, vitamin-lacking foods, drink rainwater, go without milk, go without any entertainment other than that which they could provide from amongst their own group, and perhaps worst of all, fight a running battle with mosquitoes and other insect life.

Such things were seldom mentioned in official reports to CAP headquarters in Washington. A description of the "airport" submitted November 9, 1942, in response to CAP Operations Memorandum No. 9, stressed the positive, even "stretching" the runways to lengths longer than recalled by most pilots:

> Hangar new, 60' by 60', high enough for all planes to enter. Will hold four planes. Concrete floor, well built. Administration Building formerly old hotel, completely rebuilt by CAP members, two-story, well screened and lighted; complete hospital, four beds, operating room, completely equipped, 6 foot refrigerator (gas) for blood bank; building has large lounging room on main floor, commissary, storeroom, two bedrooms, study room, kitchen, two screened-in porches, one bathroom. Second floor has radio room, plotting room, five Administrative Offices, two bathrooms, and two screened in porches. Hangar has completely equipped shop.... Main runway: East and West, 1900 feet, 34 feet wide. Middle runway: Northwest and Southeast, 1400 feet long, 34 feet wide. North South runway: 1250 feet long, 34 feet wide.

In December, the Grand Isle base got a new boss, Captain Melvin A. Smith, a gray-haired veteran of World War I who had flown antisubmarine patrols at Atlantic City and had for a time commanded the coastal patrol base at Portland, Maine. During the winter and spring, many other new men also arrived, in part to replace men who had only volunteered for thirty-, sixty-, or ninety-days of service. As the number of flight crews increased, men no longer needed to fly two or three times a day, so the new commander instituted a regimen of drill, calisthenics, and classwork to fill their time. Not everyone liked the change.

## Halsey C. Alderman

*One of the still later arrivals was Halsey C. Alderman, a native of the Tri-Cities area of New York State (Endicott, Binghamton, and Johnson City). He learned to fly in the early 1930s on First World War vintage aircraft such as the OX-5 Waco biplane. In mid-1943, while then the commander of the Tri-Cities CAP Squadron, he was asked to join the Grand Isle coastal patrol base:*

I was told that some of the pilots at Grand Isle were goofing off to some extent, landing on beaches and islands to salvage materials from sunken ships, and taking unnecessary risks in doing so. CAP headquarters wanted to send some "Yankees" down there to straighten them out. At least that's what I was told. So four others and myself went down together, driving night and day in my Oldsmobile convertible. One of them was Art Weller who later did a wonderful job as operations officer at Grand Isle.

Since I was a senior officer with many years flying experience — I was then thirty-eight — they scheduled me to begin flying immediately. I'd served very briefly at the Atlantic City base and knew something about it, so received no special instructions from the Grand Isle people. My first flight was a dusk patrol. I quickly found out that over the Gulf, when the sun went down, it got dark almost immediately. I'd done some night flying up north, and usually we had a half hour or so of twilight to get home. But when I headed home on this first flight at Grand Isle, it was dark when I reached the base. I was a good navigator (most pilots were their own navigators in those days) so I had no problem finding the base, but landing on an unlighted field was something else. When operations knew we'd be landing after dark, they told everyone on duty to go out to the end of the runway and aim those lights our way. I used the longest runway to land on, and even made the most of that by dragging in right at sea level. Though we got down safely on our first pass, my first flight was a notable introduction to flying over the Gulf.

In about a month I brought down my wife and twelve-year-old son. I think they basically enjoyed the place, and when I'd accumulated enough time off, we'd go off exploring the area by car. My son liked the slot machines at Tony's. We didn't have them back home, and the first time he pulled the handle and got back a bunch of nickels for hitting a winner he was pretty impressed. We went up to New Orleans several times, too. One of my most pleasant assignments was flying Bob Robinson, our flight surgeon, back there after his periodic visits to the base. We got to be good friends and he and his wife were great hosts when we went up to enjoy the city.

Halsey C. Alderman (left) and Arthur C. Weller inspect an above-ground crypt in the Grand Isle cemetery, photo dated June 1943. The high water table precluded in-ground interment (courtesy Halsey C. Alderman).

A couple of unusual flying experiences come to mind. I'd been out on dusk patrol in a Stinson SM8-A, and after returning and parking it for the night I pulled its fuses as required. One of them was a bar fuse, about three-quarters of an inch thick and maybe three inches long. In some way, when I removed it, one end hit the airplane frame and caused a spark about a foot from the compass. Next morning I flew the lead on dawn patrol, and it wasn't long before I recognized that the compass was forty degrees off. I radioed the base to tell my sister ship to take over (we lacked plane-to-plane capabilities) and we flew the rest of the patrol without incident. In my four months at the base, it was the only mechanical failure of any kind that I experienced.

You'd have to call the next incident a kind of pilot error. I often let my co-pilot take over the flying in order that he build up some time. On one occasion, in pushing back my seat to relax, without realizing it I must have hit and locked the toe-brakes on the rudder bars. That didn't affect how the ship flew, but when I took control to land, I hit the ground with the brakes still locked. Well, those wheels just dug into the soft, crushed shell runway and we flipped over on our back instantly. The only damage was to the propeller. We were left hanging there upside down but unhurt. It felt like we were twelve feet in the air. We had a great bunch of mechanics that got that plane flying again in no time.

Halsey Alderman's ten-year-old son, Gene, with a nice-sized sea trout fresh from the Gulf. Most of the nicer homes on the island were built on stilts as this one was (courtesy Halsey C. Alderman).

I was never afraid of flying over the water. The only difference between the flying I'd done up north and down there was in the weather. We had lots of rain and thunderstorms, and I even saw some waterspouts out over the Gulf, which we were cautioned to stay far away from, as they easily could tear a plane apart. For me, serving at Grand Isle was a positive experience in almost every way. I didn't get to know the commanding officer very well, but he seemed a fair man in his dealings with people. I continued flying after the war — only quit a few years back when I was in my eighties.

## Dr. Robert A. Robinson

*Robert A. Robinson, M. D. joined the Civil Air Patrol in December, 1941 and upon the establishment of the Grand Isle base, became its assigned flight surgeon. A pilot and part-owner of an Aeronca airplane, which he called a "powered glider," Robinson practiced surgery at Southern Baptist Hospital in New Orleans, and taught at Loyola University. He visited Grand Isle on weekends, but was on call for whatever emergencies might arise there. Asked about his duties there, he provided some detail to Colonel Lester E. Hopper in 1983:*

> The Oleander Hotel was where the big percent of the boys were housed. But the Brown Hotel ... about half a mile away was the headquarters for the patrol, and it's where I had the blood bank and the little operating room. The major injuries that we had were fractures, arms and wrists, sometimes a shoulder. Then wounds that were inflicted by stumbling around or falling out of a plane or by a propeller cut, various laceration wounds on arm or hand, or nail puncture wounds in feet. We didn't have any other major tragedies that happened while manipulating a plane. But we did have a lot of medical problems such as dysentery, respiratory infections, and simple abscesses caused by bacteria on the skin.

When word got around that Dr. Robinson came to the base each weekend, local residents began coming there to seek treatment. Finally the demand was such that he opened a separate off-base office in order to serve them without disrupting base routine:

> The Mayor of Grand Isle was Mercedes Adams — they called her Judge Adams. She gave me a room plus a kitchen where I could sterilize instruments, needles, syringes and other equipment that might be necessary. So once a week I had them gather there on a Saturday afternoon so that we could limit the visitation to the base.... There were no charges for base personnel, but these other townspeople were regular, paying patients.... I think my main accomplishment at the base was that I established certain procedures to handle serious emergencies, to get such cases to the New Orleans lakefront airport by plane and to have the Southern Baptist Hospital ambulance meet us there if needed.

Dr. Robinson figured indirectly in the last near-tragic experience suffered by Grand Isle personnel. John F. Haller from Moberly, Missouri, had flown Dr. Robinson back to New Orleans and was returning to base at dusk, when he went missing. An all-night vigil at the base radio brought no news. Four search planes went out at dawn, and at 7:32 a.m. it was Sidney L. Rosen of St. Louis who called in the heartening news: "LOCATED WRECKED SHIP IN SWAMPS ABOUT 25 MILES

NORTH OF BASE. PILOT O.K. HE IS SITTING ON TOP OF THE WRECKAGE." Finding him was easy. Rescuing him was not.

John Haller had crash-landed in dense swamp land about three miles from the nearest navigable water. The rescue party attempting to reach him on foot sunk to their knees and then to their shoulders before having to turn back exhausted and badly cut by six-foot saw grass. An attempt to reach Haller by pirogue — a native dugout canoe — also failed. A life raft packed with food, water, and first aid supplies was dropped for the downed man, but quickly sank from sight in the muck. His friends in the planes circling overhead judged from the wreckage that Haller must be seriously injured. Clearly he had no shelter from the broiling sun, no food or drink, and was under constant attack by clouds of mosquitoes. The entire day passed and as twilight fell, twenty-four hours after his crash, Haller was no nearer to rescue than he had been when first spotted.

When all seemed hopeless, a final do-or-die rescue attempt was made by Army Warrant Officer Cecil Pritchard, in the lead, Coast Guard Chief Petty Officer Chighizola, and two members of his crash boat crew. Disregarding the threats of water moccasins, coral snakes, and alligators, they reached Haller at 10:30 p.m. Though he was badly injured, Haller struggled out of the swamp under his own power. It took the group three hours to regain dry land. Base nurse Nina Cohen spent an hour bandaging him, wondering how he could have survived the cuts and bruises and prolonged exposure. The bone-weary pilot and his rescuers arrived at Grand Isle at 3:00 a.m. When he had fully recovered, John Haller continued to fly. Cecil Pritchard and Petty Officer Chighizola received citations for their part in the rescue.

\* \* \*

Only two weeks before Haller's crash and rescue, on Sunday morning, July 18, 1943, the base loudspeaker announced that there would be a meeting of all base personnel in the Administration Building. There the assembled pilots, observers, mechanics, guards, service men, and clerical staff heard base commander Smith tell them the "Fighting Nine" would cease to exist after August 31. For most the announcement had come as a total surprise.

Addis McDonald remained at Grand Isle after everyone else left, responsible for closing the base and selling all of the government-owned property to the highest bidder. Part of his job was transporting a number of unflyable airplanes back to New Orleans. He and local helpers disassembled the planes and placed them on a flat-bed truck, wings on either side of the fuselage, which sat backwards on the truck bed:

> Hamilton Landry was a big help to me and he liked to make those trips to New Orleans with me. But one time his brother Hector, who was a guard there at the base, went in his place. So when we got ready to leave, Hector wanted to ride in the airplane. I told him, "You'd be a lot more comfortable if you'd ride up here in the cab." He said, "No, I'd rather ride back there." So he rode all the way to New Orleans back there in the Fairchild, in the cabin of the plane. When we got there, he told me, "Mac, I want you to know I'm the only man in the world that ever came across the Huey Long Bridge in an airplane backing up."

This unidentified base member wears a pith helmet to protect himself against the semitropical sun (Hopper collection).

One year later, Addis McDonald revisited Grand Isle to see how it had changed. His remembrances were published in the *Civil Air Patrol News* nearly forty years later. Deserted and empty, the headquarters building and the hangar stood silent guard against blowing sand, invading fiddler crabs, and flights of seagulls no longer scared away by aircraft engines:

> I was greeted by no O. D. Missing was the noisy laughter of boys on the porch; there was no sound of busy footsteps in the hall, nor any sound from the radio room above. The screen door hung at an angle.... I walked around in back and with cupped hands drank the cool water from the cistern [then] turned and walked toward the hangar.

The board walk was still there, with grass growing high between the boards. This same grass had been placed here at the cost of many blisters and sore backs. It seemed that it desired to do its part by holding down the walk....

[In the hangar] I noticed a fluttering as if to attract my attention. It was a small piece of orange and black crepe paper hanging on a ceiling joist, tacked there by happy hands, while celebrating their new hangar. Closing my eyes I went back to Halloween night of 1942. I could see the sandwiches piled high and case after case of cold drinks and the floor full of happy dancing couples.... The sun was just setting as I started back and my body cast a long shadow along the runway. I could see a line of pelicans slowly winging their way toward Timbalier. I stopped and faced the naked flag pole standing rigidly at attention with moist eyes tightly closed. I stood this last retreat.

---

Base officers, pilots, and observers who served at least one month at CAPCP#9 and who are not elsewhere mentioned in this chapter include: Garland Anthony, Jr.,* Louis E. Armstrong, Luke E. Barber, Louis M. Bertucci,* Adrian Block, Jr., John F. Bosch, Jr., Owen E. Brennan, Jack A. Brown, Maurice A. Brown,* Marion B. Cahn,* Cleveland A. Cardino, Hiram E. Carson, Francis J. Carty,* Norman J. Chambers, Melvin M. Chatfield, Raymond L. Cook, William L. Cratty, John P. Culpepper, Harold C. Curran, Howard V. C. Davis,* Quintin H. DeClerk,* Richard H. Dewees,* Martin H. Dickey, Sigmond E. Florsheim, Adolph Freret, Francis A. Fuller, Arthur L. Galbusera, David H. Goebel,* Mortimer R. Goldsmith, James W. Griffith,* Edwin Hadley, Claude L. Hamel, Allan E. Hause,* Emile L. Hebert, Jr.,* Oscar P. Hoffman, David H. Kennedy, Fred J. Lang, James O. Lantrip, Didier B. Launey, Louis I. Metoyer, Thomas M. Miller, Lewis A. Mills, Jr.,* John Mokriski, Henry A. Muntz, Frank Orosz, Jr., James P. Phillips, John E. Peyton, Jr., Ralph W. Peyton, Mancell G. Pitts, James H. Postlewait, Harry A. Pursley, Fred W. Reno, Carl J. Ripberger,* Tom B. Robertson, George S. Salley,* John Smith, Robert M. Smith,* Clarence H. Springer, Detlef W. Stoven, James J. Sutton, Lucien J. Troxler,* Robert E. Van Gundy, Samuel R. Viterlaro,* Lloyd P. Wells, Charles E. Woolford, and Harold C. Wright. Asterisk indicates Air medal winner.

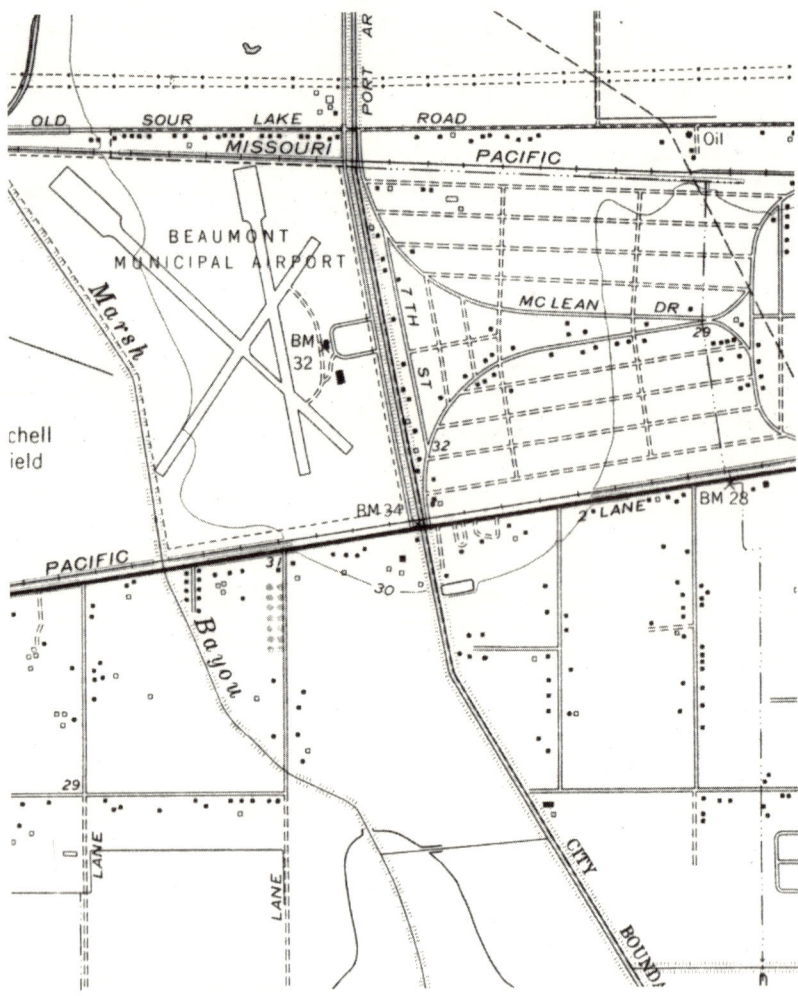

By 1960, urban development was encroaching on Beaumont Municipal Airport from the east. Expansion was limited by the railroads immediately north and south of the field, by the Willow Marsh Bayou to the west, and by the Port Arthur Fresh Water Canal to the east (source: United States Geological Survey map).

# 10

# Beaumont, Texas

Bordering southwestern Louisiana, the towns of Beaumont, Port Arthur, and Orange, Texas are often called the "Golden Triangle" because of the abundance of oil that brought them wealth early in this century.* By 1942, all three cities had deep-water ports and oil refineries, with the Neches River providing easy access for tankers and other ocean shipping via Sabine Pass to the Gulf of Mexico. Located thirty air-miles southeast of Beaumont, the mouth of Sabine Pass was a powerful magnet for German U-boats determined to blast and burn the precious cargo of the oil tankers.

The Beaumont coastal patrol was based at the Beaumont Municipal Airport, which had been built in 1932 and consisted of a rather modern-looking terminal building and three shell-surfaced runways, one hundred feet wide and between twenty-five hundred and thirty-five hundred feet long. The airport was located ten miles west of town along U.S. Route 90. The first floor of the terminal housed the airport office, a canteen, and a Civil Aeronautics Administration office. The various coastal patrol offices were on the second floor. A large all-metal hangar and a former Civilian Conservation Corps dormitory used as a recreation building were nearby. Except for a CPTP school operated by Lamar College, the coastal patrol had exclusive use of the field.

---

*Beaumont might have stayed a little farm town if it hadn't been for the gusher that blew in on January 10, 1901, at Spindletop, a salt-dome hill south of town. Suddenly the richest oil field in America, it ignited a world-wide petrochemical industry. Four hundred oil companies sprang up in the next two years, including the forerunners of Texaco, Gulf, Mobil, and Exxon.

## George E. Haddaway

*At thirty-three years of age, base commander George E. Haddaway had already lived a colorful life. As a youngster he had sat on the laps of Royal Canadian Air Force men training near Fort Worth during World War I, had taken his first airplane ride at age twelve in a Curtiss JN-4 Jenny owned by a next-door neighbor, and had joined a boy scout troop that helped moor dirigibles at the helium plant in Fort Worth. During his University of Texas days, Haddaway took flying lessons and spent summers working as a seaman. After his graduation, he did a full-time stint in the U.S. Merchant Marine before returning to Texas where he and a partner founded a monthly magazine called* Southwest Aviation. *A self-confessed "wild-eyed aviation enthusiast," he never lost that enthusiasm:*

> Gill Robb Wilson was a fraternity brother of mine, not that that made any difference, but he was a spiritually motivating man. He had been a pilot in the first World War and was one of those few who didn't agree with Lindbergh's advice to stay out of Europe's messes. At the National Aeronautical Association convention in Louisville, Kentucky in 1941, Gill told me about New Jersey's Civil Air Defense operation.... "We had nothing," he said, "no air power, no planning." Remember, President Coolidge later court-martialed Billy Mitchell who had called on the president with three or four of his fellow officers in the Air Corps. They desperately needed new airplanes. Mr. Coolidge sat there with that deadpan expression and said, "Well, men, why don't we buy one airplane and let all the boys fly it."

When the United States entered the war, Haddaway helped to persuade members of the Texas Private Flyers Association to join the CAP. The Wing-Over Club of Beaumont joined as a unit and began to fly patrols over the Gulf in February 1942. Haddaway took part in these early patrols and later became the Beaumont base commander. In September 1942, he brought his wife and infant child down from Dallas and moved into Gallinipper Gables,* "a tourist court with lots of mosquitoes":

> My main function at the base was keeping things going. I checked on patrol reporting procedures, the condition of our equipment, and handled everyone's complaints and suggestions. I knew my men were accomplished pilots and observers, but every now and then I'd ride in the back seat just to let them know I was taking some risks, too. I know all about the story that engines always ran rough once you got

---

\* The *American Heritage Dictionary* defines a "gallinipper" [origin unknown] as "a large mosquito or similar insect capable of inflicting a painful bite." Though proof is lacking, Texas legend insists that enough gallinippers could lift a human victim and carry him away to be devoured later!

forty or fifty miles out over the water. But, you know, I don't believe it. Most of my men were ... cool people. Usually those kind of guys came up the hard way. I found out that the best pilots and the best men I had down there were not millionaires. In fact, the millionaires didn't stay long. The best men I had were guys who came up the hard way and had worked all their lives.

Beaumont Base Commander George E. Haddaway before his promotion to Major. Whenever something was needed at the base, his men felt he'd accomplish miracles to get it (Hopper collection).

[If our operation seemed pretty loose] ... you have to put it in the context of the time.... We couldn't fight our way out of a wet paper sack. I couldn't get guns to train my men in the local squadron. We used wooden guns. We had a hell of a time with paperwork we had to fill out. We had a hell of a time with no pay, they were always late in their pay, and most of my people had to live on their eight-dollars a day allowance.... But as tough as things were, and as difficult as our operations were, and as bad as our airplanes and our engines and our sorry radio communications were, we still had a tremendous effect on submarines along our coastal waters.... So nobody is ever going to take that away from us.

## Kenneth J. Carter

*Air Medal winner Kenneth J. Carter grew up in the Dallas area, learned to fly at Hudson Airport a few miles northeast of Garland, Texas. He once owned a 70 hp Rearwin monoplane, in which he says he nearly killed himself, then bought another with a 90 hp engine, which "was better, but not much":*

I heard about the coastal patrol from the various Civil Air Patrol members who hung out at Hudson Airport, one of them being George Haddaway, a good friend of mine and later our base commander. I had a private pilot's license, but I didn't go to Beaumont to fly so much as to work around the hangar as a mechanic. I knew Bill Van Cleave, assistant engineering officer, and worked with him at first. He was a *real* old-timer, a contemporary of the Wright Brothers! But then I got into flying and enjoyed that very much.

I lived at the Beaumont Hotel and think I paid a dollar a night. The whole town of Beaumont turned out to help us. Some of the girls organized a kind of shuttle service to the airport. We'd go out front at 4:30 a.m. and there'd be someone in a station wagon waiting to take us out for the dawn patrol. For its day, Beaumont Municipal was a pretty good field. Some commercial DC-3s came in now and then but most of the time we had things entirely to ourselves. The field was located at "China," a tiny village on U.S. Route 90 right in the middle of some extensive "rice farms." Some of our best pilots had been in that business, planting and fertilizing rice paddies from the air. If they made a forced landing from such a low altitude, they tried to come down on the levies separating the paddies, ten or twelve feet across and barely wide enough for their landing gears. They had great incentive to be good pilots — if they smashed-up their plane, they lost their job.

I logged about three hundred and fifty hours of over-water patrol in single-engine planes and probably flew every plane we had, including our Sikorsky amphibian. In fact, three other guys and I went to Florida to fly it to Texas. There was Jimmy Marshall and "Dub" Jackson, but I can't remember the third. A lot of different fellows flew as my observer. Some were pilots while others weren't. Some had private licenses, some had only their student permits. I didn't care just as long as they had good eyesight and could use a radio. I believe I had a couple of forced landings. I ran out of gas once due to a faulty reading on a broken gas gauge. On another occasion an exhaust stack on a Waco came loose from the exhaust collector ring. It made the damndest noise I ever heard, then when I began to smell exhaust fumes, I was afraid we might catch fire so I set her down. Both times I landed on a beach, easy enough if you stay close to the waterline, where the sand is wet and hard.

During my time at the base I got to know a Coast Guard captain named Smith, and out of gratitude for the good work we did in keeping the subs at bay, he told several of us that when the time came to close the base, if we wanted to try it, he could get us a special deal with the Army Transportation Corps. George Haddaway knew Smith, and I understood that it was he who made the arrangements that sent Don Luce and I to study celestial navigation and other marine subjects at an Air Transport Command school in New Orleans. In six weeks, we were commissioned second lieutenants and assigned to sea-going tugboats operated by the Army Transportation Corps. I'd never even been aboard a boat before, let alone the captain of one, so I have no idea why the Army would have wanted me for this.

I took my tug down through the Panama Canal, where we broke a rudder, and then had to go up to San Francisco for repairs. During the six or seven weeks we were there I visited some of my buddies from Beaumont who in the meanwhile had been transferred to TTU #15 at San Jose. I remember Del Gallier and Charlie Kehoe, two of our better pilots, and how surprised they were to see me. With the repairs done, I took our 2,000 hp tug to Australia, then later up into the Pacific islands where we mostly hauled fresh water barges.

Don F. Luce of Wichita, Kansas was one of several pilots assigned to the Army Transportation Corps after they left the coastal patrol base at Beaumont — presumably because they understood the principles of navigation (courtesy Ruth Coffee Luce).

Meanwhile, back home, George Haddaway had learned that my mother had died, and wanted to let me know personally. When George learned that his old buddy Jimmy Doolittle happened to be in town, I understand that George took Jimmy downtown to the Baker Hotel and after a few drinks got him to agree to find me. I can't tell you how, but one afternoon soon thereafter when I pulled my tug up to a ravaged Manila dock there was an MP standing there. "I'm looking for Captain

Carter," he yelled, and when I replied, "You're looking at him," he said, "You've got a phone call." It was George to tell me that my mother had passed away. He was a very capable, very intelligent commander. I used to kid with him that if he wasn't such a character he could have been governor of the state.

After I was discharged and came home, I got into the brass gift business with my five brothers, all five of whom had been in service, too, and we ran it into a pretty good-sized company. Later we got into school furniture as well. I haven't been back to Beaumont since the base closed, and haven't kept track of many of the coastal patrol vets, either. Don Luce and I always remained good friends but he's dead now. "Sly" Cole was an engineer with Pure Oil who worked around the hangar, and was just a fine young man, but he's also lost now. There aren't that many of us left.

## Ruth M. Coffee

*Twelve-year-old Ruth M. Coffee (now Ruth Luce) and her nine-year-old sister Ann joined their mother and father (Ruth S. and Wesley W. Coffee) shortly after they left Wichita Falls, Texas in 1942 to serve in Beaumont, her father as a flight observer, her mother as radio and plotting board operator. When the little girls weren't in school or at home studying they were at the base. The pretty little twelve-year-old was nicknamed "Little Ruth" to distinguish her from her mother, who was better known as "Big Ruth":*

In the 1920s, dad had been a barnstormer in the Chicago area. He told lots of stories about how he and mom and another man took turns working as a team. One flew, one did wing-walking acts, and the third would stay on the ground to pass the hat for donations. It wasn't any way to make money. At one show, dad said they collected only fifty cents. After dad and mom were married, they gave it up. Dad was working for an oil company in Wichita Falls when war came. He was too old to be drafted, and since he'd been a flyer, he decided that joining the CAP would be his contribution to the war effort.

They left Ann and me behind, with a lady to take care of us, until they got an idea of what kind of housing was available in Beaumont. All the shipyards were booming and people were coming in from everywhere to work there. I can't tell you much about the base, but I do remember being alone a lot. Dad started as a guard because as a barnstormer he hadn't bothered with things like licenses and logbooks. Once they got his background straightened out, and he took some tests, they let him fly as an observer. Mom was usually gone all day, too, so I worked hard at school, and actually graduated from high school at age fifteen.

Maybe I took after mom, a woman who'd been far ahead of her time. Not only had she been a barnstormer, a homemaker, and a patriot, but after the war she got her master of arts and doctorate degrees and taught Texas history and government.

While I was in Beaumont, I met Donald Luce, who at age seventeen was the youngest pilot at the base. He couldn't have paid any attention to me then, because I was too young. But our paths were to cross again a couple of years later. When the base closed down, daddy moved to Dallas where he worked for Jimmy Marshall — another Beaumont base member — who ran Marshall Field. But that didn't take, so he came back to Beaumont to run an industrial laundry for Magnolia Refinery, a job he never especially liked. Later on he became a juvenile officer for Jefferson County — something he really enjoyed.

Ruth Coffee, age thirteen, and her sister, Ann, age ten. Because both of their parents worked at the base they spent lots of time alone at home. Years later, Ruth Coffee married pilot Don Luce who hadn't even noticed her when she was still a child at the base (courtesy Ruth Coffee Luce).

Meanwhile, I went up to Dallas to work for George Haddaway, my first job ever. Don and I started dating up there. One day he took me for an airplane ride but the weather turned bad and we had to land and spend the night at Waxahachie. When dad found out he scolded Don pretty hotly. Don just told him, "Now you be careful what you say. I might marry this girl and then I'd be your son-in-law." Dad was speechless. I think he thought well enough of Don as a kind of friend, but never dreamed of having such a brash young man as a part of the family. Don and I were married just before I turned nineteen.

While Don was in the coastal patrol, he lived at the Hotel Beaumont, and I know he won the Air Medal. From there, he served in the Army Transportation Corps as captain of an Army tug boat in the South Pacific. He and Tom Yost first were sent to New Orleans for several weeks to learn to run a tug and navigate by the stars. He was commissioned a second lieutenant and sent to Seattle, taking over a ship's crew of sixty men mainly because he arrived two days before some Officer Candidate School graduate. He hadn't had a day of actual military training, and was the youngest tug skipper the Army had. He landed in New Guinea once and ended up crossing the Owen Stanley Range* on foot. He called that the greatest challenge he'd ever faced. After Don was discharged in 1945, he got back into military aviation. We moved twenty-five times in twenty-five years and raised three children. After the military, Don spent twenty more years in private industry. Mother and dad have died, and I am now the grand matriarch of my family.

## G. Thomas Yost

*G. Thomas Yost was born and raised and got his private pilot's license in the Texas Panhandle. While visiting his grandparents who lived in Beaumont, he heard of the coastal patrol and wasted no time signing up:*

I was nineteen and the new kid on the block, so when I first got there I pulled guard duty for a while until being placed in charge of fueling the planes. After a time, they let me fly as an observer, and that was great. It's no fun being a pilot and not flying. I wasn't there long, and didn't experience any forced landings or that sort of thing. I did persuade one of my pilots to land on the beach near my grandparent's waterfront home so I could go in and say hello. I think I did that a couple of times and once even landed on the two-lane road paralleling the beach. Not all "forced landings" were really forced, you see! I feel fortunate to have had the opportunity to work with those men. Most had been successful businessmen, well into their forties and fifties, and certainly didn't have to do what they were doing.

---

* New Guinea's Owen Stanley Range rises to more than 13,000 feet. Early in the war, a narrow foot trail across the mountains between Allied-held Port Moresby on the south and Japanese-held ports on the north — impassable even to pack mules — was the scene of heavy ground fighting and high casualties. Japanese hopes of using New Guinea as a springboard to invade Australia ended there.

Once a barnstorming wing-walker, beautiful Ruth S. Coffee ran the plotting board at Beaumont and later earned a Ph.D. degree in history (courtesy Ruth Coffee Luce).

## Del Gallier

*Del Gallier was one of the few base pilots native to Beaumont. He started flying in the mid-1930s and soon was co-owner of a sporty Fairchild 22. Later he owned a Waco ZKS-7, which he took with him into the coastal patrol. When a major storm threatened the base, many planes were flown to Randolph Field in San Antonio as a precaution. But the storm path veered and destroyed or badly damaged several of them anyway. Though his Waco was lost, Gallier's insurance settlement let him buy another plane and remain at Beaumont. In 1983, he told Colonel Lester E. Hopper that what he didn't know was that lady luck wasn't through with him yet:*

> I was going on a mission to pick up an airplane in Fort Worth and hitched a ride with John Henry Dean and Dean [Robert D.] Ward. The weather was bad when we left Beaumont, and about half way there, John Henry Dean thought he'd better drop down and check the reading on a water tower to see where we were. Afterwards, he made a too-steep climbing turn, and with the weight of the three of us plus our luggage, the plane spun out over the top, and we headed straight down under full power from about four hundred feet. He got out of the spin just in time to level off and crash through a bunch of trees. Dean and Ward were both killed instantly, but I was in the back seat and suffered only bruises and a broken ankle that put me

into the hospital for a week. I couldn't fly with that ankle, and since the base was looking for an engineering officer, that became my assignment.... I was pretty well hung with that job because no one else wanted it. But I did make some missions after my leg got to where I could fly again.

My Waco was a powerful machine with a lot of lift and a short take-off run. It would almost fly up out of a well. Once we had a Stinson Voyager go down in a pasture near Cameron, Texas. A couple of pretty good-sized men with all their gear landed there with engine trouble. The pasture was maybe a thousand feet one way and fifteen-hundred the other. Their Voyager barely made it in. With J. K. West for company, I flew my Waco over to pick them up. After we landed, and I told them I'd take everybody back to the base, they said, "Man, we can't get out of this short field with all this weight!" I assured them we could. They thought I was going to go out the long way. There were some trees over on the short side, but I knew I could get out in half the distance, so I just revved her up and turned loose the brakes and headed out the short way. These guys would've jumped out if they could've got the door open! They'd evidently never been in a plane with so much power. I ran right to the trees and then just pulled it up and over as easy as could be.

Living conditions at the base were pretty good. We had everything we needed, almost. What we didn't have, well, we had people there who could get it for us. Major Haddaway was very good at getting us practically anything. We had a canteen and some good cooks and they always had three good meals a day for us. You'd go in, order what you wanted, and then pay for it, just like a regular cafe. There wasn't much in the way of recreation except for dominoes and cards. Some of the younger guys might play softball, but not us older fellows. There was a certain amount of drilling each month. I don't remember for how many hours, but everybody was supposed to do it, and most did. But nobody liked to wear those red epaulets. They were pretty conspicuous, you know. Any place you used to go in public, they stood out like a sore thumb, but we had to wear them.

When the Beaumont base closed down, Del Gallier was reassigned to TTU #15 based at San Jose, California, fifty miles south of San Francisco. He flew searchlight missions at night and simulated strafing runs during the day around San Francisco's wharves and bridges, and at the Mare Island ammunition dump. The simulated strafing runs were stopped when someone realized that even a small aircraft such as a Waco or a Stinson crashing into a stockpile of explosives might just blow up the whole city. In 1983, Del Gallier shared with Colonel Hopper some of the techniques of towing targets:

We had a pretty good-sized winch put behind the pilot's seat. You'd have to take the back seat out. The winch drum was about eighteen inches wide, eighteen inches in diameter, and carried about three thousand feet of quarter-inch steel cable. You had a trap door cut in the floor right behind the winch that was big enough to get your target out. The target measured twenty-four inches by ten feet. The bridle was made out of pipe that would fold up into halves to make a small package. It would be folded and rolled up so you had a small enough package to get out through the trap door. And your cable was coming off the winch going down to a pulley below the belly of the airplane. It'd come back in and you'd hook your target on it and drop it out. Immediately it would open up and start stringing out behind you. The winch had brakes so that you could let out whatever length needed.

Really, it was pretty safe. We never had anybody shot down. Had a lot of them scared. Had some cable shot off about half way between the target and the airplane. There's a gunnery officer that stands with each gun, and there's a post stop on the guns that only allows them to swing so far. The gunnery officer doesn't give the "commence firing" order until the airplane is beyond that stop, so there's no chance of hitting the plane. We'd fly over several different gun positions, in radio contact with them, and they'd all be firing different-colored bullets. After a number of passes, they'd tell us where to drop the targets for their easy retrieval.

We'd have a "fish" that you'd drop on the cable. It had a cup-shaped end on it that the airstream would catch and blow back along the cable to the target, where it would trip a release, and the target would fall straight down. If you dropped this fish on your cable right over where you were supposed to drop the target, it would come down within a hundred feet of where they wanted. They would examine the target and see who had been hitting it by the color markings. Then we would wind the cable back in to where we could put a new target on it. We carried a whole big box full of targets with us. You might put on a half dozen targets on one mission before you'd land for refueling and more targets. We might spend two or three days with one outfit, and wouldn't return to our San Jose base until we got through with them.

We also had some other missions out there, like hauling mail and freight for the Fourth Air Force. We'd go into a big bomber base in Nevada, flying across the Sierra Nevada Mountains and that deep snow rather than to go around by Reno and come back up through the valleys. We'd cross some ten-thousand foot high mountains on some runs.

## Willis F. Rose, Jr.

*Willis F. Rose, Jr., a nineteen-year-old from Fort Smith, Arkansas, was in the ROTC at the University of Arkansas when the war began. Angry after failing a pre-induction physical because of an alleged heart murmur, he joined the CAP unit at Fort Smith vowing to learn to fly. When one of his lieutenants told him of the possibility of active service at Beaumont, and asked if he'd like to go, he said, "Yes, sir!":*

Because of my ROTC background, I guess, I was made sergeant of the guard as soon as I arrived. That was on April 11, 1943, nearly a year after the base was activated. I had some kind of allowance for uniforms, just khaki stuff with CAP insignia added. I took a forty-five caliber Colt automatic with pearl handles, the prettiest thing you ever saw. We didn't wear any mosquito netting, although the bugs were a definite nuisance, but relied instead on insect repellent — which I think the bugs found very tasty! I came down with a case of shingles while there and at first didn't even know what they were, what with all the mosquito bites.

Willis F. Rose, Jr. as an ROTC cadet at the University of Arkansas. Because of that background, he was placed in charge of the base guards (courtesy Willis F. Rose, Jr.).

I lived in the Beaumont Hotel with some other coastal patrol people and several soldiers assigned to the base. We got a special rate. It wasn't much but it helped. The soldiers had vehicles, and I'd usually ride out to the base with one of them. I only served there for a few months but I experienced the June 14-15, 1943 race riot, and it was really scary. I had to secure the base and protect both our property and our colored employees. They weren't coastal patrol members, but people like cooks, janitors, and maids. I remember driving a Jeep around Beaumont at this time, making sure that my Colt was loaded and handy. All of us armed guards were made deputy sheriffs and authorized to make arrests.

As the sergeant of the guard, my hours were rather irregular. Guards were posted at the front gate, the terminal building, the armament shack where the bombs were stored, and down in the hangars. We were on duty twenty-four hours a day, in three shifts, and I had to come around at all hours to make sure there was no sleeping on the job. Many guards were older guys, way up in their forties and fifties, and not above taking a snooze. We fired the undependable ones. My boss was airdrome officer Charles DiDio, the owner and operator of the beauty salon, "House of Charles."

In the daytime, I often sat in on the classes given at the base, such as radio communications and semaphore signaling. I had a chance to go out on patrols several times, "sandbagging" behind the co-pilots. I was surprised at how low we flew, and that was a little scary. The pilot I went out with was a real young fellow whose dad was also a pilot at the base. For recreation I often went down to Port Arthur's "Pleasure Pier." Famous band leader Harry James — Betty Grable's husband — was a Beaumont native and played there often. I liked to dance and I never found any shortage of girls. As much as I appreciated serving with the CAP, I still wanted to be in the military, so I went back to Little Rock, to the Marine recruiting office. This time I passed my physical without a problem. I spent two years as an ordnance man in the Ninth Marine Air Wing at Cherry Point and at Camp LeJeune.

## Edgar E. Duncan

*Edgar E. Duncan was a twenty-four year old grocer from Floydada, Texas when he moved to Beaumont to join the coastal patrol. He served first as a guard at the front gate of the base, then as a service technician, and recalls the Beaumont race riot\* most vividly:*

They assigned me the job of going into Beaumont to pick up our colored cooks and driving them out to the base. I wore a loaded Colt forty-five strapped to my waist and went to the door of their houses to

---

\* Two black men and one white man were killed; hundreds of people, mostly black (among them 52 black draftees waiting at the bus station) were injured, and much property belonging to black citizens was destroyed. By comparison, the June 20-21, 1943 Detroit riot resulted in 25 black deaths, 9 white deaths, and 700 injuries; the August 1-2, 1943 Harlem riot resulted in 5 deaths, 367 injuries, and $5 million in property damages.

escort them to our car. I had to do the same thing when I took them home again in the evening. I wasn't particularly scared, but it was a touchy time. Needless to say I was glad when that was all over. Ordinarily I spent most of my time refueling the planes after they returned from patrol. It was important that they be ready to fly at a moment's notice, and gassing them up immediately was a good way not to forget that crucial step. But then I was drafted and ended up in the 60th Regiment of the Ninth Infantry Division in Europe. After an injury, I spent nearly a year in an army hospital before being discharged.

The cooks and janitorial staff supervised by Mabel Duncan, standing at far left. Her husband, Edgar E. Duncan, kneels at the far right. During the Beaumont race riot, these employees were escorted to and from work by base security guards (courtesy Edgar E. Duncan).

## Paul J. Alford, Jr.

*A father-son team at Beaumont was Paul J. Alford, Sr., a pilot, and his son, Paul J. Alford, Jr., a part-time aircraft mechanic, who talks of those days and his father:*

Dad had lost two fingers and part of his right hand in a hunting accident, but it never impeded his flying. He had been born in 1900, so by the time the coastal patrol began he was a highly experienced pilot. A doctor friend of his had a Fairchild 24 and when the doctor learned that the government would pay him so much for leasing it to the CAP, he agreed to do so, on the condition that only my dad and another fellow — whose name I forget — be allowed to fly it. So we flew down to Beaumont in the Fairchild and took a room together in a boarding house.

Dad flew patrol missions at all different hours of the day while I attended Lamar State College of Technology (now Lamar University) and worked on a part-time basis, without pay, as a sort of apprentice engine mechanic. We were only there four months, but in that time I earned my "E" license at the college, and did a lot of minor maintenance work on the planes at the base, mostly the Fairchild, as a flight line mechanic. Despite different schedules I saw a lot of dad and even flew a couple of "sandbag" missions with him — ten miles straight out, then up the coast and back. When he was out flying the dawn patrol or at other times, his safety never worried me. Kids don't think about things like that. I knew he'd be okay. My mother and my two younger brothers remained in Houston maintaining our family home.

Dad taught me to fly while we were in Beaumont, and I'd just soloed when we both left the coastal patrol and went to Curtis Field, the Air Corps training base near Brady, Texas. We were sworn into the Air Corps reserve, but reassigned as civilians, dad as an instructor on PT-13s, me as a flight line mechanic. I earned my "A" there. In early 1945, dad went back to Houston to resume work in the automobile dealership he'd been a part of before the war. I went into the Navy for two years, assigned to the Naval Air Training Command at Jacksonville Naval Air Station and later at the Corpus Christi Naval Air Station After returning home when the war ended, I earned an instrument and commercial pilot's license and continued sports flying until about two years ago. I'm still current as an A&E mechanic.

\* \* \*

Martin and Osa Johnson, the famous African explorers, were among the various celebrities who leased or sold their aircraft to the coastal patrol. One of their two zebra-striped Sikorsky S-39 amphibians ("Osa's Ark") was sold to the Brownsville, Texas base, the other ("The Spirit of Africa") to the Beaumont base. A letter from Osa Johnson to the Beaumont base commander George Haddaway began, "I hear that you are flying our old amphibian ship and that you are doing grand work on the Gulf coast. Nothing could cheer me more." Her letter provides an interesting early history of the plane:

> And I am very happy to hear again of the good plane that is so bound up in many of our adventures for the last 10 years. Sooner or later I knew that I would hear of it in the war, for it has a fighting destiny. It has flown us for at least 60,000 miles over the jungles and that should

tell you that it has a stout heart. We never even had the spurt of a motor with that ship. Both these ships, "Osa's Ark, and "The Spirit of Africa," took us from one end of Africa to the other, and from the cockpit we photographed almost every animal on the continent, and saw a large percentage of the native tribes.

They carried us up over Mt. Kenya and Mt. Kilamanjaro, Africa's highest mountains, so that we could make their portraits for the first time, and were the first planes to land on many a spot out there, including the now strategic Lake Rudolph, and got us out of many a tight spot which you can read about in the book we dedicated to them, entitled, "Over African Jungles," or see in our films, "Baboona," or "I Married Adventure." Both ships brought us happiness and success and I hope that you have every good luck.

\* \* \*

As it happened, on Armistice Day, 1942, "The Spirit of Africa" had the ultimate in bad luck, as did two downed Beaumont flyers whom the Sikorsky's crew went out to try and rescue. Del Gallier, the base engineering officer, gave this account:

On his first day at the base, James C. Taylor went on patrol with Alfred H. Koym, and we think the crankshaft on his Ranger engine probably broke, and the plane went down. Both men got out of the plane all right, and their companion plane called in their position. Visibility was not real bad, but it was windy and stormy and the waves were probably 12 to 14 feet high. James K. West and Robert F. ("Wimpy") Neel went out in the Sikorsky to get them. The landing tore the pontoon off a wing, and that wing went into the water. A Coast Guard boat picked up West and Neel, then Taylor and Koym, who by then had both drifted quite a distance away. Taylor was already dead of exposure — the men had been in the cold water for around four hours — and Koym died before they got back to land. The Coast guard boat towed the Sikorsky a short distance, but when it began to sink they had to cut it loose and watch it go down. That was the end of "The Spirit of Africa."

\* \* \*

Besides West and Neel, the Beaumont base contributed five other members to the Duck Club: captains Charles F. Kehoe, II and Sumner C. Evans; Lts. Andrew J. McCauley and T. V. Conner, Jr.; and Flight Observer J. H. Winfield, Jr. — Evans and Winfield drifted seven long hours in darkness before they were rescued. A tune written by Beaumont pilot Elbert C. Isom of Garden City, New York, may have captured the feelings of many ship captains and crews:

*And the wolf pack hovers nigh*
*When the skipper scans the ocean*
*With a grim and worried eye,*
*Then a distant sound grows louder*
*And brings comfort to his soul,*
*For he knows his ship is covered*
*By the Civil Air Patrol.*

The originial caption for this photograph describes the Fleetwing Seabird as "lost at sea in a vain attempt to save two downed flyers." Standing in front are service technicians Claud W. Moody and James W. Marshall, Jr. The others are unidentified (Hopper collection).

## John G. Atherton

*John G. Atherton was only sixteen when he served as a guard at Beaumont during the summer of 1942. He had joined the Civil Air Patrol in his home town of Emporia, Kansas shortly after Pearl Harbor, and had been training for six months when a chance for active duty arose:*

Four of us went down to the Gulf together: Harold M. Priest was a professor of English at what was then the Kansas State Teacher's College and is now the Emporia State University; George H. Phillips was also a faculty member; and Harold C. Davis was a radio mechanic. By my lights, they were "old" — Priest in his early 40s, Phillips in his late

30s, and Davis in his late 20s. The professors were going down to be guards like myself. For a summer job, the pay was pretty good — five dollars a day — and for a youngster like me, that was real good! We went down in Davis's 1941 five-passenger Chevy Coupe with all our luggage and three shotguns.

When we got there we were assigned to live in the renovated hayloft of an old barn within a short walk of the base. It wasn't that bad at all. We had the use of a new "two-stooler" outhouse, and bathed and washed our clothes in a canal that ran between the barn and the base. We ate all our meals at the base canteen. When we arrived, the base had only just been made operational, and things weren't too well organized, but the patrols were going out, and that's what counted. After a couple of days of guard duty, they pulled me off that to help out on the line servicing the planes — gassing them, checking the oil, wiping them down, and such. They taxied next to the pumps in our fuel pits, because we had no fuel truck. We did, however, have a great old fire truck, a 1911 America La France, with its steering wheel on the right, and its several gear shifts mounted on the running board. I recently saw one exactly like it at an antique show.

We were all caught up in a hurricane once, and spent much of a day knee-deep in water trying to hold down the planes left on the field. Though most were tied down, several were badly damaged when they were flipped over on their backs. One of the problems was a lack of tie-down rings. We were just in the process of installing more when the storm came. I stuck around the base most of the time, and only went into Beaumont once that summer. I hitched a ride with a civilian who had been on the base and he needed to stop at his home to pick up something before going on downtown. He took me inside where I met his wife and two young daughters. One was fifteen and very comely. I think I went to a movie. I don't really remember, but I was in uniform I know. Being in Beaumont was the first time I'd ever been in the south, but I recall no "culture shock" excepting for overhearing one of our own men tell a story of striking a Negro woman who'd brushed against his wife in a store or something. I was appalled. We were pretty peacefully integrated up in Emporia.

I had several chances to fly as an observer, but before I did I had to take a course in the use of radios and get an Federal Communications Commission radio license. My first time up was in an old Fairchild 24, which had glass fuel gauges mounted under the wing tanks like little laboratory test tubes. Well out in the Gulf, I saw that both gauges were showing empty. I knew that couldn't be right because I had personally topped-off the tanks myself just before take-off, and none had been seen escaping. Nevertheless, the pilot prudently turned for base, where we landed with the expected level of fuel remaining.

Come the end of summer, all four of us from Emporia returned there — the two professors to resume teaching at the college, Davis to resume work in a radio shop, and myself to finish high school. After graduation in 1944, I got into a West Point preparatory school, but as my appointment was delayed, I enlisted in the Army. Since I intended to be a career officer, I volunteered for the infantry, thinking it would be the fastest way to the top. Because of an accident that caused a partial loss of hearing I did not get overseas, but in 1946 was accepted into West Point. Later I went to the University of Kansas to get my law degree and still practice here in Emporia. Sorry to say, all three of my local coastal patrol colleagues are dead. But we had a lot of fun down there in Beaumont, and we all thought it was a good experience.

## Oscar Oliver Cooke

*Oscar Oliver Cooke was born in 1901 in Gueda Springs, Kansas and had learned to fly by the time he was sixteen. After taking classes at a business school in Emporia, Kansas, he bought a plane and when he wasn't working on his farm barnstormed around the state in it. He became a traveling salesman for Allis Chalmers, dropping in on prospective buyers in several states by air, and helping to develop many air strips in Missouri, Kansas, Nebraska, and Montana. Oscar O. Cooke died in 1995, but his widow Marcella Reilly Cooke, and a daughter, Macie Cooke Limpp, recall stories he told about his coastal patrol days. His daughter writes:*

My dad was too old to be drafted in World War II, so he volunteered as a pilot for the CAP. My mom says he always felt that the town of Beaumont and the people of Texas had been very good to all the men and women at the base. He made some nice life-long friendships, and kept in touch with people from his coastal patrol days for well over thirty years. When I was a young child, I remember him telling stories about flying anti-submarine patrol over the Gulf of Mexico and saying that if you had engine trouble that was the end of you. The sharks would get you before you could inflate and get into your life rafts. He told me of one special friend of his who went down, and his body was later found on shore. Many thought dolphins had rolled him up on the beach.

When the coastal patrol ended, he returned to Omaha but remained active with the local CAP squadron. I remember his describing the blackouts, and his flying a plane with a spotlight on it. He'd shine it on houses with a light on so the wardens would know who to get after. He said it got a little nerve-wracking, because he knew his wasn't the only plane flying around up there in the dark. My mom actually met dad in the Omaha Athletic Club, where he was visiting Jack Algar, the manager. He later told her that when she came in, he told Jack, "now *there's* a real All-American girl!" In 1958 he purchased the CX Ranch at Decker, Montana and he and mom moved to "Big Sky Country." His great interest was turn-of-the-century farm machinery, and his "Oscar's Dreamland, Yesteryear Museum" in Billings gets throngs of visitors annually.

Oscar O. Cooke of Billings, Montana once flew this Tri-Motor Stinson on a short check ride over Roanoke, Virginia. The control wheel was nearly as large as an automobile's (courtesy Macie Cooke Limpp).

**Henry L. Mayer**

*Henry L. Mayer was a twenty-three-year-old pharmaceuticals salesman from Opelousas, Louisiana when he joined the Beaumont base, bringing with him his wife and year-old son. His widow recalls their sojourn in Beaumont and in Gallinipper Gables trailer court as a wonderful experience, but one that was not without its budgetary problems:*

I'd been reared in New Orleans and Henry had been educated there before we moved to Opelousas. When the war came, he joined the CAP and learned to fly, and then we and our baby boy went over to Beaumont to live in a trailer court. Other men and their wives lived there as well. During the day, we mostly looked after our children and visited back and forth with each other. Some local ladies took us into town in a station wagon to shop for groceries and whatever we needed. It was very nice except for the mosquitoes and the lack of timely paychecks. They were nearly always late, and if it weren't for my parents, who helped out as much as they could, and the kindness of a humane grocer who carried us all on credit, we'd have been in real trouble.

When the Beaumont base closed, my husband was recruited by the Air Corps to give primary instruction at its base in LaFayette, only twenty miles south of our home in Opelousas. When that base closed after about a year, he tried to enlist in the Air Corps but couldn't meet the physical requirements. So Henry ended up in the Navy as a quartermaster aboard a mine sweeper, serving until 1946. For a while following the war we managed on his somewhat limited income. He was a most old-fashioned man who believed that a woman's place was in the home so I never sought work outside. After he went into investments and banking he became quite successful. We'd been married over fifty-five years when he died.

## Joe N. Summers

*Joe N. Summers was born and raised in Mission, Texas, a small town in the lower Rio Grande valley. He had joined the local CAP group, taken the various courses offered, and had earned his private pilot's license by the time he was seventeen. He volunteered for active duty as soon as he graduated from high school:*

They didn't have any openings for me at Brownsville, so I ended up at Beaumont as a guard. Though I was a pilot, I didn't have enough experience to be rated a pilot, and right then they didn't need any more full-time observers, either. At first I lived in the Beaumont Hotel but it was way too expensive so I quickly switched to the YMCA, four or five blocks away. When it wasn't rainy, and the roads weren't wet — which was seldom — I rode my motorcycle to the field. Otherwise I walked to the hotel and got a ride with the others who lived there. I flew a number of times as a fill-in flight observer. To do so, you didn't need any special training, just a good set of eyeballs! I mostly flew in Stinson Voyagers, and once in a Stinson Reliant SM-8

The airfield was way out in piney woods country, and guard duty was very routine. I was issued a forty-five automatic, and kept it loaded, but the only thing I ever shot at were some hoot-owls. As I recall, guard duty consisted of spending a couple of nights at the ammo dump, then a couple of nights up at the hangars and administration building, then back to the ammo dump. As in the Army, we challenged anyone we didn't know right away, shouting "Halt! Who goes there? Advance and be recognized," and all that stuff. On our off-duty time, we chased the girls. When you're young and your hormones are working right, what else is there? I think Beaumont maybe had about forty thousand people before the war and they were very nice to servicemen and servicewomen. I think they knew what the coastal patrol was doing.

1st Lt. John Henry Dean of Fort Worth, Texas was killed November 16, 1942 in a crash during a plane-ferrying mission. 1st Lt. Robert D. Ward was also killed (courtesy Edgar E. Duncan).

After three months, the draft began to get after me. I had a chance to become an Air Corps service pilot, but I wanted to fly fighter planes, so I opted for the Cadets. But part way through the program, I was caught up in a general reduction — about 35,000 Cadets were washed out because they just had too many — and I wound up back in radio school. After that I served with a Ferry Command unit until being transferred to the North African division of the Air Transport Command, shuttling back and forth from Casablanca, Morocco to Karachi, India, a two-day trip. After the war, I ran a machine shop, and owned a Cessna 170 tail-dragger for almost twenty-five wonderful years.

## John H. Walker

*John H. Walker was born and raised in Beaumont and learned to fly in the mid-1930s on the early Taylorcraft, a Rearwin Speedster, and an old Douglas. The Douglas, a pusher design, had an extremely low landing speed. "If you* landed against a ten or fifteen mile an hour breeze," says Walker, "you could just about set down going backwards." For a while before the war, he owned a Hispano-Suisa powered Waco, but demolished it flying through a power line while landing at Center, Texas:

The Waco had its own judgment about how and where to fly, and we managed to cut off electrical power to all that part of Texas. Aside from this one detail, it was a nice pleasant day! My friends Del Gallier and "Dub" Jackson had a lot to do with my joining the CAP. Slightly older than myself, they were more or less my special heroes. Whatever they did I wanted to do it, too. Then George Haddaway, who was a writer and publisher from up Dallas way, came to town and painted such a glowing picture of the coastal patrol that we all joined. I worked for the P&H Company at this time, supervising welding crews, so I flew for the coastal patrol only on a part-time basis. Mostly I flew a gullwing Stinson, a nice-flying airplane, but I never accumulated enough patrol hours to merit the Air Medal.

I gave the base all of my free time, as well as all of the company time I could borrow. I sometimes helped out in the operations and engineering offices, but was never in charge. I remained until the base closed, and watched as some of my friends went to California to tow targets, while others went with the Ferry Command. I stayed with the P&H Company, where I was put in charge of its dealerships and soon gained enough experience to start my own Ford Tractor dealership, which I operated here in Beaumont for over twenty-two years. I continued to fly some, but it got so expensive, and my business was taking so much of my time, that I had to pull back from it. Meanwhile, my wife and I raised two girls and a boy. The girls earned masters' degrees and my son has a doctorate in mathematics from New York University.

\* \* \*

In 1959, the men and women of the Beaumont coastal patrol base held their first reunion. For the newspaperman who reported on it, former base commander George Haddaway produced a copy of a letter he had written to a friend in late 1942. Some of it was published in the *Fort Worth Star-Telegram*:

> We have about run all the Nazi subs out of our coastal area and the freighters are moving again. It's downright inspirational to see the sailors take off their shirts and wave at you in grateful acknowledgment of the air support which they didn't have earlier in the year. I have 125 men on my base and we are living in one of the biggest stories of the war. But the whole story hasn't been told yet. My aide is 14 years old, can fly like a duck swims, and serves in every capac-

ity from yard bird to morale builder. My shop foreman is 73 years old, saw service in the Spanish war, repaired army aircraft in 1917–1918, and is the oldest A&E (Aircraft and Engine) mechanic in the United States.

We are flying all sorts of "clunkers" from old SMA-7A Stinsons to late model Howards. I've got paupers and millionaires in my command — all volunteers, of course. We are neither swan nor goose; we are perhaps "swooses." We are civilians working for the Army on anti-submarine patrol, yet in uniform and have commissions. All of us are sacrificing — and love it. And are we giving the Nazi subs hell! ... I've seen these pilots with their canvas hangars and tools and spare parts stored in wooden boxes in which canned milk had been shipped to them. Dust, rain, mud, hastily cooked chow and cots and water-barrel shower baths. But the CAP lads go off on schedule — their little planes burdened with bombs and radio sets. Planes of 90 to 340 horsepower just edging over the trees at the end of the runway to hours of patrol far out over the sea.

* * *

Interviewed years later for a story in the December 10, 1972 *Texas Star*, "the all-Texas Sunday magazine reaching more than 4,000,000 Texans each week," Haddaway compared standing off the German subs to a famous Civil War naval action at the Sabine Pass, Beaumont's shipping outlet to the Gulf of Mexico:

You might call it the 2nd battle of Sabine Pass. Eighty years before, in the summer of 1863, the Union Navy attempted the invasion of Texas with five river gunboats and 6,000 troops. Dick Dowling, an Irish saloon keeper from Houston and commander of the irregular Davis Guards, brought his 43 men to a low mud fort at Sabine Pass. Dowling had six cannon, relics of the Mexican wars, and these he zeroed in on the shallow channel. The Union Navy had to steam in single file and when they came abreast of the sticks driven into the mud flats as aiming points, Dowling's men disabled and sunk the first two with pinpoint accuracy. Men from the wrecked gunboats waded ashore and when their commanding officer laid eyes upon Dowling's sweaty cannoneers, he is reported to have said, "With six popguns and a handful of men you have captured two gunboats and sent the Union fleet, 6,000 men and a general back out to sea in the dark. You, sir, ought to be ashamed of yourself." I guess we did the same thing to the U-boats. People don't change. I believe in the volunteer spirit of America. It will always be there when needed.

* * *

Walter S. Menge (left), unknown (center), and Richard H. Winfield, Jr. prepare to make the last gesture of affection and respect to comrades lost at sea (courtesy Edgar E. Duncan).

Base officers, pilots, and observers who served at least one month at CAPCP#10 and who are not mentioned elsewhere in this chapter include: Claude I. Anderson, William R. Armstrong, Thomas W. Baker, Clarence E. Barrett,* John L. Bates, John C. Box, Jr.,* Ray J. Bradley, Jr.,* Elvon F. Brockman,* Clifford W. Brogdon,* Jo H. Cable, Hugh P. Carlisle,* William M. Cason, Altee N. Chittim, John B. Clark, George R. Clay, James B. Courtney,* Lance M. Cox, Randall E. Culver,* Rodney L. DeLange, Arthur M. Donnelly, Robert M. Dresser, Julian J. Fertitta, Lawrence O. Fisher,* Oliver P. Fullerton,* James L. Gartner, Carsie Y. Gorman, Dean A. Hammond,* Lauren B. Hapgood, John J. Healey, Edward T. Helms, Burton Holton, Dion L. Johnson, Edgar Kimball, Jr.,* Joe P. Klein, Earle J. Kuntz,* Morris Landau,* Joseph F. Long,* James G. Lubbock, John W. Lumpkin, James A. McLeod, Gilbert A. Mapes,* Walter S. Menge,* Curtis J. Metcalf, John P. Morgan, Sherwood H. Morgan, William D. Morris, Jack C. Neal,* Reginald M. Nicol,* Hubert B. O'Neall,* Francis R. Parkman,* Jack P. Pavletich, Hal B. Pratt,* Harry L. Putnam, Forrest A. Rhea,* Arthur J. Roderick, Benjamin A. Rollinson, Ansel L. Ross,* James H. Shaw,* Jack D. Shell, Vole G. Smart,* Leslie R. Stringer, Chris C. Strong, James L. Thomasson,* Ralph E. Turner, Jr., Ignatius J. Vacek, Otto M. Vehle, Robert H. Wallace, Clarence P. Welton,* Gerald H. Westby, Gus H. Whiteman, Joe R. Wier, and Lonnie O. Wilkerson. Asterisk indicates Air Medal winner.

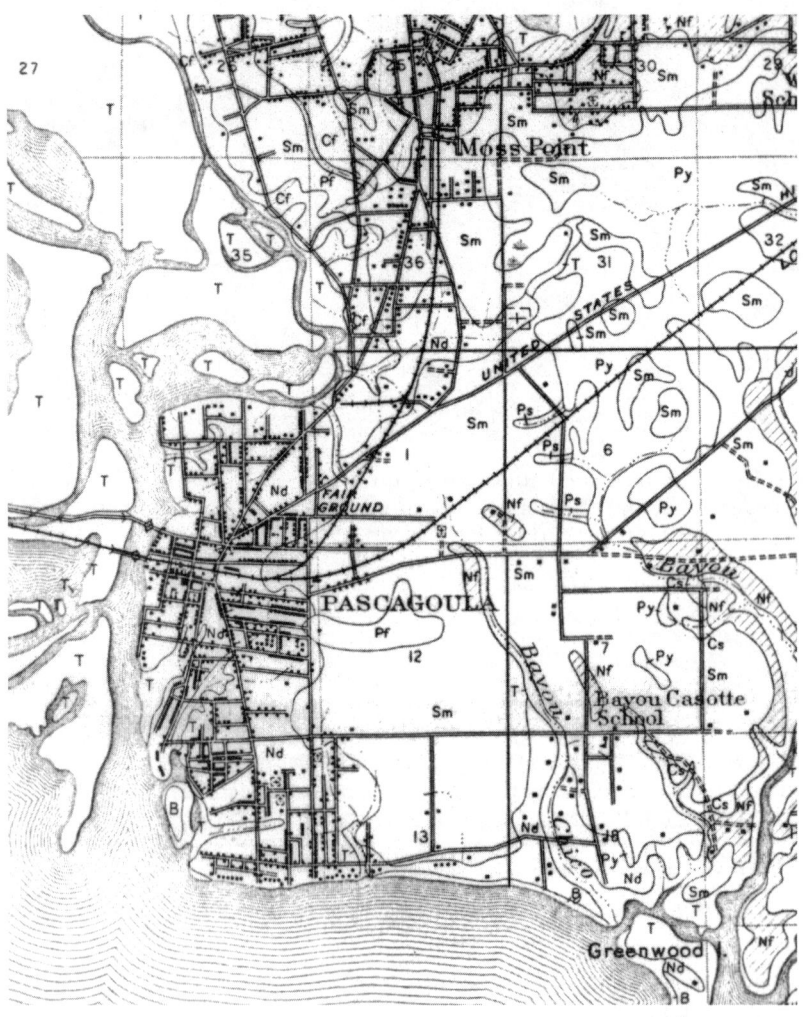

The Pascagoula coastal patrol base was located between U.S. Route 90 and the Louisville and Nashville Railroad, approximately one-half mile east of the Jackson County Fair Ground — shown on this map just above the town name, Pascagoula (source: 1927 U.S. Department of Agriculture map).

# 11

# Pascagoula, Mississippi

The Pascagoula coastal patrol base was located at Raby Field about two miles northeast of Pascagoula, Mississippi, and was activated on June 24, 1942. Owned by Jackson County, the fifty-six acre field had three runways, each two thousand feet long and over four hundred feet wide. While adequate in most respects, the drainage was so bad that it took six hours for the runways to dry out after a rain. Captain Esmond Avery, the commanding officer, in his November 14, 1942 report to CAP Washington headquarters described the physical plant in detail:

> One main hangar WPA constructed about three years ago (approximately 100' x 100'). Adjacent line to rooms attached; pilot's room (15' x 20'), operations office (20' x 20'), radio room (12' x 16'), administrative office (20' x 20'), engineering department (about 30' x 20'), radio repair shop (10' x 20'), one small laundry shack, one dining room (approximately 15' x 30') with cook wagon attached. Hangar building owned by Jackson County [other buildings owned by CAP]. Small privately-owned hangar about 30' x 30' constructed of wood and galvanized iron. Capacity of main hangar about eighteen civil aircraft. One small hutment about 10' x 12' to house kitchen help along with a trailer used similarly.

## Marion F. Parkinson

*One of the first arrivals at the base was Marion F. Parkinson, a thirty-year-old-pilot from Easterville, Iowa, who served as engineering officer. While still in high school, he and his brother bought a Jenny JN-4D with an OX-5 engine and taught themselves to fly. When World War II came along, and his fixed base operation was shut down by the government, he went to Ames, the state capital, and volunteered for the coastal patrol. A few weeks later he was in Pascagoula. In 1948 he was awarded the Air Medal, and in 1983 related many of his experiences to interviewer Colonel Lester E. Hopper:*

> We didn't know exactly what the operation was or how it was going to function for a day or so. They quartered us in a Coast Guard Artillery base that was set up on the beach with gun emplacements for protecting the shores. They had five-inch guns and we remained there for billeting until we got our quarters built on Raby Field. We picked up some buildings from an old Civilian Conservation Corps camp up in Monroeville, disassembled them, then rebuilt them on the base. Some people slept in eight-man, twelve foot square wooden hutments with sides that lifted up and were screened so that you had plenty of ventilation. The main building with toilet facilities and staff quarters was maybe eighty feet long and forty feet wide.

Captain Marion F. ("Parky") Parkinson of Easterville, Iowa, was base engineering officer, and once spent more than a week marooned on Chandeleur Island eating roast wild boar (Hopper collection).

> Ninety percent of our work was escorting convoys. About three months after the base opened, our planes were equipped with bombs, but it wasn't the possibility of dropping bombs as much as the nuisance value of our observation work that kept the German submarines from the convoys. The subs in the Caribbean were the huge 750-ton, double-walled models that could stay away from Germany up to three years provided they could get fuel and food. I believe that most of the refueling in the Gulf was done by Mexican sailboats. And food was obtained from coastal fishermen under threat of having their villages destroyed by shelling.... The subs didn't seem that interested in sinking the new ships coming out of the Ingalls ship-

yards at Pascagoula. They wanted the tankers that were carrying precious oil to Europe. We never dropped a bomb on a sub because we never found one.

The Stinson Voyager, the model 10A with a 90 horsepower Franklin engine, was our workhorse. But we also had some gullwing Stinsons, some Wacos, and a staggerwing Beechcraft that was lost at sea. Out of our group of seven little Stinsons, five of them broke their crankshafts, 80 miles from the base, over the water. The shaft would break just behind the propeller thrust bearing on the front of the engine, and on the throw, so the end of the shaft couldn't leave the engine, and the knuckling effect on the broken shaft would keep it running. Of course, the number one cylinder stopped firing, so the boys came home on only three cylinders. They'd throw everything overboard, including their shoes, then with half-flaps and full throttle they could maintain 60 mph. That brought all five of those airplanes back home.

Putting up a base radio antenna always came first, because sub-hunting patrols were pointless — and dangerous to the flyers themselves — unless constant radio contact was maintained (Hopper collection).

I remember one day when Mel Holderness was flying a Fairchild 24 and ran out of fuel while on patrol. He and his observer made it to Chandeleur Island, but on landing they hit a big log and knocked the landing gear off. I went out with Earl Stuenkel, a mechanic, to assess the situation. I picked out a nice level spot that looked like dry dirt and made a landing. But this dry dirt was just a scum on the surface of a bog and I put that airplane right out of operation! The radio was okay, so we called in, and the base sent out a Coast Guard boat with a repair crew and a cook and a tent, and we were there several days. There were a lot of wild pigs on the island then, and we shot and barbecued some of them. They tasted of fish — not good at all. The hardest work was getting the beach cleared of the logs that had washed up. After both planes were repaired, I flew one off, and Charlie Whitaker, the other.... When the base closed, the Air Corps said, "Well, we need some freight hauled." So they took most of the larger planes and made cargo haulers out of them. Put in plywood floors and sides and tie-down rings for hauling freight. Most of our pilots went into the Air Corps, too, but not with their planes. I took the airplane assigned to me to Denver and got as far as Tinker Field in Oklahoma City, where I got weathered-in. And that's as far as I ever got. I received orders to go to El Paso, Biggs Field, and fly on a search for a B-24 that had crashed in Mexico. I guess I spent two weeks hunting for the B-24 and a couple of other missing planes. Our association with the Mexican government was very friendly. Our landing place down there was at Chivawa City, about 150 miles south of the border. While I was flying out of El Paso ... I went to the Air Corps operations officer, and he got on the teletype and got my release from Washington.

## Earl E. Stuenkel

*Earl E. Stuenkel was a 32-year-old mechanic from Lawrence, Kansas where he had been the service manager for an automobile agency and a member of the local CAP squadron. Although he was classified 3-A in the draft because of his wife and two children, he says that joining the coastal patrol seemed like the least he could do for his country. Stuenkel served at the Mississippi base from almost its first day until its last. His memory of the Chandeleur Island rescue mission differs somewhat from that of Marion Parkinson:*

The Fairchild that went down on Chandeleur Island had a Warner Scarab engine that had just been rebuilt. This was only the plane's first or second mission since then, but one of the cylinders lost all of its attachment bolts and pulled the intake pipe from the engine case. "Parky" was wrong about the plane's just running out of gas, and wrong about our staying out there only "several days." I know for a fact we were out there thirteen days! When base decided that the plane be repaired and flown off the Island, Parky and I took a Stinson 10-A out to see what was needed. The downed flyers told us, "Whatever you do, don't land on the beach, it's littered with logs and other debris." We found a big level space in the middle of the Island and set her down. The wheels dug deep furrows in the sand for two or three hundred feet, and we'd almost stopped rolling when we abruptly flipped over on our backs. We weren't hurt, and except for the propeller, neither was the plane.

While we were standing there wondering what to do — even if we could get the plane upright and repaired, we couldn't take off again from there — several big fishermen happened by and suggested we use a nearby bunch of planks to lay a track to the beach. They helped us turn over the Stinson and lay the planks and that's how we did it. So then we had *two* planes to repair and get off the Island. The repair crew and equipment came out on a Coast Guard boat. I think we were out there nearly two weeks, and I went without a bath or a shave the whole time. On Thanksgiving Day, a plane from the base dropped a roast turkey to us. Apparently without thinking, they dispatched it by fast Cessna Airmaster,* instead of a slower plane, and after retrieving it we found it so embedded with sand as to be inedible. Still it was a nice gesture. Once all the repairs were completed, and the beach cleared so the planes could take off safely, the Coast Guard picked up the rest of us and we ate a fine steak dinner as their guests on the way home.

Major Esmond Avery, base commander, was from Grosse Pointe, Michigan, and had a reputation among his men as a fair but firm-handed leader (Hopper collection).

I did not have an A&E license when I came down from Kansas, but I took the tests and got one while at the base. At first I was listed on the roster as an "apprentice mechanic," and then was promoted to "mechanic." I found the living quarters comfortable, but we had some pro-

---

\* The Cessna Airmaster appeared in 1934 and promptly won the title, "World's Most Efficient Airplane." It remained in production until WW II and was the basis for the Models 190 and 195 that were introduced at war's end. The Airmaster's clean lines and its distinguishing lack of wing struts look modern even today.

visioning problems. If the Air Corps people at Keesler Field hadn't helped, we've have been hurting. I don't recall much in the way of entertainment, but I don't think I missed it either. At some point, I remember that Major Avery selected a group of us that he wanted to be sure weren't drafted away from him and took us over to Keesler to be sworn into the Air Corps reserves. I did, in fact, serve with the Air Corps after the base closed, but not for long. After the war, I joined a Cessna dealership and was active in the aviation industry until I retired.

\* \* \*

A majority of Pascagoula personnel were from Michigan and Iowa. As at most bases, there was a considerable turnover. During the life of the base, 184 different men and women filled the standard base complement of 75 positions. Sixty-eight of them came from Michigan, 52 from Iowa, 19 from Missouri, 16 from Mississippi, 10 from Kansas, and the remainder from fourteen other states. Group departures for coastal patrol duty often made the newspapers. This excerpt comes from a July 1942 *Grand Rapids Sentinel* story, "Four More CAP Pilots Leave For Coastal-Patrol War Duty":

> Four more pilots of Grand Rapids squadron 638-1, civil air patrol, have been ordered to active duty on coastal patrol and were en route to their destination Saturday under "sealed orders." Three of the local men left the Kent County Airport Friday afternoon by plane and the fourth went by automobile. Flying to duty in Leonard Ward's plane were Peter Sienko and Rodney Den Herder. They will meet Floyd Wood Monday at the unnamed destination. Den Herder and Wood have signed for active duty for the duration of the war, Ward for one month and Sienko for three months. The four hope to join another squadron pilot, Paul H. Miller, who left two weeks ago.

\* \* \*

A similar story, "Five County Fliers Will Join Nation's Patrol on Atlantic," appeared about the same time in the *Battle Creek Enquirer and News*. The newspaper was incorrect (deliberately or not) about pilots flying alone (they never did), about communicating directly with the Navy (except in some emergency they never did), and about their destination (the Gulf Coast not the eastern seaboard):

> Five members of Calhoun County's Civil Air Patrol [Harold O. Perkins, Robert Despins, Glenn Soloman, Bernard L. Coplin, and Louis E. Legg] will leave late this week by plane for the eastern seaboard where they have been ordered to join with navy fliers and other civilian pilots in the hunt for enemy submarines. They have

not yet been advised where they will be stationed on the coast, but have been told that they will survey an area extending 15 miles out to sea. They expect to be in the air for about three or four hours each day for 30 days.... Each pilot will fly alone, and via two-way radio equipment, will communicate immediately with navy authorities if he spots a submarine. Pilots who own planes with 80 or more horsepower will rent them to the government for the undertaking.

### Herman ("Skip") Dugo

*Herman ("Skip") Dugo, a native of Saint Louis, Missouri, served at the base from November 1, 1942 through October 20, 1943. An Air Medal winner, he logged two hundred and eleven patrol missions totaling 503:40 hours (including eight missions that were flown out of the Grand Isle, Louisiana base, when it was short a plane due to maintenance problems). He particularly remembers efforts to refine the effectiveness of patrol plane armament:*

Herman ("Skip") Dugo hailed from St. Louis, Missouri, and was both a pilot and a mechanic. He flew 211 missions and more than five hundred hours of overwater patrol, and in 1948 received the Air Medal (courtesy Herman Dugo).

On December 1, 1942, I was assigned a part-time duty to test and accept (or reject) a Stinson 10-A that had been equipped by the Army Air Corps armorers at Keesler Field (Biloxi, Mississippi) and Brookley

Field (Mobile, Alabama) with a bomb rack, a manually operated bomb sight, and an electrical release switch. A bomber squadron from Hattiesburg, Mississippi outlined a life-size German U-boat on the ground along the coast near Moss Point Airport east of Pascagoula for our practice bombing. We used one hundred pound demolition bombs filled with white flour. I made nine practice flights with three different pilots: three with Melvin P. Holderness, four with Everett H. Vaughn, and two with Arthur B. Billet. We made some direct hits, and enough near-misses to have done some real damage to a real sub. Later on, two hundred-fifty pound depth charges were installed, using the same aiming and release system, on our Stinson SM-8A, a Stinson Reliant, and a Waco ZQC6. I was trained on the functions and settings of the hydrostatic fuses that exploded the depth charges underwater, and then I trained the rest of the pilots at our base.

Many of the buildings for the Pascagoula base came from an abandoned Civilian Conservation Corps camp. They had to be dismantled, trucked to the base site, and reassembled there (Hopper collection).

On February 26, 1943, we lost Paul W. Davis, our flight surgeon from Saint Louis, and Martin E. Coughlin of Kansas City, when their staggerwing Beech D-17S went down in the Gulf. Along with William C. Napier of Chicago and Herbert G. Coo of Pittsburgh I flew seven hours searching for them. Neither were ever found. After this, our mechanics fitted our Stinson SM-8A with a large life raft that could be dropped to men in the water. A few months later I had a scare myself. While out on a patrol with Stanley T. Ambro of Kalamazoo, our plane broke a crankshaft in the front thrust bearing as we approached Dauphin Island. We were lucky to land on the south beach without damage or injury. Afterwards a crew came out by boat and rebuilt the engine, then Stan flew off the beach back to base.

* * *

Besides Davis and Coughlin, whose lives were lost in the Gulf, six other Pascagoula flyers became Duck Club members — ditched but saved. Five were from Michigan: John E. Dammeyer, Detroit; Arthur B. Billet, Berkley; David R. Anderson, Royal Oak; Floyd R. Wood, Grand Rapids; and Sidney Moskowitz, Jackson. Joseph W. Bush was from Nashville, Tennessee. The ditching by Dammeyer and Billet is mentioned in *Sank Same*:

> The airmen were operating far out over the Gulf of Mexico when their engine started to miss, then conked out. At the base, on the radio, they heard Billet: "Now we're losing altitude, now we have 400 feet, now we have 200 feet, we're settling fast, now we have 100 feet, now we — glug," and the gurgle of water took over. They learned later that Dammeyer crashed his ship close to a Norwegian oil tanker. The fabric peeled right off the frame when the ship struck the water, and she sank like a rock. Under water, Dammeyer couldn't find the door, so he broke out the windshield. Billet got mixed up in his safety belt and struggled beneath the surface for what seemed like hours to him; but he finally got free, and both flyers were saved.

* * *

According to Marion Parkinson, the men were flying a Stinson SM8-A and the crash occurred in August 1942 about a month after the Pascagoula base became operational. Dammeyer and Billet were picked up by a brand new, German-built tanker flying the *Swedish* flag, and went with it to wherever it was going. The men did not return to Pascagoula for a week.

## Arthur B. Billet

*Air Medal winner Arthur B. Billet was only twenty-two when he joined the Detroit CAP squadron, but already had a private pilot's license and an engineering degree from the University of Michigan in Ann Arbor. His recollection is that he and Dammeyer were flying a Fairchild 24 and were picked up by an American tanker:*

We had picked up a large tanker heading into the Gulf to join a convoy then making up. We understood from a Navy briefing that it was one of the largest of the war up until then. We were out ahead of the ship about eight miles when we apparently "sawed off" a valve, breaking it off with a piston. You could hear the piston coming up and hitting the valve — bang, bang, bang! This lasted a minute or two until everything went to pieces and we knew we'd have to ditch. The water was fairly rough that day, and we came in nose-high at stall speed trying to settle on a wave crest, but just then the wave broke beneath us and we hit the water in a full stall. The left wing was torn off and we were under water at a forty- to fifty-degree slant, nose down. We were shaken up badly, but fortunately not injured.

But the way the plane was smashed up didn't make it easy getting out. The cabin quickly filled with water as I fumbled around trying to find the door latch. John Dammeyer, a big man at six-two and two hundred and twenty pounds, managed to get turned around with his feet against his seat and his shoulders and back against the windshield and pushed it out. I could feel him surge out though at the time I wasn't quite sure where or how. By then, I'd swallowed some salt water and thought "this can't go on." With my last fumbling effort, I got the door opened and got out. The fuselage was now vertical and that's how far from the surface I was. When I popped up, John said he'd thought I wouldn't make it. I think I said as much to him. You could probably say that we had both been darned lucky.

As it happened the tanker's captain and mate had been watching us for a long time before we went down, and when we disappeared from sight they thought something must be wrong. Since they were coming toward us, they did eventually spot us with a high-powered telescope. They slowed enough to launch a fast powerboat that raced ahead and picked us up, and, in turn, was then picked up again by the ship. They gave us some dry clothes and a hot drink. After the ship joined the convoy, we were transferred to a small Navy boat and returned to a base some miles up the Mississippi. The Navy then drove us to New Orleans and dropped us off on Canal Street. Since we had very little money, we took an inexpensive room three blocks from the Monteleone Hotel, from where I called the base. It was now three a.m. and only the O.D. was on duty. I told him where we were, and he said they'd send a plane for us the next morning, which they did. Just about everybody at the base was there to welcome us when we landed at Pascagoula, and that was very gratifying. We didn't fly for a couple of days, but then it was back to business as usual. It was better to be back in harness than just sit around not flying.

## Herbert G. Coo

*Herbert G. Coo, another Air Medal winner, had a private pilot's license and his own plane, a Waco cabin, when he joined the Civil Air Patrol in Pittsburgh. His wife, Louise Coo, recalls:*

Herbert always said that the people in Pascagoula liked coastal patrol personnel and were much impressed with their uniforms, especially the red epaulets on their shoulders. One of his favorite off-duty nightspots was "The Comet Club," and he once admitted that it was there he drank too much one evening, hit a light pole on the way home, broke a tooth, and knocked out the electric power to half the town. I happened to be a dental hygienist, and that's how we met. We dated the rest of the year that he served at Pascagoula. When the base closed, he enlisted in the Air Corps, hoping to continue to fly but was instead relegated to a ground job, dropping down in rank from lieutenant to private. The same thing happened to several other coastal patrol flyers. Meanwhile, I had enlisted in the Navy Nurse Corps. When we were married in 1944 I had to resign my commission and Herbert went overseas a month later. We didn't see each other again for a year and a half.

Pilot Herbert G. Coo came to Pascagoula from Pittsburgh, Pennsylvania, and was one of the base's forty-seven Air Medal winners. Here he chats with an unidentified aircraft mechanic (courtesy Mrs. Herbert G. Coo).

## Harold P. Chadderdon

*Harold P. Chadderdon, an aircraft mechanic from Kalamazoo, Michigan, also found Pascagoula to his liking. Before joining the Kalamazoo CAP squadron, he had been living in Dearborn, and working at the Ford River Rouge plant. Then he heard that the CAP was looking for coastal patrol volunteers. Twenty years old and sick of Detroit, he thought five dollars a day and a chance to travel sounded like a good deal. When he arrived, he wasn't surprised to be assigned to live in a six-man tent because he'd been told that Pascagoula might be a "little rough." It would become much nicer:*

Later on, our headquarters people obtained some plywood and we built a number of six-man "hutments," as the Army called them, and lived at the field. We had a mess hall, where some of the wives helped out, a small detachment of Army armorers who loaded and unloaded the bombs on the airplanes, and a bunch of young fellows who pushed airplanes around and policed the area. So we mechanics were left strictly

Group of unidentified mechanics unpacking an engine newly delivered from the factory. Replacements were difficult to get, and treated like treasures when they arrived (Hopper collection).

to work on the planes. I had only a powerplant rating when I got there and acquired an airframe license later. Some of the other fellows were strictly auto mechanics. Each man brought his own tools. Our chief mechanic, Robert F. Despins, had had his A&E rating quite a while, so we could do just about everything we had to, except for some major engine overhauls, which we sent to the factory. I had five Stinson 10-As and a Monocoupe that I took care of, and it seemed like I always had one in the back of the hangar waiting for some work. Pascagoula was just a very small place with nothing downtown except for some bars.

I had a motorbike, but later went in with another guy to buy a 1937 Ford so we could drive to New Orleans and Mobile for some fun. Just about the time I got down there the draft boards were starting to breathe down the backs of younger fellows, and someone came up with an Air Corps reserve program which most of us signed up for. When the base closed up at the end of August 1943 we could either accept discharge from the CAP and become immediately eligible for the draft, or join the Air Corps, which I did. I missed the Cadet program by being one-half inch too tall, and I didn't qualify as an aircraft mechanic either. Instead, they trained me as a remote-control turret mechanic and I worked on B-29s in the Pacific for a year and a half.

### Richard P. Oberhaus

*Richard P. Oberhaus was one of a dozen young men and women from Muscatine, Iowa who made the long trip south to Pascagoula.\* He had been a CAP Cadet in high school and after he graduated in May 1943 his squadron C.O. suggested that it might be interesting to join the several Muscatine men already there. After his attempt to enlist in the Air Corps failed, a tour in the coastal patrol appeared to be a valuable way to get experience while waiting to be drafted. Soon thereafter, a grimy eighteen-year-old Oberhaus and his equally sooty friend, Paul C. Nolan, stepped down at the Pascagoula train station to face their first hot, humid day on the Gulf.*

For someone who'd never been far from home, it was very exciting. We became part of the unit that guarded the field, the planes, and the ammo dump where the bombs were stored. All posts were manned twenty-four hours a day, and we carried loaded weapons. A fellow on the base loaned me his German Luger so I wouldn't have to buy a gun. It had only a dozen parts and could be broken down and reassembled real fast. Of course, I never had to use it, nor did any of the other guards use their weapons. Guard duty was completely routine. We used a firing range at the end of a runway down by the railroad tracks, but it wasn't necessary for us to be marksmen.

\* Muscatine, a town of less than ten thousand people, was located on the Mississippi River not far from Davenport, Iowa, and produced more coastal patrol volunteers than any other Iowa city. Besides the seven mentioned in the text, Lee C. Anson, George E. and Ruth E. Moore, Vernon J. Oostendorp, and Robert L. Smith also came from Muscatine. Ottumwa accounted for six volunteers, and four each came from Davenport and Des Moines. Twenty-six others came from all over the state.

While I was there, the six-man hutments only held five men — three across the back wall and one on either side. These flimsy hutments were surprisingly comfortable and at night with the shutters open we enjoyed cooling Gulf breezes. The days were something else. You might pick up a freshly washed and pressed uniform at some downtown laundry, and by the time you got back to the base it looked like you'd dragged it all the way. The two regular Army guys, both single, who daily loaded and unloaded bombs from our planes lived on detached service in town. We all figured they had a pretty easy work day. I don't recall having any inspections or any drilling or other military formalities, such as saluting or "policing-up" the area and such.

There wasn't much to do in Pascagoula. We might go downtown and just walk around a little, look in the store windows and such. There was a nice looking roadhouse right across from the airfield, but a big sign proclaimed it "off limits." Pershing Elder and Ray Zeidler, both of Muscatine, had cars, and sometimes we'd get a gang together and go over to Mobile or to New Orleans. We also went to Biloxi and Gulfport a lot. There was a Navy base at Biloxi and Paul Nolan and I twice bummed rides to Cuba in a Navy PBY. We stayed a couple of nights, and then bummed rides back. I also flew a few missions as an observer. That wasn't scary at all, and you got to see from the air what you couldn't on the ground. Everything down there was as flat as a pancake so you couldn't see anything *except* from the air.

## John W. Bryant

*John W. Bryant was another Muscatine volunteer who served as a guard at the Pascagoula coastal patrol base. The twenty-one-year-old was a relative latecomer, arriving in May 1943, after having served in the local CAP squadron for about six months:*

I took the bus to Des Moines to meet three other fellows and we drove down from there, stopping overnight in southern Illinois somewhere. One man was from Waterloo, another from Sioux City, but I don't remember where the third man came from. They put us in wooden-sided, six-man huts, with large screened windows all around. The days were very hot down there, but at night we had cool breezes off the water and you'd need to sleep covered-up. The change in climate from Iowa didn't bother me at all. When you're young, you scarcely notice things like that. I already had my uniform from before and was able to borrow a thirty-eight revolver from one of the officers. I'm glad I never had to fire it for any reason.

Pascagoula was kind of dull, but I do remember a skating rink. We'd go there in the evenings mostly because it was a good place to meet girls. Some of us used to hitch-hike to Mobile when we had a day off. Fifty years ago, a good many Southerners were still fighting the Civil War and didn't have much use for us Northerners, but they *did* stop to give us rides. There wasn't so much to do in Mobile, either, but at least it was much bigger than Pascagoula. We'd visit some of the shops and stores, and maybe have a nice meal at Bishop's cafeteria. I think there was also a Morrisons, which was pretty popular.

Our officers were a good bunch. They were all volunteers just like us. I came down because I was 4-F but still wanted to do something for my country. I had an ear problem, which, after the war, I had repaired in a number of operations. I heard about the ditchings and the pilots who were lost at sea, but all that was before I got there. I recall several times when some Navy pilot out of Pensacola would land at our base, and one of our pilots would go up with him to try flying one of those hotshot Navy planes. They'd probably known each other in civilian life. Just before the coastal patrol ended and I came home, I had a chance to go up myself. One of our pilots was offering rides to anyone who'd never been up and wanted to give it a try. That was nice of him, and I enjoyed getting the invitation, but I didn't take him up on it.

Edwin ("Dusie") Buffington was another fellow from Muscatine. Dusie was the head of our commissary and did most of the cooking. His wife helped him and while she wasn't carried on our base roster she was paid five dollars a day just like we were. Sometimes when I wasn't on guard duty, I worked in the kitchen for fifty cents an hour. Dusie paid me, but I don't know where the money came from. We bought most of our food right there in Pascagoula. We took an old bus downtown and Dusie would buy bags of potatoes and cases of canned goods and such and we'd load them on the bus to take to the mess hall. I recall that our pay checks were always late, but that just before the base closed, they paid us all our arrears.

We never really knew right up until the base closed what we'd be doing or where we'd go. The rumors were rampant that we'd be transferred to the Yucatan. Well, of course, that didn't happen, and the base just closed. As for myself, I got into the Cadet program all right, but by late 1943 they didn't need more pilots, so I finally ended up as a flight engineer on B-17s. After the war, I flew some for fun with a friend who had a Great Lakes Trainer with a 450 hp Pratt & Whitney engine, but never earned a pilot's license. I intend to revisit Pascagoula soon — my daughter lives in Florida and my son in Texas — and relive some good memories of my time there.

### John H. Kirstein

*John H. Kirstein of Des Moines was another Iowan who went to Pascagoula as a guard. At seventeen he had already been turned down by the Seabees because of a heart murmur, so as soon as he graduated from high school in January 1943, he headed south. Because he was a member of the local CAP squadron, he had his uniform and wore it on the train. During a layover in Nashville to change trains, he took a walk around town and was amazed and puzzled by the many American enlisted men saluting him. He learned later that some British Army officers, whose red shoulder epaulets looked much like his own, were in town:*

At first I lived in the same hutments as the coast artillery men who were stationed along the coast road at the east end of town. We didn't get on so well because they knew we amateur civilians were out chasing submarines in the Gulf, while they, who had all the training and equipment, couldn't do anything where they were on land. The townspeople knew all about the ships that had been sunk, and they practically gave the coastal patrol the keys to the city. That didn't sit so well with the coast artillery fellows, either, and I was glad to move into our own housing at the base.

John S. Kirstein had this picture taken in a Biloxi, Mississippi studio familiar to thousands of Air Corps men stationed at Keesler Field (courtesy John S. Kirstein).

I took with me a twelve-gauge pump shotgun that I had learned how to use on various hunting trips, but when I got there someone gave me an Army Colt forty-five. It was enormous, much too big for my hand. I had occasion to show it just once. Across the highway from our hangar was a roadhouse known as the Airport Inn. It was off-limits to all coastal patrol personnel, but very popular with the hillbillies who moved to town from northern Mississippi and Alabama to work in the Pascagoula shipyards. Before the coastal patrol arrived, some of them had become used to staggering across the road, going under a fence, then climbing into a comfortable airplane seat to sleep it off.

One night I caught this one fellow just as he was half-way through the fence. I came up and just dropped my arm down to where he could see the forty-five in my hand. He quickly withdrew, but he was pretty drunk, and when he tried again later, I had to use my night stick to subdue him. A couple of nights after that, I was walking the same post after a real heavy rainstorm — the water was standing inches deep — when I heard a "plop" behind me. I searched and finally found a honed-down steak knife in the water. He must have thrown it at me in the dark, and fortunately for me he missed.

After I was there a while, Major Avery, the base commander learned that my father, a painter, had taught me the trade. He got me to paint a thirty-eight foot fishing boat that he and another man had purchased. After he found out that I also could handle boats, I began taking him and his friends out on fishing trips into the Gulf. I became responsible for getting food and drinks and ice, and then navigating us out through the harbor for twenty miles or so to where they could fish for sharks or whatever. We'd go down river, go under a railroad bridge and toot three times, then wait for a Navy PT boat to come up and check our IDs. After a time, the Navy boys got to know me and they'd just ask me if I had any suspicious characters on board without bothering the others. This duty was not at all unpleasant.

I saw one crash. A Cessna Airmaster was returning from patrol when it apparently ran out of gas just before the pilot could land. They came down in a grove of pecan trees adjacent to the field. They were rolling fast and when they hit a slight rise the plane went airborne again and clipped off its right wing on a tree, then slammed around and broke in half. I was sitting in a Jeep out by the main gate, and was one of the first to reach the scene. The two flyers were unhurt, and seemed to be arguing about which one of them had turned off an ignition switch too soon. I went back to Des Moines after the base closed, but stayed with the CAP twenty-five years, working up through the ranks in the Des Moines squadron and then the Iowa wing, retiring as a colonel.

## Robert M. Brocket

*Robert M. Brocket was one of the crew of service technicians who did all of the non-mechanical work on the planes, gassing them, checking their tire pressures and oil levels, washing them, and pushing and pulling them around when necessary. He was born and raised in Muscatine and lives there still:*

I joined the local CAP squadron not long after Pearl Harbor. Then I guess some of us persuaded each other that going down to Pascagoula would be a good way to serve the country. I went down by train using a series of connections that don't exist anymore. We were right on the Gulf, and while it was very hot during the days, there were usually cooling breezes off the water at night. I got used to the heat, and enjoyed myself down there, but never even considered moving there after the war. I much prefer our northern, four-seasons climate. We had a pretty good bunch of officers to work for. Many of them were millionaires, of course, flying their own planes and sometimes behaving just a "little above" us linemen and guards, but mostly they were real nice.

I was struck by the laid-back, easy-going nature of most Southerners. That was different to me, noticeably unlike the faster pace I was used to at home. Something else new was the amount of seafood we consumed. To this day I don't care much for shrimp because I ate so much of it down there. Despite the ship building boom there really wasn't much to do in Pascagoula. I'd hoped to have my wife and son for a visit, and had it all arranged, but then decided to go home and join the Army. I wound up in the Corps of Engineers serving at Bougainville and in the Philippines. Upon discharge, I stayed in the reserves to keep my rank as sergeant, largely because I'd hated KP and guard duty so much. As a result, I was called back and spent a year in Korea.

## Keith L. Vetter

*Keith L. Vetter remembers taking the train from Muscatine to Pascagoula with Bob Brocket and others from different parts of Iowa. Theirs was a cinder-filled smoky ride, and they all arrived looking rather dirty and disheveled. Born and raised in Muscatine, Vetter tried to enlist in the Air Corps, but could not pass the physical:*

Before I joined the Muscatine CAP squadron, I had started taking flying lessons on my own, but I hadn't earned a license. I was twenty-four and married, but I felt I should be doing something patriotic, so I volunteered for the coastal patrol. After I got somewhat settled at the base, I returned to Muscatine to pick up my wife. We bought an eighteen-foot travel trailer from her uncle, and towed it to Pascagoula. We rented space in a trailer court fairly close to the base, and lived there all the while we were down there. My wife worked as a secretary at the Ingalls shipyard.

Once a proper mess hall was built, base personnel enjoyed tasty meals prepared by excellent cooks. Fresh fish, shrimp, clams, oysters, and crab were staples in the Pascagoula base menu (Hopper collection).

I did the usual things a lineman does — gas the planes and keep them ready to fly on a moment's notice. We didn't have a gas truck. Instead, our eighty-octane fuel was stored in an underground tank, then dispensed from a gas pump just like at a service station. Though there were several big NO-SMOKING signs around, we were frequently cautioned of the danger involved. I particularly watched anyone that I knew who smoked just in case they forgot. I didn't smoke so it was no problem for me. We also checked oil levels and topped them up as necessary. I recall that our oil came in five-gallon cans, and that we used one-gallon containers with a long, curved spout to add oil to the crankcase, not the round cans like you see today. Complete oil changes were handled by the mechanics as part of periodic engine tune-ups. The airplane tires had recommended pressures, but I think we learned to check them just by eye. There were usually two to four lineman on duty at any one time.

When we first arrived at the base, Bob Brocket and I performed guard duty for a time, so many hours on, then so many hours off. When other men were found for guard duty, we started taking care of the planes. My wife and I really enjoyed Pascagoula, and made quite a number of friends, including some native Mississippians, with whom we've kept in touch over the years. and have visited on a couple of driving trips. I remained at the base until August 1943, then my wife and I returned to Muscatine. I attempted again to join the Air Corps but was turned down. So I got into the Culligan water business and have stayed with it for fifty years now.

Lawrence Lindhart of Humboldt, Iowa served as a flight observer and as the base bugler (courtesy Norman Lindhart).

## Orval O. Myers

*Orval O. Myers was a pilot and flight observer from Ottumwa, Iowa, who soloed at age thirty-three on August 17, 1942, the day his daughter Molly was born. In eight months at Pascagoula, January through August 1943, he flew 360:05 hours on anti-submarine patrol and received the Air Medal in 1948. Florence Myers tells about her late husband's coastal patrol service:*

His pilot most of the time was George G. Mayle of Detroit, Michigan, who died shortly after the war ended. I think the base lost several planes, but he never talked much about it. They slept in square tents with very small heaters in the middle, so during January and February it was cold, damp, and miserable. Besides Orval, there were two Ottumwa couples down there. Leo Hahn was a service technician and his wife Lucille worked in an office in town. Richard Evans was the airdrome officer, but helped out around the base mess hall with his wife Dorothy Jean. All four of them are dead now.

When the base closed, a number of the pilots went up to Fletcher Field, an Air Corps primary training center at Clarksdale, Mississippi. Orval said that he was one of only four who made it through. Most of the others were too old and set in certain flying habits and couldn't take the pressure. My husband and I made several winter trips to Pascagoula, the last one twelve years or so ago. We found the old hangar, but a hospital had been built on the south side of the field and a four-lane highway ran past it. We also visited one of the mechanics and his wife who lived in town. Orval talked with them about old times for a while, and then we moved on.

The Pascagoula base as seen from the air, looking generally southeast. The highway at right is U.S. Route 90, passing through Tallahassee to the east and New Orleans to the west. Four planes sit on the grass in the foreground, and a row of six-man tents is to the left of the hangar (Hopper collection).

> Base officers, pilots, and observers who served at least one month at CAPCP #11 and who are not elsewhere mentioned in this chapter include: Thomas M. Adams,* L. V. Antoine, Stanley Barber,* Gottlieb Bauer,* James C. Brown, Curtis M. Burbey, Frank L. Burke, Percy H. Byars,* Jack E. Crysler,* Carroll F. Day,* Squire B. Eurich, John R. Finn,* Edward Fitzgerald, Jr., Vernon J. Gingerich, Laurence F. Graham, J. D. Hammett,* John S. Hammond,* Richard N. Haynes,* Charles M. Huber, Richard L. Jacobs, George W. Jacobsen,* William D. Jamison, Loren D. Johnson, Travis E. Kallenbach, Myron B. Kemmerer, Ralph Knouse,* Alfred Kohlberg, Raymond G. Loy,* Robert A. MacVicar,* Mark T. Martin,* Leonard Miner,* A. L. Moore, Chester R. Mothershead,* Clyde H. Peabody, Samuel K. Prentice, James E. Rainer,* Joseph M. Savage, Winfred W. Scott,* Hazen H. Smart, Jack W. Squires,* Bruce L. Thomas,* Jim E. Thornton,* Bernard J. Trappe,* Walter L. Van Fossen, William H. Wells, William C. Whelen, Charles R. Whittaker,* Cyrus T. Willock,* and Gordon Wyrick. Asterisk indicates Air Medal winner.

278   From Maine to Mexico

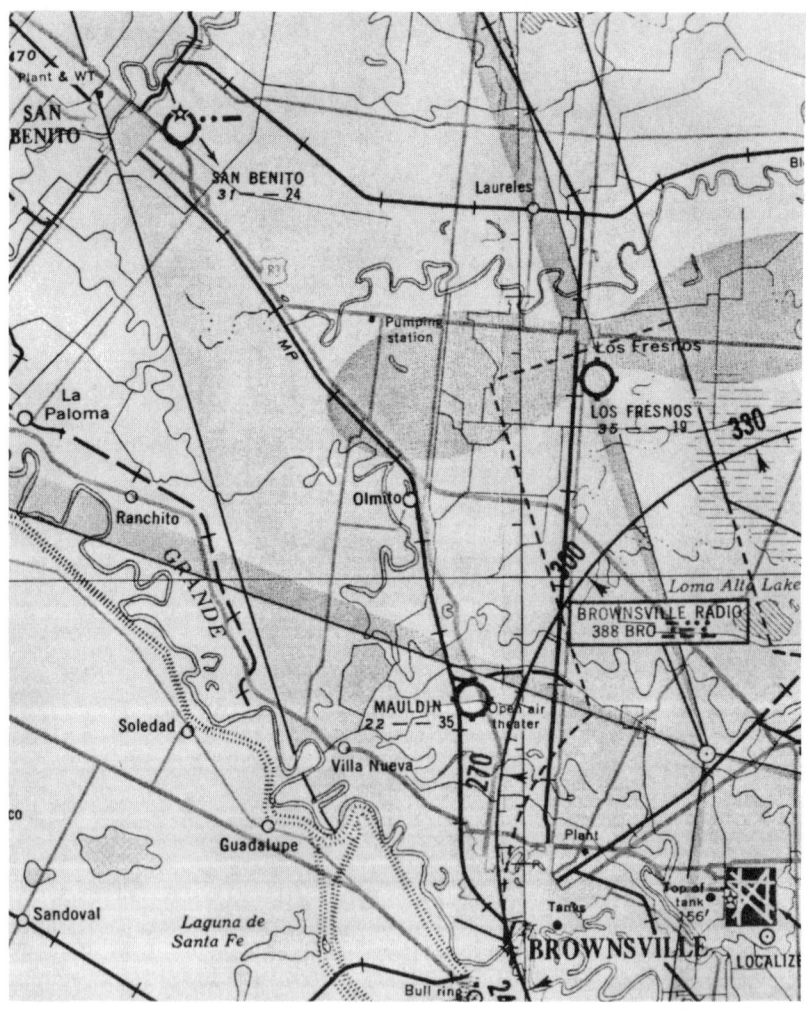

Although the "Brownsville" coastal patrol base began its operations at the Brownsville Municipal Airport (later, as in this 1952 aeronautical chart, much expanded and renamed the Rio Grande Valley International Airport), it soon moved several miles to the northwest to the smaller but less busy airfield at San Benito.

# 12

# Brownsville, Texas

Early in its history, the Brownsville coastal patrol was staffed by some of the most famous personnel to be found at any of the bases. Though the best known of them seldom stayed beyond the thirty-day minimum, among these Aviation Club of California celebrities who volunteered for Brownsville were its first intelligence officer, Henry King, one of Hollywood's all-time great directors, who would soon film "The Song of Bernadette" with Jennifer Jones; Mary Astor, one of the base's radio operators, who had just won an Academy Award as best supporting actress for her role in "The Maltese Falcon;" and Earl Wolcott, RKO sound director. The leader of this Hollywood contingent was Benjamin S. McGlashan, the Aviation Club's president. McGlashan, who at age thirty-seven had logged over a thousand hours in his own Stinson Reliant and had flown more than forty other planes including a Douglas DC-3, served as base commander until mid-1943. In addition to all of the Californians,* there were numerous volunteers from Oregon and Washington.

   * Among the base officers, pilots, and observers from California not mentioned elsewhere in this chapter were: Lloyd G. Allen, Roy H. Anderson,* Charles B. Beatie, Harry Bosshardt, Reuben B. Gilbert, Floyd W. Gladish, Clifford B. Hanson, Lewis E. Hanson, Frank H. Hasey,* Bayard S. Henderson,* Irwin H. Jacoby, Richard T. James, Leroy A. Jones, Homer C. Livingston, Thomas G. Lynch,* Clarence D. Mabey, Don J. Manning, Irven T. Miller, Frederick Robertson, Charles F. Sainsbury, Raymond D. Shock, Spencer W. Shaw, Willard E. Shepherd, John W. Smith, Roy L. Spector, Ronald A. Stewart, John P. Stripling,* Frank Tavolacci,* Frank E. Temple, Robert E. Thomason, John R. Todd, Carl J. Turner, Georg A. Turner, and Davis M. Wellman.* Asterisk indicates Air Medal Winner. Seventeen other Californians served in support roles.

## Dan C. Putnam, Jr.

*The original location of the base at Brownsville Airport was far from ideal for coastal patrol work. Dan C. Putnam, Jr. was a thirty-two-year-old from Spokane, Washington who followed Henry King as the base intelligence and supply officer. In 1986, Putnam, in his "Reminiscences of CAP Base 12," wrote of various problems, the major ones being the non-CAP traffic and erratic winds:*

> Brownsville airport was very crowded. Pan Am stopped there. I can still hear the Mexicans who prepared air flight meals in the terminal building hollering "lonches." There were continual flights of military aircraft in and out, either from the Harlingen gunnery school, or from the training base at Corpus Christi. Whole flights of AT-6 trainers would descend on the airport. And it was a regular stop for military ferry flights to South America and maybe Africa as well. In addition, the wind seemed to blow strongly from all directions at once. I remember being ordered out of George Felt's Stinson SR-7 to push on the tail to swing it around enough for a crosswind take-off.

Having been officially activated on July 8, 1942, the Brownsville base moved to another location five months later. An administration building and hangar were built at a CAA emergency field at San Benito, near Harlingen, thirty miles up the Rio Grande, and the new base opened just before Christmas. One problem the relocation didn't solve was the damage caused by hungry Texas ants and termites. Dan Putnam remembered that the base had a wooden-paneled 1936 Ford station wagon. One day when the driver was starting to town, a bunch of pilots came galloping out and leaped on the running board. They "bit the dust to a man as the whole side ripped loose." The wagon was full of termites.

Before the base moved to San Benito, Putnam put in three of the hardest working months of his life. Although he knew nothing about aircraft parts or radios, the engineering and communications officers told him what was needed, and it was his job to get it. He might be on the phone to New York, Seattle, and Los Angeles several times a day. He was more a supply officer than an intelligence officer:

> One of my first duties as supply officer was to go around to a tire place and get a bunch of truck tubes, then to an awning maker to get a bunch of big sacks made. The tubes went into loops at the tops of the canvas sacks. If forced down, a pilot was supposed to inflate his Mae West, grab this anti-shark contraption on hitting the drink, then blow up the tube and climb in. I don't think there was even a carbon-dioxide cylinder to help. What a device! Fortunately CAP 12 never had to try to use one. Not a week after I arrived on base there was a great to-do about sighting a sub. I never did get the true story, but

the impression remains that there was considerable doubt about it. And that was the last sighting CAP Base 12 ever made, so far as I (the *un*intelligence officer) know, except for sharks and sea turtles six feet long.

Intelligence officer Dan C. Putnam, Jr., his wife Esther, one of the base plotting board operators, and Martha, their five-year-old daughter, sharing a pleasant moment at home (courtesy Dan C. Putnam, Jr.).

More recently, Dan Putnam has described other aspects of his experience at the Brownsville base:

When I arrived in early summer 1942, the base seemed like a Hollywood plaything. Mary Astor was there, a very nice woman with a classic profile and pipe-stem legs. She didn't stay long and didn't do anything as far as I knew, but was horribly afflicted by chiggers. Jean Arthur had been there before I came. And some well-known Hollywood director whose name I've forgotten berated me for having talked to a newspaper reporter, because, he said, the base was supposed to be a secret. That was the first time I'd heard that! My picture had already appeared in the Spokane newspaper, along with a story about where I was going. The director threw his coffee cup on the floor and started to yell at me, but Mary Astor intervened and calmed him down. I learned years later that some people didn't want the base located in Brownsville in the first place, and that the less attention drawn to it, the better. Most people probably don't realize that we were the only coastal patrol base to have regularly flown "overseas" missions — that is, through Mexican airspace and over Mexican waters as far south as Tampico. On these flights we carried only two-dollar bills because the Germans were known to have flooded Mexico with valueless counterfeits of other denominations. I recall the time Hallice Beckett let down the wheels of his Beechcraft staggerwing and flew like that all the way to Tampico so he wouldn't outrun the slower sister ship. From then on, of course, we always kidded him that he did it so he wouldn't forget to lower his gear when he returned for landing. The captain of the Danish freighter being escorted that day begged our C.O. to continue our coverage to Vera Cruz, but that was well beyond our range.

## George H. Felt

*Before he joined the CAP in 1941, twenty-nine-year-old George H. Felt had been an instructor at the Eugene Vocational School for Aviation Mechanics. An Oregonian like so many others at the base,\* he was ordered to Southern Liaison Patrol Base #1 at Laredo, Texas to work as an A&E mechanic. But at the last minute his orders were changed and he paused at Laredo only long enough to refuel, then go on to Brownsville, arriving November 28, 1942. In 1983, he described some of his work there for Frank S. Myers, a member of the CAP National Historical Committee (and himself a former base member).*

> I was the engineering officer at Brownsville and my main job was keeping the aircraft ready for flight duty. That was difficult because our facilities were very meager, and we had a rough time getting parts for the planes. When we had engine problems, we'd often have to find parts and obtain services from local garages, because we didn't have the equipment to grind valves and do things of that nature ourselves. I remember once that we had seven Fairchild 24s out of service at one time. We had about twenty-five planes at the base, and sometimes we had a hard time keeping four of them serviceable for each day's patrols. Lots of times we'd be so short of planes that we'd use the same ones on morning and afternoon patrols, just changing the pilots.

---

\* Among those not elsewhere mentioned in this chapter were base officers, pilots, and observers William H. Anderson, Edgar A. Cummings,\* Charles T. Haas, Jack D. Hallberg, Niels Holm, Albert W. Holman, Dan A. Howard,\* William E. Lees, Jr., Allen C. Oosterveer,\* George W. Reed, James V. Rosenbaum,\* Frank H. Seal, Elmer L. Smith, Leslie V. Stiles, Frank N. Van Petten, Earle E. Voorhies, and Raymond L. Wescott. Another fourteen Oregonians served in support positions. Rounding out the West Coast representation at Brownsville were these Washington pilots and observers not elsewhere mentioned in the chapter: Charles F. Bartschat,\* Harold C. Filbert,\* Arnold M. Fredricksen, Bill Lee,\* Fred Marschante, and Gibson M. Wolfe. Three other Washington people served in support. Asterisk indicates Air Medal winner.

We also had a lot of radio problems. Of course the aircraft couldn't go on patrol unless the radios were working. We had some patrols come back in when their radios quit. The radios in the planes were of all makes, RCAs, Bendixes, and so on, whatever the planes had in them before the war came along. We had to have a bunch of different service manuals and spare parts, and our radio man did a fine job with what he had to work with. The base transmitter itself was a ham outfit that our radio man from Spokane brought to the base. That helped us a thousand percent with the radios.

After a plane was repaired, we usually flew it around the field on a test hop to see if everything was working right. But, also, on the first flight out over the water, the mechanic was required to go along as an observer.... In the long run this requirement was very successful because our base never lost an aircraft in the ocean. We had several make forced landings on the beach after running out of fuel, and in one particular case we had a cylinder blow off a Warner Fairchild about three miles out, but by all kinds of persuasion the pilot made the beach straight on.

## Dean E. Rankin

*Dean E. Rankin worked under George Felt as the assistant engineering officer, a job he describes as being the "shop foreman." Like Felt, he had attended the Eugene Vocational School where he earned an engine mechanic, or "E" rating, then stayed on as an instructor. When the twenty-one-year-old Rankin decided he didn't care for teaching, he took a job as a mechanic at a CPTP base in Klamath Falls, Oregon. Hometown acquaintances serving in the Brownsville coastal patrol recruited him and his friend Arnold Reed, another mechanic, and they joined the base shortly after it opened:*

In the shop, besides George, Arnold, and myself, I remember Elmer Molitor — we called him "Molly" — and Norris Kaldor, George Smith, and young Kenneth Johnson — we called him "Swede" and gave him an awful hard time. Max Green was there to help out too. A number of others also come to mind. Earl Wolcott was assistant operations officer. He was a sound man for RKO, and you still see his name on the credits list of many old movies. "Rachel and the Stranger" with Bill Holden, Robert Mitchum, and Loretta Young, is an example. Earl was a real perfectionist, and his airplane got plenty of attention from the shop crew.

I was pretty much in charge of the shop, because George Felt's job was mainly at a higher level as a go-between with the commanding officer. I worked some myself, but mostly I supervised the other mechanics. I was usually there from about eight in the morning until five or six in the evening. We went to work in our uniforms, changed to coveralls, then at noon changed back to uniforms for lunch downtown. Then back to our coveralls, then back to uniforms to head home. It was so hot and humid that our uniforms were always wet. They never had a chance to dry out. That's the one thing I never got used to. It was very uncomfortable, and caused some fellows an almost constant heat rash.

You know, everyone calls it the Brownsville base, but we were actually up in San Benito a good deal longer than we were in Brownsville. Four of us shared an apartment on McDonald Street, which was then the main street. There was little to do. We'd drive down to Brownsville, about twenty-five miles, and cross over the Rio Grande to Matamoras for dinner, and quiet things like that. Molitor met and married a local girl, so that kept him busy. I often returned to the base and built things we needed around the shop, like a certain kind of wiring tester. For a time, several of us went up to Del Rio, and established a shop there for use by the border patrol planes. That's when I left the CAP and entered the Air Corps. After basic training at Amarillo, Texas, I wound up as a ground crew chief with B-29s at Clovis, New Mexico. The war ended by the time we got overseas, and I wasn't discharged until July 1946. After working with George Felt for a time in our own aviation business, I went with a Caterpillar dealership, where I stayed until I retired. My wife and I raised two girls and now divide our time between our home in Eugene and a summer place on the beautiful Oregon coast.

## Lee E. Stevens

*Air Medal winner Lee E. Stevens was twenty-seven when he joined the Brownsville base as a pilot on July 20, 1942. He remembers George Felt well. "Before Felt's arrival," he recalls, "the maintenance on base aircraft wasn't so good. Afterwards, it was great. He was the best." Stevens flew his last mission from Brownsville more than a year later, having logged over three hundred hours as the pilot-in-command and another one hundred hours as an observer (he later flew nearly as many hours on border patrol from the Laredo, Texas base). He recalls patrolling the Mexican as well as the American coastline:*

To the south, the base had the job of patrolling the beach from the border clear down to Tampico, Mexico, about two hundred miles, looking for balsa life rafts that German agents employed to paddle from their submarines to the beaches. One day, Ralph C. Parker, a fellow from Portland, and myself were flying his Stinson 10-A about sixty miles south of Brownsville when we ran through a rain storm at about a thousand feet. Most Gulf coast rain storms were no more than a half-mile straight through. This one was seven miles. The spark plugs on the two front cylinders shorted-out, and we had to land on the beach. The trouble was a ten foot piece of six-by-six timber laying on the beach crossways. We hit it and flipped over on our back. We weren't hurt but the plane was badly damaged. Getting it back to base over those rugged Mexican coastal roads proved an adventure for our ground crew.

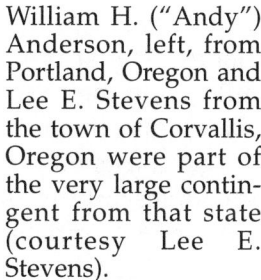
William H. ("Andy") Anderson, left, from Portland, Oregon and Lee E. Stevens from the town of Corvallis, Oregon were part of the very large contingent from that state (courtesy Lee E. Stevens).

The first four months on patrols we wore Mae Wests and carried shark sacks, canvas sacks laced to an inner tube. How we were expected to blow up the inner tubes by mouth was a mystery. I know I couldn't do it, even on dry land. Then we got one-man life rafts that we could inflate with carbon dioxide cartridges just like our Mae Wests. I was given the job of taking all flight personnel out in an Air Corps crash boat and having them jump off into the water to practice using the rafts. Some of the fatter guys couldn't get into them even after repeated practice. We didn't lose any planes in the Gulf, but had a close call when a Waco lost power because of a broken exhaust valve push rod, and landed head-on in the surf and was tumbled up onto the beach.

I don't remember any Fairchilds having problems. One came to the base using a lot of oil, however, and George Felt and I took it apart at least twice without finding the problem. We finally got a replacement engine from the Navy. This plane was flown more than any of our others, because the owner was absent. Some of our planes couldn't be flown unless the owners were in them. About eight of ours were in that category, which sometimes left us short of available aircraft for patrols.

Most of the pilots at Brownsville had always used visual navigation, looking at roads and towns and mountains, so we spent our first two weeks learning to navigate with flight computers and wrist watches. Although the war had shut down weather reports and we didn't know the winds aloft, at least in the summer we could count on the same wind day after day — as I recall it, about eight to ten knots from about seventy degrees. We flew two routes, one about five miles out, the other about twenty-five miles out. We reported the names and locations of every ship we saw, and around the mouth of the Rio Grande River we also noted the numbers of the fishing boats, because the Navy thought that some subs were being refueled by them. We didn't see any subs after the first week of patrols, but I think that our being out there kept them from sinking any more ships.

I had been married only eight months when I went down to Brownsville. My wife came down later by train (her first train ride). We had a room in a motel, along with several other pilots and their wives. Max Green, who was in charge of fueling our planes, also lived there with his wife. George Felt's wife and mine became good friends at this time. After we relocated to San Benito, most of the couples found apartments. Brownsville had bad drinking water, and was mostly inhabited by Mexicans. Only after returning from a drive across the bridge to visit Matamoras, Mexico, did Brownsville look pretty good. We liked pleasant little San Benito much better. The people were real nice to us, and on our days off we'd drive to the Gulf beaches for a swim.

## Henry E. Schurman

*Henry E. Schurman grew up and learned to fly in the Pittsburgh, Pennsylvania area, soloing a J-3 Cub in January 1941. He served at Brownsville from December 14, 1942 to August 31, 1943, and in 1948 received the Air Medal. In 1985, he recorded his reminiscences for the CAP Oral History Program, and remembered enjoying, not dreading, his first long flight over the ocean with Holt W. Warrens of Portland, Oregon, and how some morning fogs were so thick the pilots would have to taxi back and forth to create a visible runway. Some of his flights with the older more experienced pilots were quite exciting:*

> We had some real first rate pilots there on CAP-12. I remember once Bruce Barrett took me up in that old Waco he had. He went into a dive with the airspeed on the pin, past the redline, and he looked over at me and said that George Felt told him that if he went over 150 mph the wings would fall off. He then looked over at the airspeed and said, "George Felt was wrong about that." However, we did lose some fabric. Another time, Stephen K. ("Cobie") Coburn from Eugene, Oregon and I were several miles offshore and I was gazing at the water — you know how that goes — and Cobie got my

attention with a shout, "Hey, my g. d. gas gauge shows empty, what does yours say?" We were in a Fairchild 24, where the gas gauges drop down from the wings, so I looked out and told him mine showed empty, too. He radioed the base, and they admitted that the ship had not been gassed that morning.... So we headed for the beach, and crossed our fingers, and just did make it. We set down and got out and checked the fuel in the gas tanks and found none. Now this was all my fault, because I usually wet my finger in each tank. Anyway, George Felt flew over with three five-gallons cans of gas, and he dropped those three cans in a row right off the wing one, two, three. Boy, that guy sure could fly! I think he flew the bush in Alaska at one time. When we got back to the base, Cobie asked him why he hadn't put the gas right into the tanks while he was at it.

Henry E. Schurman came from Pittsburgh, Pennsylvania and met his wife-to-be Ruth Perry when he went to a party at the border patrol base at Laredo, Texas (courtesy Henry E. Schurman).

More recently, Schurman described the unusual way he met his wife-to-be, their long-distance courtship, and their marriage:

They were having a Christmas party at the Laredo border patrol base, and invited anyone from CAPCP #12 who wanted to come. Four of us — Isadore Greenberg as pilot and myself as co-pilot and two mechanics — checked out a Waco and headed for Laredo, where they flew from the parade ground at Fort McIntosh. This "airfield" was a short, dirt strip with an eight-foot wall at one end and barracks at the other. Greenberg was quite unhappy to see where he had to land. He was high the first time and had to go around. We cleared the buildings, but not by much. When the stabilizer jammed we were in real trouble.

So we lined up again, Greenberg with both hands on his yoke and me with one hand on my yoke and the other on the throttle. We went over the wall and the approach was good in all respects, but at the last minute we caught a gust and started drifting. Greenberg told me to chop the throttle, which I did, but I knew what was next. I wound down my window with one hand, and fumbled under the seat for our pint-size two-bit fire extinguisher. We ended up with the nose dug in, and one

Left to right: clerk-typist Eloise ("Sugar") Kane, pilot Henry E. Schurman, and Dolores Hilliard, head of the technical section. Kane, also a pilot, had acted in several movies prior to serving in the CAP (courtesy Henry E. Schurman).

wing tip in the dirt. I got out of the window in a flash and emptied our extinguisher into the fire coming out of the cowling. Meanwhile, a fire truck arrived, and the crew jumped around unrolling hoses and turning levers and valves, but all they got was a little dribble out of one hose. I kept screaming for them to get the carbon dioxide tanks off the truck, which they finally did, and then they quickly put out the fire.

Well, when the fire truck raced out, there was a Jeep right behind it, and in the Jeep was a good-looking blonde with about three-feet of hair trailing in the wind. Her name was Ruth Perry, and she was from Oregon. I asked her if she had a date for the party, and she said, yes, but that she'd break it for me. After I returned to San Benito, we started corresponding via the border patrol planes that landed at San Benito for refueling. Each one had a letter for me, and returned a letter for her. I managed to get transferred to Laredo but then El Paso needed a radio man and I was transferred there. Ruthie resigned her CAP post at Laredo and came to El Paso. We were married on March 1, 1944, and will soon celebrate our fifty-second anniversary.

When Schurman speaks of Brownsville, he also recalls radio mechanic Leo Hirchaut's "Lover Boy," an overly affectionate male dachshund who tried to make love to anyone and everyone. The dog also loved to fly. He would go out with one patrol, come back and jump out of the plane to look for a tree, then go out again. The pilots kept a log book for him, but Schurman says he doesn't know how many hours the dachshund accumulated. Then there was the time that a couple of pilots went over to Matamoras, had a little too much to drink and wound up broke and in jail. Schurman was sent over to bail them out. "The fine was bartered, as was everything else in Mexico," said Schurman. "They started out with some enormous sum, but after an hour or so I managed to spring them for fifty pesos each. At that time, the exchange was eight to one, so the fine was a little over six dollars each."

Schurman described his fellow pilots as well as anyone ever has: "The coastal patrol had some of the best pilots, and I guess a few of the worst. Most were the best. They could not make the military for various reasons. Most were too old. Some were color blind or needed glasses to fly. The Air Corps wouldn't take a pilot who needed glasses to fly. One border patrol pilot I knew had been an Alaskan bush pilot, and had lost both feet to frostbite. But could he ever fly! One fellow had a cork hand, and another had a metal plate in his head, and so on, and so on. By comparison to such veterans, my experience was limited, and I was proud to be part of the Civil Air Patrol."

## Ruth Perry

*Ruth Perry (now Ruth Schurman) began taking flying lessons in Bend, Oregon in June, 1942 with money saved from her job as a bookkeeper in a hardware store. When she soloed two months later, the* Bend Bulletin *described her as the first woman to to do so from the new Bend Airport. In a traditional celebration, she was tossed into the cool waters of Mirror Pond by other flying students, then taken to dinner by them. When a CAP unit was formed in Bend, she joined, and when they began recruiting staff for the border patrol, she left for active duty at Laredo in December 1942 as a clerk-typist:*

When I first went to Laredo, we were flying from the Laredo Air Corps field. As the activity there increased, we were asked to move.

Our only choice was the parade ground at Fort McIntosh. Of course I'm grateful to the Civil Air Patrol for bringing Henry and me together. How else would a country girl like me from Oregon meet a city gentleman from Pittsburgh like Henry!

Sgt. Ruth Perry broke a date to go to a dance with Henry Schurman. Later, he arranged a transfer to her Laredo base, and they were married soon afterwards in El Paso, Texas (courtesy Henry E. Schurman).

**Frank S. Myers**

*Best man at Henry Schurman's wedding was Frank S. Myers of Portland, Oregon, fellow pilot and the base's training officer. Myers had been a buyer at the Montgomery Ward mail order house and volunteered for CAP at his first opportunity. Leaving his little Porterfield CP-65 behind in storage because its engine was not powerful enough for coastal patrol, and with Howard H. Haag along as a passenger, he flew a 210 hp Waco biplane to Brownsville, making his first landing in the strong off-shore crosswind that caused many pilots trouble. He was formally enrolled at the base on September 21, 1942 by Cpl. Phyllis Layton of Marshfield, Oregon, whom he later married. Interviewed in 1983 by Capt. Hellenmerie Walker, a CAP historian, Air Medal winner Myers described many details of the Brownsville operation, among them the unusual weather and its consequences:*

> It's extremely humid, semi-tropical, a high degree of moisture in the air, and yet on occasion, a "Norther" would sweep down from the north and the weather might radically change in a matter of one or two hours, temperatures might drop forty or fifty degrees. When

this happened — given the 85-95 percent normal humidity caused by the fog and moisture coming in off the Gulf — there would be a lot of condensation in the gas tanks. Even though we tried our best, if one or two of the aircraft once in a while had to land on the beach it would be because of water in the gas. No plane at CAP 12 ever was dumped in the water, but there were aircraft that just kinda sputtered their way in for a beach landing, and usually the problem was contaminated fuel.

Each morning when we went out to fly the aircraft, the wings, the interior wing panels, and the drip holes would be dripping with water. We might take a healthy cupful of water out of the tanks, and of course we always refilled them right to the top as soon as an airplane landed.... This same condensation, of course, affected the electrical system and the mags. Fortunately, most planes were flown every day and that kept them pretty well dried out inside.

First Lt. Frank S. Myers was from Portland, Oregon, and served as the base training officer. Here he sits for the photograph used on an ID card needed for base access and other identification purposes (courtesy Frank S. Myers).

Myers had the unique experience of flying to Atlantic City, New Jersey, to attend an anti-submarine school taught by Eastern Sea Frontier personnel. There, various base training officers learned about submarines, what they might do when they thought they'd been sighted, and what coastal patrol planes should do to counter their actions. He took Ralph C. McClenahan of College Place, Washington, along as his observer, and they flew clear around the Gulf and up the east coast, stopping at every coastal patrol base en route:

> After returning to base, we marked out a target area out on Padre Island and all our pilots made repeated practice flights and became proficient at aiming and dropping practice bombs on it. At no time were we ever issued real bombsights. Each pilot made his own makeshift arrangement. This was necessary, really, because the viewing positions of the pilots and observers in each aircraft would be different depending on the design of the airplane — whether it was a low-wing monoplane, a high-wing monoplane, or a biplane. Usually a sighting was done along lines painted on the cowling. It might be on the side visible to the pilot, or it might be on the side visible to the observer, or on both sides. It must be kept in mind that we felt most of our duty was accomplished by scanning the water below for anything that could be seen. We never did, to my knowledge, sight a submarine.

As elsewhere, many coastal patrol members found things they didn't expect. When those from the green-forested northwest — Oregon and Washington — arrived on the banks of the Rio Grande they were disappointed to learn that in the summer it could be walked across almost anywhere, and it was extremely muddy all the time. Frank Myers remembers that the border towns were very dirty, and that the southern tip of Texas involved many surprises:

> That's a whole story of its own. We kept a Chamber of Commerce publication on the lower Rio Grande valley and we made a joke of memorizing the opening sentences — "clean, attractive towns and cities, broad surf-creamed beaches, golden-laden citrus orchards, broad palm-lined highways and wide vistas of green fields of vegetables glowing under the deep blue of the cloud-flecked Texas sky, create an unforgettable picture of lush beauty." When we were being trundled out to the field at five-thirty in the morning we'd sing this as one of our little jingles to entertain each other.

> The chiggers and ants were a terrible problem. The coarse grass that was common to the area was simply alive with insects of all kinds. The chiggers would bite right through the girls' nylons (then available in Mexico but not in the United States) if they strayed anywhere near the grass, and their legs would become visibly blood-stained. All the furniture in the El Jardin Hotel was made of steel because any wooden product would soon be eaten by insects. When you came into your room after dark and flicked on the light switch all the critters would run and hide. If you left a candy bar partly eaten or anything at all that could be consumed, in a drawer, or even well wrapped-up, in the morning there would be a continuous file of ants

all the way up from the ground, up the stairwells and into your room to the food.

For the benefit of several uncommitted friends back home in Oregon who wanted to know what the coastal patrol was really like, Frank Myers wrote a detailed letter that anticipated almost every question they might ask:

> Horsepower ratings are absolutely adhered to. Do not under *any* circumstances come down here without at least a 145 hp rating, but preferably a 330 rating. If possible, get a little time in a Waco cabin or Beechcraft, as they have each one here with throw-over wheels and cannot check out pilots in the ships without full dual control. For example, the Waco I brought down here I have to fly all the time, as there is no one else to do so. You will have to pay your own transportation down here, and your pay will start *after* you arrive at the base. Do not let anybody tell you different. If you have the required ratings you will get all the flying you will ever want. You do fly over water practically all the time. Much of the flying is done out of sight of land.

Unidentified man trying out a one-man life raft. Brownsville office and operations building, with "control tower," is in the background (Hopper collection).

> They have a good ground crew and seem to keep up the equipment pretty well. I believe that operations here are perfectly safe. Do not bring your wife as there is nothing for women to do in this town. You can tell your wife not to worry about you as there are no women

here you would go for anyway. There is only one place to stay and that is this hotel [the El Jardin]. It is very nice. Three of us have a room here for 73¢ a day each. Food is a little cheaper than in Portland. You won't spend very much though, as you will only have time to eat two meals a day anyway. The weather is supposed to get better. It was cool and dry the first few days here but is hot and sticky today [October 1, 1942]. Just like a steam bath. If you sign up for the duration you can be in the enlisted Army Air Corps reserve, as a private, and will be exempt from the draft. Learn all about the [handheld flight] computers, as they are used all the time. There is no hurry about it, but try to learn the international radio code so you can send 6 or 7 words a minute, as we are all going to have to learn it. You *must* have a third class license.

If possible, come down here with a ship, ferrying it here, as we did. That way you will probably be assigned to it. Otherwise you will have to act as observer for a while at least. You won't mind that though, as you can log half the time anyway. The deal on logging time is that the pilots log all the time, and the observers log half of it too. All the dope given above pertains to the Coastal Patrol, at Brownsville, as of today. It does not pertain to the Border Patrol, about which I know nothing. I know, however, that you will not get paid for transportation or per diem until you arrive. The official story as far as pay is concerned is that we are supposed to be working for nothing. We are not on salary, but are on a subsistence allowance, of $8.00 per day. They can ask you to work for 24 hours a day if necessary, and have done it in the past, but not since we have been here. The patrols will be made as ordered by the Army, regardless of anything else. The work is very interesting. In fact, it is fascinating, although there is the normal amount of bitching as on any army post. I think everyone is really more or less proud of the outfit.

You will be a first lieutenant. Here in Brownsville the Army doesn't have much use for us as our red shoulder straps give us away. About one-third of the soldiers salute us. The rest disregard us. I am told they will be instructed to accord us military courtesy. They make you salute your arm off if you go to any of the other towns around here. Don't waste a lot of time drilling. You can already drill about 5 times as good as these guys. They drill every other day. Today they are starting a new system. Pilots and co-pilots will be permanently assigned to a ship, and will have to keep it up and keep it clean to about the same extent they would if they were private pilots owning their own ships. They specialize in Beeches. Get checked out in one.

Let us know if you know of any good heavy ships for sale. The base needs Wacos, Fairchilds, Cessnas, etc. I do not mean for sale. I mean to be placed on the base for operation, for the duration. This type of ship is hard to find, and they need more of them. The Army is going to replace ships for the bases when there are no more private ships obtainable. I am enclosing a sample of the red material. The shoulder straps are covered with this material, and first lieutenant bars are worn also. The cap has a braid of the same color, or a strip of this material sewed on, so that it shows all the way around. Chutes are not worn. Any type of hunting knife will do. It does not have to have a cork handle. They furnish the life jacket and a little one-man floating device that is supposed to fool the sharks and barracuda.

## Thomas G. Somermeier

*Thomas G. Somermeier reported to Brownsville from Los Angeles where all private flying had been prohibited after Pearl Harbor. The first to fly "Osa's Ark," one of the base's two Sikorsky S-39 amphibians — so nicknamed because it had once belonged to Martin and Osa Johnson, the famous African explorers — Somermeier called it a wonderful airplane that would take-off, cruise, and land at eighty miles an hour! In 1985 he reminisced for fellow Brownsville base member Frank S. Myers what it was like to fly it:*

> One day there was a Mexican tanker coming up the coast on its way to Galveston. It was our mission to escort it and keep a lookout for German submarines.... My crew consisted of a co-pilot, who had never been on a mission before, and who, I found out later, had a problem with stammering, and two other non-rated observers in the back seat. It was a beautiful day and the S-39 was a pleasure to fly so the time passed quickly.... [finally, because I didn't know how much fuel I had left, and our relief plane never showed up] ... I told my co-pilot to call the base and tell them we were returning, and that's when I learned about his stammering problem. Just then the 300 hp Wasp gave a cough and I knew immediately what the trouble was. I told him to get on the wobble pump and I started to look for a place to land.
>
> The beach was smooth but had some debris on it, and as it was such a beautiful day and as the sea was calm, I elected to make a water landing near the beach.... I was curious to see how much fuel was left so I climbed up and took off the gas cap. Just a little vapor came out. We were on the Harlingen Gunnery School Range, and soon two AT-6s came along, the first towing a sleeve target and the second shooting at it. We wrote "NO GAS" in big letters in the sand, and soon one AT-6 wiggled his wings so we sat down to wait. About an hour later a Jeep with two sailors and a five-gallon can of aviation gasoline appeared. We then took off and landed back at Brownsville without incident.

It just so happened that I was aerodrome officer that night, and was on duty when the TWX "ding-dinged" and typed out a message from Army Air Corps headquarters in Miami reading, "Give me a full report on the forced landing of the Sikorsky today." I thought, "Isn't it fortunate that I am here and can really give an accurate and ungarbled report," which I proceeded to do. As I finished the last sentence I just couldn't resist the temptation to say "due to the ability of the pilot, no damage was done to the plane. There was a moment of silence, and then the TWX shot back — "GOOD PILOTS DON'T RUN OUT OF GAS."

## Bruce Logan Patton Barrett

*Twenty-nine-year-old Bruce Logan Patton Barrett hailed from Peoria, Illinois, and had owned three planes before joining the CAP. Along about Thanksgiving 1942, he flew his 225 hp Waco YOC, to Brownsville, there to make his first-ever landing on a paved runway. Despite his self-admitted weakness in "constructing messages in writing," by choice he manned the base teletype machine about as much as he flew:*

Upon my arrival at Brownsville, and with little or no indoctrination, I was given a set of gold bars and sent out on a patrol as an observer. I was in the air before my plane was. Waco NC 15217 was accepted for coastal patrol duty only after fatigue cracks in the landing gear system were repaired by Air Corps welders at Harlingen. On patrol we flew in pairs and maintained a strict schedule by reference to grid squares. I don't remember ever losing sight of Padre Island. I do recall once when returning to base we had to remain aloft until a front passed, and for a few minutes the wind was so strong that I flew more or less stationary in front of the control tower. Written reports had to be turned in after every patrol. Our intelligence officer was a professional artist named Putnam. One day Lt. Putnam said to me, "Lt. Barrett, you can't tell me that anyone could spell unintentionally like this! It's bad enough to read your writing, but to be expected to decipher this is impossible!" Years later, I got a letter from Dan Putnam saying, "Please don't try to correct your spelling, Bruce. It's so original that I find it a delight to look forward to."

Soon we moved up to a grass strip at San Benito, where we installed boundary lights, an open-end shed for aircraft maintenance, and a unique administration building one-room-wide and six-rooms-long, with a control tower at one end. Each room was separated from the next by large glass windows so that any room was visible from any other. Our ready room was sparsely furnished — a card table, some chairs, a wall map, and a magazine and newspaper rack. We had a base station wagon that would collect flight personnel in town each morning in time for the dawn patrol. San Benito wasn't much. Because it was at the same latitude as Miami, there had been some land speculation during the 1920s and 1930s. But it didn't pan out, and from the "Magic Valley" it became known to disappointed investors as the "Tragic Valley."

Unidentified Brownsville flyers confer on matters of offshore navigation — or perhaps where to have dinner that evening — not that there was much choice (courtesy Henry E. Schurman).

I don't rightly recall why my request for night duty was readily accepted, or why I made it. But I became the night teletype operator, and spent much of the year on night duty. It was quite agreeable because I found myself hooked up to a network of like beings. Following our base reports to our various headquarters we'd exchange nonsense messages which we eventually improvised into doing illustrations on the teletype. Though we could only visit Mexico once a month, unless we were on flight duty or standby, our time was pretty much our own. Being a church-goer I made my social life among the Christians, with many of whom I've maintained friendships through the years.

* * *

Though some base members recall an absence of socializing with the dominantly Spanish-speaking Brownsville community — perhaps because of the commander's policy of maintaining strict secrecy on the base's anti-submarine mission — others enjoyed the community, as well as an occasional trip to Mexico. Matamoras was just the other side of the Rio Grande and was easily reached by car. Frank Myers recalls many meals there, and getting acquainted with Mexican foods and drinks:

> Waterfell and Fraser, made in Juarez of dubious constituents, was the leading whiskey. And of course we learned to drink tequila in the approved Mexican fashion, with a pinch of salt in the hollow of the left thumb and forefinger, or on the back of the hand. You ate a slice of fresh lime, put your tongue on the salt, and drank the tequila straight. Montezuma and Carta Blanca were the leading beers, and they were excellent. There were lots of opportunities to buy silver knick-knacks and ornaments and what-nots to send home. We learned to enjoy trips into Mexico....

> Speaking of the Mexican nationals, some mention should be made of the guards. They were about the first persons hired at the base, because of the considerable security involved The guards were local Texans or Mexican-Americans, and they were very friendly and very efficient. We had one sergeant, I've forgotten his name, and he had a good, lively crew. As you can visualize, with our colorful, air force-type uniforms, with the silver buttons and red epaulets, we looked pretty grand, and the Mexican guards, I think, enjoyed wearing our uniforms. Probably it gave them a certain amount of prestige in their community.

### Mrs. Holt W. Warrens

*Holt W. Warrens and his wife Alice had been married about two months when they went down to Brownsville from the Portland area, he as a pilot, she as a clerk typist. In 1986, she recalled for Captain Hellenmerie Walker how little she knew about the job or the area:*

> Before I went with Holt to Brownsville, I had been working as a hair stylist, and I didn't even know what a clerk-typist was. It all happened very quickly. I got my papers on the run, and bought my uniform after we got to Texas. I understand that I was just one of more than fifty Oregonians who either went to the coastal patrol — most of them to Brownsville, but others to another Texas base and some I think to Louisiana — or to border liaison units. I was about thirty-three at the time and wasn't that some honeymoon! When we flew in, they were having a "norther." The palm trees were bent almost to the ground. I thought we'd gone to the end of the world.

> When I reported for work the first morning, the woman in charge, Dolores Hilliard, came over and handed me a big fat pack of papers to file. I didn't know where or how. When I started looking at them, they were letters from people who'd been on the base but were unhappy with the situation and left. I got absorbed and just sat there

reading them. I didn't get any directions, but I guess I must eventually have figured out where they went. I could type, but in fact I was never asked to, and before long I became one of the radio operators in the control tower.

Betty [Bernice] Stewart worked in the control tower, too. When we weren't busy we'd read magazines. Her husband Ronnie [Ronald] Stewart was a pilot, but he was also the assistant operations officer, and he came upstairs one day and told us we absolutely could NOT read magazines. It didn't matter whether we were busy or not. Then Betty started keeping them under her desk. She was a little devil!

After a regular eight-hour day, I went home to the El Jardin hotel. At first we'd had a cheaper place at a motel, but the cockroaches had been so bad we had to leave. At the hotel, we had a hot plate and I'd fix dinner and wait for Holt to get off duty. We weren't very well off financially and generally avoided eating in the hotel restaurant. He was often very tired because he flew more than most other pilots, often filling-in for those who'd partied too much the night before and couldn't go up. We didn't go to any of those parties. We were happy just to be home and together. There wasn't much to do down there anyway, and we were still newlyweds....

The biggest scare I had was one day when I heard, "Mayday! Mayday! WVV23." I said, "Oh! That's my husband's plane. Holt's in that plane!" He was out on a regular patrol with Elmo Jarrett, a pilot from Kingsport, Tennessee, and their engine had quit. Holt was a fine pilot and I knew he'd do whatever it took to get down safely. I was immensely relieved, of course, when they made the beach and landed without injury. Later, the plane was found to have had water in the gas tanks.

## Harold G. Spencer

*Harold G. Spencer, a pilot from Ogden, Utah, reported shortly after the base opened and stayed until it relocated to San Benito. Twenty-eight years old, he arrived at Brownsville leaving behind his wife, his two children in school, and his job as a locomotive crane operator for the Southern Pacific.*

I'd been active in the Ogden squadron of the CAP since it was formed. One day, the state CAP commander described the coastal patrol and suggested I ought to go down there and do something for my country, so I did. I didn't own a plane then, so I took a bus to Brownsville — about a three-day trip in those days. They were so short of pilots, that as soon as I was oriented a little bit, I was quickly assigned to flying missions. I flew my butt off. Up almost every day, and usually twice a day, six hours or more in the air. I also flew beach patrol down along the

Mexican coast. All I ever saw were porpoises. Along with virtually everyone else I lived at the El Jardin. It was a fairly modern, rather nice hotel, and we had the second floor. As I recall, almost everyone had left their families behind. Brownsville was not a particularly attractive town, and, besides, everyone was so busy it wouldn't have been much fun for the wives and children anyway. I was never a card player so the only recreation I can remember was walking down the street to a pool hall and shooting a few racks of rotation. We all took most of our meals at the hotel, and at first we were paying our own way, which was a son of a gun until pay checks started coming through.

Pilot Stephen K. Coburn of Eugene, Oregon poses for a photo with a Mexican and his burro (courtesy Frank S. Myers).

Before the war I owned a Fairchild 22. That was a parasol monoplane with an inverted Cirrus engine. It was nice! One of the jobs I had with it was to round up wild horses near the Skedaddle Mountains in northern California. Because of the short exhaust stacks coming up out of that inverted engine, the Fairchild 22 was a noisy plane, so when I got down close to a stallion I could get him going right now. I'd run the horses fifteen miles or so, and by then they'd be easy for the cowboys to herd into a prepared corral. At Brownsville I was checked out to fly both the Fairchild 24 and Beechcraft staggerwing. I could fly everything they had but never had the chance to. In recent years, I've been working as an actor, doing television commercials. You may have seen me as a granddaddy in some Chevy Cavalier spots!

\* \* \*

When the Brownsville base closed down, its personnel found themselves reassigned to three different locations. Forty-seven men and women went to SLP #1, twenty went to SLP #2 in El Paso, and seventeen others went to the Tow Target Unit #12 based at Gibbs Airport in San Diego, California. Those assigned to towing targets included commanding officer Raymond L. Westcott; operations officer Holt W. Williams; engineering officer George H. Felt; pilots Roy H. Anderson, Isadore Greenberg, Dan A. Howard, Homer C. Livingston, and Frank Tavolacci; observers James W. Fitzgerald and John C. Mattingly; mechanic Kenneth E. Johnson; service technician Robert G. Haughey; technical section head Alyce A. McGuire; and guards Eduardo Guerra, Eugenio Lopez, and Guadalupe Navarro.

---

Base officers, pilots, and observers who served at least one month at CAPCP #12 and who are not elsewhere mentioned in this chapter include: Bruce A. Bates,* William Beatus,* B. F. Bryan,* Duane L. Croft,* William R. Devenish,* Clifford J. Grube, William V. Hanley, Charles Johnson, Con R. Little, Jr., Kenneth H. Lloyd,* John E. McCollum,* Kay W. Mendenhall, Manfred D. Quinby, Wade A. Rowse,* Frank N. Van Petten, and Milton V. West. Asterisk indicates Air Medal winner.

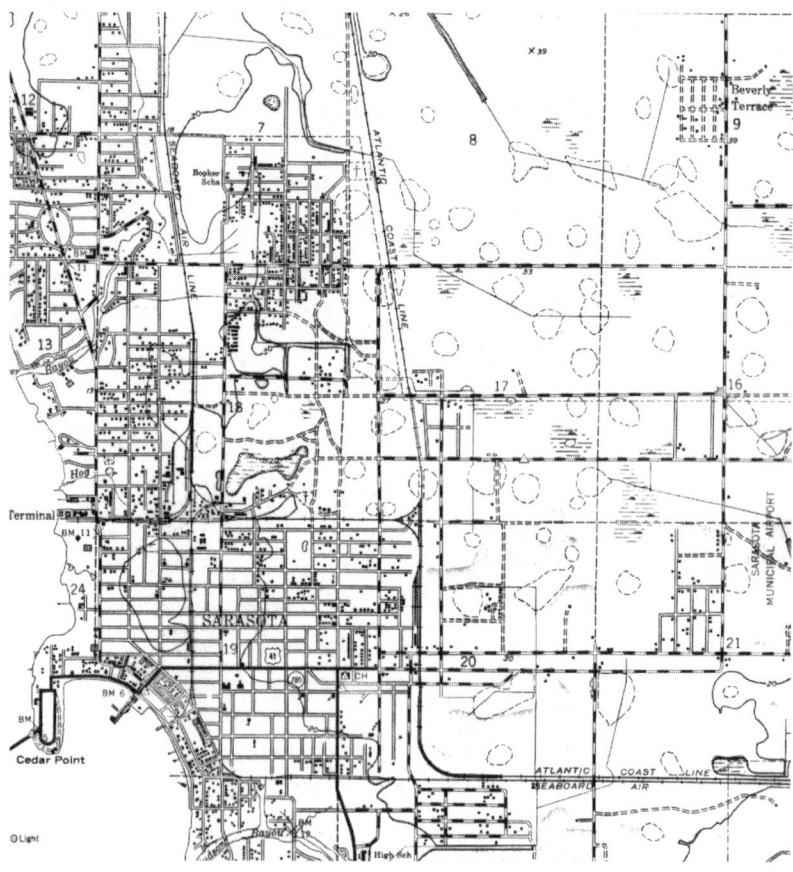

The Sarasota Municipal Airport used by the coastal patrol was located about two miles east of downtown in a then rural area pockmarked by intermittent ponds and marshy wetlands (see far right edge of map). Now a retirement mecca, Sarasota is roughly forty miles south of the St. Petersburg-Tampa metropolitan area (source: 1944 United States Geological Survey).

# 13

# Sarasota, Florida

Situated on Florida's Gulf Coast, twenty-five miles south of St. Petersburg, Sarasota is sometimes called Florida's cultural center, the "Palm Beach of West Florida," and Florida's "cradle of golf," because the first course in the state was laid out there in 1886. A yachting and fishing resort, it was for many years also the winter home of the Ringling Brothers Circus. During the days of the coastal patrol it was little more than a small village facing Longboat Key across Sarasota Bay. Interstate Route 75, which today links most of the Florida west coast's resorts and retirement communities, was not even imagined.

Commanding Officer Peter J. Sones, forty-six when he took over the Sarasota base, was born and grew up in Lacrosse, Wisconsin. In 1918, he enlisted in the Army, but the war ended while he was in Jacksonville, Florida waiting to board a ship for France. Discharged in Florida and given twenty-five dollars mustering-out pay, he bought a bus ticket for Wisconsin. During a rest stop in the small town of Haines City, on the way to Tampa, he volunteered to help a motorist with car trouble. He fixed the car and decided to stay. Before long he had his own garage, which evolved into a successful Chrysler-Plymouth dealership.

Caught up in the aviation enthusiasm of the 1920s, Sones took his first flight lessons in a Curtiss Jenny and soloed in a Stinson "Junior" in 1930. He soon was taking part in air meets throughout Florida and in 1933 won *Liberty* magazine's famed "Treasure Hunt" race over an eight-city route starting from Lambert Field in St. Louis and ending at Roosevelt Field on Long Island. Much more than speed was involved. Giant letters spelling out L-I-B-E-R-T-Y were placed at locations along the way. Finding them depended upon a pilot's ability to solve tricky riddles in rhyme. Sones won out over seventy-three competitors, and was met by 75,000 onlookers when he landed at Roosevelt Field. Some people called him "Florida's Lindbergh," and when the Sarasota coastal patrol base was established, he was an obvious choice to be its leader.

**Peter J. Sones, Jr.**

*When war came again, Sones joined the CAP in Haines City, then was asked to command the new coastal patrol base in Sarasota. His wife and his son, Peter J. Sones, Jr., remained in Haines City, but were frequent visitors to the base. His son recalls:*

I was only five years old, so I don't remember much about the base. The field itself was just a grass strip. There was nothing remarkable about it. But I sure remember the Ringling Brothers circus across the road — you could hear the lions roar over the noise of aircraft engines. In 1948, Dad was awarded the Air Medal at a ceremony in Orlando honoring the pilots and observers from the Sarasota base. Dad and Zack Mosley were good friends, and after the war, I remember that each bought a V-tailed Beechcraft Bonanza. Dad loved to fly and continued to do so almost until his death in 1978.

Major Peter J. Sones, commander of the Sarasota base, was widely regarded as "the Lindbergh of Florida" for his successful competition in several highly publicized cross-country races (courtesy Peter J. Sones, Jr.).

## Walter E. Pooser

*Walter E. Pooser, an Air Medal winner, was a twenty-three-year-old whose family had moved to Orlando from Orangeburg, South Carolina when he was six. In his teens, he took whatever jobs he could find to save enough money to afford a fifteen-minute flying lesson, which then cost about $2.50. At seventeen, he soloed in an Aeronca C-2, a tiny aircraft with miles of brace wires, which he describes as "not much more than one of today's ultralights:"*

After I got my private license, I built up a lot of time ferrying Piper Cubs from the factory in Lock Haven, Pennsylvania, to a Cub dealer in Orlando. I either went up by train or flew up with the dealer. I couldn't accept money for it — I'd have needed a commercial license for that — but I got expenses. The trip usually took three days: Lock Haven to Washington, DC and spend the night; Washington to either Savannah or Brunswick, Georgia, and spend the night; then on down to Orlando. I recall one trip where I had to land at Jacksonville because of an approaching hurricane. As I set down, the wind was blowing so hard some guys had to grab my wings as soon as I touched the runway to keep me from being blown backwards. Nothing else was in the air, and I'm sure they considered me crazy.

I'd always wanted to fly, but one of my eyes was too weak for me to pass the physical as an Air Corps Cadet, so I joined the CAP. I had two hundred hours by then, and served at Sarasota from start to finish. We were based at Peter O. Knight Airport in Tampa for two or three months before moving to the airfield across from the circus grounds. Most of our pilots were from the Orlando, Tampa, and Saint Petersburg area and many owned their own planes. We had at least a dozen, including a number of Stinson Voyagers. I was so crazy about flying I'd go up in anything with an engine in front and a propeller on it. Bomb racks had been put on our planes at the Orlando Air Corps base, but I don't think we ever carried any.

Our patrol area extended from Clearwater down to Naples, and we usually flew fifteen to twenty-five miles out in the Gulf. Our main job was picking up and escorting ships approaching the Tampa-Saint Petersburg harbor from Key West. I had more than eight hundred hours of patrol time, and I never saw a sub or a sunken ship. I saw a number of damaged vessels, but there was no way to know where and how the damage was done. Several Air Corps bases dotted the area — among them, one at what had been the Sarasota Municipal Airport and another across Tampa Bay at Mac Dill Field in Tampa. At first, they didn't take to us too much. At times, they seemed to look down their noses at us, like what we were doing wasn't worth fooling with, really. But that all changed when we saved the life of a fighter pilot who went down in the Gulf.

This pilot was practicing gunnery by himself when he ditched. He had to get out quickly because those heavy things wouldn't float more than a few seconds, but he only had a Mae West, no life raft. One of our patrol crews, I think it might have been Jim Hamlett and A. J. Brock, luckily saw him go in and dropped him a half-inflated truck inner tube that had a big canvas bag attached underneath for his legs (this happened before our base got its life rafts). Our fellows called in their position, then continued to circle the pilot until a Coast Guard boat arrived for the rescue. After this, our commander and the fighter squadron's commander became more friendly, and the rest of the people in both commands loosened up a lot.

Walter E. Pooser of Orlando served at the base from start to finish. Here he is standing by the sturdy Waco cabin plane he often flew on patrol (courtesy Walter E. Pooser).

There was a time when I might have had to ditch myself. They had just put a brand-new, rebuilt engine into one of our Voyagers, and I gave it a thorough test flight and it checked out fine. The next morning, by luck of the draw, I was assigned to fly that plane on patrol. Another pilot, Edgar Woodhams — we called him "Woody" of course — spoke up and said, "Why can't I have that airplane? Why give it to Pooser?" Woody was a lot older than me and a little grumpy, so I said, "Well, if you want it, take it." As it happened, we flew sister ships that morning, and after we'd been out on patrol for a couple of hours, I noticed Woody starting to lose altitude. He called over to report that his engine was failing. When it seized-up completely, he had no choice but to ditch. He did a good job landing, and while the plane pitched forward it didn't flip over on its back. He and his observer, Harry Ackley, got out all right but only managed to free one of their two life rafts. Harry, who couldn't swim, got into that while Woody hung on to the side. We called base, then circled around them for nearly two hours waiting for the Coast Guard. When I saw the boat, I flew to it, then returned straight to the life raft, giving the rescue boat its heading. I've always remembered that it could have been me down there.

Early in the war, the Civil Air Patrol actively recruited new members. The response was so overwhelming that the campaign was soon discontinued. This is a typical advertisement (Hopper collection).

Sarasota was just a little town then, and didn't offer much in the way of entertainment. When we weren't flying, many of us spent our time across the road watching the circus performers practice. Mornings or afternoons, we could watch the acrobats and the clowns and the animal trainers — all for free. There was a stand there, too, where you could buy something to eat. The base was only two or three miles from town, and since I owned a 1936 Ford I saw downtown Sarasota a few times. I don't think we had any social activities at the base itself. Whenever I had a weekend off I'd head for Orlando to see my family.

I think I was there about ten months. Toward the end several of us went up to Lakeland, Florida and became civilian Air Corps instructors, teaching Cadets to fly Stearman PT-17s. After a year or so I got into the Ferry Command, made several trips to Alaska, then began flying C-54s across the Pacific with the Air Transport Command. After the war I did all kinds of flying — crop dusting, charter work, ferrying new planes, and so forth. I flew for another seven or eight years but finally got tired of the traveling involved and quit in favor of a job with the Post Office. I think the CAP coastal patrol did lots of good work, just as the present CAP continues to do.

## James C. Hamlett

*James C. Hamlett, a native of Tampa, was the youngest pilot on the base. As a teenager, he did odd jobs around the local airport, and began flying when and how he could. After earning his license, he became part owner of an E-2 Cub and later had a third interest in a Waco. By the time he volunteered for the CAP, Hamlett also had a commercial license, and took with him the very first Waco YKS-7 to roll off the assembly line (NC 17452). His recall of people and events at the Sarasota base is extensive:*

There aren't many of our group left, you know. Joe Senninger, a pilot from Chicago who invented the system to prevent wasps from clogging sprinkler heads, fell from his boat off the Bahamas and drowned. Gale Haxby, a pilot from Birmingham, Alabama, died of a heart attack. Jimmy Mitchell bought a Stinson SR-5 after the war and killed himself and three passengers when he went down in bad weather. Harvey Thornton, a fellow from New Jersey, operated the Lake Wales, Florida airport after the war, and with his wife and a neighbor's twelve-year-old daughter, he took off in dense fog, decided to come back to the field and flew into a house, killing all three of them.

A brighter story is that of Edgar Woodhams, who was an American volunteer with the Royal Flying Corps in World War I. At age fifty-two, Ed was our oldest pilot and lived six months past his one hundredth birthday. He played golf several times a week virtually to the end. Harry Ackley, Ed's partner on most patrols, was probably the base's second oldest pilot at age fifty-one.

As you know, our Sarasota base actually started out at Peter O. Knight Airport in Tampa, just a few blocks from where I lived with my mother. We moved to the Sarasota field across from the Ringling Brothers' circus grounds a little later. The field was jointly owned by former circus roustabout Johnny Lowe and the Seaboard Terminal Company, and Johnny ran it. We took over one of the two hangars at the northern end of the field, plus a small operations office and a radio shack. The other hangar was used by a crop dusting outfit serving nearby Palmer Farms, the largest vegetable grower in Florida. We had three long sod runways, but the drainage was poor, and they were often wet. The Sarasota-Bradenton Municipal Airport, occupied by an Air Corps P-40 squadron, was northwest of us. I remember two P-40s colliding in mid-air near our field. One pilot got out but his chute failed, while the other one didn't get out at all, and both were killed.

The youngest pilot at the base, James C. Hamlett and his future wife, Jeanette, in front of his 1941 Buick, placarded "not to exceed 103 mph," a speed higher than many heavily-loaded coastal patrol planes could attain (courtesy James C. Hamlett).

One day my observer, Arley Brock, and I saw a P-43 from Pinellas Army Air Base in St. Petersburg go down in the Gulf. I circled around while Arley dropped him our life raft. It nearly clobbered the poor guy, but he climbed into it. When I saw a sponge boat in the distance, I flew to it and managed to get it to follow me to where the pilot was floating around. Except for his broken nose, he wasn't hurt. Brock was also my observer the day we saw a U-boat and again on another occasion, when we nearly had to ditch coming back from about forty-five miles out. Our Jacobs engine — to most pilots it was "old Shaky Jake" — had really been acting up. We barely cleared the seawall at Saint Petersburg. Despite some misleading statements about the Sarasota base in *Flying Minute Men*, I doubt that any other base flew so many hours so far from the sight of land. Gulf of Mexico coastal charts show that to reach the water depths required by subs we had to go twenty-five to seventy-five miles off shore. I'm glad for the chance to set this straight.

While we were based in Sarasota, I shared an apartment in town with Laurence Richardson, a pilot from Lakeland. I owned a 1931 Studebaker "President," a beautiful tan coupe with two seats in front, and half a seat in back — the spare tires mounted on each running board were really spiffy! I later sold it to Bert Naylor for forty dollars, which is what I'd paid for it. I was single but don't recall having time to fool around much. When we weren't flying, I think we all enjoyed crossing the road to see the circus people at work on their acts. If you liked the flavor of roaches and other exotica in your food, there was even a place to eat over there. It was *not* appetizing.

From Sarasota, James C. Hamlett went back into the Air Corps and flew in the China-Burma-India theater, even though he was supposed to be restricted to service only within the U.S. (courtesy James C. Hamlett).

When the base closed down, I went into the Air Corps — for the second time. After I graduated from high school, I passed all the tests and got into the Cadets. But when I got to Kelly Field some old scars were discovered on my lungs and I was given a 4-F medical discharge, The second time around I had some help. A flight surgeon I knew gave me a medical waiver, and I returned to the Air Force with a direct commission as a service pilot. That once meant only ferry pilot, and there was an "S" on our wings. Some called us "snake pilots" because of the "S." But later we did everything, even flying *through* combat areas if we weren't on combat missions. This distinction is not always clear. Bob Blackwood and I went to India together. He went to "fly the Hump" and I went to what was called China Sub-Sector Headquarters, and later to Tezpur where Bob was stationed. When I got to China my commander was Colonel John S. Feagan, and his deputy was Lieutenant Colonel Herbert Beeks. They had commanded the 26th Antisubmarine Wing in Florida and remembered me and knew about the P-43 going in the drink off St. Petersburg. Colonel Feagan said he'd put me in for the Air Medal, which I received only after I returned to the States. All the time I spent overseas, I was supposed to be restricted to duty in the United States only. When a sterner flight surgeon finally caught up with me, I was sent home Class A-1 priority. I resigned from the Air Force shortly after the war ended, but always made aviation my career until for health reasons I was forced to retire.

## Robert A. Blackwood

*Robert A. Blackwood was born and raised in Scranton, Pennsylvania, where he learned to fly before enrolling at, and graduating from, Rollins College in Winter Park, Florida. He was living in Atlanta and flying a Waco cabin plane when the Japanese attacked Pearl Harbor:*

There wasn't much I could do with my plane once wartime restrictions were imposed. When I heard that the Sarasota coastal patrol base was seeking planes suitable for over-water patrols I called and said I'd lease my Waco at whatever the government offered, and that I'd come with it. I flew down and reported shortly before the base moved from Peter O. Knight Airport down to the Sarasota field. While in Tampa, I stayed at the Casa del Sol Hotel on Davis Island just near the airport. After we moved to Sarasota, I took a place out on Sarasota Bay, right down from the Ringling Brothers grounds.

I flew my own plane sometimes, but not always. When I joined the CAP I didn't really know what to expect, so I can't say that I was disappointed in any sense. I don't think I expected to win the war or anything like that. There wasn't much to do except to fly — the area was very much undeveloped. Longboat Key is highly built-up today, but at that time, you needed a boat to get to it. There wasn't any bridge. Once in a while some of us would visit the circus to see what might be going on. The best times for me were when my wife came down from Atlanta to spend a weekend.

I left the coastal patrol after a short time and went into the Air Corps, at first as a service pilot, and later as a combat pilot. I flew to Africa, India, and China, and flew B-24s, C-87s, and B-29s. I earned the Distinguished Flying Cross and several Air Medals as well as other awards. After I left the Air Force I attended the University of Virginia and became a lawyer, then came back to Atlanta to practice and raise a family. I continued to fly for fun and owned several airplanes, but the law was my profession.

Edgar Woodhams, who had first served at the Atlantic City base, was Sarasota's oldest pilot. Here he is playing golf in Clearwater, Florida at one hundred years of age. Before his CAP service, he was wealthy socialite Jock Whitney's personal pilot for many years (courtesy James C. Hamlett).

## Richard L. Stacey

*Richard L. Stacey was a thirty-two-year-old resident of Sarasota who took a "mostly daytime" job as a guard, but continued to play the steel guitar with a small dance band that entertained locally. Though he had no previous experience or training as a security technician, he was a burly six-footer from the coal fields of western Virginia, and unlikely to be challenged by an intruder:*

I got down to Florida and the CAP in a pretty roundabout way — in 1940 I was playing with a group in Cincinnati when some other musicians came in to catch our show. They liked what I did with the steel guitar, an unusual Dipson "Electro-harp" with eight strings, four pedals, and a lower pitch than most ordinary hillbilly steel guitars, and they invited me down to Florida to play with them in Sarasota. That was fine, because my wife had asthma and I'd already been advised by a doctor to take her to a warm, dry place, or if not dry, at least warm. So I accepted. A year or so later, looking for the extra income from some kind of daytime job, I heard about the coastal patrol from a friend, went down and got a job as a guard.

There wasn't much to it really. I didn't carry a weapon, I don't think any of the guards did, just a billyclub. We had to provide our own uniforms, of course, but we never had to stand inspections, or march, or do anything of a military nature. Mostly I had daytime duty, because I continued to play with the band in the evenings. I drove a 1936 Pontiac to work every day down Fruitvale Road to the airfield. There wasn't any traffic in those days and it hardly took any time at all. The airfield didn't have a restaurant, but we could go over and eat lunch in the circus cafeteria. I was there about a year, but my memory is not as sharp as it used to be, and I don't remember any names or particulars.

Something I do remember, though, is flying with one of the pilots as his observer. He came by one day and said, "Get someone to take your guard post tomorrow, because I want you to go out with me." I believe he had in mind to make me his observer. I flew as a fill-in observer a few times, and coming back from a patrol one day I recall him saying, "Now, Stacey, in case anything should happen to me, I'm going to teach you to land this plane." I'd been watching him handle the controls, so I did what he did and came down and pretty much landed the plane myself. He probably helped me some, but after we'd landed he said he didn't have anything to teach me, I already knew how to fly. I can't remember his name to save my soul, but I believe his father started the chain of "White Tower" hamburger stands. Once the base closed, and my marriage failed, I went back north again and spent most of my life as a musician.

## Joseph E. Scheb

*Joseph E. Scheb was born in Scranton, Pennsylvania, and came to Florida with his family during the hard times of the 1930s. A printer by trade, Scheb was also a ham radio operator and happy to take a second job with the coastal patrol. He remembers helping to install the radio equipment at the field, then boosting the wattage to increase the effective range of the airfield station:*

I wasn't full-time at the base. I just worked there when I could. My main occupation was as a printer. I lived in Sarasota, but not that far from the airfield, which I understand was the first flying field in Sarasota, a small grassy area that was originally part of the winter quarters for the circus. My wife and our young son came out to visit me a few times, but because he was so young it wasn't easy for them to do.

Daniel H. Wallace served at both the Sarasota and Flagler Beach coastal patrol bases as engineering officer (courtesy Marti Cheesbro).

The biggest excitement I had was when one of our planes went down in the Gulf. I was on duty when the mayday call came in. We told the Coast Guard and they sent help right away. Our two men were rescued unhurt. [1st Lieutenants H. B. Ackley from Louisville, Kentucky and Edgar J. Woodhams from Great Neck, New York] I flew a number of times, mainly to check out the plane radios after some repair or adjustment had been made. I enjoyed my time at the base, and made some good friends. Unfortunately, the people I knew best are dead now, and I've lost track of the others.

Sarasota, Florida

The final act for many coastal patrol veterans came in 1948 when more than eight hundred of them were awarded the coveted Air medal for courage in action. Here, Peter J. Sones receives his from Brigadier General Frederick H. Smith, Jr., CAP National Commander (courtesy Peter J. Sones, Jr.).

Base officers, pilots, and observers who served at least one month at CAPCP #13 and who are not elsewhere mentioned in this chapter include: Maxwell K. Aulick,* N. A. Barrett,* K. E. Benson, Peter H. Brower, Jr., Myron I. Burtness, Randolph A. Caruthers, Samuel C. Coachman,* Merritt S. Craft,* Perry H. Crane,* Frederick C. Crowell, Ralph S. DeAvila,* John V. Denison,* William W. Edwards,* Jr., Donald S. Evans, Richard J. Fleck,* William A. Fraser, David M. Giltinan,* William B. Haggert, John E. Harris, Robert P. Heidbrink, Arthur C. Holman, Wallace R. Johnson,* William L. Jones, Harry E. Lisk, Charles E. McBride, Alexander C. Maxfield, Jr., Walter A. Melton, Lawson E. Mitchell,* George A. Newell, John H. Pairitz, James S. Penney, Jr.,* Eric Ravndal, Thomas H. Shreve,* G. O. Shute, Karl L. Smith,* Hubert H. Stark, Dean P. Thomas, and Wayne M. West. Asterisk indicates Air Medal winner.

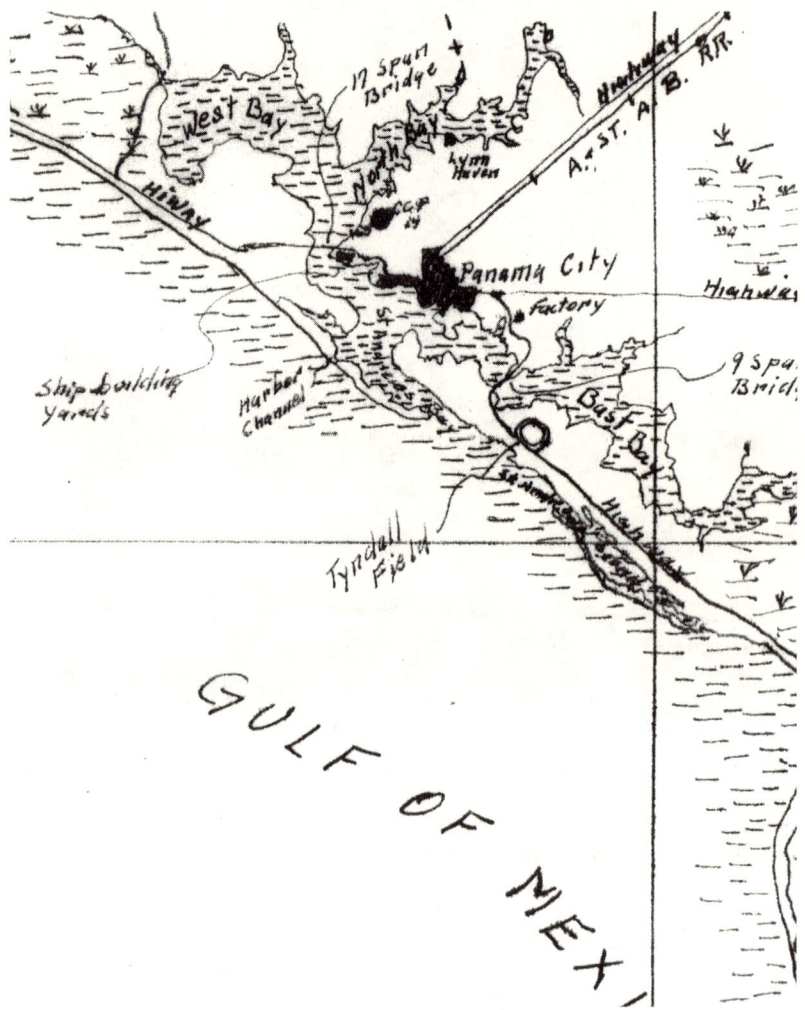

This freehand map of the Panama City area was submitted to CAP Washington Headquarters by commanding officer Robert E. Dodge on November 5, 1942. It's easy to imagine why anyone living on this self-contained base some four miles northwest of the city and surrounded by water and swamps might have felt rather isolated from the local citizenry.

# 14
## Panama City, Florida

Coastal Patrol base number fourteen was established at an abandoned airfield four miles northwest of Panama City, a hundred miles east of Pensacola and about the same distance west of Tallahassee. When the coastal patrol took over, the field was empty except for an old concrete apron with weeds growing up in the cracks, an abandoned gas pump next to it, and the outlines of three sod and sand runways, two of them seventeen hundred feet long, and the third twenty-four hundred feet long. Barracks and a mess hall, and enough extra lumber to construct administration and operations buildings and a small hangar, were brought in from a former Civilian Conservation Corps camp several miles away. Meanwhile, most base members lived in a nearby tent city and Air Corps personnel from nearby Tyndall Field provided many support services to the isolated coastal patrol base.

Forty-one-year-old Major Robert E. Dodge was base commander and his friend, thirty-eight-year-old Capt. Henry T. Cross, was operations officer until replaced in 1943 by Capt. Carl S. Clark. Dodge closed his bridge-building company "for the duration" and often worked seven days a week to improve the efficiency of the Panama City base. A member of the "Quiet Birdmen," Dodge told a *Columbus Dispatch* reporter "There are no days off in this business. Sunday is the same as any other day. Bad weather is the same to us as good weather. We fly any time the crow flies. We're out over our area at sea before the dawn breaks, and we come in with our landing lights on." Major Dodge and Captains Clark and Cross came from Columbus, Ohio as did many other base members. In fact, so many personnel were from Ohio, that the base soon became known as the "Ohio" base.

## Robert E. Arn

*The major elements of the base history are well recorded in a 1989 memoir by former pilot Robert E. Arn, who came to Panama City from Westerville, Ohio. He had finished both his second year of college and all three phases of the Civilian Pilot Training Program and was about to enter the Navy Flight Training program in the summer of 1942, when he was severely injured in a car accident. The setback almost ended his promising flying career before it began. A few excerpts from Arn's memoir follow:*

> In July, 1942, U.S. Representative John Vorys from the State of Ohio, ran a request in the *Columbus Dispatch* newspaper asking for volunteers to help in the formation of an all-Ohio CAP Coastal Patrol Base. After reading the request from Congressman Vorys, I made a visit to the office of Wing Commander Stone of the CAP. He talked me into signing up at once. I was told to report to base Commander Robert E. Dodge by August 10, 1942. The base was located on the site of a small abandoned airfield on St. Andrews Bay, about four miles northwest of downtown Panama City. The only sign that indicated this had been a former airfield was an old cement slab about seventy-five feet by one hundred and fifty feet with an abandoned gas pump at one side of the slab. Toward the end of August, 1942, a rough hangar was built behind the slab so aircraft could be repaired under cover.... Three sides of the base were surrounded by the waters of St. Andrews Bay. Our runways were sod and had a large number of sandy potholes.

> At the end of our longer runway, about one hundred yards from the mainland, there was a small island out in St. Andrews Bay called Mouse Island. We went out in a small boat, cleared off an area, then created an outline of a full-size submarine and used fifty-five gallon drums for the conning tower. This was our practice range for dropping the one hundred pound demolition bombs. We practiced making bombing runs on our "submarine" to prepare us in case we ever spotted one of the U-boats. Practice bombs, with a small powder charge, were used to improve our skill. When the operation started in late August, 1942, we had a total of eight planes. In September, we got hit by a hurricane in the Panama City area. We lost two of our aircraft on the ground. In October, six more planes were brought in. A few more planes were added each month after that.... Ready or not, our patrol duty was started in August, 1942 from base #14. The coverage area of the patrols was to be from 84 degrees longitude to about 88 degrees longitude. This gave Base #14 the vast area from Mobile, Alabama to Light House Point, Florida — three shipping lanes and all of the beach area and islands along the way.

Arn recalls that emergency procedures and equipment were virtually nil when the patrols began, and that he and his fellow flyers were "either a very brave group of men or just plain NUTS." After an Army-Navy inspection in late September, a Navy truck arrived from Pensacola with Mae Wests, one-man life rafts, sea markers, belt lights, and other emergency gear, followed by an Army truck delivering new equipment for the base radio station, along with bedding, cots, and other improvements to the base living quarters. During his months at the base, Arn experienced both highs and lows:

> One of my lowest days came in November, 1942. Lt. Milkey and Lt. Andrews took off in one aircraft. Lt. Clark and Lt. Wetzel took off in another aircraft on a dawn patrol over St. Andrews Bay. A mid-air collision occurred which resulted in the loss of Lt. Milkey and Lt. Andrews. A tug boat crew on the inland waterway rescued Clark and Wetzel after they were able to execute a semi-controlled crash landing into St. Andrews Bay. They reported that the Milkey and Andrews plane went straight in. Both pilots were killed on impact with the water. Another low occurred in January, 1943, when we lost Lt. Black and Lt. Vaughen* while they were on patrol. They were flying an "on course" track in a fairly new Cessna 145 Airmaster. The "sweep" aircraft saw the Cessna do a half roll at about four hundred feet. It hit the water in an inverted position. Neither the bodies nor aircraft were ever recovered.

Both crashes were reported tersely in Columbus, Ohio newspapers, the first under a one-column lead, "Columbus Flier Rescued in Crash: 2 Others Missing After CAP Mishap":

> Carl S. Clark, 26, son of Mr. and Mrs. Homer C. Clark, 190 Oakland Park Ave., a lieutenant in the Civilian Air Patrol, was rescued yesterday after a collision of two CAP planes over St. Andrews Bay, Fla., during a routine flight, the Associated Press reported from Panama City, Fla. He and another Ohio man, Franklin Wetzel of Lakewood, were slightly injured and two men, Lester Milkey, 50, of Sandusky, and Charles W. Andrews, 36, of Springfield, were reported missing. Clark, a graduate of Ohio State University, was assistant sales manager of the Columbus & Southern Ohio Electric Co. when he joined the Civil Air Patrol last August 4. His mother said he started flying as a hobby two years ago. His father is assistant manager of the southern district, Columbus & Southern Ohio Electric Co.

* Vaughen's death was made particularly poignant by the fact that his wife and three children were with him at Panama City. A trust fund for them was started by members of the base with a donation of $769. According to the base newsletter, "Buckeye Beacon," dated February 1, 1943, additional pledges subsequently were made by various Ohio Wing squadrons.

The account of the second crash followed the lead, "Two Ohioans Die On Patrol Duty: Civil Airmen Killed When Plane Falls Into Sea":

> Two occupants of a civil air patrol plane lost their lives when it crashed at sea, CAP officials announced yesterday. They identified the fliers, whose bodies were not recovered immediately, as Lieut. Alvie T. Vaughen, 36, pilot, of Galion, Ohio, and Lieut. Curtis P. Black, 34, co-pilot, of North Olmstead, Ohio. Lieut. Vaughen's widow and three children are now living in Panama City. Lieut. Black was the son of Mr. and Mrs. A. L. Black of North Olmstead. The ship was on a routine patrol flight, CAP officials said.

Although these losses caused Robert Arn some terrible lows, he also had some real highs:

> Christmas Eve, 1942, was very eventful. When I joined my room mate Steve Morrison and his wife for dinner at the Cove Hotel, their other guest, an old Hollywood friend, was CLARK GABLE!!

Pilot Robert E. Arn and Jackie Arn on their wedding day in Columbus, Ohio, the "high point" of his whole Civil Air Patrol career (courtesy Robert E. Arn).

In February, 1943, the Navy requested us to make simulated air attacks on LSTs [landing ship tank] while they were training the crews off of Panama City Harbor. We were told this would give the gun crews training they badly needed. We used our fastest planes, the Cessna 165 Airmasters. This type of plane also gave us more maneuverability. We sometimes would come at the crews from about 50 feet above the water — a nice change from normal patrol flights.

APRIL 2, 1943 !!!!! My very highest point. I got a leave from the base. I returned to Westerville, Ohio where I married my high school sweetheart Jackie!... We returned to Panama City and got a beach house with another newly married couple, Lt. Carl Clark and his bride Martha. The beach house overlooked the Gulf. Later, Jackie and I were lucky enough to get a little house of our own in Panama City. The house, with its own dock, was right on St. Andrews Bay.

After 179 missions and 485 hours of flying time, Arn left Panama City on June 23, 1943 and flew for two months as a civilian pilot employed by the Air Transport Command. In August he received his direct commission as a rated service pilot in the Air Corps, became an instrument flight instructor, and in September joined the 1337th AAF Base Unit in Assam, India. There he flew 106 missions and earned the Distinguished Flying Cross, three Air Medals, and several other decorations. After the war, Arn finished college, helped raise a son and daughter, and spent all his working career in private industry.

## E. Phillip Bruch, Jr.

*E. Phillip Bruch, Jr. was from Mentor, Ohio and learned to fly at Lost Nation Airport in nearby Willoughby. After his high school graduation, he enrolled at Kenyon College, Gambier, Ohio, intending to continue flying under the CPTP there. Unfortunately he was not eligible for the program until he became a sophomore, and by then the CPTP was dropped from the college's offerings. Bruch went home and got a private license on his own. On October 7, 1942, accompanied by mechanic Joe Azis of Cleveland, he flew his Stinson Reliant SR5-E, a gift from his father, to Florida and reported for active duty:*

At that time, they had plenty of pilots, so I was assigned to guard duty for a couple of weeks. We were then still living in tents, and it was hotter than hell! When we moved into the Civilian Conservation Corps barracks it was like heaven. The month after I got there Milkey and Andrews were killed so again the base needed pilots. Our boss, Major Robert Dodge, a real square-shooter, called me to his office and asked me, "Phil, do you want to fly?" I said, "Hell, yes, that's what I came down here for." Other people had been flying my plane right along, but I didn't mind that and, in fact, I didn't bother to ask for it. I enjoyed flying all the different planes. We flew routine patterns except when we followed a convoy through our area.

I was flying the sister ship that day when Alvie Vaughen and Curtis Black crashed. I'd just come around on a turn when I saw them at some distance going down in what appeared to be a power spin. I didn't see the start of it and can't imagine what happened. They went straight down and hit hard. When I got there, all I saw was an oil slick. I reported our position, and before long another plane came out to relieve me as fuel was running low. Nothing was ever found of those fellows or their plane. I was lucky. I had just one forced landing. Johnny Reaver and I were out in someone's Fairchild 24 when the engine quit. We were flying parallel to the beach at the time, so it seemed I'd have no trouble setting the plane down. At the last minute, I saw a fisherman surf casting on the beach dead ahead of me, so I had to land on the water. Fortunately, we did not roll over, and the plane sank slowly in about twenty feet of water. We got out all right and swam to shore easily. The Fairchild 24 was eventually winched out and taken back to the base, but I doubt whether it ever flew again. The salt water ruins everything almost completely. On this day, all Johnny and I had with us were our Mae Wests, so it's just as well we weren't fifty miles out over the Gulf.

Captain E. Phillip Bruch, Jr. (left) with 1st Lt. Kenneth C. Davies. Flying over water in bright sunshine made dark glasses absolutely essential (courtesy Mrs. Donald Ross).

I was only nineteen and single when I was with the coastal patrol, but I don't remember any fun and games at Panama City. It was a pretty tiring assignment. All the patrols were close to five hours' duration and I recall that once or twice a month we might fly two patrols a day. That's a lot of flying. In the evenings, most of us would sit around and drink a couple of beers while we shot the breeze, then hit the sack early. I seldom went to town, there wasn't much there anyway.

Somewhere around January 1944, I was reassigned to the tow target unit based at Glendale, California. Being out there was far more fun, because we had a social life right there in the middle of Glendale. We'd go out a couple of nights a week and hit the local pubs and restaurants, and there was all of Los Angeles for that matter. The flying was more fun, too. Soon I was drawing mostly night assignments because I had an instrument rating and the others didn't. Not too many fellows wanted night work anyway. I flew radar tracking missions at ten thousand feet, where it's really cold. I spent a few weeks working with the forest service, too. Once, during a big fire in the woods, I flew the chief forest ranger over it while he used the radio to direct his men on the ground where to go and what to do. I think I left the CAP in early 1945, and didn't fly again until 1979, when I went up with a friend in his Pitts Special and got hooked on aerobatics. I still fly my Russian-built Sukhoi 29, but my air show and competitive aerobatics days are over. Looking back, the CAP years were probably the best of my life. I had a ball.

**Mrs. Donald W. Ross**

*One of the young married couples at Panama City was Donald and Iris Ross from Columbus, Ohio. Both had been active in the CAP from its beginnings. He started flying at fifteen and soloed at sixteen. She started flying lessons and took all the courses required to be his observer. Ross joined the Florida base in August 1942, all of twenty years old and eager for as much flying as he could get, but within a month he returned to Ohio, married his sweetheart, and she soon joined him in Panama City. Mrs. Ross has contributed what she calls a "wife's version of life at an active duty base":*

Don and another married pilot, Leonard Starit, were fortunate enough to find a family who decided to rent out two bedrooms and a bath in the upstairs of their home to fellows from the coastal patrol base. Then Don sent for me, and Leonard sent for his wife Mary. We each had a room, shared the bath, and were allowed to cook on hot plates. Lacking any refrigeration, we had to shop daily. In the evenings the four of us often played blackjack, the winning couple sometimes raking in enough to go to a movie. We didn't have any money then but we did have fun. We lived from payday to payday, which was whenever the U.S. government decided to send a check. We young married couples hung together. I particularly remember Bob and Jackie Arn, Joe and Lou Gabney, Gene and Dotty Kissell, Eddie and June Hahn, and Carl and Martha Clark.

At Norton Field in Columbus, my friend Jean Dillman and I wore the first CAP women's uniforms in central Ohio, but in Panama City I didn't work at the base as some wives did. I did help out some in the operations office. It seemed Dolly Heberding, Anna Mash, and Mary Vespur could always use the extra hand. One day while driving to the base to meet Don after his patrol, this huge rattlesnake slithered across the road. I got out of the car, shot the six-foot seven-inch monster, draped it across the hood of our 1938 Buick convertible, and continued to the base. You can imagine the comments I got. I guess we young married girls were as gutsy as our men back then. That base road was nothing but sand, and we all tried to get rid of the snakes anywhere around the base because they were continually interfering with our daily existence.

Joe Azis (left) and Don Ross beside a shark-nosed Stinson 10-A. The base insignia n the fuselage behind them shows Donald Duck astride a bomb presumably headed for a German submarine (courtesy Mrs. Donald Ross).

By the spring of 1942 I was pregnant. Don and I decided to get out of that one room and find a house. Our landlady and her husband ran a real estate office, and had a client who was leaving to join her husband somewhere in service. We talked her into renting the house to us instead of selling it. What a happy day it was when we moved into that beautiful five-room house and had a place to call our own! We enjoyed lots of company then, not only the "young marrieds," but some of the single men from the base as well. One of the mechanics — I can't remember his name but he was Italian — sent home for his mother's recipe for spaghetti, which he then prepared for dinner groups. Everyone was very close then, and it was great. Don had one scary accident that I remember well. He had an emergency landing in a swamp with Phil Bruch's airplane, and the plane flipped over on its back. Don cracked some disks in his spine, but it could have been worse. After a few days of recuperation, he was taped-up and back on patrol duty. He loved to fly and nothing could stop him.

By September 1943, pilots were leaving to enter the Air Corps. Bob Arn went with the Air Transport Command out of Memphis, Tennessee, which sounded so good to Don, that he went there, too, eventually flying for many months in the South Pacific. After the war we went back to Columbus, where Don was awarded the Air Medal in 1948. We returned to Florida in 1974. We spent our fiftieth wedding anniversary back in Panama City on the beach, and visited with Opal and Johnny Reaver, discussing the old base and the people we'd known.

Jean Dillman (on the ladder) and Iris Smith wearing the first approved CAP women's uniforms, early 1942. Not long after this photo was taken, Miss Smith married Donald W. Ross and went to Panama City (courtesy Mrs. Donald W. Ross).

### John ("Johnny") P. Reaver

*Like Robert Arn and E. Phillip Bruch, most Panama City personnel came from Ohio. The three Reaver brothers hailed from Columbus: Capt. Stanley H. Reaver was a pilot and Air Medal winner, Lt. William P. Reaver was a pilot and observer, and M/Sgt. Johnny Reaver was an aircraft mechanic and occasional observer. With two other brothers — Charlie, who stayed at home but served with the Columbus CAP squadron, and Adam, an Army Air Corps instructor — they were called "The Five Flying Reaver Brothers." Johnny Reaver is now the lone survivor and lives in Panama City:*

I came down in July 1942, just about the time the base was activated. At first we lived in six-man Army tents under the trees along Watson Bayou. Then we brought up the barracks from Lynn Haven. They were fairly nice, partitioned off into a series of rooms about twenty-feet square, each with a door to the outside, and in most cases two men sharing a room. In mine we had an upper and lower bunk arrangement to save space. We had our own mess hall that served three meals a day. It was a good deal, because the meals were free, all our food rations supplied from Tyndall Field. We also went to Tyndall for our shots and for any medical care short of going into the hospital. It was over there that I met Clark Gable. He was coming out of the PX. Impulsively I said, "Hi, Clark. How are you?" Then I realized he was an officer, so I quickly corrected myself and said, "Captain Gable." I saluted him then he saluted me, and we both just grinned.

I really liked it down here, it's so nice and warm compared to Ohio,* and that was one reason I settled here after the war. In the evenings, a gang of us would jump into somebody's car and drive downtown to the U.S.O., or just to see a movie. I think we got special prices like other servicemen. There was also the beach for swimming on days off and some pretty girls to date. We threw a few parties on the base, but for security reasons were pretty careful about who we invited. There was only one road to the base, and we had guards there who insisted on seeing identification and passes. You couldn't go around the security gate because there was nothing but swamp right up to the road. We had guards there twenty-four hours a day.

We had a nice bunch of planes, too. Several Fairchild 24s, and for some reason several Cessna Airmasters, sleek four-seaters with no wing struts. We also had a Buhl Air Sedan, a large, six-place aircraft with a 330 hp Wright engine. Since I was a pilot as well as chief mechanic, I got to fly all our airplanes after they were worked on. I even flew some missions, both as observer and as pilot in command. Most of our planes could fly for four hours, but for safety reasons we planned our missions for three hours. We lost six pilots down there, but not because of mechanical problems. Les Milkey and Charles Andrews crashed after a mid-air collision, Curtis Black and Alvis Vaughen spun into the Gulf

* Among the base officers, pilots, and observers from Ohio not elsewhere mentioned in this chapter were Fred W. Binger,* William V. E. Burdick,* William J. Fowler,* Gerald R. Gray,* Fred D. King,* Robert B. Landfair III, David Laufman,* Bernard C. McCabe, Philip A. Meinke,* William H. Oliver,* Forrest V. Powers, Orin Redhead, Robert E. Rogers, George H. Sanderson, Edward D. Schott, Frank M. Slough, Kenneth G. Smith, Harry E. Studier,* Joseph Ule,* William C. Vance,* Doyle S. Varn, Ferdinand L. Weston,* and James G. Willoughby* (asterisk indicate Air medal winner). Another thirty mechanics, radiomen, linemen, guards and clerical workers were also from Ohio.

one day without explanation, and two other fellows, Gerald Owen and George Ferner, following a routine take-off had to dodge another plane, stalled, and crashed on the field. Though they were killed, their one-hundred pound bomb miraculously did not explode.

Once the coastal patrol base closed, most Panama City personnel, including myself, were transferred to Tow Target Unit #7 at Glendale, California. In early 1944 I learned that restrictions on private flying were being eased so I left the CAP and returned to Panama City to take over as general manager at what was once again the municipal airport. My brother Charlie joined me from Columbus and became a flight instructor. Our first female student was a very pretty girl named Opal Pannell who was working at the shipyard as an engineering draftsman. She earned her licenses as pilot and aircraft mechanic when only two women in the whole state could say that — we'll soon have been married fifty years! In 1946 I opened Skyland Park, my own airport, and retired forty years later with more than sixty-five hundred hours in the air. I still have my ratings and fly once in a while even at age eighty. Sometimes the younger fellows ask for some tips on spins and loops, and I help them out.

## Dolly L. Heberding

*Dolly L. Heberding (now Dolly Feigenbaum) was one of the many women pilots who volunteered for CAP duty, but were kept from flying coastal patrols because they were "too hazardous for women." While earning a degree in bacteriology at Ohio State University, she had become a member of the coed Ohio State Flying Club, and competed with its "A-team" against similar flying clubs in the 1941 National Intercollegiate Flying Club meet. Her "A-team" won the national championship that year and she was awarded the Friedlander Trophy as the outstanding woman pilot in the meet. She later earned ratings as an instructor and commercial pilot, was a flight instructor at a private airport in Columbus, and taught aerodynamics in the university's CPTP. Heberding belonged to the Columbus CAP squadron, and when the chance for active duty came, she jumped at it:*

At Panama City, I had several different jobs. One of my first was to return to Columbus to ferry a plane back to the base, which was only a small half-abandoned airport on the Bay. When we arrived we "inherited" the remains of an old Civilian Conservation Corps camp, some miles away. We begged, borrowed, and stole the trucks and tools to dismantle various buildings, move them to our base, and rebuild them for our operations office, hangars, barracks, and mess hall. Every able bodied person was involved in this construction process and in a few months most of us were living on the base — a great advantage, since we worked from dawn, when the first flights took off, until dusk when the last planes landed. In those days, Panama City was a very small town and quite crowded with Army personnel from Tyndall Field. Traveling to and from town for meals and hard-to-find sleeping accommodations had been burdensome. I've forgotten many things, but I vividly recall my first night there when I had to sleep on a cot in the business office of a hotel because there were no rooms available. I was so grateful for a bed that I didn't dare complain about the phones ringing all night. I remember another night when a chair in a hotel lobby was my bed.

Dolly Heberding learned to fly while attending Ohio State University, and was named the outstanding woman pilot in the 1941 National Intercollegiate Flying Club meet. Here she flashes her winning smile (courtesy Mrs. Dolly Feigenbaum).

We weren't exactly loved by the Army and were commonly referred to as "boyscouts" by Tyndall Field personnel. I have no recollection of interacting with them any more than necessary, nor with the townspeople, either. We were self-contained and didn't socialize much outside of our own group. One of our buildings had a living area with a large fireplace — a popular gathering place on cold evenings, because our other buildings were unheated and northern Florida is cold in the winter months. In any case, by the time we'd had dinner after a long day, we usually weren't energetic enough for any further activity.

After our buildings were completed, I suppose some of our personnel had free time to socialize outside of the base, but I can't speak for them. Occasionally some of us went swimming in the Bay but this wasn't a popular sport because of the alligators. Somehow we became acquainted with a man we called "Uncle John" who had a cabin in the woods at Dead Lake in Wewahitchka, some miles east of Panama City. He taught us to "grunt" worms out of the ground and took us to the good fishing holes. Art Greene, George Furry, Bob Dodge, and I went there when we could get a little time off. I don't think "Uncle John" had much use for me until the day he saw my twenty-two rifle. He asked if I could shoot and I said I could. He looked doubtful, but Bob knew I could, so Bob stuck a coke bottle cap up on a tree and told me to put a hole in the middle, which I did. Uncle John thought it was an accident so then *he* stuck up another bottle cap, which I also hit. From then on I could do no wrong.

The Florida woods generally, and even places around camp, were avoided in deference to the many diamond-back rattlers we had seen. We were most vigilant when we made our brief excursions into the woods to our so-called co-ed outhouse, which was more "out," and no "house," merely an empty wooden box sitting over a hole in the ground. You can understand our relief at finally getting plumbing in our barracks. This was especially true for the women, as there were only four of us and any private use of the outhouse was quite a challenge. We finally rigged up a flag signal system that was reasonably effective.

Although our women's barracks served us well, it left a lot to be desired in terms of comfort. It was unheated and was by no means weatherproof. When it rained the roof leaked and we often had to move our beds around to avoid getting soaked. We set containers under the worst leaks. We had a small wood stove just for heating our water supply and I was nominated to build the fire each morning to heat the water. The water tank was so small that anyone who slept late got a cold shower. Needless to say, I always had a hot shower.

In the beginning, my primary duty was to schedule the daily patrols and assign appropriate pilots to each flight. There were always two planes to a patrol, with a pilot and co-pilot in each plane. Frequent morning fogs, poor visibility, tropical storms, mechanical problems associated with our vintage planes and the lack of equipment and parts to repair them caused frequent schedule changes. One of our pilots, John Vorys, who was also a Congressman from Ohio and had helped to recruit many of our personnel, always called me "Simon Legree," because, he said, I was so "firm" about the flight schedules. No one would be more pleased than John to see our bit of history being recorded. Those of us who were close to him really loved that guy. Even after all these years, thoughts of him bring me warm feelings. Congress would do well to have more men like him today.

Aerial view of the airfield looking to the northwest across North Bay. In the original photo, every building stands out remarkably clear (courtesy E. Philip Bruch, Jr.).

## John Vorys

*In September 1942 John Vorys left Panama City to resume his congressional seat in Washington, a post he held continuously from 1939 until 1959. He soon wrote back to "Master Sergeant D. L. Heberding, Civil Coastal Patrol 14, Panama City, Florida" humorously deriding the secrecy surrounding any mention of the Coastal Patrol in the nation's capitol, but expressing also his admiration of its men and women volunteers. A portion of his letter follows:*

> ... On general publicity, I find the following are the rules: (1) Never say you have been on the Coastal Patrol, (2) Never say what base you were on, (3) Never tell whether your plane carried any you-know-whats, and (4) You are allowed to say that you carried knives to stab sharks with. Following these rules, when anybody asks me what I did during August, I just say, "I had a knife to stab sharks with," which, being a lie, certainly throws the enemy off the track.... My spies report you now have a wonderful office, but otherwise are as mean as ever. I also hear that the creeping paralysis which affected

the left brake of the log-wagon finally spread all over it. There is a lot of paralysis here in Washington, particularly from the ears up. I hope it doesn't spread. More seriously, I miss all of you and think of you all a lot. It's a great crowd down there and you are doing a wonderful job. In fact, I don't know of any part of the war effort which is doing so much with so little.

John Vorys, U. S. Representative from Ohio, was the only Congressman who served in the coastal patrol. Though his stay in Panama City was a short one, he quickly became one of the gang and was widely liked and respected (courtesy Joseph N. Brandhuber).

## Dolly Heberding

*In further describing her experiences at Panama City, Dolly Feigenbaum recalls pilot Henry Cross coming down from the Rehoboth Beach coastal patrol base to become operations officer, and how a subsequent tragedy overtook him:*

After Hank recovered from his ditching in the Atlantic Ocean, he joined us as operations officer, a position that Bob Dodge had been holding open for him. On my trip back to Columbus to pick up a Cessna and bring it back to Panama City, Hank served as my navigator on the return trip, as he was not yet doing any flying himself. Hank left the base some time before I did to take a job at the Atlanta Airport. I had become close friends with him and his wife Kay, so when I went home, I stopped in Atlanta to see them. They had just learned that their only child, Jim, had been killed in action on a submarine and were in deep mourning. Kay never fully recovered, and I've lost touch with Hank.

Besides my work in operations, my other main duty was taking our pilots on check flights. We had many different types of planes and our pilots had varying degrees of experience and training. Both ends of our shorter runway ended at the Bay, and the slightly longer one was limited by the Bay on one end and by woods on the other. There was little leeway for errors in take-offs and landings. To my great disappointment, flying patrol missions was strictly forbidden for women. Times have changed, but too late for me. Other than performing flight checks, and flying visitors over the area, I had little opportunity aloft.

Though she wasn't permitted to fly patrols, Dolly Heberding took her Aeronca Chief with her to Panama City "to keep her hand in." She was accepted for the Women's Ferry Command, but the program ended before she had a chance to serve (courtesy Mrs. Dolly Feigenbaum).

In general my coastal patrol experience was a good one except for the sad times that surrounded the several crashes and loss of lives we had. I think most of us felt we did a good job in overcoming the many obstacles and serving our country. I don't think the townsfolk particularly resented us, I believe they were just overwhelmed by the onslaught of all the service personnel both from Tyndall Field and our coastal patrol base. When I left Panama City, I went back to Columbus and worked for Curtiss-Wright, although not as a flyer. I applied and was accepted in the Women's Ferry Command but that service was suddenly cancelled before I could report for duty. Next day I enlisted in the Army and served two years in the Women's Army Corps — fourteen months as a Link Trainer instructor at Mather Field in California, and as a motor pool driver and dispatcher at two other California bases.

## Joseph N. Brandhuber

*Joseph N. Brandhuber came south from New Town, Ohio, not far from Cincinnati. He had been flying for many years, and with a friend was part owner of a Waco cabin plane — but because of a heart problem he couldn't pass the physical and was never a licensed pilot. When the war came, and civilian flying was curtailed he recalls that their plane had to be rendered unflyable and be guarded twenty-four hours a day. They decided to store the Waco at the Cincinnati airport and it was there that Brandhuber opted to volunteer for the coastal patrol:*

We had kept our plane on my buddy's father's farm, but that became impractical after the new restrictions went into effect. So we flew it down to Cincinnati where we heard about the CAP and the benefits of becoming part of that organization. We both joined but he stayed behind and I went to Panama City. I drove down alone. Since I couldn't fly legally, I was signed on as a guard. At first we lived in tents. The others in my tent were an FBI agent and a couple of other non-CAP men. This didn't last long though, and all the CAP men were moved into barracks up at the airfield itself. Mostly, I worked as a serviceman, gassing and washing the planes and so on. But I actually had my A&E license and also did some mechanical work. I still only earned five dollars a day.

I remember all too clearly the day that Gerald Owen, another fellow from Ohio, and George Ferner of Tulsa, Oklahoma, were killed right there at the base. Another mechanic and I were in the mess hall and heard the impact. We ran the two hundred yards to the crash site, and were among the first to reach the wreckage. It was very grisly, and they had died instantly. My understanding was that they had been chasing an Army L-5, and in trying to match the L-5's better performance, had stalled and spun in from a low altitude. There seemed to be different versions of what had happened.

When the base closed, I went back to Cincinnati, where I quickly was inducted into the Army. At the ancient age of thirty-four, I was too old for the Air Corps — they said — so I ended up in the artillery as a mechanic for L-4 spotter planes. The pilots in these little "grasshoppers" flew behind the enemy lines near enough to targets to observe the fall of our barrages and to radio back corrections that let our gunners zero-in. After our tanks and infantry captured the bridge at Remagen, I was ordered to accompany one of our pilots and land on the far side of the Rhine to set up a landing strip. We scouted around and found a good field and dropped down. I think this was the first *planned* landing of an Allied plane east of the Rhine. It was later discovered that my feet had been frozen earlier that winter, and I was invalided home. The rest is a long story but when I retired many years later, I was a financial analyst at Wright-Patterson, Dayton, Ohio.

\* \* \*

The link between home-state squadrons and their men on active duty at the various coastal patrol bases remained strong despite their considerable distances apart. Robert Neprud states in his *Flying Minute Men* that more than one thousand CAP members were among the throng that turned out in Sandusky, Ohio for the funeral of Lester Milkey after his fatal crash at Panama City. Fourteen of them volunteered to take Milkey's place for the duration. Local CAP units and civic organizations also provided financial help:

> The "Sink a Sub Club" sponsored by Michigan's Exchange Clubs raised $12,000 in three weeks' time to equip the Pascagoula base; twenty North Carolina squadrons contributed $100 each to help the Manteo base get started; a group of mechanics in the Middle West raised enough money to send one of their number to the coast for several months; and in Dallas, the High Noon Club donated a Stinson Voyager, "The Spirit of Dallas," to one of the Texas bases. Further aid came from dances, bingo parties, and other benefits put on by scores of inland units. A South Dakota squadron even staged an aerial coyote roundup and turned over the proceeds from the sale of pelts.

## Clyde B. Pinson

*Though the majority of Panama City's personnel were from Ohio, many others, like Clyde B. Pinson, were from adjoining states. Born in Huntington, West Virginia in 1911, Pinson learned to fly in the mid-1930s, and when war came he wanted to continue to fly. He and his friend were two of the first pilots to arrive at the fledgling Panama City base:*

I just heard that they needed some pilots down there. I knew a fellow from Bluefield, West Virginia, Herb Thompson, who lived there in Cincinnati, and he said "Let's buy a plane and go down there," and I said "That's a deal." Herb was the president of a small coal company, and I was in the same business. He'd heard of a Waco biplane for sale up at the Greenbrier Hotel's private airport near White Sulphur Springs. The Waco had belonged to one of the DuPonts, and we bought it for fifteen hundred dollars. But it was a bad deal because that damned airplane didn't have any generator in it. If the battery gave out, the engine would stop. Nevertheless, we bought it and flew it down to Panama City and it did all right until someone else wrecked it.

My wife and two children joined me a little later, and we rented a house in town. Panama City was one of those war-time cities with lots of things going on and the population just about doubling overnight. The Army Air Corps had an aerial gunnery school down the way at Tyndall Field, and housing was pretty tight. I remember the day an Air Corps officer berated me and my friend for not saluting him, but since he didn't have jurisdiction over us we just laughed and walked away. I had signed up for six months and returned home when my time was up. But when they kept on asking me to come back, I finally did. This time I left my family behind and lived at a hotel in Panama City until the base closed.

The field wasn't far from the coastal beaches, and after flying south for a while, you could look down into the water, and you never saw so many sharks in your life. There were sand sharks and other kinds, too. They didn't particularly worry me, but they scared some of the boys pretty bad. One fellow used to carry four or five knives with him every time he flew patrol. Ironically, he was one of several men we lost. One day out on patrol, his plane crashed into the water for unknown reasons, and neither he nor his observer were ever found. I think his name was Curtis P. Black and he was from North Olmstead, Ohio.

My friend from Beckley and I didn't fly together, because we were each senior pilots with a good bit of time — I had over a thousand hours — and they made us first lieutenants and pilots in command right off. The fellows with low time flew with us as observers. And we didn't necessarily fly our own plane, but just whatever we were assigned. We received an allowance for the government's use of the plane — I forget how much per hour — and free maintenance. Except that we ended up doing a good bit of it ourselves. We were sworn into the Air Corps Reserve, and eventually received the "certificate of belligerency" that was to safeguard us from execution as spies if we happened to be captured by a German submarine.

I never saw a sub, though one day I thought I did. When I dropped down to take a closer look, it proved to be a torpedo. We learned later that it was a spent practice torpedo without any explosive in it, and that's why it was light enough to float. We told base what we'd found and they said they'd have the Navy come out and take a look if we could tell them its location. I said what I'd do was fly due north until I hit the beach, and then marking that spot, they could come due south along that line so far and that's where it would be. The next morning my observer and I went out and found it in about fifteen minutes or so, a little farther north, but about where we said it would be. A Navy boat was just then approaching. They'd started out the night before. They were almost on top of the thing before they saw it, and did they veer away fast!

I never saw a ship sunk by a sub, but I once saw what I thought were some survivors. Close-up, there were fourteen or fifteen men — it was impossible to get an accurate count — tied together in a circle, but they were all dead. I called the base, and they told the Navy, and the Navy said, "Well, no hurry, but we'll come get them." We flew pretty low most of the time, between about four hundred and seven hundred feet. The weather wasn't bad. We had a lot of afternoon thunderstorms in the summer, but we just dodged around them. After our planes had been fitted with bomb racks over in New Orleans, we carried bombs, but I never had reason to drop one. On the whole, despite our losses, I got a kick out of the experience. After the war ended, however, I went back to West Virginia and got into the coal business again, and for all practical purposes gave up flying for good.

## Carl S. Clark

*Air Medal winner Carl S. Clark came from Columbus and was the base operations officer. He also took his regular turns at flying patrols. One of the early arrivals who helped establish the Panama City base, he remained to the end, then went to Glendale, California with TTU #7. Clark recalls the mid-air collision that killed Lester Milkey and Charles Andrews but cannot explain exactly why it happened:*

We were climbing out in clear air on a routine dawn patrol. I was flying the lead plane, with Frank Wetzel as my flight observer, and Milkey and Andrews were following as our sister ship below and to our left. Somehow they hit us and took off part of our left wing. They crashed and were killed. We also crashed, but I had partial control of our plane and struck the water softly enough that Frank and I survived. We suffered serious cuts and bruises, and my jaw was severely fractured. Our Waco sank in about fifteen feet of water, nose-down and tail sticking up in the air. We clung to that until rescued. I was flown to Columbus for surgery by specialists suggested by my brother who was a doctor. I was fortunate that they could put my jaw back together again so that I would look good. The best part of my stay in Columbus was meeting Martha, my future wife, while in the hospital. Not long after I returned to Panama City she came down and we were married in a civil ceremony in Pensacola.

I don't recall that we gave any special training in safety. Since we were all pilots and had flying experience before we got there, safety was mostly a matter of encouraging the use of common sense. As base operations officer, one of my jobs was assigning men and planes. That was never a problem. Pilots and observers paired up voluntarily. We never required anyone to go out with someone they didn't care to fly with. And which planes were assigned didn't seem to matter. We required that every pilot be checked out in each type of plane we had — Stinsons, Wacos, Fairchilds, and some Cessna Airmasters — and the maintenance on each was equally good.

Capt. Carl S. Clark, base operations officer from Columbus(left) and Capt. Francis "Gene" Kissell, from Upper Sandusky, Ohio, heading out for a patrol in 1942. Kissell died only a few years after the war (courtesy Carl S. Clark).

Besides Carl Clark and Frank Wetzel, the Panama City base had only two other Duck Club members — 1st Lt. John P. Spellerberg of Upper Sandusky, Ohio and 2nd Lt. Bernard R. Cohen of Cleveland Heights, Ohio. Ironically, the six men killed on missions — 1st Lts. Charles W. Andrews, Curtis P. Black, Lester E. Milkey, Gerald G. Owen, and Alvie T. Vaughen, and 2nd Lt. Donald C. Ferner — were by definition as *non-survivors* ineligible for Duck Club membership. Similarly, although Lts. Andrews, Milkey, and Ferner gave their lives in the line of duty, they had not yet flown the requisite number of hours on patrol missions to earn the Air Medal.

## Thomas Y. ("Tom") Bingham

*Though most pilots and flight observers came from other states, a large number of local citizens were employed as guards, service technicians, and clerical staff. Among the local recruits, but only recently arrived from Pensacola, was Tom Bingham. He had come to Panama City in 1939 as the owner-manager of a soft-drink bottling plant, then took on a second job at the Wainwright Shipyard helping to build the first Liberty ship launched there. But even that didn't seem enough:*

I was offered an eight-month deferment to remain at the shipyard as an electric-torch cutter, but I wanted to do more. I was told I could buy a plane and lease it to the CAP and then get in enough hours as an observer to qualify as a co-pilot ferrying planes to England. After getting set up in the security section at the Panama City base, I learned that

The Panama City coastal patrol base as it appeared when the first base personnel arrived — there was nothing there except for a weed-infiltrated concrete apron, an unuseable fuel pump, and the rotted remains of a small hangar (courtesy Mrs. Dolly Feigenbaum).

no additional planes were going to be leased. Meanwhile the Liberty Ship on which I'd worked was about to be launched, and it was the occasion for celebration. The base commander, Major Robert Dodge, chose me to be his bombardier to drop a bouquet of roses on the *E. Kirby Smith* as she came off the ways and floated out into the bay. We circled the ship in a Fairchild 24 and, as instructed, I dropped a wreath of roses about two hundred feet off the starboard bow as the ship went stern-first into the waters of the bay.

The coastal patrol base was on the south side of North Bay and had a large water perimeter that required protection from possible sabotage or infiltration. I was only a corporal of the guard but had intentions of buying a Cessna and eventually getting into the Ferry Command. When I couldn't, I patriotically resigned from the coastal patrol and went to New Orleans to join the Army Transport Service. At age thirty I was named captain of the Army ship *FP 144* and spent a year moving men and supplies around Pacific islands out of New Guinea. I returned to Panama City after my discharge, got into small boat manufacturing and then the oil distribution business.

## Karr C. Isenbarger

*Karr C. Isenbarger came down from Laura, Ohio, a small town about thirty miles northwest of Dayton. Most of his friends were in the military service while he was still making machine gun barrels at a General Motors plant in his home town. When a friend, who had been rejected for military duty because of extremely poor eyesight, suggested that they join the coastal patrol at Panama City, he gave General Motors notice and left:*

My friend D. W. Kissell's brother Francis was already in the coastal patrol as a pilot. They drove to Panama City together in one car and I drove their parents down in my car. Everybody lived in a tent city when we got there, but we were young and that was simply part of the adventure. I was a guard and I'm sure I carried a sidearm but what it was I don't remember. However, I do recall one of my posts being at the beach, and hearing the sand sharks splashing in the shallow water. I was only there a month, but one of the funny things that comes to mind is the fellow who stayed only one day. He came across a real big diamond-back rattler taking the sun on the tarmac, and that was enough for him!

When my draft notice came it said I'd better enlist in something quickly or be drafted, because they didn't accept the CAP as a "recognized unit of national defense." I don't know whether that was a local interpretation of the rules or what, but I went home and joined the Navy. After boot camp, I went to aviation school at Chicago's Navy Pier to learn metal-smithing and welding, then to Norfolk to work on PBYs, installing armor plate behind the pilots' seats. This was like working a nine-to-five job in a plant, and so far from my idea of military service that I soon volunteered for overseas duty. Eventually I spent a long time in the Pacific in a land-based aircraft carrier service unit, working on planes that couldn't be repaired aboard ship.

## Roy Rish

*Roy Rish, born in Wewahitchka, Florida, was one of the few southerners at the base. After learning to fly in Ocala, and just as he was about to accept a contract with the Air Corps to instruct Cadets there, he was put on hold until he could take the required course for civilian Air Corps instructors. He was urged to join the CAP somewhere and "stick there until we do have an opening, because we really want you as an instructor." He called the coastal patrol base at Panama City and was told to "come on up":*

I went there by bus, and was assigned to one of the wooden hutments on the base. I was always just a flight observer, even though I had my pilot's license, but I got in plenty of flight time all the same. We never saw a sub, never dropped a bomb. As for recreation, there was little to do, and I was flat broke besides. I didn't make much, so I didn't fool around, just stayed mostly at the base. The Panama City folks liked everyone at the base, even the northerners, because they knew very well that we were all out there trying to get rid of the subs in the Gulf. But I don't recall that they put on any socials or entertainments for us. I did go to church fairly often, something many of the others didn't do.

I left after ten months, recalled to Ocala as a flight instructor on PT-13s. At a certain point I entered the Cadet program myself, but had to start from scratch. From the first day, my main instructor and I played a game of who could fly better. He'd do a snap roll, I'd do a snap roll. I'd do a slow roll, he'd do a slow roll. It was a terrible waste of government money. The guys like me were known as "F.F.I.s" — former flight instructors — and we were all somewhat bitter about having to begin again at the beginning. With the war coming to an end, I was given a choice as between signing up for two years as a second lieutenant, or getting out. I got out. Then I attended the University of Florida, got a degree in physical education and coached different sports for a year at Chiefland, Florida, quit and flew for Johnny Reaver in Panama City for a while, and ended up as a civilian flight instructor at an Air Corps base in Georgia. After ten years of that, I'd logged ten thousand hours in the air and felt totally burnt out. I spent the rest of my work days with the state of Florida, but not in aviation.

## James G. Dossey

*James G. Dossey of Tulsa, Oklahoma joined the Civil Air Patrol in December 1941. He reported for active duty at Panama City on October 2, 1942, and subsequently accumulated enough patrol time to win the Air Medal. His wife, Billy, and their two daughters, Shari, age two, and Nancy, age five, joined* him as soon as they could. Billy traveled by troop train as a "soldier's" wife. The children loved it since the G.I.s kept them entertained and well supplied with candy, pop, and gum:

I received a wire one morning saying Billy would arrive in Pensacola at 10 a.m. the next day, so I got permission to change my flying schedule and go meet her. On that next day, Lester Milkey and Charley Andrews were in the lead ship that I was scheduled to have flown, with Frank Wetzel and Carl Clark in a sister ship, when they collided shortly after take-off. Both planes crashed in the Gulf. Wetzel and Clark survived, but Milkey and Andrews were killed.

Pilot James G. Dossey came from Tulsa, Oklahoma, and was one of relatively few men who served at two coastal patrol bases — in his case at Panama City and Brownsville, Texas (courtesy Frank S. Myers).

At first the only house that Billy and I could find was very unsatisfactory. But then we found a better one, across Saint Andrews Bay from the shipyards turning out Liberty ships, and shared it with Don and Grace Ferner, friends from Tulsa. It was interesting to watch a new ship being launched and to know that we might be protecting it for part of its trip to Europe or wherever.

One day I'll never forget was when Don brought home a pet monkey. The little thing promptly grabbed a pair of Billy's nylon stockings — rationed during the war and quite precious — and ran all over the house carrying them with Billy in hot pursuit. She finally got them back, but they were ruined. My contribution to our household "wildlife" was a baby octopus I brought home to the kids in a paper cup. It was found clinging to the the wing of an airplane pulled from the Gulf after an accident.

Only a few months later, our friend Donald Ferner met a tragic, needless fate. Jerry Owens and he had just taken off when the crew of their sister ship had to return to the field to have their radio adjusted. Jerry and Don circled and waited. About then, an AT-6 from Tyndall Field began buzzing the field, making fast low passes, then pulling up steeply into a 180-degree turn, only to dive back and across in the opposite direction. While Jerry was maneuvering to keep the AT-6 in sight and prevent a collision, he turned too steeply at low altitude. He stalled-out and the plane plunged to earth, killing both men instantly. Another pilot, Ken Davies of Cincinnati, Ohio, and I received ten-day furloughs to return Don's body to Tulsa. Ken accompanied Don's body in a plane. My wife Billy and I took Grace back to Tulsa by car.

Second Lt. Donald C. Ferner of Tulsa, Oklahoma lost his life in a crash at the base on April 3, 1943 (courtesy Mrs. Dolly Feigenbaum).

On May 21, 1943, I was transferred to the Brownsville, Texas base then at San Benito, Texas. It was something of a special experience. We again rented a house, and our girls were delighted to find our next-door neighbor had a grapefruit tree in his back yard, and that the fruits could be eaten right off the tree, and that indeed they tasted much sweeter than those purchased in stores. It was much hotter down there than in Panama City and I quickly learned to sleep in nothing but shorts. One night I woke up to see something like a little flashlight going on and off inside them. I was startled at first, but then I realized that it was only a firefly.

When the base closed, I flew some courier service until April 1944 when I went into the Air Corps. Ultimately I became an Army glider pilot, but missed combat action by a few weeks because the war ended. I was discharged from Fort Sam Houston on September 23, 1945, and headed straight home to Tulsa to work for my dad at the Dossey Lumber Company.

John M. Vorys (left) and Joseph Ule (right) support an unsteady Carl S. Clark. During the war years, the Panama City beaches were beautiful and unspoiled (courtesy (Mrs. Edith Frankel).

### Elmore H. Nord

*Elmore H. Nord went to Panama City as a truck driver, but quickly earned a promotion to radio operator. The twenty-one-year-old had joined the CAP in his hometown of Willoughby, Ohio, and when he heard that the coastal patrol needed help, he gave his employer, Parker Appliances, a one day's notice and left for Florida with others from the area:*

There were a whole bunch of us from Ohio that went down in a kind of "caravan." Two planes left from Willoughby, and we picked up others en route. We flew only when we could keep visual contact with the ground and, excepting for some who got lost, we all got to Panama City about the same time. The trip took three days, and we all pitched in at once to help build the base. The only thing there was the concrete tarmac. They assigned me to an Army "six-by-six" loaned to us from

Tyndall Field and my job was driving back and forth to an old Civilian Conservation Coprs camp to help dismantle the buildings there, and then truck them to the base and help make our barracks and other buildings from them. This was part-time work for most people, since our flight crews were already doing regular patrols. While the base was being built, we all lived in a tent city, and another of my jobs was driving truckloads of people back and forth to the base. The six-by-six had a very hard suspension and I nearly ruined my kidneys driving that thing.

Sgt. Elmore H. Nord, a radio operator from Wickliffe, Ohio, looking sharp in a new uniform (courtesy Elmore H. Nord).

Then I sort of got promoted to radio operator. There were three of us and we each worked a four-to-six hour shift, depending on the season and the amount of daylight, because none of our planes flew after dark. When we weren't at the radio, we did a little of everything around the base, even to grubbing the runways. I remember that if you dug down only eighteen or twenty inches, you could hit brackish water, the field was that close to sea level. I was working the radio the day we had the mid-air collision. Two of planes had just taken off and weren't two hundred feet in the air over the Bay. Those poor guys had no time to make a mayday call. I did, however, receive the distress calls that came in from other planes that went down.

On my time off, I took flying lessons from Dolly Heberding in her Aeronca. Then after I got my license, I went out as an observer every chance I got. I was kind of a standby, and flew several times in one of our Cessna Airmasters, the ones with the cantilever wing. I thought that in case of a ditching they were a death trap. They only had one door — on the passenger's side — and to facilitate its use quick release pins were put in and the passenger's seat was removed. The observer sat in a back seat. One of the things I remember about flying over the Gulf was how shallow and clear the water was. We thought we could actually see sub "tracks" on the bottom where they had crept along the ocean floor. I think we really did. What else could they have been?

We younger guys had a lot of fun down there. We never had a curfew like the Army and Navy guys. We could stay out all night as long as we got back to the base in time for work. The regular servicemen were peeved at us for that because as a result we got the prettiest girls in town. Some of our men dated steady, but I don't recall any getting married. I'd left a car at home, so the first leave I had I went up and drove it back to the base with the "A" ration stamps I'd been saving. I remember going over to Tallahassee a few times and up to Dothan, Alabama, but that's as far as I strayed. I served at the base until it closed, then went home, worked at Euclid Road Machinery for a while, and ended up doing commercial art work. I flew for sport for a few years, but gave it up when I married. What do I best recall of Panama City? How amazing it was that everyone got along together so well — they were just a grand bunch of men and women.

---

Other base officers, pilots, and observers who served at least one month at CAPCP #14 and are not elsewhere mentioned in this chapter include Clifton T. Bowes, Jr.,* Ray E. Carley,* Robert E. Church,* James E. Cullifer, Ernest T. Dwyer,* Michael C. Forth, Harley D. Hawes,* Wade H. Herrin,* Selwyn F. Lewis, A. H. Lisenby, Clifford C. Millergren, and Doyle S. Varna. Asterisk indicates Air Medal winner.

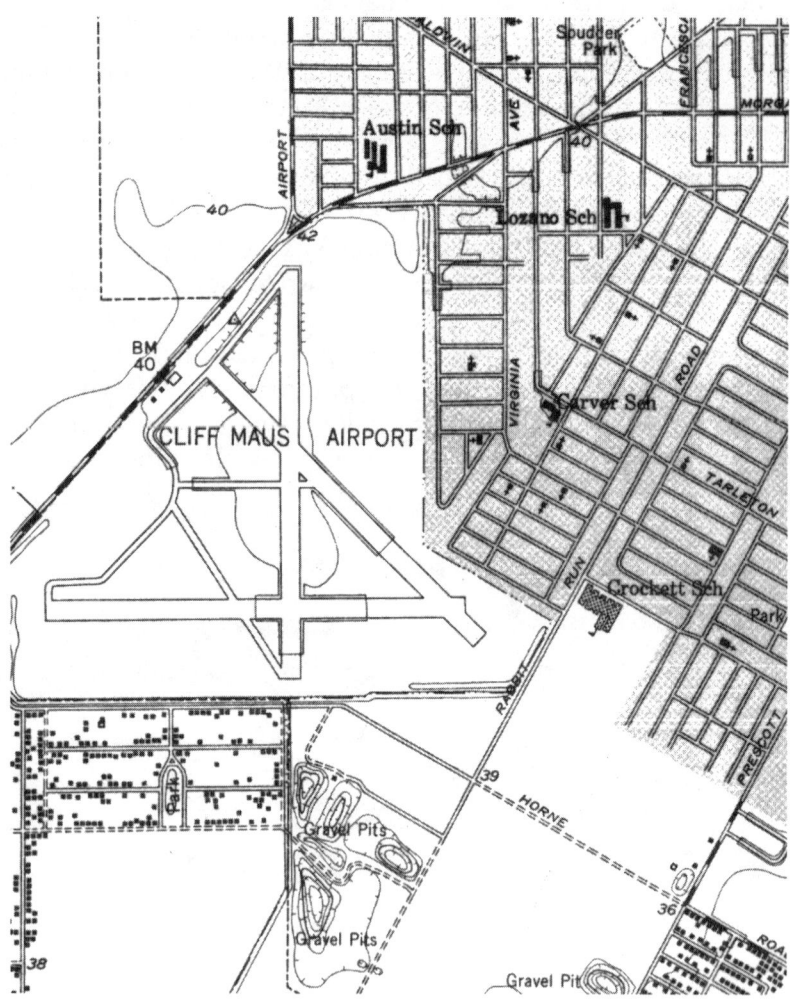

Corpus Christi, Texas was practically ringed by Naval Air Stations, so that the coastal patrol flyers operating out of what was later named Cliff Maus Airport had special flight patterns for leaving and re-entering the area (source: 1951 United States Geological Survey map).

# 15

# Corpus Christi, Texas

Along with other points on the lower Texas coast, Corpus Christi (Body of Christ) was first mapped in 1519 by the Spanish explorer Alonso Alvarez de Piñeda. Piñeda named the bay in honor of the ecclesiastical feast day on which his ship landed. Though it prospered during the war with Mexico as a supply post for the U.S. Army, the city's growth languished until the 1920s when the federal government paid for dredging Corpus Christi Bay and providing a deep-water ship channel to the Gulf. Industry was immediately attracted to the area, and was followed by the military, which established a Naval Air Station and Army depot at the bay's east end. When coastal patrol personnel arrived, Corpus Christi was a community of over one hundred thousand.

Base commander Captain William G. Green, a newspaper publisher from Tulsa, Oklahoma, in his November 1942 report to CAP's Washington headquarters, described the city-owned Corpus Christi Airport as having three runways, each more than four thousand feet feet long, with unobstructed approaches except for downtown office buildings three miles northeast and a tall smokestack a mile away. There were runway and boundary lights, a CAA radio station, a U.S. Weather Bureau station, a rotating beacon, and a control tower — all of the basic requirements of a busy municipal airport of the 1930s. The city was served by Eastern Air Lines and Braniff Air Lines, each with two flights daily, and both Army and Navy used the field for training and ferry operations.

But according to a short base history, thought to have been written by base commander Green, matters were very different when the first base members arrived in July. Not only was Cliff Maus Airport then almost completely under water due to recent heavy rains, but the first base offices had to be squeezed into the control tower where several typewriters, a teletype machine, and too many people all struggled for survival in so small a space:

> Only one building was available and it had to be completely remodeled inside before it could be used. As personnel arrived, and it was evident something had to be done, the equipment was moved within a few days from the tower to this building, and though there was more room, this move only added to the confusion as there were more people, carpenters hammered incessantly, the new paint steamed in the hot sun, and the mosquitoes came in hordes from the pools of water left on the airport after the rains. The girls sat on boxes and typed and the men cursed amd tried to fathom directives. Everyone slapped at mosquitoes, sweated and laughed, and tried to operate the teletype, which was a thing of wonder to all as it stood and clattered away by itself, bringing all kind of orders and messages.

> Shortly after this move, the base radio equipment was installed. Edward R. "Ronnie One Corpuscle" Durham and his able assistant Gilbert J. Ruiz worked day and night to create WXBU, one of the best stations on the Gulf Coast. A unique grid system for reporting locations was developed by base commander Green, observers James L. Gartner and Glenn S. Ramsay, and pilots Gerald H. Westby and Sherwood H. Morgan, and each received a citation for distinguished service from CAP Washington headquarters ["For experimentation with grid system of reporting position by latitude and longitude, which shortens the report, lessens radio traffic, and simplifies the accurate plotting and reporting of position by planes while in flight, thereby greatly increasing the efficiency of anti-submarine control. This mission was performed during the summer of 1942." Citation Order No. 1 dated November 27, 1942, signed for national CAP commander Earle Johnson by Jack Vilas, Major, A.A.F., Executive Officer]

> The first patrols went out on August 7, 1942: Fairchild NC 29010 with Gerald H. Westby as pilot and James L. Gartner as observer, and Stinson NC 31596 with Thomas R. Wingate as pilot and Glenn S. Ramsay as observer went out on the morning flights. Stinson NC 36731 with W. G. Green as pilot and Jesse L. Pate, Jr. as observer, and Fairchild NC 19104 with Phillip H. Ray as pilot and Roy E. Box as observer, went out on the afternoon flights. From this date, regular patrols and convoy escorts continued every day, except when the weather closed in, for thirteen months. The men were keenly aware of the "big" hunting they were doing, also of the danger of flying over the water in tiny ships, but no fear of any kind was ever evidenced.

## Glenn S. Ramsay

*One of the first arrivals who established the new base from scratch was Glenn S. Ramsay of Tulsa, Oklahoma, assistant intelligence officer. A twenty-six-year-old civil engineer but not a pilot, Ramsay flew over four hundred hours as a flight observer, and won the Air Medal. He recalls some highlights of his months at the Corpus Christi base:*

The state of Oklahoma, and the Tulsa area in particular, was well represented among the personnel at Corpus Christi. Three of our top men were in the oil business in Tulsa: our first commanding officer, Bill Green, was the owner of Engineering Laboratories, and his successor, J. W. McLendon, worked for the same company; our operations officer Gerald W. ("Gerry") Westby was the president of the parent Seismograph Services Corporation. I was in the business, too, doing oil exploration when the call for coastal patrol volunteers went out. I served first at Beaumont, and then at Corpus Christi, in both cases as assistant intelligence officer. I was married and had a three-month-old son, but we were very young and thought of going to the Gulf Coast as an opportunity to serve the country.

Glenn S. Ramsay, base intelligence officer, only had a student pilot license, but got in plenty of flying time as an observer. One of several men from Tulsa, Oklahoma, he is shown here holding his first son, William Glenn (courtesy Glenn S. Ramsay).

My wife Mary and son Bill remained in Tulsa when I went to Beaumont with Bill Green as his observer and navigator. Bill flew his plane, a Stinson Voyager, and I drove his car for him. As it turned out, we became part of a pool of pilots and observers and seldom flew together. My first patrol flight out of Beaumont was with fellow Tulsan, Clark Millison, on July 18, 1942. For the next week I flew at least once every day, but only twice with Bill Green. On July 25th I flew to Corpus Christi with a pilot named Wallace in Bill's plane, while Bill drove his car with our clothes and stuff. I then went home to get my family, and by the time I got back my friend Roy Box had found a small but new duplex into which we moved and settled down for the duration. My first flight from Corpus was logged on August 7, 1942, and my last on August 31, 1943. I completed 481:37 hours of patrol missions.*

I went down there with only a student pilot rating, and never did get my private license. But I got plenty of air-time as an observer and more than enough exciting times. We flew in weather that I wouldn't dare fly in now — very low ceilings and lots of sudden rainstorms. On patrol with Roy Box one day we were about ten miles out when we got caught in a fast-moving front that sucked us right up into the clouds. We couldn't see anything and the turbulence had stuff flying all over the cabin around us. Roy asked me what I thought we should do, and I suggested he just turn the plane loose. "It'll find its own way out," I told him. I knew the clouds wouldn't go clear down to the water. So Roy cut the power, and we sort of bounced our way down out of it. After we were clear, I radioed a nearby weather station to ask about conditions where we were, and they replied, "CAVU" [ceiling and visibility unlimited]. I told Roy, "Well, maybe that's so where they are, but not out here!"

An interesting thing about flying out of Corpus was that the wind seemed to average at least thirty mph every day without much let-up. On one real windy day, I watched a J-3 Cub take off almost vertically. Facing into that stiff wind with the engine at full throttle, all the pilot had to do was to pull back the stick. The J-3 didn't need to roll forward at all. After climbing five hundred feet or so, he just dropped straight down again, and called it quits. Also, I'll never forget the day a Navy cadet landed a twin-engine Beechcraft on our field with its wheels up. I

---

* In addition to those mentioned throughout this chapter, other base members from Tulsa included pilot Sherwood H. Morgan; pilot-observers Stanley J. Ehlinger, James L. Gartner, Eugene P. Neal, and James A. Price; radiomen Edward R. Durham and James E. Woodburn; and Marian E. Coffman, plotting board operator. James G. Dossey, another Tulsan, served as a pilot-observer at the Panama City and Brownsville bases. Other Oklahomans not mentioned in the chapter include Carl P. Cowan, radio mechanic from Bartlesville; Robert V. Montague, pilot from Okmulgee; Joyce E. Robbins, pilot from Drumright; Modena N. Shewey, plotting board operator from Duncan; and Allie R. Walker, flight observer from Broken Arrow. The most-played record on the juke-box in the "Fly Inn" base canteen (later christened "Nash's Hash for Cash" in honor of the proprietors, Mr. and Mrs. Nash) was "Take Me Back to Tulsa."

happened later to overhear the instructor berating the student for his carelessness. "Didn't you hear me screaming at you to put the gear down?" the instructor asked. "How could I with all that racket?" the cadet replied. That racket, of course, was the warning horn telling them the gear wasn't down.

Capt. Roy E. Box was the base engineering officer and later was part of the group that was transferred to Tow Target Unit #17 based at San Jose, California (courtesy Mrs. Violet Bumpus Rentfrow).

I suppose my main job at the base was organizing our continuing training program — radio communications and navigation, and things like that. New arrivals at the base needed orientation for over-water flying, and we gave that to them. Toward the end of 1942, Bill Blevins was the intelligence officer, and he sent Turner E. ("Dink") Hubby and I to Atlantic City to learn more about identifying ships and submarines, and about bombs and the best techniques for delivering them. When we returned to Corpus Christi, we then trained our men in turn. After that, our planes were equipped with bomb racks and some Air Corps men were assigned to us as armorers, and we began flying patrols with live bombs. We never carried depth charges.

On the earliest patrols, we noticed that all of the ports were jammed with hundreds of ships tied up or anchored because the crews would "jump ship" as soon as they could for fear of the submarines. The shipping lanes between ports were empty. It wasn't long before word got around that we were out there flying cover for them, and crews began signing-on again. It was really a good feeling to fly low alongside a ship and see many of the crew on deck jumping and waving to us. We would dip a wing in salute to them, knowing that they felt more secure with us on the look-out.

We flew rectangular search patterns, and if we were escorting a ship, we flew submarine search patterns both ahead of it and then behind it. Later, when a base was set up at Brownsville, we flew both directions. Some of us came up with what I think was a unique system of identifying and calling-in our half-hourly patrol positions in code: a rather finely gridded plastic transparency that, when placed over a regional map at a different registration point each day, would have identified the same location by different grid numbers. A certain sunken ship might be in grid 157 one day, but in grid 413 the next. A listening submarine captain would never know. If I were flying in my own airplane — a Ranger-powered Fairchild 24 with the call number WXBU-15 — I'd simply call in WXBU-15 reporting 157 or 413 or whatever.

My wife and I both enjoyed our stay in Texas. For me, it wasn't that much of a change from Oklahoma. But my wife was from Minneapolis and for her it was a whole lot different. We had met at a pre-war dance when I was an engineering student at the University of Missouri, and she was a student at Stephens College in Columbia, Missouri. In Corpus Christi our rented one-half of a duplex wasn't far from the airfield. Most of the social activity for base members was just among themselves, getting together for dinners and such. We all had a good fellowship. Individually, we belonged to churches and to other organizations, but it wasn't like anyone really had time for lots of fun and games. After the war, I returned with my wife and son to Tulsa and worked in the Douglas Aircraft Company modification plant and later in the Customer Service department until my services were no longer needed.

\* \* \*

Shortly after the base was officially activated on July 20, 1942, a twenty-page set of "instructions," described as "confidential military information," was issued to all pilots, flight observers, and radio operators. Every aspect of flying and reporting on the results of patrols was covered — even down to avoiding seagulls (but not how to do it). For example, because of the huge U.S. Navy presence in and near Corpus Christi, departure and arrival flight patterns had to be flown precisely:

> Lead ship, which is slower ship, will take off first followed immediately by second ship and both will circle airport to left and cross airport at more than 1500' but less than 3500' altitude on a true course to be continued across Mustang island to the ocean of not less than 75° nor more than 100°. The Navy orders that we stay above 1500'

and below 3500' in the 25° segment to and from the ocean. It is recommended that pilots establish a true course across this area, and by recognition of certain landmarks, determine ground speed and true heading to make good this course. From this data and air speed the wind can be calculated for use in further navigation. Upon crossing Mustang Island let down to normal patrol altitudes, that is, 400-1000', and continue out to sea for three miles. Turn northeast and parallel the coast at a distance of three miles from the shore.

In the vicinity of the wreck southeast of Cedar Bayou is the line of demarcation between the Army and the Navy practice area. At this point, using the buoy marked wreck (latitude 28°00', longitude 96°46') as a check point, turn out to sea so that upon turning back northeast again you parallel the coast at a distance of not less than eight, nor more than fifteen statute miles. Maps to be furnished show a danger line of six miles. The wreck is about seven miles offshore. The Army Air Corps is conducting tow target practice up to 9000', shooting out to sea with .30 caliber guns all along Matagorda Island. You must stay clear of them. If CAP planes are approached in air by Army or Navy aircraft, they will adhere strictly to their proper course, following, however, CAA traffic rules, unless it shall be apparent that the Service planes are directing CAP away from danger or restricted areas into which they may have unknowingly approached.

Our principal mission is to report the location of enemy submarines in our general area, but principally in the shipping lanes leading to the entrance to the Aransas Pass. In addition to this we are to take all actions within our means to destroy any enemy sighted. We should therefore look for ... [both submarines and enemy surface craft]. A periscope leaves a thin pencil wake which is usually easily identified. Investigate any crate or box floating at sea — it may conceal the periscope of a submerged submarine. Note anything unusual about surface craft such as radio equipment larger than usual, excessive speed of ordinary looking craft, unusual rigging of any kind, two craft rendezvousing at sea, blinker signals on shore to craft at sea. Inspect closely all ships not under way. We are also to look for friendly vessels in distress or survivors of such craft. Investigate any floating object and identify it satisfactorily. It might be a survivor, wreckage, or a floating mine.

## Thomas H. Hughston

*Air Medal winner Thomas H. Hughston was one of the pilots who received these instructions. Born in Olmito, Texas, just a little north of Brownsville, he joined the Corpus Christi base when an associate of his agreed to lease his Fairchild 24 to that base and wanted him to go with it. The Brownsville base itself was not yet in operation:*

I learned to fly at age eighteen through the Brownsville Junior College CPTP. I took both primary and advanced courses and received both my private and commercial ratings. Actually, I'd been aiming for the Air Corps, but I had a health problem that required an extended recovery period, and I thought flying for the CAP would be a good way to get experience while I improved enough to pass the Air Corps physical. At Corpus — nobody down there says Corpus Christi — I first stayed at the Princess Louise Hotel down by the beach on Ocean Drive. It was painted all-pink. Then I shared a kind of basement apartment with two other guys, also on Ocean Drive. Later on I rented a room in the home of Les Ellison's mother. Les was carried on the patrol roster as a "security technician," but he was actually our control tower operator. His father had just died, and having me as a guest gave his mom some financial help.

Air Medal winner Thomas H. Hughston was checked out in every plane on the base except for the Sikorsky amphibian (courtesy Mrs. Violet Bumpus Rentfrow).

At the time, Corpus was practically all-Navy, with naval air stations and supporting auxiliary fields all over the place: at Corpus, at Kingsville, at Beeville, and so on. I remember flying a lot of convoy escort duty. Small convoys of two or three ships at a time were organized at Corpus and such groups pretty much hugged the coast eastwards to Galveston. There, more ships were added, and these larger convoys went farther out into the Gulf where Navy surface ships joined them. We escorted the small convoys as far as Galveston, and often accompanied the larger convoys fifty or sixty miles out into the Gulf. In all my time on patrol, I never saw a U-boat or dropped a bomb except for practice. I doubt if our hundred-pound demolition bombs set with depth charge fuses could do much damage anyway.

We knew there were plenty of subs out there, however, and I believe that on one patrol my observer and I were responsible for the interception of a boat bringing them supplies from Mexico. We were of course instructed to watch for suspicious vessels of any kind. We saw this strange looking ship, and as we came up on it, we saw the sailors switch their flags around, and head straight out into the Gulf. We didn't *know* that it was a supply ship, but its behavior was definitely suspicious. So we called in our location, and we understood that a Coast Guard ship ran it down before it got back as far as Corpus Christi. It had been growing dusk when we first saw the ship so we couldn't follow it, but I think we gave a pretty accurate location. We didn't have the navigational instruments that today's pilots have, but we always knew more or less where we were, and reported our positions half-hourly by grid square. With a good soaking at risk one learns to be pretty accurate at dead reckoning!

I flew all the different shifts and all of the different planes — except one. We had an old Sikorsky flying boat that just about everyone was afraid of. Even so, some of us wanted to be checked-out in a seaplane, so one day when a CAA examiner came round the base, we asked him to go up with us and do the honors. Well, he inspected that Sikorsky very carefully and I guess he wasn't too impressed, because afterwards he told us, "I'll go up with you, but the wind's blowing pretty hard today, and if you shouldn't do well I fear I might be liable to take away whatever rating you've already got." We got his message loud and clear. None of us went up that day.

Other than the Sikorsky we had a bunch of good planes. Many businesses leased their corporate planes to the coastal patrol, rather than see them confiscated by the government. So we had several Beechcraft staggerwings, a Stinson Reliant gullwing, and several Fairchild 24s, as well as the familiar Stinson Voyagers. The weather was generally pretty good. We stayed home if the weather was real bad, but since we flew so low anyway only some ceiling under a thousand feet was any problem. We didn't lose any lives and had few incidents of any kind. I do recall one of our boys test flying a Howard at some inland location when the engine quit. He came down in a plowed field and went over on his back in the mud, but wasn't hurt.

I don't remember the date, but once when a hurricane was due to hit the area all our flyable planes were flown to Randolph Field in San

Antonio. As luck would have it, there was a lot of wind in San Antonio and almost none in Corpus. We lost two planes at Randolph but suffered no damage at all to the non-flyable planes left at the base. When we returned we heard that a submarine had surfaced near Aransas Pass to recharge its batteries — as if the Germans knew we had all moved inland. We also heard that it'd been discovered that subs were getting information on ship movements from a radio concealed in a vendor's hot tamale wagon set up near the drawbridge at the entrance to Corpus Christi Bay.

When the base closed, much of the staff transferred to San Jose, California to a tow-target unit, but I didn't. While I waited to be called up by the Air Corps Reserve, I went to Mexico to fly for *Aero Transportes,* a brand new airline just starting up. As it happened I stayed for about a year and while I was there, I became friendly with an American Airlines chief pilot who was there as an adviser, and in due course I also became an American Airlines pilot. Before that came about, however, I was called up and took the Air Force refresher course on AT-6s and had a commission approved as a service pilot. But by then that program was closing out, so I was dumped into an Air Force pool from which various airlines could draw pilots, and that's when I went with American. I flew for them until 1952, when I went home to assist an ailing father in the insurance business. I still fly my modified all-metal, low-wing Swift built in 1946, and maybe have logged seven or eight thousand hours altogether.

\* \* \*

The August 4, 1942 "instructions" also covered various patrol techniques, among them ditching in the Gulf of Mexico:

> In the event of improper functioning of engine or airplane, turn to closest land, radio the base in uncoded language of your difficulty and procedure. Base will call sister ship and inform them. Land at nearest airport. Contact operations at base before flying ship again. In the event of a forced landing at sea, make a stall landing three or four feet above the water. Endeavor to land as close to a buoy or surface craft as possible. Take care not to land on leeward side of surface craft, where aircraft would be subjected to down drafts. Sister ship will keep radio silence until ship in distress has landed. Sister ship will drop pigment bomb but must take care not to hit the men in the water. Sister ship will circle location until men are rescued or until relieved by another ship but, if not relieved, must leave location for nearest airport while gas supply remaining is safely adequate to make such airport.

\* \* \*

Before many weeks had passed, the Corpus Christi group became known as the "Wolf Squadron." As described in the base history:

> Though the OWI [Office of War Information] graciously attributed this to the "predatory ways of members who scour the country picking up equipment from sympathetic people" and though this was and is very true, there were other reasons. There were four star, three star, and two star wolves about and it was suggested that a significant decal be made up for the planes. This was done by pilot-observer Stanley J. Ehlinger of Oklahoma and is now one of the most original decals of any squadron anywhere. It depicts a wolf in full CAP uniform with a radio microphone in one paw and in his other a bomb ready to be dropped on a periscope rising above the water.

This black and white reproduction of the hand-drawn and crayon-colored original fails to do justice to its intricate design and eight different colors. The wolf's slavering tongue and his shoulder epaulets were the same bright red (courtesy Mrs. Violet Bumpus Rentfrow).

Whatever its true origins, the "Wolf" motif soon was seen not only as an insignia on the base's planes — even commander Green's personal plane, a spunky Culver Cadet, wore it proudly — but it was adopted also as the name of the weekly base newsletter, "The Wolf Howls," and on items such as a personnel roster of "Wolves and Wolfesses" listing hometown mailing addresses (their "permanent lair"). The first newsletter was published February 16, 1943, the brainchild of operations officer J. W. McLendon, who in June became base commander when William G. Green was forced by personal business demands to resign. The mimeographed newsletter was full of news, personals, jokes, and cartoons, and was published regularly until the base closed.

Many of the newsletter's stories were slanted towards safety — for example, a discussion of the base's "dunking classes" on how to inflate and get into a two-man raft after a forced landing or crash at sea, written by base commander Green who was a participant:

> On the first dunking expedition we took along Capt. Cowden, Capt. McLendon, Lt. Paul, Lt. Willoughby, Lt. Peden, F/O Lebman, and myself. We went out into the Bay about ten miles and anchored the boat. We broke out a Navy type raft and inflated it with the hand pump, so that everyone could see how the valves worked and how long it took to pump it up. Then F/O Lebman who can't swim a stroke went overboard with an Army type raft and inflated it in the water and then crawled into it. He was in the water only 45 seconds when his raft was inflated and he was aboard it. Then, one after another we jumped into the water and climbed aboard the rafts. Always go over the stern or hind end of the thing. You can't go over the side, as the thing will turn over. Also be sure to have the bow or front end down wind from you. Otherwise you will have trouble. All the boys practiced turning the boats over in the water. It's not difficult to right the one-man types.
>
> We then decided to see if the rafts could be rowed around, and everyone tried rowing. The Army type isn't as good as the Navy type — must have been designed by a landlubber. Anyway, the Navy type has some nice jointed paddles — and the Army type has some little ping-pong type paddles that would just get your hand into the shark's mouth if you tried using them. However, it is possible to make headway with either of them. In fact, one can row against the wind, which is a good thing to know, because if you drop something that will float, you can go back after it. Incidentally, right at this point, we found that you have to be tied to your raft — and should make provisions for that before leaving your base. And everything else has to be tied to the raft — otherwise, it'll disappear. Ask Albin where his shoes went!

Anyway, with the towel for a sail, we started smartly away from the other raft. We decided to see if we [i.e., commander Green] couldn't sail to shore — a distance of five miles. So after about an hour of very pleasant sailing, in spite of boisterous little white-caps that sometimes emptied a bucket or so water down my back, and into the boat, we sailed ashore. Incidentally, the boat will not sail nearly as well with three or four gallons of water in it. Better keep it bailed out — and that's more comfortable, anyway. Highlight of the affair was when some PBYs landed alongside to rescue us. When we sailed by, they were still sticking their heads out the hatch to see what was going on!

Clerks Ann McDonald, left, and Irene Bednorz holding onto wingtip, have their photos taken by assistant operations officer Joe A. Payne, kneeling in foreground. Other men unidentified (courtesy Mrs. Violet Bumpus Rentfrow).

## Orville Strean

*Orville Strean was born in Leavenworth, Kansas, but in 1932 moved with his parents to Chanute, Kansas, a small town in the far southeastern corner of the state. He and his younger brother, William H. Strean, both served in the coastal patrol; he as an apprentice mechanic, his brother as an A&E mechanic; he as a staff sergeant, his brother as a master sergeant. After he got to Corpus Christi, his first reaction was to turn around and go home:*

The heat and humidity was terrific. It felt like being inside a greenhouse. But the funny thing is, after a while I began to like it. I was single and took a room in a boarding house, sharing it, actually, with a civilian. I remember two Navy pilots living there also. The town was full of Navy people, but we always got along with them well. They were aware of the red epaulets that we had on our shoulders, but I don't recall any bantering because of them. Some may have speculated about what foreign nation we were from, but I never took offense at that. As I remember it, our base was southwest of Corpus Christi, and the nearest Navy base (there were several) was two or three miles away. It wasn't like we had a lot of contact with them.

S/Sgt. Orville Strean, left, with M/Sgt. Gerald K. Berman, another base mechanic. On the plane behind them is the popular wolf insignia (courtesy Violet Bumpus Rentfrow).

I worked on all the planes, generally under the supervision of an A&E. For some reason I seldom worked closely with my brother and in any event he was transferred after a few months to the Beaumont base. I did engine and airframe work, including some painting, patching, and recovering. Though I think I could have, I never became an A&E. After finishing a job, we went along on the check flight. I guess that's how they made sure mechanics didn't forget to do something. We had to purchase our uniforms, but wore coveralls at work. The uniforms were for off-duty wear. There wasn't just a whole lot to do — maybe go into town just to wander around, and maybe see a movie.

When the base ended its anti-submarine patrols, I had a choice of leaving the CAP or going out to California with others as a tow-target unit based at San Jose, thirty or forty miles south of San Francisco. Since I was still single and wanted to see what California was like I chose going out there. Around December 1943 I drove my 1936 Ford Coupe halfway across the country to San Jose. I found that California was all right but not that much different to Texas. I didn't fall in love with it like some did. The main difference was that we could live in barracks on the base if we chose, and I did. My work, however, was no different than before. Those married men whose families came west with them found living quarters off-base. I stayed there about nine months, then left the CAP and returned to Chanute.

## Wayne D. Pinson

*Wayne D. Pinson was born in Aspermont, some miles northwest of Abiline, Texas. When his father went to Corpus Christi in 1939 to help build a National Youth Administration school for aircraft mechanics, the 14-year-old Wayne accompanied him and worked as an apprentice carpenter on the same project. He was sixteen when he became a CAP service technician:*

I serviced all the planes — gassed them, checked the oil and tires, washed the bugs off the windshields, towed them around and tied them down, and just about everything else you do to airplanes. On the ground, it was pretty makeshift. We didn't even have a gasoline truck so I had to tow each plane to the fueling pit with an old Model A truck. I lived with my parents about five miles from the base. We had a wooden station wagon that would come around in the mornings and pick up people who lacked transportation. As I recall it, I only worked the morning shift, six days a week, rising at 3:30 or 4:00 a.m., getting out to the base well before dawn. I'd be off by noon or so but I'd go over to the hangar to do odds and ends the rest of the day. I fell in love with airplanes in the second grade and liked nothing better than to hear the pilot's talk about flying. We had some great aviators at that base, including one that wasn't a CAP member. "Slats" Rogers was a crop duster who kept his plane there in the city hangar. After I got the dawn patrol off each morning, I'd go down and help him get started. He was quite a guy. He'd been a barnstormer, and they say he'd once flown an airplane upside down through a whole city block in Dallas.

One of the men, Captain Ray [Philip H.], who was our engineering officer, flight-tested all the planes after anybody worked on them. He learned how much I wanted to become a pilot, so every now and then he'd come get me and say, "Pinson, let's go see how this one flies!" I got in a lot of that kind of flying, and pretty soon I began taking lessons from different fellows on the base. I don't recall their first names. Being so young I called every officer by his rank and last name — "Captain" Ray, "Lieutenant" Smith, and so on. I'd say that most of the pilots were in their mid-twenties or older. Most were ineligible for the military. I remember one pilot who was missing his left hand.

To me, working at the base was almost like any other job. It didn't seem military at all, even though we had a certain amount of marching drills, and had to wear uniforms and such. I was always comfortable in khaki so that was no big deal. Around the base, I mostly wore khaki trousers with white T-shirts. As you can imagine, it was *hot* down there.

The base newsletter, "Wolf Howls," contained both personal and war news, considerable humor, and occasional cartoons such as this one by base cartoonist Master Sergeant Larue Newby (courtesy Mrs. Violet Bumpus Rentfrow).

For a time, we were ordered to do calisthenics, but the older fellows made such a fuss that the exercise periods were abolished. It was really a pretty loose organization, but everyone did their assigned jobs without having to be pushed. And it was good job. We were still coming out of the depression down there, and one hundred-fifty dollars a month was good pay.

By mid-1942 I was only about five or six months from reaching eighteen, so instead of waiting to be drafted and risking going into the Army, I went downtown and signed up at the Navy recruiting office. I had five uncles in the Navy, and that was always my preference. I didn't realize that the CAP had become an auxiliary of the Air Corps and that I was already signed up in it. I was too dumb to know. I didn't even think of it. When I returned to base and told them I had joined the Navy, it caused one big stink! After a while, though, they said, "All right, we'll miss you, but if that's what you want, okay."

Of course, I volunteered for any kind of duty associated with airplanes. So naturally they made me a carpenter, undoubtedly because I'd had a Union card at age fourteen. I served in the Navy from August 1942 until August 1946. After my discharge, I went ahead and got my private pilot's license, and later owned an Interstate Cadet, which was like a glorified Cub but with more horsepower and more slender wings. I got married in 1947 and my wife and I have two boys and a girl, and six grandchildren. I retired in 1990 after forty-two years working in an asphalt plant. Right now, while I no longer fly, I'm carving airplanes from two by fours to sell at a Confederate Air Force show this fall. This all began with some toy airplanes I made for my grandchildren. People liked them so well they said I should make more.

## Thomas A. Manhart

*Thomas A. Manhart was a thirty-four-year-old seismologist employed by Seismograph Services Corporation when he joined the Tulsa CAP squadron shortly after the war began. The Corporation used several airplanes, and in his travels around the country on business Manhart had found it advantageous to get a pilot's license and fly a corporate aircraft. When he left his wife and young family behind to serve at Corpus Christi, he took one of the company's Fairchild 24s with him:*

I believe I reported in 1943 and most of the patrol work was pretty routine. But we still had our forced landings for one reason or another. Returning from Galveston one day, my sister ship lost an engine valve and had to land on the nearest beach. I couldn't land in the same area so I flew inland to put down as close as possible and use a telephone. It took nearly all day to get a small boat and go out and get our men — the beach being inaccessible from land — and to ascertain the problem and how to fix it. One of our fellows eventually came in with a mechanic and a replacement engine. The engine didn't quite fit, but the mechanic jerry-rigged it and they took off and got back to base safely. My patrols were otherwise rather uneventful — no ditchings or sightings or anything of that exciting nature. One thing I particularly remember is that many of our pilots weren't very good at navigation. Many were old-timers used to flying by the seats of their pants and without radios.

Some were former crop-dusters who landed on the airport apron instead of the runways. They were good pilots, but they nearly drove the commanding officers to drink. We spent a lot of time trying to teach them how to read maps and navigate with the help of maps and radios. We were lucky that one of our men from Tulsa, Sherwood Morgan, owned a printing company and we were able to make some good maps and get enough printed to go around to everybody. This was where my degree in seismology from the Colorado School of Mines was helpful. In oil exploration, you become used to drawing your own maps, and they have to be extremely accurate. That helped me in my flying, too.

Perhaps what impressed me most about the CAP was the work done by the Tulsa squadron even before the coastal patrol was established. We met two or three times a week to attend classes in navigation, meteorology, engines, airframe construction, and so forth. The Spartan School of Aeronautics was located in Tulsa, and I believe some of their instructors may have provided class leadership. The squadron developed a good class of CAP cadets at this time, and that tradition continued long after the war ended. After the base closed I tried to enter military service but my company kept on getting me deferments — on the logical grounds I'd do more good finding new oil fields than flying airplanes. I've spent sixty years in the business, and at eighty-eight I still keep an office and drill a well or two each year. I consider my greatest accomplishment, however, has been just *making it* to this age.

## Leslie W. Ellison

*Leslie W. Ellison held two jobs at Corpus Christi, one as a city employee running the airport tower, another as base communications officer, operating the base radio and grid system plotting board. Born in Austin, Texas he had moved to the coast with his family well before the war. Also a pilot, he sometimes took a turn at flying patrols with the other CAP pilots:*

I had been running the airport tower for some time before the coastal patrol arrived. It wasn't a major airport, but both Braniff and Eastern Airlines were there, and we also had some military traffic in and out, so a tower was definitely necessary. I was twenty-two at the time and had lots of energy so working two jobs was no problem. I lived near the airport, and went over in civilian clothes to do one job, then switched into my coastal patrol uniform to do the other. I was single and living with my mother, my younger brother, and two sisters as kind of the family head. My brother Jesse joined the coastal patrol base as a service technician, and was one of the ones that went out to TTU #15 at San Jose. That was his first job. Later he went with ARCO, and remained with them until he retired. I'm sorry to say that he's dead now.

Of course all our planes had radios, and we cleared them in and out of the airport just like any other planes in the pattern. There were still some trainers using the field, Cubs and Aeroncas and such, and since they didn't have radios, we used a light gun for them, green for cleared to take-off or land, red to stop, and so forth. In June, 1943, I joined the Air Corps, and went through the Cadet program, starting with a year in college at the University of Arkansas. We had two years of college in one year. After winning my wings, I did some instructing, I flew for MATS (the Military Air Transport Service) out of Kelly Field and other Texas bases. After the war, I stayed in the Air Force, accumulated twenty thousand hours flight time, and retired as a Colonel. I then became sales manager for McKesson-Robins. I was active for a time with the Confederate Air Force group, but now I dabble with real estate and have part ownership in a sizable shopping center.

Texan Leslie W. Ellison filled a security technician's position in the base table of organization, but was in fact the base communications officer (courtesy Leslie W. Ellison).

### Charles T. Heno

*Before his serving as a flight observer and navigator with the coastal patrol, Charles T. Heno had worked for the Gulf Oil Corporation in Mississippi, Louisiana, and Texas. When he and his pregnant wife arrived in Corpus Christi, housing was so scarce they rented and shared a house with her brother (who was a mechanic at the base) Warren A Smith, and his wife:*

I understand that I had more flight time than anyone at the base — more than a thousand hours. I was awarded the Air Medal and my certificate shows I served from October 16, 1942 until the base closed on August 31, 1943. But it was all as a flight observer-navigator and with different pilots and different planes. Lots of times, after a rough night, some pilots did more sleeping than flying, so I had the controls some, too. I was always just a little afraid of flying, but believe it or not, for some reason I actually felt safer over water than over land. Anyhow, I never let it stand in the way of doing my duty.

At nineteen, Irene D. Bednorz was the youngest of the several women volunteers comprising the base administrative section (courtesy Mrs. Violet Bumpus Rentfrow).

I recall a couple of significant flying incidents. One was when a pilot and I were returning from a patrol and an oil line broke and the engine started immediately to overheat. In the direction of Matagorda Island I saw the masts and flagpole of a sunken ship sticking up. I pointed and told the pilot, "After we ditch, I'm going to go up that flagpole!" Even though the engine burnt out, he kept it turning just long enough for us to make a safe beach landing on Matagorda. We had kept in radio contact with our base and they sent a plane out to pick us up. Later, they sent out a crew to replace the engine and fly the plane — a big biplane Waco — off the island and back to base.

I had another close call when my pilot and I ran into some real bad weather and got turned upside down in a bunch of clouds. We ended up in a power dive, and only barely had room to recover once we saw the water rushing up at us. After landing, we noticed that long strips of fabric had been torn from the top wing. When the base closed I went to work in the New Orleans shipyards. I thought I'd be called into the military, but I never was.

Clerk-typist Ann McDonald took flying lessons and soloed while at Corpus Christi, but she was better known for her keen musical talents (courtesy Mrs. Violet Bumpus Rentfrow).

By memorandum of August 23, 1943, base commander McLendon announced that provisions had been made to set up a Courier base in Ogden, Utah, with a staff of thirty. McLendon explained that:

> These individuals have been picked according to seniority and qualifications for the new assignment, and have been officially notified, but it is apparent that 46 of our number cannot be taken along. I wish to take this opportunity to express to you my appreciation for your whole-hearted cooperation, your loyalty to duty, and your untiring efforts to make the success of this Base possible. I deeply regret that each person who is now on our base roster cannot be taken to the new location, but Army regulations have specified otherwise, and we are not empowered to carry out our own wishes in this matter. You will receive before August 31, an honorable discharge from this Base, along with your service record. These papers will reflect to you and to every person concerned, your achievment on Coastal Patrol.

Corpus Christi personnel who were discharged from the coastal patrol still remained members of the Civil Air Patrol, and within several months many of those who were not transferred to the courier base in Ogden, Utah were reassigned to Tow Target Unit #15 at San Jose, California. Included in that group were intelligence officer William M. Blevins; assistant operations engineer Joe A. Payne; pilots John W. Corn, Rall B. Cowden, James F. Davis, John R. Moulton, Morrisette W. Horne, John R. Mouton, Raulan R. Rentfrow, Coy J. Roden, and Gordon K. Wear; mechanics Jerry Berman, George W. Cavanese, Edwin Kaufman, Charley J. Ritchey, Warren A. Smith, and Orville Strean; radio mechanic Gilbert J. Ruiz; service technician Jesse M. Ellison; technical section head Clarence E. Dietert; and clerks Ann McDonald and Violet K. Bumpus. Some of this group also served at TTU #7 based at Glendale Army Air Base in Glendale, California; at TTU #12 based at Gibbs Airport in San Diego, California; and at McChord Field, Fort Lewis, Washington.

## Violet K. Bumpus

*Violet K. Bumpus became Violet Rentfrow, wife of pilot Raulan Rentfrow, on the very day that the selected base personnel were scheduled to leave for San Jose. Their departure was delayed a day by bad weather, with somewhat frustrating results for the newlyweds. The events leading up to that final day and night in Corpus Christi are recalled by Mrs. Rentfrow:*

I was born and raised and went to school in Hannibal, Missouri. When I was twenty-one, my parents were divorced and my mother and I and my stepfather moved to Corpus Christi where his construction company helped build the Naval Air Station. Although I'd attended LaGrange Community College in Hannibal, the only positions I could find there were piddling low-paying jobs like receptionist for a doctor and clerk in a stationery store. When a friend told me the CAP was seeking clerical help at thirty-five dollars a week, I thought, "Wow! Wouldn't that be something!" That was twice what I was then earning. I rushed out for an interview and got the job, but not until they'd checked my background back in Hannibal. A fellow named Clarence Dietert was head of administration, and I became his assistant. We kept on top of personnel payrolls and payments owing to the owners of the airplanes leased by the base, insurance matters, and most of the business stuff associated with running the base. I was soon promoted to master sergeant, but we weren't very military, and I certainly never cracked the whip over anyone like sergeants do in the movies

I lived there on North Beach Avenue with my mother and stepfather, and I believe the base had a station wagon it sent around to pick up people like me who were without cars. I think I'd been on the job two days when this fellow Raulan Rentfrow arrived from the base at Brownsville. He came to my desk and said he wanted to sign up for a week. I told him he'd have to sign up for thirty days — that was the minimum. So he did and he and I just sort of went on from there.

Raulan was an excellent pilot. I remember when one of our pilots put a plane down in some of the marshlands surrounding Corpus. It was considered a good landing because he walked away from it. The problem was how to get the ship back to the base. The ground was extremely soft, and any kind of take-off run seemed impossible. Raulan announced he could do it. Well everybody thought he was a crazy braggart, but he convinced them to come help give it a try. The plane was

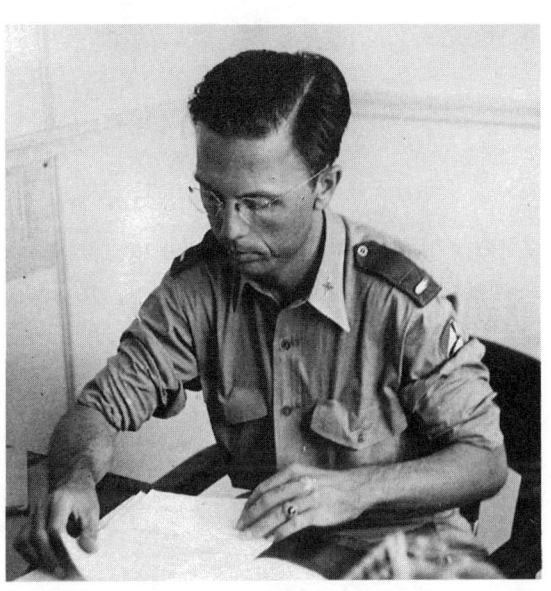

First Lt. (later Capt.) Clarence E. Dietert was a Certified Public Accountant and a perfect choice to head the base technical section, which was responsible for all fiscal and personnel record-keeping (courtesy Mrs. Violet Bumpus Rentfrow).

standing on its nose, so first all the air crews and mechanics — I think even Major McLendon — went out there and pulled its tail down and dug mud and weeds from the engine. Raulan got in the plane, and while everyone got under its wings and tail to support most of its weight he gunned the engine to full throttle and they kind of half-carried, half-pushed the plane far enough for him to get it moving and then airborne. Most of them ended up splattered with mud from head to toe. He flew the plane back to the base and it was soon back on the line ready for patrol work.

Ron and I became a pretty steady item throughout the following year and were married at 6:00 a.m. on December 5, 1943. We were scheduled to leave as part of a four-plane flight headed for San Jose at 8:00 a.m. But the weather turned bad, and our departure was delayed until the next day so we spent the night with my mother in her bungalow. My poor husband slept on the sofa in the living room.

The weather remained a problem throughout our trip west. I've forgotten who we flew with, but he had a staggerwing Beechcraft, and besides Ron and myself it was filled with typewriters, calculators, files of paperwork, and various office stuff. Our first stop was at Midland, Texas, where we'd been promised a Texas-style barbecue by Rall "Bum" Cowden, one of our pilots who owned a huge ranch there. We were

M/Sgt. Violet Bumpus Rentfrow with her pilot-husband Raulan R. Rentfrow after their arrival in San Jose, California. They raised four children, and had been married forty-three years when Capt. Rentfrow died in 1986 (courtesy Mrs. Violet Bumpus Rentfrow).

served "Rocky Mountain Oysters," which I respectfully declined. We continued across New Mexico, Arizona, and southern California, held up with bad weather once or twice more. I recall that overnight accommodations were a problem all the way. There just wasn't much. On our first night in San Jose, Ron and I slept in a barracks on the base, not much fun, either. On our second night, we found room in the De Anza Hotel. I think the hotel may still be there — but the old base is just a big housing tract now. After a bit, we rented an apartment and finally bought a little house.

We stayed there until the tow target unit broke up sometime about mid-1945. I held the same job I'd had before — assistant administrative head — and Ron flew regularly pulling targets. Some of the gunnery was awful. One day when he saw tracers *ahead* of his plane, he called the battery commander and told him to tell his men, "I'm towing this damned target, not pushing it!" He lost his target once when a bullet cut the tow cable, so the assignment was not without considerable risk. Meanwhile, I'd become pregnant, but continued working at the base. When I left work this particular Friday, I set up my schedule as usual for the following Monday and my daughter was born on Sunday. After the war, Ron and I stayed in San Jose, then just a sleepy little Spanish town, and had three more children. I still live nearby, but it's nothing like it was fifty years ago.

---

Base officers, pilots, and observers who served at least one month at CAPCP#15 and who are not elsewhere mentioned in the text of this chapter include: Paul C. Barker,* William R. Berger, Rolfe F. Carlisle, Hilliard F. Clark, Worth B. Cline,* Charles E. Courtion,* J. Frank Davis,* Gorman E. Fox,* Bernard F. Gibson, Jr., Claude W. Glasson,* August W. Gustafson, Luther B. Hall,* Alfonso B. Heath, Raymond V. Hood, Jr.,* Morrisette W. Horne,* Charles I. Jennings, Edwin L. Kain, Eugene F. Kendall, Ralph G. Lawrence, Jack P. Lindsay,* Rose G. McDaniel, Lloyd Martin,* LaRue Newby, Jesse L. Pate, Jr.,* Charles S. Polhemus,* Marion L. Quinn, Clarence M. Ranck, Richard D. Shinkle,* Stuart S. Smith, Norman D. Tucker, William D. Warren, Jr., Richard W. White, Thomas R. Wingate, and Robert C. Wolf.* Asterisk indicates Air Medal winner.

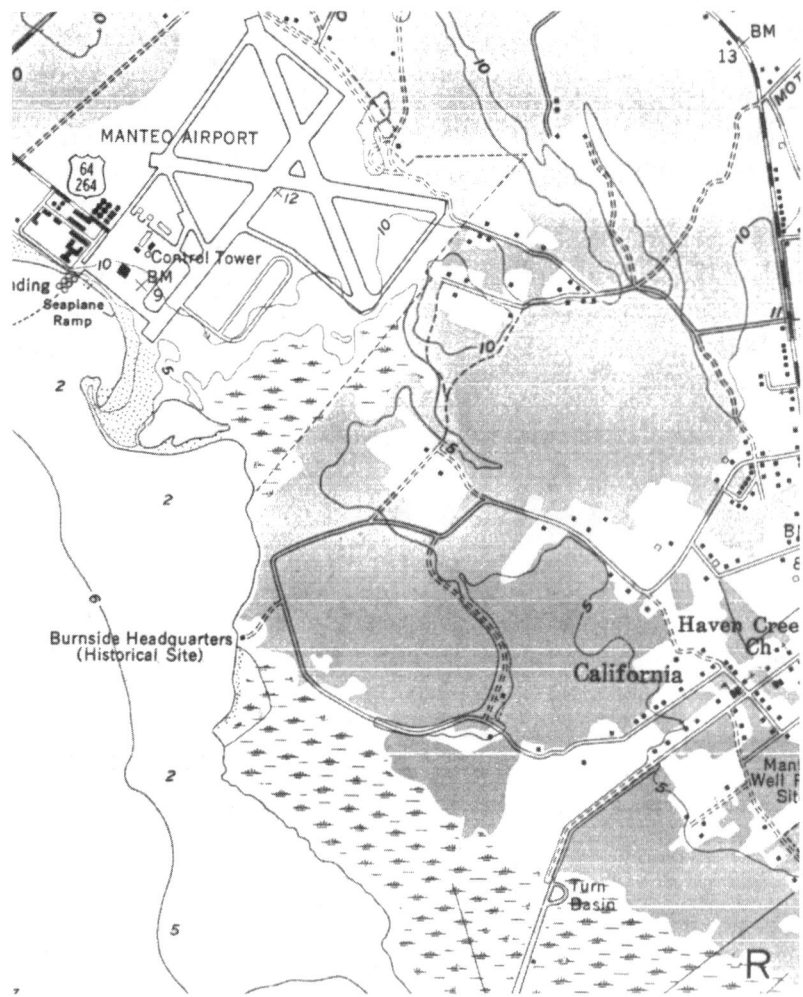

What is now the Dare County Regional Airport was originally built as the Manteo Naval Air Station. Coastal patrol personnel erected a hangar and other buildings on a small corner of the base (source: 1953 United States Geological Survey map).

# 16

# Manteo, North Carolina

None of the coastal patrol's twenty-one bases was located in a more historic place than the one at Manteo, North Carolina. Manteo is near the northern tip of twelve-mile long Roanoke Island, site of the first English settlement in the Americas — Sir Walter Raleigh's "lost colony" established in 1585, but found abandoned by a supply ship five years later. Virginia Dare, the first white child of English parents in the New World, was born on Roanoke Island in 1587. To provide living proof that the Indians were "the most gentle, loving, and faithful, void of all guile, and treason, and such as lived after the manner of the golden age," two of them, Manteo and Wanchese, were taken to England by Raleigh's captains, Philip Amadas and Arthur Barlowe, then returned on their next voyage to Roanoke Island. The island's two principal towns were named to commemorate those gentle natives.

An unusual history of the Manteo coastal patrol base exists in the form of the "security log" kept by the S-2 office. The first two entries identify the initial coastal patrol arrivals, and what they found at Skyco, an airfield of sorts at the south end of Roanoke Island.

> **22 July 1942:** A group of men arrived in Manteo, North Carolina, to begin CAP Coastal Patrol Base No. 16. The group included Captain James L. Hamilton, Lt. Allen H. Watkins, Lt. Walter M. Bryson, Lt. C. Y. Nanney, Jr., Lt. George F. Hatch, Flight Officer Raymond V. Hood, Jr., Sergeant James L. Thompson, Sgt. Lloyd W. Cook, Jr., Sgt. Clarence B. Henderson, Sgt. A. W. Greeson, Jr., Corporal Leo E. Stewart, Nurse Lottie B. Sapp, Private Bert W. Engleman, Pvt. Lester H. Yandel, Jr., Pvt. Ted E. Sellers, and Pvt. L. J. Sapp, who spent the entire week cleaning up headquarters (farm house), mowing grass, cutting

bushes, putting up radio antenna. Mosquitoes were terrific! [Fittingly, an adopted base mascot was named "Skeeter," and she was important enough to all personnel that a subsequent security log entry reported the day she had her four puppies.]

**27 July 1942**: A mass flight from Charlotte, Asheville, Elkin, and Winston-Salem, North Carolina, arrived, including eight planes piloted by Lt. Dabney M. Coddington, Lt. Paul Bridges, Lt. Claude Jarrett, Lt. Donald Hutton, Lt. Rufus A. Brown, Lt. O. A. Corriher, Lt. James E. Owen, Lt. R. Edward Church, Lt. Samuel M. Atkinson, Lt. Vernon C. Rudolph, and Lt. Paul Little. Most of the entire personnel arrived today ... a hectic day for all, especially S-2 office. The end of first week found a tired bunch of pioneers (old hands by now) ... [and] a canteen on back porch; a pilot's ready room on front porch.

## Theodore E. Sellers

*Among the first arrivals were James L. Hamilton, base commander (to be succeeded by Allen H. Watkins) and Theodore E. Sellers, a young man still in high school who had soloed in a J-3 Cub on his sixteenth birthday the year before. Sellers recalls flying to Roanoke Island with Hamilton in Hamilton's Stinson gullwing and then having great difficulty finding the Skyco airport:*

We circled and circled trying to find it. Finally, our presence attracted the attention of a number of townspeople who realized our dilemma. They drove to a long grassy field and formed two lines with their cars right along where a dirt runway was hidden under the waist-high grass. Though we landed without any problem, the scary part was not knowing what was under the grass — like maybe a deep drainage ditch, or a barbed wire fence. We were the first plane to arrive. I like to say that commander Hamilton and I opened the Manteo base. The next day we had the grass mowed as fast as we could, expecting to see more planes arriving any minute. At summer's end, I returned to high school for my senior year. In February, 1943 five of us went to the principal and asked if he'd grant us diplomas if we joined the Navy and he said okay. The Navy accepted the others, but I was rejected because I wore glasses. I contacted Major Frank Dawson, C. O. of the Beaufort coastal patrol base, and he asked me to join them as an observer, so I did.

## C. Weldon Fields

*C. Weldon Fields, an amateur radio operator from Greensboro, was another early arrival. Born in Guilford County, North Carolina on June 8, 1914, Fields had been a licensed "ham" radio operator since 1930. He says that getting Manteo "on the air" was no easy task:*

When I learned about Manteo's need for a communications system, I was working for a company dealing in radio parts and supplies. I immediately called on friends who were "hams" like myself, and we began collecting the parts for a station, gathering at my place of work in the evenings to plan what was needed. We loaded our results into a pick-up truck and took it to Skyco, where we set up in a small upstairs room in the farm house headquarters. We were assigned the same frequency as one of the Norfolk Naval Air Stations, and call letters, WXDD. From this we decided to designate our planes "DOG-1" and so on — whatever the number of the craft was. One day we received a phone call from the Navy demanding to know, "What's all this 'dog' business we hear on our frequency?" Because of their objections, we eventually got a new frequency.

The Manteo coastal patrol base was originally located at Skyco, toward the southern end of Roanoke island. It was nothing more than a farmer's field with a farmhouse for headquarters. The constant clouds of mosquitoes were unforgettable for all who served there (courtesy Harry P. Bridges).

On July 27th, about fifteen aircraft arrived from Charlotte, and the grass meadow began to look like it was ready for business. We had no hangars, so the planes were lined up near the strip, and even though they were all colors of the rainbow, they made an impressive sight, filling all of us with great anticipation of the job ahead. Of course, we had to make a lot of dry runs to check the radios and let the pilots get used to the strip. Landings could only be made in one direction and there were ground loops at first, but none serious enough to damage the planes. I believe the first patrols went out the middle of August.

When the Navy completed its base for training fighter pilots on the northern end of the island we moved up there. We built a new base of our own at the northeast corner of the Navy base even while continuing our patrols out of the Skyco strip. It had an operations building, a hangar, and a mess hall-recreation center. We had to jump to keep communications going from both Skyco and our new base and not interrupt our flights. When the base closed at the end of August 1943, I had been on duty from start to finish, and when I pulled out driving our last service truck over to Beaufort in mid-October, I left only two people still at the base, Commander Watkins and his secretary, Bernice Raiford.

Before the Manteo base closed, everyone was given an opportunity to sign up for further duty if they desired. I was the only one to do so, and that is why I was sent to Beaufort. There I learned I'd be sent to Monogram Field in Virginia as part of a tow target group that would also provide planes for night-flying and tests of anti-aircraft battery tracking techniques. We were preparing for the move when a welder's spark inside the hangar set fire to one of the planes. We lost every plane, except for a few outside on the line. Since the control tower was attached to the burned hangar, I lost all of my radio gear that I'd used at Manteo and planned to use at Monogram.

Towing targets was a whole new ball game, especially for our pilots. Getting a folded or rolled up target into a plane was difficult enough, and we only had a couple of planes with enough power to pull them once they were unreeled. We pulled targets during the day and flew tracking missions at night. We all were barracked with a Seabee battalion and ate Navy mess, which was different too. We were at Monogram until April 15, 1944, and the job was mostly routine — with one terrible exception: our loss of flight officer Norman L. Buckey and 1st Lt. Alfred C. Kendricks on a January 22, 1944 night tracking mission. We never really knew what caused the crash. Something went wrong as they were taking off, I saw an explosion just off the end of the runway, and the radio went dead. They were both good pilots and great friends.

## William Paul Bridges

*Another of the first arrivals was eventual Air medal winner William Paul Bridges, age thirty-three, who had been born on a farm near Shelby, North Carolina. In 1983 he told Colonel Lester E. Hopper of the hazards of the early patrols, and about the base's first fatal ditching at sea:*

We usually plotted our patrols as going from this buoy to that buoy to the next buoy. I remember one day our lead ship seemed to mistake one buoy for another and ended up heading straight out to sea. I told my observer I thought he was headed wrong, and after following him for half an hour, I signaled and turned back, and he followed. We were all sort of green pilots back then, and it was pretty easy to get lost. I knew one fellow who'd been a bus driver and knew every bend in the road from Charlotte to Manteo. I told him, "Listen, where you're going you ain't going to see any landmarks like that. You've got to learn to watch your compass and fly that compass and your watch. If you don't, you ain't coming back from out there, maybe."

As for our first fatalities — I think I might know what happened. There were a lot of people back in those days who didn't know about carburetor icing and how to handle carburetor heat. Sometimes if you pulled on partial heat, it would create freezing conditions in the carburetor throat and choke off the fuel mixture supply, the very thing the heat's supposed to prevent. When he flew with me, I had occasion to tell Mr. Cooper to quit fooling with the heat setting. Either pull it all the way on, or push it all the way off. He was the one flying the night of the tragedy, and it was one of the coldest, rainiest, and windiest days I can remember.

The hourly sequence of events was recorded in the base security log for December 21, 1942:

Today at 1640Q Aircraft DD4, NC 36782 forced down at sea at 3540-7526 two miles off beach one half mile south new river inlet. Crew Pilot Julian L. Cooper and observer Frank M. Cook. Sister ship DD11, pilot Story and observer Moore, stood by until fuel exhaustion forced a beach landing. Flight took off 1430Q due in 1730Q. Flight at south end of north patrol. South patrol #20, #12 Arnette-Simpson and Stradley-King came upon scene at 1650Q returning from south patrol. Crew #4 got out of ship apparently unhurt and got in flotation. #11, #12, #20 dropped slicks and flares keeping survivors in sight at all time. #1 Capt. Watkins with Hatch observer flew to scene dropping flares, etc. until darkness. #11, #12 landed on beach due to fuel exhaustion; #19 dispatched to beach pilot Fenner and observer Corriher with emergency gas. All three ships left on beach due to debris and darkness. #11 and #20 dropped flotation gear. #3 pilot Black and observer Geaslen dispatched to drop flares, slicks. Regular procedure followed CGEC advised by telephone as well as CG stations on beach, Langley, Norfolk, New York and Washington advised by teletype; NYC and Norfolk called to verify sea landing. Navy blimp, PBY and scouts stood by at scene. Rough sea prevented rescue; survivors last seen at dark.

First Lt. Frank M. Cook died at sea during the night of December 21, 1942. His would-be rescuers circled him as long as there was light, but by the next morning he could not be found (courtesy Harry P. Bridges).

The Elizabeth City *Daily Advance* reported the tragedy on December 26, adding details about the last sighting of the two men in the water and of the attempted rescue by Navy and Coast Guard boats:

> The evening was bitter cold. No human could withstand the cold for long. The spray that flew over the heads, shoulders and arms of the two men froze almost as soon as it struck them, making them helpless to fight for life. It is reported that one of the men apparently was numb before the companion plane left, as his head was dropped over his shoulder while the life jacket still kept him afloat. The other waved to the companion plane as its pilot left and headed back to the base.

> Every Naval and Coast Guard unit in this area was striving to rescue them.... the Negro crew at Pea Island fought heroically to launch their boats. They were the nearest the scene of the accident. Each time they would thrust their boat into the breakers it would be thrown back at them overturned.... every crew of the stations named [including Nags Head, Chicamocomico, and Oregon Inlet] made all possible human efforts to get to sea. The wind and the tide and the relentless breakers would not let up for even a few minutes

It was not until March 11, 1943 that Frank Cook's body was found floating face down in the water just north of the shoals off Cape Lookout, near the coastal patrol base at Beaufort, North Carolina. The discovery was made by a pair of patrol planes searching the area on a special mission for the Navy to find and record ships sunk in the area. The body was quickly recovered by a Coast Guard boat.

In the 1983 interview, William Bridges also talked of moving to the Manteo Naval Air Station near the northern end of Roanoke Island. Although squeezed into a far corner of the newly-built base, coastal patrol operations actually began before Navy operations did. Bridges then described the little town of Manteo, saying "down here," because by 1983 Manteo had become his home:

> It was a fishing town mainly. There's a lot of fish caught down here in the sound. Nags Head, over on the beach, now that's a vacation town, but there was an old wooden bridge betwixt here and the beach. You crossed that thing in the morning and them planks went "yackety, yackety, yackety." There were several teams of oxen pulling two wheeled carts down here at that time. The natives, they're clannish type people, but once they know you and begin to like you, you've got a friend for life. We've got some of the best friends down here as we've got anywhere in the world.

First Lt. Julian L. Cooper died along with Frank Cook on December 21, 1942. The storm-lashed Atlantic was too rough to launch a rescue boat or to land an amphibian airplane (courtesy Harry P. Bridges).

Bridges recalled no big problems with Navy and coastal patrol planes flying the same airport traffic patterns and using the same runways, even though some of the Navy boys might hot-shot around out of sight of the control tower. Asked if the weather restricted flying from Manteo, and whether the base was well run, Bridges replied:

Of course we didn't fly instruments, but we flew in weather that we shouldn't have flown in, really. But most of the time we flew. Yes, I'd say that the base was well run, and turned out as well as anyone could expect under the circumstances. I think we carried out our mission about as good as it could have been done. Yes, we took a band of disorganized civilians and turned it into a pretty good military organization. It puts me in mind a whole lot of the battle of Kings Mountain, with them sharpshooters coming up there on top of the mountain, you know.* You could compare it with that, I'd say.

First Lt. William Paul Bridges was flying long before the coastal patrol came into being. Here he is suited-up to handle an open cockpit two-seater, probably a Stearman PT-17 (courtesy Harry P. Bridges).

The airport rules and regulations as set forth in an operations memo from Lt. Robert E. Church, assistant operations officer, were relatively concise and traffic control for coastal patrol aircraft was largely accomplished by the use of signal lights:

> (1) The traffic control area will be area one and one half miles from field and below fifteen hundred feet. (2) When tower lights are not being used, white flag on tower will indicate an open field, and red flag will indicate closed field. (Red flag will be displayed only in case of emergency.) (3) At night a light in the wind sock will indicate

---

* A remarkable defeat imposed, October 7, 1780, on a British raiding party by a diverse group of frontier riflemen. Situated near the South Carolina line, west of Charlotte, the battlefield is now part of the Kings Mountain National Military Park established 1931. The analogy to the coastal patrol "Flying Minute Men" is clear.

open field. No flag or lights on traffic control tower will indicate tower is not operating. (4) All turns will be counter-clockwise. (5) No right hand turns below fifteen hundred feet or within three miles of the field. (6) A steady red light means "Stop." (7) A flashing red light means "Return to line." (8) A flashing green light means "Land and stay on the ground." (9) A steady green light means "Clear for take-off or clear to taxi."

Naval and coastal patrol personnel were compatible on the ground as well as in the air. Though physically located at opposite ends of the airfield the men and women from both bases socialized at dances and parties, and the men competed at sports. The favorite game was softball. Hand-lettered notices announced an after-hours, late afternoon game on May 5, 1943, between the CAP "Fallen Angels" and the NAS "Hogs" — the Navy flyers' nickname for their heavy, gas-guzzling Corsair shipboard fighters. The notice signed by coastal patrol pilot Louis Gross advised base members that "any ball players who fail to appear for other than duty reasons will be thrown into the sound three times and dragged out twice." The coastal patrol won this game 6-5.

The Bridges family, left to right: Dixon, father William P., Tillie, infant son Harry, mother Vetus, and Tommy. Harry followed in his father's footsteps and became both a pilot and long-time CAP member (courtesy Harry P. Bridges).

A companion notice advised "AND A GOOD BALL GAME IS NOT ALL. At 2000Q — not one — but THREE moving pictures will be shown. All Coastal Patrol personnel are invited to see these shows at the Naval Air Station, 5 May 1943. You'll enjoy them. Be sure to go!" Having won this challenge softball game, 6-2, a few coastal patrolers may have opted to celebrate in some more robust fashion.

## Carl O. Swaim

*Carl O. Swaim, a native of Winston-Salem, was thirty-one and already had a radio repair business on Roanoke Island when the coastal patrol arrived. Though he installed radios in many of the CAP aircraft, and helped set up the base's communications system, he resisted becoming a member of the base until Allen Watkins took over as its commander in December 1942. From then until the base closed, M/Sgt. Swaim was one of the four radio operators who manned the base communications center every day from 4:00 a.m. until dark. As he told Colonel Lester E. Hopper in 1983, Swaim preferred the morning shift, and getting the dawn patrol away:*

> They'd take off, two of them going south, two of them going north, and you'd give them permission to take off in the morning at dawn, soon as it was light enough for them to see, and get them out, and then they'd come back and give you their coordinates every fifteen minutes, where they were, and they would go further out to sea. Also they had a rule that each plane had to fall back behind the other at intervals to see if anything was wrong with the other airplane. All the time they would do this, and you'd ask him if his sister ship was all right, and if he saw anything, and the other one too.... We had a map of the whole area, and kept tabs of the exact latitudes and longitudes of all the planes.... They became pretty good navigators. When they first started down here it was kind of a haphazard thing. They used buoys offshore. They'd say we are at buoy so-and-so.... They were comical sometimes, in the remarks that they made. They were a pretty happy-go-lucky bunch of people to be out there where they were in planes.

Swaim was off duty the day Julian Cooper and Frank Cook had to ditch off Kitty Hawk, but he was well aware of the circumstances — the surf so high that the Coast Guard couldn't even launch its rescue boat. After that tragic loss of life, he recalled that flights would be canceled if the ocean were so rough as to prevent such launchings. Swaim was one of the relatively few CAP personnel to see a ship sunk by enemy action:

> Oh, yes. I saw them from the shore. I stood over in that old casino on Nags Head one night in the winter time when it was cold, and I saw

one of those tankers right close to shore go up just like a firecracker, and you could see the men flying out of it, and the oil burning on top of the water.... I saw two or three blow up, just standing looking. I mean we were just standing there talking, looking out the window. People don't realize how hot the enemy action was here, and the coastal patrol did a world of good. I began to really admire them afterward, after I got with them, because I knew what they were doing — it's the only thing we had.

They'd call in and say they saw a submarine, when I was on duty and we had a teletype to the Navy in Norfolk, and I'd call the Navy and tell them they had seen a submarine, which is what we were supposed to do, and where it was, the location of it, and the Navy said, sorry, there's one PBY flying and he's off Florida someplace. From Florida to above Norfolk, they had one PBY flying at a time. They covered that whole coast. We had no protection. We didn't have anything. And if our coastal patrol planes hadn't helped the Navy, the Germans could have come in any time they wanted to. They didn't know how little we had.

## Everett C. Long

*Everett C. Long was born and raised around Newton, North Carolina, and learned to fly Piper Cubs and Stearmans at Lenoir-Rhyne College where he earned his private license under the auspices of the government's Civilian Pilot Training Program. When he arrived at the Manteo base, he had been checked out in Wacos and Stinsons and was ready to fly whatever he was assigned:*

I was single then and several of us had rooms in town with a lady whose name I forget. When we came back from the movies, we had to scrape the mosquitoes off with a pine brush before we went into the house. Our first base was just a long dirt strip way south of town, out in the country down near Wanchese at the southern tip of Roanoke Island. The poor boys who stood guard duty out there really had to battle the mosquitoes! Later on, we moved up to the Manteo airport, which had paved runways. We used one end of the field, the Navy used the other end. We put up some of our own buildings with salvaged lumber from a former Civilian Conservation Corps camp.

Most of the people at the base were North Carolinians. All the first bunch of pilots were, but later we got some flight observers who weren't. Allen Watkins couldn't be beaten as a C.O. He brought his own plane with him, a four-place Curtiss Air Sedan, something like a Robin. We flew twice a day — up the coast as far as Norfolk, and south to a little island inhabited only by wild animals.

I had one forced landing. We were about thirty miles out one day, when smoke started coming back from under the engine cowling. The boy with me shouted, "Put 'er down, put 'er down, put 'er down." I told him, "No way!" I nursed the Waco back to Nags Head, a few miles across Roanoke Sound from Manteo, and landed in a field covered by tree stumps. Would you believe that the good Lord let me put that plane down among all those stumps without so much as a scratch!

I remember once flying up to Norfolk to watch a demonstration of radar. I learned that one of the submariner's tricks to avoid detection was to get up real close under a surface ship's stern, so that only one radar blip would be seen, not two. Another time I flew to Rocky Mount to buy the Navy fellows some liquor, and I also recall flying out to Pittsburgh to pick up a radio for the base. The ceiling was so low I flew right past the high-rise Pittsburgher Hotel where I stayed that night.

Manteo was just a little village then, but the people were very accepting of us. There wasn't much to do except go to the movies. I don't remember any base beer parties or blowouts like that. I think we played bridge and rook and other kinds of cards. I was never much good at socializing, and I didn't pay much attention to the other activities around the base. I pretty much minded my own business and did what I went down there to do — which was to fly. The weather was usually good and we flew most every day. I don't think we had an amphibian for rescue work but relied on the Navy boys for that. I remained at Manteo until it closed, then went down to Camden, South Carolina, as a civilian flight instructor for the Air Corps. In 1948 I received the Air Medal.

## William M. Gantt

*William M. Gantt was from Albemarle, North Carolina and learned to fly — the first eight hours for fifty dollars — at Concord, North Carolina, where he volunteered for the CAP in mid-1942. When he went to Manteo later that year, he went as a guard and did not begin flying until April 1943, and then only as an observer. In 1986, he recalled for Colonel Lester E. Hopper many highlights of his nine months at the base:*

> I lived in Manteo itself. Various people took in boarders, and I lived in the home of Mrs. Theodore Meekins, one of the oldest residents there. She had a three-story house, and I lived on the top floor. Out front was a Captain's Walk, where you could overlook the ocean. You got back and forth to the base the best way you could, usually hitching a ride with someone. There was no food at the base so you'd go to the drug store and bring food out there in paper sacks for your meals.... I learned that you could put a pimiento cheese sandwich on a piece of wax paper on top of a hot fifty-five gallon oil drum

stove and that the sandwich would toast up without burning, but the minute you picked that sandwich up off the wax paper, the paper would catch fire. The trick was to pick up sandwich and paper and turn them over together.

We had to have a private pilot's license to get the job as observer, and they did that for us while I was down there as a guard. They had a school and they got a guy to come down and give us a test, and we all passed our written exam, and then I went back home to Charlotte and got my private license there and came back. They had all of us practice landings on the windiest days they could find just to be sure we could land particular airplanes. But I remained an observer. I never went over to the left seat the whole time I was there. I flew a lot with Tommy Thompson, Hank Fenner, Martin Bernstein, and Milton Arnett. I was pretty much of a nosey kid. I was young, and I know I made the mistake a lot of youngsters do, I asked too many questions and talked when I should have been listening. I realized this as I got older, but I got on well with those guys.

This aerial view of the Manteo coastal patrol base — located in one corner of the Manteo Naval Air Station — resembled nothing so much as a World War I base with a squadron of Spads or Nieuport monoplanes sitting about (courtesy Harry P. Bridges).

According to my log book, I flew just over one hundred hours down there. I remember that the radio work was just about like in the old movies. You'd say something, then repeat it without being asked.

Our radio antenna was a hundred feet of copper wire covered in leather that we'd reel out and let trail behind. Our call letters were WXDD. The planes were numbered XD such-and-so. We didn't have any formal training. We'd just call in, "XD8 calling WXDD, and Carl Swaim would reply, "Slow it down, Bill, I can't keep up with you." The radios were affected by atmospheric conditions, and sometimes you had a real hard time hearing. We had a map with a grid on it, left side numbers, letters across the top, and that's how we'd report our positions. When we came back in, I had to reel in that hundred feet of wire. For a little skinny guy, who's right-handed, using his left hand to reel in that wire, which had a little cone on the end of it to keep it stretched out, would get me winded and sometimes the pilot would have to take over.

\* \* \*

Gantt remembered that most of the guard group with whom he worked when he first arrived at Manteo furnished their own weapons, mainly thirty-eight caliber revolvers, but many couldn't use them, and no arrangements were made for target practice. A number of older townsfolk worked at the base, filling in wherever needed. One was the man who had sent the telegram to tell the world that the Wright Brothers had sustained mechanical flight. Gantt also talked about the high winds that often swept the base:

We had no grass on the airport, so when these high winds blew — I'm guessing that some were thirty-five to forty knots — the sand would blow up to a thousand feet right over the base. It'd cover the whole airport and you could see that column of sand forty miles out to sea. You didn't have to navigate, you'd just aim at that column of sand. When you landed, they lined up eight guys, four on each side of the runway, right at the end. When the airplane quit rolling, the nearest man on either side would wrap his arms and legs around the wing strut, and they'd all hang on until you taxied over to the tie-down and were secured. The Stinson 10A was the worst, because with that big tail and deep fuselage, the plane would weathervane and the wind could move you around pretty good.

Regarding our insignia ... We didn't like the wings they issued. They looked rinky-dink, so everybody would go in to Norfolk to buy their wings. There was a store that had observer's wings, with a circle in the middle, a round hole. They sold a half of the wing, too, probably as an observer on a balloon or something, and we'd go buy those and come back and our sign painter artist would take the CAP three-bladed prop and would cut that thing out and solder it in those wings, and that's what everybody had for wings. About the only really ingenious thing we did was to make those home-made wings.

## Anthony Wietholter

*Anthony Wietholter was born and raised in Newport, Kentucky, across the Ohio River from Cincinnati. Drafted in 1942 he took Army basic training at the Aberdeen Proving Ground, and became a specialist in handling bombs and ammunition. Later he was chosen, with three other soldiers, to report to the coastal patrol base near Wanchese:*

It was nothing but a cow pasture, with a farm house as headquarters. The mosquitoes were *unbelievably* bad. The worst in years people said. When a plane returned from patrol and the mechanics added engine oil, it took one man to pour the oil, and two men with spray guns to protect him! Sergeant George Moore was in charge of our detachment, and we all boarded at Miss Bell's up in Manteo. We were on "rations and quarters," which in the Army is a good deal, because you drew a daily allowance and could choose your place to eat and sleep, and drove back and forth to work in the big Army truck we brought from Savannah. The truck was needed to transport our bombs and fuses from Elizabeth City. Sergeant Moore carried a thirty-eight caliber government-issue revolver, required whenever we were working around the bombs.

When we first got up there, there wasn't much for us soldier boys to do, because we didn't have any bombs or anywhere to store them, nor were the planes yet equipped with bomb racks and release mechanisms. Then we moved to the airport at Manteo, and had all the work we wanted. We pitched in with everyone else to help build the new facilities. Trees were cut down and hauled to a makeshift sawmill, and an old fellow named Ed ran the circular saw with a power take-off from an old farm tractor. A derelict truck was found, and after we got it running I drove it to haul the logs. Those coastal patrol fellows did a heck of a job building their own base, I'll tell you. They worked their butts off!

We used some of the new lumber to build a revetment in which to store the one-hundred pound demolition bombs that we eventually got. It didn't matter that the new lumber was green, because we covered the whole thing deep below ground anyway. I think we never stored more than ten bombs at a time. Our ordnance crew gave the flyers formal instruction on bombs and fuses and how they worked. I believe only two were ever dropped at sea, and we never had depth charges. Our crew reported to Major Watkins, the base commander, who told us, "You fellows know what you have to do, just go ahead and set your own hours and do it." He was a fine man and treated everyone swell. He called me "Weatie" just like the other men did.

Three of us soldiers, including myself, were single when we arrived in Manteo, and the other fellow's wife was at home having a baby. Later, one of the other fellows and myself got married, and we brought our wives up and we four shared a rented cottage right near the base. Our landlord was Paul Bridges, one of the pilots, who had just bought the house. Our wives didn't work, though some wives did. I bought a used Model A from a local fellow who'd just had it all fixed up, and my wife and I sometimes drove over to Elizabeth City to see a movie or do some shopping. We also drove up to Norfolk several times to see her brother, who was a sailor and was in a Navy hospital for burns he got in an accident there. I recall going to some dances and other entertainment at the "Brass Rail," but mostly Manteo was pretty quiet. We'd been there only about a year when the base closed.

## Bernice Barbour

*Bernice Barbour (now Mrs. Bernice Raiford) was born in Hampton, but mostly grew up in Franklin, Virginia. After high school, she was trained as a bookkeeper by her father, a C.P.A., and worked in his automobile agency. She then moved to Greensboro, North Carolina to work for another agency. When the war began, she wanted to serve in some manner, but had just had knee surgery and was still hobbling around with a cane, so couldn't do anything very physical. Her next-door neighbor, who was an amateur pilot, suggested she consider the Civil Air Patrol:*

I was brought in as a clerk-typist and assistant to the administrative chief of the base. In the beginning, no one knew exactly what was needed or how to set up the records. After a few weeks of struggle we had a workable solution. The administration section head returned home, and I was given the job and promoted to Master Sergeant, the highest coastal patrol rank a female could hold. I don't recall what my pay was — it was certainly minimal — but out of it I had to buy the summer and winter uniforms I had to wear while on duty, and pay for my own meals and living quarters.

When I took over as chief, no one worked for me directly, but later I had a secretary. I believe the base complement totaled seventy-two, of whom seven were women, all of them younger than myself. Several of them were the wives of the pilots. It was far from an eight-to-five job. We did whatever we had to, and a few nights I was still there in the office at two o'clock in the morning. We were supposed to have a day off a week, but it didn't always work out that way.

I worked directly under our base commander, Major Watkins. Two stories will help explain my experiences with him. Twice a month I had to make payroll requisitions to Washington. That meant typing a form with a great deal of information on it for each member of the base. Of course, everything had be in seven copies! The heading on each form was very long, beginning with "Major Allen Watkins, Base Commander." I was a hunt and peck typist so for the first requisition I prepared I took what I thought was a good shortcut. I wrote "Major Allen Watkins, B.C." Soon after I put them on his desk for signature he stormed up to my desk, threw them down, and said "I am *not* 'Before Christ.' Do them over!" I learned not to take shortcuts.

M/Sgt. Bernice Olivia Barbour (now Bernice Raiford) was head of the technical section and commander Allen H. Watkins's administrative assistant. She remembers him as tough but fair (courtesy Harry P. Bridges).

The second story is about our first check from Washington for expenses. It was for about thirty thousand dollars. I quickly pro-rated this to make payments to all our creditors, wrote the checks and ran to the post office. Later that day I almost had a heart attack when I remembered that Major Watkins had to co-sign them! They were the first checks I'd written and I had forgotten that. When I admitted my mistake to him, he was quite concerned that we didn't really have the money. When I assured him we did, he said, "Oh that's all right, then. I thought I was going to have to put it up." He was always fair with me, but he did not suffer fools gladly.

Yes, originally, the base was down near Wanchese on the southern end of Roanoke Island. As it happened, I reported for work on the very day that the operation was relocated to the existing airport up near

Manteo. It was Thanksgiving Day, 1942. The Navy had its training base at one end of the field, and we built the new coastal patrol base at the other end. Our pilots flew so many hours a day, then came in and cut the boards, and erected the hangar and other buildings. I stayed until Thanksgiving the following year. The base had closed earlier but I remained to handle visitors and the disposition of property. It was definitely lonely being the only one left on that big field.

Manteo was only a tiny town then, with maybe five hundred people. We all saw lots of first-run movies, because the town was so far from the next nearest theater — there was a kind of rule that gave such isolated towns a high priority. I was back living in Greensboro for a year before any movie came through that I hadn't already seen! There was also a little town hall where we held get-togethers and dances.

Left to right: M/Sgt. Bernice O. Barbour, plotting board operator Cpl. Evelyn E. Davis, and an unidentified woman, possibly clerk-typist Cpl. Katherine P. Smathers (courtesy Harry P. Bridges).

I had some dates with the Navy boys. One of them, after finishing his training at Norfolk before heading for the Pacific, made a training flight to Manteo to see me. After landing — without permission — he came across the field to invite me to go flying with him. "Sure," I said, "if Major Watkins will let me." We weren't long on protocol there, so for effect I entered his office very military-like, clicked my heels, and said,

"Major Watkins, Sir! Lieutenant Freeman has asked me to go flying with him in his SNJ, Sir! May I go, Sir!" Major Watkins looked at me kind of amused, and after a moment said, "Well, if the Navy doesn't care, I don't guess I do." We flew for about thirty-five minutes, and that boy showed me every combat maneuver he knew. I loved it. Our pilots, with hundreds of hours in the air, said they'd have been sick as dogs.

The people of Manteo were very kind. Most of us took rooms or apartments in town, even though it was several miles from the base, too far to walk. I took a room in Edna Bell's boarding house along with many others. Three soldiers attached to our base had one room. Beverly B. Fowler and Helen R. Poovey had the room next to mine. Margaret P. ("Polly") Overcash and her pilot-husband Marvin B. had another room. Quite a few of us were there. I think I paid about four dollars a week for the room.

The remarkable thing was how everyone gave us credit from month to month until our paychecks came. And they were *always* late. Many of us put everything on the cuff — rent, meals, gasoline, and other purchases — knowing we'd pay when we could and no hard feelings. Most of us had given up their regular jobs to come with the coastal patrol, and were living on a shoestring. One needy young man often waited for me when I reported in the mornings to ask me, "Have the checks come in yet?' It was embarrassing. I believe the checks were late because the war was still so new, and the government hadn't yet geared up to handle us. My overall experience at Manteo was one that I wouldn't take anything for. I met and enjoyed so many more people than I could've otherwise — people from all walks of life and with all kinds of interests. I found it a wonderful, unforgettable experience.

## Dorothy Graham Wescott

*One of the young women who worked in the office with Bernice Barbour was Dorothy Graham Wescott. Born and raised in Edgefield, South Carolina, she graduated from Howard Business College in Raleigh, then worked eight months in private industry, where one of her co-workers happened to be a member of the CAP. Dissatisfied with her job and unwilling to oppose parental objection to her going overseas with the Red Cross, she joined the CAP and asked for active duty with the coastal patrol. In a 1983 interview with Colonel Lester E. Hopper, she said she'd never even heard of Manteo:*

> The base was located at a little place called Skyco and headquarters was a little two-story farm house. The landing field, from which our coastal patrol personnel had cleared the undergrowth and trees, was across a dirt road from the farm house. When our linemen went out

to service the planes, they'd have to wear mosquito netting over all exposed parts of their bodies in order to tolerate the bugs. The men told jokes about how big the mosquitoes were and what they would say to each other like, "Shall we eat him here or drag him off to the swamp?" One lineman said he'd put several gallons of gasoline into what he thought was our number five airplane until he realized it was a mosquito.... We had a little lunch counter there, where we did our own cooking, soup and things like that. We had one girl who was an excellent mechanic and ran the parts shop — Polly Overcash — and she rode a motorcycle out to the base. One day she begged me to go with her, and I went, but one trip in that sand was enough for me!

When we first got down to Manteo you could see ships burning off the coast almost every night. You couldn't walk on the beaches out around Nags Head for the litter from the ships that had been torn apart, from the cases of fruit and the cases of vegetables that had come in from the ships, and the sailors hats, and all these things. You could not walk on the beach anywhere in Dare County at that time. And the people who've never experienced this and have never been told the story of this do not realize how close that war was to our shores. We hated to see a moonlight night, as pretty as the ocean is when it shimmers and sparkles, because we knew that the moonlight silhouetted the ships for the U-boats. I remember that on one occasion we were all called back to the base because it had been reported that landing craft had been spotted. And we wouldn't dare strike a match or hardly breathe, but we stayed at base all night and nothing materialized. I don't recall where we thought the landing craft were supposedly coming from.

After about three weeks I got my first day off and went to see Norfolk, Virginia. In those days the sailors, of course, outnumbered the civilians and it was disgusting to me to see signs on the lawns saying "No Sailors or Dogs Allowed" and things of that nature. And I said, "Good Lord, if you'll take me back to Manteo, I promise you I'll never complain again." I came back to Manteo and was very happy to be here, after visualizing and having seen Norfolk in person.... I wore my uniform, which was the basic Army Air Corps uniform except for the red epaulets and the insignia. We had the submarine and bomb on our sleeves, and our dress uniforms were forest green. Our work uniforms, either skirts or trousers, were khaki.... I had always done my duty to the best of my ability, but after my visit to Norfolk, I was even more eager to do it....

I remember Cooper and Cook very well. I happened to be playing cards with them just as they were called to take the flight on which they were lost. They never did find Lawrence Cooper, but Cook's body washed up on March 23rd of the following year down near Beaufort, in a good state of preservation because the water was cold. We were all very devastated.... We had another plane go down, but it was near enough to the shore that the pilot and the observer were able to come in on their life raft by themselves unassisted to the beach.... I'm very proud of the time I spent at Manteo, and I believe that every volunteer we had on the base felt the same way.

\* \* \*

The possibility of an enemy landing on the Outer Banks near Manteo was always a real threat in many minds. The events of the night remembered by Dorothy Wescott — March 12, 1943 — were recorded in the base S-2's security log for that date, but no subsequent explanation was ever noted:

Alert called 2105Q by Lt. Nickleson, Camp Va. Dare, 111th Inf., Manteo, N. C., stating that seven unidentified boats had been sighted one-half mile offshore and one-half mile north of Bodie Island Coast Guard — possibility that landing had been made from one boat. Call taken by Sgt. McNaully at 2105Q. Sgt. McNaully called 66W Captain Watkins and found he was gone to Greensboro on extreme emergency. [after various subsequent calls, Sgt. McNaully reached Lts. Alston and Thomasson who] made quick contacts of all personnel that could be found by telephone or messenger, and then came quickly to Base. Practically all personnel contacted had arrived at Base from 2200Q to 2230Q. Alert called off by Lt. Nickleson at 2300Q. Base personnel released to depart from Base at 2320Q.

Four other Manteo men, all North Carolinians, were members of the Duck Club: Glennon H. Shields and Kermit F. Stubbins, both of Greensboro; Rhonda L. Story of Lenoir; and John J. Healey of Raleigh. Pilot Story and Flight Observer Stubbins ditched May 29, 1943 at 9:25 a.m., and were picked up were picked up by a Coast Guard boat from Nags Head at 10:15 a.m. Pilot Shields and Flight Observer Healey landed in the water the very next day at 6:00 a.m., also victims of engine failure. A security log entry indicates that they were picked up at 7:45 a.m. by a Coast Guard boat. There were no injuries, but both planes were lost.

## L. J. ("Jeff") Sapp

*One of the husband and wife teams at Manteo were Jeff and Lottie Sapp who came down from Concord, North Carolina, he first, and she a little later. Upon his arrival at Skyco, Jeff Sapp was a student pilot, and worked as a service technician until he earned his private license. He then began flying as a flight observer, and ended up as acting operations officer. Lottie Sapp was a public health nurse, and served the base as such, though she appeared on the roster as a plotting board operator because there was no table of organization position for a nurse. Jeff Sapp recalls:*

I learned to fly in a friend's Piper Cub in 1941, and had about thirty-five hours when I reported in at Skyco Airport near Manteo. My first job was as a service technician, gassing-up the planes, checking the oil, tying them down, and so forth. After I got my private license I began flying regularly as an observer, and later I became acting operations officer. My only "near-ditching" came on a routine patrol about twenty-five miles off shore when a pilot buddy told me to fly our plane while he had his sandwich and Coke. As usual, he popped open the cap against something on the dash — except that his hand slipped. When the bottle accidentally hit the ignition switch, the engine quit dead at about seven or eight hundred feet. Startled by the sudden silence, and not realizing what he'd done, he hit everything in sight, and finally the ignition. The engine started right up, but for a few moments we were both scared.

You thought about the water each time you flew a patrol, but not enough to really bother you. Losing Cook and Cooper within sight of the beach resulted in an important new procedure. We called the Coast Guard stations each morning to check the surf. If they said they couldn't launch a rescue boat, we didn't fly. Cooper was from my home town of Concord and I knew him well. He was never found. Cook's body washed up months later. His wife and small son were on the road to Manteo for a Christmas visit when the plane was lost. Someone met them at the bus depot to tell them what had happened. They stayed that night and returned to Concord the next morning.

Two of my best friends at the base are dead now, along with a good many others. Johnny Rehder and his wife lived in the same building with me and my wife, and we often went to the movies during the week, or to our local nightclub on Saturday evenings. Vernon C. Rudolph was a real good friend and after the war helped me to get started in the bakery business. Vernon had founded Krispy Kreme Doughnuts at age twenty-one, and he often told me, "When the war's over, I want you to go to work for me." When Manteo closed, Vernon went into the Air Corps, but he called me at home one day, and offered me a job. I said, "I don't know anything about doughnuts." And he said, "Well, you know how to count money don't you? Go down to Winston-Salem and tell my accountant that you're going to run the place." I did that until 1947, then started my own doughnut business, which I eventually turned into a fully rounded bakery. I'm sorry to say that Vernon died about a year ago. We're all getting up there, you know.

## Lottie B. Sapp

*After Jeff Sapp joined the coastal patrol, his wife Lottie missed him so much that she joined, too. She recalls it all as an exciting adventure:*

Manteo seemed pretty primitive back in the early nineteen-forties. Roanoke Island was served by one physician, a sweet old guy named Johnson. He agreed to "sponsor" me so I could give shots and whatever else might be necessary in an emergency. Jeff and I lived in "The Restover," a great big boarding house jointly owned and operated by two couples, Max and Ruby Man, and James and Helen Balance. The ladies were sisters. Jeff and I had meals with them but the other boarders had to walk a few blocks to Fearings Restaurant, more or less in the center of town. Jeff and I drove back and forth to the field in my brand new 1941 Plymouth, a real beauty in a robin's egg blue trimmed with lots of chrome, for which I'd paid nine hundred dollars. I matched my schedule to his, so if he was flying early, I went out early, too.

At first, we drove down to Skyco every day, that's where the mosquitoes were so bad. In the half-light of mornings, the men servicing the planes for the dawn patrol were the most grotesque things you ever saw — with their pith helmets and netting down to their shoulders they resembled creatures from outer space. Fortunately, malaria had been stamped out years before. Living on an exposed island in wartime was a little spooky at times. We expected German agents to sneak ashore from a U-boat any time. When we went to the movies at night, we did so in little groups, and kept our voices low because you never knew who might be lurking in the shadows. But it could be funny, too. I remember one night there was a group of us that included David Black, a pilot from Alabama. He walked up an unseen telephone pole guy wire, straddling it in full stride. He changed from a bass to a tenor real quick!

I remember flying in our Piper Cub to the scene of a crash, when one of our planes went down in some woods. The plane was torn up pretty good, but the crew was okay. Just like in a movie, the first thing each asked for was a cigarette. I also recall ducking for cover when a Navy fighter crashed at the base, killing the pilot and the resulting fire spewing live ammunition in all directions.* Jeff and I hadn't been married long before we went down to Manteo and didn't have a family. But then I became pregnant and when he was sent to Norfolk as our liaison

---

* The pilot was Ensign Sam Carlton whose Corsair fighter had lost power on takeoff and who then made the fatal mistake of turning back to the field at low altitude. Carlton was training with what became the most famous Navy fighter squadron of the war. *The Jolly Rogers: The Story of Tom Blackburn and Navy Fighting Squadron VF-17* (Orion Books, New York, 1989) gives a young naval aviator's viewpoint on Manteo and surrounding area.

officer with the Navy, I went home to Winston-Salem to have my baby. Jeff and I had a really wonderful time at Manteo. You couldn't find that kind of camaraderie today.

### James S. Bryan

*Though she never worked at the Manteo base, Elizabeth Bryan joined her husband of only a few months, James S. Bryan, after he had already gone there to serve as a pilot-observer. Bryan, an Air Medal winner, died in 1993, but Elizabeth Bryan has his logbook and lots of memories of Manteo:*

James had been in the Cadet program but received a medical discharge after experiencing blackouts. We met in New Bern, not far from Beaufort, North Carolina, where he was with Western Union Telegraph as a regional supervisor, and I was a secretary in a contracting firm that was helping to build the Marine Corps air base at Cherry Point. He had learned to fly as a civilian and joined the local Civil Air Patrol before volunteering for active duty, but his logbook shows that his first flight at Manteo was on May 13, 1943. We were married two months later.

We lived in a big boarding house in Manteo, where we had a nice little nook on the second floor in the rear. A porch had been glassed-in, and that was our bedroom. But we had a kitchenette and bathroom, and I cooked all our meals there. As one of the eight children in my family I certainly knew all about that. A local bank offered me a job, but as it appeared we might not be there very long, I declined it. James was twenty-four at this time and I was twenty-two, and we were, after all, honeymooners! I enjoyed Manteo. We had some friends with a car, and on Saturday nights we drove over to Nags Head to go dancing. After the base closed, some strings were pulled and James got back into the Air Corps, not as a pilot, but in communications, probably because of his experience with Western Union. When James was discharged in 1945, we came back to New Bern and while we raised a son and daughter, he worked with an uncle who sold industrial supplies.

### Bruce G. Wagoner

*Bruce G. Wagoner was born in High Point, North Carolina in 1907, served as a pilot-observer with the coastal patrol in early 1943, and distinctly recalls the little cluster of coastal patrol buildings in one corner of the Naval Air Station and the long, paved runways. Wagoner never saw a sub but on his first mission he was excited about spotting a whale just beneath the surface:*

I flew mostly with Charles E. Bailey of Madison, North Carolina. He was near deaf in one ear, and wore a hearing aid, but was a good pilot — after the war he was killed at an air show in Norfolk while flying a plane across the airport upside down. Our patrols, some of them as far as sixty miles out, consisted of our meeting and escorting merchant ships through our territory until they were picked up by the coastal patrol escorts to our north or south. I'm sure they were glad to see us! We would fly up ahead of them scouting out the waters, then come back and circle them until they were out of our territory.

Pilot Bruce G. Wagoner remembers base commander Watkins telling his men, "If you go down sixty miles from shore, I want you to be so tough that you can swim back!" Fortunately, Wagoner never had to try (courtesy Bruce G. Wagoner).

I remember the day Mr. Bailey and I almost had to ditch. Stinson No. 9 had been having some engine problem and the crew had been working on it the day before we flew it. While doing preflight checks at the end of the runway, we called in to tell the Navy tower the engine didn't sound right. They said sit there a while and let the engine warm up some more (it was February, and very cold). Well, to make a long story short, we took off all right, but about five miles from base, the engine began acting up again, so we turned for home and barely made it, the engine stopping and starting several times on the way. It would have been a cold dip, because ice already rimmed the shore.

We didn't have much night life in Manteo, but there was one occasion that I will always remember: a memorial service held for two pilots lost at sea, Julian Cooper and Frank Cook. I understand they died of exposure and that only one of them was ever found. This was one of the reasons commanding officer Watkins wanted us to be in as good a physical condition as possible. He'd say, "If you go down sixty miles from shore, I want you to be so tough that you can swim back!" That was the main reason that he'd have the idle pilots take our truck and go chop some firewood for the pot belly stove in the barracks. Unluckily for me, while that was fine exercise, I developed a serious back problem, and had to go Baptist Hospital in Winston-Salem for treatment. I never returned to the base.

## John P. Calligan

*John P. Calligan was a twenty-two-year-old apprentice mechanic from the cotton mill town of Gibsonville, North Carolina. He joined the Manteo base on September 11, 1942 and stayed until January 11, 1943. Aside from all the hard work, the youthful Calligan also had a lot of fun:*

I went down to Manteo as a result of knowing the McLean family who had a farm, a sawmill, and a flying field very close to where I lived. When I got out of school during the week and on Saturdays and Sundays I'd go over to help out whenever I could. One of their boys, Marchal Edwin McLean — we called him "Red" — went up to Greensboro and got his A&E license, and then came home again after two of his brothers were killed. After Pearl Harbor, "Red" went down to a coastal patrol base in Florida. When the Manteo base opened, he returned to North Carolina to set up the maintenance operation there under our first commander, Jim Hamilton of Charlotte. "Red" asked me if I'd like a job there, and in two days I had one.

McLean and I had rooms in Manteo with Mrs. Grace Davis in her boarding house just across from the fire station. "Red" had a car and plenty of "B" gas ration coupons, and that's how I got back and forth to work. The people in Manteo took us right in, and treated us like any of the other servicemen who came into the USO there. I remember going to some dances, and ganging together to go swimming over at Nags Head. There were a couple of bridges, as well as a ferry to Englehard. Every time a nor'easter came in, the little home-made ferry would sink and have to be repaired. The water in Roanoke Sound was so shallow that a big storm would blow out enough that you could practically walk across to Kitty Hawk. In most places it was only three or four feet deep to begin with. But there was good fishing to be had. It was fall when I was there and the striped bass were running. We'd fish for them along the side of the bridge, where they'd come in among the pilings to eat the mussels that grew on them. If we wanted something bigger, we'd take a boat out and troll the channel, and maybe get some good sea trout. We took our catch to a restaurant, and they'd clean and cook it for us. Later in the year, we went duck hunting on the Sound. For that we had to have gun permits from the Coast Guard, but we didn't need to buy "Duck Stamps" like hunters do today.

Thirty-one-year-old Capt. Alan A. Alston was from Charlotte, North Carolina and served as the base intelligence officer (courtesy Harry P. Bridges).

I had time for such things because I usually worked the morning shift — getting out to the field by three o'clock in the morning to get the planes set for the dawn patrol — and had the afternoons off. I didn't get my A&E until after the war, but I had a student pilot license since 1941, which made me eligible to go up as a flight observer. What I remember best was flying down to Cape Hatteras, only sixty miles away. That was really a ship's graveyard. Each way you'd look you could see a sunken ship — a mast sticking up, or a bow, or a stern. I counted at least twenty-five or thirty. It was a great hunting area for the subs. Our dawn patrols were designed to surprise them just before sunrise when they normally re-submerged for the day after spending the night recharging their batteries and sucking in fresh air on the surface. Our problem was that they could see us a long time before we could see them.

My friend McLean had gone home for Christmas (against the express wishes of Allen Watkins, who had replaced Jim Hamilton as our commanding officer) two days before we lost Cooper and Cook in the ocean. The weather on the morning of that tragedy was terrible — cold and blustery, and that morning I remember cleaning sleet off our planes' wings and tail surfaces. The morning flights were canceled, but someone decided to send them out at noon. I don't think either one of the pilots knew much about using carburetor heat, and they'd certainly have needed it. I'm also convinced that if my hot-tempered Irish buddy McLean had been on the base he would have insisted on canceling that flight. When he got back from visiting his wife and family, he never resumed duty. Instead, he went to his friend Alan Alston, our intelligence officer, and obtained releases for himself (and me) to transfer to another coastal patrol base. After that base closed, we both worked as civilians at an Air Corps training center until the end of the war. I remained in aviation for a number of years, but spent the final part of my working life in private industry. "Red" McLean died a few years ago.

## Raymond V. Hood

*Raymond V. Hood was a twenty-four-year-old pilot from Charlotte who served as an observer at the North Carolina base. His claim to have been the first to arrive at Skyco stems from his having driven James Hamilton's car there the day before the base commander flew down:*

I had my private license before I reported to Manteo, but not many hours flight time, so I served as a flight observer throughout my time at the base. My wife and baby daughter came with me from Charlotte, and we found a pleasant place to live right in town. We all liked Manteo and fit into the community and became part of it. I certainly remember mowing that high grass at Skyco, and marking out what passed for runways, and of course the hungry mosquitoes, and cutting lumber and helping erect our buildings at the naval air station on the upper end of the island. I remember both Jim Hamilton and Allen Watkins, and have a hazy recollection of going fishing with Paul Bridges and his wife. I know we had a good bunch of pilots there, and I guess I flew enough to earn the Air Medal. I was never involved in any unusual flying incidents, at least not at Manteo. When the base closed, I got into the Cadet program and eventually ended up with the Air Transport Command. I got out of the Air Force in 1947 but was recalled in 1951 and served in Korea. I stayed in the Air Force, specializing in logistics and missiles, retiring as a major in 1984. I went back to Manteo in 1950 to take a look around. Now I'd like to return again to see the coastal patrol museum they have at the airport. I hear it's great.

\* \* \*

William Bridges's son, Harry P. Bridges, was twelve weeks old when he came to Manteo with his family, and has lived there off and on ever since. He became a permanent resident in 1974 and his present home is only a half-mile from the former coastal patrol base and Naval Auxiliary Air Station. A private pilot and Civil Air Patrol member, Major Bridges planned and helped to build, as a tribute to his father and other base veterans, both CAP and Navy, perhaps the most complete combined Coastal Patrol-Naval Auxiliary Air Station Museum in the United States. Open daily, this fine museum is located in the administration building of the Dare County Regional Airport. Included are smartly-arranged and identified displays of uniforms, equipment, photographs, and other artifacts. A fifteen-minute video of the base's history, including rare footage of coastal patrol operations, is also available.

---

Base officers, pilots, and observers who served at least one month at CAPCP#16 and who are not elsewhere mentioned in this chapter include: Homer K. Barnes, Raymond L. Beeson, Floyd J. Brown, Joseph R. Bull, Jr., Paul W. Callahan,* Plumer G. Carson, Jr.,* Dabney M. Coddington, James E. Cole, William E. Crowell, Parks A. Davis,* John W. Dickens,* Roscoe L. Ford, Jr., James C. Gwynn, Victor S. Holcombe,* Paul B. Houston,* Robert G. Lee,* Lucius K. Long, John L. Lyerly, Jr.,* Walter R. MacPhail,* Clifford C. Mercer,* Robert V. Montague,* Robert L. Moore,* Carl Rehder,* James C. Smathers, Joseph J. Smith,* Howard L. Thompson,* Lyle B. Turner, George H. Vaughn,* George D. Washburn, and William H. Watkins. Asterisk indicates Air Medal winner.

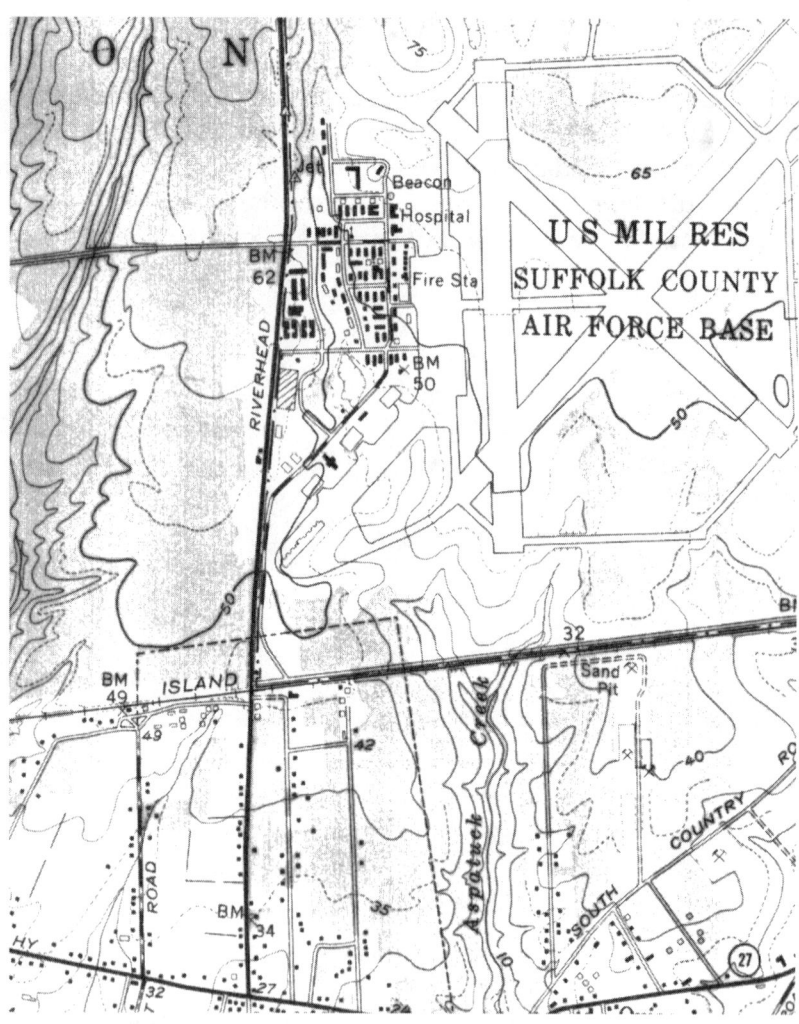

By 1956, the Army Air Corps base that adjoined the Riverhead coastal patrol airfield in 1943 had been expanded and renamed Suffolk County Air Force base. The famed Long Island Railroad runs east-west just to the south of the base (source: United States Geological Survey map).

# 17

# Riverhead, Long Island

When on July 1, 1942, Captain Ralph Earle of Haverford, Pennsylvania was invited by Civil Air Patrol headquarters to organize and command a coastal patrol base near the eastern end of Long Island, he worked so quickly that the first patrol missions were flown August 18, only six weeks later. Earle was more fortunate than many base commanders because he had alternate base locations from which to choose. A large field north of East Hampton, later to be nicknamed Ricksen Field, was one. The Hampton Airport farther west at Watermill and two large farms, each with natural mile-long grass runways, were possibilities, too. The final choice was Suffolk Airport, situated about four miles south of Riverhead and three miles north of Westhampton, selected for its excellent facilities, all-weather sand surface, and unobstructed runways. By the last week of August, five patrols were flown daily. The base history describes a "typical day of patrol missions":

> The sequence for all five was first, dawn; second, morning; third, noon; fourth, afternoon; and fifth, dusk. Each patrol covered a flying period of three hours. The large ships, Stinson Reliants, Wacos, and Fairchilds, stayed out the entire period, while the little Stinson Voyagers returned to the Base for refueling half way through the patrol period.... While flying was continuous for fifteen hours per day, opening up at five in the morning and finishing at eight in the evening, the flying personnel were assigned overlapping schedules. Eight men were chosen for dawn patrol on a rotating basis. They constituted the crew for the first and third patrols. Upon completing the noon mission, they were through for the balance of the day.

The remaining Pilots and Observers presented themselves for roll-call and drill at eight in the mornings. From them were selected the crews for the morning, afternoon, and dusk patrols. All remained on the post until the last flight landed. The dispatch with which everybody cleared out ... following the return of the dusk patrol, constituted a perfect technique for an expedited evacuation. Even though the day was long and each one was scheduled for at least two patrols per day, enthusiasm never seemed to wane. This was objectively evidenced by the fact that everybody gathered on the apron for each take-off and landing.

## Joseph N. Hettel

*Air Medal winner Joseph N. Hettel was born and raised in the Camden, New Jersey area, and while attending a junior college near Atlanta, took flying lessons and soloed the day after Thanksgiving, 1935, at Candler Field, Atlanta, Georgia. While earning a degree in economics at Guilford, a Quaker college in Greensboro, North Carolina, he often returned to Candler Field to gain more flying time:*

On weekends, I'd head for Atlanta to fly. In those pre-war days, dual time cost seven dollars and fifty cents an hour, solo time six dollars an hour. Eventually, a friend and I bought an E-2 Cub for four hundred dollars. That was the one with the square wing tips, a square tail, and a 37 hp engine. Ken Roney borrowed two hundred from a finance company, and my dad gave me two hundred. We earned our private and commercial ratings in that plane, and even taught ourselves to fly at night in it. It was wired for navigation lights, and we bought a back-up light at a Pep Brothers auto parts store and rigged it up on a wing strut as our landing light.

Later I worked for the Flying Dutchman Air Service at the Somerton, Pennsylvania Airport, where I washed planes, ran errands, and did all kinds of odd jobs, but still had time to earn my instructor's, commercial, and instrument ratings. Then I went to Memphis, Tennessee as a pilot for Chicago and Southern Airlines for one hundred-ninety dollars a month. About this time I applied for the Civil Air patrol, not even knowing much about it. Soon afterwards when I flew into New Orleans the airline station manager said he had a telegram for me. When I opened it, it said "Report immediately ... to Riverhead, Long Island." I told the manager, "I quit." He asked "When?" I said, "Right now."

At Riverhead, I asked the executive officer, Wallace D. Newcomb, from Wallingford, Pennsylvania, what my duties would be. I already had three thousand hours of flying by then — quite a lot for those days.

He said, "I dunno, go get a pair of suntans and a set of first lieutenant's bars and come back." He assigned me to go out as an observer on a few flights, and then to start making patrols as pilot-in-command. Later, when I was promoted to captain and became base operations officer, it became my job to test-fly any aircraft that had major mechanical work and to schedule all our patrols. I tried to even it out so that everyone got flight time, and at least one day off a week. A good many fellows flew twice a day.

There were plenty of regulations for when and how patrols would be conducted. As I recall, the so-called "dawn patrol" was to begin a half-hour before sun-up, and the "dusk patrol" was to end a half-hour after sun-down. We brought the dusk patrol in early, regardless of the regulation, because if someone went into the water with little or no light left, we'd never have been able to find them.

We had a very good man as our engineering officer, and a darned good shop with a lot of well qualified mechanics. Warren E. Moody was not only good with aircraft, but he had a first class radio operator's license, too. One of our mechanics, Carl ("Slim") Hennicke, who lived near Riverhead, had been in Charles Lindbergh's crew when he made his famous trans-Atlantic flight to Paris. "Slim" was one darned good mechanic. Ruth M. Shaffer was one of our radio operators. She joined the WASPs when the base closed. Bennett Cerf's daughter, Katherine, was another radio technician and a teletype operator. She was a good-looking kid. We called her "Cindy, the incendiary blonde." We stood retreat every night, at least the boys who didn't sneak off did. And we had role call every morning, which was no problem, but everybody *hated* the half hour of calisthenics afterwards.

I was checked out in our Sikorsky amphibian, but never had occasion to fly it on a rescue mission. It was always kept out in front of the other planes, ready for a fast take-off. In the winter, it was kept in the front of the hangar so there wouldn't be any delay rolling it outside. Our base commander, Ralph Earle, had bought the amphibian from the late Jake Ruppert — he died in 1939 — owner of the Ruppert Brewery and the New York Yankees, specifically for such work. We flew it on patrols now and then to keep it exercised and ready to go.

I remember the day that Captain Guy de la Rigaudiere and Lieutenant Peter Lafen went out to rescue a couple of our pilots. Neither of them had much experience in seaplanes, but they went out with the Sikorsky and got away with it anyway. They landed in the ocean fine. The only trouble was, after they got our two men aboard, they couldn't take off again. I don't think they knew the technique, which is a little different than with a land plane. You have to haul back hard on the yoke to start with, and get the boat up on its step, hold her pretty level for a while to build up speed, then sort of ease her off. So they taxied the Sikorsky all the way back to Floyd Bennett Field, transferring the two other guys to an Army crash boat along the way.

The boys in the water had used their raft, so they were okay, except for being wet. When I arrived at Riverhead, we didn't have anything, not even the Mae West life jackets. What we had at first were called "barracuda bags." They were just automobile inner tubes with a four-foot white canvas bag attached so that a downed flyer could step into them and be protected to some extent from sharks or whatever. I don't think anybody ever used one, nor do I know whether they'd work or not. We borrowed the idea from one of the Florida bases. The concept went back to prohibition days when bootleggers sometimes had to abandon their ships offshore and had to have protection against the voracious barracudas down there.

We were only a mile and a half from the Atlantic Ocean, and in the winter the field was cold and windy. We ran a tractor back and forth scraping off what snow we could, and then laid down a center line with the marker material we used for dropping into the water around downed planes. The stuff was like shredded aluminum and came in containers about the size of croquet balls. We broke the containers open and when the marker material was sprinkled on the remaining snow it looked more or less black from the air.

In the summer, the beach was handy, because we could go down and swim when we were off duty. A place called the "Swordfish Club" provided us with showers and lockers but unfortunately no bar. Some of the men's wives went with them, and maybe one or two of the girls that worked at the base as radio or teletype operators. Having a restaurant right next to the back of the hangar was a nice convenience, too. I recall that a woman and her daughter ran it. John Reilly — we called him "Ace" — was the biggest pilot at the base, and he used to eat anything that wasn't nailed down. He'd finish an enormous meal, then lean back and say, "Not bad for a light snack!"

A lot of the fellows are dead now: James Boudreau, who wrote the history of the base; Gordon Pyle, who was killed just after our base closed when he plunged into New York harbor while flying tracking missions from a station in Flushing; "Ace" Reilly, and many others. After my coastal patrol service, I continued to fly for the airlines for another thirty-five years or so, working up from DC-3s, DC-4s, and Avro Yorks for British South American Airways to Boeing Stratocruisers for British Overseas Airways Corporation. I didn't get married until 1950 because for me flying always came first.

## Guy de la Rigaudiere

*As the first operations officer, Guy de la Rigaudiere's main responsibility was setting the daily schedule of who would fly patrol and who would not. A native of Unionville, Pennsylvania, a small town near Kennett Square, he held ratings both as instructor and commercial pilot, and was licensed to fly multi-engine aircraft as well:*

I hadn't personally known Major Earle, our commanding officer, but he was an excellent administrator, and absolutely matchless in terms of procuring anything needed for the base's success. We disagreed on certain matters, and there were times I probably irritated him very much. The best example may have been his withholding approval for me to designate a specific someone to fly the Sikorsky amphibian he'd purchased for use in emergency rescues at sea. Both Joe Hettel and I had flown the plane several times. Hettel was a great pilot and handled it very well. I told Earle that we needed a designated pilot but he'd postpone a decision, and never go any farther. Maybe he just liked to look at the thing sitting there.

As it happened, when Donald Leas and Ted Palmer went down, I was on duty when the mayday came in, and I immediately grabbed an observer and jumped in the S-43. Fortunately, the sea was fairly calm and I landed okay. Leas and Palmer had gotten out of their plane and were rising and falling in the swells and the good Lord got us together so we could haul them in. However, I did fail to get airborne again — and you've heard the rest of that story. Joe Hettel would have gotten the plane off the water with no trouble. When I finally returned to base, Major Earle started hollering at me, saying there'd be no decorations in it for me, and so on, and so forth! I never even thought of a decoration. I've always suspected he was mad as hell because I hadn't asked him to come along as observer. But he was a good boss most of the time.

I continued to fly missions even after I was named operations officer, and flew enough hours to be awarded the Air Medal. My wife came with me to Riverhead and we rented a nice beach house at Westhampton. She gave birth to our baby while we were there and I remember it as an elegant area even then. I don't think we had time for much social activity, although we took a train into Manhattan a couple of times. Occasionally I played chess with Wallace Newcomb, our executive officer from Philadelphia. My favorite "recreation," if you want to call it that, was taking time on our Link Trainer. I really fell in love with that thing and Pat Brooke was a tremendous instructor. About this time I felt I had to leave the CAP to seek a better income, and I ended up flying for a Central American airline for a time. After that I returned to the United States and joined All American Aviation — Richard DuPont's line — based first at Wilmington, Delaware, then at Harrisburg, Pennsylvania.

**Warren E. Moody**

*Warren E. Moody was born in Philadelphia in 1912, and learned to fly in a 1917 Fairchild Challenger with a Philadelphia motorcycle policeman named Joe Campbell as his instructor. Moody served as the Riverhead engineering officer from June 1942 until the base closed in January 1944. His wife, Cpl. Ann C. Moody, was a secretary at the base. Moody joined the coastal patrol after an Army Air Corps general told a meeting of private and commercial pilots at Wings Field, Ambler, Pennsylvania, of the seriousness of the submarine attacks along the east coast:*

He told us of the large loss of life and valuable cargoes of war materials that were being sunk every day within sight of people on shore, admitting that the Air Corps had no way to fight the U-boats. He said that most of his first-line planes had been destroyed by the Japancse while his second-line planes, which might otherwise be assigned to anti-submarine patrols, were being sent overseas for critical war zone operations. He invited pilots who owned large planes to enlist in the Air Corps as a second lieutenants and to lease their airplanes to the government for anti-submarine warfare.

A "cracked-up" Waco cabin plane that Warren Moody's crew of mechanics would soon repair. The mechanic in the photo may be Sidney M. Field (courtesy Warren E. Moody).

Since I had both an excellent low-time Stinson SR-5 and a private license, I volunteered. Then, because I had A&E and commercial radio licenses, they picked me to be an engineering officer. I distinctly recall that the Air Corps general said we could join the Air Corps as second lieutenants and we were all sworn in as such. Quite some time later, word came down that we would not be commissioned in the Air Corps, but rather only as a member of an Air Corps auxiliary. To protect us under the Geneva Convention, should we be captured by the enemy we would be registered in Switzerland as active combatants.

Frankly I think we were badly short-changed. After the war, none of us were ruled eligible for veterans benefits, not even for Veterans Administration hospital care. In my case, after three years of service flying coastal patrols over the ocean in single-engine planes, flying searchlight and radar training missions over Washington, DC, and towing targets for fighter plane gunnery practice, I certainly expected more from my government.

**Farwell W. Perry**

*In mid-1942, Farwell W. Perry was a 22-year-old student at Yale, a member of the wrestling team and captain of the pistol team, when he learned he might be dropped from ROTC and drafted. Since he knew of the coastal patrol, he hopped in the Stinson Voyager his older brother had passed down to him (when their father had given him a newer plane) and flew to the Bar Harbor base to join up. He discovered that the commanding officer was a man he'd had disagreements with, so he said to himself,"the hell with this":*

Then I heard of the base at Riverhead and flew over there one weekend to see if they could use me. The commanding officer, Major Ralph Earle, said, "Well, this is a Pennsylvania base, we're nearly all from there, but since you've troubled to come over here, come back in a couple of weeks and we'll take you." I was still attending Yale at the time, so I went back to New Haven and asked both my dean and the draft board if I could join the CAP, and they said okay. I was graduated from Yale a month before the rest of my class, and returned to Riverhead.

Out there, most everyone acquired their own digs, and I rented a cottage in town. This was in November, 1942. Though I had my private pilot's license, I had just the minimum number of hours required for the coastal patrol, so I was commissioned as a flight officer and performed only co-pilot and observer's duties. One day, still extremely new at the base, I was flying a patrol with William Walter, and we were about ten miles out headed for Montauk when the engine quit cold. This was before we had any life-saving equipment other than our Mae Wests, and an inflated truck inner tube in the back of the cabin. I thought Walter was kidding, and that he'd turned off the switch just to scare me. When he saw my indecision with the radio and shouted at me to declare a mayday emergency, I thought, oh damn, this is for real. We'd been up around a thousand feet, but I'm telling you it didn't seem any time at all for that plane to get down on the deck. Just before I was sure we'd hit the water I thought, if I were the pilot, I'd be switching off the ignition right now. But I wasn't, so I didn't. However, I did turn off the radio I'd been using to call base, and just then the engine went "br-room, bup, bup, bup, bup, and br-room, bup, bup, bup, bup," and we then managed to hedge-hop to shore not more than fifty or seventy-feet off the water. We landed right there on the beach, and that was the nicest ground I ever felt in my life!

What happened was that the plane's ignition ran off a battery — like a car's ignition system — and we hadn't noticed that the ammeter showed it discharging. Turning off the radio allowed the battery's last little gasp of spark to reach the engine. After we landed, there was still enough juice left for me to call the base and tell them where we were. It really made me angry that the engineering officer, Captain Warren Moody, then told us to quit fooling around and bring that plane in. He should've been with us!

I cared a lot about safety, even though I noticed that many others didn't. One day, months later, I was out on patrol with Don Leas, when I noticed the cabin door on my side was frozen closed. It was Don's plane, so I asked him if it would be all right if, when we got back, I told the mechanics to have the door fixed. While they were at it, I also arranged that they equip his plane with a life raft behind the cabin outside the fuselage where it would be quickly accessible. I believe that may've saved his life.

Some time later — I had the day off and missed the whole thing — Leas was on dusk patrol about five to ten miles off the Hamptons when the engine of his Stinson Reliant quit and he ditched in the Atlantic. Ted Palmer was flying as co-pilot and Palmer told me later, "If my door hadn't released, and that life raft hadn't been easy to get off, I don't think we'd have made it. The minute we hit the water, everything was pitch dark. I got out and here was the life raft looking right at me. The nose of the airplane was straight down, and the compartment with the raft in it was right at eye level. Don had been knocked unconscious and didn't come up, so I had to dive down, unbuckle him, and bring him up." The ship sank immediately and the two weren't rescued until an hour later. Our Operations Officer, Captain Guy de la Rigaudiere, went out and got them with the "Duck," our Sikorsky amphibian. Rigaudiere had never landed it on water before, but he pulled it off.

After his duty with the coastal patrol, Air Medal winner Farwell W. Perry flew as a Service Pilot for the Air Corps's Flight Control Command (courtesy Farwell W. Perry).

Leas never thanked me, but he did help me get a promotion to Second Lieutenant. One morning, assigned to dawn patrol, Leas and I had just taxied out for takeoff, when he said, "God, I've got a headache like you wouldn't believe. Do I have a hangover!" I said, "Don, get the hell out of your seat and let me fly this mission." And he did. I didn't think any more about it at the time, but shortly thereafter I was surprised to see my name on the bulletin board with a promotion. I remember another fellow, John Grubb. He was all of eighteen or nineteen, but he already had a commercial rating and had taken the grommet out of his hat to give it that "thirty-mission crush" and thought he was about the hottest pilot around. I was with him one day when he took his plane about thirty miles straight out into the Atlantic. Fifteen miles out, I reminded him that our regular patrol lane was only ten miles out. I said, "You know, Lieutenant Grubb, if the engine on this plane quits, we're both dead." He just reached up and patted the cowling in front of the stick and said, "Don't worry. Good old Betsy won't let us down." I thought to myself, *oh sure*. Well the next day, Grubb took his plane out with another fellow, Ed Allen, and they weren't out but twenty minutes before the engine quit over Montauk Bay and they had to ditch. Even though Grubb's Waco stayed afloat for twelve minutes, the water was very cold and their experience extremely hazardous. By the time they were rescued, Grubb bobbing around in the water unconscious, it had been a pretty close call for both of them, but especially Grubb. To finish the story, a few months later I flew as co-pilot with Lieutenant Grubb again. And it wasn't in "good old Betsy," because "good old Betsy" was at the bottom of Montauk Bay. Much subdued, he flew the whole patrol pretty close to the beach and I never said a word.

M/Sgt. John Warwick, a base mechanic from Milmont, Pennsylvania, astride his Harley Davidson near the Suffolk County Airport (courtesy Allison G. Catheron, II).

It always amazed me that everyone seemed to need to have a really scary experience before they could visualize what it was like to go into the water. Later on, we got the big cumbersome "zoot suits," something like a diver's wet suit — a head-to-foot rubberized outfit in which you could float a long time without freezing. Most pilots hated them. I didn't. I was tickled to death to have just that much more insurance against drowning. I didn't give a damn about how hot they were as compared to the alternative of finding myself in the water unconscious and without one. I knew I wouldn't last long like that.

I didn't get involved in much socializing at the base. I was kind of a hermit while I was there, partly because of a young lady back home that I was expecting to marry. I remember playing softball a few times. I was just over five feet, seven inches, and was slender, so I didn't hit any home runs. They let me pitch once, and I was surprised how hard it was to get the ball over the plate. So I used most of my spare time to study for my commercial rating. It took great effort, and everyone at the base told me not even to try, but I got it.

I stayed at Riverhead until Guy de la Rigaudiere — we'd become good friends — left to join All American Aviation, Richard DuPont's fledgling airline. Guy asked me to go with him and I did. I obtained my instrument rating at Harrisburg, Pennsylvania and had just completed my final check ride when their air mail pick-up service ended and I was let go. After that I tried to get into the Air Corps and the naval air service, but failed physical after physical. As a kid I'd had crossed eyes that, though long-since corrected, left me with only partial depth perception. Eventually I was accepted as a service pilot for the Flight Control Command, the "federal aviation administration" of the Air Corps, and I continued to fly until five years ago, at age seventy, when a health problem grounded me. I still have and cherish my Air Medal from coastal patrol days, and I'm glad I had the chance to serve.

## Allison G. Catheron, II

*Allison G. Catheron, II, was one of the base radio operators. He was barely nineteen when he went on active duty, March 17, 1943, after more than a year of training with the CAP squadron at Norwood, Massachusetts. He was first assigned as a guard under Lt. Edwin L. Mayberry and Sgt. Charles H. Leibfried. He was temporarily shifted to a service detail and then permanently moved to the intelligence unit under Capt. Gordon M. Pyle, promoted to sergeant, and made radio operator:*

Our base was located on a flat, sandy plain on the eastern end of Long Island several miles south of Riverhead. Many of us stayed in the Henry Perkins Hotel, whose manager, Mrs. Van Brunt, treated us with kindness and consideration. We were also well treated at the local U.S.O. We were located next to an Air Corps gunnery school. The main road ran by both bases and both supplied people to guard the road at night and shared a common guard post. Our men flew at least two patrols a day. As a radio operator, I took position reports every fifteen minutes and posted them on a large grid map on the west side of the radio and ready room. I remember that the lifebelts of the captured German saboteurs who landed at Amagansett were piled up there. Our flight personnel actually used them until they were issued their own Mae Wests.

The most serious times were when an aircraft went down at sea, and our Sikorsky amphibian — the "Duck" — went out to find them in the cold and sometimes shark-infested waters. But we had fun, too. Several of us, like Lieutenant George Mercurio, were enthusiastic fishermen and went after stripers in the Moriches and Great South inlets along the southern shore of the island. George sometimes forgot the time and would be late for patrol, which earned him displeasure from Major Earle. I fished a lot for flounder in Peconic Bay with Sergeant Albert Penny, a Long Island native. We also had a softball team and competed with other teams in the area, and took classes in subjects such as radio procedures, instrument flying, and other military and technical skills. Sergeant Pat Brooke was one of our main instructors. I remained at the base until coastal patrol activities were halted, and then was reassigned to a tow target and tracking unit at Flushing Meadows, Long Island. Captain Gordon Pyle was our commanding officer until he was killed when his plane crashed into New York harbor. Though there was excellent regard between most officers and enlisted men, there wasn't the stricter military discipline I later found when I trained with the 82nd Airborne Division in 1950 after earning a degree and a commission at the University of Maine.

## William H. Walter

*Like so many others at the Riverhead base, William H. Walter was born and raised in Pennsylvania.\* A native of Allentown, he first flew in 1936 and had three hundred hours flight time when he arrived at Riverhead, where he would go on to win the Air Medal:*

My most vivid memory of flying with the coastal patrol was the time my sister ship had to ditch just south of Fire Island. Don Leas and Ted Palmer were flying lead plane in Leas's Stinson Reliant and I was flying a Stinson Voyager with Enoch Raysor as my observer. I was to the right and behind when I noticed Leas start to descend. I did likewise to stay with him, not knowing his intentions, until I saw that he was going into the water. The sea was calm, and when the plane hit, the landing gear caused it to tip over on its nose. After it settled back, I watched both men get out, then free a life raft from the Stinson's exterior luggage compartment.

This was the last patrol of the day and I was afraid we might lose them from sight. They weren't very visible. So I flew a wide circle and

---

\* Among other base officers, pilots, and observers from Pennsylvania not elsewhere mentioned in this chapter were John R. Betters\*, Stanley E. Cortright, Guy Giordano, Edwin L. Maberry, Matthew D. Mackie, Frank H. Mitchell\*, Elmer E. Renninger, Roger S. Robbins, Victor W. Shaub, and John O. Schweitzer (asterisk indicates Air Medal winner). Also from the Keystone State were another forty-two mechanics, linemen, guards, and clerical workers.

had my observer drop clay marker bombs every ninety degrees around. We radioed our position to the base and continued to circle them until the Sikorsky "Duck" came out to pick them up. We were still there about an hour later when the amphibian arrived. What I've never been able to understand, and which I think was remarkable, was how the dye from those four marker bombs seemed to blend into a full circle through a kind of wave or tidal action or something. After the men were picked up, Guy de la Rigaudiere and Peter Lafen in the "Duck" were unable to take off again, but as they taxied for shore, an Army crash boat met them and took Palmer and Leas aboard for the trip back.

Sometimes a ditched plane could be retrieved from shallow water. Here a fishing trawler brings in what looks the remains of a Stinson 10-A (courtesy Warren E. Moody).

When I first came to Riverhead I stayed at the Henry Perkins Hotel. This was shortly after four German saboteurs had been landed from the German *U-202* on the beach at Amagansett. Many residents out that way on Long Island thought the whole German Navy was going to be right behind them and moved into New York. This made it possible for some of us, including myself, to rent big furnished houses at a reasonable cost. My wife Katherine took a leave of absence from her teaching job in Allentown to join me, then volunteered to be an aircraft spotter for the Office of Civil Defense. Before the war she hadn't been interested in flying or airplanes but recording every airplane she saw during her "spotting shift" — its type, altitude, and direction of flight — whetted her appetite for flight, and after the war she became an avid flyer. Another thing I remember about Riverhead was the clamming. Coming in to land at the base, we'd often fly over Peconic Bay, and I'd see all these little boats down there, guys standing in them using long rake-tongs to scratch the clams from the bottom. The water was probably only waist deep. I went over to the docks one day to see them unload their catches, and learned I could buy a whole bushel basket for three dollars, and how I love clams! I once bought three bushels of clams to take back to Allentown. My sister and brother-in-law had a nice big yard with a built-in fireplace, and we all had a great clam bake!

When I arrived, the base didn't yet have a full complement of pilots and we flew our butts off. In four months I think I flew about six hundred hours. Toward the end — I stayed even past the time the base closed for coastal patrols and became a tow target unit — the pace slowed considerably. Our C.O., Major Ralph Earle, pulled some strings and borrowed for our use a Link Trainer from the State of Pennsylvania. His brother was the Governor. This was a great opportunity, and I was happy to pay for Link Trainer time from my own pocket as a step toward getting my instrument rating. I spent almost all my spare time at it. When I went to Harrisburg to take the required flight test, I passed readily, and became the first at Riverhead to have an instrument rating.

After a stint of pulling targets over Long Island, our group was transferred to Hyde Field, just outside the nation's capitol, and I was assigned to flying courier service between there and the aeronautical chart plant in Saint Louis, Missouri. In those days, that was a two-day flight, with an overnight stopover. I guess I flew about two thousand hours for the CAP, and by then I'd really had a belly full of flying, so after the war I got into marketing house trailers — then a pretty new thing — and developing trailer courts, including one in Saint Croix. Life has been good to me, and the coastal patrol was surely one of my personal highlights.

## Carl L. Walter

*Air Medal winner Carl L. Walter — no relation of fellow Riverhead pilot William Walter — was born in 1916 in Scranton, Pennsylvania and soloed in a Waco biplane when he was fifteen years old. After he finished high school, his family moved to Lake Wallenpaupack in the Pocono Mountains, where he went to work for his father in the automobile business. In 1941, he took a position with the Campbell Soup Company which required his moving to Philadelphia. There he became active in sports flying, and familiar with most of the airports in the region. He recalls much hangar talk of forming a CAP-like organization even before the war began, and, afterwards, seeing CAP recruiting posters tacked to airport bulletin boards:*

As far as housing went, I think I probably had the best deal of anyone at the base. Soon after I arrived in Riverhead I met an infantry colonel on his way overseas. He wanted to rent his beautiful beach home in Quoque, near Westhampton, to a military person while he was away. I got it for just fifty dollars a month. My wife joined me then, and we enjoyed swimming that summer right off our front lawns. There was little socializing — maybe a dance or a bridge party somewhere.

I was a flight observer. It was really a very routine job, with no problems. But *never* boring. I had never flown over water, but it didn't bother me at all. What it comes down to is that the airplane doesn't know if you're over land or water. That's what I told anyone leery about it. I said, "*You* may be leery about it, but the *airplane's* not!" I saw one submarine for sure. It was just below the surface with its periscope up. I saw it as clearly as could be. I think the guys in our sister ship saw it, too. We reported our sighting to base, and I think the Navy came out to take a look, but I never learned of the outcome.

In the winter we wore zoot suits over our regular uniforms, but only put them on up to our waist, letting the rest hang down. Otherwise, they were so doggone hot you couldn't stand them. If we'd ever had to ditch, I don't know how we'd have gotten them fastened up. I don't think we ever flew the same plane twice in a row, but I remember that I loved the Stinson gullwing best. After a time, I began to give a lot of ground instruction at the base. I knew something about tower operations and was excellent at Morse Code, with which a lot of fellows had trouble. After the war I built and operated an airport in the Poconos for seven years. Then I flew some for Van Dusen Aircraft Supplies and for Piper Aircraft, but in 1959 I moved down here to Florida and haven't flown much since then.

## Norman W. Rehrig

*Norman W. Rehrig was born and grew up in Lehighton, PA, twenty-five miles north of Allentown. In 1937 he soloed in a Taylor Cub. Rehrig was a member of the CAP's Allentown squadron when his friend, Paul Knepper, another member, suggested they join the Riverhead coastal patrol. Rehrig wasn't the first to report, but he stayed until the base closed, and later was awarded the Air Medal:*

At first we were housed in the Henry Perkins Hotel in Riverhead with just about everyone else. Later on, the married men found apartments and homes in the area to rent. The majority of the men didn't have their wives with them, or were single, and stayed at the hotel throughout. I didn't own a car, but transportation to the base was provided. I usually ate breakfast at a diner across the street from the hotel. I took lunches at the field restaurant (thirty-five cents) and dinners back at the hotel. Base commander Ralph Earle arranged credit for us at the hotel and at the diner, and we paid our bills when our paychecks came through. It was a manageable arrangement.

Captain Norman Rehrig admitted that his first flight over water was a little scary because of the lack of refined navigational equipment (courtesy Mrs. Harold E. Wallin).

We had Stinson 10-As with the 90 hp Franklin engines. They were easy to start, and we did much of our winter flying with them, most especially the dawn patrols. We also had some Waco cabins, Stinsons, and Fairchild 24s. It was entirely a sand field, not even any grass. There were no marked runways, we just knew where they were and we had plenty of space. Though I had well over two hundred hours flight time before going there I was one of the "kids" at Riverhead. But I flew nearly every day and my air time built up quickly. Before leaving the base, I had over six hundred hours on Stinsons alone. I enjoyed it very much at the time. It was a thrill partly because we got to fly planes that we'd never otherwise get to fly, the bigger, heavier, more powerful Wacos and Stinsons.

I'd never flown over water before, and that was a little scary. My first flight was something else. We had to radio-in our positions each half hour, and when initially I had some trouble figuring it out, my pilot laughed and asked me if I didn't know where I was. I told him, "No, I *don't* know where I am!" We were beyond sight of land most of the time so there weren't any navigational landmarks.

We had three ships go down, but didn't lose anybody. On one patrol, my sister ship, flown by John Grubb and Ed Allen, ditched. I circled them quite some time before they were picked up — Grubb bobbing around in the water and Allen frozen to a buoy. They had to cut him loose. It was a near thing, because both men had started to turn blue, the water was so cold. We started out wearing only Mae Wests, then we got zoot suits. They were clumsy to fly in, and hot and sweaty. The feet were weighted so as to help keep you upright in the water. But we followed orders and wore them.

When the base closed, some of us formed the 17th Tow Target group, and were sent to Hyde Field, Clinton, Maryland, a few miles south of today's Andrews Air Force Base.* Mostly we flew night missions at around ten thousand feet with our running lights turned off so the anti-aircraft searchlight batteries could practice picking us up with their radar. When they did — which was seldom — a blinding white light filled the cabin and could be very disorienting. You had to keep your eyes on the instrument panel and not look out. After some of us were reassigned for tow target work at what had been the Rehoboth coastal patrol base, I became the commander, and it was off Rehoboth that I had my first and only ditching.

\* \* \*

Altogether, the Riverhead base had seven Duck Club members, Besides the four already mentioned — Allen, Grubb, Leas, and Palmer — there was 1st Lieutenant Robert E. Ricksen, Jr. and 2nd Lieutenants Richard T. Lancaster of Collingsdale, Pennsylvania and Theodore R. Prokopovits of Philadelphia.

---

* The thirty-one base members who went to Hyde Field were operations officer Joseph N. Hettel, assistant operations officer Arnold L. McNeal, engineering officer Warren E. Moody, and communications officer Carl P. Temple; pilots James C. Boudreau*, Hibbard S. Evans*, Kevin Fitzgerald*, Howard E. Haines, William S. Hall*, Philip E. Hoffmeister*, Joseph Kapey*, Peter Lafen*, George Mercurio*, Wallace D. Newcomb*, Norman Rehrig*, Albert J. Sidlow*, Harold E. Wallin*, and William H. Walter*; observer Louis J. Damasco; mechanics M. M. Cooper, Sidney M. Field, Leon H. Snyder, James C. Tallman, Joseph T. Thayer, and John Warwick; radio technician Robert L. Hartung; service technicians Alison C. Catheron II and Curtis W. Maunder; guard Harry R. Pohle; technical section head Charles L. Turbett; and clerk William E. White. Asterisk indicates Air Medal winner.

## Henry W. Herbert

*When pilot James C. Boudreau wrote the base history he was ably assisted by flight observer Henry W. Herbert of New York City. Herbert, then in his early thirties, had been active with the Manhattan CAP squadron until his friend Boudreau persuaded him to accept active duty at the base and take all the photographs for the history before the base shut down. He was not only a pilot with a keen sense of what scenes might make aviation history, but a professional photographer as well:*

I learned to fly in an open-cockpit Kinner Fleet with a five cylinder radial engine out at Roosevelt Field on Long Island. After I got a license, my first passenger was my wife of three months. While I served in the coastal patrol, I owned half of a Rearwin Cloudster. A clipped-wing job with no landing flaps, it landed at about seventy-five mph and you had to stay with it. It wasn't any good for missions, however. When I was recruited to take photographs, it was made clear to me that I would also have to fly missions, and I certainly did so.

I flew at least three hours a day, six days a week, for three months. Because of my age — I was thirty-three — and because my wife and two daughters were out there with me in Westhampton, I was spared the dawn patrols. After the war, in 1950, we moved to Florida where I continued to fly incidental to my photography business, often helping other photographers do aerial shots and surveys. My flying ended in 1983 due to a heart condition, but I've had a great life combining both of the things I love to do.

\* \* \*

When gradually it seemed that the submarine attacks on coastal shipping had ended, the rumor mills that are always busy around military installations began to grind out possible next tasks for base personnel. The base history provides a humorous summary of them:

- We were being trained to take over Coastal Patrol in Mexico.

- If we didn't go to Mexico, we would surely be transferred as a unit to the Caribbean area as there was so much sub activity down there.

- Brazil would be our real duration assignment, thus protecting the jumping-off point of our South Atlantic shipping.

- We were scheduled to go to a cold climate, either Alaska or the Aleutians, or perhaps, Iceland. No one was ever quite sure which it would be.

- Our patrol training was so complete and successful we would soon be going to England to relieve the British Coastal Patrols who were to be given combat assignments in the R. A. F.

- Following the appearance of large units of American Troops in Northern Africa, it was practically a fact that we would soon "go over." Our job would be to patrol the African Coast, of course.

- There was to be a call for trained volunteers to do Coastal Patrol in the Far East. While this would be optional, the inducements coupled with the glamour would probably see the Base go as a unit.

- We were to be retained for Border Patrol, either Mexican or Canadian; we could not be sure which. Everyone would carry an automatic and all ships would be equipped with machine guns and bombs. The important question of the design and payload of our civilian ships never found a place in our discussions.

- A "detail" was to go to Alaska to search out and bomb "wolf packs." Col. Johnson said so — well, he mentioned something about the possibility.

- When we had completed our "Missions" at Westhampton, we would be assigned to "Courier." Where to? Take your choice. Denver, pretty high altitude — 1 mile; the Northwest, very cold; several spots in Texas — that's a big state. Rome, not Italy, but New York; Middletown, Pennsylvania, too close to the Alleghenies to be comfortable. Maybe most of our service would be eastward — certainly hoped so. Flushing, Long Island, five cent subway fare to the big city — not bad! The rumors grew hot or cold, according to whether or not one minded the Northern winters.

## Harold C. Fletcher

*Harold C. Fletcher grew up in Charleroi, Pennsylvania, thirty miles south of Pittsburgh. In the late 1930s, he joined a local flying club there and soloed in a J-3 Cub. When the war came and he received a pre-induction notice to report for a physical examination, it was determined that childhood polio had left one of his legs smaller than the other, and he was rated 4-F. When he heard about an opening in the coastal patrol, he gladly took that opportunity to do something for his country:*

When I first reported at Riverhead I was made a guard. After I was there a while, and did some things they liked, I became more or less a mechanic, though I did not have an A&E license. And still later, I did occasionally fly as a back-up observer, never with that rating or pay, but only as a reserve. I think I arrived there pretty much when the base opened, and I stayed to the end. I was single and lived in the Henry Perkins Hotel. Some men took short-term leases on houses out on Long Island's southern shore.

After the coastal patrol ended, about half of our base personnel were assigned to Hyde Field in Clinton, Maryland, where in December 1943 we were renamed tow target unit seventeen. Joseph Hettel and Peter Lafen were sent to tow target unit twenty-one at Monogram Field in Driver, Virginia, where Joe was named the commanding officer. We flew more tracking than tow-target missions, mainly providing practice for the anti-aircraft radar and searchlight batteries around the nation's capitol. At night we'd fly out of radar range then come back into the area with our navigation lights off to test how quickly they could lock onto us with their searchlights. I believe that a few planes and air crew were sent to Fort Bragg, North Carolina, on a kind of detached service, to perform mock strafing maneuvers. I then went to tow target unit five at Otis Field, Falmouth, Massachusetts, where several fellows from other east coast bases joined us. One of them, Francis C. McLaughlin from Flagler Beach, took over our group there. He and I are still friends and neighbors here in Peoria, Illinois. At Otis, our pilots towed targets for both aerial and ground gunnery practice. Some of us later moved to the Baltimore Army Air Base at Sparrows Point. I'll soon be eighty-two years old, and I may have forgotten a lot, but I believe our coastal patrol and tow target units did excellent work and deserve far more recognition that they've received in the past.

## Leon H. Snyder

*Leon H. Snyder was born and raised in Carbon County, Pennsylvania, just south of the Pocono Mountains. After earning an aircraft engine rating, he went to work for fellow Pennsylvanian Paul Knepper, who was an engineer, a pilot, and a licensed A&E mechanic. Together they built the prototype Knepper KA-1, a two-place, tricycle landing gear, high-wing monoplane, the first of its design in America, and possibly the world. It is displayed, along with a Piper J-3 Cub, in the State Museum in Harrisburg, Pennsylvania:*

We had reached the point of planning to produce the KA-1 when the war came along. We'd uncovered and disassembled the prototype preparatory to making the jigs needed for production and were seeking sources for the parts and materials we'd need. They quickly proved unavailable. Knepper belonged to the local CAP group and learned of the base being established at Riverhead. He volunteered for active duty there, suggesting I also do so. Once there, Knepper saw the dire need for mechanics and suggested to the base commander, Ralph Earle, that I be invited to join the staff. I reported two weeks later and remained eighteen months. Counting my service after the coastal patrol ended, I was in the CAP for three years, September 1942 to September 1945.

Riverhead had a pretty good hangar, sand runways, and a blacktop apron where the planes were tied down. Our Sikorsky amphibian was kept inside the hangar, but up front, where it could be rolled out quickly in case of an emergency. The "Duck" was my main responsibility, probably because despite my youth I was the most experienced mechanic on the base. Some fellows who'd graduated from the Rising Sun School of Aeronautics couldn't match what I'd done with Knepper — helping to build a plane from scratch then disassembling it again. My boss was Warren Moody, our engineering officer, a fine man for whom I developed great respect.

We usually got off one day a week, but it wasn't unusual to work several weeks, maybe even a month, in a row, and then get three or four days in a row off. Norm Rehrig was a neighbor of mine back in Pennsylvania and we would sometimes go home together when we had enough time off coming. We'd take the Long Island Railroad to Penn Station where we'd change for Allentown. We wore our uniforms, red epaulets and all, and certainly met no derision — despite any stories you might hear from others along those lines. I was married in my CAP uniform and proud of it!

When the coastal patrol ended, most of us went down to Hyde Field outside Washington, DC. The air crews flew night missions over the nation's capitol so the searchlight and anti-aircraft boys could practice their skill. I remained a mechanic, but sometimes went up as an observer as well. Paul Knepper left the CAP at this point. He had developed very painful sinuses, and was excused on medical grounds. He went to work at a fighter aircraft plant in Allentown, and soon became a main mover in getting things done. After the war was over, he left the field of aviation and became an authority on the care and restoration of antique automobiles. After his death five years ago, his widow had his collection of old auto parts auctioned off for over a million dollars.

Leon H. Snyder and his bride, Lorraine. They have been married now for more than fifty-two years (courtesy Leon H. Snyder).

As for myself I went from Hyde Field to another CAP group at Rehoboth Beach — not to the coastal patrol because it was long gone, but to another tow target unit. In January 1945, I was reassigned to the Baltimore Army Air Base. There all the airplanes that had been leased by the government for CAP use were made ship-shape before being returned to their owners. I had to make all the moves from place to place because I'd signed up "for the duration." Not every CAPer did so. I very much enjoyed my time with the CAP, learned a lot, and thought I did my share for my country. I can't praise the pilots enough. They did a helluva job! They went out over the cold, cruel ocean flying from dawn to dusk, and you'd never hear a single complaint.

## Lester S. Holden

*Lester S. Holden was born in Brooklyn in 1895, and with his family moved to Southampton well before World War I. There he married a local girl, just before enlisting in the Army and serving in France, where he was gassed and invalided home. He learned to fly in the late nineteen-thirties, and turned to the coastal patrol as a means of serving his country in World War II. He died in November of 1944 still a young, handsome, and robust man. His son, John I. Holden, remembers his dad's early interest in aviation:*

I don't recall exactly what got him interested, but he began taking lessons at what everyone called "Frog's Flying Field," because a fellow named "Frog" Chapman operated it. Chapman had a hangar and rented planes such as my Dad used. Sometimes I went with him and took some lessons myself. I think this was the same field taken over, then further developed, by the coastal patrol. In any event Dad volunteered and served two years — most of it as Assistant Intelligence Officer at the Riverhead base. My father was a patriotic man, who was very proud of his coastal patrol service.

Gassed in World War I, and ineligible for service during World War II, Lester S. Holden turned to the coastal patrol (courtesy John. Holden).

## Abner F. Ney, Jr.

*Abner F. Ney, Jr. became a member of the Chester, Pennsylvania squadron in November 1942. The squadron meetings usually were scheduled for the Buckman Airport just outside Chester, and squadron headquarters were in the Chester Armory. Ney's interest in flying began in the summer of 1942:*

One of the men I worked with at General Electric in southwest Philadelphia began taking flying lessons and telling me all about it. I went with him one day and had my first half-hour lesson. But then all civilian flying within 150 miles of the Atlantic coast was suspended, so that was the end of that. I joined the Riverhead base on March 31, 1943 and remained until August 31, 1943, serving as a guard. More than a half century has dulled my memory of names, but various faces and events come readily to mind.

CAP personnel were expected to study such subjects as navigation and the Morse Code. This is pilot Harold E. Wallin hitting the books prior to joining the coastal patrol (courtesy Mrs. Harold E. Wallin).

We guards, or security technicians as we were known officially, laughed about our job "fighting the battle of Suffolk" because that was the name of the airport and the county in which it was located. We had a little guard shack with a set of windows all around at eye level with a "duck your head" door facing the driveway entrance. It was affectionately called the "Jap Trap." A potbelly coal stove kept us warm in the winter, and we had a hand-cranked telephone that connected us to a central guardhouse. Lt. Edwin L. Mayberry was our commander and Charles H. Liebfried was our sergeant of the guard. Some of the guys whose names I recall were Donald Krupp, Curtis Maunders, and James Gardner — and lots of other faces come to me but with their names rubbed off. Local men were recruited now and then to keep the ranks filled. One of them, Leonard Grabowski, owned a store in Riverhead, and another, Salvatore Bongiorno, was a barber from Brooklyn.

Being interested in flying, I naturally spent a lot of off-duty time at the base watching and trying to learn whatever I could. One of the attractions for base personnel and visitors alike was our Link Trainer. We were likely to have been the only base to have one. Visiting pilots would come by and say, "I hear you've got a Link Trainer here." Commander Earle then would introduce them to our chief instructor, Sergeant Pat Brooke, who'd give them a ride in the Link. All usually went well while he explained things with the hood up and all the instruments "behaving." But once the hood came down, most of them would last about thirty seconds, then the thing would make some strange noises and the turning motor went into high speed. They had gone into a spin! Then Pat would tell them to forget the seats of their pants and rely on their instruments: "Center the needle, center the ball, check the air speed." He called the Link his "little deflator." But he certainly helped a lot of base personnel get their "fog tickets," and likely saved some lives.

Some years later, about 1948 or 1949, we held a dinner reunion at Riverhead, and a visit to our old base. Getting there, I flew as a passenger with Arnold Tegler, a former pilot-observer, and we stopped at the Flushing Airport on western Long Island to pick up Pete Lafen, another former pilot-observer. From there we picked up the south shore, then flew at about two hundred feet over the Atlantic all the way to Westhampton. On the way to a landing, I noticed the flags all flying at half-mast. Later I learned it was a day of national mourning to honor General John J. ("Blackjack") Pershing who had just died. The base operator had a couple of good-looking Stearman PT-17s sitting on the line so I checked one out and just flew around the area for an hour. It brought back some great memories.

---

Base officers, pilots, and observers who served at least one month at CAPCP#17 and who are not elsewhere mentioned in this chapter include: Adolph M. Backstrom,* Eugene L. Brown,* Paul V. Cline,* Hibbard S. Evans,* Herbert G. Fales, Frederick S. Gilley,* Joseph F. Gunster, Seth R. Jagger, Norman R. McCandless,* John L. Milton, Jr.,* Paul F. Nagel, Hyman V. Paul, and August L. Thiede.* Asterisk indicates Air Medal winner.

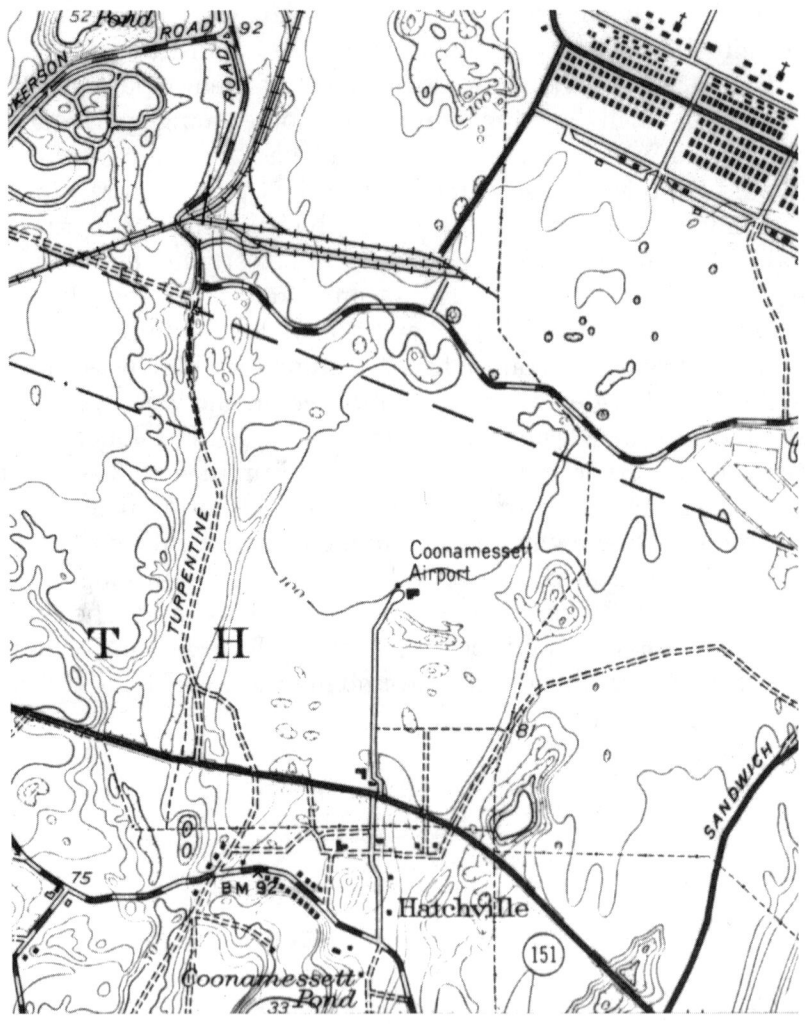

This 1953 United States Geological Survey map shows what was then known as the Coonamessett Airport just north of Hatchville and nearby Coonamessett Pond. The southern boundary of Camp Edwards is to the north and Otis Army Air Base is just off the map to the northeast. Falmouth is approximately six miles to the southwest.

# 18

# Falmouth, Massachusetts

In mid-1942, the Falmouth Airport, located about seven miles northeast of Falmouth near Camp Edwards, was used mainly by a flight school for the advanced phase of the Civilian Pilot Training Program. Once war was declared with Japan, and most civilian flying near the coasts curtailed, the operation was relocated to another airport. When taken over by the coastal patrol — the Falmouth base was activated on August 25, 1942 — the airport had three sod runways, and two large, heated hangars with concrete floors and integral maintenance shops. The field had boundary and obstruction lights, but no beacon. Two Camp Edwards water towers rose a mile to the north while the main road to Falmouth and a small lake were to the south. The field was leased from the Coonamessett Ranch Company, a private enterprise. Except for occasional drainage problems, the field was generally adequate.

## Everett L. King

*Air Medal winner Everett L. King was born in 1916 in the same house in East Taunton, Massachusetts where he and his wife live today. He likes to say he was born on an airport, because when he was only three years old, a former first World War Army Air Service pilot based his plane in his dad's cow pasture. He adds that there's been an airplane at the farm ever since, and right now it's his little pre-war Taylorcraft. King still has his license, and gives some dual instruction:*

Starting from 1919, several planes were based here and dad ran what became a small airport. I began by gassing the planes and carrying water out for the OX-5 engine on the veteran's Jenny and some other water-cooled old-timers. When I turned old enough I learned to fly. I had six or seven hours in a Hess Warrior-Argo, which was like a Fleet biplane, and then I bought a damaged single-place, 26 hp Aeronca C-2. My mother helped me to rebuild it, and I asked some of the airport fellows to test hop it for me. They said, "Oh, you can fly that, Everett," so I kind of checked myself out by taking her up.

When the war came, of course, all private flying within a hundred miles of the ocean was prohibited, and we closed down the airport. Until then, working around the planes was about all I'd ever done. I was 4-F because I was blind in one eye, and ended up in a factory in Boston putting the fabric covering on the control surfaces and tail assemblies of the big Waco gliders that were to be used in the invasion of Europe. A friend of mine, who knew I was a flyer — I had about a thousand hours by this time — suggested I go down and join the fellows at the Falmouth coastal patrol base.

Outside the base hangar on a late summer day in 1943. Men who had already gone into the military (such as Roger Antaya) and those on patrol at the time are absent (courtesy Mrs. William R. Kordas).

The day I walked into the base commander's office to see about flying there, I realized I knew him. It was Captain Gordon Gibbs, owner of the well-known Katherine Gibbs Secretarial School. Captain Gibbs had invested in an airport in Rochester, Massachusetts and I had flown in a couple of air shows for him. He was very cordial, remembered me, and engaged me right away as a First Lieutenant, pilot-in-command. I always called him *Captain* Gibbs, though I think some of the fellows called him "Kitty."

Every trace of the field we flew from, then called Falmouth Airport, is gone now. I think it had been used for polo matches. It was a great, large grassy expanse, with no marked runways, but a windsock, and we landed and took off according to where the wind was. About a month before the base closed in October of 1943, a fire destroyed our original sixty-by-eighty-foot hangar and four of our aircraft. The remaining hangar was disassembled and moved to Glen Falls, New York, and the T-hangars were sold and moved to a new airport in East Falmouth. When we left, nothing remained but the administration building, and it was eventually moved elsewhere, too. Today the property is part of the Francis A. Crane Wildlife Refuge.

When I first reported, September 14, 1942, I lived with many other coastal patrol personnel in the Wellsmere Inn, right on the water near Falmouth. I paid for my room and meals and uniforms out of my fifty-six dollars weekly pay. I got my uniforms from a local Army-Navy store. My wife Olga and I were married while I served at Falmouth, and we then shared a house with another couple from the base. Both of us had cars, and Olga worked at the Falmouth Hospital. I also had a motorcycle, but Olga didn't like it, and I didn't use it much.

We weren't very military, though we might have had an occasional inspection. I flew everything on the base, including the Sikorsky amphibian we used both on rescue and regular patrols. We had a lot of fog and flew under some pretty low ceilings. We pilots didn't decide when we flew, the operations officer did. We didn't have and didn't really need direction-finding equipment. We weren't always very far out, and if the weather started to look bad, we'd head in, and we'd be in sight of land pretty quickly. I'd flown a lot around the Cape Cod area before joining the coastal patrol and it helped that I knew the shoreline pretty well. After the coastal patrol left Falmouth, I transferred to Hyde Field, Clinton, Maryland, to fly with the tow target unit there. After the war I resumed running the airport in East Taunton, and I've been here ever since.

\* \* \*

The most exciting thing that Everett King recalls was being the first to spot a big oil slick that proved to come from a German submarine that was later sunk by Navy destroyers. The incident is written up in *Sank Same*:

[On the morning of January 9, 1943] the Army and Navy ordered a search of the area south of Block Island for suspected enemy submarine activity, and although the fog was heavy, six planes were sent aloft. Fifty miles out to sea from the island, two of the planes, carrying Everett King, former Taunton airport operator, Louis Ferrari and Walter Murphy, of Boston, and Don Reed, of Fort Madison, Iowa, spotted a long narrow slick which showed traces of all the colors of the rainbow. Both planes were nearly out of gasoline, so the observers dropped aluminum marker bombs over the slick and the planes headed back to the base.... [Though the U-boat was not found that day, other coastal patrol planes from Falmouth found a fresh oil slick the following day, and this time Navy ships arrived in time to hunt down and sink it].

## Georgia Ransom

*Georgia Ransom (now Georgia Watkins) of Mattapoisett, Massachusetts doesn't remember how she heard of the coastal patrol's need for teletype operators, but she was between jobs and looking for work. She was interviewed and hired, and has never forgotten her experience at Falmouth. She describes what for her was a typical day at the base:*

Three a.m. and the damn alarm clock would go off. It seemed like I'd just gotten into bed, and I sometimes had. My roommate was on the office shift and didn't have to get up until 7:45 a.m., so I tried not to wake her. Having dressed and made-up in the dimmest of lights I'm sure I must have looked ravishing at the Wellsmere Inn breakfast table but then everyone was too sleepy to notice anyway. Most of the boys ate a hearty meal, though how they could at that ungodly hour I don't know. Most of them were always eating. With all due respect to Benny, our cook, his coffee was something to avoid. I swear that some mornings it was strong enough to make the spoon stand straight up in the cup with no human hand touching it. But as I had only fruit juice and coffee, I managed to get the stuff down. We all generally ate in silence.

After we finished eating and carrying our own dishes to the kitchen, we all gathered in the lobby to see who was taking whose car that morning. I usually had mine, because my stretch at the teletype was done before the boys finished their flying for the day, and if I didn't drive, it meant a long wait for someone to give me a lift back to the hotel. We all kept a lookout for Don Reed at that hour. Often we'd find his cottage dark, and we'd wait until he tumbled out wondering where he was — especially if he'd had a few beers the night before.

Sometimes the moon would be shining in all its glory as we hit the road for the base, and the little airport looked pretty in the moonlight.

The Officer of the Day would have a light on — if we didn't get there too early and find him still asleep. But the guards were always on the job, and would have a light on in their shack to help guide us. The hangar crew would have some planes out on the apron ready for a pilot to jump into and start up. The teletype machine would have a couple of yards of messages on it when I came in, but usually only one for us. Our intelligence officer decoded it before briefing the dawn patrol.

There was always a thrill in seeing the planes take off. Everyone would watch and comment, and then the stand-by crew would either sleep, eat, or work on some personal job as they wished. After sending out certain morning reports on the teletype machine, I'd be more or less free until the half-hourly aircraft position reports had to be plotted in the intelligence officer's office. The radio operator had to be especially alert for any reports of our aircraft with engine failures or other problems. Thanks to a good engineering officer and a fine crew of mechanics, we experienced but two emergencies and neither resulted in serious injury. Our total hours flown, and our record for safety, equaled any other base our size in the coastal patrol.

Things would begin to stir again when the dawn patrol was sighted coming back to the field. The landings were watched as closely as the take-offs had been, and the pilot unfortunate enough to have made a poor landing heard about it from all sources. Our little clunkers never let us down, and I never tired of watching them take off and land. There was always some suspense about it, even though nobody ever expected anything at all to happen.

Once in the office, the crews were questioned by the intelligence officer. Except for special patrols, there'd be a lull until the dusk patrol took off. The returning crews headed for the canteen, then went into the tents for their share of shut-eye. As I remember it, the office force arrived at 9:00 a.m., and the dusk crews appeared about 10:00 a.m. At 1:00 p.m. the dusk patrol went out and at 2:00 p.m. the dawn patrol went home. The office force quit at 5:00 p.m. and at about 7:30 p.m. the base closed for the day. For me, it never got monotonous. I wish we were all back there — flying, griping, drinking, and living under the command of our swell leader, Captain Gordon Gibbs. It was a great life!

\* \* \*

Georgia Watkins still keeps the post card receipt for her application for Civil Air Patrol employment. Dated October 20, 1942 and signed by the National Commander, Major Earle L. Johnson, it reads:

> Your application for enlistment as a volunteer in the Civil Air Patrol has been received. Your patriotism is deeply appreciated. Upon re-

view and preparation of your service record and identification material, your papers will be forwarded to the Wing Commander of your State, who will in turn notify you of assignment to organization and duty. Please assist by patience. Do not write letters. Everything possible will be done at National Headquarters to expedite your assignment. The serial number assigned you is 1-4-1106.

Air Medal winner Lieutenant William R. Kordas was from Taunton, Massachusetts (courtesy Mrs. William R. Kordas).

### Roger J. Antaya

*Roger J. Antaya, another Air Medal winner, was born and raised in Springfield, Massachusetts. The youngest pilot at Falmouth, he had soloed at sixteen and had earned his private pilot's license two years later. When he reported to the Falmouth base in September 1942, he was all of nineteen. Like most other bachelor pilots, he lodged and dined at the Wellsmere Hotel:*

I recall shortly after my arrival, Lieutenant Jay H. Bushway of Marblehead, one of the organizers of the base, flew a group of us out over the waters we'd be patrolling. This was very exciting, and it was a great experience for me to make new friends with the same interests as mine. I felt everyone was great, the administrative staff, the radio operators, and the terrific ground crew. The base itself was sod-covered, and for a short time during the spring thaw of 1943 it was too muddy to fly from, so we flew out of the Army's Otis Field. That was part of Camp Edwards, which was located adjacent to the Falmouth Airport, and it had paved runways. Some B-25s of the 126th Anti-Submarine Command flew from Otis Field, and that gave our gang a chance to compare notes with the pilots, who were great guys. Many claimed they wouldn't *at all* care to fly over water in single-engine planes like we did.

We patrolled the large area from our base north to Cape Ann, about forty miles northeast of Boston, and south to Long Island's Montauk Point. The bee-line flying distances were about seventy-five miles in each direction. Winter was the most dangerous time of year. Survival time in the water, should you have to ditch, was brief because the water was so cold. We did get the rubberized zoot-suits, which covered us from head to toe with just a little of our faces showing, but they would have provided just a slightly longer survival time.

Being young and foolish, some of us took other kinds of chances. On our way out to fly patrol one day, the pilot of my sister ship, a Lieutenant Michael F. Sullivan, from Palmer, Massachusetts, hand-signaled that he was going to fly under the three bridges across the Cape Cod Canal connecting the Cape to the mainland. I asked my observer if he was game, and when he nodded okay, Sullivan and I flew our planes under all three: the Bourne, the Sagamore, and a railroad bridge. The first two were fairly high, but the railroad bridge was a vertical-lift span that could be lowered for a train or raised for an ocean-going ship. The Army Corps of Engineers maintained the canal, and they were *very unhappy* with our performance. They reported us, and we were reprimanded and nearly grounded. We were told the coastal patrol was serious business and not to forget it!

I remember a particular patrol on February 16, 1943, well out over the water, when snow squalls developed. Our patrols were always flown in pairs, and we both turned and headed for shore as quickly as we could. Because of the poor visibility we got down on deck and just skimmed the water. We got over land near Peabody, where there were industrial smoke stacks sticking up all around at our own level. Rather than risk such flying all the way back to base, we decided to land as soon as possible.

My partner in the other plane, First Lieutenant Everett King — a superb pilot, by the way — picked a spot beside a highway just large enough to get into, and had no problem in landing. By now the ground was snow-covered and slippery, and after I landed, I skidded into the highway embankment, damaging the plane considerably. I cut my lip, and Lieutenant Ralph DeAvila, my observer, was shaken up, but otherwise we were fine. I loved flying, but in March, 1943, I left the base to join the Navy (which is why I'm not in the group photograph of base personnel taken somewhat later). The Navy gave me a rating as an aviation machinist mate, and sent me to the South Pacific. I returned to flying after the war and flew for twenty-five years as a private pilot.

\* \* \*

## Sloat F. Hodgson

*Sloat F. Hodgson grew up in the West Falmouth area and was a mechanic at the Falmouth base throughout its operation. He recalls it, "in its entirety, a very strange place," and wonders whether anyone who wasn't there could possibly capture the flavor of its trials and tribulations:*

The base was the story of how a nation, caught short without adequate protection, turned to a rag-tag and bobtail collection of civilians to guard its shores during a time of serious trouble. From Cape Ann to Block Island, the job was ours. How the Germans would have laughed if they had known who was flying those silly little Stinsons with their stout-hearted Franklin engines. At first we called them our "Little Treasures," or just plain clunkers, but by the end of 1942 our sarcasm completely disappeared. They went out on schedule over the water and, more importantly, they came back.

Corporal Sloat F. Hodgson was listed in the base table of organization as an apprentice mechanic, and later promoted to Sgt. (courtesy Mrs. Janet Bosworth).

The personnel consisted of wealthy aristocrats, everyday people, draft-dodgers, people trying to escape their ex-wives, guttersnipes, 4-Fs, and you name it. One ex-bootlegger left the base to get into black-marketing. They were all ages. Some had houses or lived in town, but a large group took over the Wellsmere Hotel. We were a pretty rowdy bunch, perhaps best described by a teletype message that came from another base: "Base 18, where every night is Saturday night, and Saturday night is New Year's Eve!" But we were proud of our record, and in fact thought ours was the only base that amounted to anything. And we felt that way right from Gordon Gibbs, the only boss we really acknowledged, down to the lowliest of us.

## Mrs. Janet Hodgson

*Mrs. Janet Hodgson was born in Chicago, educated at Bryn Mawr College, and from age three spent her summers on Cape Cod where her parents owned a home at Woods Hole. Fred Hodgson's family summered in West Falmouth, and Fred and Janet met there. Married in Japan in 1932, they honeymooned in Korea then lived there for five years. After two years spent in South Africa, and their return to the United States following the Japanese attack at Pearl Harbor, her husband joined the Navy. She resettled on the Cape close to her brother-in-law, Sloat Hodgson. The following is how Janet (now Mrs. Janet Bosworth) happened to join the coastal patrol:*

Sergeant Janet Hodgson was born in Chicago and educated at Bryn Mawr College. At Falmouth, she was a radio and plotting board operator (courtesy Mrs. Janet Bosworth).

There was a large Air Corps base in Falmouth and many of the officers from there spent their evenings at the Coonamessett Inn. One evening in order to entertain some guests, I took them to the Inn and there we met a Civil Air Patrol officer who told us he was signing up personnel. One of my friends was a stunningly beautiful girl, who unfortunately for the CAP had to return to Atlanta the next day, but I went myself to the base and was hired as a radio operator. Believe it or not, it was the same field at which I'd earned my private pilot's license when I was eighteen, just before I married. My husband-to-be, Fred Hodgson, was a pilot, a fact that encouraged me to take lessons. As radio operator, I never had to guide a plane in through foggy weather, or instruct one to wait and circle, or anything like that, but I received reports from each of the two planes on patrol in all navigable daylight weather, and recorded them. We never sighted a suspicious sub, though several oil slicks were reported and one of our planes made an emergency beach landing due to engine trouble. Our pilots were skilled and careful fliers, and we had excellent mechanics, and these are the only incidents that I can recall. Our radio signals were said to be the bane of other coastal patrol bases within range, because ours were the stronger and blocked theirs out. I developed a gift for hearing and understanding our men's voices over almost all static and interference — something, now that I'm very deaf, I really marvel at.

The base insignia consisted of an impish figure riding a bomb down toward a sinking German submarine. Six different shades of emroidery thread were used in this beautiful hand-sewn version. The original is five inches in diameter.

When I took flying lessons there, the airport had two grass runways, though I can recall only one being used by the coastal patrol. Our administration building had a basement level with a small dining room and tiny kitchen. Public-spirited town ladies brought and served lunch every day, but we were also free to make sandwiches and get snacks at any time. A larger downstairs room was used as a classroom for teaching Morse Code and other things, and the rest rooms were on this lower level as well. Upstairs, one entered a fairly large room with desks for the pilots and anyone on duty. To the left of this was our commanding officer's office and his secretary's desk. Our second-in-command also had a desk there. To the right was the teletype connecting us to Otis Air Corps base, the radio, and the intelligence officer's desk. Outside was our hangar and in back of it was a kind of common quarters for the guards and mechanics. Just beyond this was a parking area and the guard post. We were surrounded by stands of scrub pine, and the little village of Hatchville, a part of Falmouth, was nearby.

I think what some said about our operation — "nearly every night was Saturday night" — was close to the truth, but I don't remember a single instance of anyone coming in late, and the morning shift reported *very* early, soon after daybreak. I myself recall plodding through deep snow drifts in the dark when the snow was too deep to drive. We were young and enthusiastic, starting with the gatehouse guards who wouldn't let us in until we showed them our passes, right up to the commanding officer. A bad hangover, and I suspect there were many, never interfered with the performance of our duties!

## Erwin T. Mellor

*Erwin T. Mellor, from Chicopee Falls, Massachusetts, was a twenty-two-year-old pilot who had learned to fly J-3 Cubs at the metropolitan airport in Palmer, Massachusetts when dual time cost eight dollars an hour. His Air medal shows that he reported to the Falmouth base on September 16, 1942 and that he remained until the base closed on August 31, 1943:*

Most of the single men lived at the Wellsmere Hotel. A pilot by the name of Norman Tucker from Fitchburg, Massachusetts, who was in the oil business, came down and arranged to lease the whole place. We paid for our rent and meals, and as I recall they had two pretty good cooks. We didn't have that much seafood, really, except when another pilot, Louis Ferrari, went out to fish and dig clams and then brought them back to the cooks to prepare. Louis ran the Moosehead Inn in Scully Square in Boston, and he knew seafood as well as anyone around. Once we had to fly a spare radio transmitter up to Bar Harbor, and the plane returned chock-full of Maine shrimp. They were smaller than Gulf shrimp, but tasty. We had shrimp dishes meal afer meal after meal! The Wellsmere was an old place, quite warm and comfortable, but it's gone now, destroyed by some hurricane long after we left.

As for the flying, the weather was always a problem. On one patrol, I was clear down around Block Island, when I was advised that fog was developing at the base, and that I should land at Fall River, or somewhere around that area, so I wouldn't get trapped above an impenetrable layer of the grey stuff. Occasionally we did search and rescue work. One morning we were briefed about a fishing boat that was disabled somewhere east of North Truro. We were scheduled for the north area so we flew toward where the boat might be, getting into a fog bank some fifty miles off shore. We soon came upon a large fishing boat flying the American flag upside down. It appeared to be dead in the water. We called in its position and continued circling overhead until we a saw a Coast Guard vessel in the distance. We flew back and forth between the two until they were close enough to see each other, then left the rescue to the Coast Guard.

Lt. Erwin T. Mellor was from Chicopee Falls, Massachusetts, and served nearly a year at the Falmouth base (courtesy Erwin T. Mellor).

Another time, closer to base, fog had already rolled in. You could look down through it and see the ground, but when you got down to come in for a landing it built up ahead of you so you couldn't see. Fortunately they had an old Sikorsky amphibian at the field that someone took to one end of the runway and revved-up to blow an open path down the runway for us. I don't know who thought of it, but it sure was a good feeling to see that cleared area. The Sikorsky was mainly used for rescue work, but I recall flying patrols in it as co-pilot a few times. Only one man was officially checked-out to fly it, Carl Davis of Detroit, Michigan, an old Ford Tri-Motor pilot. I flew regularly and accumulated over five hundred hours on patrol, but we had some time off, too. My home was only three hours' drive away, so I'd leave the evening of my last day on duty, perhaps for a long weekend. I don't remember any base parties or dances. There were only a couple of girls working at the base, and not many of the married men brought their wives, so there wasn't much sense having a dance. Clifford and Bill Allen, brothers from Nantucket Island, would sometimes have their wives over for a visit, and Arnold Larson, who was also from the Island, did the same. Long after the war was over there was a big banquet at which Air Medals were distributed and everyone celebrated getting home safely, but I think that was the only social occasion attended by all base personnel.

After the base closed, I served a year as a civilian instructor in the War Training Service Program in Burlington, Vermont, then for another year as a technical representative at the Bell Aircraft plant there, all the while in the Air Corps Reserve. After being called up for active duty with the Air Transport Command they told me I was too young for it, and I was put into the Cadet program. I was four weeks from graduation when the war ended, and, given a choice of continuing or being discharged, I went home. After flying some for pleasure, I let my license lapse until my son turned thirteen and wanted to fly. So I got myself re-licensed, bought a Cessna 172, and helped him learn in it. I retired here to southwest Utah not long ago, but still fly occasionally.

## George A. Eaton

*George A. Eaton and his older brother Albert J. Eaton were born and raised in Auburn, New Hampshire. Albert, a licensed aircraft mechanic, reported to the Falmouth base when it was first activated and George, whose work experience had been mainly automotive, joined the base later as an apprentice mechanic. Albert is dead now, but George, who returned to Auburn after the war, remembers his time at Falmouth very well:*

I brought some tools with me, but I was buying some of what I needed as I went along. When I left for the Navy I gave what I had to my brother, and his and mine were lost in a hangar fire. I worked on all our different planes doing whatever was required. The hangar was comfortably heated in the winter and pleasant enough to work in. Only the planes under repair were inside. All the rest were tied down outside, which meant they had to have engine covers and be externally heated before they'd start in real cold weather. There were two shifts, each around eight hours a day. If you came in for the dawn patrol, you would be done by noon or so. Come early, leave early, or come later and leave later. We worked in coveralls, but had to have uniforms anyway. That was no problem. They weren't very expensive.

Falmouth seemed like a good-sized town, with a lot of businesses. I used to go to the movies pretty often, but I didn't drink, so I skipped the bars, and since I didn't have a car, I didn't chase the girls. I fished a lot, though. Another fellow and I rented a boat and went up the Cape Cod Canal to catch "stripers." They're big fish — anywhere from ten to fifty pounds — and we'd sell them to the local fish market for thirty cents a pound. We had good luck at the time, but I think the Canal is all fished out now. I don't remember too many of the people at the base by name. I recall Ev King because he was always riding his motorcycle around the base, and Georgia Watkins because of her bright red hair.

Sgt. George A. Eaton from Auburn, New Hampshire filled a table of organization position as a service technician, but was actually an appentice mechanic (courtesy George A. Eaton).

As I said, when the base closed I went into the Navy. To save time I went up to nearby Camp Edwards to take my physical examination, and the Navy accepted me immediately as an aviation machinist mate. I served three years, including nineteen months in the Gilbert and Marshall Islands in the Pacific. When I got back home to Auburn, I belonged to the local CAP squadron for a while but when I married I gave it up. I still have my CAP jacket and such, but I can't wear them anymore. Back then I was a size forty-two, now I'm a size forty-eight and weigh over two hundred pounds. Times and people *do* change.

## Donald V. LaCouture

*Donald V. LaCouture was born and raised in Marlborough, Massachusetts, and learned to fly there. When he joined the CAP, he was nineteen and on his way toward commercial and instructor ratings. He flew as co-pilot on the first patrol out of Falmouth and over a year later, as a pilot, made the very last landing of the last patrol from the base. He also won the Air Medal:*

At Falmouth I shared a room at the Wellesmere Inn with Ev King, a good friend and great pilot. Getting to and from the base was no problem. We each owned a car *and* a motorcycle, Ev had an "Indian" and I had a "Harley-Davidson." What we took each day depended on the weather: when it was good, we drove our bikes. The flying weather around Falmouth was pretty spotty, with fog the usual culprit. I don't think our base had any ditchings, though I'm sure we had some off-base landings. I never had any problem. I just went out and did a job every day. After maybe three months or so, we started to get a day a week off. Ev and I bought a little lapstrake-built sailboat with a center board just to fool around in. I sailed it over to Martha's Vineyard one day by myself, seven or eight miles. Looking back on it, that was pretty stupid. There were rip tides in that area, but at the time I didn't understand how dangerous they could be. To me it was just great sport.

After the base closed, three of us went down to an Air Corps base at Douglas, Georgia as civilian flight instructors. But we didn't like our reception so we quit and accepted a similar assignment at an Air Corps base in Burlington, Vermont. After a year, I was transferred to Arizona and then to Langley Field in Virginia where I picked up some co-pilot time in C-25s, B-25s, and B-17s. After the war ended I returned here to Marlboro, and I'm now the fixed base operator at the airfield where I learned to fly almost sixty years ago and where my son is the chief pilot. I also have four daughters, each of whom has at least soloed. At one time, some of us from the Falmouth base got together once a year, but there aren't enough of us left now, and we've sort of drifted out of touch.

## Ronnie L. McLane

*Ronnie L. McLane was born and raised in Falmouth and lives there still. McLane was twenty-four, married, and had two young children. While working nights as a guard at the base, he worked days as a carpenter:*

Our whole company of the Massachusetts State Guard (created after the Massachusetts National Guard was called to active service) served as airport security guards. We had a captain, two lieutenants, and various sergeants and corporals and privates like myself. We'd been training for a year, learning military discipline and drill and how to fire our thirty-caliber Enfield rifles. Everybody but the captain held regular jobs because we couldn't support our families on State Guard pay. I think we were the only State Guard company in the state assigned to guard an airport, although I know that some other companies were active in the Boston area, mainly up around the docks. I recall that several of our men were excused from guard duty for "hardships" of one sort or another, and that we had three eight-hour shifts to provide round-the-clock security at four different posts: the main gate guardhouse, the flight-line area, the hangars, and the administration building. The man in the administration building was also the night time teletype operator. We were all from around Falmouth except for several who came from down Barnstable way.

Base pilot William Kordas snapped this photo of two waitresses outside a soda shop-drug store in Falmouth. The townspeople were happy to have the coastal patrol folks in their midst (courtesy Mrs. William R. Kordas).

I never had occasion to challenge anyone out at the airport. About the only thing that happened would be some local hunters might drive onto the airport at night looking for deer. We all knew what they were doing, and it was okay. There were so many deer around we'd sometimes have to chase them off the runway so the dawn patrol could take off. The guards didn't mix much with the other base personnel. Having to work two jobs to make ends meet you don't have much time for socializing. The base had a cafeteria that was open twenty-four hours a day. That was nice because those of us on night duty could wander in and get coffee and a snack whenever we wanted to. At night it was operated on the honor system. Since nobody was there, if you had a coffee or a donut, or whatever, you'd put what it cost in a can. The fellows on day duty usually ate lunch there.

Falmouth was just a little town then. It still is. But we had a theater and a U.S.O. and they were popular with the soldiers down from Camp Edwards. Many of the coastal patrol people from the base lived in Falmouth or nearby in the Wellesmere Inn, and we didn't think of them as visitors as we did with the boys from the Army camp. When the base closed I joined the Navy. Since the State Guard wasn't part of the U.S. Army, they had no ties on me. I got as far as Pearl Harbor and served there about a year and a half before the war ended and I was discharged. It was good duty at Pearl, but I was more than glad to get home again and rejoin my family.

**Bruno L. Tassinari**

*Bruno L. Tassinari was born in Sandwich on Cape Cod's northern shore in 1908 and at age thirty-five was one of the older mechanics at the Falmouth base. He and his brother and sister were running a garage in Falmouth when he joined the base:*

Frank Kimball [Capt. Francis A.] from Lynn, Massachusetts was our chief mechanic, and we had eight or ten men to work on all those airplanes we knew nothing about, but tried to keep in the air! We all supplied our own hand tools, but the bigger stuff belonged to the base. We had a spirited bunch of people at the base and some good times. It seems like we were only paid every couple of months — the pay was always late — but when it came through we'd have a big bang of a party at the Wellsmere Inn where most of the single guys lived. We'd have beer or whatever anyone wanted to bring, and sit around and tell stories and jokes all evening. Sometimes we'd have a deer feast along with it. Some of the local fellows were assigned as guards at the airport, and they'd shoot deer out there and bring them in. We got all the butter we wanted out at the base, without any coupons or anything, and we'd cook that venison until it was just right. We didn't hang it for aging, we ate it the next night!

When the base disbanded, I went up to Concord, New Hampshire and worked for the CAP up there. About the time I was scheduled to take the tests to get an A&E license, I joined the Marine Corps. But my CAP experience helped me make crew chief on a Martin B-26 and earn a tech sergeant rating. My squadron had just departed San Diego in a ship bound for Japan when we heard that the Japs had quit. The ship turned and headed up along the West Coast, and I think they were trying to decide whether to go ahead and send us overseas or call us back.

Well we went ahead, but I got off in Honolulu where I learned that anyone who was thirty-five or older could get an immediate discharge just by asking. I asked, and it took three months, providing me, incidentally, with the total time in the service later needed to qualify for a Massachusetts veteran's bonus. All I did while I waited was eat and sleep and get fat, and listen to the World Series. At home again I resumed as service manager at our family automobile dealership and we grew large enough to sell about a hundred cars a year. In a small town like ours that was very good. After we sold out in 1969, I took a temporary job as a clerk with a local lumber store and stayed twenty-six years. I'd spend six months in Florida, and each spring when I got back they'd say, "When can you start?" I've been lucky all my life, and at eighty-eight I'm still feeling great!

Part of the scene after the terrible hangar fire that destroyed a Stinson Reliant and three Fairchild 24s. This skeleton appears to be that of the Stinson (courtesy Erwin T. Mellor).

### Robert E. Durand

*Robert E. Durand was, in his words, "just a kid from Marlboro, Massachusetts" when he joined the coastal patrol base at Falmouth. Although he later served at the War Training Service base in Concord, New Hampshire, and for a time at the coastal patrol base in Beaufort, North Carolina, his memories of Falmouth are the most vivid:*

The group in Falmouth was a high-flying, live-it-up bunch, including the women. I remember one pilot who apparently misplaced the location of one of the five aircraft he owned, and on his off time would take another of his planes and go off looking for the lost one. He sometimes took me along as an observer to help him look for it. Another otherwise very quiet and proper pilot took me along when he went to Boston for weekends to see a burlesque show at the Old Howard. He had a season pass and knew some of the girls. It was very exciting for a young fellow like me, and quite a change from my work in the hangar to keep a lot of aircraft in flying condition. But then came the fire in the hangar and in seconds the whole place was a roaring mass of flames. Everything in there was lost — the Stinson plus three Fairchild 24s, all our tools and equipment, and the radio repair shop. What with the doped fabric, fuel and oil, and rubber tires, you can imagine how hot and incredibly smoky it was. I guess we were very lucky that nobody was trapped inside and burned to death. Some months later I enlisted in the Air Corps. What's kind of unusual is that three years ago my wife and I bought and moved into a house only a few miles from where the Falmouth base used to be.

## William A. Allen

*William A. Allen and Clifford W. Allen were brothers from Nantucket Island and both already had their commercial licenses when they entered the War Training Service Program to obtain instructors ratings to teach in that program. Although Clifford, the older by a year and a half, did his WTS training in Vermont, William did his in Massachusetts. While waiting for assignments, they joined the CAP and reported to the Falmouth base at about the same time. William recalls:*

When the war came, I was part of the family restaurant business on the Island. I owned a Fairchild 24, which the government made me take apart so it couldn't fly, then later the coastal patrol came down and put it together again and rented it for the duration of the war. I'd paid three thousand dollars for it, which was big money in those days. A year or so after the Falmouth base closed, I received a check in the mail for that amount. I thought that was pretty wonderful.

I never had any forced landings or anything while a member of the patrol, but I had a good scare one day when my engine nearly stopped *three times*. I was half way between Long Island and Martha's Vineyard on a cold, windy day in winter. I had dropped down to about three hundred feet on one occasion before the engine revved up enough to get me back up to a thousand feet. I figured that it was carburetor icing, but after I managed to limp into base I found that a hole I'd previously reported in the exhaust manifold had not been fixed. As you can well imagine I was upset — thinking you're going into that icy water three times, you know, was no fun! I told the mechanic I absolutely wouldn't fly that machine nor would anyone else until it was properly fixed.

My brother Clifford and I lived in a private home in Falmouth until the base leased the Wellsmere Inn and then we shared a room there. My wife remained here on the Island taking care of our son, and unfortunately I was unable to get home much to see them, even though it was only fifteen or twenty miles across the water. There wasn't really much to do in Falmouth except have a drink with the other boys — which was more or less obligatory. Turn someone down and you might not be asked again. I smoked on patrol, by the way, and so did everyone else. There was certainly no order against it. I didn't begin on cigarettes until I reached twenty-seven and I sure wish I'd never started.

Lt. Ramon F. Lawrence was a pilot from New Bedford, Massachusetts, and presumably was used to all the snow (courtesy Mrs. Janet Bosworth).

Cliff and I left before the base closed. I was assigned to a War Training Service school in Montpelier, Vermont, and instructed there until the war ended, accumulating thousands upon thousands of hours in the air. My teaching schedule was ten students a day, each for one-half to an hour's time every day. After the war ended I worked as an electrician in a Providence, Rhode Island shipyards for six months, then returned to Nantucket to continue in the family restaurant business. When we sold it in 1968, I retired. My wife is gone, but my son lives nearby and sometimes we fish a little. At eighty-eight I don't get out too much. No, I never flew again. After the grind at Montpelier I'd had enough.

## Clifford W. Allen

*Clifford W. Allen's experience with the Falmouth coastal patrol was somewhat like his younger brother's except that he came even closer to becoming a Duck Club member:*

My observer Cedio Salterelli and I were returning from patrol, coming south over Massachusetts Bay, when a Coast Guard PBY came alongside and we had some fun hand-signaling back and forth to one another. Cedio was a very, very nice Italian boy from Buffalo, New York, and I think he did all of the signaling. Just about then my engine decided to quit. Fortunately we weren't far offshore so I drifted away, and managed to land safely on the nearest beach. A mechanic came by later and fixed the problem and I took off from the beach again that afternoon. I thought I'd run out of fuel, but in fact, one tank had run dry, while the other was full and just hadn't fed properly. I don't remember whether this happened in the winter but I know I felt lucky not to have ditched. Even in the summer the water up here stays pretty cold.

Like William, when the war ended I returned to Nantucket to help out in the family restaurant business. As a company, we owned a number of planes over the years and I flew them all. I think we once had a Cessna and a Navion, and somewhere in there was a Luscombe. I love Nantucket — the people are great, and it's one of the most beautiful places in the world — but it started to get pretty expensive to live there, so when we sold the restaurant in 1968, I retired and came here to Hyannis. As the crow flies I'm only fifteen miles from the Island but at my age I don't travel much so it's been quite some time since I've been back.

---

Base officers, pilots, and observers who served at least one month at CAPCP#18 and who are not elsewhere mentioned in this chapter include: Henry D. Arvisais, Charles W. Aspinall,* M. A. Bentley,* Raymond F. Brune,* Archie C. Burnett, Jr.,* George Defren,* Alfred J. DePadua,* Kenneth G. Fletcher, Clifford J. Grube, Carl F. Gulat,* Milton B. Hall,* Charles H. Haskell, Blair G. Johnson,* Richard B. Lavallee, Joseph K. McCarthy,* Howard J. McMurray, William G. Marx,* Theodore S. Messinger, George H. Miller, Edwin J. Nilsson,* Anthony Ricciardiello, Charles H. Shepard, Edwin P. Tripp, Jr., Frank T. Weinz, Harry J. Welch, Jr., and Robert B. Winslow. Asterisk indicates Air Medal winner.

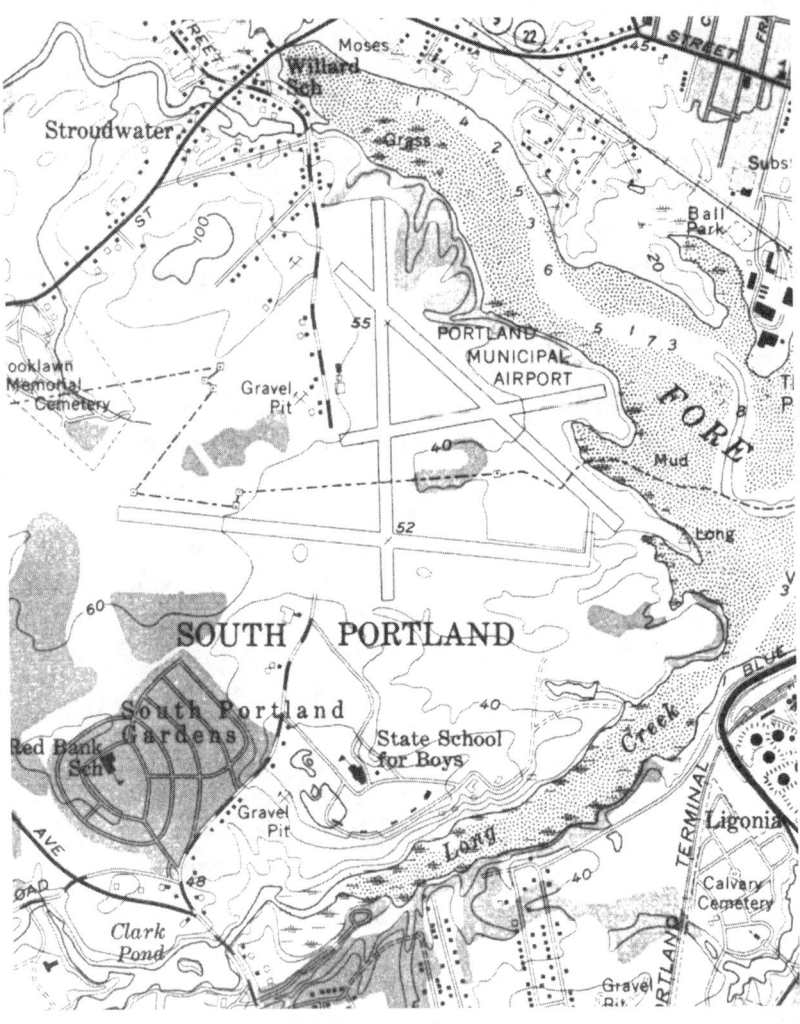

Portland Municipal Airport was just southwest of downtown Portland. Urban development still stopped at the northern banks of the Fore River, and the Maine Turnpike, which now skirts the western edge of the airport, had not yet been envisioned (source: 1956 United States Geological Survey map).

# 19
# Portland, Maine

With an average of more than thirty foggy days a year, Maine may be the "foggiest" state in the nation. The winters are also *very* cold! For those who were responsible for getting the dawn patrol away, standing around in minus-twenty to minus-forty degree temperatures waiting for a balky aircraft engine to make up its mind to start was no fun at all. As it happened, most Portland coastal patrol personnel came from the upper New England states and presumably were inured to such extremes. But the weather, even apart from below-zero temperatures, was inimical to patrol work as some excerpts from the base history suggest:

> After nearly one year of operation, the 19th Patrol Force has encountered nearly every type and condition of weather in the book. Being located on the north-east corner of the continent, we are in the midst of the final dirty work kicked up by the highs, lows, and fronts as they leave the coast and start across the Atlantic.... [though fog was the worst problem, there were others] ... Winter cold brings troubles and hardships, chief among which is the zoot suit; a devilish rubber union suit which successfully prevents all attempts to remove anything from the pockets, or to scratch. Unfortunately for the pilots, Lt. Pothier's brain child engine heater, which we called "Gunga Din," was so very efficient that our aircraft nearly always started, and we had to venture forth into the land of frost on the wings, icy runways, carburetor icing, high seas, strong winds, and that draught that always gets in and works around to the back of your neck.
>
> High winds and strong gusts are ever present, and are responsible for several of the Waco pilots becoming members of that fine organi-

zation, the Tattered Wingtips Club. Thunderstorms cannot always be skirted, and even if you are successful in this, they have a habit of working between you and the base as you come in on your last few gallons of gas. Besides the rain and poor visibility, these storms are accompanied by extremely rough air, and many of our flight personnel have found that even a tight safety belt will not prevent a dented noggin if you tangle with a half-grown cumulo nimbus.... Yes, the weather has heated us, chilled us, surprised us, and scared us, but one thing it couldn't do, and that was stop us.

The coastal patrol base grew out of the two local CAP squadrons that had been operating from Portland Municipal Airport since shortly after Pearl Harbor. They were then merged as Portland CAP Squadron 111, and Major Milton V. Smith was named as commanding officer. Members took two hundred hours of instruction in thirty different subjects, so that when they were activated as a coastal patrol base on August 18, 1942, they were "raring to go." The base history speaks humorously to the least popular part of the training they received:

> Of course in any military group there must be some semblance of discipline and there is only one way to attain that goal, drill, drill and more drill. Col. David Hayes of the Maine State Guard offered the services of his group to train us in the art of executing the proper turn at a given command. Lt. Gammon and Sgts. Wooley and Rumery were detailed to this training and after a short talk by the Colonel we started on the first training that every good soldier must have. Drill was held at the Armory on Stevens Avenue and all the stories and jokes about the raw recruits of our armed forces were brought very vividly to our minds as we all made right turns when we should have been making left and many of us thought that flank movements were something to do with cows and cattle. After a great deal of sweating by us and mild cursing by our instructors we began to look more and more like soldiers. Before long we were able to stand review for the visiting officers from various branches of the armed services.

Compared to the many makeshift airports used by other coastal patrol groups, Portland Municipal Airport, three miles southwest of downtown, was safe and well-equipped. There were three gravel-surfaced runways, the shortest of which was three-thousand feet long; one 50' by 120' hangar used by the Navy; and two hangars for the use of the coastal patrol, one 50' by 60' and the other 80' by 112'. As cold as the 1942-1943 winter may have been, most of the staff, except for the Maine State guardsmen who had barracks on the base, slept in their own warm beds at night.

## Louis R. Furlong

*Born and raised in Clarion, Pennsylvania, Louis R. Furlong was the twenty-six-year-old Operations Officer who scheduled the patrols and flew a regular turn himself — more than often enough to win the Air medal. He learned to fly from a barnstorming pilot based at Kramer Airport in Clarion, a stop on the first Cleveland-New York airmail route, soloing in a Monocoupe in 1935. By late 1941, he had flown over fifteen hundred hours:*

When the war came, I volunteered for the Ferry Command, as many of my friends had done, but I wore glasses and couldn't get past the physical. And waivers weren't being granted then, as they were later in the war. So another friend, Bill Culbertson, who owned a Bellanca, but who didn't have many hours, told me he'd commit his plane to the coastal patrol if I'd go along with him, so I did. The original operations

Base commander Major Milton V. Smith in civilian clothes before his appointment to the coastal patrol post in Portland, Maine (courtesy Cynthia Bessey Oakman).

officer at Portland was Glenn Rossman, a practicing local doctor who told me he couldn't spend all his time at the base, and asked me to give him a hand. After three or four months as a part-time operations officer, I was given the job full-time by the base commander, Milton V. Smith, and I served as such until the base closed.

After my arrival, I found and shared lodgings close to the airport with Wylie Apte, an old-timer who ran his own airport in North Conway, New Hampshire. For exercise I walked the three-quarters of a mile to the base each morning. I had breakfast in the canteen, which opened early enough to serve the men who had the dawn patrol. Portland Airport was a fairly new facility, and served us well. We had an excellent safety record. No lives were lost, and we had only a few minor mechanical problems. I once blew a cylinder head on a Jacobs engine and on another occasion lost part of an engine cowling but got back safely each time. As a base we totaled about twelve hundred hours of patrol time a month, averaging forty hours a day, virtually every day, even in some deplorable weather.

We didn't have a great amount of time for fun and games, but we did establish a little club in one of the Portland hotels. They kindly gave us an upstairs room, and we set up a bar and tables and chairs for playing cards and such in the evenings. We also tried to arrange a party every once in a while, sometimes at the hotel, sometimes at the base. Portland offered lots of girls to chase. Though the competition from the Navy was fierce, I think our boys did all right. Most of our fellows were older and married, so girl chasing was left to the young single guys.

When the base closed, Milt Smith asked me to do some flying for him, and I spent three months at Moosehead Lake flying seaplanes. Then I went out to California as a test pilot at Douglas Aircraft for a time. I was also the fixed base operator at Long Beach Airport for several years. Along the way I picked up an A&E license and started to fly for the airlines. After logging thirty-thousand hours flying time, I became vice president for operations of Overseas National, a charter carrier out of New York. I've been retired for some years but am now busy building a six-place amphibian I hope to fly when it's finished.

## Lucille M. Dingley

*Lucille M. Dingley and her husband Henry M. Dingley were both pilots, and were operating the airport in Auburn, Maine when the war came and put a halt to all general aviation activity within one hundred-fifty miles of the Atlantic coastline. For a time Mr. Dingley remained busy instructing CPTP students, and Mrs. Dingley was free to respond to a request that she help set up the Portland coastal patrol. Listed on the base roster as flight observer, she was, in fact, commanding officer Milton V. Smith's administrative assistant, passing along orders, preparing reports for CAP headquarters, and directing the office staff doing the base paperwork:*

When I first went down to Portland, I stayed in a hotel. Several months later, when my husband became one of the base pilots, we rented a house. Henry leased his two Waco cabin planes to the base and as part of the deal brought along our fine mechanic, Merritt R. Roakes, who was later named our base engineering officer. At the outset, the biggest problem we had was to find pilots and airplanes. Maine was then a backward state in terms of aviation development, and finding qualified pilots, and planes suitable for patrol work wasn't easy. However, the Portland Airport, while not exactly new, was perfectly adequate for our purposes, and the kind of aircraft we flew. We had no big planes

From left: Lt. C. V. Watson, intelligence officer; Lt. Louis R. Furlong, operations officer; Capt. M. V. Smith, commanding officer; Lt. William C. Mudgett, U.S. Army Ordnance Dept.; Mrs. Henry M. Dingley, base administrative head; and Lt. Edwin Nelsson, assistant operations officer (courtesy Louis R. Furlong).

requiring longer runways. Major Smith was a relaxed individual. He'd been at the airport for some years, operating a flight school and running charter flights, so he certainly knew the area and the problems our flyers would face along the coastline. My husband and I had known him because we were all pilots. Most of us at the base considered ourselves civilians, which we were, and didn't take wearing uniforms too seriously. I had a bunch of stuff on my jacket, but I don't remember if I had a "rank" or what it might have been. I bossed six girls altogether, four clerk-typists and two plotting board operators. They were a good bunch, and I believe that we had a fairly smooth operation right through until the base closed at the end of August 1943.

My husband went into the Navy then, and I served as a WASP for several months. While we were away, the Navy leased our airport and used it as an auxiliary to its Brunswick base. When the Navy pulled out in 1945, I ran the airport until my husband came home from service in 1947. I'd earned my private license long before the war, and as long as we ran our airfield I flew a lot. When we got too old to run the business we sold out. I'm eighty-five now, and Henry died about eight years ago. We'd been married for fifty-four years.

Pilot Henry M. Dingley (left) filing a report for assistant base intelligence officer Clifton S. Robinson. On the wall behind Robinson is an aircraft identifcation chart (courtesy Louis R. Furlong).

### Edward K. White

*Air Medal winner Edward K. White, a native of Belmont, Massachusetts, attended Dartmouth College, where he played football, captained the swim team, and received All American honors in the breast stroke. Three days after his graduation with the class of 1938, he went to work for one of the largest dairy firms in the eastern United States, and settled in Portland, Maine as a salesman. His flight training was gained through the CPTP after leaving college:*

In mid-1940, Bernice, my bride of three weeks, and I decided to compete for the limited number of openings in the brand new CPTP. More than two hundred of us completed a three-hours-a-night, three-nights-a-week, three-month study period, and both Bernice and I were among the nine admitted to go through the program to a private license. When Bernice soloed before I did, I was forced to explain that, after all, I had to work five days a week. I keep a story from the front page of the *Portland Press Herald*, headlined "June Bride First Woman To

Solo-Hop Here, Bernice White Masters Plane In Two Weeks," featuring a picture of her one-hundred pounds sitting in a parachute behind her instructor in a tandem Aeronca. Her husband (me, that is) was mentioned as *also* being in the program.

I then went on to take the CPTP course for instructors. Upon completion I was supposed to serve as a civilian instructor for the Air Corps. To get out of that I exited the graduation hall through a bathroom window and with rating papers in hand, drove to Portland where I was enrolled into the CAP immediately. This temporary shelter gave me almost six months to get needed flying hours, and to enjoy being with my wife and Judy, our newborn. Bernice settled into homemaking and teaching at a local elementary school. Her only piloting came later as my co-pilot on various planes we owned.

Edward K. White was an All-American swimmer at Dartmouth College. After coastal patrol service, he joined the Navy, and this is the photograph used on his ID card (courtesy Edward K. White).

I started flying regular anti-submarine patrols out of Portland Municipal Airport around August or September 1942, right when the base started up. There was a large hangar containing a minimal amount of office space, a fueling dock close to the hangar, and extensive tie-down space where most of our planes were kept. Our routine was pretty simple: put as many ships as possible in the air on three-hour patrols throughout the day. Sometimes a pilot and his observer could get in three patrols a day. I loved it, because I was logging lots of flight time, working with some really fine pilots and mechanics, and confident that I was contributing to the war effort. I was also home every night with a wonderful wife and a baby daughter. This was to change later as some boredom set in, and the urge to get closer to the war finally prevailed.

The usual patrol encompassed a triangular area limited in size by the speed of the aircraft, the slowest being the Stinson Voyager. Its 80 mph cruise around the triangle still covered nearly two hundred-fifty miles, almost all over water. Our half-hour fuel reserve was occasionally needed when a quick Maine fog made locating the field a real problem. At such times, if flying up the Fore River to our base didn't work, there was always Old Orchard beach to the south or Sanford Airport to the west. Few of our pilots were instrument rated, and our planes were inadequately equipped for instrument flight. Dead reckoning was still the order of the day.

Radio mechanic Earle B. Whittemore and the Portland "radio station." In the 1940s, transmitters and receivers were cumbersome masses of tubes, coils, condensers, and other parts — now long since replaced by miniaturized electronics (courtesy Cecil Tyler).

Speaking of Old Orchard beach, a favorite pastime when returning from the south leg of a patrol was to drop down and touch our wheels onto the hard-packed sand and "run the beach" until we pulled up and flew over the famous wooden pier that extended well out beyond the surf. We even had some claims of having flown under the pier at low tide, but this was never verified. Our fooling around was done only in the winter months, of course, when the place was deserted. As we heard of and occasionally saw sinking ships off our coastline, our zeal to pick up those periscope trails intensified. All entrances to Portland harbor were either blocked off or sealed with underwater anti-submarine nets. Most of the North Atlantic convoys were made up there, and a large naval presence was always on hand. A convoy would grow as tankers and cargo vessels crept up the coast out of New York and Boston. They hugged the shore, and their crews often cheered us as we flew low over them. Little did they know that the only weapons we had were Colt forty-fives and radios.

But the radio was an effective weapon, and often used. When we were convinced of a periscope sighting, we called in our position, and destroyers out of Portland and bombers from Brunswick Naval Air Station thirty miles north responded while we circled the spot of last sighting. The eruption of depth charges pumped our hearts as we searched for tell-tale debris. We never found any, but we took solace in the unquestioned fact that we were forcing the subs to stay well out of our designated patrol territory.

On one occasion, my co-pilot and I actually sighted one on the surface. The crew saw us at about the same time and were probably tempted to shoot us out of the sky — which would have been an easy enough exercise — but they chose instead to dive. We breathed easier as we called in our position.

During my six months with the coastal patrol, we got rubberized flotation suits and our planes were armed with small bombs. We heard that a bomb would have to explode within ten feet of a sub's conning tower to do major damage. Our chances of executing that maneuver were pretty remote. When worn, the rubber suits covered our bodies completely. Only our faces were showing. The black rubber was about an eight of an inch thick, and zipped up the front. Since the suits didn't "breathe," you were a welter of sweat in no time. They were usually discarded after the second try. Besides, there was an unconfirmed rumor that two pilots were lost at a base north of us despite their wearing the suits. They only helped you survive a *little* longer.

In February 1943 I went to Boston and signed with the Navy for special orders to fighters. To make a long, disappointing story shorter, after a few days at Corpus Christi, Texas, I was assigned as a flight instructor at Bunker Hill Naval Air Station at Peru, Indiana for the next ten months, and after that was a ferry pilot. I left the Navy after the war and rejoined the dairy company I'd left, retiring thirty-three years later as executive vice president.

Though we now live in Florida, we usually spend our summers in Maine, and I'm happy to say that Portland is once again the charming city it was before the war came and turned off all the lights at night.

\* \* \*

The Portland base history provides the best last words — none of them very flattering — on "zoot suits" and "Barracuda Bags":

> Did somebody say safety equipment? That is something we knew little about until long after. The old faithful "Mae West" was our only comfort in our ocean voyages for several months. They did give us "Barracuda Bags" which are supposedly a sort of life boat and protection from sharks. But considering the fact that we don't have sharks in these waters and the fact that to our knowledge nobody has ever been able to get into one of the things once he was in the water, our faith in them was very limited. Then too, the kit bags which were filled with everything from a pint of brandy to a needle and thread and were attached to the bags practically made it impossible to remove the whole conglomeration from the ship before it reached the bottom....
>
> Finally, right in the middle of zero weather, some superbrain thought up the "zootsuit" or, in other words, an all-rubber refrigeration covering for the flying personnel to wear in flight. A more miserable cold weather garment was never invented, but orders were orders and we wore them much to the disgust of all concerned. After a flight we felt like some mongrel addition to the clam family.... Probably the highlights of the "zootsuit" escapades were "The Man from Mars" (alias Ed White) and the midwinter swim of Bob Norton, Bill Mallory, and Walter Soule off the shore at Captain Watson's house on the Cape. They claimed they were as warm as they would have been on a day in mid-July, but knowing the boys fairly well we have our doubts. Anyway, they had a pint from the sea kit and the seal was broken, so you know what happened.
>
> Finally, after having flown these ocean patrols through six months of freezing weather and continued pleading by influential and interested officials, we were furnished with rubber life rafts which have really put our minds at ease and made the prospects of a forced landing at sea seem more like an afternoon picnic than the nightmare that had followed us hour by hour over the water. However, safety equipment or not, our flight personnel carried out every mission assigned to them with an efficiency envied by all.

## Cecil A. Tyler

*Cecil A. Tyler, a thirty-seven-year-old from South Paris, Maine, was one of the base's most experienced A&E mechanics. He began flying from a grass strip near South Paris as the part-owner of an OX-5 powered, open-cockpit*

*Waco biplane, and became an adept pilot even before obtaining his student pilot license. In the coastal patrol, however, he worked only as a mechanic, having learned the basics through an International Correspondence School course, then gaining practical experience on various previous jobs. He passed his A&E exams while serving with the coastal patrol. Tyler died in 1987, but his son Cecil A. Tyler, Jr. recalls his father's time at the Portland base:*

I was nearly eighteen, and hung around the airport quite a bit, watching Dad work, and meeting many of the people there. When Dad first joined the coastal patrol Mom and I remained in South Paris while

Sgt. Cecil A. Tyler, from South Paris, Maine, was probably the most experienced mechanic on the Portland base. Here he sits in the Waco GXE in which he first soloed (courtesy Cecil A. Tyler, Jr.).

he lived in Portland near the airport. We visited him on weekends. Once I'd enlisted in the Navy, my Mom moved down there to be with him. The Portland Municipal Airport was located on the shore of the Fore River in the "Back Bay" area — where the Portland International Airport is today. The best field in the state at the time, it had a sizable administration building, with the usual dinette, waiting room, and ticket counter for airline passengers. There was also a U.S. Weather Bureau office. The end occupied by the coastal patrol had previously been Northeast Aviation Company headquarters, as it was again after the war. The company was owned by M. V. Smith, who became our base C.O.

People at the base were real gung-ho. I remember that everyone wore their uniforms all the time, and looked real sharp. Dad always described it as an exciting period of his life, and said that he enjoyed every minute of it. One of the things I remember happened right as the base was closing down. It seems that either the Army Signal Corps or the Air Corps — I can't recall which — gave the base three brand new Taylorcraft L-2Ms. When the base was deactivated, my father bought one of them and, later, when I left the Navy after a year and a half in naval air ordnance, I came home and flew it extensively. The L-2M was a great airplane, but I don't know what the CAP used it for. Perhaps they were to be used for search and rescue over land, instead of seeking submarines. The rear seat swiveled, and with the huge expanse of windows all around, the observer had an unparalleled field of vision.

When the base shut down, Dad remained and worked as a mechanic for Northeast Aviation in the same hangar where he'd worked with the coastal patrol. He stayed with Northeast for many years, but finally the cold Maine winters became too rugged for him, so he moved to Florida and went to work as an A&E for Showalter Flying Service in Orlando. Dad made many lifelong friends in the coastal patrol and often exchanged visits with them. They'd go see him in Florida and he'd come up here with Mom to visit them. Walter Moore was a friend who later became the champion aerobatics pilot in Maine. After the war, I more or less followed in Dad's footsteps, learned to fly his Taylorcraft, then went to Florida to get what is now called the A&P license at Embry-Riddle in Daytona Beach. I returned to Massachusetts and taught aviation mechanics for forty-two years at the East Coast Aero Technical School, located at Hanscom Field near Lexington.

## Wylie Apte

*Wylie Apte was already forty-seven-years-old when he flew with the coastal patrol. Because of his age and craggy appearance, some of his fellow pilots at the base nicknamed him "the old man of the mountain." Born around North Conway, New Hampshire, Apte caught the flying bug at an early age and when he was only sixteen he built a full scale Bleriot-type airplane from drawings he saw in* Popular Mechanics. *He trucked it around and exhibited it at country fairs for five cents a person. The following year his father bought an engine for it, and young Wylie soon flew the plane successfully. His son, Wylie Apte, Jr., recalls his father's keen interests in aviation:*

Dad wasn't a stunt pilot or a wing walker or anything like that, but he was locally well known for devilishness when it came to flying. For example, when his father bought him an engine for the plane, friends said that its weight-to-horsepower ratio was too high for the plane to fly so he modified the plane and engine until it *could* fly and flight tested it himself. By the 1930s, Dad had developed his own airfield and called it White Mountain Airport. When the war came along, he had to close the airport, and because he was too old for service, he volunteered for the coastal patrol as a pure act of patriotism. Going down to Portland, he took his own Waco YKS-7 with him. His Air Medal shows that he served on coastal patrols from September 16, 1942 to October 31, 1943.

Mother didn't seem to object to his serving with the coastal patrol. It was wartime, and certain sacrifices were just sort of expected. I was eight or nine, and recall visiting Dad a couple of times at the base, and seeing him at work on the planes. He was a licensed A&E mechanic and did a lot of maintenance on the planes. I went into the hangar once and there were airplane parts scattered all over the floor. One of my best

"Eyes, right!" A lot of practice must have gone into looking this good on parade. Administration building in background (courtesy Cecil A. Tyler, Jr.).

memories was the time I had an emergency operation for appendicitis: when I came to in the hospital recovery room, there he was standing beside the bed still wearing part of his pilot's gear. He had come straight off a patrol, and to the hospital as quickly as he could.

After his service with the coastal patrol, he returned to North Conway and reopened his airport. Besides flying charter work, he began offering special "mountain scenery flights" across the northern New Hampshire ski area. When I was old enough I learned to fly there, and went on to fly for TWA — everything they had, up to and including the 747. Meanwhile, Dad's business grew steadily through the '50s, '60s, and '70s. When Dad died, I took over a thriving fixed base operation. As it has often happened, however, the urban development around the airport eventually made land so valuable that the taxes forced us to sell out. Dad was proud of his time with the CAP coastal service, and proud of the other men and women he served with.

## George S. McGowan

*George S. McGowan was twenty-nine when he joined the Portland base as a flight observer. Born in northern Maine near Ashland he had started flying lessons even before entering Colby College at Waterville. There he obtained a private pilot's license in the CPTP then left to obtain his commercial license in Schenectedy, New York. Despite his ratings and experience when he joined the coastal patrol he found they didn't need senior pilots, so he spent his year at the base flying patrols in the right-hand seat:*

By this time I was married and had a family and was working in Portland as an engineer with the Portland Gas Light Company. I flew enough patrols to win the Air Medal, and probably flew in all of the different planes we had. My wife didn't work, because we had a baby boy, but I believe that she came out to the base once for a hangar dance. That's the only socializing I recall now. I remember our having a bunch of Wacos, and our patrols seeming fairly routine. The only scare I had was with a little engine trouble one day. My pilot and I were well out over water when the engine began backfiring and missing and carrying on but it keep going and we got back to base all right. My only thoughts were *where* we might go in, not about surviving the experience or anything. We were wearing those rubberized affairs they called zoot suits. The C. O. was a stickler about that.

When the coastal patrol ended, I became a civilian flight instructor at an Air Corps base in Arcadia, Florida — Carlstrom Field, I believe — and I was there until the war was over. I then returned to Portland Gas Light Company, but flew on the weekends an instructor, earning four dollars an hour. One day just after take-off with a student, I became so ill I had to ask the student to take over. When he said he'd only had an hour or two, I managed to turn around and come back in. But that fright, and the fact that I wasn't getting rich at instructing and now had a bigger family to support, caused me to give up flying for good. But it's always fun to think back on my days with the coastal patrol.

## Richard D. Frost

*Richard D. Frost has lived in Portland all his life. With all the water in that part of the country, the bays and inlets of the Atlantic, and the many lakes of all sizes, he got into the boat business in 1928, and remained in it until early 1996, selling out at age eighty-five. He learned to fly, then naturally enough bought a Cub Coupe float plane and kept it on a local lake. When war came, he sold the Coupe to a buyer in New York State:*

When I volunteered for the coastal patrol I could have gone in either as a pilot or as a mechanic. They had plenty of flyers and I felt I could do more good as a mechanic. I wasn't a licensed A&E, but I'd been a mechanic by trade from way back. Mostly I worked on four-cylinder in-line engines like the Franklin, but also worked some on the flat-six used in the Bellanca. I didn't work on radial engines at all.

We kept the planes in such good shape that I can remember only one plane almost lost because of an engine failure. He got back to the beach, but his wheels were mighty close to the water line when he landed! We had a good place to work, a regular commercial hangar before the coastal patrol took it over, but it was a long day, more or less from dawn until late afternoon, or whenever the last flight returned from patrol. I was married, and had two children at the time, and brought my own lunches.

Our head mechanic was a good man, and I learned a lot about aircraft engines from him. We had an occasional PBY from the Brunswick Naval Air Station drop by, coming in on the runways wheels-down, but of course we did no work on them. Most of the time our coastal patrol had the exclusive use of the field.

After my discharge from the coastal patrol, I was employed by a local shipyard to work on marine engines. Then I was with the Raytheon Corporation as the first mate of a small harbor boat that carried a specially-trained crew to repair and maintain radar equipment aboard Navy ships based at Portland. We did most of our work overnight, mostly on destroyers. Forty or fifty called Portland home base. They'd come in at night and go out the next morning. I remember when the battleship *USS New Jersey* arrived. Completely blacked-out in a blacked-out harbor, it seemed enormous. We must have climbed thirty or forty feet just to get aboard. Motor launches circled it constantly during the night, and we were sharply challenged before coming alongside. That's all a long time ago now, but some memories always stick with you.

\* \* \*

## Homer A. Olsen

*Homer A. Olsen was born in 1913 on a farm outside Falmouth, Maine. A platoon sergeant in the Maine State Guard, he was assigned, along with ten or twelve of his company, to guard the base. As the head guard, he reported to the base commander, Major Milton Smith:*

Our uniforms and weapons were provided by the Maine State Guard. We all lived together in one barracks on the base itself. I stayed there, too, because I might be needed at any hour of our round-the-clock surveillance. The men took eight-hour guard watches and were rotated weekly as to shifts and posts. We had men at the base entrance, at the hangars, at the administration building, and one or two men who roved among the planes outside. I had been assigned a Jeep, and used it to get around and check on everybody to keep them alert. I left before the base closed, but while I was there, I can't recall any trouble of any kind — no attempts at sabotage or theft or anything out of the ordinary.

Capt. Merritt Roakes (left) and S/Sgt. Arthur Pothier with the engine warmer nicknamed "Gunga Din" devised and built by Cecil A. Tyler. Without it, some winter flights might never have left the ground (courtesy Cecil A. Tyler, Jr.).

Most of the guardsmen were young and single. I believe we had most of our meals at a base cafeteria, and did our own washing and ironing and such in our barracks. Our self-containment was a hardship in the sense that we didn't have much opportunity to get to know the other personnel at the base. I did, however, have a chance to go up with one of the pilots, but at the time I wasn't interested in flying and declined. My wife sometimes visited me at the base, taking time off from her job as a secretary for a local greenhouse. We didn't have children, so it was no problem for her, and I think she enjoyed seeing what was going on. Because my previous background was in heavy construction, when I left the coastal patrol I enlisted in the Seabees, and spent nearly all the rest of the war in the South Pacific teaching men in construction battalions how to use heavy equipment.

After the war, I remained in the construction business, and — strange to say — when I hit sixty, a friend took me up in his sports plane, and I was hooked! I began taking lessons in a Piper Cherokee and was half way to my private license when I decided to buy my own plane, a Cessna 172 on floats. After I got my ticket, I ended up living in a house on Little Sebago Lake, just northwest of Portland, with my Cessna sitting on the beach out front. I guess I had the plane for five or six years but my flying made my wife pretty nervous, so I finally gave it up. My present love of flying may have started with the coastal patrol, even though I declined that free ride so many years ago!

## John E. Howe

*John E. Howe was born in Bryant Pond, Maine in 1906, and spent most of his early years working on cars and planes. When a friend suggested that he join the local CAP squadron, he did. Shortly afterwards he was called to active duty with the Portland coastal patrol as an apprentice mechanic:*

Though I'd been a mechanic for years, and had my own tools and such, I was never a licensed A&E. But they needed aircraft mechanics pretty bad and I seemed to suit them — they had me work a double shift my very first day. I was married and had a son and a daughter, but they were old enough that we could leave them with my mother and her aunt while we took an inexpensive place to board in Portland. Our second son, who came along much later than our first two children, was actually born during our stay in Portland. I seem to recall the base having hangar parties every so often, with food and refreshments, and all off-duty staff were expected to attend. My wife and I went to several of them and enjoyed ourselves with the others.

I worked on most of our planes at one time or another, and usually went up with them for a check flight afterwards. I didn't particularly enjoy the flying, but then I didn't dread it either. It was just part of my job. I think they gave us surplus Army uniforms at practically no cost, and we had to sew on the red shoulder epaulets. I wanted to keep those uniforms, but as soon as I was discharged, and while I was waiting around for a couple of days for a ride back to Bryant Pond, somebody emptied my locker. They must have thought I was already gone. I liked everyone at the base, and didn't experience anybody who wasn't good to work with. I was assigned for some time to Claremont, New Hampshire, where I recruited Cadets for both the Air Corps and the CAP. I'm no longer in touch with any people I knew at Portland. Most of them were older, and are gone now.

**Thomas Z. Winther**

*Thomas Z. Winther was born and raised in Portland and was about twenty-four when he served with the coastal patrol. While working full-time days at the Bath Iron Works, he took and passed a difficult written test to win a scholarship for the CPTP, then had studied nights and flown when he could to obtain a private pilot's license. When war was declared, he became a member of a local Portland squadron and was soon taken into the new anti-submarine service. Winther was one of the few coastal patrol flyers to spot a sub close-up:*

Before my pilot and I went on this particular patrol, we'd been given a chart with an oblong-shaped area drawn on it, showing where we might expect to see U.S. Navy submarine activity. What I saw was definitely outside this area, so I'm reasonably positive it was an enemy submarine. We were flying at about five hundred feet when I saw a periscope wake as plain as day. There was no doubt about it at all. But then the sub submerged and the wake disappeared. We remained in the vicinity, however, and shortly I saw the periscope reappear. This time we dove on it, even though this was before the base had been given any bombs. Again we had a positive identification of the moving object as a periscope plume, and we saw the shadowy underwater outline of what could only have been a sub and no whale! We immediately radioed-in what we'd seen, but as it happened, the base intelligence officer was in town at a meeting and at that time no one else on base was authorized to notify nearby Army and Navy bases. So we stayed in the area without being able to do anything. By the time the intelligence officer returned, the sub was long gone. You can imagine how frustrating that whole thing was!

I wasn't involved in any forced landings, but it's a wonder, considering the weather up there. You wouldn't believe what we flew in. Fogs and fronts rolling in unexpectedly. Losing trailing antennas while feeling our way home was commonplace. Get under the ceiling and hope for the best! One joke concerned a pilot asking another pilot where he'd lost his antenna. "Believe I snagged it at the corner of Main and Chestnut Street" was the second pilot's reply.

When the weather was right, and they had time, base personnel might play some softball right on the base (courtesy Louis R. Furlong).

One of the things I remember best is going about six months without a nickel of pay. That was rough. I had quit a pretty good job in the shipyard and my wife and I weren't really prepared to tough it out that long. No one seemed to know where our pay was supposed to come from. But I stuck it out until the base closed, winning the Air Medal for persistence I suppose, then got into the Cadet program. I was still under the age limit. I finished the program, but to my chagrin was assigned as an instructor and spent the rest of the war at several Texas bases. I had badly wanted to go somewhere and fly fighters, but maybe it was just as well that I didn't. I left the Air Corps as soon as I could and went to work for the Portland Flying Service, running the Pittsfield, Maine Airport and instructing. After three years, I took a position with a non-profit trust concerned with historic preservation and land development, and remained with that until retiring eleven years ago.

## William W. Mallory

*William W. Mallory learned to fly while earning his BS degree in history at Bowdoin College in Brunswick, Maine. His first job out of college was as the fixed base operator at Brunswick Airport, while also instructing in the CPTP at Waterville, Maine. When the war came, he was twenty-six, owned a Piper Cub Coupe, but bought a Stinson Voyager to take with him when he went into the coastal patrol:*

I was there when it opened and there when it closed. Besides the flying, for which I earned the Air Medal, I helped out in other ways. Mainly I'd describe myself as a kind of expediter, helping to obtain certain hard-to-find parts and supplies. As the fixed base operator at Brunswick, I'd gotten to know a lot of people and I just got on the phone with so-and-so and said here's what I want, when can you send it? As a pilot I didn't experience much excitement other than for one forced landing on Little York Beach off Boone Island. The plane came to a stop with one wheel on the sand and one wheel in the water. It was lucky we didn't have to ditch, because this happened in December, and the ocean was colder than hell.

The chunky Waco cabin plane was another of the mainstay aircraft used for coastal patrol at nearly every base from Maine to Mexico (courtesy Louis R. Furlong).

There was one occasion where something worse might have happened. One of the Florida coastal patrol bases had lost a couple of Stinson Voyagers when the spinners flew off into the arcs of the propellers and splintered them. So orders came down to remove all the spinners — as far as I know, with no research into the matter at all. I argued with our chief mechanic that taking off the spinners would only expose the propeller hubs to rain and water, causing them to swell on their shafts and split. His response, naturally, was that orders were orders. Some time later, I was out on patrol when my engine seemed to start running rough so I returned. The prop had just been varnished, but sure enough there was a nice big "lift" to the varnish the whole length of the prop where a crack had begun to develop. I asked the chief how he was going to argue that away. After forty-five minutes of wedging that swollen prop off the shaft, he had to concede I was right. Within two hours, all our Voyagers had their prop spinners replaced.

When I first went to Portland, I lived for a while with a private family, then moved into the Eastland Hotel. The airport had a regular restaurant, and I took most of my meals there, though I sometimes ate at different places around town as well. Brunswick is quite near Portland, so I knew the town well, and I generally liked it. The municipal airport was not the greatest — although it was the best in Maine. The weather, as everyone knows, wasn't so hot, either. There was fog and more fog, and we often flew in minimal weather, *and below.* I had previously known Milt Smith, our commanding officer, and he was tops. Though we never lost a man flying out of Portland, one of our pilots, Raoul E. Souliere, later lost his life while flying a searchlight mission down in Virginia.

When the Portland coastal patrol ended, I flew some courier service for the Navy out of the Brunswick Naval Air Station, then spent two and a half years in Burma as a volunteer ambulance driver for the American Field Service. The war was over when I returned home, and I married in January 1946. I flew no more and neither did my little Stinson Voyager — while I was in Burma, a local CAPer did something he shouldn't have done and crashed in the ocean, killing himself and destroying my plane. I got into the insurance claims business, and wound up living in New Haven and Greenwich, Connecticut, and working in Manhattan.

## Paul M. Bessey

*Paul M. Bessey, a graduate of the Lawrence Academy at Groton, Massachusetts, earned his pilot's license at age eighteen at the Portland Airport, then managed by his older brother Edward C. Bessey. The year was 1934. The following April, through no fault of his own, the young Bessey suffered the only ditching of his long aviation career. As described in local newspapers:*

> Pounded and lashed by giant combers that threatened disaster at any moment two young Portland fliers were rescued from their water-logged airplane off Sea Point Beach, Me., late today by the Portsmouth station of the coast guard. The plane, owned and piloted by Paul Bessey, 19, of Portland, and with Arnold Morris of 72 Chestnut street as passenger, was en route from Boston, where Bessey purchased it today, to Portland. Off Whaleback Light motor trouble developed from a clogged fuel line, and then the engine failed. Bessey set the ship down among the giant seas that were still raging from the recent northeaster. The ship, an amphibian, landed all right, in

spite of the high waves, and he let go the small anchor, hoping that it would hold until help arrived.... [it did not, and just before the plane struck the rocks] ... The partially undressed men were taken off the seaplane by the coast guard none the worse for wear just as they were ready to plunge into the water and swim for the beach  The plane was only slightly damaged and taken to Portland by truck.

Not many men have flown open cockpit biplanes in 1920s-style raccoon coats, but Paul M. Bessey was something of a free-ranging spirit (courtesy Cynthia Bessey Oakman).

Paul Bessey is dead, but his daughter, Cynthia Oakman, has kept his flying scrapbook, and parts of his coastal patrol experience are highlighted in it, namely, that he joined the Portland base on September 28, 1942 and remained until February 16, 1943. In less than six months, 1st Lt. Bessey flew more than two hundred hours of patrol missions, easily earning one of the Air Medals that were awarded individually to twenty-two members of the Portland patrol base at an August 12, 1948 ceremony in Portland's Lafayette Hotel. All medals were presented by Colonel William G. Booth, National Deputy CAP Commander.

In February 1943, Bessey enlisted in the Navy, then earned his naval aviator's wings at the Corpus Christi Naval Air Station. After service at several other stations, he was with the Navy's Air Ferry Squadron One shuttling planes up and down the east coast and between the Atlantic and Pacific until the war ended. He remained in the Naval Reserve and was recalled during the Berlin Airlift as an instructor at NAS Pensacola. He left the Navy in 1959, then worked in private industry until his death in 1984 of "Lou Gehrig's" disease.

As did many coastal patrol aviators, Paul M. Bessey went from that service into one of the branches of the military — Bessey chose the Navy (courtesy Cynthia Bessey Oakman).

---

Base officers, pilots, and observers who served at least one month at CAPCP#19 and who are not elsewhere mentioned in the text of this chapter include: Hiram W. Berry, James F. Black,* Edgar P. Cate, Fred S. Catir,* Ellsworth H. Chadbourne,* Lester P. Chick,* George C. Clement,* Charles L. Cragin, Edward G. Dube, Jr., Roger P. Dube, Raymond D. J. Fortin,* Prentiss Godfrey, Audrey L. Goodheart,* Elbert C. Isom,* Howard B. Kaler, Charles S. Kohler,* Norton H. Lamb,* William N. Lacourse,* Charles P. Loring,* Kenneth W. MacKenzie, James G. MacPherson, Loring E. Miller,* John B. Nutter, Robert D. Palmer,* Carroll E. Philbrick,* Albert M. Reese,* Clifton S. Robertson, Arthur J. Roderick, Eldon L. Skillings,* Willis L. Stahlman, Edwin P. Stiles,* Hebert Sutton,* Edward Tomlinson,* Guy B. Walker, and Reginald H. Williams.* Asterisk indicates Air Medal winner.

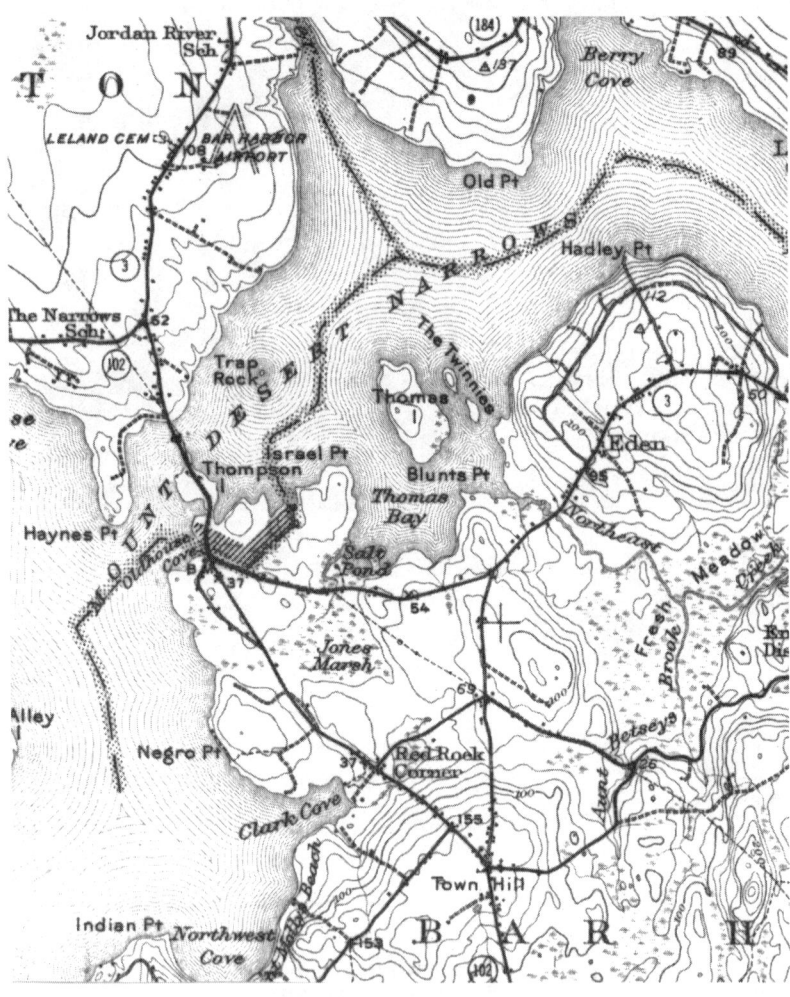

The triangular symbol for the Bar Harbor Airport can be located on this map just north of the Mount Desert Narrows in the town of Trenton, not Bar Harbor. Given the frequent fogs that shrouded the Maine coast, Bar Harbor coastal patrol flyers had to be pretty good at dead-reckoning navigation (source: 1942 United States Geological Survey map).

# 20
# Bar Harbor, Maine

The northernmost of all the patrol bases, the one at Bar Harbor, Maine covered the Atlantic coast from the Canadian border southwestward to the limits of the Portland coastal patrol area, a bee-line distance of approximately one hundred and twenty miles. Unlike their more fortunate counterparts at southern bases, the airmen from Bar Harbor could expect to find no wide sandy beaches or welcoming warm waters awaiting them should trouble develop while on patrol. Instead, they were confronted by a rocky coastline continuously and deeply indented by bays and inlets and marked by numerous large and small islands — and water too cold for swimming even during the summer months.

The Bar Harbor base was activated on August 22, 1942, and its first missions were dispatched on the fifth of September. The field was actually at Trenton, Maine, nine miles northwest of Bar Harbor. It was built in 1934-36 and consisted of two short runways and an eighty-foot by one hundred-foot hangar. In May 1942 the Civil Aeronautics Administration began building three new runways, and the Navy, well aware of the location's strategic value, leased the airport and four hundred additional acres. On December 12, 1943 the airfield would be commissioned as an auxiliary of the Brunswick Naval Air Station.*

Meanwhile the men and women of the coastal patrol took over and began creating a fully functional base out of practically nothing. A two-page Bar Harbor base "history" included in the excellent Portland base

---

* Brunswick Naval Air Station included both a seaplane parking apron with a ramp into Frenchman Bay and a mooring mast for blimps. British Fleet Air Arm Corsair fighter squadrons used the field at times in 1944 and 1945 to practice simulated carrier landings. Today, as the Hancock County-Bar Harbor Airport, nothing remains of the World War II base except for the seaplane ramp, now used only for boats.

history describes what the first arrivals found:

> There was plenty of space, and beyond that the magnificent view that Maine is noted for, but little else. This was during the last week in August, 1942 and the [base operations] log reads that the entire facilities of the Base included one hangar, a canteen, a small building used by the guards, and outdoor sanitary (in)conveniences. Even this list sounds more impressive than it really was. There was a canteen, to be sure, but no staff to manage it, and therefore, no food in it. The hangar looked even larger than its floor measurement [would indicate, because] there was little inside it! But there was plenty of room for improvement, and soon, the improvement began.

Everybody pitched in. As new men arrived, each was assigned to help build the necessary new structures — an administration building housing the base commander, Major James G. King of West Allis, Wisconsin; a combined operations-intelligence building containing a radio room, pilots' ready room, and canteen; and guard, radio, and supply shacks. The base "history" continues:

> The entire time of the personnel was not spent in the building program. Daily classes, supervised by Major George Noland, AAC, who was assisting in the formation of the Base, were preparing the crews for routine patrols. Regular hours of duty were an unheard-of luxury. A pilot dug a few yards of ditch — and Maine digs hard — helped shingle part of a roof, attended a class, flew a patrol, and then grabbed a sandwich and a few cups of coffee, and took over Officer of the Day duty. If the guards weren't there, he stood guard; he carried wood for fires; he did everything and anything that needed to be done. A pilot in name only! The canteen problem was solved by Red Cross volunteers from neighboring towns, who assumed preparation of meals and lunches, arriving at the Base with a trailer packed with home-cooked food, and improved the morale of the personnel considerably.

## Oscar H. Ginnow

*One of the early arrivals at the Bar Harbor base, and an eventual winner of the Air Medal, was twenty-eight-year-old pilot Oscar H. Ginnow of Omro, Wisconsin, a village twelve miles from Oshgosh, now famous for hosting the world's greatest air shows. A serious accident in a home-built sled powered by an engine-driven propeller encouraged him to begin taking flying lessons:*

What the hell, I'd already been smashed up sledding. My first lessons were at Leonard Larson's airport, only a mowed-down hay field, that I'd been told was the first airfield in Wisconsin. I soloed in a little 40 hp plane that cost six dollars an hour for lessons, then later rented larger planes to improve my ratings. After a lot of hours, I took a test flight with Steve Wittman, the famous aircraft designer and race pilot, and he gave me some instruction on spinning a Waco. When Pearl Harbor came along, I had my ratings in a 215 hp SM-80 Stinson and in a 220 hp Waco biplane. Classified 4-F due to damage from my sledding accident, I joined the CAP and, with my wife, made the long trip to Bar Harbor.

The scene there was quite unique: the streets were dark because of the drawn shades at all the windows, the top halves of all the automobile headlights covered with black masking tape, and every business dark at night. It was altogether eerie by comparison to our home in Wisconsin. If these things were not done, of course, the light from the city might silhouette ships passing by in the night and make them easy targets for waiting German submarines. My wife and I lived in part of a two-story frame house in Bar Harbor, and Gardner Reed, a flight observer and native of Bar Harbor, lived nearby. We enjoyed long scenic drives on Mt. Desert Island, visiting Cadillac Mountain, Eagle Lake, Southwest Harbor, and so forth — all part of Acadia National Park.*

Many of the roads were closed off by the Army, but the guards recognized our uniforms, and soon our faces, and we could go wherever we wanted to. Our best friends during our stay there were H. Garner ("Nick") and Dottie Nichols, and Roy R. and Viola Fontaine. We swam at the swanky Bar Harbor Club, went canoeing, and hiked all over the place. I have a photograph of Gardner Reed posing with the "bear" that probably shortened the life of Leslie Eichler, a pilot from Milwaukee, Wisconsin,** by several years and gave him some gray hairs. Some of the boys who were on guard duty one night thought they would have some fun so they hung this bear skin rug over a saw horse, and set it in front of a door that Les would come out of. The boys of the guard will never forget that night, and I guess Les won't either.

The weather and visibility at that latitude were often pretty bad, and fog and possible carburetor icing were constant hazards. Roy Fontaine, a milkman from New Haven, Connecticut, and I were out on

---

* Two-thirds of this beautiful island off the Atlantic coast (some 31,000 acres) were designated as the Acadia National Park in 1919. From the top of its 1,532-foot Mount Cadillac, an early morning visitor will see the first rays of sunrise to fall on the United States every day. During the war, the mountain summit was closed to civilian visitors and an Army squad posted there made sure no spies used the mountain to broadcast messages to enemy submarines.

** Besides the C.O. James King, and pilots Oscar Ginnow and Leslie Eichler, five other Wisconsin natives served at Bar Harbor, all as pilots: Elroy P. Campbell of Marinette, Ralph A. Klatt of Beaver Dam, and Clarence J. Nielson, Archie R. Fuller, and Walter M. Petersen, all of Racine. Klatt and Petersen were Air Medal winners. Four other Wisconsin men served at Saint Simons Island, and one served at Atlantic City.

patrol one day when it turned bad. This meant high seas and poor visibility. In a short while, we were advised to return to base. Some hours later the weather cleared and the same plane we'd had was dispatched again. Welles Bishop of Meriden, Connecticut and William Hites of Jamestown, New York were flying it, and they went down in the sea. Our flight surgeon said that they couldn't have survived more than twenty minutes, even in their zoot suits. Rescue boats arrived after about two hours and found one of the men. In attempting to retrieve the frozen body with grappling hooks, the straps of the Mae West broke and the body slid back into the sea, never to be found again.

Pilot Oscar H. Ginnow was one of several Wisconsin men serving at Bar Harbor. Because of injuries resulting from a sledding accident, he could not meet Army Air Corps standards and opted for the coastal patrol (courtesy Oscar H. Ginnow).

I only had one little problem myself. Out on patrol I noticed that my engine suddenly sounded different. I checked the magnetos and found one inoperative. I called the base and told them what the trouble was, and told them I thought I could get back home. They thought otherwise and told me to land at a desolate intermediate air strip where we would stay overnight. But then, after we landed, two Jeeps arrived, one with men to stand guard over the plane, the other to take us back to the airfield. As it was dark by then, we were dropped off at an inn in Cherryfield for the night, and next morning the fellow in the Jeep picked us up again for the ride home. Again, one hazy summer morning when

I was flying wing position I saw that my lead ship hadn't noticed an oil slick, so I dropped down for a close look and became pretty certain that a sub had just submerged in the area. I called base to ask that a Navy blimp with listening devices be sent out to check.

Observer Gardner A. Reed poses with the fearsome beast that in the dark of night confronted a very "tenderfoot" officer from Wisconsin — the bear rug mounted on a sawhorse looked convincingly real (courtesy Oscar H. Ginnow).

However, the blimp crew had just returned to base, as the morning was the best time for it to land. A submarine was thought to have been seen in the area several times that day, but I don't know what actions the Navy may have taken. Since we shared the same base, we coastal patrol fellows were often called out early in the mornings to help land the blimp. Plenty of men were needed to hang onto the long lines that hung down from it, and lead it to its mooring place.

Something unique to the Bar Harbor base, I suspect, was our dropping packages to lighthouse keepers and their families. Theirs is such a lonely business that our friendships began just by our flying past close enough to wave to them. In time we wrapped boxes of candy, newspapers, and other items to drop to them, and I know they greatly appreciated it. The lighthouse tender at Machias Seal Island, a collection of rocks barely larger than a football field, and about twelve miles from the mainland, was a fellow named Harvey M. Benson. After the war, when I visited them, his wife and son told me that the foghorn and light might not be turned off for six weeks at a time. No wonder they enjoyed the distraction of our gifts from the sky.

* * *

The two-page base history elaborates most humorously on "the long night of the bear and Les Eichler" mentioned by Oscar Ginnow:

> On a certain evening, very early in the spring of 1943, a pilot hailing from the gullible West reported for night O.D. duty. Darkness came early those days, and the nights were long and lonely. Our pilot was armed, however, and ready for whatever might happen. Strangely enough, something did occur that needed his entire attention and bravery. Nearing midnight, and time to take weather observation, stepping out into solid blackness, the pilot aimed his flashlight in the general direction of the weather box and sighted two bright eyes. He immediately stepped back into the office to reconnoiter. That didn't look good to him. Giving the matter consideration, he decided to confirm his suspicions, and if he was right in his surmise, to get help. One more quick look proved he was right, a bear was waiting just outside the door. The O.D. decided the bear couldn't be waiting for him, so he called the guardhouse and asked for some help. The guards later said that before calling them, the pilot had made two or three feeble attempts to fire his gun at the animal, but lost either courage or aim. The guards arrived, assured the O.D. that a bear that size wasn't worth ammunition, and rolled up their sleeves, grasped a knife and advanced to the sawhorse, overthrowing the bearskin they had previously draped there.... One O. D. will never hear the last of the bear facts.

## Lawrence A. Pidgeon

*Lawrence A. Pigeon, originally from East Windsor, Connecticut, served at both the Atlantic City and Bar Harbor bases, but longest at Bar Harbor where he was operations officer. Pigeon began his coastal patrol assignment in Atlantic City on April 24, 1942 and ended it at Bar Harbor on March 25, 1943 with more than enough hours on patrol to win the Air Medal. Years later, he recalled two incidents at the Maine base:*

> In the late fall of 1942 I was in charge of flight operations and preparing to close the base at sundown. A flight of two Navy SNJs had just departed their base in Rockland, Maine. A short time later, just as darkness was setting in, one plane returned and reported that his sister ship had ditched just off shore about one hundred yards, and about twenty miles down the coast. I dispatched a search plane equipped with flares and the navy pilot aboard to locate the area. In the meantime I was able to contact our base commander, Captain

King, who had gone into town. He immediately organized a search party from the Naval Base to drive down the coastal highway to the accident scene. A flare from our search plane was seen and the search party rescued one pilot who had made it to shore but was unconscious, suffering from hypothermia, but who later made a complete recovery in the Naval base Hospital. [Pidgeon's account is unclear as to what happened to the other naval aviator.]

The second event occurred late in the winter of 1942-43 when I was on duty in flight operations. The weather was poor all up and down the coast, with poor radio communications on 3105 K.C.s. Our radio operator called me into the radio room to listen to a plane a long distance down the coast coming in clearly, obviously on skip-distance. The plane was trying to contact his base with a mayday call to report a plane ditched at sea. When it was obvious he was not receiving or reaching anyone, I started to relay all his transmissions on a "priority one" on our teletype to Coastal Defense Command. A short time later, Defense Command answered that a rescue mission was on the way. Later they called again to announce a successful rescue and to say we were the only ones who had received the distress calls.

## Mrs. Lawrence Pigeon

*Not long before reporting to the Bar Harbor base, twenty-seven-year-old Lawrence Pigeon had married Dorothy Ellsworth, also a native of East Windsor, Connecticut.\* He arranged ahead of time that his bride would become one of the base's two plotting board operators. Dorothy Pigeon now recalls:*

I believe it was fall when we got to Bar Harbor and rented a house there. I definitely remember that Larry and I spent a lot of time stoking the coal-burning furnace (it went out once while we were at work, and what a time we had starting it again). The house had an extensive library, and that was great because we both spent many evening hours reading, and listening to the radio. Many of the people socialized among themselves quite a bit, but after our long days at the base we weren't reluctant to retire early, especially if we had to be at the base for the dawn patrol. Driving at night on icy or snow-covered roads was a little tricky, so we had to leave early, and go slow.

\* More Bar Harbor base officers and air crewman came from Connecticut than from any other state, including the host state of Maine. Among those not otherwise mentioned in this chapter are Theodore B. Coleman, William B. Day, Charles E. Drazen, Sumner H. Foster, Meyer E. Garber, William T. Gilbert, Jr., Raymond H. Goodrich, George R. Gyurkovics, Louis C. Hall, Frederic S. Harold, Michael Jellen, Gilbert Lamb, John L. Maloney, Ernest L. Markham, Clarence A. Martel, Elliott P. Miller, Bruno A. Oskinis, Sherman Rocklen, Pascal C. Stannard, Raymond V. Thomas, Richard Van Lear, and John T. Walker. Jellen, Van Lear, and Walker were Air medal winners. Seventeen enlisted personnel were also from Connecticut.

The other plotting board operator — I think her name was Ruth Bedford — and I took turns, if I did the morning shift, she did the afternoon shift, or vice versa. My task was to move toy metal airplanes around on a grid map mounted on a large table according to the grid coordinates the crews called in every half hour. There wasn't much to it. I remember spending much of my time just gabbing with other people. I wasn't allowed to help out at the radio because I didn't have a radio license. In December, we had a terrible fire, and our radio and plotting board operation was relocated temporarily to a makeshift office in a corner of the hangar.

Larry and I left the base about the end of March 1943, basically because he wanted to get his multi-engine rating. I know Major King hated to lose his operations officer, but he didn't stand in Larry's way. I don't remember too many of the fellows, but Briggs Cunningham, one of the pilots, comes to mind mostly because he was a wealthy Philadelphia "mainliner" who treated the entire base to a lobster dinner on one occasion. That was fun. And who could forget "Mose"? I think his name was Moseley, and he was a genuine character. In any case, Larry got his multi-engine rating and began flying to Alaska and the Aleutians with Northwest Airlines for the Air Transport Command. That was pretty rugged flying. After the war, he flew thirty-three years for Northwest, and amassed tens of thousands of hours. Over the years we raised five children, and owned several planes. Larry died in 1995, and he was always proud of his service with the coastal patrol.

\* \* \*

The awful fire recalled by Dorothy Pigeon occurred December 10. The calamity and its aftermath are described in the short base history:

> December 10, and the entire personnel electrified by an alert! "Come to the Base — at once!" What could have happened? Many feared the worst, and were not disappointed. They arrived to find those cherished buildings on which they had counted every shingle — every nail — a mass of smoking ruins. It was a low point in the morale of Base 20, but before the day was over, the smoking timbers had been dragged to a snow bank, the ground was cleared, and plans were underway for the erection of new buildings.
>
> This time, experienced pilot-carpenters and observer-painters were ready for the job, and before spring, CAP 20 was comfortably housed in well-built offices, with a real pilot's lounge, radio tower and canteen. During the building operations, no official duty was slighted; no possible patrol missed, and all routine work kept up-to-date. If the alarm clock failed on a dark, snowy morning, as they sometimes

do, the latecomer knew the routine. He reported in, took an ax or saw and started for the woodpile. Usually the alarm clock worked better the next dawn duty! The neatness of the grounds by spring testified to the numerous "details" assigned by Operations. Every man was proud of the Base, and willing to make it "tops."

Other aspects of the rebuilding are told in *Sank Same*. There the story goes that base commander James King immediately took his men into the woods where they cut enough logs to start reconstruction the next day, while the townspeople of Bar Harbor and Ellsworth were so impressed by the members of the coastal patrol base that they raised five hundred dollars to help buy the things which couldn't be found in the woods — like nails, hardware, roofing paper, and plumbing supplies. During it all, base personnel assisted in the midwinter rescue of a Navy flier down at sea far off the rocky Maine coast:

> A nearby naval air base notified the CAP unit that Lieutenant John Shelley, of Wellesley, Massachusetts, had been missing since early afternoon, and that his last radio report to the base had been made from somewhere off to the north of Bar Harbor. An icy wind blew across the field from the Narrows as Dave Emerson, of Coventry, Kentucky, and Lewis Pfouts, of Burghill, Ohio, took off in the dark, roared over Hulls Cove just skimming the tops of the cottage roofs and headed out across Frenchman Bay. The lights of Winter Harbor twinkled at them from off to the left, and down below, near Bar Island, a little white sloop beat a laborious course for home through the scud kicked up by the cold wind. It was no night for anybody to be down at sea.
>
> Once out over the tumbling ocean, the fliers dropped down until they were only fifty feet above the water. Even at that altitude, it would be almost impossible to spot a swimmer in the darkness, and difficult even to see a plane, if the plane was still afloat. But they could try. Flying on parallel courses a half-mile apart, back and forth, back and forth, they covered a hundred and fifty square mile section of the ocean. They were about to turn back when they spotted the Navy amphibian, badly broken up, wallowing in the trough of a big sea. Surface craft, notified by radio, picked up the aviator and his plane, and the CAP fliers returned to their base. They got home at 4 a.m., groped their way down through the blackness to make a safe landing, wrapped themselves in blankets, and turned in right there in the plane. Next morning they were working once more with hammer and saw.

This somewhat tamer version of the same search and rescue appeared in the February 19, 1943 Civil Air Patrol "Bulletin":

Lt. John Shelley of Wellesley, Mass., was saved off the coast of Maine last week after his plane had been spotted in the water from CAP planes, according to an Associated Press dispatch. A companion Navy plane came into a CAP field and the Navy men were flown as observers in two CAP ships to search for the missing aircraft. After it was found, a CAP plane went out to drop flares. Thus guided, 6 townsmen from Surrey, Me., drove along icy highways and went out in a small boat to rescue Lt. Shelley. The CAP pilots on the missions were Lts. David Emerson, South Coventry, Conn., and Lewis Pfouts, Burghill, Ohio. They took off after dark without landing lights and returned to a dark field. Naval authorities commended CAP for its part in the rescue which is one of many incidents along the coast in which CAP has saved personnel of other services.

## Julian P. O'Leary

*Julian P. O'Leary, a twenty-two-year-old pilot from South Dartmouth, Massachusetts, came to the base after serving as an American Field Service ambulance driver for fifteen months with British forces based in Egypt. His learning about and joining the base could almost be called coincidental:*

I'd come up to Bar Harbor in the spring of 1943 on my honeymoon, and while I was there I heard about the coastal patrol base and their need for pilots. Since I'd got my private license way before the war, soloing a Piper Cub when I was sixteen, I applied and was accepted at once. My new wife was all in favor of my decision and we rented an apartment in Bar Harbor. At that time, there was plenty of space available. The local people treated all of us coastal patrol people beautifully. While the coastal patrol was supposedly hush-hush, everyone knew what our mission was and could guess at the dangers involved with over-water flying. My wife and I missed the fire at the base, but we heard a lot about it.

I flew mostly Stinson Voyagers, and I remember having only one scare. Returning from a mission, we seemed to run out of gas, and I landed on a narrow strip of sandy beach. It was probably a matter of carburetor icing. After sitting there a while, I got the engine going again, and we flew back to base with no further problem. What little I knew of it then was, that if you took off without carburetor heat, you'd usually come back down in a hurry! The base had other forced landings, but they were all "good" because everyone walked away from them. When I was there we didn't wear zoot suits, just life preservers, but I was never really worried about flying over water. There was no point to worrying. You just did it. When the base closed, I became re-associated with the company I'd been with before the war, a cordage manufacturer in New Bedford. I continued to fly, accumulating a thousand or so hours flight time and owning several airplanes over the years. I remember my time with the coastal patrol as a very pleasant part of my life. The flying was always great, even when it was challenging. We enjoyed a good airport with paved runways, a pilot's lounge, well-maintained airplanes, and good leadership. It's a pleasant surprise to learn that someone's finally writing the whole coastal patrol history.

The 20th Patrol Force base emblem was this frock-coated radio operator-pilot astride a bomb falling on a German submarine. The original artist is unknown (courtesy Ms. Sharron L. Nance).

## David T. Farrelly

*A good account of the early days at Bar Harbor is David T. Farrelly's monograph, "How I Got Into World War Two." Born in 1917 in Woodstock, Vermont, Farrelly learned to fly in 1936 on a 40 hp Taylor Cub. After frustrated efforts to fly for the Lafayette Escadrille (prior to the 1940 fall of France), the RCAF, the RAF Ferry Command, and finally for the U.S. military, he joined the CAP, drawing serial number 1-3-32: 1st Corps Area, 3rd state (Vermont) and personal number 32. His orders to report for active duty at the Portland base came September 3, 1942, but when he arrived he found that Bar Harbor needed him more, so he drove north the next day:*

> I arrived at Bar Harbor Airport about 5:00 p.m. as they were winding up the day. The commanding officer, Major James B. King, told me, "Go find a place to live and come in tomorrow and we will sign you up." So I went back to Ellsworth, Maine with a few of the other pilots who had found lodging there. One of them was renting a room from the wife of the County Sheriff and they had another room over the garage. I took it. The only hotel in town had been taken over by the Army Reconnaissance Detachment that patrolled the coast roads in Jeeps to "prevent," or at least observe, any German landings. So we all stayed in tourist homes in Ellsworth, or places in Bar Harbor town. We never had barracks. I reported the next morning at 8:00 a.m. as ordered. At 8:30 a.m. I held up my right hand and was sworn in by Commander King and his adjutant. I was commissioned a First Lieutenant and pilot. I was finally officially in World War II....
>
> So I was now a pilot and ready for duty. At 10:00 a.m. I was assigned to a Fairchild 24 as an observer with an experienced pilot to get acquainted with the patrol area. We were assigned to the Northern Patrol Area that contained the Bay of Fundy, out past Cape Sable at the southern tip of Nova Scotia and extending as far south as Isle Au Haut and back to the Maine coast. The pilot was a Yale student in the Navy Reserves waiting to be called up. He was an excellent navigator and used a slide rule, which impressed me very much.... He showed me the lighthouses, islands, power lines, and rocks we might try to make with engine failure. With this patrol we flew as high as a thousand feet — primarily to get radio communications with base as we still had the old pre-war radio the planes came equipped with. I had very little radio experience and all I heard was hash. I was to get used to it and learn to read the faint voices through the static, but it took some time. There was a lot of "Say again!" We didn't say "Repeat" as that was an artillery command to keep firing. I wish I could remember dates and names as well as I can remember incidents and trivia. This patrol was my first one and my first time out of sight of land over a real ocean. I was too interested to have any fear....
>
> My second day started early in the morning but I was not on the dawn patrol yet. This time I was assigned to pilot a Stinson 10-A and was wing-man to another pilot. This time we got a little further into the Bay of Fundy, up to Eastport where the tide was out and some ships were grounded a couple of miles from water. With those forty foot tides and the tidal "bore" this was normal. We were briefed that German subs would get into the Bay and lay on the bottom during

daylight sometimes, to come out at dusk to find convoys and ships making solo runs. Most of the few encounters we had with subs was near the mouth of the Bay....

The third day of my World War II duty I was again posted on the second morning patrol in the north area. By this time I was considered a "veteran" and was assigned the Stinson 10-A as lead pilot with a new pilot for wing-man. Whoo boy!!! I now really had responsibility. Not only to get my own plane and observer back, but another plane and crew too! I was supposed to find any enemy in the area and protect our own ships at sea. And I hardly knew where I was or what I was doing there.... Three days before I had just been a member of CAP with no rank whatsoever. I had a minimum of uniforms. Can't even remember when I got my 1st Lt. bars. Maybe somebody gave or loaned me a set....

Group identified in Ginnow photo album as "Flight Crew F." At far left is Sherman T. Nance, and at far right is Oscar H. Ginnow (courtesy Ms. Sharron Nance, Sherman Nance's daughter).

After the first three days we settled into more or less routine. We did get some more pilots and observers. We had one amphibian, a single-engine Sikorsky "Duck" belonging to Briggs Cunningham who, if I remember right, was one of the originals at Atlantic City. He was very wealthy and had a summer home at Bar Harbor. He brought with him a couple of one hundred pound practice bombs on his wing struts, but we had not been authorized or cleared for bombs yet. As one of the three seaplane pilots on the base, I occasionally took the "Duck" on patrol. Because of its long range, we used it when we had to take a convoy, or one of the "Queens" making a solo run, north to where the Canadian patrols out of Nova Scotia took over.... Come winter, Briggs took his Sikorsky to Florida, possibly to Panama City, I'm not sure, and there was commended for saving the lives of a ship's crew. Later, he won an America's Cup Race for the United States and raced his own car, the "Cunningham," at Le Mans.*

\* \* \*

More recently, David Farrelly, Air Medal winner, has added anecdotes about particular pilots he knew at Bar Harbor. One concerns Oscar Ginnow and twenty-five other base members who were sent on their way to Fort Lewis, Washington to reorganize themselves as TTU #17.** Pilots and flight observers flew in three-plane formations, while most of the ground personnel drove out. Bad weather held back the flyers so that those who went by car got there first. Farrelly recalls his friend Ginnow flying through a high mountain pass in bad weather, determined to catch up with his wife:

Our flight from Missoula, Montana to Spokane, Washington called for negotiating Lookout Pass (4,725') through the Bitterroot Range near Mullan, Idaho. After two days of waiting for the ceiling to lift enough to try the pass, Ozzie was the first to take off. The weather was closing in by the time we started up the canyon to the pass, and when he hit the crest the ceiling was down to a hundred feet. He went through anyway, and according to the CAA weatherman, Ozzie practically taxied through the pass and almost hit his parked car. I was fifth in line going into the pass, and was it narrow! A creek, a railroad, and a highway squeezed together, competing for room. We were all flying right under the bottom of the overcast. The plane behind Ozzie turned around, as did the next two. To avoid a mid-air collision, I had to execute a wingover. There was no time even for a sharp turn. We all got back to Superior, Montana, and spent another two or three days in the one restaurant-bar there trying to date the local girls. But Ozzie had made it!

---

\* Born in Cincinnati, Ohio, Briggs S. Cunningham was thirty-five and living in Green Farms, Connecticut, when he reported to CAPCP #1 on May 18, 1942. He stayed there until August 4, 1942 then served a short time at CAPCP #3 before transferring to Bar Harbor and taking his Sikorsky amphibian with him. CAP records show that he stayed with the coastal patrol until August 31, 1943, and was awarded the Air Medal in 1948, but do not mention any details of his service at Bar Harbor.

\*\* Led by base commander James B. King, they were operations officer George Farr; engineering officer Michael Jellen; communications officer Chester W. Sprague; pilots Tom V. Conner, David T. Farrelly, Oscar H. Ginnow, Vincent M. Guilfoyle, Ralph A. Klatt, Frank E. Light, Frederick F. Ludwick, Jr., Peter C. Romero, Albert P. Stock, and John T. Walker; observers Harold G. Nichols and Gardner A. Reed; mechanics Leslie C. Brewer, Irvin H. Hammond, Michael Popovich, Clarence B. Rand, Arthur L. Seavey, and Clifford W. Whalen; technical section head Alton L. Marshall; and clerks Harold F. Carter and Gladys M. Pier.

Farrelly has also added various recollections of over-water navigation and his need to learn more about it:

The first few patrols I didn't have any problems. As I remember it, the incident that really got me into taking navigation more seriously was in my second month. I was the lead plane in our flight and we started over the mouth of, and into, the Bay of Fundy and then out to Cape Sable, Nova Scotia, where we started a search pattern southward. We knew of no convoy this day, but our intelligence officer did not always alert us to one on its way. So we made wide sweeps out into the steamer lanes. This made us a little late heading for home.

S/Sgt. Harold F. ("Fritz") Carter, Jr. and Sgt. Prisicilla Bailey both worked in the administrative section. Duckboard sidewalks reflect the temporary nature of the base (courtesy Oscar H. Ginnow).

In twenty minutes we should have raised a lighthouse. It wasn't there. It wasn't there a half hour later either. But I knew I had another twenty or thirty minutes of gas, and I'd learned not to quit a course that would eventually hit a landmark, even if it wasn't the right one. So I kept the heading that I thought would bring us to the bay entrance on the north side of Mt. Desert Island. I knew we had some headwind, so I told my wingman to follow me, and got down closer to the water and throttled back. Just then, a headland showed right ahead. Unfortunately, it looked more like the mountain on Isle Au Haught, almost fifty miles from home. How could I be that far off?

There was a beach on the north side of the island so I headed around to the right. We were well below the peak, and didn't have much visibility, but it was the right move. The Marine Corps was running a trans-Atlantic radio station for the Navy at the entrance to the bay I was aiming for, and as I came around the point there it was! But it wasn't quite over. We were twenty minutes overdue and still thirteen miles from the airport. I didn't push it, just stayed down low and throttled back some more. I made it with a gallon of fuel to spare and my wing-man had maybe a cupful more than that. What we hadn't known was that the visibility had dropped from five miles to a half mile, while a headwind had risen from ten knots to twenty-five knots. When searching for periscope wakes, you usually couldn't notice a gradual loss of visibility or increase in wind velocity. After this close call, I began studying radio range navigation right away.

Farrelly also recalls, with some humor, his first blimp ride, which occurred when the Navy began using the base for refueling purposes:

Once on a day off I went out on a blimp patrol that I knew would be returning the same day. Now a blimp is not exactly lighter-than-air, but is supposedly about four pounds heavier-than-air. It takes off with a run down the runway and then noses up like a plane to get off. I learned later that the Navy boys loved to climb about fifty feet then chop the throttle. To an airplane pilot, of course, that meant a crash and probably a fatal one. But a blimp only drifts. They pulled this nasty trick on me and another pilot taking our first ride, smirking and finally laughing out loud at us as we sat there white-knuckled, holding our breaths waiting for a crash. Later on, we laughed about it, too.

## Norman L. Ring

*Norman L. Ring, born in 1909 in Portland, was another of the older men at Bar Harbor. He grew up building and rebuilding all sorts of radios, starting with crystal sets in the 1920s. In 1940, Ring became an FCC-licensed radio ham. When war came, he and his brother owned a plumbing and heating business in Yarmouth. Although he was married and had two children, he thought he might still be drafted, and volunteered to be a radio technician in the CAP. In short order, he found himself in Bar Harbor:*

They listed me on the roster as a "security technician," but I really did radio installation and maintenance. The base already had a radio so I left my set behind, removing a key part (a tube or coil or something like that) so some enemy agent couldn't capture and use it to talk with off-shore submarines. Disabling unattended radios was required by government regulations. Our base radio was set to four hundred cycles, a very low frequency that isn't even used today. Our antenna must have been a quarter to half a mile long! I worked on all the plane radios too, and usually went up in the planes afterwards to see how the radios worked. I enjoyed the flying, but I never did it myself.

Left to right, observers Howard G. Nichols and Roy R. Fontaine, and pilot Oscar H. Ginnow enjoy a sunny but cold Maine afternoon (courtesy Oscar H. Ginnow).

I went up to Bar Harbor without my wife and pre-school age children, but within the week I got pretty lonely, and brought them all up. We rented a place on Cottage Street in Bar Harbor. My wife was a very outgoing person, and made friends quickly, and in no time at all our kids were playing with the neighbors' kids and so on. Mike Popovich, a mechanic from Waterbury, Connecticut, and his wife were friends who lived near us. And I remember a character we called "Mose." But at eighty-seven my memory isn't what it used to be. My wife died last year, and now my daughter's sixty-four and my son's fifty-seven. He's a stunt pilot, but *not* when I go up with him!

There were certainly subs around when we were there. Some attempted to sink the Liberty Ships coming out from Bath, where they were built. One came up to charge its batteries during the night, and our guys spotted it on a sand bar. They immediately called in their position, but by the time Navy boats arrived, the tide had come in and the submarine escaped. Everybody was pretty mad that we still weren't carrying bombs at the time.

The Navy shared our base, and operated a number of blimps from it. Our people at the base helped them moor. The blimps had two length of lines, long ones and short ones. As a blimp came in, they'd drop those lines and we'd grab hold of what we could, trying to maintain a "V" shape, and then pull her down. They warned us repeatedly that if the lines started to pull us up, we were to let go immediately. Other bases had lost some men who hung on, and finally fell off to their death from hundreds of feet up. They had a mobile mooring mast there, and while we hung on they'd drive the nose of the blimp into it, and make fast. The blimps kept carrier pigeons aboard for sending messages back to base without breaking radio silence.

I met many people at the base and in the town, enjoyed the restaurants there, attended hangar parties and movies with my family, and fished a lot on my days off. The base lost a plane and two men before I got there, I think because of engine failure. Some of the planes were not the best. We called one plane, I believe it was a Fairchild, the "vibrator" because it was so shaky when in the air. There's not too much more that I remember. It seems like a long time ago, and I guess it was.

### Matthew A. Donner, Jr.

*Matthew A. Donner, Jr. was the thirty-two-year-old airdrome officer from Hamden, Connecticut, a New Haven suburb. A Colgate graduate (BA 1932) with a major in business administration, he was division sales manager for Liberty Mutual Insurance Company and taking flight lessons when the war came and put an end to all civilian flying:*

Civil Air Patrol representatives came down to the southern Connecticut area recruiting, apparently because there weren't enough planes and pilots from Maine to staff both Portland and Bar Harbor bases. Even though I had a wife and three small children, I wanted to do something in the war. I'd wanted to join the Navy, and could have gotten a direct commission thanks to my college degree, but my wife wouldn't have it. However, she did agree to accompany me to Bar Harbor, and we rented a house with an antique central wood-burning furnace. We left the children with their grandmother.

When I arrived, the base consisted of a hangar and something that looked like and probably had been a hot dog stand. That's where we set up our offices. My assignment was as supply officer, responsible for ordering and maintaining the stock of everything needed to keep a coastal patrol base in business, from paper clips to plane parts. Technical section head Alton Marshall and clerk technician Harold ("Fritz") Carter worked in the office with me. I left the base before either of them — my wife became seriously ill and I had to take her back to her family home in Albany, New York — but I understand that when the base closed, both were assigned to TTU #20 at Gray Field, Ft. Lewis, Washington.

Bar Harbor police chief George Abbott (right, in dark jacket) with some of his men assigned to the base. Their uniforms were a strange mix of police department and Civil Air Patrol (courtesy Oscar H. Ginnow).

My memory is so bad that I can't remember many of the details of my time in Bar Harbor, but I do recall the terrible winter of 1942-1943 when two of our men went down in the Atlantic and froze to death. I don't believe anyone ever feared being shot down by a submarine, but we were certainly fearful of an engine failure of any kind — and I say "we" because I also flew a number of missions as an observer. Aside from losing Welles Bishop and William Hites, I have nothing but warm feelings about my time and friends at the base. They were a good bunch and did a great job. I later returned to the insurance business, retiring here to Florida twenty years ago. I never did get my pilot's license.

## John Kief

*John Kief was one of the local men hired to guard the base. Born and raised in Bar Harbor, like many of the other guards, he was married and at age thirty-one had five children. He remembers quite clearly how he happened to get the airport security job:*

Our chief of police, George Abbott, had been asked by the coastal patrol fellows to set up security out at the airport. When I stopped in the police station one day, George said to me, "I've got a job for you if you want to take it," and I asked what it was. He said, "Security out at the airport. The CAP'll pay you five dollars a day." Well, that was more than I was making, so I took it. The chief's brother, Art Abbott, was another one of the guards. I believe there were six of those Abbott boys altogether, and now they're all gone. In fact, most of the fellows who were guards are gone, like my friends Ed Cameron and Vern McQuinn. We bought our own uniforms and supplied our own weapons. I carried a forty-five automatic and most of the others had thirty-eights. There were four of us to a shift: at the gatehouse, the administration building, out at the hangar, and down where they stored the bombs.

Mt. Desert Island was a welcome sight to returning flyers. This shot looks eastward from Southwest Harbor in the foreground to Northeast Harbor across the bay (courtesy Oscar H. Ginnow).

It wasn't too exciting except for the night a four-man Army reconnaissance team riding around in a Jeep decided to have some fun with us. They apparently came to check the security around the island and over at Winter Harbor. They went into the Bar Harbor police station and asked the chief about security at the airport. He told them, "If you know when you're well off, you'll stay the hell away from my boys." Well they came on out there anyway. I was on duty at the gatehouse and my cousin was down at the hangar. He yelled out to me he saw a vehicle with its headlights on driving down the runway toward him. I told him to get out there and wave it down with his flashlight. He did so, but they wouldn't stop. So I drew my forty-five and put a couple of rounds out there in front of that Jeep. The only ammunition I had for it were tracer bullets, and you should have seen how quickly those Army boys turned tail to head the other way!

Though many members of the coastal patrol came from other states — a large group were from Connecticut, and their commander, Major King, was from Wisconsin — there wasn't any friction between them and us. New Englanders may have a reputation for taking a long time to warm up to newcomers but that wasn't the case in Bar Harbor. I got to know some of the men real well, and even took them hunting on my time off. One of my cousins had a real good coon hound, so we went after coons as well as deer. You couldn't hunt deer on the island, but the Airport was off the island at Trenton, and there were plenty of deer up that way, too. I remember loading a freshly dressed deer into a plane that came in one day, maybe from the Portland coastal patrol base. Deer meat was a staple in our part of the country, especially as meat was scarce in the stores due to rationing.

I was on duty the night we had a fire at the base and lost a building and a lot of office equipment. We didn't have a fire hydrant, and knocked down the fire with hoses and water from a tank truck. We got the fire out before it spread much. No one was injured. Some of our local fellows were hired to help in the rebuilding. When the base finally closed, I was asked to go along to Fort Lewis, Washington where they were being sent to tow targets. I wanted to go, but couldn't because of my family. I still live in Bar Harbor, and at age eighty-five I have twenty-four grandchildren and twenty-six great grandchildren. Do you know of anyone who can beat that!

### Jerome M. ("Jerry") Lamont

*Jerry Lamont, at nineteen, was the youngest man on the base. Though he had his private pilot's license, he was assigned as a flight observer. He signed up for and stayed only ninety days, but did plenty of flying in that time:*

My log book is full of pilot's names, fellows I flew with and who certified the number of hours I was out with them on patrol. Casimir Lawrynovicz, from Danbury, Connecticut — like myself — was one of those I flew with a lot. Cassy and I went to Bar Harbor together and shared a room at a motel only a half mile from the airfield. We had a fireplace and a daily supply of dry logs that burned so hot we feared we'd set the place on fire. A small restaurant next door was where we usually had breakfast before walking to the base. If we had the dawn patrol, we'd have doughnuts and coffee at the base canteen. We had to be careful walking the road at night because of all the skunks we'd meet.

Cassy died a few years back, but I remember a couple of missions we flew together. We were out in a Ranger-powered Fairchild 24 one day when we iced up so bad I doubted we'd get back without going into the water. There was ice on the wings and struts, and the engine was icing up, too. We kept turning the carburetor heat on and off, and after we were back over land and away from the cold and heavy ocean mist everything slowly got back to normal. But it was a little hairy because it was a real rough day and the waves were running high. Cassy and I had another unusual patrol: we spotted what looked like a fishing boat, but when we dropped lower to make closer examination its deck was covered with fifty-five gallon drums. That was pretty suspicious. We'd been briefed that there might be subversives secretly refueling German submarines offshore. So we radioed-in, and the Coast Guard came out and picked them up. We never got a report on the outcome.

Jerome M. Lamont at nineteen was the youngest pilot at the Bar Harbor base. He went on to become a much-decorated Air Force veteran (courtesy Jerome M. Lamont).

In my log book, I see that I flew several times with Briggs Cunningham in his Sikorsky S-39 amphibian. Briggs lived at Green Farms, Connecticut, and was a very wealthy man. In my logbook, I can decipher also the signatures of pilots Vincent Guilfoyle of Branford, Connecticut; David Emerson of South Coventry, Connecticut; David Farrelly of Woodstock, Vermont; Melvin Goldstein of New York City; and Lewis Pfouts of Burghill, Ohio.

There were probably more pilots from Connecticut than anywhere else, and that's because somebody from Bar Harbor came down and recruited us. Every airport along the coastal area was within a designated "defense zone" where after the Japanese attack at Pearl Harbor private flying was banned. When the man showed up at the Danbury

Airport one day to ask who'd be interested in flying for the CAP he quickly found his volunteers. I was single, footloose and fancy-free, and all I wanted to do was *fly*. But at Bar Harbor I enjoyed myself in other ways, too. Several local men took us deer hunting, for example, and we usually had several deer "hanging" near the mess hall waiting to be cooked. There was plenty of sea food, and it wasn't unusual to have clam chowder, fish soup, or fresh lobster for lunch. There weren't any hangar picnics or beer parties or that sort of thing. When we weren't flying we were busy building the base. Besides which, it was too cold, and too many people had to get up early for the dawn patrol.

I left exactly ninety days after I arrived — November 28, 1942 — to enter the War Training Service Program, a course designed for pilots with their private or commercial ratings who wanted to get instructor's ratings in order to teach in that program. I got the rating, but was hired by an Air Corps primary flight school instead. Later I served for thirteen months in the China-India-Burma theater as a "Hump" pilot. I returned to the States for a year of ferrying planes to South America and elsewhere, then flew a C-47 from Dallas, Texas to Calcutta, India, a two-week trip. I stayed some six years, flying for Orient Airways in India and into Java, where I helped break the Dutch blockade in the Dutch-Indonesian War, and into Northern Kashmir commanding an airlift during the Indo-Pakistan war. In India, I married an English girl and our first two children were born there. I have stayed in aviation all my life, running up almost 29,000 logged-hours and setting three world records. I'm still flying, which makes fifty-six years, dating from my first solo in a Piper Cub Coupe in 1940. It's been a wonderful lifetime since my coastal patrol days, but I certainly haven't forgotten them!

---

Base officers, pilots and observers, who served at least one month at CAPCP#20 and who are not elsewhere mentioned in this chapter include: Harley L. Arnold,* Henry M. Bergeron,* Harold K. Congdon, Charles E. Coo, Alvin U. Hatch,* Robert H. Kemp,* Eric B. Lammert, Melvin J. Larsen, Frank E. Light, Orrin B. Maxwell, Charles C. Morrison, Sherman T. Nance,* Gus P. Nonweiler, Albert J. Packett, Peter C. Romano,* Elmer E. Sawyer, George E. Shivers,* and Alfred L. Speckman.* Asterisk indicates Air Medal winner.

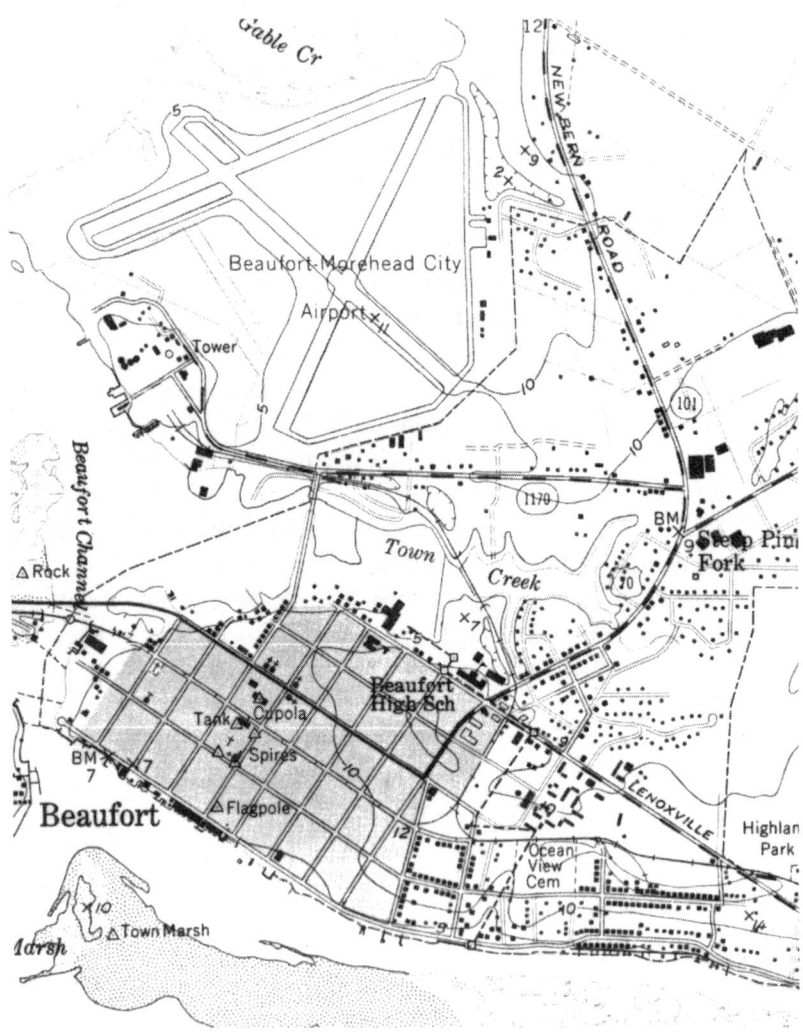

As this 1949 (development revised to 1983) United States Geological Survey topological map shows, the airport tower and various buildings were located immediately on the Beaufort Channel. Walking from town to the base was possible, but seldom done.

# 21

# Beaufort, North Carolina

The last coastal patrol base activated — on September 7, 1942 — was that in Beaufort, North Carolina, then a decidedly ante-bellum community with stately 1790s Southern mansions lining the main streets. The Sea Island cotton trade bestowed immense wealth on local planters, who built grand homes in Beaufort, at the time a thriving port. During the Civil War these splendid mansions were spared from General Sherman's firebrands only because of Beaufort's having been lost early to occupying Federal troops. Its Southern traditions persisted, and the men and women of the coastal patrol found Beaufort residents still offering gracious hospitality even in the midst of a world war.

The base history, *CAP Coastal Patrol Base Twenty-One,* written by Captain Melvin J. Warner of Rocky Mount, North Carolina and Lieutenant George W. Grove of Hickory, North Carolina, the base intelligence officers, provides an excellent description of the base and its personnel. Like many others, the patrol base was created by the coastal patrol volunteers themselves:

> The field at Beaufort had been used as an airport, of a fashion, but when the men arrived at Beaufort and asked for directions to the airport, few local people knew where it was. And good reason why. The 75 CAP volunteers finally located it growing waist-high in swamp grass, and full of stump pine. About half the field was under water at high tide. The only evidence of human effort of living in the area was a tiny, two-room homestead in the northeast corner of the field. Later this house was moved and became the headquarters building for the base. Soon, through almost superhuman effort, two runways

were mowed out on the highest ground, the longest only 2300 feet in length. It still wasn't an airport, probably resembling more the air strips from which many of our military planes are forced to operate in the South Pacific. On September 30, 1942, the first organized patrol took off, and except for periods of bad weather, similar patrols were in the air every day until the base closed on August 31, 1943.

Warner and Grove's history of the base chronicled many specific highlights and hardships that they felt helped mold personnel base into one effective unit by the end of their first month at Beaufort. Among them:

• The construction and dedication of Bert Hellmeuller's Outside Memorials (plumbing was unheard of in the community), so named because Bert's impression served as a pattern, his dimensions being slightly reduced on the second building.
• The remodeling of the house consisted of taking the kitchen sink out and installing Operations, closing in the front porch and installing Intelligence, and building on a back porch and installing Communications.
• Building the radio tower, a memorial to the efforts and unsurpassd cussing ability of Joe Josephson and his hard-working crew of guards and servicemen.
• The building of the Pilot's House, Harry Thompson's lumber camp having been brought from Williamson, N. C., and serving as the main section.
• The building and stocking of the canteen, where Flight Officer Curley Sykes first showed his ability as an electrician, an accomplishment which later became one of the major contributions in the construction of the base and made it possible for us to have many of the conveniences which might not have been possible otherwise.

## Charles R. Russell

*Air medal winner Charles R. Russell was born and raised in Raleigh and learned to fly there under the CPTP about 1940 in a J-3 Cub. He and his wife Margaret were flying in his 40 hp Taylorcraft the morning the Japanese attacked Pearl Harbor, first learning about it from excited ground crewman after landing. Within the month they had joined the CAP squadron established at Raleigh Municipal Airport, and in early September 1942 answered the call to serve at Beaufort, he as pilot, she as secretary to the commanding officer:*

You know that we built the base ourselves, the hangar, the pilot's ready room, the whole thing. On our first patrols, all we had were some soaked German life preservers. I was told they were off sunken subs.

Later on we had Mae Wests and barracuda bags. I doubt that I could even have got those things out of the plane. With all the equipment we carried and the short runways we used it's a wonder we got into the air at all. We had at least one fellow that didn't abort his take-off in time and just went straight on out into the bay. Even more powerful planes like the gullwing Stinsons had trouble. The airfield was right at the edge of the water.

Base radioman David Stephen Williams was killed, with base engineering officer, Capt. H. Leonard Lundquist, in a crash at the airfield on June 27, 1943 (courtesy Harry P. Bridges).

I was watching the day we lost two men in the same plane I'd just flown on patrol. It was one of those strutless Cessnas, a bright red job with the 165 hp Warner Super Scarab engine, and man was it fast! When my observer and I were out there both the engine and the radio had been acting up, so I brought her back in. After some work was done, Captain H. Leonard Lundquist, our engineering officer, and Steve Williams, one of our radio technicians, went for a check ride. Len was a highly skilled pilot who'd flown in air shows, and I think had served in the first World War. When he got to the end of the runway he pulled up steeply and hung that plane on its prop. Just then the engine quit, and they pitched straight down into the ground. It seemed like it happened in slow motion. I was standing on the runway, waiting, thinking I'd take the plane out again as soon as they returned. I ran up there and was the first man to reach the crash. Both men had been killed instantly.

When I first got to Beaufort, the subs were sinking so many ships the sky was lit up all night. They were sinking Liberty ships from the Wilmington shipyard almost as fast as they were being built. One practically blew up in my face — it hadn't got a hundred miles from launching. Coming back from around Montana Shoals one day I saw something behind the sand dunes along shore. After going down for a closer look, it proved to be a large life raft. We gave base its location and later, after someone had checked it out, I was told it was German equipment, all slashed and cut up for no apparent reason. To this day no one knows how many German spies might have been landed in the United States without our knowing it.

Base commander Major Frank E. Dawson was later the North Carolina CAP Wing commander and a leader in the postwar effort to obtain full veteran's rights for former coastal patrol flyers (courtesy Harry P. Bridges).

Our commanding officer, Frank E. Dawson was really a good guy, firm, but friendly and fair. He ran a happy base where everyone got along together with everyone else. Albert Barden, a chap older than my father, was the base handy man. A professional photographer, he also took most of the photos for the base history, and ran the concession stand. "Pops" Barden was a fine gentleman who just wanted to do his part. Mel Warner, who wrote the history, is dead now. He had been a reporter for a newspaper his father owned in Rocky Mount. I think he took it over when his father died. Carl Lucas from Erwin, North Carolina was the base cut-up who kept everybody laughing. Herman "Zero" Reid married one of the local girls and returned to live in Beaufort after the war. We had a great bunch and I'm sorry to say that I've lost touch with those who are still with us.

Toward the end of my stay at Beaufort, we spent a lot of time surveying the location of wrecks and sunken ships. We didn't have much navigational equipment, but we usually knew where we were, at least we thought we did. I remember getting caught in a big storm a hundred miles off shore. The magnetic compass went crazy so we didn't know where we were, we just guessed. We got back to base, but it was hairy. We had just *hoped* we were going in the right direction! Afterwards, I enjoyed flying Hob Anderson's Stinson gullwing — with its radio direction finder — even more than before. You might not get where you were going in the shortest distance, but you'd get there.

When my wife Margaret and I arrived in Beaufort in 1942, it was already September so we took an apartment in town. In the summer of 1943, we shared a waterfront house in Atlantic Beach with Ed Howard, our operations officer, and his wife. Somewhat older than the rest of us he'd been around more and seemed to know everyone in the world. To get to Atlantic Beach, a "resorty" place on the Outer Banks across from Beaufort, you crossed a lift bridge over the Intracoastal Waterway to Morehead City, then went across a causeway to the Banks. After a barge struck and extensively damaged the lift bridge, we "commuted" via Coast Guard boat for about a month while repairs were made. Though the Coast Guard boys were very considerate of us land-lubbers, it made for a long work day because our beach house was a real hike from the nearest landing pier. For me the best part of living on the Banks was the superb fishing. You could catch anything you wanted to in twenty minutes, even a bushel of crabs.

Some time in December 1943, well after the base had been shut down as a coastal patrol unit, many of our personnel went to Monogram Field, Driver, Virginia, to tow targets and carry out tracking missions. I wasn't one of them, but instead entered the Air Corps Cadet program, starting right from the beginning. They said, "Here's a plane, go instruct yourself." When the war ended I could have taken either a commission and assignment to Japan, or a discharge. Since my wife was pregnant, I took the discharge. For a while I taught flying but soon joined the U.S. Post Office. Before retiring in 1972, I supervised some sixty-two post offices in North Carolina.

## Robert F. Boone

*Robert F. Boone, born in 1912 on a farm in Duplin County, North Carolina, still recalls the day in 1927 when his family moved into nearby Wallace. His job was to lead an obstinate Jersey Cow the fifteen miles to town. The trek took them all day. He chuckles and says, "You know how slow a cow walks. I tell friends I made a slow entry into Wallace." In time, Boone and his good friend Steve Williams became well-known radio hams and when the new coastal patrol base opened at Beaufort they were suddenly in big demand to set up the radio station there:*

There was this big government official from Washington who came down and told us we were needed on a secret mission but wouldn't tell us what. Steve and I met with Major Frank E. Dawson, the commander of the new base, at the Morehead Villa Hotel in Morehead City, and there he explained the mission to us, namely, to establish and maintain the base radio station. This job had to be done before any anti-submarine patrols could be flown, so we were there right at the start. We took our radios and tools with us, then found we had to change the frequency on our transmitter to 496 kilocycles in order to match the aircraft receivers. Our workshop was in the hangar but it was nothing special, only a workbench and some space in a corner. I never had any formal training in radio. I just picked it up out of handbooks and manuals.

Base radioman Robert F. Boone was a radio "ham" from the early days of radio. After serving in the coastal patrol he went with the Philco Corporation and helped develop airborne radar equipment (courtesy Robert F. Boone).

I guess there weren't many radio hams in those days. You have to remember that in 1942 long-range voice radio was still relatively new. Before we went to Beaufort, Steve and I had been members of the local CAP squadron, so we knew of the need for radiomen at Beaufort, and were glad to go. We left wives and children behind but as the base was less than a hundred miles from Wallace it was easy to visit back and forth. I lived right in Beaufort, with another hometown friend by the name of Lawrence Cavenaugh, an aircraft mechanic. When Lawrence brought his wife down, they rented a house and let me stay with them.

We generally had dinner out and could go to a popular restaurant in Morehead City or a couple of places in Beaufort. The seafood was wonderful. Beaufort had one theater, and a few bars, but that was about it for recreation.

Things were going real well, when one day my friend Steve Williams was killed in a plane crash during a routine flight to check out a plane radio he had just repaired, something we always did. The plane faltered and spun-in from low altitude after take-off. Neither he nor the pilot had any chance. Then there was a hangar fire that destroyed our radio transmitter. I never got a dime from the government for it and ended up installing a substitute out of my own pocket. After that I finished up my tour of duty at the base, but I really never went back to ham radio again.

When the base broke up, a bunch of people went to Driver, Virginia as Tow Target Unit #21.* I went into radar engineering with the Philco Corporation in Philadelphia, working on the refinement of airborne radar equipment. Later, I returned to Wallace to continue in the retail business I'd started with a friend before the war, and to concentrate on raising a family. My wife and I have two daughters, five grandchildren (four of whom graduated from the University of North Carolina) and two great grandsons who, with no regard at all for my eighty-four years of age, keep me busy taking them to the ball games!

## Paul L. Sigmon

*Paul L. Sigmon was born and raised in Mount Holly, North Carolina, and learned to fly at Plaza Airport in Charlotte while still a teenager. He had his private pilot's license when he joined the coastal patrol but so few hours in the air that he was accepted as a service technician rather than a pilot:*

I was a poor country boy working for a living when I started taking flying lessons. Daddy didn't have thirty cents, and I didn't have ten. In my spare time I traded mechanical work on the planes for flight time. I went to the Southeastern Aeronautical Institute in Charlotte until it shut down because of money problems about the time the Beaufort base was

---

* Led by commanding officer Murray W. Keeler, they were operations officer Edwin T. Howard; assistant operations officers Darlin D. Duncan; engineering officer John H. Sellers; communications officer Robert E. Dawson; assistant engineering officer Bert J. Hellmueller; pilots Benny H. Baxter, Jesse J. Coletrain,* John Lindsay,* C. B. Robinson,* James M. Teachey,*and Walter F. Woodward; observer Thomas L. Hooper;* mechanic Woodrow L. Marshall; radio mechanic Billy G. Haire; radio technician Weldon C. Fields; service technicians Herman B. Gilbert, Jr. and Carl E. Lucas; clerks Ethel H. Gerald and Elizabeth G. Stem; and guards William D. Fussell, John F. Garrett, Jordan K. Rouse, and Fred W. Tucker. Asterisk indicates Air Medal winner.

setting up. As it turned out, Harry L. Lundquist, who was to become the base's engineering officer, taught at the Institute and several of us went with him to the base. I remember Wayne Wilson and Tyler Dunlap going down as mechanics and there might have been others. Wayne and I rode there on his motorcycle. I found a room with a Mr. and Mrs. Jones (Mr. Jones ran the local Western Auto Store) and Wayne found lodging two blocks away. All the people in town took someone into their homes. They knew what the patrol was trying to do and were very supportive. I pushed the planes around, gassed them, did anything to them that needed to be done. Once in a while we'd wash them down, just like you'd wash a car, using soap and water. We'd use ladders to get to the top wing and the top of the fuselage. That wasn't necessary too often, because rain and drizzle and fog keep them rinsed clean. Salt spray wasn't a problem, except after the boys buzzed the beach where the girls sun-bathed. Some flew so low their trailing radio antennas skipped across the water. Planes were always refueled as soon as they returned from any mission, so they'd be ready in an emergency.

When we first got there, the base was just an open field. It was privately owned by a farmer who had cleared only one dirt strip for himself, and so many of our take-offs and landings were crosswind. The area was so low that on several occasions water covered the field, and our planes used the Marine auxiliary field near Bogue. That field had four-thousand foot runways and a swell operations building, which the Marines graciously allowed us to use.

Being a service technician was no nine-to-five job. We had to be there for the dawn patrols and we were there all day. In theory, we were expected to wear our uniforms off duty (dungarees to work in) but that rule wasn't strictly enforced. I wasn't there long before I bought a car despite the fact that our pay took forever to come through. I'd sold the one I had at home because I didn't know what serving at Beaufort would be like. I'd used up what little savings I had long before getting paid — others faced the same situation — but we explained how it was to the local people and they gave us credit without hesitation. There weren't many ways to spend money in the town. I remember hanging out at a drugstore a lot, but I don't recall a U.S.O. or even a theater. There was an outdoor theater as well as some nice beaches over on Harker's Island, and on days off we'd take a mail boat over in the morning, spend the day with our girls, and come back that evening. I went pretty steady with one girl, but when the base closed I went away into service for three years. When I returned, I went back to see her, but things had changed and it didn't work out.

While I was at the base, I got to fly occasionally. I'd do some extra mechanical work on somebody's plane, and they'd let me take it up. Before he was killed, Captain Lundquist let me fly his old Fairchild KR-21 biplane, which he kept at the base just for fun. I didn't build up many hours, but I flew whenever I could. When the base closed I got into the Air Corps Cadet program but washed out. I ended up as the flight engineer on a B-17 crew, and we were ready to go overseas just when the war ended. After the war, I flew some with a friend, but didn't pursue aviation as a career.

### Edward A. Scholtz

*Edward A. Scholtz, another Charlotte native, served at Beaufort for about six months as a flight observer. He had served in an Air Corps glider school long enough to have earned his private pilot's license, and a staff sergeant's rating, but then was discharged on grounds of the Air Corps's having too many glider pilots. When later he tried to enlist again, he was rejected as being physically unqualified:*

That was when I joined the coastal patrol and moved down to Beaufort with my wife. We didn't have any children, and my wife didn't work, so we just enjoyed ourselves a lot. We rented a house in Atlantic Beach, right on the ocean, and that was great. We swam a lot and were happy just watching the breakers roll in. Nowadays, people pay a fortune to rent a place like that. Robert Cartier and his wife, from Hickory, North Carolina, were good friends, and we often played cards in the evenings, or went out together for dinner and such. To tell the truth, I don't remember much about my time there, except that the officers seemed very much on the ball and that we all flew an awful lot. After the war, I came home and flew a little, but I nearly killed myself one day flying solo in a rented plane and after that I never flew again. I'm seventy-five and retired but I enjoyed a long, pleasant career in the nursery business, selling trees and plants to people right here in Charlotte.

\* \* \*

The Beaufort base history provides a chronology of important events and the following are just a few of them:

### October 8, 1942
Pilot Clay Swaim and Observer Manfred Mashburn were forced down at sea off Bogue Inlet today at 12 o'clock. They climbed out on the wing of the plane, which sank in 5 to 8 minutes. The sister ship circled, then lost them, picking them up again approximately five miles off-shore. The Coast Guard was notified and picked them up

in good condition at 1400. Pilot Swaim reported that water in the gas tank caused the trouble.

**October 11, 1942**
No patrols for the past few days due to bad weather conditions. It doesn't take much to cover the runways in inches of water and "ground loving" Stinsons make no bones about needing plenty of room. We were notified by Cherry Point, Langley Field and the Coast Guard at 0800 this morning that we could expect a 75-mile-an-hour wind from the Southeast in about an hour ... then came the wind and the rain and down went our beautiful new radio tower, the pride of Joe [Myrton M. Josephson, assistant engineering officer] and the boys, victim of a floating dead man [a buried log to which a guy wire was attached] that had not been properly covered.

**November 16, 1942**
[Pilot Guy T. Cherry, Jr. and observer George W. Grove ditched at 10:40 a.m. about 15 miles southeast of the Cape Fear lighthouse].... A navy PBY was sent to the scene but reported that it was too rough for a water landing. Lts. Cherry and Grove were finally picked up about dark and taken to Cherry Point hospital. Lt. Cherry had been dead for some time. Lt. Grove had strapped Cherry's body to his own to keep him afloat. It was a terrible shock to us all, the first time we had to face death since being together ... and none was dearer to us than Guy Cherry. [Nineteen-year-old Cherry, of Kinston, North Carolina, was the youngest pilot to lose his life on coastal patrol.]

**November 19, 1942**
The funeral was very impressive; an outstanding contribution was the Major's prayer at the graveside. It was as beautifully sincere and as heartfelt an utterance as a human could make. As many members from the base attended as possible and still keep up the patrols. The Rocky Mount Squadron, of which Guy was a member, was there as a unit.

**February 4, 1943**
While Flight Officer Nicholson [Newlin B.] was reporting to Intelligence that he had been stopped and thoroughly questioned on the highway, deputy sheriff T. M. Thomas came in to inform us that German saboteurs had landed last night in the Bogue Inlet area. A Coast Guard patrolman spotted a group of men on the beach and after no response to his challenge he shot into the group. The men disappeared into the dunes and wooded section of the beach near-by. In connection with this activity it was reported that a submarine was sunk off Beaufort Inlet at this time and that two or more survivors got ashore. All guards on duty were sent home so that the full comple-

ment could go on duty at night for a while. The Base Commander decided that it was necessary to deputize a few of the base personnel so that traffic near the base could be more easily handled. Lts. Edwin T. Howard, Melvin J. Warner, Edgar R. Zimmerman, Jesse J. Coltrain, and Darlin D. Duncan went before the sheriff and were made deputy sheriffs of the county.

**March 20, 1943**
Pilots Arthur Rose and Charles Robinson and Observers Milton Brock and Manson Arrowood were went out this morning to escort a freighter coming north. These two planes, bright yellow with large Civil Coastal Patrol insignia painted on wing and fuselage, met the mission just off New River. Using the prescribed technique in approaching a friendly vessel, the planes circled in to within about a mile and a half of the freighter. As they circled the boat, at about 600 feet, they noticed tracer bullets crossing their paths. The pilots immediately dropped to a lower altitude so as not to cross the path of the fire, and as they did, the gun crew on the ship tracked the planes with their continuous fire. The planes were forced to leave the vicinity, since the mission could not be completed under such hazardous conditions. This was reported to the Navy, who later met the captain of the boat in Lookout Bight and severely reprimanded him for allowing such action to take place. He said that the crew was only practicing. Now we don't mind flying these puddle-jumpers out over the water and doing most anything else for these convoys, but the "clay pigeon" idea is just too much!

**May 17, 1943**
Pilots Russell [Charles R.] and Ellen [Bruce P.] and Observers Wagstaff [Robert L.] and Permenter [Jesse B.] took off on a routine North flight today. While flying at 1500 feet they saw what appeared to be the wake of a ship at about ten miles distance. Assuming that it was the small Coast Guard boat that usually patrols up around buoy six, they proceeded to go down and identify her. Upon approaching the position, they noticed that there were two wakes, one fore and aft with a black object in the center and soon the whole thing disappeared.... The Navy slapped a negative evaluation on the report.... Although we know we are inexperienced and we realize that the Navy at Norfolk has the ability to weigh facts and learn the truth, we still question some of their decisions on happenings down here, happenings which we see with our own eyes. After all, we patrol this area every day, we know whether certain wrecks give off oil or not, we know whether they are above the surface or not, and we are pretty darn sure that none of them bob up to the surface now and then. I wonder what it'll take to convince them.

**June 4, 1943**
Pilot Stowe and Observer Permenter, flying Fairchild NC 16891, joined the Duck Club this morning at 1010. They were on convoy flying at 800 feet when the motor started to miss and then cut out completely. The ship landed in the water off Bogue and with a calm sea and little wind, Pinky made a perfect water landing. The crew got out of the ship in a couple of minutes, got up on the wings, inflated the rubber boats, tied them together and made themselves comfortable while waiting for the rescue. The plane continued to float for fifteen minutes. The sister ship circled the spot waiting for relief ships to appear ... [Stowe and Permenter were picked up by a Coast Guard boat at 1129.]

Aerial view of the Beaufort airfield. Operating conditions were relatively primative, and the runways sometimes were under six inches of water (courtesy Harry P. Bridges).

**June 16, 1943**
Observer Wagstaff is being billed as the "Human Doughnut," for this is the second time he has been dunked. He and pilot Williams made a forced landing in the water off Bogue today at 1410 in the "old graveyard of CAP planes." Neither was hurt and they were picked up just forty minutes afterward by the good old Coast Guard. There's nothing to it now, but let's not let it become a habit. It's get-

ting to be downright peculiar the way we lose ships in that same location.

**June 27, 1943**
It is Sunday and the worst has happened! Captain Lundquist and Steve Williams have just been killed. They were taking off in the Cessna for a routine radio check flight. It was just to be a casual flight. There was enough wind. The weather was right. The Cessna roared and looked trim as ever and Len and Steve were in the best of spirits. Len taxied her down, turned into the wind and gave her the gun. The plane climbed to approximately 200 feet and then seemed to hang there on the prop. She nosed down for just an instant, then fell off on the right wing and crashed into the ground head on without giving Len a chance to pull her out. We all rushed out, but soon found that human help was not needed....

## Theodore E. Sellers

*Theodore E. Sellers, the young man who, with base commander James Hamilton, had "opened" the first Manteo coastal patrol airfield, found his further coastal patrol work at Beaufort to be both interesting and rewarding. Several incidents stand out in his memory:*

Perhaps the most exciting few moments for me came on a routine flight with my pilot, Jim Teachey. When he suddenly observed a long dark object under the surface of the ocean, Jim shouted for me to throw out a smoke bomb to mark the spot while he made a sharp turn to come back around to identify the object. As we approached it, it seemed to bend in the middle — and so proved to be a large school of fish. What a disappointment! Well, we'd tried! On another flight, a fast-moving front rolled in and we were advised by base to land at the Army Air Base near Wilmington and stay the night. The Army entertained us and put us up in their bachelor officers quarters. The next morning as we were preparing to take off, three P-47 Thunderbolts appeared and put on a show. Then they landed, taxied in, and climbed down. When they took off their helmets and shook out their hair we realized that they were women pilots of the Ferry Command.

After the base closed, I again took and this time passed the Navy physical exam. I was aboard a train to my first assignment three days after returning home from Beaufort. I volunteered for and won my wings as an aerial gunner and was assigned to — guess what? — anti-sub duty in South America. After the war I went to college under the G.I. Bill, married, and had a family. I worked for Ford Motor Company and General Motors in middle management before retiring in 1980.

Left to right: Sgt. Jefferson M. Rhodes; 2nd Lt. Francis W. McComb, Jr.; observers Edward A. Scholtz, Theodore E. Sellers, and Thomas L. Hooper, August 30, 1943, the day before the base closed (courtesy Theodore E. Sellers).

## Wyatt A. Keever

*Wyatt A. Keever served at the base as a guard, but only for a short time — March 10, 1943 until June 1, 1943. Born near Charlotte, he was working in a textile mill in Gastonia when he joined the local CAP group:*

I went to a squadron meeting one Friday night, where someone announced they wanted six volunteers for the Beaufort coastal patrol base. I said I'd go if I could have two weeks to give notice at the mill and get my affairs in order. They said that was all right, but they called me sooner, and said I must report immediately. Me and a boy from Lowell, Edward Fraley, drove down together, and shared an upstairs room in the home of the local Ford dealer. When I was on guard duty, I carried both a twelve-gauge double-barreled shotgun and a thirty-eight caliber revolver. It was about this time that the subs were landing people as saboteurs. There were two or three alerts just while I was there.

Toward the end of my stay, a new airport was being built right next to ours, but closer toward town and to the ocean. Our landing strip tended to flood whenever it rained hard and we guards often had to help clear the drainage ditches around the field. That was real hard work.

Your shirt would get soaked with sweat, then when you took it off your back would get blistered from the sun. We didn't have much to do in Beaufort, and I recall Paul Sigmon and I driving home together on our occasional weekend off duty. I had a 1928 Ford, and Martha Fraley, Ed's wife and the base cook, sometimes went with us. We dropped her off at Lowell, which was right outside Gastonia.

But me and my overseer had a falling out, and I quit. He said I couldn't quit, and that if I did the Army would get me. Well, I was married (my wife stayed behind in Gastonia to keep on working at the mill) and thirty years old, and it didn't look like I'd be drafted, so I quit regardless of his threats. My brother-in-law gave me a job running one of the dime stores he owned, and then I got into selling used cars for a while, then later I started up a furniture store, which my son now operates here in Gastonia. I'm eighty-three and have lost my sight but my wife and I are otherwise in good health. I thank God for some slight side vision, enough to move around, but straight-ahead it's just black.

### Joseph R. Bull

*Another Gastonia volunteer was Joseph R. Bull, who served as a base mechanic from September 9, 1942 until August 31, 1943. Single, he took a room in town with Leonard Lundquist, the base engineering officer, and his family. Bull had worked for Lundquist and his son Harold back in Gastonia:*

The Lundquist house was about four miles from the base, and I walked it a few times just for the heck of it. I was just a young kid, not a licensed mechanic, but I'd studied under Captain Lundquist in Gastonia and I learned fast. When a real high tide came in, we could count on our landing strip to be anywhere from four to six inches underwater. At one point we stopped flying for two weeks until the runway could be built up. We requisitioned trucks from nearby Fort Macon, and everyone helped haul stone and build up the runway. Fort Macon, by the way, was really just a Civil War historic site, housing only a few hundred soldiers with whom we had little contact, though we might see them in Beaufort now and then. The four Army guys who put the bombs on our planes came from Fort Bragg.

During the two weeks we weren't flying from Beaufort, I accompanied another mechanic and a group of pilots, and we established a temporary base at a U.S. Marine emergency airstrip at Jacksonville, North Carolina, near Camp LeJeune. We all slept in the small operations building. Though we were roughing it, we were all young and considered it an adventure, not a hardship.

I remember working on all the different planes at the base, and I think we felt that as long as we had two planes flying south and two planes flying north, we were keeping up on our work. But we were kept hopping. When several new mechanics that we didn't know came in to help, Captain Lundquist made it a rule that the mechanic responsible for any major work on a plane had to go up on its first test flight. That kept everyone sharp. As you know, Captain Lundquist was himself killed checking out a plane on which some radio repairs had been done. As busy as we were, however, we had some time for fun. Mostly we dated local girls and went over to the Banks to swim and play and picnic on the beaches.

Flown by another pilot, Bruce P. Ellen's beautiful #63 Stinson Voyager was destroyed in a crash that he witnessed. The coastal patrol's "old reliable" Voyagers accounted for more hours over water than any other aircraft used for patrols (courtesy Bruce P. Ellen).

As far as I know, there weren't any marriages at the time, but there might've been after the war. When the base closed, many of the people went to Virginia and became a tow target unit. Instead I went home and was drafted — having had four deferments during my coastal patrol time at Beaufort. I was assigned to the Air Corps, and spent the rest of the war as a mechanic with a P-38 training squadron on the West Coast. As a civilian again I worked a short while as a railroad telegraph operator then went home to Gastonia and got into the truck repair business. My involvement with aviation pretty much ended with my Air Corps experience, though I still have cherished memories of good friends at the coastal patrol base, especially Harold Lundquist whom I saw last year in Detroit.

## Leonard Harold Lundquist

*Nineteen-year-old pilot Leonard Harold Lundquist began his coastal patrol enlistment at the Flagler Beach base, later transferred to Beaufort and lived with his father and stepmother in a rented house not far from the water. He was born in Minnesota, but grew up mostly in Detroit. In the mid-1930s, fighting to earn a living in the depth of the Great Depression, his father received an offer "too good to refuse" and moved to Charlotte, North Carolina to run the Joe Cannon airport. The younger Lundquist also worked there as a dollar-a-day "flunkie," but got an hour's free flight instruction every day. He reported to the Flagler Beach base on May 20, 1942 and subsequently served at Beaufort until August 16, 1943:*

We lived on Ann Street extension in one of the new homes on the far side of the one-block "downtown" toward the water. The breakers were clearly visible from our kitchen window. We had a hurricane while I was there and I don't really see how the house withstood it. We had warning enough to dig in the planes as best we could. At the time, Dad and I were co-owners of a Curtiss Robin, and we dug holes for its undercarriage so the fuselage was just about on the ground and then we lashed the plane down as securely as we could. But to no avail. The hurricane tore the plane loose and completely destroyed it. Dad was killed some time after that, and since I was still a minor I was unable to collect the insurance payment until I turned twenty-one. By then I was in the Air Corps.

For the most part, the fellows at Beaufort were a happy-go-lucky bunch, and liked to play tricks on one another. That included the times when the pilot of the faster of a two-plane patrol might come up behind the slower lead plane and put his wing tip over its wing tip and give it a gentle tap. That was really pretty silly *and* dangerous, but when you're young, you do things like that. On one occasion, I was flying the lead ship, and pretty certain that my sister ship was going to pull that on me, so I said to my co-pilot, "Let's have some fun with them. I'll trim up the plane so it will fly hands-off, we'll get in the back seat, and when they get close to us, we'll stage a fist-fight." That's just what we did and when those other guys flew close enough to see us flailing away at each other, did they get out of there fast!

While I was still flying from the Florida base I saw a number of submarines, and once my sister ship and I each dropped bombs on one. My sister ship missed but my co-pilot and I actually clipped one. Although there was a lot of debris and an oil slick, it was impossible to know if we sank it. The action was practically right off the end of the runway at the Banana River Naval Air Station. I recall looking right down at the NAS tower and radioing in the clear for help, because this was an emergency, and I thought we really had a chance to do something. The Navy did nothing. But we hung around and pretty soon a couple of Lockheed Hudsons from an Air Corps base in Miami showed up. They dropped a few bombs but got no confirmable sinking, either. The coastal patrol may not have gotten any kills, but we sure helped keep the subs under water.

When the coastal patrol came to an end, rather than risk being drafted into the "walking Army," I took various Air Corps tests and got a direct commission as a service pilot. I think I flew about everything they had and ended up in the CBI flying the "Hump." I made 89 round trips, or 178 flights, across the mountains, and I can tell you I still think coastal patrol flying was far more hazardous. I'm no hero, but we honestly *were* "flying minute men," and I'm very proud of that. In 1948, I received a wire from President Harry Truman inviting me to Daytona Beach to pick up an Air Medal for my coastal patrol service. By then, however, I was married and had a couple of kids, and already had several Air Medals from the Air Corps, so I didn't go.

## Bruce P. Ellen

*Bruce P. Ellen, a pilot from Canton, North Carolina, served at the base from November 25, 1942 through its closure on August 31, 1943. In that time he flew 386:05 hours on over-water patrol and in 1948 would be awarded the Air Medal along with thirty other airmen from the Beaufort base:*

I left Asheville just before Thanksgiving 1942 and after three days weathered-in at Charlotte, I landed in Beaufort on a *very* windy afternoon. It was certainly not what I expected. The rest of the day was spent on paper work and making an orientation flight up the coast. It was hard to believe the number of wrecks and oil slicks I saw. Back in town, I learned that all the housing in private homes was gone, but base personnel had persuaded the Morehead Villa management to open their then-closed hotel. I was given a single room and a pledge of adjoining rooms when my wife and two-year old son came down after Christmas.

Upon my arrival I turned over my beautiful red Stinson 10-A Voyager to base maintenance and a few days later, except for her numbers, I didn't know her — she'd been stripped for patrol duty. The operations staff loved her long-range tanks, but we pilots hated the six-hour flight endurance they gave us, because that meant we were scheduled for the longer patrols. I flew as an observer for a few days to learn the ropes. All of our planes used fixed-length antennas wound on deep sea fishing reels and unwound behind us once in flight. The observer's job was to reel in the antenna before descending to land. As it happened, our final approach to the one usable runway was over twenty-four hundred volt powerlines. Coming in from my second patrol as observer, the plane seemed to hesitate on final, and a distinct smell of ozone filled the cabin. The pilot advised me out of the corner of his mouth, "Let that be the last time you forget to reel in your antenna before landing. We don't have the money to spend on new ones."

Bruce P. Ellen had the misfortune to see another pilot crash Ellen's beautiful Stinson Voyager into the water. The plane was a total loss, but its crew escaped serious injury (courtesy Bruce P. Ellen).

Like gasoline, sugar, meat, and some other staples of life, whiskey was also rationed in those dark days. On a trip to the local ABC store one day I engaged in some conversation with the clerk, who informed me that he had several cases of White Horse Scotch in the rear that he'd let go wholesale because the local residents all drank "pop-skull." Most of the fellows I knew preferred Scotch because it spared them hangovers, and the bar stash at the Morehead Villa was "low grade." So I quickly rounded up enough ration tickets to purchase a case, with the promise that we would take the rest as soon as our remaining tickets became valid.

Winter dawn patrols were "the pits" because we knew if we went down we wouldn't last for rescue. My beautiful Stinson, now painted with a big number "63," had been on the line most of the time since my arrival at the base. It was set for dawn patrol on February 19, 1943, with Jack Bryson as pilot and Roger Faulkner as observer. I flew another Stinson as sister ship and thus followed them for takeoff. We usually rolled at once behind the lead ship, but when I lifted my eyes from the muddy runway, old number "63" seemed to have an awfully steep angle of attack. All I could see was the complete top of her wing and fuselage.

I aborted my take-off as "63" went into the Bay and flipped over. Out of the steam from the hot engine I saw Bryson and Faulkner pop up out of the waist-deep water. Neither was seriously injured, but I was devastated at what happened to my plane. The bright side was that my accident insurance covered the loss, with enough left over to buy our first house when my wife and I went home after the base closed.

From the left: First Lt. Herman M. Reid, Bruce P. Ellen, and Ted Sellers in front of a Stinson Voyager (courtesy Theodore E. Sellers).

Late that spring, I contacted friends who had cottages over on the Banks but couldn't use them on account of travel restrictions. One friend gladly rented us his cottage for two months, but after "eating and sleeping sand" for two months we both declared "no more beach houses!" In early August we found a sublet in Beaufort and moved back to town, aware the base would probably soon close. About this time the Signal Corps announced it needed service pilots, so Frank Davis and I applied. We passed all the paperwork and the physicals and were called to Greensboro to take flight tests on AT-6s. It turned out they had only one AT-6 and it was under repair, so we returned to Beaufort. The plane was still off-line two weeks later, and I'd had it with the military — my family had to eat. Without going into the details, I went into private industry and did very well. I also kept flying. I owned a nice Stinson in the 1950s and a beautiful Cessna Skylane in the 1960s and 1970s. I quit flying following my heart attack in 1980, but I'm otherwise active, and right now I'm planning a trip down the Intracoastal Waterway from Norfolk to Saint Augustine.

## Oscar E. Shouse

*Air Medal winner Oscar E. Shouse was a twenty-six-year-old pilot from Winston-Salem when he reported for duty at Beaufort on September 14, 1942. When his wife delivered their second son only a week later, he went home to be with her, then returned to the base ferrying a Stinson Voyager. He recalls how he happened to join the Civil Air Patrol before heading for Beaufort:*

When it looked like we were going to have to fight, and we didn't have the planes or pilots we wanted to have, the government started a program where they'd teach you to fly if you wanted to. I didn't pay anything and got all my lessons free and earned a private pilot's license. They said they'd expect me to volunteer if they needed me. Later they said they wanted me as a glider pilot for the war in Europe. I volunteered for the coastal patrol because I thought it'd be safer, which it was. Some of my buddies later were killed flying gliders.

Air Medal winner Oscar E. Shouse, Jr. was from Winston Salem, North Carolina, and remembers more than one occasion when the Beaufort airfield was covered by four to six inches of the tidal Atlantic Ocean (courtesy Oscar E. Shouse, Jr.).

The Beaufort flying field wasn't much. I'll tell you this — when it got to be bad weather in the winter, that field became so muddy we'd have to taxi to the very farthest end of the runway, where a bunch of fellows held on to the plane while we revved the motor to full power. When they let go, we got airborne as fast as we could to avoid the worst of the gooey stuff. For a few weeks we couldn't use our field at all, so we went down to the Marine auxiliary field at Bogue. After a couple of winter storms I remember that our field was covered with about four to six inches of water. About the time the base was due to close they finally got around to paving our "runway." They trucked in loads of gravel and rolled it out so the runway was somewhat higher than the surrounding ground. That might have been after we'd left, I'm not real sure.

In the coastal patrol, officers and enlisted men fraternized without the restrictions observed by the military services — as attested to by this mixed group of pilots and ground crewmen (Hopper collection).

When I first went down, I stayed at some hotel. When my wife and two boys joined me, we got lucky and found a small house on Front Street. It was over a hundred years old, and a little decrepit, but livable, and there we remained until we went home. We rented space to another Winston-Salem man, Herman Reid. He married a girl he met down there and after the war returned to Beaufort to live, though when she died, Herman returned to Winston-Salem and lived the rest of his life here. While we were in the coastal patrol, we bought an outboard motor and Herman and I often went fishing in a borrowed boat. We lived right on the Intracoastal Waterway, and we'd troll up and down for bluefish, sea trout and maybe an occasional red snapper. We'd bring them home for my wife to cook, and were they good!

I recall several flying incidents. On one patrol, I noticed my sister ship having trouble, and some oil and smoke coming from her. She had to ditch, so I circled and called the base and pretty soon a Coast Guard boat came out and got the pilot and observer. They were okay. The worst thing was losing Guy Cherry. He and George Grove had flown down the coast to escort some ships coming out of Wilmington. I was on patrol down that way, too, and when the base told us Cherry and Groves had ditched, we began searching for them. Though we weren't the first to do so, my pilot and I found them. Again the Coast Guard came out, but by this time Cherry was already dead. Some time later, George Grove told me he thought Cherry had undone his seat belt too soon and had been thrown through the windscreen, suffering fatal injuries.

When the base closed, I returned to Winston-Salem and my former job as a mail carrier for the Post Office. I did little flying after that. I rented a plane once in a while but that cost more than I could afford so I gave it up. Eventually I quit the Post Office and went into business with a couple of friends. That didn't work out, so I became a salesman for another friend who owned a print shop. I retired too soon, and un-retired and worked some more until 1989, when I turned seventy-three. My wife and I eventually had four children, three boys and a girl. We now have twelve grandchildren and three great grandchildren. I've lost touch with all my friends from the good old Beaufort days, most of whom, like Herman Reid and Pinkney Stowe, have passed away.

* * *

The Beaufort base history records the sharp disappointment of all concerned upon learning that the base would be closed:

**July 18, 1943**
Now comes the announcement to end all announcements. At the end of church services today, the Major read a letter from Lt. Col. Johnson stating that with the completion of the Dusk Patrol on August 31, all coastal patrol bases would be closed. What's the idea? Our work has been praised by high officials in every branch of the service. The Office of War Information has just published a glowing account of CAP Coastal activities. We've completed almost all the missions assigned by the Navy. We've found their boats when they couldn't. In fact, we thought we were doing a mighty fine job....

**August 31, 1943**
This is the end. Everybody has been invited to a final banquet at the Villa tonight at eight-thirty. The personnel will be the guest of the Base Commander and quite an elaborate program has been arranged. In the morning everybody but the mechanics and four pilots will pack up their things and head for home. The mechanics will be kept on to repair the planes and it is rumored that the base will be moved and continued as a maintenance base to repair ships for other bases on express duty.... So ends the activity of CAP Coast Patrol Base 21 as a Patrolling unit.

As activity at the base wound down, pilots Alfred C. Kendrick of Gastonia and Carl B. Sloan of Greensboro penned the "CAPCP Base 21 Ballad," a parody bidding a not-so-fond adieu to the plane base airmen flew the most, the Stinson Voyager. Full of joking sentiment, and sung to the tune of "The Prisoner's Song," these are some of the many verses:

> *Now I'd like to tell you the story*
> *Of some famous flying bricks.*
> *They are put together with some mucilage*
> *And some old discarded sticks.*
>
> *They take damn near all the runway,*
> *Their motors spit and spew.*
> *And the boys who haven't chewed their cushions*
> *Are distinct, in fact damn few. . . .*
>
> *Now we are sure going to miss Harkers Island*
> *And the barefooted babes galore.*
> *But we are sure as hell glad of one thing,*
> *We won't have to ride those damn Voyagers no more.*

Left to right, in foreground, Lts. John M. Brock, Herman M. Reid, and George F. Hatch assembling crates to ship base equipment no longer needed for patrol work (courtesy Theodore E. Sellers).

Tragically, Lt. Kendrick was killed a few months later, on January 22, 1944, when his plane crashed on take-off on a night tracking mission from Monogram Field in Virginia. In total, seven airmen were killed flying tow target and tracking missions. Besides Lt. Kendrick, three others had previously served in the coastal patrol: Capts. Clifton K. Hyatt of Miami, Florida; Gordon M. Pyle of New York City; and Raoul E. Souliere of Biddeford, Maine.

The base historians, Capt. Warner and Lt. Grove, nicely summed up what they considered the prime motivation of all their members — plain old-fashioned "Minute Man" patriotism, that special spirit pervading the men and women of the coastal patrol everywhere:

> The pilots and observers didn't come to Base 21 only to fly planes. The mechanics didn't come only to keep those ships flying. The servicemen didn't come only to service planes. The guards, the office workers, the communications staff, the officers didn't come only to do a job at the base. They came, instead, to avenge enemy action as only they knew how. They came to help America maintain what fighting strength it had until more men could be trained, more equipment built, more supplies shipped to strategic points of action. They succeeded admirably.

---

Base officers, pilots, observers who served at least one month at CAPCP#20 and who are not elsewhere mentioned in this chapter include: William F. Ashworth,* Ernest Behre,* Robert H. Cooper,* Herbert O. Crowell,* George F. Hatch,* Carl R. Johnson, Paul J. Little,* Gordon W. Love, Francis W. McComb, Jr.,* Millard W. Makepeace,* Wilbur A. Raynor, Frederick Robinson, Charles R. Russell, Jr.,* Lawrence W. Spencer,* Julian A. Wiggins, Barthwell L. Williams,* and Lester H. Yandle.* Asterisk indicates Air Medal winner.

"The Civil Air Patrol grew out of the urgency of the situation. The CAP was set up and went into operation almost overnight. It patrolled our shores and performed its antisubmarine work at a time of almost desperate national crisis. If it had done nothing beyond that, the Civil Air Patrol would have earned an honorable place in the history of American air power."

General Henry H. Arnold
United States Air Forces

# Epilogue

Most of the coastal patrol veterans who went into one of the regular armed services sought discharges and returned home when the war was over. Some of those who joined the Air Corps remained to follow a career in the Air Force, while a few others found a career in naval aviation. Coastal patrol volunteers who hadn't been eligible for the armed forces generally resumed their civilian employment.

Unlike other war veterans, those members of the coastal patrol who did not go on to serve with the regular armed services were denied the normal benefits accorded to war veterans — such as government health care for service-connected injury or illness and the various assistance programs provided by the G.I. Bill. Some members of Congress feared setting a precedent: if Civil Air Patrol volunteers were granted veterans' benefits, how many other volunteer groups might seek them?

Other members of Congress felt differently, certainly about those Civil Air Patrol volunteers who were called to active duty with the coastal and border patrols, the tow target units, and the Army courier express. Senator Robert R. Reynolds of North Carolina, in a powerful speech to the U.S. Senate on November 21, 1944, stressed the military nature of the coastal patrol:

> The veterans of the C.A.P. volunteered for one thing and were commanded to do another by the War Department, but because of their original intentions, there exists an opinion in high places that they are just civilians like many that watched for forest fires or spotted airplanes. Unlike many other civilian organizations which performed admirably, these veterans not only performed their civilian functions, but were futher commanded to seek out and attack an armed enemy and to engage him in mortal combat. Upon being commanded to engage the enemy, these men ceased to be civilians and became combat troops.... These veterans of the C.A.P. were instructed carefully about prescribed uniform insignia, because in the event of capture

by the enemy they would be treated as soldiers only if such insignia were properly displayed. This would not indicate a status of either civilians or guerillas according to the concepts of international law. There is one and only one answer to their status; that is, they were soldiers of the United States, and as such they are entitled to all rights and privileges pertaining thereto. Regardless of the original intentions ... these men were by command of constituted authority made combat troops and so used in the conduct of this war.... To deny these men veteran's status on the grounds of establishing a precedent for others to seek similar status is a denial not based on justice nor even on practical considerations. These men are comparatively few in number and regardless of deaths, wounds, injuries, or personal sacrifice in line of duty, these men were made combatants not by choice of their own, but by command of the War Department.... These men did not question the right of the War Department to make them combat troops; now who has the right to question whether or not they were soldiers?

Though Senator Reynold's early efforts at securing legislative recognition for active duty CAP veterans were unsuccessful, the fight continued when a number of these veterans banded together to help themselves. Organized as The Association of Civil Air Patrol Veterans, Inc., with Frank E. Dawson, formerly C.O. of the Beaufort coastal patrol base as national commander, the association's letterhead carried a motto "For the Welfare of the Widows and Orphans of Our CAP Members Who Served on Active Duty." Seeking additonal members, a March 13, 1945 letter from commander Dawson to all ex-active duty CAPers noted that:

> For your information, THE ASSOCIATION OF CIVIL AIR PATROL VETERANS, INC. are the sponsors of HR Bill #2149, introduced in the House of Representatives by Representative Joe W. Ervin of North Carolina, and Senate Bill #381, introduced in the Senate by Senator Claude Pepper of Florida, whereby the Civil Air Patrol members who served with the above units [coastal and border patrols, tow target units, and Army courier service] on active duty would be entitled to the rights of a Veteran, and that their widows would recieve compensation and their orphan children be taken care of.

These bills did not pass, and the Association of Civil Air Patrol Veterans eventually just faded away. Many coastal patrol veterans feel it is not too late to redress this oversight and that, at the very least, appropriate benefits should be awarded to the surviving families of the men who were killed on active duty — twenty-six in the coastal patrol, seven in tow target and tracking service, six in courier service, and two with the border patrol.

# Bibliography and Source Notes

At the heart of this book are the stories attributed to over 270 individuals. Seventeen of them are my edited excerpts from unedited transcripts of 1983-1986 interviews — thirteen conducted by former National CAP Historian Colonel Lester Hopper, (William P. Bridges, Marilou Eggenweiler, William J. Fandison, Del Gallier, William M. Gantt, George E. Haddaway, William L. Heim, Addis H. McDonald, Marion F. Parkinson, Robert A. Robinson, M.D., Hugh R. Sharp, Jr., Carl O. Swaim, and Dorothy Wescott) and four conducted by CAP Historical Committee member Captain Hellenmerie Walker, (George H. Felt, Ernest G. Helms, Vernon S. Hickman, and Frank S. Myers). The remaining stories result from (1) several written memoirs, (2) in-person and/or telephone interviews I conducted during 1995-1996, or (3) from an exchange of letters between myself and the persons quoted.

Throughout the book all excerpts from interviews conducted by Colonel Hopper and Captain Walker are double-indented, as are all longer excerpts from other sources — notably the books *Flying Minute Men* and *Sank Same*, various base histories, and other published sources. The stories I collected have normal indentation and appear without quotes.

I tried to clarify what might be ambiguous or repetitive recollections, rearranged the sequence of events related in some interviews so as to create more readability, and corrected ungrammatical language except where it was clearly colloquial or regional in nature. I took great care to avoid changing anyone's intended meanings. Most contributors had the opportunity to see and amend the stories attributed to them. Many found and corrected errors, and often added new material of even more interest.

I made no systematic attempt to verify what I was told. I'm almost as old as many of my respondents and am myself well aware, as so many of them reminded me, that it's easy to mis-remember events more than half a century removed. Still, nothing I heard struck me as impossible or as a deliberate enhancement of what really happened. I'm fully content that the stories are as true and trustworthy as the human condition allows.

My next most important source of information was the large amount of archival material collected by Colonel Lester Hopper during his long tenure as CAP National Historian. Although he had just resigned that post and had already transferred the original material to CAP Headquarters at Maxwell Air Force Base, when I visited his home in 1995 he kindly allowed me free access to his own collection of material relating to the coastal patrol.

To me, the single most useful item was a typed roster of nearly three thousand men and women who served at any of the twenty-one coastal patrol bases long enough (one month or more) to qualify for the so-called "Certificate of Belligerency." I looked up all of them in a computerized national residential telephone directory, and either wrote or telephoned (sometimes both) more than a thousand individuals who I thought might be the "right" one.

Colonel Hopper also allowed me to acquire copies of many of the photographs he had collected over the years. Those reproduced herein are credited as being from the "Hopper Collection." The other photographs that appear are credited simply to the persons who loaned them to me, because the actual photographers were mostly unknown. In all I borrowed or was given well over a thousand photographs, and the selection of those for this book was difficult. I sometimes used a poorer rather than a better photograph in order to illustrate a point that would not otherwise be covered.

Though I wrote to numerous local librarians and historical societies (those that replied are listed in the acknowledgments), their holdings relative to the CAP Coastal Patrol were, on the whole, disappointing. And so were the contents of contemporary newspaper and magazine accounts. I sampled a number of those listed in the Civil Air Patrol Historical Monograph Number Eight, "Civil Air Patrol, 1941-1991: A Chronological Bibliography," but then made no futher attempt to scan such periodicals systematically. For general background, however, the following books were quite useful:

Blair, Clay, *Hitler's U-Boats War: The Hunters, 1939-1942*, Random House, New York, NY, 1996.

Cremer, Peter, in collaboration with Fritz Brustat-Naval, translated from the German by Lawrence Wilson, *U-Boat Commander: A Periscope View of The Battle of the Atlantic*, The Naval Institute Press, Annapolis, MD, 1984.

Johnson, Robert E., *Guardians of the Sea*, Naval Institute Press, Annapolis, MD, 1987.

Mellor, William B., Jr., *Sank Same*, Howell, Soskin, Publishers, New York, NY, 1944.

Neprud, Robert E., *Flying Minute Men: The Story of the Civil Air Patrol*, Duell, Sloan and Pearce, New York, NY, 1948.

Pisano, Dominick, *To Fill the Skies with Pilots: The Civilian Pilot Training Program, 1939-1946*, University of Illinois Press, Urbana, IL, 1993.

Schoenfeld, Max, *Stalking the U-Boat: USAAF Offensive Antisubmarine Operations in World War II*, Smithsonian Institution Press, Washington, DC, 1995.

Wilson, Gill Robb, *I Walked With Giants*, Vantage Press, New York, NY, 1968.

---

Special note: The author will be happy to answer any reasonable inquiry addressed to the publisher and accompanied by a stamped and self-addressed envelope.

# Index

Air Medal, CAP qualifications for, 49

Air Transport Command, 24, 41, 68–69, 91, 158, 253, 325, 400, 441

Aircraft Owners and Pilots Association, 67, 111, 158

Army Specialized Training Program, 174

Arnold, Lt. Gen. Henry H. "Hap," 3, 83, 524

Atlantic City, NJ Convention Center, used for airmen training, 22

Aviation Club of California, 279

"barracuda bags," critique of, 464

Beau, Maj. Gen. Lucas B., 172

Beck, Thomas H., 3

"blimps," 164, 378, 479, 490

Bradley Air Museum, 51

Civil Air Patrol (general)
- active duty oath, 6
- headquarters personnel, 2-3, 7, 9, 15, 20-22, 74, 87, 145-146, 209, 331, 348, 433, 511, 522
- personnel identification numbers described, 11
- recruiting poster, 307

Civil Air Patrol Coastal Patrol
- aircraft leasing, 80
- aircrew qualifications, 65
- base insignia, examples, 67, 357, 438, 445, 485
- base table of organization, 65
- certificate of service, 169
- duck club, 74-75
- personnel per diems, 80

Civil Air Patrol Coastal Patrol, oral histories [SPECIAL NOTE: The following are the names of ONLY those coastal patrol members whose stories are told through interviews or by surviving family members.]
- Alderman, Halsey C., 223–225
- Alford, Paul J., 244-45
- Alison, Landon E., 120–122

Allen, Clifford W., 449
Allen, William M., 447–449
Anderson, Herman L., 161–163
Antaya, Roger J., 434–435
Apte, Wylie, 462–464
Arn, Robert E., 318–321
Arnold, Harry R., 186–187
Atherton, John G., 247–249
Barbour, Bernice, 388-391
Barres, Robert F., 167–169
Barrett, Bruce L. P., 292–297
Bates, Aubrey R., 148
Beilman, Robert D., 158–159
Bessey, Paul M., 471–473
Betchen, Maury H., 57–58
Billet, Arthur B., 265-266
Bingham, Thomas Y., 338-339
Bird, Bruce H., 52–54
Blackwood, Robert A., 311–312
Blocker, Walter E., 221
Boone, Robert F., 503–505
Bouknight, Robert M., 187
Bowes, Clifton T., Jr., 171–173
Boynton, Ralph S., 81–82
Brandhuber, Joseph N., 333–334
Bridges, William Paul, 376–380
Brocket, Robert M., 274
Bruch, E, Phillip, Jr., 321–323
Bryan, James S., 396

Bryant, John W., 270–271
Bull, Joseph R., 513–514
Bumpus, Violet K., 368–371
Burnham, Isaac W., II, 9–10, 85–89,
Bush, Joseph W., 265
Calligan, John P., 398–400
Carter, Kenneth J., 233–236
Catheron, Allison G., II 413–414
Chadderdon, Harold P., 268–269
Clark, Carl S., 336–337
Coffee, Ruth M., 236–238
Coleman, Thomas G., 82–83
Coo, Herbert G., 267
Cook, Glen P., 42-44
Corley, Brady F.,187–188
Creasey, Frederick K., 11–14
Crescenzo, Marilou, 19–22
Crim, Omar W., 219–221
Custer, Randall M., 31–35
Custer, Ray C., 29-30
Datz, Robert J., 26–29
de la Rigaudiere, Guy, 407–408
Denham, Nicholas F., 204–207
DiCarlo, Louis J., 207–211
Dingley, Lucille M., 454–456
Donner, Matthew A., Jr., 492–493
Dossey, James G., 340–343
Dugo, Herman, 263–266

## Index    531

Duncan, Edgar E., 243–244
Durand, Robert E., 446-447
Eaton, George A., 441–442
Egan, Russell P., 166–167
Ellen, Bruce P., 516–518
Ellison, Leslie W., 364-365
Englert, Lawrence G., 211–212
Fandison, William J., 203–204
Farrelly, David T., 485–490
Felt, George H., 283–286
Fields, C. Weldon, 374–376
Fletcher, Harold C., 421-422
Flint, Wyly F., 145–146
French, Charles B., 126–127
Frost, Richard D., 465
Fuller, Edward R. II, 93–94,
Furlong, Louis R., 453–454
Gallier, Del, 239–241
Gannt, William M., 384–386
Gassaway, Owen, 62-63
Gautreaux, Alvin H., 201–202
Ginnow, Oscar H., 476–480
Gray, David F., 124–125
Haddaway, George E., 232–233
Hairgrove, Arthur L., 55
Hamlett, James C., 308-311
Harper, Marshall B., 163–165
Heberding, Dolly, 327–3333
Heim, William L., 199–201

Helms, Ernest G., 135–137
Heno, Charles T., 365–367
Herbert, Henry W., 420
Hettel, Joseph N., 404–406
Hickman, Vernon S., 183–184
Hinnant, Carl R., 184–186
Hodgson, Janet B., 437–439
Hodgson, Sloat F., 436
Holden, Lester S., 425
Hood, Raymond V., 400
Howe, John E., 467–468
Hughston, Thomas H., 353–356
Hull, Clyde K., 127–128
Hurt, Robert H., 165–166
Isenbarger, Karr C., 339
Keever, Wyatt A., 512–513
Kief, John, 493–495
Killmon, Alvah B., 99–100
King, Everett L., 429–431
King, Wallace R., 79-80
Kirstein, John H., 272–273
Kloth, Carl M., 26-28
Kraemer, Luverne A., 16–18
LaCouture, Donald V., 443
Lamont, Jerome M., 495-497
Lankalis, John F., 30-31
Lawrence, James S., 119-120
Lawrence, Thomas P., 104
Long, Everett C., 383-384

Loux, Paul R., Jr., 89-91
Lovelace, Brooks W., 140–142
Low, Chester F., 22-23
Lundquist, Leonard H., 515-516
Mallory, William W., 469–471
Mangum, Joe O., Jr., 143–144
Manhart, Thomas A., 363–364
Mann, Billings L., 103
McClain, Raymond B., 216–219
McDonald, Addis E. 215-216
McDonald, Addis Holly, 214
McEvoy, James A., 192
McGowan, George S., 464
McLane, Ronnie L., 443–445
Mears, William Edward, 107-108
Mellor, Erwin T., 439–44
Metz, Jack W., 137–138
Meyer, Jack L., 173–174
Meyers, Hugh L., 189-189
Minshew, Grey S., 190–192
Minter, Irwin D., 23–24
Moody, Warren E., 408–409
Mosley, Zack T., 75–79
Myers, Arthur R., 91–93
Myers, Frank S., 290-295
Myers, Orval O., 276-277
Ney, Abner F., Jr., 425–427
Nord, Elmore H., 343–345
Northam, Robert P., 104–105

Oberhaus, Richard P., 269-270
O'Day, Roland W., 38-41
O'Leary, Julian P., 484–485
Olsen, Homer A., 466-467
Ozenberger, Norman T. and Lois L., 212–213
Parkinson, Marion F. 257–260
Perry, Farwell W., 409–413
Perry, Ruth, 289–290
Phipps, Henry E., 41–43
Pigeon, Lawrence A. and Dorothy, 480–482
Pilgrim, Samuel W., 181–183
Pinson, Clyde B., 334–336
Pooser, Walter E., 305–308
Prescott, John S., 68–69
Putnam, Dan C., 280–282
Ramsay, Glenn S., 349–352
Randles, Wesley C., 170-171
Ransom, Georgia, 432–433
Rast, John A., 188–189
Reaver, John P., 325–327
Rehrig, Norman, 417–419
Reynolds, Wiley R., Jr., 73–74
Ring, Norman R., 490–492
Rish, Roy P., Jr., 340
Robinson, Robert A., 226–227
Russell, Charles R., 500–503
Sapp, L. Jeff and Lottie B., 393

Index    533

Rose, Willis F., 242–243
Ross, Mrs. Donald W., 323–325
Rowland, John S., 154–155
Royce, Robert G., 159–161
Savage, Clarence L., 106–107
Scheb, Joseph E., 314
Scholtz, Edward A., 507
Schurman, Henry E., 286–289
Seiferd, Charles E., 14–15
Sellers, Theodore E., 374, 511
Sharp, Hugh R., 49-52
Sherwood, Sidney L., 101
Shouse, Oscar E., 519–521
Shurley, Fletcher R., 147–148
Sigmon, Paul L., 505–507
Simpson, Gustavus S., Jr., 24–26
Smith, Whitemarsh S., 178-179
Somermeier, T. G., 295-296
Sones, Peter J., Jr., 304
Spencer, Harold G., 299–301
Stacey, Richard L., 313
Strean, Orville, 359–361
Stuenkel, Earl E., 260-262
Summers, Joe N., 251–252
Swaim, Carl O., 382–383
Tamm, John R.,122–124
Tassinari, Bruno L., 445–446
Taylor, Nancy B., 102–103
Tegg, Henry W., 44–46

Thompson, David R., 69–73
Thomson, Alexander D., 65–66
Thoroughgood, Joseph W., 54-55
Townson, George W., 46–47
Tucker, Harry H., 192-195
Tyler, Cecil A., 460–462
Vetter, Keith L., 274–276
Vorys, John M., 330–331
Wachter, Elmer E., 138–140
Wagoner, Bruce G., 396–398
Walker, John H., 252–253
Wallace, Wesley C., 115–116
Walter, Carl L., 416–417
Walter, William H., 414–416
Warrens, Alice S., 298–299
Weatherman, Ferrell E., 96–99
Weeks, Charles, Jr., 66–68
Wescott, Dorothy G., 391–393
White, Edward K., 456–459
Wietholter, Anthony, 387–388
Wilson, Gill Robb, 1–3
Winther, Thomas Z., 468–469
Witte, Edward E., 151–153
Wolcott, George A., 118–119
Worth, Arthur T., 55–57
Yost, George T., 238
Yuengling, Richard L., 98-9

Civilian Pilot Training Program, purpose of, 97

Coffee, Harry, 2

Confederate Air Force, 362

Doolittle, Col. James H., 142

DuPont, Richard C., 37, 50

Evans, Floyd, 2

Florida Defense Force, 61–64, 66, 75, 111

"Flying the Hump," 24, 123, 145–146, 173, 517

"Flying Tigers," 40

Gable, Clark, 321, 326

Gannett, Guy P., 3

Hitler, Adolf, 1

Hopper, Col. Lester E., 18, 48, 74, 135, 183, 198, 203, 213, 239, 241, 257, 377, 383-384, 391

Intracoastal Waterway, 141

Ishihara, test for color blindness, 23

Johnson, Martin and Osa, 245-246

King, Admiral Ernest J., 71

LaGuardia, Mayor Fiorella, 3

LIFE magazine, story on CAP, 16

"Li'l Miss De-Icer," 76, 88

Link, Ed, 10

Lusitania, 107

Manteo Coastal Patrol Museum, 401

McLemore, Henry, columnist, 78–79

McMullen, A.B., 2

Morris, Les, 2

Morrison, Grace K., 61

National Aeronautics Association, 2, 111

Quiet Birdmen, 111

Racial incidents, 89, 243

Radio Berlin, 10

Ringling Brothers Circus, 311

Roosevelt, President Franklin D., 3, 49, 148–149

Sherif, Fred, 2

"Sink a Sub Club," 335

"Snake Pilots," 310

Southern Liaison Patrol, 149–150, 183, 186, 284, 287, 301

Tanker Protection Fund, 86-87

Texas Private Flyers Association, 232

Tow target Units (TTUs)
    list of locations, 126
    TTU #1, 18, 21, 31, 34, 220
    TTU #5, 125-129, 421
    TTU #7, 164–165, 323, 327, 337, 368
    TTU #12, 368
    TTU #15, 240-241, 364, 368

Index    535

TTU #17, 350, 419-424, 431, 488

TTU #20, 493

TTU #21, 376–377, 421, 503, 505

U.S. Coast Guard, 7, 13, 48, 91, 93, 103–104, 138, 178 182, 189, 208, 219, 227, 235, 259, 261, 307, 378–379, 382, 393, 440, 499, 507–508, 510

U.S. Merchant Marine, 42, 55, 121-122, 167

Virginia Protective Force, 93, 104

War Training Service Program, 448, 497

Walker, Hellenmerie, 290, 298

Weidenfeld, Gregory F., 31

Works Projects Administration, airport construction aid, 86, 88